THE RISE OF THE AMERICAN FILM

THE RISE OF THE

AMERICAN FILM

A CRITICAL HISTORY

BY LEWIS JACOBS

HARCOURT, BRACE AND COMPANY *hb* NEW YORK

COPYRIGHT, 1939, BY
LEWIS JACOBS

[e·7·47]

Designed by Robert Josephy

PRINTED IN THE UNITED STATES OF AMERICA

TO

MY WIFE LILLIAN

PREFACE

HUNDREDS of motion pictures are made each year, tons of news-print commend them, millions of people see them. And there in a sense the whole thing comes to an end: the films disappear from sight, leaving behind little more than the wholly incalculable effect they have had on their multitudinous audiences. Astronomical numbers of tears have been shed, pulses have quickened, unrealized associations have been set up, but a medium that bears so transient an appearance does not readily enjoy respect or provoke reflection, since it is about as difficult to compare one dream with another as to measure film against film in recollection.

The liveliest and most popular art of the twentieth century, however, deserves better than this. Politics and history itself are ephemeral, but are not ill-considered or neglected for that reason: and for that matter the motion picture is by no means an inconsiderable element in contemporary society. More than this, in a most curious and striking way the film actually reflects contemporary history as it flows. Primarily the motion picture is a great popular art and, as such, concerns the art-student first, but it is also the concern of the historian and the sociologist. There need be no fear that their interest will in the least detract from the pure and only semi-reflective enjoyment of the normal filmgoers. It is remarkable, too, that there is nothing the average film enthusiast seems to enjoy more than discussing the movies of yesteryear both for their own sake and for a certain highly personal and nostalgic quality they possess. To the average adult today, his own past can be most quickly recaptured or recalled through the medium of old phonograph discs and old films. But to hear the discs and see the films again is not to recall one's past: that is achieved better by pure recollection of past music and past movies. Actually to hear and to see again what pleased one so much in music or in photographic imagery is, rather, to get a sharp critical slant on one's own past. That was what one enjoyed ten years ago: this is what seemed the most exciting or beautiful thing in one's adolescence? *Cabiria* and *Male and Female* and "I Must Have That Man" have not changed: it is we who have changed, and the world we live in.

A book such as Lewis Jacobs's history of the American film possesses, then, an assortment of attractions of a purely human kind. Beyond this, it has its own sharp and intrinsic value since it reviews, sums up, and judges something absolutely new in human experience which has had a profound if unknown influence upon humanity. The motion picture is barely fifty years old. No major art had previously reached us since remote times, and it cannot but be fascinating to learn how this new thing came into existence, how it grew and what nourished it. Perhaps the idea that art is something particular and for the few has to be further dispelled before we can approach the film honestly, for there has been some shame about its immense popularity. Yet if *Measure for Measure* and *The Birds* and the Elgin marbles have only a restricted appeal today, these revered art-expressions were *created* to be popular, were made to be enjoyed by the maximum number of people at the time. If Byron is tedious to study in school, he was desperately delightful to clumps of fascinated readers and listeners among his contemporaries. The motion picture is in good company in its popularity.

"The Rise of the American Film" is really a romance. It is the colorful tale of as typical a group of Americans as one could hope to hear of, men and women of every possible kind of nature and origin irresistibly drawn into a new kind of creative expression suited to a machine age. Despite all that other countries have contributed to the steady stream of film production since 1895, the film has become essentially an American expression and its history is part and parcel of the national life. Here in a new setting appeared new pioneers, robber barons, martyrs. Mr. Jacobs in telling his vivid tale has done well to stress the financial structure of the motion picture industry for, although the complete story is yet to be told, this is one of the most fantastically absorbing and most utterly American of sagas imaginable. But his principal interest is, very properly, in the film itself about which, actually, so little is known. There was a very great need indeed for such a book, and in many respects the author is bravely breaking new ground. There have

been no more than three or four histories of the American film
and fewer critical histories: and Terry Ramsaye's admirable "A
Million and One Nights" was published long before sound came
to the screen, Hampton's book goes little further, and only Gilbert
Seldes's delightfully provocative books are readily obtainable today.

There is another reason for such a history being cordially welcome. During recent years more and more people, including a
growing number of young folks, have begun to take the motion
picture seriously and there is a very definite trend towards studying
it as one would study, say, music or the drama. This was curious
because actually it was probably rather more difficult to study the
motion picture than it was to launch oneself into Egyptology or
Romanesque Architecture—there was considerably less physical
material available for study. After all, the least privileged schoolboy
with a bent in that particular direction could make a start at informing himself about the home life of the Pharaohs by the simple
expedient of dropping into one of our great public museums,
whereas his companion with an itch to delve into early Metro or
primitive Warner would have found, with two exceptions, nothing
whatsoever to give him a start along that particular line of arche-
ology. He could not, unless very exceptionally, have seen a single
film over ten years old, although he could fairly simply have
examined at least a reproduction of the most cryptic of the architectural decorations of the great Romanesque edifices at Ravenna
or at Kilpeck.

To some very considerable extent, this curious situation—that
there was virtually no means of informing oneself about the
medium of expression which appeals to the greatest number of
people—has lately been partly remedied. One of the most active
departments of the Museum of Modern Art in New York is its
Film Library, created four years ago. With the co-operation of the
motion picture industry itself, the Museum has gathered together
a very large number of films of all kinds representing practically
every sort of material that has been produced since 1895. One does
not have to go to the Museum to see them, either, although films
are regularly shown there. This Film Library provides films to
students in colleges, museums and other cultural institutions all

over the country, so that it is no longer necessary to wonder what the first films were like or what kind of fare the cinemas offered in the nineteen twenties—it is possible to see them for oneself. There is an infinite fascination in witnessing the birth of a new art, and this highly enjoyable type of study now has its addicts in tens of thousands.

Certainly to me the most admirable chapters of Lewis Jacobs's book are those that recapitulate the history of motion picture technique from first-hand re-examination of those films which actually *made* history, since this is essentially a story of adventure and of daring. A film is, basically, only a succession of ordinary still photographs like the ones we take with a dollar camera. At first, it was enough that restless and inquisitive men had made a machine which would take such pictures continuously and a machine which would then project them on a screen so that an illusion of movement was created. Audiences paid gladly just to see this curious new replica of life and, if the inventors themselves as well as the customary wiseacres believed that this novelty would quickly fade and moving pictures soon be thrown into the discard, it was not without reason; had this been all that the film did it would doubtless have long been obsolete. It was the adventurers and experimenters who turned a semi-scientific novelty into something much more, and who found out by patient trial and error (and sometimes by accident) how to make the photographic images *mean* something. It seems now a very simple matter to compose a film of long shots and close-ups and medium shots, and to arrange them in such an order that the very juxtaposition adds meaning not visibly apparent in the assembled shots themselves. This, as Mr. Jacobs explains so admirably, is the very essence and art of the motion picture, but it was not arrived at naturally or easily and it is not the product of complicated machinery or great production corporations but of the artist-artisans who actually make films. There are, of course, a large number of very inferior and even of badly made films, but I doubt if there are proportionately nearly as many bad films as there are bad oil-paintings—in this respect at least it is certainly an advantage that films are relatively so costly to make. And the really great and creative films—like *The Birth of a Nation* and *Potemkin,* for instance—remain even after the passage of years infinitely exciting because in their composition and creation a new technique for expressing ideas and emotions as well as for dramatizing pictorial action was being evolved.

What may not be immediately apparent, but must not be overlooked, is the immense amount of research which has gone to the making of this cross-section through half a century of American life. The author became a pathfinder through this tangled realm of the film's course. He has gone back to the original material and the original documents, dispelling many strange beliefs and false traditions concerning both influences and events: he has uncovered a mine of new and arresting facts as well as recovering forgotten ones. The result is not journalism but scholarship. Only the most devoted and inspired energy, as well as a monumental degree of hard work, could have produced a book so valuable to the student and so illuminating to the general reader.

It would be needless to say that I disagree here and there with some of Mr. Jacobs's critical and social interpretations of motion picture history—I think he entirely underestimates and misunderstands the work of Chaplin, for instance—because this is as it must be. There are no authorities in this field as yet, so that we are all free to form our own judgments now that it is possible actually to see (and not merely to recall or to read about) the films of the past forty-odd years. Some readers will be almost exclusively interested, as they re-examine the birth and growth of this new art, in its innate esthetic. Others will be fascinated by its technique, and others again by the effective use of this technique as it works upon the mentality of audiences and individuals. There will always be the faithful souls who, more simply, love films and love the personalities who have appeared in films or who have created them. And a very different group of people will continue, as now, to esteem the film not for its own sake but because in it we can see at first hand a truthful (if not always obvious) reflection of the *mores* of the society that produced it and that enjoyed it. For all of these different tastes I believe that "The Rise of the American Film" will be a cheerful guide, a stimulant, and an eye-opener.

IRIS BARRY

ACKNOWLEDGMENT

I WISH to record my thanks to those persons who have given me valuable assistance in the preparation of this book. In particular I am extremely grateful to Miss Lillian Willis, who has been unsparing in giving me the benefit of her knowledge of the American movie. My thanks go also to Miss Iris Barry, Mr. Jay Leyda, and Miss Helen Grey of the Museum of Modern Art Film Library, for their generous helpfulness; to the Museum for the opportunity to re-view films of the past in their collection; and to the Federal Writers' Project in New York City, which made accessible the files used by the Motion Picture Bibliography unit in the compilation of the first volume of their *Film Index*.

I also wish to thank Mr. Lee Simonson for his efforts to make this book a reality.

LEWIS JACOBS

CONTENTS

Part Five INTENSIFICATION (1919-1929)

Part Six MATURITY (1929-1939)

ILLUSTRATIONS

PART ONE

FADE-IN (1896-1903)

I

FIRST STAGES: TRADE, TECH-NIQUE, PICTURES

DURING the past half-century American movies have become a major industry, a new art growing out of science and the older arts, and a powerful social agency peculiar to modern times. Born in the laboratory, organized as a medium of expression, exploited for the entertainment of the masses, the motion picture has developed through the co-operation of scientist, artist, and business man. Each has contributed to the rise of the film, shaping its character and strengthening its effectiveness.

The years 1896-1903 saw the genesis of the movie. At first a minor commercial commodity, the motion picture groped toward a larger future—a broad business base, a technique of its own, and a mass audience. By 1903 it had achieved in some measure all these aims.

It was on April 23, 1896, that the moving picture as we know it today was seen for the first time in America. On the following day *The New York Times* [1] described its première at Koster and Bial's Music Hall (now the site of R. H. Macy & Company) in New York:

When the hall was darkened last night, a buzzing and roaring were heard in the turret and an unusually bright light fell upon the screen. Then came into view two precious blonde young persons of the variety stage, in pink and blue dresses, doing the umbrella dance with commendable celerity. Their motions were all clearly defined. When they vanished, a view of the angry surf breaking on a sandy beach near a stone pier amazed the spectators. . . . A burlesque boxing match between a tall, thin comedian and a short, fat

[1] April 24, 1896.

3

one, a comic allegory called "The Monroe Doctrine," an instant of motion in Hoyt's farce "The Milk White Flag," repeated over and over again, and a skirt dance by a tall blonde completed the views, which were all wonderfully real and singularly exhilarating.

The wonder aroused by the new invention was general. People regarded its performance as miraculous. Everyone was startled by the lifelike umbrella dance, awed at the sight of waves breaking on the screen, amused by the reproduction of vaudeville comic routines, won by the skirt dancers. "An object of magical wonder," rhapsodized W. K. L. Dickson, an associate of Edison, "the crown and flower of nineteenth century magic." [2]

Moving pictures had, in fact, already existed for some time in another, cruder form. Penny arcades had been featuring peep-show cabinets at which one person at a time, paying his penny, could revolve a drum and give a motion picture effect to fifty feet of tiny pictures that passed before his eyes. A popular form of cheap amusement, this peep show had suggested to its owners that, if many people at one time could watch the moving pictures, greater profits could be made. What was needed was a machine to throw the pictures onto a large screen. The development of the projector made such a feat possible and established motion pictures as a new kind of group entertainment.

When the projected "wonderfully real" motion pictures at Koster and Bial's created an enthusiastic stir, other vaudeville theatres throughout the country rushed to present this latest of novelties. Wherever shown, movies won immediate popularity. Lasting only a minute or two, their movement made them a "marvelous" sight, evoking awe and admiration for their faithfulness to "true-life action." Horses jumping over hurdles, Niagara Falls with its torrents plunging to rocky depths, trains rushing headlong across the screen, cooch-girls dancing, vaudeville acrobats taking their falls with aplomb, parades, boats and people hurrying or scurrying along—any isolated bit of movement became part of the movies' repertory.

Before long motion pictures had become an accepted feature on variety programs, and were occasionally gaining notice in print. Tucked away in newspaper vaudeville columns would appear such

[2] *History of the Kinetograph, Kinetoscope and Kinetophonograph.*

items as "The Vitagraph surprised its admirers by exhibiting colored pictures which were marvelously true to life." [3]

Toward the end of 1900 a single event sharply revealed the strong popular appeal and commercial value of movies. Vaudeville managers had combined into a trust to keep down the wage scale of actors. To meet the challenge, actors organized into a union, called "The White Rats" after the London actors' organization, and the union called a strike. Caught unawares, many vaudeville theatres closed. Others, determined to keep open at all costs and beat the strike, began to feature moving pictures. For the first time programs consisting solely of movies were offered to the theatrical public. To the theatre managers' great astonishment, people came —and came again. Before long the vaudeville trust declared the motion picture to be its surest weapon against "the dissolution, bankruptcy and humiliation" engendered by the strike.

Its success as a scab for vaudeville was convincing evidence of the movie's own appeal. This first substitution of movies for vaudeville anticipated by a quarter of a century the eventual near-disappearance of vaudeville itself. But the vaudeville managers lacked the imagination to take advantage of their new opportunities; it was the arcade owners who were to develop the money-making possibilities of the new medium.

Most movies had hardly advanced beyond their first attempts and continued to show similar subjects with the same reproductive technique. As the initial fascination and wonder of the audiences waned and the strike ended, managers of the better-class vaudeville theatres either abandoned the novelty entirely or presented it at the end of their programs, so that the people who did not care to see it could leave. Movies became disdained throughout the theatrical world as "chasers."

The penny-arcade owners, who had done good business with the peep-show cabinets, had constantly tried to obtain projectors and films. But in the attempt to keep it exclusive equipment had been sold only to vaudeville theatres; equipment was, besides, scarce and expensive. When the vaudeville managers sought to sell their pro-

[3] *The New York Journal*, January 1, 1900. Such colored pictures were tinted by hand.

jectors and stocks of films despite the movies' successful reception by the public during the actors' strike, arcade owners eagerly bought them. In the rear of their amusement parlors they closed off a section, filled it with rented chairs, and set up a screen for their exhibitions. They charged ten cents admission—less than vaudeville prices—and advertised "animated moving pictures."

People were at first suspicious of the darkened, partitioned area of the arcades and doubted that a real movie show would be offered at such a cheap price. Thomas L. Tally, an arcade owner in Los Angeles, thought up a scheme to convince prospective customers that his offering was genuine. He cut a hole through the partition so that people could see for themselves, before paying admission, that movies were actually being shown on a screen. The ruse worked; news of it spread, and the practice was adopted widely. Moving pictures became before long the most popular attraction in the arcades, arousing even greater enthusiasm and proving to have a far more lasting success here than in the vaudeville theatres.

The patrons of the amusement parlors were of a poor class and had little theatrical knowledge or critical judgment. They were spellbound by the jerky shadows that mysteriously evolved into a scene of a foreign land, shouted with genuine fear as the screen showed a train hurtling toward them, and were speechless at the sight of President McKinley's inauguration. The sheer impressiveness of the motion on the screen, the intrinsic eloquence of pictures which even a child could appreciate, captured their imaginations. The simplicity of movies made literacy unnecessary for understanding or enjoyment, and the cheap price put this new entertainment within the means of most wage-earners. The result was that movies became established as a cheap form of amusement for the masses; the ground had been broken for the broad base on which motion pictures were henceforth to be built.

In the next three years motion pictures ventured beyond the arcades of the cities into the hinterlands. Traveling showmen peddled movies on the open road, at street fairs, picnics, county benefits, church socials, medicine shows, in one small town after another, and they found a warm welcome everywhere. In the rapid spread of enthusiasm for films the future of the industry was vaguely foreshadowed.

In 1902 Thomas L. Tally, the man who had convinced Los Angeles customers to see movies, led the way in establishing moving pictures as distinct feature attractions. Finding them the most profitable of all his arcade amusements, he discarded other novelties, transformed his arcade into an auditorium, and began exhibiting films only, charging ten cents admission. He advertised his venture as "The Electric Theatre. For Up-to-Date High Class Motion Picture Entertainment Especially for Ladies and Children." [4]

Other arcade owners watched carefully for the outcome of Tally's enterprise. It appeared for a time that the Electric Theatre was to be none too popular. Tally, sensing a possible misunderstanding because of his theatre's title, added to the title the explanation "A Vaudeville of Motion Pictures," and he gave matinee showings at five cents. The Electric Theatre now became an auspicious success, and Tally promptly opened a second theatre.

Rumors of the success of this new type of theatre, showing movies exclusively, circulated through the country. Soon hundreds of arcade owners, showmen, and business men were converting their arcades or empty stores into movie theatres.

The following year a third innovation pushed movies further on the way toward capturing the mass-entertainment market. At the St. Louis Exposition, George C. Hale, ex-chief of the Kansas City (Missouri) Fire Department, built as a sideshow a motion picture theatre in the shape of a railroad car, patterned inside and out after a typical coach of the day, with the ticket collector dressed as a train conductor. This attraction, "Hale's Tours and Scenes of the World," began with a clanging of bells and a mechanical rocking of the theatre, simulating the motion of a train. The coach was darkened and motion pictures of landscapes, which had been taken from the rear platform of a speeding train, were flashed upon a screen. The illusion of travel was thus produced for the delight of Hale's customers.

Hale's Tours was a startling success at the Exposition. The ability of the movies to arouse strong feelings was made doubly effective

⁴ *Los Angeles Times,* April 16, 1902.

through the illusion of train travel, then an uncommon and exciting experience for ordinary people. After the Exposition closed, Hale's Tours traveled the country triumphantly. Hale himself made about two million dollars in two years' time.

With the success of store theatres, traveling picture shows, and Hale's Tours, the exhibition of movies as a specialized form of popular amusement had become securely established by the close of 1903. Disdained by more sophisticated audiences, movies were delighting the common man and were well on the way to becoming a people's art.

Rapid improvements in exhibition created a steadily increasing demand for pictures. Business men, seeing opportunities for getting rich quick through the novelty, pushed into the growing trade. Despite the attempts of many entrepreneurs to establish themselves as movie manufacturers, however, three American companies were able to monopolize the field. Edison and Biograph, which had been in the business since the peep-show days, had each bought separate key inventions at about the same time and owned the patent rights to cameras and projectors. Vitagraph had come into the field in 1899, although two of its founders, J. Stuart Blackton and Albert E. Smith, had been operating together since 1896 when Thomas Edison, not realizing how profitable movie making was to become, sold a projector to J. Stuart Blackton, a newspaper artist who had come to interview him. Blackton, with his friend Albert E. Smith, a professional magician, had converted the projector into a camera.

These three pioneer manufacturing companies served almost the entire market and schemed to keep the new and expanding field under their joint control. They refused to sell cameras to others, and Biograph was at first willing to rent only its projectors. With the mounting demand for equipment, however, other business men found ways of entrance into the trade. Some imported cameras from Europe; others disguised American inventions and sold or rented them as their own; still others, unable to get cameras, resorted to trading in ready-made films, imported and domestic. The first newcomers to get into manufacturing were William Selig and George K. Spoor of Chicago, and Sigmund Lubin of Philadelphia.

Riley Brothers and George Kleine became at this time the leading jobbers and importers.

Making movies was not yet an extensive business. A business office, a camera, and enough money to pay for the film and to cover the cameraman's modest salary were the only necessaries. Films were sold outright to the exhibitors, largely by mail order, the prices ranging from 10 to 25 cents a foot. The average film, at first running from 50 to 100 feet in length, eventually increased in length to 500 feet. Each manufacturer or jobber sent out catalogues listing his wares under major classifications, as "Views," "News Events," "Vaudeville Turns," "Incidents," "Magical Pictures." Jobbers often added to these film subjects song slides and stereopticon views. The films were described in detail and graded according to their physical condition, as the following excerpt from Riley Brothers' 1901 catalogue indicates:

These films listed are the very best quality and adequately perforated. They are clean and sharp and full of vigor. They are properly treated in the course of manufacture and do not leave the celluloid. . . . None of the subjects have been "faked." All are genuine photographs taken without prearrangement, and are consequently most natural.

Usually the selection of a program was left to the manufacturer or jobber, the exhibitor specifying only the length and general character of the subjects he wanted.

Pictures were made in the streets. There were no studios, and only crude laboratories behind the business offices. The making of pictures depended entirely upon the ingenuity and ability of the cameraman. He was director, photographer, laboratory expert, and sometimes even the leading actor. In these early years, America had few movie cameramen—at most, six. Three of these were to become important figures in the history of American motion pictures: Edwin S. Porter of the Edison Company, soon to become the leading directorial figure in the American screen world; J. Stuart Blackton of the Vitagraph Company, later an outstanding pioneer director; Billy Bitzer of Biograph, yet to be famed as the cameraman of D. W. Griffith. All worked during these years in anonymity, unknown even within the trade, but mastering the camera and the rudiments of motion picture making. The first cameraman to show individuality of technique was none of these three Americans, however, but George Melies in France. His films, particularly those from 1900 on, pointed the way for a creative technique and led to the discovery of film dramatization, which was to change the whole course of movie making.

The early cameraman's problem was simply to get a picture. Acquaintance with the tools of his trade was for the time being his main objective. The moving picture camera was bulky; its machinery often got out of order. Carrying it through the streets and around the countryside was a laborious enterprise in itself. Once set up for shooting, the camera was seldom if ever changed for another viewpoint; the whole subject was photographed in one shot, without any shift in the camera's position. A mechanical device was finally invented to overcome this rigidity of technique. It was a flexible tripod head on which the camera was supported, and it made possible the "panning" of the scene. By this means a camera could be made to move from side to side, thus photographing a wider angle of view or a moving object. The picture so taken was proudly classified in the catalogues as a "Panoramic View." One of the earliest records of such a picture appears in the Edison Catalogue for 1901-1902:

New York in a Blizzard. . . . Our camera is revolved from right to left and takes in Madison Square, Madison Square Garden, looks up Broadway from South to North, passes the Fifth Avenue Hotel and ends looking down 23rd Street West.

The same company's description of *The Great Bull Fight* proudly advertised that "with the aid of a specially designed panoramic camera . . . we are able to keep the bull within the field of our lens during the entire fight."

Not only was the camera unwieldy, but cameramen had to work in the face of other deficiencies. Lenses were slow; raw film was slow. Very bright light was needed to get a photographic impression of anything in motion. Electric light had not yet become common or adaptable enough for use. Consequently pictures were made in the strong sunlight, which produced sharp contrasts and generally harsh photographic effects. Chemical operations involved in printing and developing the film presented as large a problem as that posed by photography, and were equally as primitive. Companies maintained only the crudest of laboratories—inefficient, home-made affairs, often partitioned off from the business office. Developing and printing were unregulated, being done on hand contrivances; the finished print was coarse, scratchy, grainy, without decent photographic quality.

Made under these conditions, the first pictures to reach the screen could show hardly more than simple movements. Nothing was too trivial to photograph: people walking, trees swaying, trains speeding, horses jumping, were esteemed as good subjects. Gradually, however, movies began using larger subjects—parades, auto races, scenes of national interest. As photographic techniques improved, it became possible to film news events, sham battles, political inaugurations, prizefights, police and fire department activities. But not until about 1900, when the imported films of George Melies startled American producers, was the theatrical potentiality of the new medium realized.

One of the first American movies to attempt a dramatic presentation of a subject was *Tearing Down the Spanish Flag* (1898). In a lecture at the University of Southern California in 1929, its director, J. Stuart Blackton, divulged how it had been made:

It was taken in a 10-by-12 studio room, the background a building next door. We had a flag pole and two 18-inch flags. Smith operated the machine and I, with this very hand, grabbed the Spanish flag and tore it down from the pole and pulled the Stars and Stripes to the top of the flag pole. That was our very first dramatic picture and it is surprising how much dramatic effect it created. . . . The people went wild.

Such an approach indicated a realization—soon to become more widespread—that the movie need not be dependent upon passing events for its material nor limited to mere reporting of events.

So movie subjects began to evolve from bits of passing movement toward simple real-life scenes, from staged scenes toward drama. By 1903 movie makers were staging events and soon were to acquire the ability to tell stories of their own making.

These earliest American pictures set a precedent for all future pictures, though producers scarcely realized it at the time, by responding to the shifting interests and activities of the public. Such attention to contemporary events and fashions makes the motion picture one of the most accurate and richest sources for information about past and present. In the subject matter of movies for the last forty-odd years, can be gleaned the changing values, standards, and points of view of twentieth-century America in flux.

The content of American motion pictures since their inception has been, in fact, not only an important historical source but a stimulant and educator to American life itself. Besides offering a social occasion and an emotional experience, they supplied audiences with information and ideas. Immigration was at its peak in 1902-1903, and the movies gave the newcomers, particularly, a respect for American law and order, an understanding of civic organizations, pride in citizenship and in the American commonwealth. Movies acquainted them with current happenings at home and abroad. Because the uncritical movie-goers were deeply impressed by what they saw in the photographs and accepted it as the real thing, the movies were powerful and persuasive. More vividly than any other single agency they revealed the social topography of America to the immigrant, to the poor, and to the country folk. Thus from the outset movies were, besides a commodity and developing craft, a social agency.

Most of these early films were simple reports of international events, world figures, foreign countries, headlines of the moment, and local interests. Through short one- and two-minute movies, film journalists expressed the prevalent optimism, the pride in American progress, the new interest in the common man, the rising assertiveness of labor, America's mounting interest in foreign affairs, and the foibles of the newly recognized "machine age." The two wars being waged on the international front were exploited colorfully if not authentically. The Boer War appeared on the screen in a number of pro-English films. That these were aimed at influencing American popular opinion is evident in the manufac-

The forerunner of the movie theatre, a Kinetoscope, Phonograph, and Graphophone Arcade
about 1900. Peep-show cabinets run by hand
were discarded for the moving picture projector.

Tableau 4: The pumpkin changes to a carriage, from George Melies' *Cinderella* (1900), the picture which first showed the theatrical possibilities of "real life motion pictures" to America. It was widely "duped" by local producers and sold under their own imprint.

turer's description [5] of *Arundel Castle Leaving for Transvaal with British Troops:*

British soldiers waving and bidding adieu to friends and dear ones left behind. This picture never fails to deeply impress any observer with any loyalty in his veins.

English Army in the Battlefield depicted the "humanitarian work of the English Army in South Africa after a battle." [6] *Boers Bringing in Prisoners* was presented to show how frightfully brutal the Boers were.

The other foreign war, the Boxer Rebellion in China, interested America more directly. Dewey, Hay, and the Open Door were perhaps the most talked of people and issues of the day, and movies helped to keep the pot boiling. The Edison Catalogue [7] boosted its *Boxer Massacres in Pekin* on the grounds that the event had

turned the eyes of the civilized world toward China. Public interest was intensely aroused and people eagerly appreciate any pictures that relate to the locality in which the war in China was prosecuted.

The objectivity of *Scene in Legation Street, Shanghai,* showing "a number of Europeans and Americans being driven down the thoroughfare in native rickshaws and wheelbarrows" [8] was countered by the bias in *Street Scene in Pekin:* "Scenes taken on the ground in front of the Legation showing British police dispersing a crowd of unruly citizens." [9]

Such attention to the foreign wars inspired recognition of the movies by newspapers, and a realization of the impressiveness of the motion picture. *Leslie's Weekly* [10] editorialized:

The American Biograph is taking a prominent part in the two wars now occupying the center of the world's stage, and the pictures which are being shown at Keith's Theatre in New York and other leading houses throughout the country, are of intense interest. . . . We are promised some vivid, soul-stirring pictures of actual, gruesome war. A written description is always the point of view of the correspondent. But the Biograph camera does not lie

---

[5] Edison Catalogue, 1901.   [6] *Ibid.*   [7] For 1901.
[8] Edison Catalogue, 1901.   [9] *Ibid.*   [10] January 6, 1900.

and we form our judgment of this and that as we watch the magic of the screen.

Such a pat on the back for the crude movie, coming from a contemporary of the noted war correspondents Stephen Crane, Frank Norris, and Richard Harding Davis, was tribute indeed.

Activities of the United States in the West Indies and South America, and then the Spanish-American War, were likewise reflected and discussed on the screen. *Tearing Down the Spanish Flag* was posed to stimulate national patriotism. *The Campaign in Cuba* series included scenes of American sailors *Landing Under Fire* and *The Battle of San Juan Hill* and the ensuing victory, *Our Flag Is There to Stay!* This series was presented to the public as genuine, but Cameraman F. L. Donoghue, recalling those days years later,[11] said that almost all war scenes in this film, as in others, were manufactured on the shores of New Jersey. The Edison Catalogue of 1901-1902 diplomatically informed exhibitors:

We are indebted to the fearless activity of our artist, Mr. William Paley, for the following war views taken on Cuban soil. Under the protection of a special correspondent's pass given by the United States Government, he improved the occasions as they presented themselves with gratifying results, as shown in the excellent films we are now offering the public.

The Pan-American Series indicated the United States' desire to promote friendly relations with Latin neighbors. It offered "a condensed film trip around the Pan-American Exposition for the purpose of viewing the exterior of the buildings with as little fatigue as possible." [12]

Views of foreign countries and foreign notables in the limelight of news events were popular on the screen. The Dreyfus case reached American shores in the imported pictures of George Melies: *Dreyfus' Court Martial, Devil's Island, Suicide of Colonel Henry, Landing of Dreyfus at Guileron, The Degradation of Dreyfus*, and *Dreyfus Leaving the Lycée for Jail. The Funeral of Queen Victoria, King Edward, The Kaiser Reviewing His Troops*, and *Czar Nicholas Walking in His Summer Palace* pointed the interest in

[11] *The New York Journal*, January 29, 1937. [12] Edison Catalogue, 1901.

England and Germany and Russia. These films were reinforced by views of foreign scenery. In the words of the Edison Catalogue,[13]

The established popularity of moving pictures led Mr. Edison to believe that a series of views photographed in various parts of the world would prove a most valuable addition to our list of subjects, thus combining instruction with interest. . . . We therefore sent an efficient corps of photographers on an extended tour, and the results are now placed before the public.

One of the biggest news events in 1902, the eruption of Mt. Pelée on Martinique, was faked for the screen by photographing a beer barrel exploding in the sun: an informative if not an actual depiction of the event.

As for America, movies highlighted national figures, news events, and local affairs and interests. The career and personality of President McKinley became commonly known through *McKinley's Inauguration*, *Speech at Panama Pacific Exposition*, and *Funeral Cortege*. Such headline catastrophes as the *Destruction of the Standard Oil Company Plant at Bayonne* (1900) and the *Galveston Cyclone* (1900) were scoops indeed for these early film journalists. They pointed with particular pride to their activities in the cyclone disaster:

At the first news of the disaster by cyclone and tidal wave that devastated Galveston on Saturday, September 8, 1900, we equipped a party of photographers, and sent them by special train to the scene of the ruins. Arriving at the scene of desolation shortly after the storm had swept over that city, our party succeeded at the risk of life and limb in taking about a thousand feet of moving pictures. In spite of the fact that Galveston was under martial law and that photographers were shot down at sight by the excited police guards, a very wide range of subjects have been secured.[14]

Popular interest in the great metropolises at the turn of the century was exploited to the full. That interest was evidenced in an editorial in *Leslie's Weekly*[15] which regretted the "tendency of our population to drift toward cities and to abandon the pleasant and healthful surroundings of country life." People were fascinated

[13] For 1901.   [14] Edison Catalogue, 1901.   [15] February 3, 1900.

by New York City in particular. Hundreds of films fed their appetite with views of *Herald Square, Madison Square, Skyscrapers, Central Park, Hotels, The Ghetto, The Bowery, Chinatown.* Such movies helped to establish New York in the minds of Americans as the Mecca of culture, opportunity, art, industry, and finance, as well as the Melting Pot of the World.

A detailed account of the metropolis was prepared by the Kleine Optical Company in 1903 for a film-slide-lecture on "The Lights and Shadows of a Great City." Pictures included such features of the tenderloin as *Pool Playing, Card Playing, 10-Cent Lodging House, Arrest for Thieving, Pawn Shop, Police Patrol Wagon, Panoramic View of the Ghetto, Dancing on the Bowery, Bowery 5-Cent Shine, The Burglar on the Roof, A Charitable Institution.* Accompanying subjects for the lecture were moral tracts on drink (comparing the anatomical diagrams of *The Stomach of a Drunkard* and *The Stomach of a Temperate Man*); on labor (*The Factory, Labor Agitators*); on the home (*A Happy Home*); and on the church (*The Church*). Before long movie exhibitors were to use such moral tracts to the exclusion of almost everything else.

Besides the growth of large cities, movies recorded for the eye the latest industrial inventions, the newest express trains, the most recent fire apparatus, automobiles, bicycles, skyscrapers, the improved electrically driven street cars, the Atlantic City boardwalk, bathing and shooting the chutes at the beaches. Hundreds of films were devoted to the newly organized fire and police organizations, showing their dangerous and heroic activities and mirroring the prestige such civic functionaries had in the eyes of the populace. Movie catalogues for these years list scores of pictures of city fire and police departments rescuing the imperiled, dashing off to fires, catching criminals, parading, showing off their latest equipment. *The Boston Horseless Fire Department, Parade of the Philadelphia Volunteer Fire Department, The Fire Department of Albany, South Orange,* etc., *Morning Fire Alarm, The Life of an American Fireman, A Quick Hitch,* are representative titles.

Movies of sports events, seasides, trains, waterfalls, winter scenes, bathing, coach riding and horses, combats, summer resorts, and vaudeville skits reveal other popular interests of the day. Among the most popular subjects were the *Jeffries-Ruhlin Sparring Contest* (which was sold in separate rounds, about 200 feet to each round, the whole series being 1,100 feet long). *Shamrock Yacht Races, Bicycle Parade,* and *Great Bull Fight* (fought in Mexico City before President Diaz and his cabinet, February 2, 1902) were other well-liked films.

At a time when *Leslie's Weekly* [16] was able to report,

> All . . . variety theatres and especially the all-day houses like Proctor's, Keith's and Tony Pastor's, find it difficult to accommodate the crowds of pleasure-seekers that visit them, especially in the evening,

the screen naturally recorded in great numbers the most popular vaudeville acts: of acrobats, jugglers, magicians, and dancers; of Eva Tanguay (*Her Sambo Dance*), Cissy Fitzgerald ("her famous wink adds to the interest of the picture" [17]), Kid Foley and Sailor Lil (*The Tough Dance* . . . "the popular dance of the Bowery in which they claim to be the champions" [18]), and Fatima (*Coochee-Coochee Dance.* "This is the lady whose graceful interpretations of the poetry of motion has made this dance so popular of recent years." [19])

Improvised incidents and short skits, which began to occupy the screen before movie story-telling was invented, are as revelatory of these years as most historical documents. In these short movies the ideas, aspirations, and social issues of the day were given lively expression. The adventures, pornography, fairy tales, religious spectacles, and slapstick foolery that graced these pictures testify to the outlook and naïveté of the non-theatrical movie audience.

The central figure of adventure comedies was always the common man or woman—the farmer, fireman, policeman, housewife, stenographer, clerk, servant, cook, rube, or old maid. Such characters were selected because the audiences and film makers alike were themselves of this class, and because of the growing popular interest in the everyday person. As Mark Sullivan pointed out,[20] "the eleva-

[16] May 26, 1900.   [17] Edison Catalogue, 1901.   [18] *Ibid.*
[19] *Ibid.*   [20] In *Our Times,* "The Turn of the Century," page 363.

tion of the common man appeared in most of the discriminating
discussions [in periodicals in 1900] of what had been accomplished."

The tramp reappeared time and again as the hero of screen adventures. How much such figures were in the public eye is suggested by an item in *Leslie's Weekly:*[21] "New York's Army of
Paupers. It Numbers Over 100,000 and Is Larger Than the Population of Several Important Cities and Some of Our States."

Typical of the tramp pictures were the Weary Willie and Happy
Hooligan series. According to the Edison Catalogue, the Happy
Hooligan series told how "a most disreputable-looking tramp has
a number of wonderful and side-splitting adventures, from which
however he always emerges triumphant, only to get into trouble
by a new prank." This series, one of the most popular, included
such tales as *Happy Hooligan with the Summer Girls, Hooligan
Causes a Sensation, Hooligan Assists the Magician, Hooligan Takes
His Annual Bath, Hooligan's Narrow Escape.* Each was from 50
to 75 feet long, consisting of a single incident with a climax. *Happy
Hooligan Has Troubles with the Cook* is typical:

Mr. Hooligan introduces himself to the audience and also to a
large juicy apple pie which rests temptingly on the window sill.
Happy Hooligan slouches around the corner of the house, and
spying the pie, gets outside of it. Having finished the pie, he turns
his attention to a large pan on the window sill, full of ready mixed
batter and flour. This he pulls over on his head and is immediately
enveloped in a cloud of white flour dust just as the cook appears
in the window and discovers him. She promptly douses poor Hooligan with water.[22]

Other popular series were *The Adventures of Jones, The Farmer
(The Farmer and the Bad Boys, How Uncle Josh Defeated the
Badgers), The Rube (Two Rubes at the Theatre, At the Moving
Picture Show), The Old Maid,* and *Grandma and Grandpa.* All
caricatured the foibles of everyday life in comic-strip style.

Considerable pornography was sneaked into some of these early
staged films. They were called "Teasers." *Making Love in a Hammock, Love in a Broker's Office,* and *Lovers Interrupted* were

21 February 10, 1900.   22 Edison Catalogue, 1901.

humorous skits of illicit lovemaking, with the wife arriving or the hammock collapsing at the climactic moment. *Lover's Scene* and *The Kiss* series (featuring a May Irwin-John Rice kiss and the "Bowery Kiss" by Kid Foley and Sailor Lil) were more pictorial presentations of "leading exponents of the art of artistical embraces."

Pictures of the strictly off-color variety soon began to diminish in number. Emphasis turned more and more to magical effects, particularly after the success of Melies' fantastic and satiric pictures was noted. *Cinderella, The One-Man Band, The Christmas Dream, Red Riding Hood,* and *A Maiden's Prayer* were all in the fairy-tale tradition. *What Is Home Without a Boarder* and *A Trip to the Moon,* on the other hand, expressed quite as fantastically a growing cynicism, particularly in regard to supernatural scientific wonders then being prophesied extravagantly.

Other films catered to the religious interests of audiences. Movies of Bible stories glorified humility, charity, virtue. One of the longest films of 1903 was *The Passion Play,* totaling 2,150 feet, more than ten times the length of the average movie of that year. From the prolific camera of George Melies came religious subjects treated more imaginatively if less reverently. *The Devil in a Convent, Christ Walking on Water, The Seven Capital Sins,* headed an entire section in Melies' catalogue devoted to religious subjects.

Fewer in number were movies taking up social topics of the day. Even in this early stage of the movies' existence, such subjects, surprisingly enough, found their way onto the screen. With Mrs. Catt, Susan B. Anthony, and Carrie Nation in the forefront of the women's movement for independence, with leading newspapers and periodicals incorporating special women's sections in its pages, with writers satirizing the "new woman," movies likewise took up the issue. *The Kansas Saloon Smashers* and *Why Mr. Nation Wants a Divorce,* films a little more than a minute long, ridiculed woman's demand for political rights and showed what would happen to the home if she got them.

No newspaper editorial could have been more forceful than these two films. *The Kansas Saloon Smashers* showed a gilded saloon with a fancy bar behind which a nobby bartender is dispensing drinks. An Irishman enters and has a huge pail filled with beer. Then Mrs. Carrie Nation and her followers burst into the saloon with their hatchets. One of the followers jams the Irishman's hat down over his eyes and another douses him with his own pail of beer. In the meantime Carrie Nation and her gang wreck the saloon, smashing mirrors, bottles, cash register, and fixtures. The bartender plays a stream on Mrs. Nation, and as she backs away from the counter a policeman enters and proceeds to hustle out both raiders and raided.[23]

Equally hilarious and not less pointed was *Why Mr. Nation Wants a Divorce:*

The scene opens in a bedroom of Mr. Nation, husband of the famous Carrie Nation, the Kansas Saloon Smasher. Mr. Nation suddenly arises from the bed and picks a crying infant from a cradle, and walks it up and down the floor to subdue its squealing. He suddenly steps upon a tack and becomes infuriated, throwing the baby back into the cradle. Then a small boy in the bed demands his attention. The overworked husband becomes exasperated, and seizes a bottle of spirits which happens to be in the room. Just then Mrs. Nation enters and is horrified at seeing her husband drinking from a bottle. She smashes the bottle to the floor, and turning her husband over her knee spanks him soundly.[24]

Such films were among the first attempts to dramatize current affairs. In picturing the world about them, they naturally presented points of view and prejudices, suggesting, informing, and persuading, and became one of the most vital influences in their times.

American values and standards in social conduct, from clothes to goals in life, began to be expressed, not always intentionally. *Weary Willie in the Park* amused the audience by showing

a seat almost full of ladies and gentlemen. Dirty tramp approaches; squeezes in; lady next to him leaves immediately; tramp moves up, and each lady and gentleman leaves in turn until the tramp has the seat to himself.[25]

Mingled with the humor here was the patent lesson that a tramp is a social outcast. If the picture flattered the audience by hinting

---

[23] Edison Catalogue, 1901.   [24] *Ibid.*   [25] *Ibid.*

that they were better people than Willie, it also intensified their subconscious determination never to sink to such a low condition. The difference between the appearance of the "dirty tramp" and the "ladies and gentlemen" was, although secondary to the comedy, exemplary.

Thus movies from their beginnings presented more than cheap entertainment. From the outset, as can be seen, they were three things: a commodity, a craft, and a social force. These different aspects of the new medium were to affect the course, character, and development of one another. Being a commodity, the movie depended for its existence primarily upon the money it made; as a potential art, it demanded new techniques; as a social force, it was to represent both business and art, with an influence proportional to its own genius and vitality.

In 1895 W. K. L. Dickson had said: [26]

From what conceivable phase of the future can the movie be debarred? In the promotion of business interests, in the advancement of science, in the revelation of unguessed worlds, in its educational and re-creative process, and in its ability to immortalize our fleeting but beloved associations, the kinematograph stands foremost among the creations of modern inventive genius.

The next years were to see this prophecy begin to take the form of reality.

[26] *History of the Kinetograph, Kinetoscope, and Kinetophonograph.*

II

GEORGE MELIES: "ARTIFICIALLY ARRANGED SCENES"

IT is with a Frenchman that the American film as an art begins. The first to exploit the medium as a means of personal expression, George Melies started movies on a new course, broadened their scope, and focused attention upon their creative potentialities. Imported into America when American movies, derisively nicknamed "chasers," were simply pictures of events, his innovations were revolutionary. George Melies, imaginative, resourceful, skillful, was the movies' first great craftsman and the father of its theatrical traditions.

Melies discovered magic in the motion picture camera. He turned its lens away from reality—from mere reporting—to fantasy and genuine creation. He also brought to movie making, with his system of "artificially arranged scenes," a conception of organization which was to change the haphazard, improvisational methods of the Americans and fertilize their technique. He enriched movies by introducing many theatrical elements: costuming, settings, professional actors. To these formal elements he added a new source of subject matter, literature, which widened the range of film subjects.

In 1896 George Melies, thirty-four years old, was a jack-of-all-trades—caricaturist for an anti-Boulangist paper, theatrical producer, actor, scenic painter at the Théâtre Houdin, and professional magician. This was the year in which he turned to moving pictures. From then until the outbreak of the World War he devoted himself to his adopted art. "Film making," he wrote,

offers such a variety of pursuits, demands such a quantity of work of all kinds, and claims so sustained an attention, that I did not hesitate to proclaim it the most attractive and fascinating of all the arts.[1]

At first Melies roamed the streets with his camera, "shooting" people, trains, soldiers—anything that moved—for the mere pleasure of it. One day while he was photographing a Paris street scene his camera jammed; the film had caught inside the aperture gate. Melies cleared the gate, readjusted the film, and resumed shooting. When the film was projected later, he was surprised to see on the screen a bus suddenly turn into a hearse. The bus he had been photographing when the camera jammed had gone its way while he was readjusting the camera, and in its place a hearse had appeared. When Melies had started shooting again, the camera had taken a picture of the hearse on the same bit of film and in the same place where the bus had been photographed.

Being a professional magician, Melies was greatly excited by the coincidence. He at once visualized the superior "supernatural" capacities of the moving picture as compared to the ordinary magician. Investigating camera possibilities further, he discovered many more devices for trick effects—effects that were to astound the movie world for many years.

He now went into movie making in earnest. By 1900 he had made over two hundred "magical, mystical and trick films," each a minute or two long. Imported into the United States, these unique and amazing movies were immediately singled out by the public and became the most popular of all screen entertainments. So popular were they, and so unmatchable, that American manufacturers made copies or "dupes" and sold them under new names as their own.

Melies' aim in these films was to mystify and startle. His prowess as a magician found curious expression in his earliest efforts: *The Vanishing Lady, The Haunted Castle, The Laboratory of Mephistopheles, A Hypnotist at Work, Cagliostro's Mirror, The Bewitched Inn, Conjurer Making 10 Hats in 60 Seconds.* These films showed people disappearing magically, cut in half, flying through the air; apparitions taking horrible shapes; animals turning into human beings, and human beings into animals. Typical of his

[1] Quoted by Stuart Legg, in *World Film News*, March 1938.

method was his 185th film, *The Devil in a Convent*, a religious fantasy

to illustrate the Triumph of Christianity over Satan . . . while it is quite fantastical and religious, there is not the least action in the film which would be obnoxious or shock the most sensitive audience.[2]

The movie opened by showing the Devil, followed by an imp, jumping from the font of holy water in the interior of a convent.

Both are transformed into a priest and choir boy. They then summon the nuns to service and while preaching change themselves back to their natural shapes, frightening the nuns out of their wits. The Devil then transforms the church to resemble Hell and the nuns flee for their lives. Many imps appear and dance wildly round the Devil, but are finally driven off by the ghosts of departed nuns, leaving only the Devil. Suddenly an apparition of St. George appears and in a struggle with His Satanic Majesty overcomes him, driving him off to Hell and ending the film with a cloud-burst of smoke.

Picture-card sermon though it was meant to be, the film displayed Melies' ingenious and individual flair for the unreal and his unusual perception of the camera's capabilities. Like all other films of that day, its entire action was confined within a single scene, as if it were a stage presentation. Unlike others, however, it was distinguished by the camera tricks that only Melies had mastered: double exposures, masks, stop-motions, reverse shootings, fast and slow motion, animation, fades, dissolves. Such effects, which made American producers sigh with envy, were not to become generally understood until years later.

His skill developing, Melies undertook ever more elaborate and more ambitious enterprises. From single scenes he turned to stories, written by himself or adapted from literature, and including many scenes. Such undertakings required preliminary organization of the subject matter: scenes had to be planned and staged in advance so as to tell a story logically. Melies himself called the method he devised "artificially arranged scenes." A novel and advanced ap-

[2] Melies "Star" Catalogue, 1900-1901.

proach to movies, it was to work profound changes in the methods of American film makers, who as yet neglected prearrangement of the scenes and, in fact, boasted that none of their subjects were "faked."

Melies' first outstanding and successful realization of his new method, *Cinderella,* appeared at the close of 1900. This picture was an unprecedented accomplishment, a remarkable advance beyond the formlessness of other current films. High lights of the fairy tale, in a series of twenty "motion tableaux," as Melies labeled the scenes, had been selected, staged, and photographed progressively. Following is Melies' original plan: [3]

1. Cinderella in the Kitchen
2. The Fairy
3. The Transformation of the Rat
4. The Pumpkin Changes to a Carriage
5. The Ball at the King's Palace
6. The Hour of Midnight
7. The Bedroom of Cinderella
8. The Dance of the Clocks
9. The Prince and the Slipper
10. The Godmother of Cinderella
11. The Prince and Cinderella
12. Arrival at the Church
13. The Wedding
14. Cinderella's Sisters
15. The King
16. The Nuptial Cortege
17. The Bride's Ballet
18. The Celestial Spheres
19. The Transformation
20. The Triumph of Cinderella

This effort of Melies illustrated rather than re-created the fairy tale. Yet, primitive though it was, the order of the scenes did form a coherent, logical, and progressive continuity. A new way of making moving pictures had been invented. Scenes could now be staged and selected specially for the camera, and the movie maker could control both the material and its arrangement. Movie making,

[3] As given in his "Star" Catalogue, 1900-1901.

heretofore an unselective process, became with "artificially arranged scenes" a creative enterprise, involving planning, selection, direction, and control of material and instruments, and the fusing of all to produce a single effect. Possible material which had heretofore been ignored was now recognized as being within the movies' range.

Cinderella introduced, moreover, devices of the stage. Elaborate settings, special costumes, carefully composed tableaux, professional acting, and many "dissolving scenic effects, ballets, and marches" gave the film a theatrical grandeur that distinguished it above all its competitors.

In America *Cinderella* was received enthusiastically. The public, rejoicing in the familiar rags-to-riches fable, was enthralled by its elegant backgrounds, spectacular staging, and magical camera effects. Vaudeville managers ran the movie again and again on their programs. Even better-grade theatres which had stopped showing "living pictures" exhibited *Cinderella* with pride. American manufacturers hastened to "dupe" the film and sell it as their own. The unusual success of the picture, in fact, not only spurred American movie makers to improve their own product but, at a time when movies needed encouragement, improved their reputation.

Success made Melies the more ambitious. He busied himself with a variety of stories with more elaborate "artificially arranged scenes," more imaginative conceptions of theatrical values. *Joan of Arc* was in twelve scenes, with "500 persons enacting the tableaux, all superbly costumed." *The Christmas Dream* had twenty scenes, "dissolving effects, tricks, spectacular tableaux, snow scenes, ballets, night effects and marches." *Off to Bloomingdale Asylum* was a fantastic tale that might have come out of a surrealist's anthology:

An omnibus drawn by an extraordinary mechanical horse is driven by four Negroes. The horse kicks and upsets the Negroes, who falling are changed into white clowns. They begin slapping each other's faces and by the blows become black again. Kicking each other, they become white once more. Suddenly they are all merged into one gigantic Negro, and when he refuses to pay his carfare, the conductor sets fire to the omnibus, and the Negro bursts into a thousand pieces.[4]

4 Melies "Star" Catalogue, 1902.

The Seven Deadly Sins, Bluebeard, Red Riding Hood, The Maiden's Paradise, were other pictures with picturesque content, imaginative camera treatment, and theatrical effects.

Unique and effective though these films were, Melies in 1902 produced another that surpassed any of his previous achievements. This movie, called *A Trip to the Moon,* established him conclusively as the dominant creative imagination in motion pictures. His four-hundredth film, it was 825 feet long, twice the length of *Cinderella* and at least three times the length of the average movie of the day. It was advertised in his "Star" Catalogue of 1902-1903 as "Ten extraordinary and fantastical cinematographic series in thirty scenes." Certainly it was an eloquent display of his fertile imagination and the graphic possibilities of the motion picture camera for fantasy and satire.

Based on *From the Earth to the Moon and Around the Moon,* the Jules Verne story, *A Trip to the Moon* charmingly lampooned the scientific and mechanical interests of the new century. Melies' experience as a caricaturist enabled him to depict wittily the lunar dream world of the professors and the fantastic hopes of some of the scientific societies. The astronomers who take the journey to the moon are foppish; their preparations are ridiculous. The start from their textbook world with solemn ceremonies, their entry into the moon—right into its eye—and their meeting with the Selenites were nonsense of a high order. Their inglorious return to earth and their reception as heroes—they are crowned and decorated—ends the extravaganza, dispelling the dream atmosphere that has been carefully created.

The scenario for *A Trip to the Moon,* written by Melies himself, indicates his order of "artificially arranged scenes," but the bald listing hardly suggests his imaginative intent, the film's rich visual effects, the ingenuity of the camera devices, or the quality of the film's unique style. The scenario follows: [5]

1. The scientific congress at the Astronomic Club.
2. Planning the trip. Appointing the explorers and servants. Farewell.

[5] From the "Star" Catalogue, 1903.

3. The workshops. Constructing the projectile.
4. The foundries. The chimney-stacks. The casting of the monster gun.
5. The astronomers enter the shell.
6. Loading the gun.
7. The monster gun. March past the gunners. Fire!!! Saluting the flag.
8. The flight through space. Approaching the moon.
9. Landed right in the eye!!!
10. Flight of the shell into the moon. Appearance of the earth from the moon.
11. The plain of craters. Volcanic eruption.
12. The dream (the Solies, the Great Bear, Phoebus, the Twin Sisters, Saturna).
13. The snowstorm.
14. 40 degrees below zero. Descending a lunar crater.
15. Into the interior of the moon. The giant mushroom grotto.
16. Encounter with the Selenites. Homeric flight.
17. Prisoners!!!
18. The kingdom of the moon. The Selenite army.
19. The flight.
20. Wild pursuit.
21. The astronomers find the shell again. Departure from the moon.
22. Vertical drop into space.
23. Splashing into the open sea.
24. At the bottom of the ocean.
25. The rescue. Return to port.
26. The great fête. Triumphal march past.
27. Crowning and decorating the heroes of the trip.
28. Procession of Marines and the Fire Brigade.
29. Inauguration of the commemorative statue by the manager and the council.
30. Public rejoicings.

In every respect *A Trip to the Moon* towered above the standard production of the day. American pictures, despite two years of competition with Melies' films, were still absurdly poor. Porter's efforts for the Edison Company were still confined to reproductions of vaudeville skits and scenes of local interest. Blackton of Vitagraph, when not turning out comic-strip novelties, was continuing to make his fake news events; Bitzer and McCutcheon of Biograph were shooting similar subjects. In comparison with such "camera copying," Melies' films were monumental, quite unmatched for style, ingenuity, and imagination.

Some idea of the intricate creative labor that went into *A Trip to the Moon* can be gathered from a letter Melies wrote in 1930 to Jean LeRoy, who asked for details: [6]

I made myself the model sculptured terra cotta and the plaster moldings. . . . The entire cost was about 10,000 francs, a sum relatively high for the time, caused especially by the mechanical sceneries and principally by the cost of the cardboard and canvas costumes made for the Selenites . . . all those articles being made especially and consequently expensive. . . .

There were not yet stars amongst the artists; their names were never known or written in bills or advertisements. The people employed . . . were entirely acrobats, girls and singers coming from the music halls, the theatrical actors having not yet accepted to play in cinema films, as they considered the motion pictures much below the theatre. They came only later, when they knew that music hall people gained more money in performing films than themselves in playing in theatres. . . . Two years after, my office was, every night, full of theatrical people coming for asking to be engaged. I remember that . . . the Moon (the Woman in the Crescent) was Bleuette Bernon, music hall singer, the Stars * were ballet girls, from Théâtre Du Châtelet—and the men (principal ones) Victor André of the Cluny Theâtre, Delpierre, Farjaux-Kelm-Brunnet, music hall singers, and myself. The Sélenites were acrobats from Folies Bergère.

Not only had Melies rewritten Jules Verne's story, designed and painted the sets, acted the principal character, directed and organized the film, but he had personally taken care of the business problems. He had hired the cast, designed the costumes, overseen the developing and printing of the film, and financed and sold the production. A prolific and original worker, Melies was also a precise and forward-looking one.

American manufacturers, pouncing on *A Trip to the Moon*, "duped" it over and over again. Melies tried to halt such infringements by publishing in his 1903 catalogue to the trade the following warning:

George Melies, a proprietor and manager of the Theatre Robert Houdin, Paris, is the originator of the class of cinematographic films

[6] Now in possession of the Museum of Modern Art Film Library.

which are made from artificially arranged scenes, the creation of which has given new life to the trade at a time when it was dying out. He conceived the idea of portraying magical and mystical views, and his creations have been imitated without success ever since.

A great number of French, English and American manufacturers of film who are searching for novelties, but lack the ingenuity to produce them, have found it easier and more economical to advertise their poor copies, that is, duplicate prints of Melies' original film, as their own original conceptions. This accounts for the simultaneous appearance in several issues of a well-known New York paper of advertisements of the celebrated *Trip to the Moon* by four or five different concerns, each pretending to be its creator. All these pretensions are false. . . .

This modest enough document sheds light on Melies' awareness of his importance in the motion picture world and spotlights the brazen practices of his competitors.

For the next two years Melies continued to startle movie-goers with similar "fantastical fantasies." *Gulliver's Travels, Beelzebub's Daughters, The Inn Where No Man Rests, Fairyland or The Kingdom of the Fairies*—the first movie to have a musical score at its opening—and the amazing *Damnation of Faust*, inspired by Berlioz's celebrated song poem, were among the most imaginative and resourceful of the hundreds of distinguished films Melies produced. Still emphasizing artificially arranged scenes as his unique style, these pictures intensified the envy among American movie makers and stirred them to scrutinize their own pictures more closely.

In 1904 appeared Melies' most ambitious and costliest ($7,500) undertaking, *The Impossible Voyage*. This film, like his *Trip to the Moon*, was a satire on scientific societies, but it was far more self-conscious. In forty "motion tableaux" and 1,233 feet of film—Melies' longest to date—its incredible story told of

The Institute of Incoherent Geography and how they discussed the proposed voyage of a new machine which must surpass in conception and invention all previous expeditions of the learned world.[7]

Its farcical intent is apparent not only in the names Melies gave his savants but in their ludicrous adventures. "Under the Presidency of

[7] Melies "Star" Catalogue, 1904-1905.

Professor Polehunter, assisted by Secretary Rattlebrains, and Vice-President Humbug, the Institutes plan a trip of the world."

The conception is in the best Disney fashion, with the scientists poring madly over maps, studying fantastic charts, and examining machines in "Engineer Crazyloff's machine shop." With a great flourish, the learned group finally take off, "employing all the known devices of locomotion—automobiles, dirigibles, balloons, submarines, boats, rockets, etc." And now their adventures begin. "At three hundred miles an hour," they visit the rising sun and the aurora borealis, pass through a solar eruption, get frozen in a heavenly embankment, are thawed out by an explosion, and eventually land on earth again to receive decorations for their brilliant voyage.

This film expressed all of Melies' talents. In it his feeling for caricature, painting, theatrical invention, and camera science became triumphant. The complexity of his tricks, his resourcefulness with mechanical contrivances, the imaginativeness of the settings, and the sumptuous tableaux made the film a masterpiece for its day.

Though superior to his former efforts, *The Impossible Voyage* was overshadowed by the debut of a far more revolutionary film, Edwin S. Porter's *The Great Train Robbery*, which had come to the screen some months earlier but was still commanding the attention of the public. This American film, itself inspired by Melies' contributions, was more vigorous in both style and content than any of the Frenchman's pictures, and its subject matter was more intrinsically interesting to Americans. Melies' position as the leader in motion pictures was now taken by Porter. The Frenchman's films, until now enormously popular, began to fall behind the more dramatic productions of the American.

Melies continued to make pictures until the outbreak of the World War. But each year after 1904 saw his reputation failing before new techniques, new men, new ideas. He was gradually all but forgotten. Struggling to meet a growing American competition, he turned away from his own unique style and subject matter to imitate, futilely, those of the Americans. *Humanity Through the Ages*, made in 1907 at the time of the Hague Peace Conference, and *The Conquest of the Pole*, made in 1912, were among his last distinguished efforts to regain some of his former prestige.

Melies was defeated not only by innovations in movies themselves but by innovations in their distribution. The rental method of distribution was proving its efficiency. Melies, who still sold his films outright to exhibitors, found it difficult to recoup even his costs. An added burden fell upon him when his branch in America was robbed of three hundred negatives.

Everywhere competition forced Melies to the wall. Disdaining American business methods, he failed to keep up with them. By 1914, retiring more and more from the main scene of competition, he had become just a novelty- and travel-picture producer. When war broke out four years later, his place of business in France was commandeered by the government. He was now in a desperate plight: too poor to rent a new office or to move his stock of negatives, he was forced to sell his films to a junk dealer and quit the business.

For fourteen years thereafter no one heard of Melies. Then in 1928 he was recognized in the streets of Paris selling newspapers. Friends bought him a tobacco-and-candy kiosk. In 1933, when he was too old to run his small stand any longer, the Chambre Syndicale Française du Cinématographe, which he had founded in 1897 and of which he had been president for ten years, sent him to a home for destitute actors. He died January 22, 1938, at the age of 77. The expenses of his funeral were defrayed by French and English film workers.

The significance of Melies in the life of the motion picture industry can hardly be exaggerated. His discovery of the camera's unique resources and his "artificially arranged scenes" freed the movie art from the slavery of dull imitation. He was the dean of motion picture directors, the pioneer in film organization, the first movie artist. He brought new subject matter and many theatrical devices to films, endowing everything he touched with individuality and flavor. Never low or cheap in appeal, his films never exploited the off-color gag or the vulgarities of the "embarrassing situation," favorite resorts of his competitors. He was the first artisan in the industry to merit serious attention; his efforts earned for the motion picture respect and admiration, and were to exert for years an elevating influence on American productions. It was through this ingenious Frenchman's achievements that American movies in 1903 could begin to take on the qualities of an art.

PART TWO

FOUNDATIONS (1903-1908)

III

ART: EDWIN S. PORTER AND THE EDITING PRINCIPLE

IF George Melies was the first to "push the cinema toward the theatrical way," as he claimed, then Edwin S. Porter was the first to push the cinema toward the cinematic way. Generally acknowledged today as the father of the story film, he made more than fictional contributions to movie tradition. It was Porter who discovered that the art of motion pictures depends on the continuity of shots, not on the shots alone. Not content with Melies' artificially arranged scenes, Porter distinguished the movies from other theatrical forms and gave them the invention of editing. Almost all motion picture developments since Porter's discovery spring from the principle of editing, which is the basis of motion picture artistry.

Significant for his genius for structural technique, Porter is equally noteworthy for his eye for content. Unlike Melies, who made fantasies, Porter turned to the real world for subject matter. He dramatized what he saw, reflected and commented on contemporary American life, illuminated many of the issues and interests of his time. His efforts to make real occurrences dramatic by means of editing widened the scope of movies, educated its technique, and through the introduction of the story film made the industry boom.

In 1896 Porter, a mechanic with an enthusiasm for machinery, had come to Edison Company as a general handy man, wondering whether or not he should have gone instead into the newfangled business of making horseless cars. Even after he had become a cameraman for Edison, he still seriously considered quitting the movies, for like most others he felt that popular interest in "living motion photography" would soon subside. He remained with Edison simply because he needed a job.

Porter's career in motion pictures lasted seventeen years. It was within four years that he transformed motion picture art. During the years 1902 to 1906, he discovered the principle of editing (*The Life of an American Fireman*) and developed its methods to include direct story construction (*The Great Train Robbery*), contrast construction (*The Ex-Convict*), and parallel construction (*The Kleptomaniac*). In these years also he reached out daringly for new social subject matter (*White Caps, The Miller's Daughter*), explored more carefully the use of camera devices (*Dream of a Rarebit Fiend*), and enlarged the scale of production (*Uncle Tom's Cabin*).

Superseding Melies with these innovations, Porter became the dominant figure in the industry. Film makers imitated him zealously until 1908, when D. W. Griffith, bringing still greater talent to filmdom, became the most admired of movie celebrities.

By 1902 Porter had a long list of films to his credit. But neither he nor other American producers had yet learned to tell a story. They were still busy with elementary, one-shot news events (*President McKinley's Inauguration, McKinley's Funeral Cortege, The Columbia and Shamrock Yacht Races, The Jeffries-Ruhblin Sparring Contest, The Galveston Cyclone*), with humorous bits (*Grandma and Grandpa* series, *Happy Hooligan* series, *Old Maid* series), with vaudeville skits (cooch dancers, magicians, acrobats), scenic views (*A Trip Through the Columbian Exposition*), and local topics (parades, fire departments in action, shoppers in the streets). None of these productions stood out from the general; literal and unimaginative, they are significant today mainly as social documents. Porter himself made such pictures for six years without showing any notable signs of originality.

It was his contact with Melies' fairy-tale films that struck the spark in Porter. He would probably have continued his prosaic, unenthusiastic career had he not been startled by the Frenchman's unusual pictures. In the laboratory Porter had the opportunity to handle and examine the "magical films" of this French director at first hand. Impressed by their length and arrangement, he scrutinized them closely, noting that they contained more than one scene or camera shot and that the scenes were strung together progressively to illustrate a story. Porter hit upon the idea that he also might make stories by cutting and joining, in a certain order, scenes that he had already shot.

Excitedly he determined to try, and his employers, seeing a chance to increase the sale of their product, encouraged him. Porter rummaged through the stock of Edison's old films, searching for suitable scenes around which to build a story. He found quantities of pictures of fire-department activities. Since fire departments had such a strong popular appeal, with their color and action, Porter chose them as his subjects. But he still needed some central idea or incident by which to organize the scenes of the fire department in action.

Now Melies' pictures were all "magical," "mystical," "fantastic," often seasoned with humor and whimsey. The realism of fire engines and firemen had nothing to do with fantasy and humor. Porter therefore concocted a scheme that was as startling as it was different: a mother and child were to be caught in a burning building and rescued at the last moment by the fire department.

Tame though such a plot sounds to us today, it was then revolutionary. No film of a dramatic nature had yet been made in this country. Movies to date had been mere reports of events. The incident as shown on the screen lasted no longer than in real life. Porter was now about to attempt a drama of more than one scene, covering a longer period of time in real life than on the screen. The scheme not only involved a new application of the movies but necessitated a new kind of form.

Porter's next step was to stage such additional scenes as his plot demanded. Having completed them, he set about assembling all the shots into a dramatic arrangement. First there was exposition: a fire chief dreams of an imperiled woman and child. Then came an incident: the fire alarm is rung. Action was next: firemen, hearing the call, rush off to the fire. Suspense was created: will the firemen get there in time? A crisis was depicted: the burning building. The climax is reached: the helpless fire victims are about to expire. And, finally, there is resolution: the rescue. Joining the scenes together

in this order, Porter created the dramatic continuity which he called
The Life of an American Fireman.

This first American dramatic film was unique, depending for
meaning upon its combination of shots into scenes. The scenes had
two functions: to communicate the action and, more important, to
relate it to the next action so that a meaning was given to the whole.
The scene thus became a unit dependent upon all the other units;
to be fully understood, it was inseparable from them. This process
of cutting film, recombining and rearranging its units, is now known
as editing, and is what makes a film expressive.

The scenario for *The Life of an American Fireman,* published in
the Edison Catalogue of 1903, after the film was completed, reveals
the dramatic arrangement of its scenes and the new born technique
of editing. The advance over Melies' artificially arranged scenes is
evident. Melies merely listed scenes and roughly described their
content, but Porter specified for the first time not only a full description of the dramatic action, but details of location, camera position, and transition. Porter's script, which follows, is the primitive
of the continuity form used to this day in Hollywood:

THE LIFE OF AN AMERICAN FIREMAN

Scene 1: THE FIREMAN'S VISION OF AN IMPERILED WOMAN AND CHILD
The fire chief is seated at his office desk. He has just finished reading his evening paper and has fallen asleep. The
rays of an incandescent light rest upon his features with a
subdued light, yet leaving his figure strongly silhouetted
against the walls of his office. The fire chief is dreaming,
and the vision of his dream appears in a circular portrait
on the wall. It is a mother putting her baby to bed, and
the impression is that he dreams of his own wife and child.
He suddenly awakens and paces the floor in a nervous
state of mind, doubtless thinking of the various people
who may be in danger from fire at the moment.
Here we dissolve the picture to the second scene.

Scene 2: CLOSE VIEW OF A NEW YORK FIRE-ALARM BOX
Shows lettering and every detail in the door and apparatus
for turning in an alarm. A figure then steps in front of the
box, hastily opens the door and pulls the hook, thus sending the electric current which alarms hundreds of firemen

and brings to the scene of the fire the wonderful apparatus of a great city's Fire Department.

Again dissolving the picture, we show the third scene.

Scene 3: SLEEPING QUARTERS

A row of beds, each containing a fireman peacefully sleeping, is shown. Instantly upon the ringing of the alarm the firemen leap from their beds and, putting on their clothes in the record time of five seconds, a grand rush is made for a large circular opening in the floor through the center of which runs a brass pole. The first fireman to reach the pole seizes it and, like a flash, disappears through the opening. He is instantly followed by the remainder of the force. This in itself makes a most stirring scene.

We again dissolve the scene to the interior of the apparatus house.

Scene 4: INTERIOR OF ENGINE HOUSE

Shows horses dashing from their stalls and being hitched to the apparatus. This is perhaps the most thrilling and in all the most wonderful of the seven scenes of the series, it being absolutely the first moving pictures ever made of a genuine interior hitch. As the men come down the pole and land upon the floor in lightning-like rapidity, six doors in the rear of the engine house, each heading a horse-stall, burst open simultaneously and a huge fire horse, with head erect and eager for the dash to the scene of the conflagration, rushes from each opening. Going immediately to their respective harness, they are hitched in the almost unbelievable time of five seconds and are ready for their dash to the fire. The men hastily scamper upon the trucks and hose carts and one by one the fire machines leave the house, drawn by eager, prancing horses.

Here we again dissolve to the fifth scene.

Scene 5: APPARATUS LEAVING ENGINE HOUSE

We show a fine exterior view of the engine house, the great door swinging open and the apparatus coming out. This is the most imposing scene. The great horses leap to their work, the men adjust their fire hats and coats, and smoke begins pouring from the engines as they pass our camera.

Here we dissolve and show the sixth scene.

Scene 6: OFF TO THE FIRE

In this scene we present the best fire run ever shown. Almost the entire fire department of the large city of Newark, New Jersey, was placed at our disposal, and we show countless pieces of apparatus, engines, hook-and-ladders, hose towers, hose carriages, etc., rushing down a broad street at top speed, the horses straining every nerve and evidently eager to make a record run. Great clouds of smoke pour from the stacks of the engines, thus giving an impression of genuineness to the entire series.

Dissolving again we show the seventh scene.

Scene 7: ARRIVAL AT THE FIRE

In this wonderful scene we show the entire fire department as described above, arriving at the scene of action. An actual burning building is in the center foreground. On the right background the fire department is seen coming at great speed. Upon the arrival of the different apparatus, the engines are ordered to their places, hose is quickly run out from the carriages, ladders are adjusted to the windows, and streams of water are poured into the burning structure. At this crucial moment comes the great climax of the series. We dissolve to the interior of the building and show a bed chamber with a woman and child enveloped in flame and suffocating smoke. The woman rushes back and forth in the room endeavoring to escape, and in her desperation throws open the window and appeals to the crowd below. She is finally overcome by the smoke and falls upon the bed. At this moment the door is smashed in by an ax in the hands of a powerful fire hero. Rushing into the room, he tears the burning draperies from the window and smashes out the entire window frame, ordering his comrades to run up a ladder. Immediately the ladder appears, he seizes the prostrate form of the woman and throws it over his shoulders as if it were an infant and quickly descends to the ground. We now dissolve to the exterior of the burning building. The frantic mother having returned to consciousness, and clad only in her night clothes, is kneeling on the ground imploring the fireman to return for her child. Volunteers are called for and the same fireman who rescued the mother quickly steps out and offers to return for the babe. He is given permission to once more enter the doomed building and without hesitation rushes up the ladder, enters the window and after a breathless wait, in which it appears he must have been overcome with smoke, he appears with the child in his arms and returns safely to the ground. The child, being released and upon seeing its mother, rushes to her and is clasped in her arms, thus making a most realistic and touching ending of the series.

Two scenes are of particular significance because they reveal a feeling and a striving for an extension of structure to be achieved later. In Scene 2 a close-up is used for the first time, dramatically and logically, to advance the story. It preceded by at least five years Griffith's use of the close-up and the establishment of the close-up as an integral part of movie technique. The last scene also is noteworthy, for it actually comprises three different shots: (1) the arrival at the fire, (2) the imperiled woman and child, (3) the descent down the ladder. This is one of the earliest signs of a realization that a scene need not be taken in one shot but can be built by a number of shots. It was not until ten years later, however, that the shot as a single element in a scene of many elements was to be fully understood and used by film makers.

Porter himself, having had no background or experience in art, was aware of few of the implications of what he had attempted. Unacquainted with either literature or the theatre, he would have been shocked to learn that he had combined elements of both to create another art.

The Life of an American Fireman aroused excitement wherever it was shown. Audiences, as if viewing a real crisis, could not remain passive. They identified themselves with the fireman and the rescue on the screen. The fire engines simply *had* to get to the fire in time! The mother and child *must* not perish! Such intense personal reactions to a movie were unprecedented.

The immediate influence of *The Life of an American Fireman* upon other film makers was, nevertheless, negligible. Since nickelodeons did not yet exist at the time the film was released, its success was limited and its importance was overlooked by the trade. But Porter suspected that he had hit upon something novel, and he wanted his next film to develop his dramatic idea even further. He reasoned that if he could build a good story out of edited stock scenes, he could make a much better one if he planned it beforehand and photographed scenes specifically for it.

Porter's hunch was to make history. When a friend suggested making a picture similar to a popular road show of the day, *The Great Train Robbery*, Porter was impressed by the timeliness of the subject: train robberies were being reported in the newspapers almost daily. The robust and provocative title, moreover, stirred his imagination. He saw at once what an admirable chance the theme presented for dramatic effects: a daring train holdup, a brave and desperate pursuit, and a thrilling last-minute capture.

But his next film was not to be *The Great Train Robbery*. Edison assigned Porter to numerous other films, among which was an adaptation of the play *Uncle Tom's Cabin*. This film turned out to be the largest and most expensive picture yet made in America, running the extraordinary length of 1,100 feet and including fourteen scenes and a prologue. His heart being set on *The Great Train Robbery*, however, Porter did *Uncle Tom's Cabin* perfunctorily, without any of the originality displayed in *The Life of an American Fireman*.

Uncle Tom's Cabin followed the Melies pattern, with scenes arranged in logical order and photographed one after the other just as they are played on a stage. The advertisement made a virtue of the method: "The story has been carefully studied and every scene posed in accordance with the famous author's version." What the advertisement went on to call "a departure from the methods of dissolving one scene into another by inserting announcements with brief descriptions" was in reality a return to the lecture-slide method.

Finally in the fall of 1903 Porter made *The Great Train Robbery*, the primitive classic for which he is venerated today. This film has been called the first story film made in America; it was, more accurately, the most successful and influential of early story films. Nickelodeons, which were to spring up a year and a half later, opened with *The Great Train Robbery* as their initial attraction. For years *The Great Train Robbery* was the nickelodeon's most widely exhibited picture, and it is said to have insured the permanence of the movies. It became the Bible for all film makers until Griffith's films further developed Porter's editing principle. The efforts of all movie makers to imitate its form and content stimulated the industry as nothing—not even Melies' films—had ever done before.

In the script of *The Great Train Robbery* one sees improvements over the cruder editing that distinguished *The Life of an American Fireman*. There is a scene-by-scene construction of a dramatic narrative in straightforward style. Longer by 250 feet than the earlier film, *The Great Train Robbery* had more room for supplementary scenes, for more shots. It is therefore not so brusque and jerky as Porter's earlier work. Each scene is more skillfully conceived in relation to its neighbor; the narrative is closer-knit and flows more smoothly. Above all the story is executed from the sum of its edited parts. This unifying conception characterizes every shot except the last, Scene 14, a close-up of the outlaw leader taking aim and firing point-blank at the audience. Tacked on to the film for no other purpose than to startle the movie-goer, this scene was recommended to exhibitors as an opening or closing stunt for the performance. The other scenes as a group show excellent editing, and established that operation as the basis for future motion picture development.

The scenario is taken from the Edison Catalogue of 1904:

THE GREAT TRAIN ROBBERY

Scene 1: Interior of railroad telegraph office. Two masked robbers enter and compel the operator to get the "signal block" to stop the approaching train, and make him write a fictitious order to the engineer to take water at this station, instead of "Red Lodge," the regular watering stop. The train comes to a standstill (seen through window of office); the conductor comes to the window, and the frightened operator delivers the order while the bandits crouch out of sight, at the same time keeping him covered with their revolvers. As soon as the conductor leaves, they fall upon the operator, bind and gag him, and hastily depart to catch the moving train.

Scene 2: Railroad water tower. The bandits are hiding behind the tank as the train, under the false order, stops to take

water. Just before she pulls out they stealthily board the
train between the express car and the tender.

Scene 3: *Interior of express car.* Messenger is busily engaged. An
unusual sound alarms him. He goes to the door, peeps
through the keyhole and discovers two men trying to
break in. He starts back bewildered, but, quickly recovering, he hastily locks the strong box containing the valuables and throws the key through the open side door.
Drawing his revolver, he crouches behind a desk. In the
meantime the two robbers have succeeded in breaking
in the door and enter cautiously. The messenger opens
fire, and a desperate pistol duel takes place in which the
messenger is killed. One of the robbers stands watch
while the other tries to open the treasure box. Finding
it locked, he vainly searches the messenger for the key,
and blows the safe open with dynamite. Securing the
valuables and mail bags they leave the car.

Scene 4: *This thrilling scene shows the tender and interior of the
locomotive cab, while the train is running forty miles an
hour.* While two of the bandits have been robbing the
mail car, two others climb over the tender. One of them
holds up the engineer while the other covers the fireman,
who seizes a coal shovel and climbs up on the tender,
where a desperate fight takes place. They struggle fiercely
all over the tank and narrowly escape being hurled over
the side of the tender. Finally they fall, with the robber
on top. He seizes a lump of coal, and strikes the fireman
on the head until he becomes senseless. He then hurls the
body from the swiftly moving train. The bandits then
compel the engineer to bring the train to a stop.

Scene 5: *Shows the train coming to a stop.* The engineer leaves
the locomotive, uncouples it from the train, and pulls
ahead about 100 feet while the robbers hold their pistols
to his face.

Scene 6: *Exterior scene showing train.* The bandits compel the
passengers to leave the coaches, "hands up," and line up
along the tracks. One of the robbers covers them with a
revolver in each hand, while the others relieve the passengers of their valuables. A passenger attempts to escape,
and is instantly shot down. Securing everything of value,
the band terrorize the passengers by firing their revolvers
in the air, while they make their escape to the locomotive.

Scene from George Melies' *The Impossible Voyage* (1904), one of the wittiest pictures of the first creative motion picture director. The inventiveness, painting skill, and ingenious theatrical conception of this Frenchman are apparent even in this photograph. Note the copyright mark on the train, a practice resorted to to prevent "duping" of Melies' films by others.

Museum of Modern Art Film Librar

A rare record of early American movies: frame enlargements from the first native story film, *The Life of an American Fireman* (1902), by Edwin S. Porter. These prints were made by William Jamison, an associate of Edwin S. Porter at the Edison studio, immediately after the film had been completed. From left to right, the continuity of pictures shows the first use of editing to tell a screen story. Note also the double exposure "dream balloons" in the first two shots and the logical use of the close-up in the next two.

Scene 7: The desperadoes board the locomotive with this booty, compel the engineer to start, and disappear in the distance.

Scene 8: The robbers bring the engine to a stop several miles from the scene of the "hold up," and take to the mountains.

Scene 9: A beautiful scene in a valley. The bandits come down the side of a hill, across a narrow stream, mounting their horses, and make for the wilderness.

Scene 10: Interior of telegraph office. The operator lies bound and gagged on the floor. After struggling to his feet, he leans on the table, and telegraphs for assistance by manipulating the key with his chin, and then faints from exhaustion. His little daughter enters with his dinner pail. She cuts the rope, throws a glass of water in his face and restores him to consciousness, and, recalling his thrilling experience, he rushes out to give the alarm.

Scene 11: Interior of a typical Western dance hall. Shows a number of men and women in a lively quadrille. A "tenderfoot" is quickly spotted and pushed to the center of the hall, and compelled to do a jig, while bystanders amuse themselves by shooting dangerously close to his feet. Suddenly the door opens and the half-dead telegraph operator staggers in. The dance breaks up in confusion. The men secure their rifles and hastily leave the room.

Scene 12: Shows the mounted robbers dashing down a rugged hill at a terrific pace, followed closely by a large posse, both parties firing as they ride. One of the desperadoes is shot and plunges headlong from his horse. Staggering to his feet, he fires at the nearest pursuer, only to be shot dead a moment later.

Scene 13: The three remaining bandits, thinking they have eluded the pursuers, have dismounted from their horses, and after carefully surveying their surroundings, they start to examine the contents of the mail pouches. They are so grossly engaged in their work that they do not realize the approaching danger until too late. The pursuers, having left their horses, steal noiselessly down upon them until they are completely surrounded. A desperate battle then takes place, and after a brave stand all the robbers and some of the posse bite the dust.

Scene 14: A life-size [close-up] *picture of Barnes*, leader of the outlaw band, taking aim and firing point-blank at the audience. The resulting excitement is great. This scene can be used to begin or end the picture.

The limitations of *The Great Train Robbery* were those of youth. The action of every scene was told in one shot instead of a number of shots. Every shot, moreover, was a long shot, its action being confined to the proscenium-limited stage area. With the exception of the scenes in which the passengers are lined up outside the train, the robbery of the mail car, the hold-up of the engineer, and the battle between the posse and the bandits, the action was played in profile before the camera. Foreground and middle ground were equally ignored, the background alone serving as the acting area. The camera never moved from eye level. Tension and excitement were achieved by a quickening of the players' movements rather than by variation of the lengths of the shots. Within this simple framework, however, the kinetic possibilities of the new technique were convincingly demonstrated.

The success of *The Great Train Robbery* established Porter at once as the outstanding figure in the movie world and initiated an American film style of vigor, movement, and melodrama. A series of similar films, all utilizing the editing technique and similar subject matter, flooded the market. The heretofore unrivaled Melies and his "magical" films fell back to second place.

Despite the success of *The Great Train Robbery*, Porter was still regarded as a mechanic by his employers. Held to a rigid production schedule, in the next three years he made hundreds of films patterned more or less on *The Great Train Robbery*.

In 1905 he made two further contributions to motion picture technique. To the editing principle as evolved in *The Life of an American Fireman* and *The Great Train Robbery*, Porter now added the corollaries of contrast and parallel construction. As if instinctively he was applying to the movie certain principles that had long been established in other arts.

Like the discovery of the editing principle, these innovations were prompted by the needs of the subject matter. In *The Ex-Convict*, for instance, a wealthy manufacturer refuses to give an ex-convict work. It was necessary to contrast the two men's life situations in order to emphasize for the audience the drama of their encounter. Porter therefore employed the formal device now known as contrast editing. Scenes of the poverty-stricken home of the ex-convict were opposed to scenes of luxury in the manufacturer's household, and thus by implication and inference the sympathy of the audience was directed. This new application of editing, not straightforward or direct but comparative, pointed to future subtlety in film expression. Not until years later, however, was contrast editing to be properly valued and developed.

Although Porter himself could not have explained what he had done, he believed that he had significantly extended his editing technique. After *The Ex-Convict* he made another film in which he refined his contrast editing and ventured into a third kind of technique: parallel editing. This new film, *The Kleptomaniac*, like *The Ex-Convict* protested against social injustice. The story told of two women, one poor and the other rich, who are caught shoplifting and arrested. The rich one is freed; the poor one is jailed. The story's effectiveness depended on the paralleling of the causes of the actions and fates of the two women. The picture was perhaps Porter's most interesting achievement, and in technique and content it was the most advanced picture yet produced.

Porter divided the story into three parts: two parallel sequences and a resolution, to which was added his own ironic comment in an epilogue. The first sequence showed a wealthy woman shoplifting some trinkets from a department store, and then her arrest. In the second sequence a poor woman stealing a loaf of bread to keep from starving is likewise arrested. The third part brings the two women together, arraigned in a police court. The judge orders a chair for the rich woman, who is placed away from the crowd; the poor woman is herded with other arraigned unfortunates. When the poor woman is called before the judge, she pleads in vain for mercy; he sentences her to jail. In the meantime the rich woman's husband, a banker, has come in with a lawyer. When they appear for her, the judge ignores the evidence offered by the store detective and discharges her.

Porter could have ended his film there, as in *The Ex-Convict*, leaving the audience to draw its own conclusions. But he added his own comment in an epilogue which served to sum up all three sequences. A figure of Justice, blindfolded, is shown holding a scale. On one side of the balance is a bag of gold; on the other, a loaf of bread. The balance moves in favor of the gold. Then the bandage over the eyes of Justice is removed, revealing her with only one eye—a glittering eye, fixed on the gold.

Original and highly expressive, *The Kleptomaniac* revealed further possibilities of film technique. Movies could now appeal to the minds of the audiences as well as to the emotions. Contrast and parallel editing not only heightened the movies' dramatic values but made it more than just a story. The picture was an interpretation of one aspect of life in society, and became in itself an agency of protest against that aspect of life.

From ramifications of editing, Porter turned to examine the camera more thoroughly. In 1906 he made what might have been a trivial picture but was actually a most imaginative one through his intelligent manipulation of camera devices. *The Dream of a Rarebit Fiend* pictured the fanciful nightmare of a man who, before going to sleep, has Welsh rarebit and a few bottles of ale. We see the man asleep. His shoes mysteriously creep out of the room; then his table and chair become animated and quickly disappear. From the dreamer's head a large, steaming chafing dish appears, and three devils jump out to beat a lively tattoo on his head. Soon the bed comes to life and, after a lively dance, spins through the room like a top, then shoots through the window and sails high above New York, past bridges, rivers, skyscrapers, with the dreamer clinging desperately to the bedposts. A sudden wind capsizes the bed and the sleeper spins through space, at last catching on a weather vane atop a church steeple. There the wind blows him around and around until he loses his balance and falls again. He crashes down through the ceiling of his own room and lands on his bed, awake, and realizing that he has been dreaming.

As Edison Company advertised, "Some of the photographic stunts have never been seen or attempted before, and few experts will be able to understand how they were done." The technical tricks which Porter put into this film did lift it to a level which no similar film had attained. The picture still looks fairly good today despite more recent mechanical and technical progress. Obviously stemming from Melies' magical films, *The Dream of a Rarebit Fiend* had a cinematic style more advanced and distinguished than the Frenchman's. Both men used a variety of camera devices—stop-motion, double exposure, masking, moving camera, dissolves—but Porter's knowledge of editing gave his effects a fluency and rhythm lacking in Melies' work.

After 1906 Porter did little to advance either his reputation or the movie medium. Still the leading director in the industry, he continued to turn out some of the most spectacular films and participated actively in an industry enjoying its first boom. The demand for pictures increased a hundredfold during the mushroom growth of nickelodeons; it was all Porter could do to keep pace with production requirements, though his company had given him two new assistants. There was neither time nor need to experiment for the enthusiastic movie-goer. Thus the hundreds of pictures Porter turned out became more and more routinized. Film after film repeated the dramatic method crystallized in *The Great Train Robbery*. Porter's urge to social criticism, moreover, waned as his personal fortunes flourished.

In the next two years other movie makers rapidly assimilated Porter's contributions and, following the editing principle, flooded the market with story films. Turning out a movie became a formula, followed with little imagination or enthusiasm; speed and quantity of production were deemed more necessary.

Not until about 1910, when D. W. Griffith came to the fore, did the industry take a new turn. Outrivaled by the experimenting Griffith but still securely established, Porter left Edison in 1911 to head Rex, his own company, and he became a leader of the independents. After competing more than a year with his former employer, he pioneered with Adolf Zukor's Famous Players Company, directing their first feature picture. To have been selected for such a momentous venture was a signal honor and indicates the rank and respect Porter commanded.

His first feature film for Zukor, *The Count of Monte Cristo*, was not released; a rival company beat it to the market with a similar picture. With his second feature, *The Prisoner of Zenda*, Porter distinguished himself. W. Stephen Bush, critic of *The Moving Picture World*, paid tribute to his craftsmanship: [1]

The skill of a talented and ardent master of the cinema silent drama is apparent at every turn. Mr. Porter knew the possibilities of his instrument and made the conquest quite complete. He has disarmed and delighted the most captious critics by the daring but entirely successful use of all those advantages which are peculiar to the motion picture.

For three years Porter remained with Famous Players as their Director-General. An influential figure in the broadening screen world, he formulated the production policy of the company and directed many of its biggest stars, including Mary Pickford (*Tess of the Storm Country*), John Barrymore (*The Dictator*), Pauline Frederick (*Sold*). When the Italian film *Quo Vadis* made Americans spectacle-conscious, Porter with a company of players went to Rome to produce what was America's second big film spectacle, the first having been Griffith's *Judith of Bethulia*. The film Porter returned with, *The Eternal City*, was his last. After its presentation in 1915 he retired from the industry, wealthy and with an honorable career behind him.

At heart still a mechanic, Porter gave himself to the hobby of tinkering with machinery. The crash of 1929 is said to have wiped out most of his investments. Today he is working in the machine shop of a mechanical-appliance corporation, modest, self-effacing, difficult to see, forgotten by the industry he set on the road to success and affluence.

But Porter's flexible inventions endowed movies with new capabilities of technique and form, opening the way for other craftsmen to follow. The movie would have remained a novelty with little social or artistic significance had not Porter, or someone else, discovered the film's adaptability to being cut up and rejoined for narrative and interpretive purposes. During the past thirty-odd years of movie making, the principle of editing has remained fundamental and peculiar to the motion picture art. It has been developed, enlarged, and reinforced by the application of other arts—theatre,

[1] *The Moving Picture World*, March 1, 1913.

painting, literature, music—but has not been essentially altered. It is the method by which the latent power of photography is released, by which a series of pictures can become impressive, eloquent, and significant. Without editing a film is dead; with it, alive. The intensity and subtlety of a director's editing are the indices of his craftsmanship.

Pointing the way to a cinematic *art*, the content of Porter's films was seasoned with a strong social feeling. Porter's interest in the streets and their humanity affected his technique and accounted partly for the popularity of his productions. Alert and sharply critical, he sympathized with the poor (*The Miller's Daughter, A River Tragedy*), consciously agitated for social justice (*The Ex-Convict, The Kleptomaniac*), and awakened the populace to a better understanding of America in the new century (*White Caps, Desperate Encounter, Capture of the Yegg Bank Burglars*). By accenting the bravery and courage of firemen and policemen, by dramatizing the hardships and misery of the poor, by showing the personal maladjustments that lead to crime and the difficulty of rehabilitation, Porter made his audiences aware of heroism in their lives and stimulated the already growing interest in the common man.

To the non-theatre-going audience, movies had to be physically compelling, melodramatic. Images on the screen had to suggest the slang and profanity of back streets. Stories had to elucidate, criticize, or acclaim their own narrow settings. Porter understood these things earlier and better than anyone else, and his films had a forthright style adapted both to theme and to audience. His technique and choices of content introduced the movies to the great task of dramatizing reality.

I V

BUSINESS: TOWARD NATIONAL EXPANSION

THE remarkable success of story films—*The Great Train Robbery* in particular—caused a fresh outpouring of capital into the motion picture trade. Between 1903 and 1908 the movies ascended from the level of petty commerce to that of a large, permanent business, with three distinct phases which were eventually to grow into big separate industries. The introduction of the exchange system of distribution, special movie theatres, and large studios made the "flimsy upstart," as movies had been termed in 1903, a bonanza for entrepreneurs. Demand for films mounted phenomenally: the movies now were becoming a commodity for the masses.

The wide adoption of the exchange system facilitated and quickened the commercial development of the industry. The "jobber," handling many products from various manufacturers, was then a novel figure in the mercantile world. When he entered the movie business, he made its rapid expansion possible. Until now exhibitors had bought their films, and their investments had been so heavy that they had begun exchanging pictures among themselves. The jobber was to develop an efficient system of exchange out of this awkward method of distribution.

Among the first to become aware of the need for a business which neither made nor showed films, but distributed them, was a free-lance cameraman, Harry J. Miles. With his brother Herbert, he established early in 1903 what proved to be one of the most important and profitable developments in the motion picture industry: a film exchange. Miles Brothers' Exchange bought films from the manufacturers and rented them to exhibitors at one-fourth the pur-

(*Top*) The dance-hall scene from Edwin S. Porter's *The Great Train Robbery* (1903), the most influential of early American films, both for subject matter and form. Note the painted sets.

(*Bottom*) D. W. Griffith (*foreground*) before he became a director, playing the leading role in Edwin S. Porter's *Rescued from an Eagle's Nest* (1907). Whenever scenes were shot in the open, as in this picture, the players moved forward and back rather than from side to side as on the stage.

From D. W. Griffith's *The Lonely Villa* (1909), the movie which introduced the "switch-back" or "last-minute rescue" to American technique.
Characteristically pre-war in staging, lighting, and camera position. Mary
Pickford, not yet America's Sweetheart, can be seen in the background as
one of the children.

chase price. Such a plan was welcomed heartily everywhere. The exchange man could continue to rent out films long after they had more than paid for themselves: his profits were large. Manufacturers now had one large customer who practically guaranteed to buy most of their output at higher prices; and they enjoyed an increased market for pictures because exhibitors, paying less for pictures, could more frequently change their programs. To exhibitors the plan meant programs at much lower cost. A variety of films from several manufacturers could be collected under one roof, and thus the time and trouble involved in the selection of pictures would be reduced. The frequent changes of programs now possible, moreover, would stimulate their business.

So successful was the Miles exchange that the entire movie business was quickened and the Miles brothers soon were competing with a dozen rivals. Some of the larger established manufacturers set up exchanges of their own. By 1907 there were over a hundred film exchanges in thirty-five key cities throughout the United States. Thousands of new store theatres had sprung up, and their owners were being supplied with programs daily through the new distribution system. Programs were sometimes changed so frequently that *Views and Film Index* [1] was able to report that

A year ago and even less, two changes a week in motion picture programs was considered fair and three changes considered good. Today it would be hard to find a nickelodeon in the country that is not furnishing a change of program every day. In some instances . . . two changes a day are offered—one in the afternoon and one in the evening.

The immediate effect of the exchange was to set up a new standard of market value for a picture. Exhibitors outbid each other to get the latest pictures first, and rental prices soon began to be graded according to the picture's showing or "run." A "first run," for instance, cost the exhibitor twenty times as much as a "twentieth run." Rival exchanges, realizing the advantage of getting the newest pictures before competitors, offered more money to manufacturers for the privilege of first choice. Selling prices as well as rental rates soared higher and higher as exchanges, by fair means

[1] December 28, 1907.

or foul, sought to get even one day's advantage over rival exchanges in buying and booking pictures.

Keener competition and the wide demand for new films quickly produced dishonest and underhanded business tactics. The exchanges took up one of the most common practices of the day, "duping." They would buy a film, have a negative made from it, and from the negative make prints which they rented as originals. In this way manufacturers were cheated of the profits of their products. Unethical though it was, the practice became so widespread that *The Moving Picture World* [2] editorialized: "We want to warn our readers against being duped by 'dupe' films. The number of copied films which are being offered for sale as originals is increasing."

Since programs were ordered largely by mail, exchanges often took advantage of the exhibitor by sending him pictures other than he had ordered, or prints that had been so worn by use and careless handling that they were hardly fit for showing. The exchange Harstin & Company, to emphasize its dependability, took the slogan "the old reliable firm" and advertised: [3]

IF YOU ARE HELD UP in the streets you lose your purse, but if you are HELD UP by the misleading method of advertising, unexperienced shipping clerks, poor selections of films and songslides, you will lose your *entire business*.

Many of the exhibitors in turn devised schemes to defraud the exchanges. A group of theatres under one ownership, or associated for mutual profit, would rent a picture for one theatre but so arrange the schedules of screenings in the other theatres that a boy on a bicycle could race with the same print under his arm from one theatre to the other. This "bicycling" of prints saved money for the theatres and became a popular ruse.

Such tricks of the trade abetted the jealousies, ruthlessness, and confusion which were becoming notable characteristics of the booming industry.

Meanwhile exhibition, spurred by the exchange system, took on a new form. 1905 saw the introduction of a new type of movie

[2] July 6, 1907.   [3] *Views and Film Index*, October 12, 1907.

theatre, the direct forerunner of the movie theatre we know today. In Pittsburgh John P. Harris and his brother-in-law Harry Davis, like hundreds of others, converted an empty store into a movie theatre. But unlike others these men had the cunning to add glamor to their showmanship and to give their establishment a catchy name which soon swept the country and became a part of the English language.

With discarded and surplus grand-opera accessories, Harris and Davis gave their store-theatre a luxurious appearance which distinguished it from other store theatres and arcades and impressed the spectators. They added the innovation of piano accompaniment, which increased the grand air of the show. Then, to advertise their theatre's cheapness and at the same time maintain its dignity, they named it the "Nickelodeon." With *The Great Train Robbery* featured on their opening program, their venture was a brilliant success. The catchy name of the place, the colorful surroundings, the musical renditions, and the story picture combined to keep the ninety-six seats of the Nickelodeon creaking with the excitement of customers from eight in the morning until twelve at night. Nickels poured into the cash box so rapidly that soon the receipts were averaging over a thousand dollars weekly.

News of this latest get-rich-quick scheme swiftly spread throughout the United States, and a nickelodeon boom began. Penny arcades, store-theatres, and empty stores blossomed forth as nickelodeons overnight. Within a year a hundred nickelodeons appeared in Pittsburgh alone, and in such big cities as New York, Chicago, St. Louis, Cincinnati, Los Angeles, and Philadelphia, competition became frenzied.

In some of the crowded quarters of the city the nicelet shops as they are called are cropping up almost as thickly as saloons, and if the nickel delirium continues to maintain its hold there will be in a few years more of these cheap amusement places than saloons. Even now some of the saloon keepers are complaining that they injure their trade,

reported the *Views and Film Index*, October 5, 1907, quoting a newspaper journalist. The New York Board of Aldermen passed a special ordinance to categorize nickelodeons as "common shows," and thus exhibitors were able to obtain a license for $25 the first year, while a full theatrical license cost $500. Licenses were granted at the rate of one a day in Manhattan alone.

By 1908 there were between eight and ten thousand nickelodeons operating in the nation. Colorful posters at their entrances advertised the excitement, adventure, and thrills to be experienced from the current showing. An additional allurement was their fanciful names spelled out in electric lights: "Bijou Dream," "Nickolette," "Dreamland," "Pictorium," "Theatorium," "Jewel," "Electric." Concentrated largely in the poorer shopping districts and slum neighborhoods, nickelodeons were disdained by the well-to-do. But the workmen and their families who patronized the movies did not mind the crowded, unsanitary, and hazardous accommodations most of the nickelodeons offered, and they volubly enjoyed the programs.

Lasting from twenty minutes to a full hour, the program often included a single-reel melodrama, a comedy, and a novelty. During the showing of the main film occasionally a "lecturer" explained the story to the ill-educated and stirred up excitement at the climaxes. This practice, popular at first, gradually died out as film makers and audience became more familiar with the medium. The films were frequently followed by a ballad singer who, accompanied by illustrated "hand-colored" slides, crooned the popular songs of the day—"Dreaming of You," "Without a Wedding Ring," "Would You Care?" Throughout the programs children tramped the aisles, selling "Peanuts, popcorn, soft drinks, candy." Their shouts often interfered with the singing but not with the enjoyment. Often the programs were further interrupted by slides carrying intimate information to individuals in the audience: "A Woman Who Left a Baby Carriage Outside Is Wanted Immediately"; "Please Do Not Stamp, the Floor May Cave In"; "Keep Your Child from Crying"; "Lady, There's Someone Behind You, Will You Kindly Remove Your Hat." The most disturbing message was "One Minute Please While the Operator Repairs the Broken Film." Then the audience whistled, stamped, and applauded with impatience.

The operator of the projector was, as a rule, underpaid, worked long hours, and constantly disturbed because of fire hazards, the possibility of film breaks, and the general discomfort of his quarters. "What is an operator," asked a letter to *The Moving Picture World*,[4] "a machine, a slave, a dog to be kicked or a man to whom some consideration should be shown?" The operator had no union to protect him, and his pay was docked for breaks in condensers, negatives, slides. The letter writer proposed an operators' league for mutual protection. This was the first move that led to the subsequent strong unionization of almost every branch of the industry.

Profits from nickelodeons were quick and large but depended upon a constant turnover of customers. Since nickelodeons could accommodate only one to two hundred people at a time, programs had to be short and were run continuously from morning to midnight. Changes of pictures had to be made as often as possible so that people would come again. Sometimes nickelodeons changed their programs in the middle of the day.

The nickelodeon boom boosted the demand for pictures so greatly that manufacturing of movies became the most important branch of the business. As in the other branches, competition rapidly intensified. Production plants spread out from New York City, Chicago, and Philadelphia to New Jersey, as far south as Florida, and as far west as California. Older companies such as Edison, Biograph, and Vitagraph enlarged their plants. New companies, the most prominent of which were Lubin, Selig, Kalem, and Essanay, pushed into the field.

Studios, then called "factories," were in a constant flurry of activity to meet market demands, for nickelodeons swallowed up motion pictures faster than they could be made. Pictures sold at a good price regardless of quality; speed of output was all that mattered. How much money was being made by manufacturers in these years is suggested by the fact that Kalem, one of the smallest and newest companies, starting in 1905 with a cash investment of only $600, by 1908 was clearing $5,000 a week profit. They were producing only two pictures a week at a cost of $200 each.

Trying to outdo each other in the speed of their operations, manufacturers expanded their equipment and quarters. The three pioneer companies were the first to abandon the streets for skylight lofts and roofs of tall buildings. Then the development of mercury-

[4] March 9, 1907.

vapor lamps for artificial lighting, in about 1906, made indoor "studios" possible. The first to be especially constructed for motion picture production was that of Edison Company in the Bronx. Its size and equipment set a precedent for the others.

Vitagraph, keeping a watchful eye on its formidable rival, quickly moved to a large tract in Flatbush, Brooklyn—as far from its competitor as cars could carry it. Biograph meanwhile made what proved to be the wisest move. It leased a brownstone building on East Fourteenth Street, Manhattan, in the heart of theatrical activity, close to Broadway. This location put it in an advantageous position to engage professional actors, a major need of all movie makers.

During these years the lesser manufacturers could not afford the upkeep of a studio with such sets and artificial lighting facilities as were maintained by the three big companies. They continued to make their pictures entirely on "location" in city streets, in country lanes, at public parks—at any outdoor place with interesting scenery or atmosphere—or at small hotels providing the necessary "props," "extras," and "interiors." With nature for background and with a small personnel, these companies produced a picture at a minimum cost, often $200 as against the $400 to $500 spent by their larger rivals.

The making of motion pictures was still a rather mysterious affair. Every studio was a guarded stronghold, located far from others. Since several companies used the Edison camera without paying royalties and without legal permission, they naturally took great precautions against being watched or discovered. Every company, fearing that others might discover its methods and ideas or steal its personnel, sold its pictures by trade-marks alone. Movie makers thus worked in anonymity, with no opportunity to pool their discoveries or help one another in their problems. Improvements in the industry were therefore slow and accidental.

Despite this isolation and jealousy, all the companies made pictures by approximately similar methods. The standard length for a story film became one reel: 800 to 1,000 feet. The entire picture was made in a day. Action was divided into scenes, and these were photographed in consecutive order. The number of scenes was limited to seven or eight, each 100 to 150 feet long, in order to keep the story within the 1,000-foot length in which the raw film came. When the film was running short the last scene would have to be rushed before the film gave out. The cameraman cranked slower so as to make the film last until the action was completed. This slow cranking made the hurried acting appear even more hurried, so that often the film ended in a ludicrous last-minute burst of activity. Such faults were rarely corrected unless they were extremely bad; usually the picture could be sold as it was.

Increased production necessitated more people and a division of duties to speed the output. By 1908 directing, acting, photographing, writing, and laboratory work were separate crafts, all of equal status. Each worker regarded himself as a factory hand, lacking only a time-clock ritual for concrete evidence of his position. No one received any screen credit for the work he did, for, as the employers realized, a public reputation would mean higher wages. Besides, most of the directors, actors, and cameramen who had come to the movies were more or less ashamed of their connection with them; they stayed in their jobs because they needed work, and they gave little thought to the medium's possibilities or opportunities. Nearly everyone still regarded movie making as a shabby occupation.

The director was the pivot of production. The idea for the film was his or was suggested to him. Having roughly plotted its action, he would meet the players, the technical crew, and the rest of the force in the morning; then he would select his cast and decide on locations, always observing the strictest economy. During the shooting he not only told the actors what to do but supervised the cameraman. It was the director, finally, who edited or cut the finished film.

The first school of American directors evolved uncredited by their own profession and unheralded outside of it. Of the pioneers in the new craft, Edwin S. Porter of Edison became, through his discovery of editing, the leader. Other prominent directors were "Old Man" McCutcheon of Biograph, who had directed some of the first "Mutoscope" peep-show movies; J. Stuart Blackton of Vitagraph, who was to become renowned for his patriotic war films; and Sidney Olcott, now with Kalem, formerly an actor and

writer at Biograph, who in 1923 was selected as one of America's
ten best directors. Another prominent director was J. Searle Dawley, an actor, hired by Edison Company to assist Edwin S. Porter
and introduce "dramatic methods into screen production," as well
as to interest additional stage actors in movies (later he became
famed as the director who made "Famous Players Famous"). G. M.
Anderson of Essanay, who as "Broncho Billy" achieved a high
reputation; Francis Boggs of Selig, freshly recruited from the stage;
and Arthur Hotaling of Lubin, who had been with "Pop" Lubin
since his peddling days, completed the major list.

Most motion picture directors were not particularly inspired by
their medium. Under constant pressure to produce at least two pictures a week, they had little time even if they had the inclination
for experiments. They worked in the narrative style introduced by
Melies and Porter, consolidating their contributions into a simple
technique. Limited means, ignorance of the medium, and unimaginative imitation of stage methods had established conventions which
were the movie director's stock in trade, a sign of his profession-
alism.

Scenes were always shot so that the complete setting and all the
actors were visible. If one of the actors happened to be cut off, as
is common today in close or medium shots, it was considered in-
artistic and amateurish and the scene was rephotographed. Some
other conventions of the day were the following:

1. Every scene must begin with an entrance and end with an
exit, just as on the stage.
2. Players must face the camera and move horizontally, except
when the movement was rapid, as in a chase, or prolonged, as in a
fight. At these times action was in diagonal relation to the camera
in order to give the players more area.
3. Any action in the background must be slow and greatly exaggerated so that it would "register" on the audience.
4. Pantomime must be exaggerated and over-deliberate; e.g., a
stare had to be held; a start must be violent; speeches must be
mouthed with pronounced slowness.

Ludicrous though these conventions seem today, they were then
accepted standards.

With the director supervising production, cameramen became of secondary importance. They were relieved of all duties except photography and lighting, still mainly manual problems. Cameramen like others had to work according to schedule, shooting a picture in a day. Every shot had to count, since shots were never done over unless the laboratory work went awry or some accident to the actors during the shooting made a retake imperative. There was no time, even if there had been imagination enough, to move the camera nearer or further away during the shooting of a scene. No attempts were made for angle views or lighting effects, and "composition" was still an unknown quality. The camera viewpoint was limited to that of an audience watching a play on a stage.

Actors who appeared in motion pictures kept their business secret: holding it in contempt, they stooped to it only while waiting for an opportunity with the "legit." Getting actors who were dependable was, therefore, a major problem for producers. To solve the difficulty Vitagraph formed a stock company. Actors were promised steady work and a regular salary of twenty to forty dollars a week—a strong inducement. As it turned out, however, these stock players when not acting were put to such tasks as carpentry, scene building, sewing, prop making. Even the leading actress of the Vitagraph studio, Florence Turner, helped to sew costumes. The grumbling of the shamefaced actors was finally climaxed by the open rebellion of the reputable Maurice Costello: "I am an actor and I will act, but I will not build sets and paint scenery." Temperament won the day: screen acting as a specialized craft became acknowledged, not only in the Vitagraph studio but throughout the other studios.

Story films being the rage, screen writing also became a specialized, "well-paid" profession. By 1906 studios were paying $5 to $15 for picture ideas. The first screen scenarists were people in the business: J. Searle Dawley, Frank Marion, Sidney Olcott, Gene Gauntier, and D. W. Griffith, to name a few of the more notable, were particularly successful. Since there were still no copyright laws affecting the screen, these actor-authors helped themselves to poems, short stories, current plays, and classics, which they condensed and translated into simple plots for the screen. This material was outlined for the director in a rough continuity of scenes; he then proceeded to work from this script improvising the details as he went along.

By 1908 all branches of movie making had expanded remarkably. Companies were producing hundreds of pictures yearly; specialized studios and specialized personnel were becoming established as conventions; a crude routine of movie making had been formulated. The growth of the industry was signalized in 1906 by the birth of the film industry's first trade paper, *Views and Film Index*, a weekly newspaper, "devoted to the interests of motion pictures, stereopticons, lantern slides, slot machines and allied industries." Synopses of advertised films, accounts of new inventions, advertisements of motion picture accessories, song slides, and lists of distributors appeared in the new publication; but there was no mention of directors, technicians, or players. The magazine was sold for five cents a copy.

Underlying the steady growth of the industry was a strong internal dissension. Competition produced petty jealousies, endless arguments, cutthroat practices, and many violations of law and ethics. In addition to the duping practices of exchanges and the "bicycling" of prints by exhibitors, all kinds of patent disputes were going on among manufacturers. Considerable time and profits were spent in bitter quarrels and lawsuits. Big and little concerns battled continually over the rights to inventions, improvements, and accessories. Accusations of theft and copying multiplied enmities throughout the trade.

While undergoing these strains of bitter competition and national expansion, the industry was suddenly threatened by outside agencies: attacks on motion pictures became frequent. One of the first indications that the movies had made powerful enemies was an editorial in *The Chicago Tribune*. Under the objective title "The Five Cent Theatre" it condemned the nickelodeon as

ministering to the lowest passions of children. . . . Proper to suppress them at once . . . influence wholly vicious. . . . They cannot be defended. They are hopelessly bad.[5]

[5] Reprint in *Views and Film Index*, April 20, 1907.

Substantiating the attack was a letter from a judge which followed:

Those nickelodeons indirectly or directly caused more juvenile crimes coming into this court than all other causes combined.

Throughout the country movie-baiting became common. From property holders, ministers, theatre critics, and social reformers came shrill cries of protest. Declaimed the *Christian Leader*, "A set of revolutionists training for the overthrow of the government could find no surer means than these exhibitions."

Eloquent though these critics were, the chief motive underlying the flood of abuse was not disguised. Dressed in moral terms, it was essentially economic: movies had suddenly become a competitor of church, saloon, and vaudeville. Their tremendous popularity had put all these out of pocket. The church collection plate had lost much of its jingle; the corner saloon had to offer variety programs with more acts and novelties; business men complained that real estate had been boosted to prohibitive highs by nickelodeon owners who "readily pay rents from $10,000 to $25,000 a year. . . . No retail store can pay such rentals and live." As for vaudeville owners, *The Moving Picture World* [6] reported:

We know the rapid advance made in public favor of the 5¢ theatre is a bitter pill for theatrical men to swallow, and that receipts have gone down considerably with many houses owing to the growing desire of the discriminating public to see the pictures.

Confronted with such a formidable competitor, several such social institutions cloaked their economic fear in moral censure and by that subterfuge sought to smash the movies. But they were up against an irrepressible force; and the motion picture men, seeing their livelihood endangered, did not sit idly by. George Kleine of Kalem Pictures, one of the largest distributors of foreign films, realized the danger to the industry before anyone else. In *Views and Film Index* [7] he thrust the issue boldly before the trade:

In view of the increasing attacks upon the users of motion pictures throughout the country, we think it well that all those inter-

[6] June 15, 1907.   [7] April 20, 1907.

ested be aroused to the situation. . . . We would suggest to owners of Nickelodeons in cities where there are located a number of them to form a local association for mutual protection and defense against such attacks. . . .

A few weeks later Carl Laemmle, then an owner of film exchanges, backed up Kleine's clarion call for mutual protection in an advertisement in *Views and Film Index:* [8]

They claim motion pictures are corrupting the morals of boys and girls. Stuff? Yes, it's stuff all right, but calling it stuff won't do any good. We can't laugh it off. . . . Personally I don't believe there's one theatre in a hundred that's showing pictures of a questionable or harmful character—but what I believe and what you believe won't count. It's what the people believe that will affect the cash drawer one way or another.

Laemmle attempted to profit from the situation by assuring his exhibitor-customers that if they rented pictures from Laemmle, "educational and catchy" advertising copy would be included to offset the evil influences of the reformers.

Views and Film Index [9] ironically editorialized on the question:

The next thing we may expect is that when a citizen ventures out on Sunday he will be kidnaped and spirited away, taken to church and made to sing, and pray with an armed guard at the pew.

Among persons unprejudiced by economic fears, the attitude toward movies was generally favorable. Jane Addams of Hull House pointed out that motion pictures "rightly conducted are a benefit and not a menace, especially to the poorer classes," [10] and she proposed to regulate rather than condemn the new entertainment form. Charles Sprague Smith, of the People's Institute of New York City, answered the attack by suggesting that "There are more things rotten in New York than motion pictures." In Philadelphia Dr. McClellan, a prominent pastor, took a progressive stand, going so far as to suggest that the movie be utilized by the church to attract non-church-goers:

[8] May 4, 1907.　　　　　　　　　[9] April 27, 1907.
[10] Quoted in *The Moving Picture World*, May 11, 1907.

We must appeal to the working man and his family. . . . Let us raise ten, twelve, fifteen thousand dollars that our church may be so enlarged and reconstructed . . . whereby . . . we could have motion pictures . . . on a Saturday night when our streets, playhouses and saloons are crowded, to be conducted with gospel services of a practical sort. . . .[11]

Even more positive support was expressed by Barton W. Currier in *Harper's Weekly:* [12]

Many moral lessons are to be had from these brief moving picture performances. Most of the slides offer you a quick flash of melodrama in which the villain and the criminal are always getting the worst of it.

The upshot of the conflict was that the opposition, realizing they were waging a losing battle, changed their tactics: instead of fighting their competitor, they formed an alliance with it. Taking up Dr. McClellan's constructive suggestion, churches discovered that an occasional movie not only brought old members back to the fold but attracted new ones as well. Vaudeville managers found that when movies were added to their program of higher-priced "artistries" their gallery patrons increased. Enterprising drinking places inaugurated screen shows for table drinkers. But the final seal of propriety was placed upon the movies by the police when it was announced that the capture of a notorious criminal, Rudolph Blumenthal, was made possible when he was spotted in a movie of a crowd of spectators at a horse race. Henceforth the agencies that had tried to destroy the movies turned them more and more to their own service.

Although now condoning the motion picture, professional reformers and social workers pointed out the desirability of regulation. In 1909 the People's Institute of New York City, in co-operation with the newly formed Motion Picture Patents Company, formed the first National Board of Censorship of Motion Pictures to insure respectability and good citizenship principles in future films. The name of this organization was subsequently changed to the National Board of Review and is still active in "carrying on a

---

[11] *Views and Film Index*, October 5, 1907.
[12] Quoted in *The Moving Picture World*, June 15, 1907.

constructive program having to do with community co-operation in the advancement and uses of the art." [13]

The issue of censorship has never been entirely solved and flares intermittently. The movement for legal control has thus far resulted in only six states (Pennsylvania, Kansas, Maryland, New York, Ohio, Virginia) adopting some form of local government censorship. Special pressure groups within and without the industry, however, have a strong regulatory influence on motion picture content.

Secure on the moral front, the close of this period saw the business foundations of motion pictures laid. Expanding nationally in three directions—in production, distribution, and exhibition—movies were no longer a novelty trade but a permanent mass-production industry. Studios, exchanges, and nickelodeons had multiplied. Producers, despite their quarrels and litigation, enjoyed steadily soaring profits. Coming years were to see the movies' commerce under the stimulus of the war, realized beyond the producers' most fantastic hopes.

[13] *National Board of Review Magazine.*

V

SOCIAL: FIRST AMERICAN STORY FILMS

THE refinement of motion picture form through editing made it possible for film makers to dramatize the moment, to give it perspective and interpretation. The popularity of stories ended the production of the trifling one-minute "report" or "incident" films that had filled the movie repertory in earlier years. Whatever movie makers saw, heard, or read they now quickly converted into crude, straightforward action pieces. Half-remembered anecdotes, newspaper headlines, cartoons, jokes, domestic affairs, social issues, economic tribulations—all sorts of everyday American ideas and activities—found their way to the screen. No occurrence was too trivial to be filmed so long as it could be made into a story. Unabashed in their still limited capabilities, movies during these years concentrated on dramatizing reality.

It is significant that despite the popularity of Melies' "magical," fantastic films and the desire of American film makers to emulate them, the Americans rarely left their own backyards and streets even when they were technically able to do so. Fairy tales, fantasies, story-book romances, were far removed from their immediate interests. Subject matter was derived from American life—from the exploits of the policeman and burglar, cowboy and factory worker, farmer and country girl, clerk and politician, drunkard and servant girl, storekeeper and mechanic.

To represent the common man in the arts was still a novel if not a daring venture. Even in literature, to depict the man of the streets as a protagonist or even as a human being was to invite censure. Stephen Crane, Theodore Dreiser, Frank Norris, and Jack London

were being greeted with reprimands or disapproving silence in their
appraisals of mean lives. But since the critical fraternity never ventured out to the nickelodeons, they could not be expected to realize
what was happening in the motion picture art.

Movies of these years, particularly those of Edwin S. Porter,
were unwittingly representing to movie-goers the conditions of
society, with little attempt to explain or justify the facts. With a
certain unpolished vigor they presented stories of crime, poverty,
headline events, fads and foibles, domestic life, the West, American
history. Not until later did they take up the practice of lifting their
subjects from famous literary works.

These first American story films had a kind of disarming honesty.
Their emphasis being entirely on action, they were forthright and
realistic, but unconsciously so. Never longer than one reel, made
with little forethought, each film was fairly typical of hundreds
of others. Told simply, the stories were blunt and extreme; the
outlook that produced them was unsophisticated and frank, as their
objective and unadorned titles show.

The first successful story film, *The Great Train Robbery*, showed
at once the startling film possibilities of crime and violence and so
struck the keynote for movie production. Burglary and looting, increasing with the growth of cities, had become dramatic news
items. The famous pursuit and desperate suicide of the outlaw
Harry Tracy had filled the newspapers of the country during the
summer of 1902; the press continually featured such news. *The
Great Train Robbery* reflected this national concern with crime:

> This sensational and highly tragic subject will certainly make a
> decided "hit" wherever shown. In every respect we consider it ab-
> solutely the superior of any motion picture film ever made. It has
> been posed and acted in faithful duplication of genuine "hold-ups"
> made famous by various outlaw bands in the far West, while the
> East has been recently shocked by several crimes of the frontier
> order, which will increase the popular interest in this great head-
> line attraction.[1]

Crime and criminals thus became one of the leading subjects of
film stories. Subsequently classified as "gangster" pictures, these

[1] Edison Catalogue, 1904.

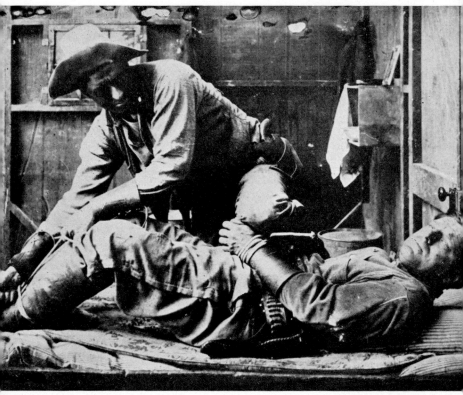

Broncho Billy, the precursor of all "western" stars, fastened to the cot. The title of the picture is unknown but it was produced before 1912. Note the opaque shadows and overhead lighting, indicating an outdoor set-up with daylight as the source of lighting.

The celebrated Keystone Cops in Mack Sennett's
In the Clutches of a Gang (1913). Ford Sterling
is at the telephone, Fatty Arbuckle, Al St. John,
and Hank Mann are in the line ready for action.

stories viewed crime from every angle, depicting holdups and robberies (*An Attack on the Agent, The Car Man's Danger, The
Thieving Hand, The Little Train Robbery, Hold-Up of the Lead-
ville Stage, The Great Bank Robbery*), outlaws' lives (*Bandit King,
Raffles, the Amateur Cracksman; The Female Highwayman, Burglar
Bill*), the work of detectives (*Trapped by Pinkertons, The Capture
of the Yegg Bank Burglars*), pursuits of criminals (*Tracked by
Bloodhounds, A Desperate Encounter*). The directors of such pictures tried painstakingly to make them authentic. Says the typical
preface to the *Capture of the Yegg Bank Burglars:* [2]

At the Annual Convention of the International Association of the
Chiefs of Police, held at St. Louis, Mo., June 6th to June 11th, 1904,
a paper was read by William A. Pinkerton, of Pinkerton's National
Detective Agency, entitled "The Yeggman" or the "Bank Vault and
Safe Burglar of Today." Using the above as a foundation, together
with additional information, and suggestions by Robert A. Pinkerton and G. S. Doherty of the Pinkerton National Detective Agency,
we offer the following picture in 15 exciting scenes, showing the
life and methods of the "yegg bank burglar."

The outlaws themselves were rarely condemned or criticized; in
fact, if there was any bias displayed it favored the burglar. He was
shown to have a spark of goodness (a baby redeems *Burglar Bill*),
or to be the victim of circumstances (*The Jail Bird*). At times the
films made the criminals characters of courage and loyalty (*Bandit
King*). *The Little Train Robbery*, for example, ended with a final
scene of

the entire gang of bedraggled and crestfallen robbers tied together
with a rope and being led away by police. Two of the police are
loaded down with revolvers, knives and cartridge belts, and resemble walking arsenals. As a fitting climax a confederate steals out of
the woods, cuts the rope, and gallantly rescues the "Bandit Queen." [3]

Poverty and the struggle for existence also were favorite dramatic
subjects. The desperate need of the average movie-goer for money
was expressed on the screens of the nation, now in serious and now
in comic terms. Hundreds of pictures discussed "its need and its
lack, its power and its curse."

[2] Edison Catalogue, 1904.   [3] Edison Catalogue, 1905.

The Need of Gold dramatically related how a miner on his sick-bed dies from lack of money for food and medicine, while his daughter, disguising herself as a man, holds up a stage coach.

Upon learning that she held up the coach to save her dying father, the posse decides to release her— The posse then take up a collection and leave it for the grief-stricken girl.[4]

The Miser's Hoard demonstrated that miserliness leads but to the grave, while on the other hand a poor widow with her destitute family,

. . . unable to pay her rent, is dispossessed. She goes to the woods to gather kindling wood to sell and incidentally finds the log containing "The Miser's Hoard," thereby bringing relief to her destitute family.[5]

A Desperate Encounter related tragically how a burglar steals because of acute necessity. *A River Tragedy* was a pathetic drama of a girl who cannot find work, and in desperation commits suicide. *Nobody Works Like Father, She Won't Pay Her Rent, Neighbors Who Borrow, Free Lunch*, though comic in tone, were equally frank discussions of the necessity of money.

Films not only dramatized poverty but, in endless reiterations, deplored it. The poor were continually beset by troubles; life was not only hard but complicated. Pictures portrayed how the poor found themselves in one difficulty after another, helpless victims of circumstances. *The Eleventh Hour* was the story of a typical unfortunate:

An honest Italian attending to his peanut stand is bothered by a bully. The Italian resents this and a fight results during which the bully falls and strikes his head, which kills him. The Italian is arrested, convicted of murder and sentenced to die. Wife makes a plea to the governor, who turns a deaf ear. She comes home overcome with grief. Her children are stirred to action. They go to the governor, and beg for the life of their dad. . . . At last the governor's human nature is touched and he hands a pardon to the two tots. They lose no time in delivering it and reach jail as the

---

4 *Views and Film Index*, December 7, 1907.
5 Advertisement of Vitagraph Films in *Views and Film Index*, December 28, 1907.

father is led out to meet his fate. The pardon is delivered at the eleventh hour. Happy reunion.[6]

How dire conditions could become for those without economic security was dramatized in *The Ex-Convict* (1905): [7]

An ex-convict is found out and fired from his job. He tries to get other work but his past is held against him and he fails . . . On the way home he saves a child in a wealthy residential section from being run over. He refuses to give his name to the policeman and disappears in the crowd. Returning home, he becomes acutely aware of the poverty of his single-room home, sick child and starved wife. He cannot stand their poverty and determines upon some desperate action to get necessities. He comes out and begins to beg (snowing night) but is refused. He peeps through the windows of a warm mansion and on the spur of the moment decides to rob it for the sake of his wife and child. Inside, he searches for valuables and accidentally knocks over a vase. The noise awakens the household. He is caught redhanded by the owner who covers the burglar with a pistol. As he calls for police his daughter comes down in her night clothes and recognizes the burglar as the man who saved her life that morning. Police arrive but the father saves the burglar from arrest. He sends presents to the house of the ex-convict who thanks the callers for their kindness at a time when most needed.

The simple realism of such a drama was soon to be colored by a moral lesson, as in *The Eviction*, reviewed as "an overwhelming success. . . . A new era in American films" by *Views and Film Index:* [8]

A poor woman is awaiting her husband outside the factory. He comes out with comrades, preferring their company to his wife's, and goes with them to a saloon where he gambles and gets drunk. Drunk, he dreams that his wife has sold her wedding ring to save their home and furniture. Awakening, he is restrained from going home by his comrades, who induce him to get drunk again. Again he dreams, this time that his family is being evicted. On awakening he hurries home to the poor tenement where they live, in time to see the landlord removing his furniture, his wife and child watching

[6] Advertisement of Essanay Film Mfg. Co. in *Views and Film Index*, November 23, 1907.   [7] Edison Catalogue, 1905.   [8] December 21, 1907.

in sorrow. Their distress is so great that passers-by chip in to pay the rent. Their furniture is thus restored. The husband repents, the wife forgives, and a new life has begun for the family.[9]

Sympathy for the poor was matched by a distrust of rich bankers and politicians. How deep the feeling was is suggested by the titles of some pictures: *Crooked Banker, Bank Defaulter, Miser's Fate, The Politician, The Grafters. The Kleptomaniac* strikingly painted a picture of American justice in the hands of the wealthy. *The Money Lender* is typical:

An avaricious old miser makes a business of lending money. One of his clients, in his teens, gets into great difficulties through borrowing money and being unable to pay it back. He is just about to steal money from his own father to pay back what he owes when his mother discovers him in the act and he confesses everything to her. His father forgives him and then visits the money lender, and after paying what the son owes him gives the old villain a deserved thrashing.[10]

Newspapers were now full of reports of how women were gaining "new freedom." Jobs for women were opening in offices and factories. The Majestic Theatre in New York was employing women ushers for the first time. "Beauty shows" were being inaugurated in commercial expositions, and the "ten-twenty-thirts" were depicting *Bertha, the Sewing Machine Girl* and *Nellie, the Beautiful Cloak Model*. Movies exploited this theme in *Why Girls Leave Home, The Path of Folly, A Danger Signal,* and *Nellie, the Pretty Typist, or a Romance Among Skyscrapers.* Not only did such melodramas reflect a few of the growing issues of the times; they taught lessons which were fresh to the unsophisticated movie-goers of that day. Typical moral teaching was offered in *The Miller's Daughter* (1905), in which a girl runs off with a city artist, only to return "in distress." Not until she repents, becomes a church member in good standing, and marries the country boy just before her child is born, is she forgiven.

Films presently began to sum up the moral code of the day, and this trend was to have great vogue in the next period. The prevalent

[9] December 21, 1907.   [10] *Views and Film Index*, March 21, 1908.

attitude was expressed by Grover Cleveland in his articles in *The Ladies' Home Journal* in 1905: "The relative positions to be assumed by man and woman in the working out of our civilization were assigned long ago by a higher intelligence than ours." In keeping with such attitudes, *Woman's Devotion* described the utter loyalty proper to woman. *A Tale of the Sea* closed with the scene of the wife who, after being presented with diamonds and treasures her husband had acquired in his many varied adventures, "brings from the room a more precious gift—a tiny baby." [11] Relatively few though these domestic dramas still were, their moral tone set the standard that movies were soon to follow in earnest.

Drink and agitation for prohibition also were claiming public attention; temperance and reform movements were gaining momentum. Movies, seizing this popular theme, depicted the results of drinking both comically (*Sight-Seeing Through Whiskey*) and seriously (*The White Caps*). The latter film told of local enforcement of temperance by vigilantes and the punishment of a habitual drunkard. The Edison Catalogue (1905) objectively declared: "We have portrayed in motion pictures, in most vivid and most realistic manner, the methods employed by *The White Caps* to rid the community of undesirable citizens."

The sordid and depressing settings of most of these dramas were counterbalanced by hundreds of comedies on fads and foibles of the day. How a French nobleman got a wife through *The New York Herald* became the film *Personal Column*. The *"Strenuous Life," or Anti-Race Suicide* made fun of the Roosevelt philosophy by showing a business man and his four babies kicking the doctor out of the house. *The Whole Damn Family and the Damn Dog* pictured the comic characters widely advertised on posters, on mailing cards, and in vaudeville skits. *Laughing Gas* showed the disastrous effects of the new anesthetic. The novelty of the automobile (in a day when people were being shown the correct and the incorrect way of entering it) was the subject of hilarity in *His First Ride*, *Purchasing an Auto*, and *Automobile Thieves*.

Many movies accented the growing popularity of sports (*How Brown Saw the Baseball Game*, *The Football Craze*, *The Little*

[11] *Views and Film Index*, December 14, 1907.

Coxswain of the Varsity Eight, The Vanderbilt Cup). *Cohen's Fire Sale* found humor in a new business practice of the day. Other current matters comically handled were *Buying a Cow, The Servant Girl Problem, Babies Will Play, Oh! That Limburger, Where Is My Hair?, When Women Vote.*

Risqué comedies burlesqued the trials and tribulations of domestic life (*Gaieties of Divorce, Honeymoon at Niagara, If You Had a Wife Like This, Waiting at the Church, Married Again, Engaged to Another*). Love frequently furnished occasion for amusement (*The Proposal, A Race for a Wife, Cupid's Pranks, Fight for Love, Love Microbe*). Out-and-out sexy teasers were extremely popular (*Old Man's Darling, A Seaside Flirtation, Beware, My Husband Comes, College Boy's First Love*). A number of films were made frankly for "smoking concerts" (*Bride Retiring, Courageous Husband, Honeymoon Trip, Kissing in a Tunnel, Ladies of the Court Bathing, Love at Each Floor, Parisienne's Bedtime*). Such pictures as these, together with the crime films, increased the general agitation for censorship of the screen.

The movie's sense of humor did not overlook the populace's major hardship: work. Sympathy for the employer was common. *Sunday with the Boss* showed him as a "regular guy" on his day off. *Work Made Easy*, temptingly advertised as a "picture for the lazy," toyed with the new notion of a robot replacing the worker and performing the most difficult and arduous tasks. *Vive la Sabotage!*, an extremely witty and popular French importation, was translated by its distributor as *Union Workers Spoil the Food*, a title which disparaged the film's pro-union theme.

A lively and popular subject for films both comic and serious was the various racial and national minorities in America. Movies tried hard not to give offense, since the immigrant population included many customers, but prejudices against the foreigner did appear. *The Masher* showed a lady-killer rebuffed by everyone with whom he flirts. Finally he is successful, only to discover that his conquest is a Negress; whereupon he runs for dear life. *Wooing and Wedding of a Coon*, "a genuine Ethiopian comedy," poked fun at Negroes. Such themes were carried over from vaudeville.

Perhaps the most violent prejudices against foreign racial groups were those registered in *Fights of Nations*. The Mexican was caricatured as a treacherous "greaser"; the Jew as a briber; the Negro as a cake walker, buck dancer, razor thrower; the Spaniard as a romantic, foppish lover; the Irishman as a quarrelsome beer drinker. The film ended with a tableau designed to fix the prejudices in the audience to stimulate their chauvinism:

America then serves as an appropriate finale. The scene is magnificently decorated with emblems of all nations, the American eagle surmounting them. In harmony, peace, and good will the characters of the different nations appear, making it an allegorical representation of "Peace" with the United States presiding at a congress of Powers.[12]

A flood of Western pictures began soon after a few companies moved West. *Views and Film Index*, February 23, 1907, ran the following trade note:

The Polyscope camera man has just returned from a stay of two weeks in the heart of the Rocky Mountains. The results of his work, coupled with that of the Selig Pantomime artists, will shortly appear in the market under the title *The Girl from Montana*. The Selig Company says that the film will unfold a pretty love story, typically Western in its characters and environment; in the way of adventure it promises something new and novel. Well, Selig knows what's what in pictures.

The Life of a Cowboy, *The Cowboy and the School Marm*, *Prospectors*, *The Adventures of an American Cowboy*, were a few of the hundreds of Western films that followed. Typical of the current style was the story of *The Pony Express* (1907), relating the capture of a rider by "greasers." The rider's horse runs away and "tells" a group of cowboys, who gallop to the scene, put the "greasers" to flight, and save the heroic rider.

American history offered an inexhaustible, colorful variety of subjects. The past was re-enacted in a series of patriotic films, hundreds of which solemnly educated the immigrant audience: *Saving His Country's Flag*, *Paul Revere*, *The Boston Tea Party*, *The Colonial Soldier*, *Days of '61*. These films always ended with a close-up of Old Glory billowing proudly in the breeze, "inspiring the

---

[12] *The Moving Picture World*, March 9, 1907.

beholder with pride for his adopted land." To dramatizations of the country's traditions, films of activities of the United States Army and Navy were added. *The Moving Picture World* [13] noted that "the United States government is trying to get recruits for the Army and Navy by exhibiting in interior towns and cities moving picture representations of the daily life of the soldiers and sailors."

The tremendous demand for stories forced movie makers to turn to stage and literature for completed material. Every possible source was ransacked; short stories, poems, plays, operas, popular best-sellers, and classics were condensed into one-reel screen presentations. *Parsifal, Uncle Tom's Cabin, The Lady and the Tiger, Ben Hur, As You Like It, Hiawatha, Evangeline, Dr. Jekyll and Mr. Hyde, The Merry Widow, Way Down East, Monsieur Beaucaire,* and *The Scarlet Letter* were some of these pioneer adaptations. In 1907 *A Curious Dream*, by Mark Twain, was accompanied by the following advertisement—probably one of the first testimonials of its kind in motion pictures:

Gentlemen: I authorize the Vitagraph Company of America to make a moving picture from my "Curious Dream." I have their picture of John Barter, examining his gravestone, and find it frightfully and deliciously humorous.

(Signed)   *Mark Twain*

The adoption of fiction and plays was quickened by the censorship attack that flared up in 1907-1908. Producers could feel certain that material taken from decorous literary works would provide critics with little excuse for further attacks. It is a policy that is still followed.

As movie makers became more fluent as well as affluent, they grew more self-conscious. Their range of interests broadened; their films imitated the purposefulness of literary sources. Movies began to present morals, preach sermons, advocate standards of conduct. *The Moving Picture World* [14] declared:

The human heart goes out to these pictures because they recall scenes that are dear to the poorest patrons of these shows. Surely

[13] March 23, 1907.   [14] June 29, 1907.

Charlie Chaplin, the bane of cops, turned "copper" for his celebrated *Easy Street* (1917), in his plea for the rights of the individual in a crass world.

Thomas H. Ince's *Typhoon* (1914), one of the
first story films to re-create a catastrophe of
nature for dramatic purposes.

an agency that draws out all that is good in human nature and shows the disastrous effect of wrong-doing is an agency that makes for good citizenship, higher education and better morals.

During the following years the moralistic quality of motion pictures was to become pronounced.

At the close of their first five years of story-telling movies had thus advanced from "sensation, grotesque humor and every-day life" to morality dramas, the early West, American history and literary adaptations. The succeeding years were to see movie producers, more self-conscious in their efforts and purpose, develop these sources in addition to those of contemporary news events.

In 1908 thousands of people were attending the nickelodeons weekly. Movies were by this time acknowledged not as just an innocent novelty but as a powerful medium of social expression. Observers outside the industry began to note that films were becoming for children and the uneducated one of the chief sources for new ideas, points of view, attitudes toward government and society, habits of mind, standards of taste, conduct, morals, canons of convention, culture. As many reformers and agitators for censorship were insisting, the imagery of the movie was significantly impressive to the populace. How powerful a social agency the motion picture could be was still, however, to be realized.

PART THREE

DEVELOPMENT (1908-1914)

VI

THE STRUGGLE FOR CONTROL

THE years 1908 to 1914 were a time of feverish activity and confusion in the industry. Bigger money stakes, keener competition, momentous innovations in technique, and experimental themes kept the business unsettled. This period saw, moreover, a ruthless struggle for the control of key vantage points in the motion picture world. Two events in particular affected the whole future course and form of motion pictures. One was the establishment of the Motion Picture Patents Company trust which, though doomed to eventual failure, dominated and influenced all motion picture activity for four years. The second event was the introduction of the long "feature" picture, which was soon to be firmly established and to revolutionize the business. These new developments spurred the industry into an awareness of its powers and into its third stage of expansion, that of big business.

The phenomenal growth of the demand for pictures produced a bitterer and widening competition. The number of manufacturers, importers, and exchange men in the industry mounted to between fifty and one hundred, and nickelodeons into the thousands. Manufacturing was a wide-open field, although the only manufacturers with a legal right to the patents were the three pioneer companies, Edison, Biograph, and Vitagraph. With lawsuits multiplying, cutthroat practices undermining the trade, and enmities spreading, the situation grew ever more critical.

In a desperate effort to stabilize the business and to forestall further unsettling competition, nine leading manufacturers and the major distributor and importer of foreign films banded together

81

and announced, on January 1, 1909, the formation of the Motion Picture Patents Company. The company comprised seven domestic manufacturers, Edison, Biograph, Vitagraph, Essanay, Selig, Lubin, and Kalem; two French companies, Melies and Pathé; and the distributor George Kleine. All pooled their patent claims, and each received a license to manufacture motion pictures. It was agreed that no additional licenses were to be issued; movie making was to be restricted to these initial nine companies. Edison, acknowledged as the owner of the basic patents, was to be paid a small royalty in return for the use of the instruments. To strengthen their plan to control and monopolize the production of all motion pictures, the Motion Picture Patents Company contracted with the largest manufacturer of raw film stock, the Eastman Kodak Company, to supply only the licensed members of the pool with raw film.

To regulate exhibition as well as production the Motion Picture Patents Company set up a system of taxation. Exhibitors were charged $2 a week for the right to use projectors and to rent films from the licensed members of the trust. Any exhibitor who dared to show a film made by an "outlaw" company was threatened with the confiscation of his projectors and stoppage of service. Theatres were classified and the rental rates of pictures were standardized accordingly, each exhibitor paying according to his class. Rates for the highest class were $100 to $125 weekly for a daily change of program; the cheapest rate was $15. When a system of booking films was framed, it was provided that the exhibitor could not change the date or selection of pictures once they had been arranged for. Violators were to be either fined or wholly deprived of the film service.

Bitter opposition from all quarters greeted the trust combine. Manufacturers and exchange men who were outside the pool refused to be victimized without a struggle. Bootlegging of films and projectors began; an underground business between independents and exhibitors was soon flourishing. Although over 10,000 small exhibitors signed with the Patents Company, all regarded the $2 tax as a dictatorial raid on their profits. To fight the trust many protective organizations (similar to "the Patents Company without the patents") were formed: the National Independent Motion Picture Alliance, Chicago, Illinois; the Associated Independent Film Manufacturers, New York City; and most important of all, the Motion Picture Distributing and Sales Company, with Carl Laemmle as president. The latter company was prepared to sell and ship "bootleg" products of any independent producer. It collected fees, and deducted a percentage from its members' receipts for a common defense fund in the battle against the trust.

The Motion Picture Patents Company, to secure its monopoly control, was soon forced to establish a national film exchange. For that purpose the General Film Company was formed in April 1910, and it swallowed up all licensed exchanges. If a licensed exchange did not want to sell, its license was revoked or suspended, so that it could not do business "legitimately" with trust pictures. By January 1, 1912, all the principal exchanges—fifty-seven out of fifty-eight—had been bought out. The one company that did not succumb was the Greater New York Film Rental Company, owned by William Fox. Powerful enough to withstand such threats because he himself owned many theatres in New York City, Fox became one of the leading opponents of the trust. He undertook the production of movies and instituted a lawsuit against the Patents Company as an unlawful conspiracy in restraint of trade. The lawsuit eventually resulted in the Patent Company's dissolution by the courts.

With the Motion Picture Patents Company monopolizing production, with exhibition regulated, and with the General Film Company controlling distribution, it appeared for a time that the trust had cornered the motion picture business. But despite its ingenious schemes and its apparently formidable strength, the trust was doomed from its birth. Instead of killing competition, it engendered more. "Outlaw" companies multiplied, flourished, and continued making pictures. So steadily did independent manufacturers increase in number and in stature that, by 1912, Fox, I.M.P., Rex, Nestor, Thanhouser, Bison, Keystone, Mutual, Powers, Lux, the New York Motion Picture Company, and dozens of lesser firms were offering stiff opposition to the trust. Besides, many other foreign manufacturers had appeared, Great Northern, Itala, Ambrosio, and Eclair being in the lead.

Independents, boldly advertising in the trade papers, pointed out to exhibitors the "dangers entailed in paying blackmail." They encouraged defiance of the trust, offering not only cheaper prices but better products. The trust countered with midnight raids on "hideout" studios, with sabotage of equipment, with subpoenas and injunctions to uphold their dictatorship legally. But it proved virtually impossible to police the numerous and active independents. For almost five years guerilla warfare, with open violence as well as lawsuits, raged between the monopoly and the independents, no strategy being overlooked by either side.

Never entirely successful, the monopoly was finally destroyed sooner than anyone had reckoned. In 1912, when strong antitrust sentiment was crystallizing under the progressivism of Woodrow Wilson, the time was propitious for those fettered by the movie monopoly to obtain "justice for the rights of the little man." William Fox's accusation that the trust was violating the Sherman antitrust law brought the trust into the courts in 1913. Though the hearings dragged on in the courts for years, disintegration within the Patents Company was rapid. Not legally declared dead until 1917, the trust had actually become wholly ineffectual by 1914.

The bitter and acute conflict had important effects, artistically and economically, on the motion picture industry. In the first place, competition focused attention on self-improvement, and the quality of motion pictures was raised. Secondly, Hollywood was discovered and established as the home of production: a move which was to have far-reaching economic and social results. Thirdly, the "star system" as a factor in profits, production, publicity, and appeal was invented; this development was to become increasingly influential in the industry. All three of these effects of the conflict entailed minor changes that were no less vital. Together they made the industry self-conscious artistically, economically, and socially.

While the licensed companies were standardizing and cramping their pictures, the independents sought in every way to better the quality of theirs and so gain patronage. They lured away many of the trust's experienced film makers by offering them higher wages; in production they encouraged experimentation, originality, inventiveness. Made almost always "on the run," the independents' pictures had the virtue of new and interesting locales and fresh subject matter. Before long it became apparent to the conservative members of the trust that the impact of the independents' competition was due in no small measure to their superior products. The trust members thereupon began to budget their pictures higher, increase their personnel, raise their own standards, allow their directors greater leeway. A race for quality now went on side by side with the race for quantity. Higher artistic standards, technical improvements, and a more ambitious state of mind finally led to the acceptance of the most significant advancement of all, the "feature."

The establishment of Hollywood as the production center of the industry was prompted by the independents' desire to avoid the attacks of the trust. Independents fled from New York, the center of production activity, to Cuba, Florida, San Francisco, Los Angeles. Cuba proved to be disease-ridden; Florida, too warm; San Francisco, too far from the Mexican border. The safest refuge was Los Angeles, from which it was only a hop-skip-and-jump to the Mexican border and escape from injunctions and subpoenas. Other advantages soon showed this location to be even more desirable than New York: good all-year-round weather, cheap labor, a rich variety of topography, and the ready co-operation of business and real-estate interests in the community. Independent companies soon were flocking to Los Angeles, and the bigger licensed companies were attracted there occasionally for seasonal reasons. As California's desirability became more apparent, the big companies, too, began to settle there. By 1913 a suburb of Los Angeles was so completely developed as the home of motion-picture making that it was separated from Los Angeles proper and given the legal name of Hollywood.

The colonization of Hollywood at that particular time was fortunate in many respects. The availability of all production needs and advantages made it possible to produce better pictures more regularly and more efficiently. Movie makers now had space to work in; the pressure of financial supervision was lighter; getting dependable acting talent was easier. With the financial offices separated from the production studios, film directors were more independent, could use their ingenuity and ideas more freely. The centralization of all production agencies created an *esprit de corps* and a competitive spirit that stimulated ambition, personal rivalry, and creativeness. The effort of each company to impress its neighbor and its Eastern offices often resulted in a refinement of its product. Before long, in fact, the designation of a picture as "a Hollywood production" was a commercial asset, since it meant that the picture had met a high professional standard.

Perhaps the most important outcome of the trust war was the establishment of the "star" and the "star system." Movie patrons by 1910 were favoring certain players and expressing their preferences, although as yet the names of their screen idols were unknown. Manufacturers diligently kept such information secret, reasoning that any public recognition actors received would inspire demands for bigger salaries. Companies paid no attention to what they termed "Who?" letters from inquiring movie-goers who wanted to know the names and habits of prominent players. The public had to identify favorites according to the company in whose pictures they appeared (the "Biograph girl," "IMP girl," "Vitagraph girl"), according to their screen names ("Little Mary," the "Husband," the "Banker," the "Waif"), or according to some distinguishing physical trait (the "Girl with the Curls," the "Thin Woman," the "Man with the Sad Eyes," the "Handsome Indian"). No manufacturer was shrewd enough to see that this mounting curiosity in movie enthusiasts could be turned to his own advantage.

It was Carl Laemmle, head of IMP, the leading independent, who made the first "star." Casting about for a means of drawing customers away from his licensed rivals' pictures, he acquired the exclusive services of Florence Lawrence, one of the most popular players of the day, "the Biograph girl." He offered her the advantages not only of an increased salary but of widespread publicity as well. Being a firm believer in advertising (his campaign conducted by Robert Cochrane against the trust was perhaps the most colorful salesmanship of its kind), Laemmle introduced Florence Lawrence to the American public through a daring ruse, imitated by others often since.

St. Louis citizens awoke one morning to read in the newspapers that the former Biograph player Florence Lawrence (this was the first time her name was publicly used) had died in a St. Louis street-car accident. Immediately after this melancholy notice was published, there appeared an advertising blast by Laemmle declaring that the story was a false rumor spread by the trust. His half-page advertisement in *The Moving Picture World* [1] raged:

WE NAIL A LIE

The blackest and at the same time the silliest lie yet circulated by enemies of the "Imp" was the story foisted on the public of St. Louis last week to the effect that Miss Lawrence (the "Imp" girl, formerly known as the "Biograph" girl) had been killed by a street car. It was a black lie because so cowardly. It was a silly lie because so easily disproved. Miss Lawrence was not even in a street-car accident, is in the best of health, will continue to appear in "Imp" films, and very shortly some of the best work in her career is to be released. We now announce our next films: *The Broken Path . . . The Time-Lock Safe. . . .*

A follow-up advertisement announced that, to put at rest all doubt in the public's mind, to satisfy America that Florence Lawrence was alive, King Baggott, I.M.P.'s leading man, would escort her to St. Louis in person.

The Lawrence-Baggott visit to St. Louis was the first "personal appearance" of movie players. King Baggott and Florence Lawrence were greeted at the station and theatre by a riotous crowd. Admirers "demonstrated their affection by tearing the buttons off Florence Lawrence's coat, the trimmings from her hat, the hat from her head." [2]

So the screen star was born.

Other independent companies soon began publicizing the names of their players. Campaigns to establish the "stars" as drawing attractions got under way. A typical advertisement to exhibitors argued,

What is the earthly use of showing pictures posed by amateurs and unknowns when you can get the very best known stars of the screen by using that Universal Program? No concern on earth is

[1] March 12, 1910.   [2] *The Life and Adventures of Carl Laemmle*, p. 141.

strong enough to engage the services of such high-priced talent as that which is seen every day in the week in Universal Pictures. . . .[3]

At first the licensed companies opposed this innovation and remained aloof from it. Many of their actors promptly began to leave, seeking the publicity offered by the independents. The trust now angrily ruled that if an actor was discovered to have left a licensed company for an independent, he would be blacklisted in all trust studios. But the trek toward "stardom" could not be halted. The roster of players who were glad to become stars included, besides King Baggott and Florence Lawrence, Florence Turner, John Bunny, Marguerite Snow, James Cruze, Alice Joyce, and J. Warren Kerrigan, to mention a few. By 1911 the flow of talented players into the ranks of the independents had left Biograph so weakened that, when *His Daughter* was released in 1911, it was news for a critic to comment in surprise that "the picture has something of the spirit and character of the old Biograph stock company's work."

Vitagraph, Lubin, and Kalem were the first of the licensed group to adopt the star policy. Biograph protested that it had won the esteem of the public as an institution, and the value of its pictures did not depend on any individuals. But Biograph, too, was forced into line. *The Moving Picture World*, April 12, 1913, reported a "change of policy in Biograph when this week's posters were issued bearing photographs and names of a score of members of their acting department. . . ."

Biograph varied the usual scheme by giving the players less publicity than it gave the directors and cameramen. David W. Griffith, whose films had become the models of the industry, led the list as "David Belasco Griffith"; Dell Henderson was next for his farces and comedies; Tony O'Sullivan was third for melodramas; Billy Bitzer was mentioned for photography. The cast of players was relegated to the end of the list.

To develop the star policy most companies turned to showmanship. They sold exhibitors trade photographs and stereopticon slides of players. Posters of favorites were placed in theatre lobbies, and "star post cards" were distributed to the inquirers, now dubbed

[3] *The Moving Picture World*, October 3, 1913.

"fans," who wrote the once-despised "Who?" letters. Ambitious players sent out personally autographed photos on their own initiative. Fan letters were encouraged and promptly answered.

The star policy was more securely established by a new type of publicity medium, the "fan magazine." J. Stuart Blackton of Vitagraph started the fashion by financing the first popular screen publication, *Motion Picture Magazine*, which he believed would glorify Vitagraph pictures and Vitagraph players. At first the magazine was distributed by the Vitagraph sales department to exhibitors who were showing the licensed companies' pictures, and through the exhibitors to their audiences. The demand for the magazine was so great, however, that soon it was being successfully sold on newsstands. It summarized Vitagraph stories and commented on Vitagraph stars; only subsequently were other licensed companies' products and players mentioned so that the magazine would appear to be non-partisan. In October 1912 an unenlightened reader wrote to the editor:

Inasmuch as there are more theatres showing independent films than licensed, I should think it would be more consistent to picture more independent players. . . . Surely such players as Pauline Bush, Warren Kerrigan, Vivian Prescott, King Baggott, Marguerite Snow, Flo La Badie and many other stars are as popular as those pictured in your book.

Other companies, not slow to see the commercial possibilities of fan magazines, followed with their own publications or enthusiastically co-operated with independent publishers in similar ventures. The next years bore a large crop of these magazines, which centered attention ever more upon personalities and "star" importance. Gradually the stars became well known through colorful anecdotes, legends, and myths that were interesting if not altogether true. Now becoming the focus of public attention, in the next period the stars were to become the pivot of production. Incorporated into the planning of movies, the star policy gradually evolved into a regular system for production. This became of increasing importance as the industry developed and exists today as one of its major factors.

With the three new attributes the trust war had brought to

motion pictures—quality, Hollywood, the star system—the industry was energized at a crucial point in its development. Production, distribution, and exhibition expanded constantly despite litigation, dissension, and other hindrances. What in another business might have proved fatal hardly slowed the upward surge of this business. With ten thousand nickelodeons and with ten to twenty million people going regularly to movies, profits skyrocketed.

During the monopoly war still another innovation affected the industry vitally: the multiple-reel picture. This, which gave the fatal blow to the patents trust, was introduced from abroad, and an independent first adopted it as a regular device. Before 1911 few productions had been longer than one reel: the full thousand feet had been reserved only for special subjects. An occasional longer picture from Europe, usually of a religious or dramatic nature, as *The Passion Play* and *The Dreyfus Case*, had aroused surprise in the exchanges; but few producers and exhibitors in America had thought about making or showing pictures of more than one reel. Then suddenly two-, three-, and even four-reel subjects began coming over from Europe. These were released by the American exchanges in installments, one reel at a time, despite the break this caused in the story. Finally Griffith's *Enoch Arden* (1911), one of the first domestic two-reelers, appeared. It was released in two parts, but public demand for a single showing was so strong that the exhibitors were forced to present the two reels together. Thus a two-reel film was exhibited as a unit for the first time in America.

More longer films were now attempted. Within a year pictures two and three reels long, known as "features" to distinguish them from the one-reel "shorts," were familiar to movie audiences. Long pictures were not yet in strong demand, but *The Moving Picture World*[4] had a shrewd eye on their future: "The two and three reel subject is indeed a necessary product of the higher ideals. It is bound to come and in two or three years will be the rule rather than the exception."

It was oddly enough an exhibitor, not a manufacturer, who became the first regular producer of features in the United States.

[4] June 17, 1911.

In 1912 Adolph Zukor imported a four-reel French film, *Queen Elizabeth*, starring the internationally famed Sarah Bernhardt, and its unusual success in his own theatres proved to Zukor that movie-goers would accept feature-length pictures. Fired by the possibilities of the idea, Zukor tried to interest the Motion Picture Patents Company in it. When they ignored him, he undertook the venture on his own. Failing to enlist D. W. Griffith, Zukor engaged the second major director in the business, Edwin S. Porter, and persuaded Daniel Frohman, one of the biggest theatrical producers, to lend his name, prestige, and affiliations to his enterprise: The Famous Players in Famous Plays Company.

The movie world viewed the project skeptically; the theatrical world, on the other hand, was deeply stirred. Stage people and business men immediately organized similar movie companies to make feature-length pictures starring stage celebrities. Within a year there were several such companies, including the Helen Gardner Picture Corporation, Pallas Pictures, Morosco Pictures (allied with the stage producer, Oliver Morosco), and most important of all, the Jesse Lasky Feature Play Company. The latter, with the name of David Belasco to add prestige to its features, consisted of Jesse Lasky, a vaudeville producer; Cecil B. DeMille, a playwright; and Samuel Goldfish, a salesman—three men who were to become important figures in motion picture history.

These new developments appeared quickly. What the trade called the "feature craze" caught on despite the General Film Company's resolute refusal to distribute features. Lacking exchange facilities, the independent feature companies sold exhibition rights to individual distributors representing the various states. This practice became known as "states' rights distribution."

The supply of feature films was swelled in 1913 by feature-length importations from Europe. One of these foreign products was greeted with such enthusiastic acclaim that it proved beyond the shadow of a doubt, even to the most conservative American producer, that the feature picture was the picture of the future. The film that decided the issue and marked the beginning of a new kind of movie making was the Italian *Quo Vadis*.

Nine reels long, the first of the great "spectacles," *Quo Vadis* held its audiences over two hours, although no movie had been thought capable of sustaining interest more than a half hour. Opening April 21, 1913, in the Astor, *Quo Vadis* had the distinction of being the first motion picture to be presented in a "first-class" Broadway theatre. The $1.50 admission instead of the usual fifteen cents lifted the presentation out of the nickelodeon class. Not since the movies' debut at Koster and Bial's Music Hall in 1896 had such a fashionable crowd been attracted to see a motion picture.

Imaginatively conceived and produced, *Quo Vadis* surpassed all of the stage's attempts at "spectacle." Its two and a half hours of "splendid acting, beautiful photography, realistic effects, and uncommon elegance" provoked the audience into "loud and prolonged applause." Scenes of the burning of Rome, hundreds of panic-stricken people, houses tottering, the charge of Romans among Christian martyrs, the struggles of Roman gladiators, bacchanalian orgies, gave the film a lavishness and splendor beyond anything the screen or the stage had ever seen. By the middle of the summer twenty-two road shows in the United States and Canada were showing *Quo Vadis* in former legitimate theatres. The widespread popularity of the film convinced producers that the feature length and a lavish production scale would hereafter have to be the standards of movie making.

Any lingering doubts were dispelled by the welcome given to similar feature-length spectacles that came from Italy soon after *Quo Vadis*. *The Last Days of Pompeii*, advertised as "having 10,000 people, 260 scenes, costing $250,000 to produce," was in eight reels. Equally long and sumptuous in production values was *Antony and Cleopatra*, of which Vachel Lindsay, the poet and critic, said,[5] "Viewed as a circus, the acting is elephantine in its grandeur. All that is needed is pink lemonade sold in the audience."

That same year the longest film yet produced was imported from France: *Les Misérables*, in twelve reels. Never shown continuously, it was released in four sections of three reels each. Louis Reeves Harrison in *The Moving Picture World*[6] pronounced it the "film of the century":

[5] *The Art of the Moving Picture*, p. 55.   [6] April 26, 1913.

Never in the history of Kinematography has there been attempted a production of any of the literary classics on a scale so stupendous. The adequateness and completeness of this picture is such that the largest and best theatres may feature it on a par with the greatest theatrical stars at regular first-class theatres.

Though none of these follow-ups of *Quo Vadis* had that film's impact or enjoyed its extraordinary success, the popularity of feature pictures could no longer be questioned or allowed to go unheeded.

The final endorsement of feature pictures came in 1914 with a significant business consolidation. W. W. Hodkinson, a successful exhibitor through better-class motion picture theatres, together with other independent theatre owners and "states' rights" distributors, formed the Paramount Pictures Corporation to finance and distribute feature-length pictures to be regularly produced by affiliated independent studios. In this way the exhibitors would be assured of a steady supply of features and the studios of a steady market for their products. The first producers brought into the scheme were Zukor and his Famous Players Company, original sponsors of the feature; Lasky's Feature Play Company, and Pallas Pictures and Morosco Pictures. W. W. Hodkinson became president of the new enterprise, later to be replaced by Adolph Zukor.

Paramount opened special exchanges throughout the country, and a nation-wide campaign was launched to win exhibitors for the feature film. The advantages of the new, enlarged picture form were hammered home to the trade in such slogans as "Selected pictures for selected audiences," "Long runs for good pictures." With four companies specializing in feature production, Paramount proceeded to sign up exhibitors, guaranteeing to give them two five-reel pictures every week.

The battle for survival between shorts and feature-length films was on. A new era of film making and of film makers was imminent; the end of motion pictures as a trade and its beginnings as a large-scale enterprise were foreshadowed. The development of Hollywood, of stars, and of feature films, together with the building of bigger and better theatres and ambitious advertising campaigns, was to urge the industry forward and bring new groups into its current.

By 1914 the tremendous expansion in movie production, distribution, and exhibition, stimulated by the trust war and the new excitement over features, had shaken the industry to its roots. The upheaval had overthrown the trust and swept out with it many of the movies' pioneers. The independents whom the licensed companies had attempted to suppress were now in a stronger position than ever before. The time was not far off when many of the trust members were to be forced out of business and a new and more powerful trust, composed of the former independents, was to be established in its place.

VII

D. W. GRIFFITH: NEW DISCOVERIES

THE third major figure in the rise of the American film, David Wark Griffith, did not want to make motion pictures. No contradiction proved more ironic for, in the entire history of the American screen, no other director achieved greater success, none won more esteem. This "enigmatic and somewhat tragic" figure, as Gilbert Seldes describes him, secretly cherished the ambition to become famous as an author and counted the moments until he should have sufficient money to quit the "flickers" and write. Ashamed of "selling his soul," he changed his name on entering the movies, only later to retrieve it and make it as familiar as the term "movie" itself.

Griffith further developed the art of Melies and Porter, contributing devices of his own that made for greater unity, clarity, and effectiveness. Sensing from the beginning the need for a body of technique to catch and control the emotions of the spectator, he did more to realize a method and a viewpoint than any other man of his day. Although he was himself a former actor and playwright, he repudiated theatrical conventions and evolved a method of expression peculiar to the screen.

Griffith came to films at that propitious moment when they were in the plastic beginnings of artistic development. To them he brought new elements of form and a variety of resources, and added at least two great productions to American motion picture achievement. The most revered and influential movie creator of his day, and perhaps of all motion picture history, he justified the new medium to the world. His productions became models for directors wherever films were made, and to this day stand not only as important achievements in themselves but as the source of central motion picture developments.

In temperament Griffith was a conventional product of his origins and upbringing. Born into an impoverished family in Kentucky in 1880, nicknamed "Sugar," he was inculcated in his earliest years with Southern prejudices, Victorian sentiments, and a local social viewpoint which he never outgrew. His father, a former Confederate colonel known as "Thunder Jake," because of his roaring voice, filled him with tales of Johnny Reb, the old chivalrous South, and Confederate bravery, subjects romantic enough to fire a boy less imaginative and emotional than Griffith. This grand mural of a departed glory was later to appear time and again in Griffith's one-reel cameos of plantation life, Civil War battle episodes, and vignettes of Southern chivalry, and finally to culminate in that powerful film of secessionist bigotry, *The Birth of a Nation*.

The sentimental bias implanted in Griffith by his father was reinforced by the boy's love of poetry in the Victorian manner. His adolescent dallying with the works of Browning, Kingsley, Tennyson, and Hood was later to be recalled and readapted for the screen in such films as *The Taming of the Shrew*, *Sands of Dee*, *Enoch Arden* and *Song of the Shirt*. Griffith's romantic values and poetic ideals persisted even after the rest of the world had abandoned them. Many of his films were saturated with the saccharine sentiments and homilies characteristic of *Godey's Lady's Book*. Even when on occasion he took up the cause of justice, tolerance, and sympathy for the downtrodden, he could not refrain from becoming maudlin. Whether as fictioneer or pamphleteer, Griffith was a man of sentimentality. That accounts in part for his phenomenal pre-war success and his swift post-war eclipse.

Griffith's romanticism determined not only his choice of subject matter but his choice of players. His persistence in casting mere slips of girls, fifteen or sixteen years old, blond and wide-eyed, was due as much to Southern ideals of femininity and his immersion in Victorian poetry as to the camera, always absolute in its demands for pulchritude. All his heroines—Mary Pickford, Mae Marsh, Lillian Gish, Blanche Sweet—were, at least in Griffith's eye, the pale, helpless, delicate, slim-bodied heroines of the nineteenth-century English poets.

But Griffith had a strong creative urge that could divert attention from his weaknesses. This quality of his character was in evidence long before he came to movies. Sent to work at an early age, he was dissatisfied with his short experience as a dry-goods clerk and bookstore salesman; he aspired to become a writer. At seventeen he got a job as newspaper reporter on *The Louisville Courier*. Soon he became ambitious to write plays, and following the advice of a friend who told him that all great playwrights had been actors, he left home to join a traveling stock company.

During the next few years, while acting, Griffith wrote continually, sending out poems, plays, and short stories to various editors and occasionally making a sale. Once, when both acting and writing failed to give him a living and he was stranded in California, he became a hop-picker. This experience he immediately turned into a drama of an itinerant laborer, called *A Fool and A Girl*, which in October 1907 played for two weeks in Washington and Baltimore. Lukewarm though the newspaper criticism was, it throws light on the outlook in the play later to appear in his films:

. . . if one wants to tell the old and beautiful story of redemption of either man or woman through love, it is not necessary to portray the gutters from which they are redeemed.[1]

The little money and slight public recognition that the play gave him made Griffith more than ever determined to win fame as a writer. Some of his poems and short stories were published in *Leslie's Weekly*, *Collier's Weekly*, *Good Housekeeping*, *Cosmopolitan*. He finished another play called *War*, based on first-hand information from soldiers' diaries and letters which he diligently studied at the Forty-second Street Library in New York City. The play proved to be unsalable, but years later its data were put to use in his screen drama *America*.

His creativeness is testified to by his wife, who recorded that he tried to make every minute in his life count. When he was not acting or writing he was inventing things. With his restless tem-

---

[1] Quoted by Mrs. D. W. Griffith, *When the Movies Were Young*, p. 26.

perament and experimental turn of mind, he would astonish his wife time and again with ideas for "non-puncturable" tires, schemes to harness the energy of the sea, methods of canning cooked foods —inventions that he thought might make him suddenly rich. This flair for attempting the impossible, or the improbable, later led him to discover new methods and devices in film making, to thrust aside the objections made by technical men and to open up new resources of the film medium.

Original and profound as a craftsman, Griffith however was never to outgrow his Southern sentiments and Victorian idealism. When his creative genius was most vigorous, it could lift him from sentimentality to dignity and art; when he surrendered to his emotional impulsiveness, his films became orgies of feeling. This accounts for the incongruity between the discipline of his structure and the lack of restraint in his sentiment that mars even the best of his works.

Griffith's screen career falls into three periods: development, maturity, and decline. His years at Biograph Company, which he began with The Adventures of Dolly (1908) and continued through some hundreds of films to Judith of Bethulia (1914), can be characterized as his apprenticeship period. He was then alert and active, displaying a critical and fertile mind. He not only learned all there was to know about the technique of motion pictures, but added to the existing technique a host of new elements. His quick intuition discovered the camera as a dramatic tool and developed its devices as integral properties of film language: the full shot, the medium shot, the close-up, the pan shot, and the moving camera. In addition his employment of such narrative transitions as the cut, the spot-iris, the mask, and the fade contributed importantly to the art of continuity in films. But even more important than such integral devices was his contribution to editing: an awareness of tempo and the device of parallel and intercutting, which greatly expanded and enriched the internal structure of movie art.

It was in 1907, when out of work in New York City, that Griffith first learned of the opportunities in movies. An actor friend, Max Davidson, advised him to apply to the American Mutoscope and Biograph Company for work to tide him over during the slack spring and summer months. Griffith applied for employment and found that he could make $5 a day for acting and $10 to $15 for story suggestions. Working hard, he acted and wrote a number of Mutoscope films. Among these were *Old Isaacs the Pawnbroker*, a bitter diatribe against the amalgamated association of charities then being muckraked; *The Music Master*, strongly reminiscent of Belasco; *At the Crossroads of Life; The Stage Rustler;* and *Ostler Joe*. At this time he appeared also in several Edison pictures. But like other movie craftsmen of that day Griffith was ashamed of his occupation and attempted to conceal it from his friends.

Poet, playwright, actor, inventor—a more fitting background for a motion picture director would be hard to define. Yet when an opportunity came to direct, Griffith debated with his wife: [2]

"In one way it's very nice . . . but you know we can't go on forever and not tell our friends and relatives how we are earning our living."

He argued with his employers: [3]

"Now if I take to this picture directing and fall down, then, you see, I'll be out of an acting job."

The vice-president of Biograph, Henry Marvin, reassured him:

"If you fall down as a director, you can have your acting job back."

With this promise to hearten him, Griffith accepted the assignment, continuing with the name he had taken for stage purposes, Lawrence Griffith. He had told his wife that his real name was David Wark but that he would only use it when he became famous.

His plan was to make enough money in movies to enable him to quit them and return to his real interest: writing. But Griffith never was to leave the movies. From June 1908, when he undertook to direct his first picture for Biograph, he was to remain in the field for more than twenty years. Commenced apathetically, almost unwillingly, his directorial career was to bring to him personal fame and fortune, and to the movies, fresh respect and importance. Medium and master had at last discovered each other, although neither suspected it.

[2] *Op. cit.*, p. 43.   [3] *Op. cit.*, p. 47.

Griffith took his first directorial job, *The Adventures of Dolly*, seriously. Before going to work on it he asked Marvin to run off a few films for him to study. What he saw was not very impressive, and he left the projection room confident that he could do better.

His talent for innovation was revealed at once. Stopping a stranger on Broadway because he recognized in him the type he wanted, Griffith selected his first leading man off the street. His intuition was later vindicated: the stranger, Arthur Johnson, became one of America's first screen idols. For the leading female role Griffith chose his wife, Linda Arvidson, who had been playing background bits; and for the role of a villainous gypsy he persuaded a stage actor, Charles Inslee, to play in the "flickers." Having selected his cast with more care than was customary, he went to work.

The film that began Griffith's career as director was 713 feet long, a naïve tale picturing "kind providence thwarting the gypsies' attempt to kidnap a child for revenge" (all films of the day had to point a moral lesson). A synopsis of *The Adventures of Dolly* in the Biograph press sheet [4] reveals its quaint story as typical of contemporary productions:

On the lawn of their country residence sport mamma, papa, and baby Dolly. Near them flows a picturesque stream where mamma and Dolly watch the boys fishing. A band of gypsies . . . whose real motive is pillage, offers mamma some goods for sale. Her refusal rouses the ire of the gypsy and he attempts to steal her purse. Papa is attracted by her screams and comes on the scene with a heavy snake whip, lashing out at the gypsy unmercifully, driving him away with revengeful venom in his gypsy heart.

Later the gypsy gets his chance and kidnaps Dolly. Hiding her in a water cask, [the gypsies] put it on their wagon and speed away. As they pass over a stream, the cask falls off the wagon and into the water, where it is carried by a strong current downstream, over a waterfall, through seething rapids, finally to enter the quiet cove of the first scene. Fishing boys hearing strange sounds from the cask break it open and discover Dolly. Soon she is safe in the arms of her overjoyed papa and mamma.

[4] July 1908.

In discussing *The Adventures of Dolly* years later, Billy Bitzer, the cameraman, said: [5]

He showed it to me and I told him it was too long. Too long! In the light of a completed scenario today, I can readily say that Griffith was years ahead of us.

Novice though Griffith was, *The Adventures of Dolly* compared favorably with the Biograph productions by more experienced directors. The company must have liked the picture for they quickly had him sign a contract at $45 a week and a royalty of one mill for every foot of film sold.

Feeling his way in the new medium, Griffith turned out five pictures in the next four weeks, each within a reel: *The Red Man and the Child*, *The Stage Rustler*, *The Bandit's Waterloo*, *The Greaser's Gauntlet*, *The Man and the Woman*. All were in the conventional style and showed no deviation from the form initiated by Porter. Whatever distinction they may have had was due to greater care in the selection of the casts and in execution, for Griffith insisted on rehearsing scenes before shooting them, a procedure then uncommon and considered a waste of time. Dubbed the "once-again" idea, it was later to be taken up by others.

The experience of directing these pictures and learning the rudimentary principles aroused Griffith to an awareness of the movies' limitations. He saw the need for a means whereby action could be developed and emphasized, characterizations built, atmosphere evoked, the whole story expressed with more fluidity and variety.

But it was one thing to be aware of a need and another to fill it. Resolved to experiment with his next assignment, Griffith chose Jack London's *Just Meat*, changing its title to *For Love of Gold*.

The climax of the story was the scene in which the two thieves begin to distrust each other. Its effectiveness depended upon the audience's awareness of what was going on in the minds of both thieves. The only known way to indicate a player's thoughts was by double-exposure "dream balloons." This convention had grown out of two misconceptions: first, that the camera must always be fixed at a viewpoint corresponding to that of a spectator in a

[5] *New York Journal*, January 29, 1937.

theatre (the position now known as the long shot); the other, that a scene had to be played in its entirety before another was begun (this was a direct carry-over from the stage).

Griffith decided now upon a revolutionary step. He moved the camera closer to the actor, in what is now known as the full shot (a larger view of the actor), so that the audience could observe the actor's pantomime more closely. No one before had thought of changing the position of the camera in the middle of a scene. Simple as this solution appears now, it was daring then.

The innovation was portentous, for it introduced the exploitation of camera mobility and the custom of breaking up a scene into separate shots. Such new methods would further the movie on its own course and free it from its crippling reliance on the stage. A closer view of the actor would make extravagant gestures, thought necessary on the stage, unnecessary—not to say unnatural and ludicrous—in the movie. Realizing this wonderful advantage of the full shot, Griffith saw that henceforth the movie must be weaned from the stage and given independence for self-development.

Excited at the effectiveness of his experiment and what it foreshadowed, Griffith employed the full shot throughout the many films he made in the next three months. Of these the most outstanding were *The Heart of Oyama, The Barbarian, Ingomar, The Vaquero's Vow, Romance of a Jewess, Money-Mad*. Gradually the full shot became a regular device in the director's yet limited repertory.

The next logical step was to bring the camera still closer to the actor in what is now called the close-up. With this in mind, in November 1908 Griffith had Frank Woods, soon to become known as the film's major critic, make a screen adaptation of Tennyson's *Enoch Arden*. Biograph opposed the story on the ground that it had neither action nor a chase, the two conventional requisites for all films. But their arguments were unavailing. Griffith was aiming for something which to him was more important than gross action: in the quiet ballad he saw the chance to use his new device, the close-up. His hunch, bringing a new concept into the technique of editing, made movie history.

Not since Porter's *The Great Train Robbery*, some five years before, had a close-up been seen in American films. Used then only as a stunt (the outlaw was shown firing at the audience), the close-up became in *Enoch Arden* the natural dramatic complement of the long shot and full shot. Going further than he had ventured before, in a scene showing Annie Lee brooding and waiting for her husband's return Griffith daringly used a large close-up of her face.

Everyone in the Biograph studio was shocked. "Show only the head of a person? What will people say? It's against all rules of movie making!" With such naïveté was the close-up greeted.

But Griffith had no time for arguments. He had another surprise, even more radical to offer. Immediately following the close-up of Annie, he inserted a picture of the object of her thoughts—her husband, cast away on a desert isle. This cutting from one scene to another, without finishing either, brought a torrent of criticism down upon the experimenter.

"It's jerky and distracting! How can you tell a story jumping about like that? People won't know what it's all about!"

Griffith was ready for all dissenters.

"Doesn't Dickens write that way?"

"Yes, but writing is different."

"Not much. These stories are in pictures, that's all."

But Biograph was greatly worried. It rechristened the film *After Many Years*, sent it out, and watched its reception closely. To the company's surprise it was immediately singled out as a masterpiece and proved to be among the first American films honored by foreign markets as worthy of importation.

Griffith's instinct had been right. In the close-up he had made use of one of the most valuable attributes of the moving picture camera, and in "cutting" from Annie Lee to her husband thousands of miles away, he had broken away from the rigid one shot per scene continuity, and disclosed a more fundamental method of film construction. Not only was the scene made up of several shots, but one scene followed another without waiting for it to end. Not connected by time, separated in space, the shots were unified in effect by the theme. Thus Griffith proved not only that the basis of film expression is editing but that the unit of editing is the shot, not the scene.

Before the year was over Griffith had introduced other radical innovations. Ever since movies had been made in studios, the use of electric light had been considered a necessary evil. A scene was always lit from above, and it was considered bad taste and amateurish to leave any portions of a scene shadowed. There was no regard for any possible tonal or dramatic value that lighting might provide. To his two cameramen, Marvin and Bitzer, Griffith complained of the haphazard and disastrous results of lighting. The cameramen did not know what could be done, since the raw film was both "slow" and "color-blind"; very strong light was needed to make any image on the film emulsion. The clumsiness of the lighting devices themselves—mercury-vapor lamps—complicated the problem.

Griffith deliberately chose a story that involved a problem in lighting, *The Drunkard's Reformation*. In one scene the actors were to be illuminated by a fireside glow. The cameramen protested that the film would not take an image if they followed Griffith's directions—or that the peculiar lighting would cast ugly shadows on the players' faces. But Griffith disdained all their objections, and Marvin and Bitzer photographed the scene under his direction. Projected the next day in the studio, the scene was greeted with a murmur of admiration, and the cameramen were perhaps the most surprised and approving of all. From then on lighting was regarded more seriously as a means of enhancing the dramatic effect of a film story.

Aiming above the obvious and absurd "chase" melodramas of the day, fighting repeatedly for the privilege of making films that would force the stage, the critics, and the discriminating public to approve of the young art, Griffith realized that pictures could become significant only if their content was significant. He therefore led a raid on the classics for his material. Before his first year as a movie director was ended, he had not only adapted works by Jack London and Tennyson but had boldly brought to the screen Shakespeare, Hood, Tolstoy, Poe, O. Henry, Reade, Maupassant, Stevenson, Browning. Among the hundred or so pictures of this first year were *The Taming of the Shrew*, *The Song of the Shirt*,

Resurrection, Edgar Allan Poe, The Cricket on the Hearth, The Necklace, Suicide Club, and *The Lover's Tale.*

Griffith soon saw that acting must be more natural, less a matter of "artistical attitudes." He canvassed theatrical agencies for fresh talent which could adjust itself to a more realistic style. Since it was not easy to persuade better-grade actors to appear before the camera, he paid as high as $10 a day for the services of such professionals as Frank Powell (later famed as the director and discoverer of Theda Bara), James Kirkwood, and Henry Walthall, a triumvirate which became, under Griffith, America's earliest anonymous screen idols. When $10 did not prove to be enough to attract Broadway talent, Griffith raised the offer to $20. Pitifully small though this salary appears today, it was then ridiculously high. By the end of the year, however, Griffith's pictures were being pointed out for their "more natural" performances as well as for their better stories and originality.

The climax of his early efforts was the film he directed just about a year after he came to Biograph: *The Lonely Villa.* In this he extended the editing method initiated in *After Many Years* and added to his technique one of its most unique and effective devices: intercutting. The story of *The Lonely Villa,* in a last-minute rescue, offered a more complex development of the chase pattern. To thwart a robbery and save his wife and children, a husband rushes home in a race against time. Griffith built suspense by prolonging the situation, intercutting from the helpless family and burglars to the speeding husband in ever-shortening intervals. The effect of such back-and-forth movement was to prolong the suspense and create a mounting tension in the audience, as they experienced by turns the fears of the family and the anxiety of the husband. Their relief at the rescue was therefore all the more pronounced.

So effective was this intercutting that it was immediately taken up by other directors, who honored its discoverer by calling it the "Griffith last-minute rescue." (Technically the device became designated as "the cross-cut," "the cut-back," "the switch-back.") It solved a major problem of story telling in films. Heretofore, to depict two actions taking place simultaneously at different places, directors had resorted to the double-exposure "dream balloons";

or they had given up the attempt to present any such simultaneous action at all. Griffith's *After Many Years* had been a step toward freedom from such a rigid method. Now, cutting back and forth before a scene was completed solved the space problem and, moreover, brought in the element of time to aid the director.

Until now the duration of a shot had been determined by the time the action would take in real life. *The Lonely Villa* proved that the duration of a shot need not be dependent upon its natural action but could be shortened or lengthened to heighten its dramatic effect. This manipulation of the time element not only increased the story's effectiveness but enabled the director to give his shots pace and rhythm.

Having within one year accomplished important innovations in technique, extended the scope of movie content, and improved motion picture acting, Griffith was regarded with mounting admiration in Biograph and in the industry generally. Everyone at Biograph now hastened to carry out his directions, wondering what great new thing he was now evolving, glad to have a hand in it. Rival directors would slip into theatres to watch his pictures and then hurry back to their studios to imitate them. Audiences and critics as well were singling out pictures with the "AB" trade-mark, the only distinguishing insignia of Griffith's films (as yet no individual credits were being given). In *The Moving Picture World* [6] the high regard for Griffith's pictures is expressed:

· The other afternoon when I sat in my accustomed seat at the Bijou Dream on 14th Street and the title of the Biograph subject, *The Way of a Man*, appeared on the screen, there was a sudden hush. . . . Now this picture held the attention of the audience right up to the very last foot of film because the Biograph Company have got down to the root idea of a moving picture. . . . Their photographs are not mere snap shots or rapidly taken groups of small parties of puppets moving about on the stage. No. They are active photographs of thinking men and women. . . . Now all of this is indicative of progress in the making of moving pictures, in which the Biograph Company prominently shines. It is clear as day that all the other manufacturers will also have to advance. . . . The photographer does his work to perfection. He puts his camera

[6] July 3, 1909.

near the subjects and the lens and you see what is passing in the minds of the actors and actresses. The total combination is that you get as perfect a picture play from the Biograph studio as it is possible in the present stage of moving-picture making to get.

Signing his second contract with Biograph in August 1909, Griffith little realized that all he had achieved so far was only a preparation for what he was yet to do. From the outset his second year with Biograph was triumphant.

For months he had been trying to convince his employers to let him make a film based on Browning's poem *Pippa Passes*. But it was not until a month after his new contract was signed—a busy month in the pastoral atmosphere of Cuddebackville, New York, where he made two mementos to the Revolutionary era, *Hessian Renegades* and *Leather Stocking*—that permission was granted him to film *Pippa Passes*.

Production began in mid-September 1909. Griffith at once turned to experiments with lighting. No doubt the success of his lighting effects in *The Drunkard's Reformation* had motivated his desire to do *Pippa Passes*, for the latter presented a complex lighting problem. Divided into four parts, Morning, Noon, Evening, Night, the film involved a more organic and dramatic use of lighting than Griffith had yet attempted. To his staff Griffith explained the problem and the kind of lighting effects he wanted. Cameramen Bitzer and Marvin were once again dubious, but Griffith—neither cameraman nor mechanic in his own right—laid out the procedure they were to follow for the first sequence, Morning. In her book *When the Movies Were Young* [7] Mrs. Griffith records her husband's plan:

He figured on cutting a little rectangular place in the back wall of Pippa's room, about three feet by one, and arranging a sliding board to fit the aperture much like the cover of a box sliding in and out of grooves. The board was to be gradually lowered and beams of light from a powerful Kleig shining through would thus appear as the first rays of the rising sun striking the wall of the room. Other lights stationed outside Pippa's window would give the effect of soft morning light. Then the lights full up, the mercury tubes a-sizzling, the room fully lighted, the back wall would have become a regular back wall again, with no little hole in it.

[7] P. 128.

Marvin, remembering Griffith's past successes, was half inclined to give the new lighting scheme a try. Bitzer was wholly skeptical. Griffith, expecting more enthusiasm, exclaimed, "Well, come on— let's do it anyhow; I don't give a damn what anybody thinks about it."

The cameramen followed his orders grudgingly.

During the projection of the rushes there was great tension: "At first the comments came in hushed and awed tones, and then when the showing was over, the little experiment in light effects was greeted with uncontrolled enthusiasm." [8]

This was another victory for Griffith's imagination. When *Pippa Passes* reached the public in October 1909, *The New York Times* [9] commented enthusiastically:

Pippa Passes is being given in the nickelodeons and Browning is being presented to the average motion picture audiences, who have received it with applause and are asking for more.

This unsolicited praise had an immediate effect upon Griffith. His earnest struggles to master the medium were being recognized and approved by the world at large. No approbation could have been more heartening, nor could it have appeared at a better moment. It marked the turning point in Griffith's attitude toward the movies. Formerly oppressed by the thought that the motion picture had little future and that his attempts to better it would never bring him renown as an artist or writer, he now felt that his endeavors must have some significance after all.

Griffith's new hopes, however, were not quite free from doubts. When he went to a stage play, his new optimism and deepening conviction about the future of movies would be dissipated. He would go home in a temper, his high resolves about movies shattered. Even the sweet success of *Pippa Passes* did not rid him of nostalgic yearnings to be an author. He would reproach himself for giving up the only thing he really cared about, and became embittered at his own inability to leave the movies. Finally he would console himself with the money he was making and the

[8] *When the Movies Were Young,* p. 129.   [9] October 10, 1909.

A scene from the Reconstruction section in D. W. Griffith's impassioned *The Birth of a Nation* (1915), the film that proved Griffith's artistic maturity and aroused a storm of social protest.

D. W. Griffith smilingly directing a scene for *Intolerance* (1916). Billy Bitzer is behind the camera, Dorothy Gish watches in the background. It is interesting to compare the simplicity of their production methods with the intricacy and magnitude of methods in use today as demonstrated in the still for *Juarez* (see p. 516).

secret thought that when he became a famous author, nobody would know that David W. Griffith, the author, was once Lawrence Griffith of the nickelodeons.

Griffith was never to free himself from the labor of movie making. The more money he made, the more he seemed to need. Before the end of his second year he was earning $900 to $1,000 a month in royalties alone, but he kept putting off his impulse to quit the business. The more he worked, the more obstacles he saw to be overcome and the more willing he became to accept their challenge. Mechanical crudities, the lack of good stories, untrained and inexperienced actors—these, and the prevalent unconcern for quality and good taste, made his prospects dismal, but he kept on. Perhaps he was more suited to the new medium than he cared to admit even to himself.

About this time California had become the mecca of the independent movie makers. Griffith, seeing the pictures made there, was impressed with the landscapes and pictorial possibilities the state offered. Upon investigation he learned that not only mountains and beaches but historic missions, tropical vegetation, and deserts were easily accessible. His love for the picturesque, his eye for the sweep of scenery and his enthusiasm for "artistic" backgrounds, urged him to leave New York and go West. Weather conditions, moreover, always a serious problem in the East, seemed better in California: they would help him to meet his expanded production schedule.

In the winter of 1910 Griffith took his company of Biograph players to California, and on the outskirts of Los Angeles he improvised a studio. Wanting for his initial production a theme that would impress the Biograph office back in New York, he wrote a religious story about the old San Gabriel Mission. This film, *The Thread of Destiny*, proved notable for three reasons. It featured Mary Pickford; it employed a new lighting effect that was both "dim" and "religious"; and, most important, its editing demonstrated conclusively that the shot is the basis of scene construction.

Griffith desired to imbue the film with as much of the Mission atmosphere as possible. He photographed the Mission in great detail, with its weatherbeaten walls, decorative interiors, stairways, choir loft, and cemetery—shots which were not called for in the plot but which, when carefully edited, created an atmosphere and background that greatly reinforced the narrative and action of the story. No one, not even Griffith himself, had as yet taken shots of the various details of a setting to build a scene. Any shot which did not present a major phase of the scene's action had always been regarded as impeding, even intruding upon, the flow of the story; it was "a waste of footage" in the usual one-reel film. Griffith's realization that the details of a background could not only enhance a scene's mood and strengthen its action, but could also be basic in a scene's construction, was a daring step forward in the refinement of movie technique.

It was now clear to Griffith that the director must use the camera not only to take the total content of a scene, but to select details within the scene that bear relations to the content of the film as a whole. This meant that a shot need not be regulated and restricted by an imaginary proscenium: freed from this spatial bondage, the camera could be stationed at any point, according to the director's desire to select details and angles of the content that would lend strength to a scene's structure and intensify its interest. This liberty to direct attention to a vital element of a scene, to vary time and space relationships for the sake of emphasis or contrast, gave the director a powerful means of stimulating the spectator's responses. Griffith suddenly understood how the art of the movie director differs from that of the stage director: in movie making, guiding the camera, even more than directing the actor, is the trick.

Acceptance of this new principle meant that hereafter the screen story would have to be conceived from a new point of view. Griffith had hit upon a truth with implications that all motion picture directors since then have been trying to command. It is that the primary tools of the screen medium are the camera and the film rather than the actor; that the subject matter must be conceived in terms of the camera's eye and film cutting; that the unit of the film art is the shot; that manipulation of the shots builds the scene; that the continuity of scenes builds the sequences; and that the progression of sequences composes the totality of the production. Upon the composition of this interplay of shots, scenes, and sequences depends the clarity and vigor of the story. Here, Griffith saw, is the epitome of motion picture method.

Working under commercial pressure, producing pictures at a steady pace in California throughout the winter of 1910, Griffith strove to apply what he had divined about camera composition, lighting, shot details, scene construction, transitions, and other phases of film technique. He constantly tried, moreover, to weld these elements into a personal style. The pictures he turned out during this period were *The Converts, The Way of the World,* and *The Two Brothers,* utilizing the missions and topography of California; semi-historical pieces such as *In Old California, Love Among the Roses, The Romance of the Western Hills;* and *Ramona,* romanticizing Dons, Señoritas, and Indians.

Ramona provoked the most public excitement. For the privilege of adapting it Griffith had paid $100, an extraordinary sum for a story in those days. Biograph issued a specially illustrated folder which declared proudly that *Ramona* was the most expensive picture ever made. In this film appeared what Griffith subsequently was to call "the extreme long shots." These were shots of vast, distant panoramas and were intended to emphasize the spaciousness of the scene as a dramatic foil to the close shots.

Ramona was followed by a series of film sermons told in the idiom of the day: *Gold Is Not All, Over Silent Paths, The Gold Seekers, Unexpected Help, A Rich Revenge, As It Is in Life,* and *The Unchanging Sea.* The last is remembered as the "first masterpiece" of Griffith's West Coast series.

Returning to New York in the spring, Griffith set himself to work so industriously that Biograph's president, Arthur Marvin sighed, "He'll die working." Besides editing his Western-made pictures, Griffith kept up with a production schedule more ambitious than ever. *In the Season of Buds, A Child of the Ghetto, What the Daisy Said, The House with the Closed Shutters, The Sorrows of the Unfaithful, The Call to Arms,* and *The Usurer* led a colorful array of dramas too numerous to list. The hard-working director's activity was constantly spurred by the increased attention of the trade papers to his pictures. The growing demand of exhibitors for Biograph products, and the new phenomenon of fan letters singling out Griffith's pictures for praise indicated his increasing ability to outshine his contemporaries.

In the summer of this year Griffith signed his third contract with Biograph. This contract stipulated the relatively high salary of $75 per week and one-eighth of a cent per foot royalty on all films sold. What made this agreement significant for Griffith was not so much the raise, however, as the fact that in it he abandoned his pseudonym "Lawrence" and for the first time used his real name, David. At last he was wholeheartedly accepting his career. From now on he was to work under his own colors. Happy over his decision, he set his face toward future accomplishments.

In 1911, again in California, Griffith produced *The Last Drop of Water, Crossing the American Prairies in the Early Fifties, The Lonedale Operator, The White Rose of the Wilds,* and *The Battle of Elderberry Gulch,* the last being released under the shortened title *The Battle.* All these films were distinguished from the general run of contemporary pictures by their content, careful attention to detail, and freshness of treatment. But in these pictures Griffith was seeking to master something new: movement of the action. Without knowing it, all he had discovered thus far had been an approach to it. Now he set about deliberately to create it by all the means he knew, and in *The Lonedale Operator* he was most successful. This was the usual last-minute rescue type of story, stemming from *The Lonely Villa.* A girl held captive in a train depot telegraphs her father and sweetheart, railroad men, for help, and they commandeer a train and speed to her rescue. In filming the scenes Griffith seized every opportunity for emphasizing movement. Not only was there action within the shot, but the camera itself moved—not as in a pan shot, but by being placed on the moving train. The cutting back and forth from the speeding train to the captive gave momentum to the whole. The fluency of action which Griffith achieved by these devices brought a new kinetic quality to the screen.

Now Griffith began to chafe under the arbitrary limitation of a picture to one reel. One reel was hardly adequate to unfold a complete story; the limitation hindered development, curtailed incidents, and proved a general barrier to the choice of deeper themes.

If the movie was ever to become a vital medium, reasoned Griffith, its length would have to be increased. But just as Porter in 1903 had had to convince his doubting employers that the public would sit through a picture a full reel in length, Griffith now had to struggle with Biograph's reluctance to lengthening films to two reels.

Finally disregarding protests, he made a two-reel picture, another version of the story which had already proved successful in one reel, *Enoch Arden*. Biograph refused to release the film as a whole; it was sold in two parts. But the movie audiences, unsatisfied after viewing only one reel, forced exhibitors to obtain both reels and show them one after the other. Biograph in turn had to comply with the requests of the exhibitors, and so the two-reel film was introduced.

The American two-reeler appeared none too soon, for almost immediately afterward two-reelers from European studios appeared. Their reception by audiences was anxiously watched by American producers. So enthusiastic was it that by 1912 two- and even three-reelers were acknowledged by the trade as inevitable.

Now allowed to expand his stories whenever he felt that they demanded more length, early in 1912 Griffith made two films which, for size and content, were his most ambitious efforts up to that time. Unlike any of his previous pictures, the first of these, *Man's Genesis*, was produced by a definite esthetic urge, not a commercial one. The seriousness of its theme, "a psychological study founded upon the Darwinian Theory of the Evolution of Man," indicated Griffith's lack of concern for so-called entertainment values and his desire to do something "worth-while." Needless to say, his employers were strongly opposed to the undertaking.

The philosophical and scientific aspects of the theme were dramatized in the conflict between the intelligence of "Weak-hands" and the body of "Brute-force." In the struggle brain finally conquers brawn. Though the film seems naïve to us today, it was then considered very advanced. The picture turned out to be one of the most discussed films of the year, provoking Vachel Lindsay to declare in his book *The Art of the Moving Picture:* [10]

[10] P. 10.

It is a Griffith masterpiece, and every actor does sound work. The audience, mechanical Americans, fond of crawling on their stomachs to tinker their automobiles, are eager over the evolution of the first weapon from a stick to a hammer. They are as full of curiosity as they could well be over the history of Langley or the Wright Brothers.

Griffith's intuitive choice of such a serious subject was proved sound, for it inspired deeper respect for the screen among those who had been wont to scoff.

Encouraged by this response, Griffith next ventured an ambitious historical re-creation of Custer's last stand, called *The Massacre*. Like *Man's Genesis*, this film was to be more than another program picture. Griffith went far beyond his budget in the production, paying no attention to the pained protests from Biograph's Eastern offices: he was determined to turn out a film greater than any he had yet done. With its casts, costumes, and sets on an unprecedentedly lavish scale, with its "hundreds of cavalrymen and twice as many Indians," the production forced Griffith to reach a new high in his series of technical triumphs. The film abounded in mass scenes, detailed shots of close fighting, vast panoramic pan shots, all skillfully blended and given a rapid continuity in a manner that presaged his later style in *The Birth of a Nation*. *The Massacre* was, in a sense, America's first spectacle film; for Griffith it was the beginning of a new and profounder turn of his talents.

But before the picture was released the American film world was disconcerted by a sudden and unexpected influx of European pictures of such dimensions that everything which had preceded them faded into insignificance. These foreign pictures, three, four, and even five reels in length, elaborately produced, with classics for subject matter, and starring such world-famed figures as Sarah Bernhardt, Helen Gardner, Asta Nielsen, Mme. Réjane, stirred America deeply. *Queen Elizabeth*, *Camille*, *Cleopatra*, *Gypsy Blood*, *Mme. Sans Gene*, in their length and power of conception, dwarfed contemporary American productions. The American companies, particularly those in the motion picture patents-trust group, regarded the invasion with mixed feelings of contempt and jealousy. Trade papers uneasily exhorted American producers to oust the foreigners. The aloof legitimate theatre itself turned a fearful eye upon these new threats of celluloid. But the climax came with the startling announcement that a young arcade and nickelodeon up-start, Adolph Zukor, had signed a contract to feature "Famous Players in Famous Plays," all to run the foolhardy length of four reels. The industry was aghast.

In the midst of this excitement Griffith's *The Massacre* was re-leased. Much to Griffith's chagrin, it was overlooked. Other events of momentous meaning had caught the attention of the movie world; in some quarters the anxiety over the rising popularity of long features, the foreign productions, and Zukor's Famous Players verged on hysteria. Everyone was wondering and fearing what would happen next. Griffith himself wanted to return to New York to view the foreign "miracles," but Biograph's winter production schedule kept him in California.

Smarting with the realization that foreign producers had thrust him into the background, Griffith set to work angrily on the pro-duction of what he called his masterpiece, *Mother Love*. His im-patient disregard of time and money threw Biograph into a panic, but he insisted on his way: this new film was to be his answer to the European invaders. His entire personnel sensed his anxiety; they worked like demons, hoping to make the production come up to Griffith's expectations. But their industry was in vain. Like *The Massacre*, *Mother Love* was scarcely acknowledged in the sweeping course of events. Even before the picture was completed, word reached Griffith of a new sensation, the Italian picture *Quo Vadis*, by far the most elaborate and best motion picture made to date. The news was a shock to Griffith: twice now, with staggering sud-denness and finality, he had been outclassed.

His ambition reinforced by intense envy, Griffith now resolutely planned a reprisal that would force the world to acknowledge his supremacy. His new production would be of such dimensions as the world had never seen. To prevent rumors of his vast under-taking from spreading to the rest of the industry, he took his com-pany to the town of Chatsworth, miles from the Los Angeles pic-ture center. Not unnaturally, everyone working with Griffith was highly curious. What was he up to? Never before had he taken so many shots or been so exacting; never before had there been so much activity and so little known of its nature. He was rehearsing scenes over and over again, photographing and rephotographing unceasingly. How many pictures was he making, anyhow? What had inspired his new meticulous firmness? What was he driving at? Why was he so secretive? But to all questions Griffith maintained an unbroken reserve. Bitterness and envy rankled deep in him. His only concern was to achieve a triumph so outstanding that every movie ever seen before would, in comparison, seem like trash.

Finally in 1913 the secret production was completed: the first American four-reel picture, *Judith of Bethulia*. And once again the coincidence of events interfered with Griffith's hopes for an overwhelming success. *Judith of Bethulia* was not released until almost a year after its completion, when, ironically enough, Griffith had already forgotten it in an undertaking of far greater consequence.

As it turned out, *Judith of Bethulia* became Griffith's Biograph swan song. When it did appear in 1914, it proved to be an extravagant treatment of the Bible story rewritten by Thomas Bailey Aldrich, and without question the ablest example of movie construction to date. Though it appeared too late to overshadow *Quo Vadis*, it was a far better film. Even if Griffith had done nothing further than *Judith of Bethulia*, he would still be considered a sensitive and outstanding craftsman. A comparison of the usual puny American film of 1913 with the opulent and vigorous *Judith of Bethulia* proves Griffith's stature conclusively.

The unusual form of *Judith of Bethulia*, modeled on the four-part pattern of Griffith's earlier *Pippa Passes*, presaged the form of Griffith's future masterpiece, *Intolerance*. The four movements were in counterpoint not unlike a musical composition; they reacted to each other simultaneously, and the combination produced a cumulative, powerful effect. The individual episodes had a tight internal structure. The imagery was not only lavish in detail but fresh in camera treatment and enhanced by expert cutting.

The picture was produced in a deliberate effort to surpass the splendors of the Italian spectacle *Quo Vadis*, which, in fact, Griffith himself had not seen. *Judith of Bethulia* was crammed with colorful mass scenes and tremendous sets in a style that was later

to be embraced by other American directors, notably Cecil B. DeMille. Such episodes as the storming of the walls of Bethulia, the chariot charges, and the destruction of the Assyrians' camp by fire "out-spectacled" any movie yet produced in America.

Satisfied with his completed achievement, Griffith returned to New York to learn that Biograph, now in a new and modern studio in the Bronx, had contracted with the theatrical firm of Klaw and Erlanger to film their successful stage plays after the policy introduced by Zukor. During Griffith's absence a new tempo had been felt in the industry; the air was full of exciting predictions that the stage and the screen were henceforth to work together. European features had made America conscious of her own movie and stage talent and had started a craze for stage names and plays. All the Eastern companies were negotiating for stage alliances.

Griffith was now notified by Biograph that, because of his reckless extravagance with *Judith of Bethulia*, he would in the future supervise production instead of direct. Angered at his employers, bitter at being misunderstood, envious of the acclaim given the foreign pictures, Griffith decided to leave Biograph. He saw in a new company, Majestic-Reliance (Mutual), the opportunity to carry out a fresh and a more elaborate artistic offensive.

After getting his bearings and studying the foreign pictures for a time, he dramatically announced his break with Biograph. The announcement, listing all his technical discoveries, appeared as a full-page advertisement in *The New York Dramatic Mirror* for December 31, 1913. On October 29 the trade papers had already broken the news that Griffith was henceforth to be with Mutual Movies, and they had heralded a new era for the "Belasco of the Screen." The advertisement in *The New York Dramatic Mirror* confirmed what in October had been thought to be a mere rumor.

Asked at this time by Robert Grau, film and theatre critic, whether a knowledge of stagecraft was necessary to a command of motion picture direction, Griffith replied:

No, I do not. . . . The stage is a development of centuries, based on certain fixed conditions and within prescribed limits. It is needless to point out what these are. The moving picture, although a growth of only a few years, is boundless in its scope and endless in its possibilities. . . . The conditions of the two arts being so different, it follows that the requirements are equally dissimilar. . . .[11]

Griffith perceived what so many producers have since often forgotten: in the theatre, the audience listens first and then watches; in the movie palace the audience watches first and then listens.

"The task I'm trying to achieve," said Griffith, "is above all to make you see."

Griffith's apprenticeship had ended. Only five years ago he had entered the industry, skeptical and even contemptuous of it; now he was America's ablest film craftsman. He stood sure of himself, eager for new achievements and a still higher reputation in the industry to which he had already made such remarkable contributions.

[11] *The Theatre of Science*, p. 86.

VIII

FIRST SCHOOL OF DIRECTORS: SPECIALIZATION OF CRAFTS

IF the trust war opened the floodgates of competition in movie making, the ensuing deluge during the pre-war years carried the motion picture into new technical and artistic channels. Competition forced producers to strive for a distinctive quality in their work that would defeat rivalry. The innovations of D. W. Griffith in particular, and of the foreign producers in general, further quickened the qualitative development of the film.

The efforts of this period were focused on the task of raising the standards of moviecraft: every element of movie making was improved and new elements were added. Direction, photography, acting, writing, and criticism, no longer professions of low reputation, were now rationally adapted to the possibilities of the medium. In construction methods there was a definite shift away from the rigidity of the preceding era. The unique nature of the screen medium was more thoroughly explored, related crafts became better understood, and the expressiveness of the film was intensified. These years of discovery, marked by self-consciousness, saw the art of movie making recognized in its full significance.

In the making of pictures the tack of the preceding era was continued. Despite the swift commercial expansion of the industry and its effects on distribution and exhibition methods, the tactics of production were still largely those of a small enterprise. As studios expanded and budgets increased, however, movie craftsmen grew more and more self-conscious of their personal contributions and began to regard themselves as artists. Their ambitions waxed and intensified as, toward the close of the period, the practice of giving screen credit became more common. The early spirit of haphazard, anonymous production was passing.

Of prime importance in the changing scene was the role of the director. Once the mere mechanic operating the camera, he had become in eight years the dominant figure in production, supervising every detail. All talents were his to co-ordinate and to resolve into their proper function in the whole. Although ideas and suggestions were often contributed by others, the finished movie was now the product of a single mind.

As the trust-defying independents pushed into the production field, the need for more directors grew. If offers of more money to the directors of the licensed companies failed to induce them to desert to the independents, assistants of the original Big Three— Porter, Blackton, McCutcheon—or craftsmen who had worked for them in some minor capacity, were hired as full-fledged directors. Anyone who had ever been in a moving picture studio could find work with the independents. Though there were perhaps not more than ten directors at work in 1908, by 1912 there were three times as many, and several companies were employing a staff of two or more directors to meet the production demand. Epes Sargent, in *The Motion Picture Annual* for 1912, pointed out the importance of this progress: "There is a growing tendency to give a director more time on a subject and this helps a photoplay. . . . The script may be studied more carefully and the finer points brought out."

The advance of D. W. Griffith pushed the older men—Melies, Porter, Blackton—into the background. Blackton functioned at this time more as a supervisor and teacher than as a director. His concern began to center largely on the business of production and less on its technique. Leaving direction to other men under him, he inaugurated a method which Thomas Ince was to later expand— that of overseeing many productions at once.

Besides Griffith there were new men whose films equaled and even surpassed the efforts of the pioneers. These men, watching Griffith's innovations, were quick to adopt them and to pattern their films after his. Of these newcomers three in particular stood

out: Sidney Olcott, George D. Baker, and J. Searle Dawley. Eager
and aggressive, they struck out in new directions, their pictures becoming notable for detail and characterization, unity, and pictorial
quality. Collectively these three men possessed talents that Griffith
had individually.

Sidney Olcott was perhaps the most talented. Among the first
stage actors to become associated with pictures, he had begun with
Biograph films in 1904 and, after two years, had quit Biograph to
become Kalem's first director. Fortunately for Olcott, Kalem produced most of his films on location: unconfined by stage sets, Olcott
could season his films with plenty of action and movement. But his
particular flair appears to have been to use dramatically the people,
local color, and history of the territory in which he worked. His
pictures stood out from others because of their flavor and authenticity. By 1911 Kalem pictures had won a reputation for their local
color.

Planning his action carefully, Olcott routed the movement of the
actors in a sort of "shooting scenario." This enabled him to proceed
with the photographing rapidly and efficiently, and then to edit the
finished film accordingly. When his company was in Florida, Olcott
insisted on having the film sent back from New York after processing, so that he could edit it himself according to his plan. Like
Griffith he wanted to know all there was about the medium; unlike
Griffith at this time he felt that movies were a serious and worth-
while undertaking, and would in time command the respect enjoyed
by the stage.

Olcott directed literally hundreds of pictures, and the quality of
his output was naturally uneven. One of his most notable productions was the spectacular *Ben Hur* (1907), which gained considerable notice, made a huge amount of money for Kalem, and incidentally brought the already irritating copyright problem to a head.
One of the first "costume" dramas produced by American film
makers, it led the movement toward more ambitious undertakings
and indicated Olcott's own anxiety to dignify the movies. At a time
when the possible themes of pictures were regarded as limited, *Ben*

Hur broke through the limits and showed that there were large subject areas yet to be explored.

During the winter of 1908 Kalem, seeking new locales, sent Olcott to Florida. Olcott's first Florida film, *Florida Crackers*, dealt with poor whites living outside Jacksonville. Jacksonville citizens, aroused by this document, threatened to prevent the production of any more films in the locality unless Olcott chose to show its more attractive aspects. During the next two years, however, Olcott made similar films, including *Judgment* and *The Deacon's Daughter*. He also made Civil War pictures from the Southerner's viewpoint (*Adventures of a Girl Spy*, *Another Hitch*) and the usual action melodramas of the day (*The Miser's Child*, *The Indian Scout's Vengeance*).

Taking advantage of Olcott's eye for regional subjects and color, Kalem sent him with a stock company to Europe, to do with European atmosphere what he had done in Florida. Olcott's first stop was Ireland, and here he made seventeen pictures during an eighteen weeks' stay. His first efforts centered on the trials and dangers of the Irish rebels of 1790 (*Rory O'More*, *Ireland the Oppressed*). Because of their controversial political material these provoked much disturbance in the home office, and Kalem wanted to recall Olcott. Promising to keep clear of explosive subject matter, Olcott remained in Ireland and turned to the plays of Dion Boucicault, American playwright of the Irish people. He filmed *The Colleen Bawn*, *Arrah-na-pogue*, *You Remember Ellen* (from Tom Moore's poem "The Mayor of Ireland"), and *The O'Neil* (from "Erin's Isle").

Olcott now went to the Continent. Touring fifteen countries during the next two years, he sent back to Kalem folk tales, dramas, and travelogues. When he reached Jerusalem he made what was perhaps his best effort at this time, *From Manger to the Cross*. When Kalem saw this religious film they were bitter because they assumed that a religious picture would not be profitable. Angry at the vast amount of money Olcott had spent on such a venture, they forced Olcott to resign. All credits were removed from the film and publicity was withheld. But a few trial showings of the film brought such a favorable reaction that Kalem decided to release it.

American critics hailed Olcott's work. Said Stephen Bush (*The Moving Picture World* [1]): "I can only pause to commend the fine reverent spirit of the master hand which directed this production." W. H. Jackson of the same periodical declared, "The masterpiece of cinematography is at last realized."

In England the religious aspect of *From Manger to the Cross* produced an agitation that was said to be directly responsible for the establishment of film censorship in that country. The picture was eulogized and condemned by pulpit and public alike; English men of letters engaged in a bitter controversy over it. The lobby of the theatre at Queen's Hall, where the film ran for eight months, displayed Israel Zangwill's opinion of the picture: "An artistic triumph; the Kinema put to its true end." This comment by a distinguished writer helped to silence most of the protests.

One of the most discussed pictures of 1913, *From Manger to the Cross* is still in circulation, on 16 mm. film.

Back in America, and now on his own, Olcott made two pictures: the Civil War drama *A Daughter of the Confederacy* and an excursion into psychic phenomena, *In the Power of the Hypnotist*. These films were lost in the confusion of change now prevalent in the industry; all attention was being focused on the feature. But the aggressive sincerity behind Olcott's work at this time did not diminish. Olcott's co-worker, Gene Gauntier, admiringly wrote of him: [2]

He would work like a Trojan, giving all his strength and vitality . . . shouting, threatening, cajoling . . . but after the scene was over, it was always the same, an arm thrown over the shoulder, compliments, enthusiasm.

Now considered second only to the mighty Griffith, Olcott suddenly dropped entirely out of the film world. Years later, in 1920, he reappeared as the director of one of Will Rogers' most hilarious comedies, *Scratch My Back*. Again he rose to prominence, directing the leading stars of the post-war period in many of the most outstanding films of the day: Marion Davies in *Little Old New York* (1921), George Arliss in *The Green Goddess* (1923), Gloria Swanson in *The Humming Bird* (1923), Pola Negri in *The Spanish*

[1] March 1913.
[2] *Blazing the Trail*, manuscript at Museum of Modern Art Film Library.

Dancer (1923), Rudolph Valentino in *Monsieur Beaucaire* (1924). All these films had, like Olcott's first short dramas, the color and atmosphere of fresh locales.

In 1927, having become one of the ten top-ranking American directors, Olcott left the United States to become production director for British Lion Film Company. When sound pictures were becoming popular in 1929, he left the industry again, whether for permanent retirement or to readjust himself to the innovation is not yet known. Sidney Olcott has been, in any event, a serious and sincere contributor to motion picture art, a director of individuality and merit, during two formative periods of the American film.

George D. Baker had begun his directorial career at Vitagraph under J. Stuart Blackton. Like his instructor, Baker had been an illustrator before entering motion pictures, but in addition he had been in the theatre as actor, writer, and director. Combining his propensity to "see" and his stage knowledge, he took advantage of the movie art's possibilities in composition, atmosphere, and acting. So genuine was his appreciation of the powers of the camera, however, that he insisted upon learning it thoroughly; he turned to scenario writing later. This was a happy evolution for a director, for it taught Baker how much a film depends, for its unity and meaning, upon continuity, and it carried him through a long and successful career. His flair for the picturesque and his concern for "tight" construction in these earlier days distinguished his efforts.

Baker first sprang into prominence as the director of the John Bunny-Flora Finch comedies. Commencing in 1910, for three and a half years Baker kept movie-goers chuckling over the antics of a "lovable fat man and his skinny spouse." These comedies, the most representative of their day, were smooth in development, and the careful planning behind them was clearly evident.

From domestic comedy Baker turned to romantic adventure, a field in which his experience as an illustrator enabled him to become one of the first directors to make the most of exotic and picturesque locales. *The Dust of Egypt*, *A Price for Folly*, and *Tarantula* set a new precedent for pictures. The stylists Maurice Tourneur, Rex Ingram, and Josef von Sternberg, each of whom later developed the picturesque to higher levels, could look back to Baker as the primitive in their special aspect of the art.

Baker left Vitagraph to become director-general of the new Metro pictures. Here he supervised the work of other craftsmen, directing the major stories himself. *The Wager, Outwitted, The White Raven* (starring Ethel Barrymore), and *Toys of Fate* (starring Nazimova) earned him a reputation within the trade. Esteemed for his knack for smooth continuity, pictorial effects, and "different" locales, he was then considered by many as "a good director to study." In the tremendous turnover of personnel in the late twenties, Baker, as many of his contemporaries, was replaced by newer talents.

J. Searle Dawley also came to the movies from the stage. Joining the Edison Company in 1907, he acted, wrote scenarios, and finally became a director under Porter. In five years he made over three hundred films, writing most of the stories himself. In deference to Dawley's stage background, Porter would let Dawley direct the "emotional" stories, keeping the "action" kind for himself. It was an equitable arrangement but it kept Dawley from ever really getting at the basis of his craft. Relying as he did upon the acting to make the film effective, he unconsciously neglected other abilities which he might have developed. To him the camera always remained a mechanical instrument; he never could understand Porter's tinkering with it. Movies, like the stage, were to him an actor's art.

Noted for his ability in characterizations, Dawley was among those signed by Zukor in 1912 for Famous Players Corporation. Henceforth Dawley became more widely known, winning the title of "the man who made Famous Players famous" by his direction of such stage stars as Minnie Maddern Fiske, Cecilia Loftus, Bertha Kalich, House Peters, John Barrymore, and Mary Pickford.

Though Dawley created no outstanding pictures, he tried always to lift film acting to dignity and importance, and he strongly influenced stage actors to accept the movie as a worth-while medium. His attention to details, to the staging of scenes and their enactment, helped to refine, if not define, the actor's craft. Although in the vanguard of feature picture directors and at the height of his career during the war period, Dawley was to be gradually left behind in the upsurge of newcomers during the post-war years. When sound arrived, Dawley, like Baker, had already been long forgotten.

There were, besides these three directors, a number of minor directors of lesser talent who helped to consolidate the discoveries of Griffith and advance the industry. Among these were Francis Boggs, Alice and Herbert Blache, Albert Capellani, Oscar Apfel, Romaine Fielding, Raymond B. West, John Noble, Barry O'Neil, Marshal Farnum, Edward Le Saint, William Parke, Hal Reid, Harry Meyers, Frank Powell. Commencing too late in this period to be considered influential in it were a number of others who in later years were to emerge as important individuals: Thomas Ince, Mack Sennett, Maurice Tourneur, Herbert Brenon, Clarence Badger, J. Gordon Edwards, and Allan Dwan.

As the technique of direction progressed swiftly under the spur of rivalries, auxiliary crafts—acting, writing, photography, criticism —likewise advanced toward maturity. These underlying elements of the screen medium, until now relatively neglected, came into the foreground.

With the advent of the "star" in 1910 and of Famous Players in 1912, the actor in particular began to assume increasing importance. Trained and untrained people who had formerly been dubious about joining movies, or ashamed to join them, now responded to the lure of larger salaries ("sometimes as much as fifty dollars a week"), publicity, and the improving reputation of the screen. The question that had worried them most, "Would pictures hurt a stage career?", was dispelled when, toward the close of the period, many famous stage celebrities and picture producers became allied.

A letter supposedly sent in 1911 to David Belasco by William C. DeMille (brother of Cecil B. DeMille and later to become an eminent film director in his own right) reveals the diffidence regarding movies that was now becoming obsolete. DeMille was worried about the future of the rising young actress Mary Pickford:

. . . throwing her whole career in the ash-can and burying herself in a cheap form of amusement which hasn't a single point that I can see to recommend it. There will never be any real money in these galloping tintypes and certainly no one can expect them to develop into anything which could, by the wildest stretch of the imagination, be called art.

I pleaded with her not to waste her professional life and the opportunity the stage gives her to be known to thousands of people, but she's rather a stubborn little thing for such a youngster and says she knows what she's doing.

So I suppose we'll have to say good-by to little Mary Pickford. She'll never be heard of again and I feel terribly sorry for her.[3]

No doubt DeMille would be the first to smile at this letter today.

The presence in filmdom of such distinguished actors as Sarah Bernhardt, James K. Hackett, Mrs. Fiske, Lily Langtry, and Dustin Farnum tended to dignify the screen and reassure doubting film actors that in gaining a foothold in the new art they were lucky rather than lost.

It was Griffith who first forcibly pointed out the difference between acting for the footlights and for the camera. His insistence upon adapting the players to camera technique—Griffith himself had been schooled in stage and screen acting—was greeted at first with hostility. But when it was seen that he could take untrained people—photographer's models, clerks, minor players—and obtain better screen performances from them than from professionals of repute, acting for the camera began to be acknowledged as requiring a technique different from that of the stage.

In one of the first books on motion picture acting, by Frances Agnew,[4] the comedian John Bunny—second only to Broncho Billy in popularity—revealed rare foresight:

I wanted to be with the "shooters" . . . so I canceled my thirty weeks' contract with the Shuberts, threw aside all the years of experience and success I had had, and decided to begin all over again. I went down to the Vitagraph studio . . . and frankly told them I wanted to work in the pictures. . . . I . . . offered to work in my first picture for nothing.

[3] *Stage*, August 1936.
[4] *Motion Picture Acting;* Reliance Newspaper Syndicate, 1913, p. 99.

Though Bunny was making at the time $150 a week as a stage actor, he accepted $40 a week in the movies, explaining that "they offer a field day for the ambitious which is not simply for this day and generation but for the infinite future."

Acting in general was still poor—too close to stage technique. Action and story were of more importance than a performance; characterization was rudimentary. The actor depended on clothes to establish the person, silks denoting the well-to-do, cotton the worker, satin the gadabout, and gingham the virtuous. Characterizations were few, being limited for the most part to types or, rather, symbols: the Banker, Workingman, Loafer, Cowboy, Good Girl, Bad Girl, Poor Girl.

Acting for the movies before 1908 meant physical action, feats of daring, exaggerated and violent gestures. Shadow players were animated puppets, never pausing for a moment; their acrobatics were more important than their acting. Under Griffith's influence natural behavior on the screen became more common. Pantomime instead of palpitation became the slogan, and toward the close of the period, particularly under the direction of George Baker and Searle Dawley, the personality of an individual and more realistic gestures began to be exploited.

Like acting, photoplay writing developed under the stimulus of commercial rivalry. "Stories" until 1908 had consisted of brief notes, or listings of scenes which were rarely so specific as even the scenarios of Porter's films. The director carried in his mind all the action, the development of plot, and the continuity of "shots." But as competition intensified and pictures lengthened, directors felt the need of writers to create full stories and prepare them for efficient production.

The requirement for stories was readily satisfied: the reservoir of best-selling fiction was tapped. Rex Beach, Jack London, Richard Harding Davis, and Elbert Hubbard were among the first to see their books come to life on the screen. The settling of the *Ben Hur* litigation in favor of the author and publisher, however (the judgment cost the film maker $50,000), taught the movie companies that thereafter they would have to observe the copyright law and buy whatever material was not in public domain.

The practice of using best-selling fiction was encouraged by *The Moving Picture World:* [5]

WELL-KNOWN WRITERS TURNING TO A NEW FIELD—THAT OF WRITING FILM SCENARIOS

When such writers as Richard Harding Davis, Rex Beach and Elbert Hubbard . . . turn to this fast growing field of amusement as a market for their composition, it clearly demonstrates to the minds of the semi-skeptical that the "survival of the fittest" will maintain its time-honored position. The advent of such writers in this new departure not only assures us better subjects, higher themes, more elevating pictures and an increased popularity throughout the country, but they are now finding themselves confronting a new era in amusement reviews.

The demand for photoplays and photoplay writers was becoming so acute that manufacturers widely advertised that they would gladly train writers in scenario techniques. Vitagraph, inaugurating a scenario department headed by Sam Pedon and Rollin S. Sturgeon, announced that "All scenarios submitted will be read and filed for future use. Applicants will be interviewed with a view towards training."

S. Lubin peppered the trade papers with advertisements like this: "S. Lubin Mfg. Co. is in the market for first class photo-drama ideas, and will pay good prices."

Demands for screen authors soon overflowed from trade publications into the fan magazines, in which individuals and schools advertised that they would "train you in motion picture writing in a few easy lessons." Correspondence courses and books on movie writing multiplied:

Make $100 monthly writing moving picture plays in spare time. Experience unnecessary.

Why don't YOU write a photoplay? We train you in ten easy lessons.

One man sold a photoplay for $30 that he wrote on his cuff. . . . This book will open up a new world and a new profession for you. Price $1. Postage Free.

[5] January 29. 1910.

The growing awareness of the necessity for skill in story writing for the screen was evident. Said an editorial in *The Moving Picture World:* [6]

It is a great accomplishment to produce a good scenario for motion pictures, either drama or comedy, with all the necessary requirements of story, interest, sequence, logic, etc. . . . . Out of the 2,000 submitted manuscripts received from all parts of the country by Vitagraph Co. . . . about 2 per cent were accepted and only four of these were practical working scenarios.

In response to the need for skilled scenario writers *The Moving Picture World* in December 1911 established a department to teach the craft. Functioning under the direction of Epes W. Sargent, it was called "The Scenario Writer." (This was perhaps the first time the term "scenario" was applied to screen writers in a publication.) These magazine articles explaining the principles and technique of movie construction were, although rudimentary, subsequently incorporated in the book *Technique of the Photoplay,*[7] which was one of the first of its kind and which crystallized a method and bred many subsequent scenarists.

As scenario writers developed a terminology of their own—a terminology even more technical than that of stage direction—the task of constructing "working scenarios" became more and more a specialized skill. New camera techniques as well as story continuity were specified in the script. Specifications of camera positions and types of transition to be used—the cut, dissolve, fade, iris, and especially the leader (title)—were becoming necessary parts of a scenario, making the writing of a film scenario a special craft.

Thus by 1914 screen writing was established as a distinct and individual craft, a branch of literature and drama. A marked advance had been achieved in the quality as well as the quantity of scripts. Though screen credits for script writing were still withheld, prices were advancing: "$50 was by no means uncommon and $100 is known to have been paid for a photoplay." Efforts to engage well-known writers, the use of copyrighted material, and in particular the establishment of a secure contractual relationship instead

[6] March 5, 1910.   [7] Chalmers Publishing Company, 1913.

of a free-lance arrangement between studio and screen writer, all helped to improve the technique and quality of movie writing.

The first school of scenarists emerged largely within the motion picture field itself or from the field of journalism: they were former actors, critics, or newspaper writers. For being among the first to convert stories into an effective screen idiom, Gene Gauntier, C. Gardner Sullivan, Edmund Jones, Eustace Hale Ball, Frances Marion, Frank Woods, and Jeanie MacPherson deserve special mention. Griffith, welcoming newspaper writers at Biograph, developed two of the industry's most successful scenarists, Frank Woods and George Terwilliger. Roy McCardell had already added scenario writing to his newspaper work. The field was generally wide open, and many writers who seized their opportunities later found themselves at the top in the subsequent "bull market."

Like the writer, the motion picture cameraman was called upon to develop and refine his work. As photography itself became a more responsible job, division of labor became common; the laboratory work was now done by the cameraman's subordinates under his supervision. That the cameraman, now a man of position, wielded great influence in production is pointed out by Gene Gauntier, writer and actress of that day:

It was the cameraman who held down the temperamental director and usually had the final authority on what could or could not be done. . . . Even as late as 1915 at Universal . . . there was a brief interval when the cameramen were given full authority over all phases of production. There were some 25 of them banded together in a tight little union. If they decided the light was good for photographing, a flag was run up on a high flagstaff, a triangular white cotton cloth on which was lettered "Shoot." And if that flag did not fly not a camera crank was turned on exteriors scheduled for that day, no matter how directors and unit managers might fume or what might be the resultant loss in time and money.[8]

Camera technique depended on good lighting and sensitive film. Lighting had been a most difficult problem, and it remained one as the practice of manufacturing movies in studios spread. The mercury-vapor lamps threw off a cold, hard light which bared every

[8] *Blazing the Trail*, manuscript.

flaw in the scene and could not be balanced for tonal effects. Many attempts were made, notably by Griffith, to dramatize lighting to enhance the story, but progress was slow and difficult. As for the raw film stock, it still remained "contrasty" and slow; it could not register subtleties in tone. The scene painters were therefore often obliged to make up the settings and do the paint jobs so as to minimize lighting problems.

As new companies went into production, more cameramen entered the field. Henry Marvin, Max Schneider, Herman O'Brock, and H. Hyman Broening were notable. Others, too, became famous. William Bitzer made successes out of Griffith's "crazy schemes." Tony Gaudio, cameraman for I.M.P., had a less creative director to work under but was perhaps more sensitive to the variability of the medium, and lasted longer than Bitzer in the industry. Working with many directors, E. Cronjager, Charles Rosher, Dean Faxon, Victor Milner, and John Seitz also made their start and today are still esteemed for their work.

With all phases of motion picture technique advancing rapidly and features becoming more important, books devoted to the movies as an art began to appear. *Moving Pictures* (How They Are Made and Worked),[9] by Frederick A. Talbot, appeared in 1912. Eustace Hale Ball's *The Art of the Photoplay*[10] was published in 1913. Other books were *Making the Movies*,[11] by Ernest A. Dench (1914-1915), *Theatre of Science*,[12] by Robert Grau (1914), and the two first really critical and significant works—*The Art of the Moving Picture*,[13] by Vachel Lindsay (1915), and *The Photoplay: A Psychological Study*,[14] by Hugo Munsterberg (1916). Such writings helped to make the movie world, as well as outsiders, conscious that under their very eyes was emerging a new art of vast significance.

Film publicity and criticism likewise flourished in this period. News of events important in the trade formerly had been scattered through popular periodicals such as *Harper's Weekly, The Literary*

[9] J. B. Lippincott Company, Philadelphia.
[10] G. W. Dillingham Company, New York.
[11] The Macmillan Company.   [12] Broadway Publishing Company.
[13] The Macmillan Company.   [14] Appleton Company.

Digest, The Scientific American, and *Popular Mechanics.* In 1906 appeared the industry's first trade paper, *Views and Film Index,* largely devoted to the needs of exhibitors and containing reviews of current releases and forceful editorials aimed at bettering all phases of production and exhibition. Not until 1908 did a critique of the movies appear in a periodical other than a trade paper. In June of that year *The Dramatic Mirror* inaugurated, under the title "The Spectator," a regular department of film reviews and criticism written by Frank Woods. From the outset Frank Woods impressed the movie makers: they read his column steadily, respected his opinions, and often acted upon his advice.

Other trade papers, notably *The Moving Picture World* and *The Motion Picture News,* likewise established regular departments devoted to movie reviews and editorial criticism. The establishment in 1909 of a regular motion picture column in *The New York Morning Telegraph,* a leading newspaper with theatrical news, set a significant precedent. Newspapers began to take notice of the new art, and occasionally even a feature article describing movie making and some movie personalities appeared. Fan magazines, springing up in 1910, began to popularize these personalities. They only rarely ventured into criticism, but this restraint was not prolonged. *Photoplay Magazine,* in the next period of movie development, set up new standards for fan journals by vigorously applauding the best pictures and staunchly condemning the mediocre.

Too much credit for the improvement of the movie art cannot be given the trade-paper critics of this period, especially Stephen Bush, Louis Reeves Harrison, Epes Sargent, and Frank Woods. These critics constantly agitated for higher standards. In a typical editorial by Louis Reeves Harrison,[15] the integrity, idealism, and general enthusiasm of critics for the movies of their day is apparent:

The new art was without tradition. None of us could go back to masters of other days and learn the rules of what had never been. . . . No man could look deeply into the subject without realizing that motion pictures were bound to become a power in working upon the human spirit and no man of heart would desire that influence to be an evil one. . . . In setting up standards I have

[15] *The Moving Picture World,* October 1913.

been accused of favoring what is new and spontaneous, but this is a slight misconstruction of what I have consistently advocated. It seems to me that a photodrama should deal with what affects people of today in preference to centering on a theme of former concern that is not of strong present interest. (It may be that an ancient environment could be more effective than a modern one.) There are social and political questions of the hour that have come up at other periods with dramatic results that could be strongly enforced by showing what happened then. . . . I simply advocate that some of the hundreds of questions now agitating civilized people would be considered rather than what is no longer of vital importance. . . . Let us go deep into the social problems that are deeply affecting us at this moment! Let us probe the ignominy of our political system! Let us search for truth even if it is as deep as a well! For truth is truth to the end of reckoning!

By 1914, then, a remarkable evolution of the motion picture had occurred. The first school of American directors had emerged, and the original crafts had been subdivided and new ones had been added. Specialization of effort and the earnest advice of critics were refining the techniques of expression. The establishment of features had opened a wide and rich field for experimentation. More manufacturers were becoming aware that the artistic quality of motion pictures would in part determine their acceptance by the public. In the next period of motion picture development this realization was to result in greater freedom for directors and in a persistent demand for better stories, better casts, better photography. And with the practice of giving screen credits, rivalry among the artists was to become keener and to produce higher standards of work in every field of motion picture production.

IX

PRE-WAR FILMS: SIGNIFICANT TRENDS

HAVING refined their story-telling technique and lengthened their films, American producers during the years 1908-1914 probed deeper into contemporary life and into various kinds of literature for their themes. Literature had been raided previously for subject matter, but it now became more inviting for at least two reasons: it was likely to be safe from the increasing threats of censorship, and it was likely to be known and popular with movie audiences. From popular magazines, famous novels, and successful stage plays, plots were taken in part or as wholes; locales were changed; names of characters were altered; ideas were shaped down to fit the movie mold. Excerpts from novels by Jack London and Frank Norris, William Thackeray and Charles Dickens, Rex Beach and Anthony Hope; from plays by Dion Boucicault, David Belasco, and Clyde Fitch; from short stories published in *Collier's, McClure's,* and *Cosmopolitan;* from poems by Robert Browning, William Shakespeare, and Alfred Tennyson—all these were remolded into film tales (the original sources seldom, by the way, being credited).

At first the novel, short story, play, and poem were utilized at intervals to reinforce material from the newspaper, anecdote, and popular joke. But fiction came to be relied upon more and more, and real life less and less. This was true particularly toward the close of the period, owing to the influence of Griffith's film adaptations of famous literary works, Zukor's picture versions of famous plays, and the foreign films of historical dramas. The movement was facilitated by the establishment of scenario departments staffed by professional writers. The final effect was to make screen stories more artificial: even subject matter chosen from contemporary life was given a literary color which all but transformed fact into fancy.

Whatever their source—current events, plays, novels, or short stories—all film stories took on a quality characteristic of the temper of pre-war America: a high moral tone and strong didactic purpose. Politics had swung toward progressivism; "causes" had become fads; social sentiment was saturated with humanitarianism; the muckraker had been superseded by the reformer and uplifter. Even in those days the motion picture industry had its finger on the public pulse, and it naturally gave its productions an appropriate air of purposefulness. Film makers followed the policy suggested by *The Moving Picture World:* [1] "No better field lies open to insert entirely without the person's knowledge a few grains of profitable and instructive matter within their [movie-goers'] interest and comprehension."

From 1908 to 1914 motion pictures preached. Current events underwent moral and often sentimental inspection, and the outlines of facts tended to become blurred by the enthusiasm of the movie makers. Literary works were shaded to emphasize the rightness of current popular doctrines. Novices who aspired to write for the movies were advised to take their themes from newspapers but to utilize them to "show justice and teach goodness and happiness with a happy ending whenever logically possible." Trying honestly to be what they were advertised to be, "dramatically strong and morally effective," movies were intensely conscious of what they said, how they were saying it, and the public effect of what they were saying. As Rev. William Henry Jackson emphatically exclaimed,[2] "What responsibility rests upon those who are controlling the 'world's' motion picture!"

Strict late nineteenth-century attitudes were the values and homilies preached and defended in films. Though more than a decade had passed since the movie, with all its possibilities of realistic portrayal, had first amazed Americans, those attitudes still persisted on the screen. Producers themselves, having been educated under the influences of Guffey and his school, saturated their films with cor-

---

[1] January 28, 1910. [2] *The Moving Picture World,* June 4, 1910.

responding doctrines. They were behind rather than in advance of the populace in their response to the changing political outlook in America, to the shattering of nineteenth-century ideas by the impact of science and industrialism, and to the new viewpoints which were peculiarly twentieth-century in their implications.

When the motion picture turned to twentieth-century themes, with their appeal to the head and conscience as well as the heart of the audience, it hardly abated its moral vigor. Behind these more "modern" films was the producers' conviction that entertainment must be stressed no more than enlightenment—a conviction in keeping with the new age of mass production in books and newspapers, multiplying public schools and libraries, and lavish private endowments of institutions for the advancement of culture and learning. With earnest persistence the movies pointed their moral lessons, exposed corruption, pleaded causes, elaborated their sociological and religious sermons—as the manufacturers, conscious of their high mission, were quick to advertise.

Still dealing mainly with the working man's milieu, the motion picture made much of his spiritual nature. The struggle for existence and the tribulations of being poor, which figured so largely in the earlier movies, were now presented as less important in life than inner goodness. Pictures preached that wealth alone does not bring happiness (*Gold Is Not All*). The poor were shown as endowed with compensations of a higher order than money: they had children (*More Precious Than Gold*), love (*Tale of a Tenement*), kindness (*As It Is in Life*). The rich, on the other hand, were portrayed as selfish (*Greed of Gold*), penurious (*Secrets of a Miser's Cave*), immoral (*Gold and Glitter*), or dissipated (*Father Gets in the Game*). The working populace were taught that it is better to be poor and good than rich and wicked (*Plain Mame*, or *All That Glitters Is Not Gold*). *The Usurer* dramatized the proverb "What doth it profit a man . . . ," and *The Violin Maker of Cremona* sermonized that to give was better than to receive, and no matter how poor you are there is always someone still worse off. The poor but pure were reassured that they have first claim to heaven.

Good and evil were made the pivotal issues in most productions:

every picture ended with sin punished and good rewarded. Divine Justice meted out final punishment and reward in the next world if not in this (*Heaven Avenges; The Sorrows of the Unfaithful*). Death was shown as the final leveler of all men. *The Conscience Fund*, for example, told the story of a detective who, finding that his own father has defrauded the government, demands that his father refund in full, whereupon "The honor of the family is saved and death kindly furnishes oblivion." No matter what the circumstances, a last-minute change always demonstrated that the wages of sin are death, and that faith and goodness always provide a happy ending after trouble.

Numerous pictures illustrated the Bible (*The Life of Christ, The Life of Moses, From the Manger to the Cross, The Black Sheep*) or, in the form of morality dramas, preached Victorian ideals of virtue (*Honesty Is Its Own Reward*), charity (*The Way of the World*), loyalty (*For Her Sweetheart's Sake*), duty (*Wife's Devotion*), self-sacrifice (*Friends*), tolerance (*Judge Not That Ye Be Not Judged*), and kindness (*Tempered with Mercy*). Love was regarded not as an expression of sex but as a spiritual bond. Not only love of a woman, but love of a son, a parent, a friend, or a fellow worker, was glorified. Love of country, wealth, power, learning, and religion were also represented with due reverence or disapproval. When love was worthy, it brought happiness; when love was meretricious, as love of wealth or power would be, it always brought deserved punishment.

The earnest emphasis upon spiritual values required an optimistic tone, and this was supplied liberally. Instead of depicting the poor as overcome by one disaster after another, films now preached that Providence took care of the stricken but good when circumstances were most dire. Commented *The Moving Picture World* in 1909: "Why is it necessary to reproduce these atmospheres of gloom and sorrow? Isn't it worthwhile to try at least to create an impression of hopefulness, if not of joy?"

The new optimism was poured forth in a series of pathetic and heart-rending dramas in which some unforeseen occurrence at the last moment always converted despair into happiness. *An Unexpected Friend*, in typical style, told of a poor man who was arrested for passing a counterfeit coin, although he was unaware of its falsity, but was saved at the eleventh hour by a policeman's unexpected help. *A Child of the Ghetto* taught, in the words of a reviewer, that "The hand of Providence is ever ready to aid the helpless and afflicted; to stay the incitant of injustice—though conditions may appear contradictory." [3] *In the Watches of the Night* preached that in the "clouds of despair" there would always be found a "silver lining."

Movies demonstrated that every man, no matter how low he had fallen, could regain his lost spiritual possessions. The means to re-demption were usually through self-atonement (*The Expiation*), "a woman's pure love" (*The Transformation of Mike, Salvation Sal*), children (*And a Little Child Shall Lead Them; Child as Benefac-tor*). A common treatment was that of *The Taking of Rattlesnake Bill:*

This is a very pathetic story which induces sympathy for the outlaw. The bad man is not all bad, and when a child's life is at stake, self-preservation, the first law of nature, ceases to be a con-sideration. [4]

Movies assiduously moralized that the way of the transgressor is hard, that the paths that lead to downfall are thorny.

The usual extremely melodramatic terms of such lessons appear in *The Rocky Road:* [5]

Ben Cook had been a man of intelligent energy, but meeting with reverses, went the way of so many others, that is, became addicted to drink. Falling lower and lower, . . . [he becomes] a drunken loafer. In return for his wife's tearful entreaties, he gives abuse, and finally desertion, leaving his native town for parts unknown. Land-ing in a strange village, he seeks and obtains employment in a saw-mill, where he resolves to brace up. Meanwhile his poor wife, learning from her husband's company of his flight, becomes unbal-anced in mind, and taking up her little three-year-old child, starts out in search of him.

The story proceeds to relate how the wife loses her little girl, who is adopted by another family. Years later the girl becomes engaged

[3] *Op. cit.,* June 11, 1910.   [5] *Op. cit.,* January 8, 1910.
[4] *Op. cit.,* October 11, 1913.

Storming the gates of Babylon, from D. W. Griffith's epic film, *Intolerance* (1916).

Charles Ray in *The Coward* (1916), the film
that made his reputation, directed by Thomas
H. Ince, renowned for his "soul fights."

to her own father, not knowing who he is. The mother, learning by accident of the impending wedding, hurries frantically to the church:

The ceremony had just begun when she rushes in. Oh, God! What a terrible revelation! She has just strength enough to make the truth clear when she falls into her husband's arms, dead. Thus, in a flash he is made to feel the weight of the hand of Divine Justice in the horror and mortification of the situation.[6]

In similar violent strain *A Drunkard's Child* and *The Drunkard's Fate* preached against drink and the horrible disasters it brought. Other factors pointed out as leading to spiritual downfall were evil companions, discontent, and greed. *A Change of Heart, Led Astray, Driven from Home* preached how wicked associates can wreck an innocent and guileless person's life. *Fools of Fate* and *A Corner in Wheat* taught that tragedy and death are the final rewards of avarice.

Love, marriage, family life, and woman's virtue were favorite moral themes. Marriage was upheld and venerated as an institution; childbearing was its unquestioned purpose. Incompatibility or maladjustment between husbands and wives—situations which were to become familiar on the screen in later years—were but rarely presented as causes of domestic conflict. The film woman accepted her position as a dutiful, docile wife whose place was in the home. On the other hand, it was proved dramatically that jealousy on the part of the husband leads only to unhappiness (*A Victim of Jealousy, Jealousy and the Man, One Can't Believe One's Eyes, The Price of Jealousy*). The wife was usually represented as being loyal and content (more content than wives in later films), and if any triangle situation occurred it was always due to the wicked intrusion of another man. Even the comedy *Love Your Neighbor as Yourself, but Leave His Wife Alone* expressed grave disapproval of the "third person."

All films of domestic life focused on the children: the care and upbringing of sons and daughters was the paramount concern of parents. *For Her Son's Sake* and *A Mother's Grief* were typical sermons in motherly devotion. *The Marked Time-Table*, striking a

6 *Ibid.*

different key, was "a powerful lesson to over-indulgent mothers, whose maternal love works a most disastrous effect on their children." Other movies pointed out the responsibility of parents to see that their offspring mingled with the right people and were not led astray. Children were taught that obedience to parents was essential to their own happiness. Filial disobedience brought inevitable disaster, as in *The Face at the Window:*

> The young man, having graduated at college, goes into the world, meets and marries an artist's model, and is disowned by his father. Later a victim of drink, he deserts his wife and child and goes the usual road. . . . The child grows into manhood, and on the day of his graduation . . . the face of the tramp appears at the window. In a lark, they bring the tramp in, and find him none other than the boy's father.[7]

In this vein films urged children to obey the dictates of their parents in such vital matters as love and marriage. Whenever a son or daughter acted against the wishes or orders of the parents in choosing a mate, degradation and sorrow followed. Parents had a wisdom that seemingly was infallible.

Romance was not yet regarded as a prime necessity for marital happiness. More important were such factors as social equality, earning ability of the husband, chastity of the wife, mutual respect, and general uprightness. *Her Romance* was a typical warning, showing the tragedy that befalls a rich young girl who, against her mother's wishes, marries her music teacher instead of "a wealthy swell." In *To Save Her Soul* a curate shoots his fiancée when he discovers her at a "banquet attended by young swells." *In the Firelight* related how Nellie, lured to the big city by a stranger, is finally deserted by him. The prayers of her stepfather lead her brother to her, and he brings her home, a repentant prodigal. *A Country Girl's Peril* and *First Love Best* were variations on the same theme.

Virtue and money became the elementary conditions for marriage, and the rightness of marrying the home-town boy was deeply impressed upon the country girl beset by temptations of the city.

Morality dramas were paralleled by films glorifying America as

[7] Biograph Advertisement in *The Moving Picture World*, June 18, 1910.

the land where true worth and ability would always triumph—a democratic nation where opportunity was open to all, where fame and fortune were not based on education or background but on good, ambitious, and just character. Grammar, formal education, family—none of these old-world standards mattered in America. Many of the country's great men had risen from humble beginnings; hard work and competition made everything possible; within every man was the power to be a superman. The true slogan for life was "Let the best man win." The essential was that a man be equal to, and ready for, every opportunity. Eloquent of this credo of rugged individualism were such films as *The Best Man Wins*, *From Cabin Boy to King*, *A Self-Made Hero*, and *The Stuff Americans Are Made Of* (a "stirring picture that makes one realize that heroism exists all around one").

But get-rich-quick schemes were condemned. Popular interest in big business and million-dollar enterprises was restrained by films which taught one to beware of too easy successes. The American spirit of hard work, honesty, patience, was the best and surest means to success; in fact, according to the movies it was the infallible means. The urge to grab a fortune all at once was proved to be disastrous in *A Corner in Wheat* (lifted from Frank Norris's story), which showed that ruin followed "ill-gotten spoils." *A Plot for a Million* and *The Counterfeiter's Fate* presented like lessons. *A Pitfall of the Installment Plan*, suggested by the new method of credit buying then becoming fashionable, and *Caught by the Coupon Craze*, warned movie audiences against too much reliance upon the promises of others. *The Dream of Dan McGuire* pointed out that "even the humblest man has the liberty of his thought," and that a hod carrier can dally with millions "in his sleep."

Dozens of movies portrayed the American ideal of stalwart virtue. Most vigorous were the new "Westerns." In 1908 the cowboy, a fresh and colorful character, was introduced in the Broncho Billy series, which set a fashion and continued for years. The sweep and action of the frontier produced much more physical exhilaration than other types of films. But with time the frontier became more than a picturesque and exciting locale for movie dramas. By 1909 it was a forceful expression of democratic feeling and moral standards—more forceful, perhaps, than the deliberate morality dramas.

Rugged individualism and the triumph of the best man were epitomized in the world of open spaces, where men ruled by democratic community, action, and a sense of honor. In the West everyone had the same opportunities to find his level; hard work and honesty were the needed qualities. Value was in action; deeds spoke louder than words. No one asked where a man came from or where he was going; it was up to him to prove his accomplishments. Material possessions, clothes, etiquette, and eloquent talk were trivialities as compared with uprightness, the ability to defend oneself, the love of justice. Always the Western hero was busy righting wrongs, doing the seemingly impossible through determination and fearlessness, protecting the weak, and thus winning fortune and the girl he loved.

Broncho Billy, the screen symbol of the best in American manhood, was taken to the heart of America. *Broncho Billy's Adventure, The Bearded Bandit, The Heart of a Cowboy, The Forest Ranger,* and *The Sheriff's Sacrifice* were only a few of hundreds of films in the series: over a period of years a new Broncho Billy picture appeared each week. Toward the close of the pre-war period Broncho Billy was overshadowed by two other "cowboys," each cherished for his particular personality, both having in common the basic traits of dauntlessness and honesty. Next to Broncho Billy Tom Mix, with his dazzling horsemanship and his wily ways in dealing with enemies, was perhaps the best-known cowboy. *In the Days of the Thundering Herd, The Long Trail, The Trimming of Paradise Gulch,* and hundreds of similar pictures attested to his noble and numerous virtues.

William S. Hart, the strong silent man of the movies for ten years after 1914, was in this same tradition. His steely gaze, adamant honesty, determination and daring, and hearty goodness were passionately enjoyed week in and week out by old and young. *Two-Gun Hicks, The Return of Draw Egan, Hell's Hinges,* and *The Silent Man* are a few of his films which old-timers well remember. As one reviewer exclaimed, "What punch and character in these names—'Blaze' Tracy and 'Silk' Miller!" These were the broad terms in which all his films were couched. Always he was "a one-woman man, nature's nobleman who fights a mob to victory single-handed." "Quick on the guns as William S. Hart" became an American proverb.

Counterparts of Broncho Billy, William S. Hart, and Tom Mix have appeared in every period of movie development up to the present day. Some of the most famous "sheiks of the saddle" have been Harry Carey, Hoot Gibson, George O'Brien, Buck Jones, Tom Keene, Ken Maynard, Bill Boyd, and Gene Autrey. But the West and the cowboy are themes which have withstood change both cinematically and conceptually. Since the advent of the talkies, only one new feature has been added to Westerns: cowboys now sing and strum guitars.

Hand in hand with frontier morality went military patriotism. As in earlier years, films about the Army and Navy and American history enjoyed an unslackening popularity. The building and fortification of the Panama Canal, the policing of the Philippines, the spread of American influence in South America, and the question of national defense were made urgently interesting to movie-goers.

The Hand of Uncle Sam vividly described the "patriotic" activities of the government in South America:

Based upon the supposed interest of an American in one of the vest-pocket republics of South America, it is chiefly interesting because of the opportunity it affords of learning how the hand of Uncle Sam can reach forth and snatch a man from before the rifles of the firing squad (even though the man was conspiring to overthrow the republic in favor of a dictator with U. S. capitalist money). . . . The closing scene, where the American is restored to his wife's arms, with the American flag waving above them, arouses strong emotions.[8]

The courage and loyalty of the soldier and sailor were convincingly dramatized in film after film. *A Day with the Soldier Boys, The Girls in the Barracks,* and *Up the Ladder with Bowline,* made with the approval of the government, were in effect recruiting pictures.

The American Revolution and the Civil War were rich and colorful backgrounds for the patriotic spirit, as in *Rally Round the Flag,*

[8] Advertisement of Essanay Film Mfg. Co., *The Moving Picture World,* March 26, 1910.

For Flag and Country, and *Faithful unto Death*. Patriotic bravery was eulogized in *The Banner Carrier*, *In the Line of Peril*, *None but the Brave Deserve the Fair*, *George Washington Under the British Flag*, and *Swords and Hearts*. The inevitability of militarism was proved in *Half a Hero* and *Destiny Is Changeless*. As a critic remarked in 1910, "By their appeal to the imagination they [these movies] help one to see beyond the pictures and observe something which stirs emotions otherwise dormant."

In teaching reverence for flag and country, and conscientiousness in the line of duty, movie producers missed no opportunity to show the Stars and Stripes. Since the display of the Flag at the end of a picture was certain to evoke applause, wily producers often made films with nothing more to commend them than a shot of Old Glory. Declared *The Moving Picture World:* [9]

The grandeur of the American flag was never more in evidence than in the portrayal of its birth as presented by the Vitagraph company in the feature film *Old Glory* . . . the standard of 90 millions of people enlisted under its protecting colors. All the great and famous men who had to do with freedom's cause in the 18th, 19th, and 20th centuries, are brought before us in motion pictures, and the almost living presence as they fight the battles of the past on sea and land, before powers and principalities, in councils of war and state to raise the Star Spangled Banner, an emblem of prosperity and Peace among the nations of the earth.

On the international scene, movies took up only the most spectacular subjects. "Help the starving Armenians!" became the national cry. *Auction of Souls*, stirring up powerful sentiment by its dramatization of the famine in the Near East, was influential in the raising of funds for the unfortunate victims of the Turks: "The sympathetic interest evoked by its awful revelations helped, perhaps more than any other factor, in materially adding to the large sums that were subscribed to this cause."

The attitude toward Russia can be seen from *Russia, the Land of Oppression*, advertised as

An unusual picture. Leo Tolstoi has aroused the civilized world with his protest against Russian pogroms, persecution and massacre.

[9] July 2, 1910.

This picture is an undying appeal to humanity, worked out in unerring detail by people who have spent years in the land of the knout and saber.[10]

Old films of Mexico and new staged ones were advertised as authentic documents of the Mexican revolution. In editorial subtitles a three-reeler made by Universal took a definite stand against a liberal Mexico by showing Madero's troops as "cruel and ruthless." So biased was this production that *The Moving Picture World* [11] discreetly commented, "Some of the reflections upon the existing administration in Mexico would probably be libelous in this country." When the picture was submitted to a Board of Censors in an effort to quiet protests against its bias, the Board conceded that there was much in it to offend, but that it had no authority to suppress it, since the Board's province "encompassed moral, not political, issues."

A few movies about Mexico were less prejudiced. *A Mexican Tragedy* showed a federal spy bribing an innkeeper's daughter to influence the revolutionary general and stop the revolution. *The Clod*, adapted from the famous stage play, showed that only long tyrannical treatment of the Mexican peasant by the government turned him into a revolutionist. Said one reviewer, "The picture's mistake lies in the failure to turn the man into a consistent revolutionist at the end." The conclusion of the film showed the peasant going mad because of the revolution.

On the local scene popular progressive sentiments prompted the movie producers to take up current social problems—the woman suffrage movement, white slavery, political corruption, capital-labor issues, and the tribulations of immigrants and racial minorities.

In deference to the power of feminism, many motion pictures portrayed the "new woman" not unsympathetically, as in *Her Face Was Her Fortune*, *The Romance of a Trained Nurse*, *The Factory Girl*, *A Female Reporter*, and *Female Sleuth*. Suffragettes and suffrage for women, however, continued to be mocked and condemned (*For the Cause of Suffrage*, *Her Duty*, *The Fatal Vote*, *Suffra-*

[10] *The Moving Picture World*, June 4, 1910.   [11] April 1913.

gettes). The plight of the working girl was realistically described. In *The Road to Happiness*, for example,

Rhoda is a salesgirl, one of the victims on the altar of trade. The heat of the long summer days, the incessant lifting and measuring, and the aggravation of unreasoning customers all help to bring about the breakdown that attracts the attention of the welfare secretary of the story.[12]

In the end, Rhoda finds "the road to happiness is down the path of love" with a farmer whom she meets in the country where she is sent for a vacation. This solution was to become the common happy ending of all such tribulations.

The constant influx of rural women into the cities, often into slums and tenement districts, was being marked by increasing prostitution and white slavery. Public interest in the series of vice investigations which led to the eventual passage of the Mann Act gave movies better reason than ever to warn girls against the lures of the city. One of the first such films, *Traffic in Souls*, was a sensation throughout the country. Widely advertised as having the unqualified approval of the District Attorney's office, the Board of Censorship, and societies crusading against vice—sanctions since employed with many such films to give them moral standing—*Traffic in Souls* depicted white slave conditions in New York, "that vicehole of America," with gangsters recruiting innocent victims from ships arriving with immigrants, from railroad stations, and from the slums. The sex theme was so heavily emphasized that many observers maintain it was this film which set the precedent for "sex in movie content." *Traffic in Souls* was quickly followed by a crowd of such pictures, *The Inside of the White Slave Traffic* and *Damaged Goods* being perhaps the most daring.

Movies continued to expose the wickedness of politics and politicians. The stories represented local corruption (*The Grafter*), political machinations (*How They Got the Vote*), and questionable political ethics generally (*One Is Business, the Other Crime*). No attempt was made to demonstrate how politics could be of service; the public was urged to be wary of politics in general and politicians

[12] *The Moving Picture World*, June 18, 1910.

in particular. Politics, a nasty business at best, was properly avoided by decent people.

Adjacent to political issues was the growing public interest in labor problems. During these years wide-flung private and local organizations were forming to relieve poverty in the laboring classes, and conservation of human resources as well as natural wealth was being established as a policy of government. Unionism was one topic on which the movie men pounced eagerly. They discussed it frequently in their films, pointing out that union men were mere dupes. *Pete Wants a Job*, for instance, showed how an unprincipled politician gains power through false leadership of the workers.

Pete tries numerous jobs without success. Then he becomes a strike organizer, leading several strikes successfully. Within a year he becomes, through his power over the workers, a leading politician, then finally a government minister.[13]

In this picture the interrelation between labor and politics was made clear, the politician being the man who, unable to get a regular job in private industry, uses others for his own selfish ends. *The Moving Picture World*,[14] after reviewing the picture, expressed the hope that it would not furnish a suggestion to ambitious scoundrels generally. It is notable that this film attempted to convince the public that workers who listen to labor leaders are listening to rascals who seek only self-aggrandizement.

Despite prevailing sympathy for the laboring man as a person, his assertion of rights as a worker was still deemed presumptuous. The American Federation of Labor, whose membership had increased to over two million by 1914, and the I.W.W., which was extremely active especially in 1912-1913, were still viewed with suspicion by the public and, in particular, by the movie producer. The tacit assumption was that labor had no rights except those granted by the employer. Conflicts between laborer and employer were always resolved on the screen by the patronizing generosity of the boss, who always forgave the "lazy" or "misled" workers (*Lazy Bill and the Strikers*, *The Loafer*, *The Iconoclast*), or by the

[13] Condensed from *The Moving Picture World*, May 14, 1910.
[14] May 21, 1910.

"impartial" intervention of the church on the side of the employer (*Capital and Labor, The Two Sides, The Helping Hand*).

The *Iconoclast*, subtitled "How the seed of discontent is sown," showed a "lazy, drink-sotted printer" who becomes infuriated when his employer

escorts a party of his friends dressed in sables and silks through the establishment. In a show of anarchism the printer attempts to strike his employer. For this he is discharged. By this time he is ripe for anything and, drunk-mad, sets about to take a fool's method of leveling ranks.[15]

The film now shows the employer at home,

in despair over the intelligence that his child is an incurable cripple. This is the scene that greets the printer as he is about to wreak his vengeance upon the boss. . . . The fortitude of the child trying to walk makes a stronger appeal than moral suasion, and the printer turns from his purpose. The publisher, however, sees him, and reasoning that now is the turning point in the man's nature, detains him to persuade him to mend his ways. . . . The employer gives him another chance by restoring his former position.[16]

That labor unrest is due to jealousy, laziness, or drunkenness was a common premise in such movies.

Capital vs. Labor persuasively urged that the church could do more to help workers than they could do themselves by organizing. Advertised as having a "soothing charm of a most delicate love story" in which "the man of heart and moral courage proves superior to the man of power and violence," the film told how

The daughter of a capitalist is courted by a young officer of the militia, and . . . a young clergyman. . . . She is undecided whom to marry. A strike at her father's manufacturing plant sends the threatening strikers, incensed by agitators, toward her home, where the officer is visiting. He dares not face them singlehanded and leaves to get the aid of his regiment. In the meantime the mob attacks the home, breaks the doors and windows and forces an entrance into the house, demolishes the furniture, and threatens her father, in whose arms she is clasped. While the fury of the mob is at its height, the young minister rushes into the room, checks and

[15] *The Moving Picture World*, October 8, 1910.   [16] *Ibid.*

silences the strikers, and gains from their employer all their claims
and privileges. Naturally the young clergyman has won the respect
of the capitalist, the cause of labor, and the heart of the young
girl.[17]

The message of the film, that capital would accede to labor demands if approached properly by the right people, prompted *The
Moving Picture World* to call the film "one of the most extraordinary motion picture dramas of the year . . . powerful in its purpose."

Film after film condemned organized action by workers as "mob
violence," inspired by foreign agitators, led by anarchists, gaining
nothing for the workers and resulting only in destruction. *An
Anarchist*, *Anarchists on Board*, and *The Bomb* are representative
of dozens of pictures that smeared the labor movement. Although
these pictures often showed the miserable conditions that provoke
labor unrest, they not only condemned labor unions but failed to
suggest any substitutes. *The Strike*, for instance, showed how a
"blackguard" union organizer, by getting men to strike for better
conditions, ruins a town. The factory owners move their plant elsewhere to teach "workers a lesson never to listen to agitators."

But during these years progressives were loudly expressing dissatisfaction with labor conditions, and pro-labor sentiment was
gaining strength. While the conflict of opinions was raging, an ex-
university professor quietly stepped into the White House. Liberals
hailed the new leader, a man who would strike "in favor of the
small folk" and the "new freedom." Shortly after his nomination
for the Presidency, Woodrow Wilson had promised that his party
would strive for "restoration of the lower middle class, hard-pressed
farmers and working people of the cities, to their rightful authority
in Washington."

A remarkable film, provocatively titled *Why?*, reflected progressive opinions. It broached the questions "Why do we have children
at hard labor?", "Why do we have men who gamble at race
tracks?", "Why are trains run so fast that fatal accidents occur?",
"Why does Capital sit easily at dinner with Church and Justice,
and with the Army, while Labor is outside starving?" These ques-

[17] *The Moving Picture World*, July 2, 1910.

tions were ingeniously presented in the form of a motion picture parable, which was executed with stylized sets, symbolism, and unusual dream sequences.

A wealthy hero takes a journey through the world and is struck by all the hardships of labor. When he discovers children at work on a treadmill, he shoots their taskmaster, who at once turns into a bag of gold to show that it is impossible to kill capital. Then he is invited to come to dinner with capital, and while they are feasting the laboring men revolt, demanding a seat at the table. The frightened capitalists rally around the generals as they shoot the people . . . who fall beside the food-laden table. The climax comes with the burning of the Woolworth Building and lower Manhattan by the workers promulgating that what is theirs they can destroy.

The Moving Picture World [18] wrote of the film,

It is such as will excite all who see it; it will get into their blood, especially if they are sensitive; and they will remember it. Yet we cannot say that the picture teaches anarchy. It is far from being a philosophical study.

Now that movies were showing a tendency to take sides on social issues, certain interests began to use them for outright propaganda. *Fight for Right* was an attack on prison labor, demonstrating that it competed with private business and was a menace to industrial workers. The film proposed that convicts be employed at outdoor and other tasks outside the sphere of organized trade unions. The proposal was supported by the assertion that outdoor work would build clean, vigorous bodies and strong minds. In another vein, *Photoplay* reported in October 1912 that Cleveland had made a movie to support its campaign for a million dollars for dispensaries, nurses, and medicines to alleviate slum conditions. The Cleveland picture exposed the evils of tenement life and pointed to the need for clinics, doctors, and nurses.

Progressivism began to appear in the movies' treatment of minority groups in the nation. A genuine effort was exerted to represent most minorities, native and foreign, by more human and realistic interpretation instead of the conventional vaudeville comic caricatures. The new attitude was due, no doubt, not only to the generos-

[18] May 31, 1913.

ity of the movie makers but to the fact that the minorities themselves were growing wealthier and more important in community
life.

The Jew, for instance, long treated as the usurer, was now viewed
with sympathy and understanding. *The Heart of a Jewess, Child of
the Ghetto*, and *The Patriarch* indicated that the Jew has finer
qualities than mere thrift. *A Man's Man* was advertised as showing a
Jew different from the "stage Jew"; he was "not burlesqued," but
had "manhood, sentiments and convictions."

Solomon's Son acknowledged dignity and intelligence in the Jew.
Elaborate historical films such as *The Life of Moses* promoted toleration and cordiality toward the sect. The persecution and sufferings
of Jews were dramatized with respect. *Bleeding Hearts*, or *Jewish
Freedom Under King Casimir of Poland*, showing the machinations
of one of the king's noblemen, who bears a grudge against Jews,
was exceedingly effective in winning public sympathy. By and large
the stage Jew of the derby and gesturing hands was being replaced
by the human being.

The film treatment of Italians was likewise being liberalized: in
the "new" Italian there was less comicality and villainy, more virtue,
than in the pre-1908 Italian. The stiletto-carrying murderer and
member of the Black Hand gang was being transformed into a "regular guy" who struggled manfully for his living like other Americans. In *Little Italy* and *An Eye for an Eye* the Italian was vindicated. The exceedingly popular *The Italian* portrayed the Italian
as taking care of his family despite the duplicity of an American
city slicker, and as rising above the adversities faced by most immigrants. Such films contributed no little to a better understanding of
the character and resources of the immigrant population in America.

As for the Irish, their traditional trade-marks of shiftlessness,
clay-pipe smoking, and the kettle of beer were likewise discarded.
You Remember Ellen, Kerry Gow, and *The Colleen Bawn* meta-
morphosed the "begorrah and b'gosh" comedian into an authentic
social being moved by real emotions. Irish pride of heritage and the
injustices of Ireland's past were explained in such films as *The
Mayor of Ireland, The O'Neil, Rory O'More*, and *Ireland the Oppressed*.

Other minorities—Mexicans, Orientals, American Indians, Negroes —also began to appear on the screen with qualities superior to those of villains and cheap comedians. *The Seminole's Trust* and *The Red Man and the Child* were two of many films portraying the faithfulness and trustworthiness of the Indian. *The Red Man's View* even went so far as to indicate that perhaps the Indians had been victims of persecution by the whites. Like the Indian, the Negro was awarded the attributes of devotion and faithfulness, as in *His Trust*. In *A Persistent Suitor*, one of the first films to deal with Negroes as human beings, the plea for "social justice" and the sermon that "whatever the clime, or race, or color, the course of love seldom runs smooth" had strong democratic feeling.

This encouragement of tolerance toward minority groups in America, the high moral tone of the morality dramas, and the didacticism of films on social problems all bespoke the idealistic American outlook during these pre-war years.

Hardly less rich in information about everyday life in the period than the dramas were the hundreds of comedies. These not only "clowned" human foibles but pointedly satirized them. Even in the comedies the didactic disposition of the producers was in evidence. *The Moving Picture World*, commenting on the comedy *The Rival Cooks*, remarked, "Perhaps there is a bit of satire here which is intended to show how impossible it is to keep a secret in a small community."

The motion picture found in everyday human activities infinite possibilities of ludicrous mixups, mistaken identities, headlong chases, rough-and-tumble burlesques. It poked fun at the telephone (*The Troublesome Telephone*), the trolley car (*Accidents Will Happen*), cigarettes and cigars (*Tobacco Mania*), the latest fads (*The Marvelous Cure, He Joined the Frat, The Fallen Idol*), civic institutions (*Officer Muldoon's Double, The New Chief*). Everyday experiences became the butt for humor in *All on Account of the Milk, Adele's Wash Day, Brown's Moving Day, Gee, I'm Late!, The Unmailed Letter, How to Get a City Job, How the Landlord Collected His Rents*.

Romance and domestic life were travestied constantly. The escapades of the "hubby" while the wife is away in the country, the experiences of a man trying to act like a "swell" on his vacation, the absurd complications of married life that result when a husband tries to gain the admiration of his wife (*How Hubby Made Good*) or when there is a plethora of *Wedding Presents* were exploited to the limit. Risqué incidents in married life were numerous, as may be inferred from such titles as *A Hot Time in Atlantic City, Their Chaperoned Honeymoon, The Bridegroom's Joke, The Old Maid's Valentine, A Happy Widower, The Bride and Groom's Visit to New York Zoological Park, An Absent-Minded Cupid,* and *A Cure for Bashfulness.* Such comedies were found on every program.

Throughout these years evidence of the great potency of motion pictures as a social force had piled up steadily. How readily they could indoctrinate the public with special ideas and ideals was now being realized. Even the censorship advocates and other reformers of earlier years had not exaggerated the power of the screen. An impressive instance of the movies' influence was noted in the case of Harry Thaw, who had been condemned for the killing of Stanley White in 1907, had been paroled, and subsequently had broken the parole. The film *Escape from the Asylum* argued sympathetically on his behalf; it ran for an entire week in half a dozen New York vaudeville theatres. Observers generally believed that this movie converted many people to the belief that Thaw had been sufficiently punished and that he deserved sympathy.

The hardly matched effectiveness of the movies as a means of relaxation after daily work also was being realized. Humanitarians and reformers throughout the country approved of the nickelodeons as "places of relief for the poor, of enlightenment for the illiterate, of dissemination of culture to the nation at large." It was proposed that some philanthropist could do great social good by subsidizing a theatre for free movie showings three times a week. It was urged that a speaker be provided to read the titles for illiterate spectators.

By 1914 a number of new significant trends in the movies were thus in evidence. Subject matter had been broadened by the resort to literature and contemporary life for themes. Purposefulness and self-consciousness, later to become more pronounced in the selection and manipulation of material, were now prominent qualities of movie art. The morality of the nineties was being transformed into the new progressivism. The motion picture's participation in current issues was becoming bolder. Movies were more responsive to modern social conditions and more astute in reflecting them.

Toward the end of the period a number of new developments in the industry—feature-length spectacles, large theatres in fashionable neighborhoods, and a closer alliance with the stage—began to bring into the movies' sphere a broader and new type of audience. Not only was the importance of the film as a social agency thus increased, but its content was appropriately altered. Victorian preaching and didacticism began to fall back before the questioning attitudes and freer thinking of the more educated audiences. Having until now dealt mostly with the working man and his world, the camera turned toward the middle class. In the future it was to concentrate not on interpreting the working man's world, but on diverting him from it by showing the problems of the economically fortunate, which problems would interest him as entertainment rather than as sermons. Henceforth the movies were to return only sporadically to his milieu, and then only during national economic crises.

PART FOUR

TRANSITION (1914-1918)

X

LARGE-SCALE OPERATIONS

WHEN war broke out in Europe in 1914, American motion picture production constituted more than half of the total movie production of the world; by 1917 America was making nearly all the world's motion pictures. Owing to the strain of the World War, between 1914 and 1917 the motion picture industries in France, Italy, Germany, Sweden, Norway, and England, countries that had been America's strongest competitors, collapsed. For American producers the European disaster was a stroke of fortune, since it gave them a virtual monopoly of the world movie market. Despite mounting costs, particularly of chemicals necessary to the manufacture of film and other accessories, the American movie industry participated in the general war boom. This was the period during which the industry, becoming big business, lost its pre-war self-consciousness and acquired a new self-assurance.

Increased profits, increased costs, rapid expansion in every direction, and then chaos—these were the features of the mammoth adolescent industry which the war boom nourished. Showmen and business men now fought more bitterly and ruthlessly than ever for the control of it. One corporation after another burst on the scene, only to disintegrate because of internal dissension or to fail to meet prevailing bitter competition in the trade. Hardly a week went by without dramatic announcements of new companies, revolutionary policies, fantastic successes or failures. Movies were the latest get-rich-quick bubble. Hollywood became the destination of a gold rush in which the mad enthusiasm of the old forty-niners lived once more.

In 1914 the movie business was at a turning point in its development. With a suddenness and finality that startled even its backers, the feature length was capturing the public's taste and becoming the vogue. Theatres showing the Paramount features found that even though features cost more, they produced more profit than the General Film Company's "shorts." By 1916 two- and three-reelers had fallen so far in public favor that *Photoplay* [1] was moved to remark,

> Mr. and Mrs. Sidney Drew, who have more laughs to their credit than any other producing unit in picturedom, may retire from the screen, because it seems impossible to make exhibitors understand that a short picture may have a bigger drawing power than a long one.

Before long Paramount was releasing as many as three or four features a week to some 5,000 theatres. Within a few years the company could boast of rentals as high as $700 a week for a single picture, whereas before 1914 the highest prices received by the members of the patents trust had been $150 a week. Conservative producers who pinned their faith to the short picture dwindled rapidly. The General Film Company, once the largest in the business, shrank to insignificance. Features produced by other companies soon were so standardized and familiar that people could not recall when they had not been so. "Shorts" survived only in the form of comedies, cartoons, newsreels, or novelties that were used to round out a feature program.

The overwhelming success of the feature film, together with the war boom, sent some companies to the peaks of success and others to oblivion. Many of the pioneer concerns were wiped out. Kalem and Melies, not seriously attempting to meet the new demand for features, dropped out of the business. The Edison Company sagged, discontinued production, and in 1918 finally sold its studio. Biograph, which had nurtured more of the contemporary film notables than any other company, drifted through a few unsuccessful experiments and expired. The Motion Picture Patents Company and the General Film Exchange, unable to resist this final blow of

[1] June 1916.

features, gradually wasted away. As the volume of business for "shorts" shrank before the competition presented by features, one company after another succumbed, only to be supplanted by newer and larger ones with sufficient capital to enter feature production.

In the fight for survival some former antagonists pooled their resources just as other producers had done in forming Paramount. Vitagraph, Lubin, Selig, and Essanay merged under the company name of VLSE. Mutual and Kessel and Bauman formed a coalition of production units under one distribution and financial head. This organization, known as Triangle (later, Fine Arts), had the three leading directors of the industry—Ince, Griffith, and Sennett—in charge of its production studios. Universal Company, headed by Carl Laemmle and Robert Cochrane, built up a steady clientele among the small neighborhood movie houses. William Fox and his Fox Corporation, acquiring sufficient capital to meet the demands of enlarged production, soon jumped into the forefront of movie making.

The vogue of feature-length pictures caused revolutionary changes in every department of the industry. Movie making now had to be a large-scale operation predicated on a mass market. The achievement of an organization and techniques to meet the new conditions now became the goal of the producers. The following years, therefore, saw fundamental changes in production, exhibition, and distribution methods.

The old Bronx and Flatbush studios in New York, until now the home of several companies, were now obviously inadequate and had to be abandoned. The passage in 1917 of the Wheeler Bill in New York, providing for the taxation of manufacturers, confirmed the growing feeling among producers that California and Hollywood might be more congenial and convenient. As the migrating companies settled in Hollywood, magnificent new studios were erected. Companies tried to outdo each other in the size, scope, and equipment of their new palaces of production. Inceville, Culver City, and Universal City sprang up. Huge tracts of land and enormous studios were now necessaries for movie makers who had formerly worked in small offices, in the streets, and in improvised lofts.

Costs likewise became grandiose. Picture negatives alone now cost from $12,000 to $20,000 for a five-reel feature—a sharp advance from the $500 to $1,000 cost of the completed picture of a few years before. (Even these large amounts were to double and triple in the post-war years.) Salaries, too, were mounting. Stars were paid $250 to $2,000 a week. Payments for stories, screen rights, and plays averaged from $1,000 to $10,000. The specialization of crafts, more necessary than ever in the new era of mass production, involved the establishment of new departments and an increase of personnel to include story editors, musical experts, costume designers, and research experts.

Producers were now faced with the difficult puzzle of how to standardize production. Standardization was essential to large-scale operations; but how could standardization of the product be avoided? The problem had to be solved before business could be carried on successfully. Henry Ford could manufacture thousands of cars exactly alike; here sameness was a virtue. But every movie had to be different; otherwise the movie audiences would not appear at the theatres again and again.

In popular personalities, the "formula" picture, and publicity campaigns the producers found their answer. The star soon became a prime means of stabilizing production. Pictures in which a reigning favorite appeared could be counted on to attract moviegoers fairly regularly; they could be manufactured faster and hence more profitably. Producers therefore deliberately went about creating new stars and strengthening the popularity of the reigning ones. So eager were producers to "sign up" prominent players that their bidding often set the salaries far beyond the actors' true merits. Companies outbid each other sometimes not for an "arrived" star but just to be sure that rival firms would not possess potential stars. How much importance was given to names was indicated in a lawsuit brought by Mary McLaren against Universal in 1917: it revealed the provision in her contract that, if she left the company, she could never use her name with another concern. Thus, being the mainstays of the business, and being "proved" by their fan mail, some stars were regarded worthy of any price. When Zukor announced in 1914 he had signed Mary Pickford at a salary of $104,000 a year—exactly double her previous salary—he shocked some producers; but he set a new gauge for scaling stars' wages.

Requiring a steady supply of stars, producers turned to Broadway for players with stage reputations. So zealous was their competition for stage luminaries that it seemed everyone who had ever been on Broadway reached the screen during these years. But it turned out that the movie audiences, by and large, were little impressed by stage reputations: they judged and applauded simply what they saw on the screen. Producers could only guess whether or not some well-known, high-priced stage star would be a popular screen favorite.

Producers did discover, however, that if they could not depend on established stage players for star material, they could groom popular players for stardom just as they manufactured pictures. A fairly pleasing personality could, by shrewd strategy and training, be "built" into a star. The process consisted mainly of the use of a player in film after film, in particular roles, until the audience became so familiar with him (or her) that they enjoyed recognizing him and welcomed his reappearance. Clever publicity campaigns turning on the player's career made the public so conscious of his name, habits, home life, tastes, and ambitions that they believed they knew him intimately.

Producers with minor stars sought to convince the public that their players were just as good as Mary Pickford, Charles Chaplin, and Douglas Fairbanks because they were paying them just as much money. Salary figures quoted for publicity purposes ran into figures beyond all credibility. A star became "great" because he enjoyed a high salary. So inflated did salaries become toward the end of the war period that the producers feared the star system, which they had invented themselves, would in the end be their undoing. For the players became more important than the business itself; some of them incorporated themselves and became "wildcat investments." The star system was, needless to say, castigated as "preposterous," anarchistic, insidious, evil, and disastrous.

The "formula" picture, the second means of standardizing production, was simpler than the star problem. Dramas (or melodramas), romances, action pictures, Westerns, "shockers," comedies, were categorized and exploited as such. These classifications became the staples on which movie producers depended for year-in-year-out profits. After 1918 there was not a studio that did not plan its year's output to include a number of films in each category.

The themes of these formula pictures were trivial. Stereotyped in pattern and treatment, they required only a certain amount of conflict, suspense, and credibility before the happy ending. Such formalization made wholesale production easy, since everything that went into the picture could be standardized—the plot, the direction, the star, the acting, and in fact the rendition as a whole.

Large-scale advertising campaigns, the third instrument for standardizing production, operated to stabilize mass consumption by keeping demand active. Producers aimed now to make movie-going a national habit, so that people would attend the theatres regardless of the presentations offered. The advertisements toward the close of the war period described the movies as "entertainment for the entire family." Publicity and ballyhoo became as centrally important in the movie business as in the toothpaste or automobile industry. Every feature of the motion picture was publicized to make the world movie-conscious: Hollywood, personalities, the pictures themselves. All sorts of rumors were circulated, and whether they were favorable or unfavorable did not matter: the only consideration was publicity—getting into the public eye.

Meanwhile it became clear to the movie magnates that capital investments were valuable only when in use. Production must be expanded. But continuous large-scale production was practicable only if there was corresponding large-scale distribution and consumption. As economists argue that not the amount of money, but its speed of circulation, is the better index of a nation's prosperity, so the producers argued. They saw that it was necessary to speed the marketing of their films to keep their production pace from being slowed down and to insure continuous outlets for their pictures. Movie distribution, thus taking on a greater importance than ever, entered a significant phase in its development. It was no longer the business of middlemen who competed for the ownership of a film; it became an effective means for the producers to consolidate their forces, eliminate rivals, and control the market. Production itself became secondary to distribution. Quantity distribution, recognized as the prime requisite for profit making, was tackled by the competing producers on a vast scale.

Paramount, whose initial championship of features had made them the leading movie makers, devised a unique producer-distributor plan that became the model for the fast-growing industry. The Paramount plan was based on "block booking." Under the plan the exhibitor contracted in advance to buy a stated number of films to be made within a definite time, and Paramount promised quality and attractiveness in the films. To show his good faith, the exhibitor advanced a certain sum of money on account.

Such a method of distribution was then advantageous to both theatre owners and Paramount. The exhibitor was above all glad to know that he would have a regular supply of feature pictures. He found it much better to patronize a single company that supplied him weekly with at least two new pictures of uniformly good quality than to run to the various exchanges and worry about selecting and obtaining a program himself. For Paramount the plan stabilized business generally: it assured a steady outlet for pictures, enabled them to schedule production, helped pay the costs of production in advance, and minimized the risk of their investment.

Block booking, quickly adopted by all producers in the business, had vital consequences in the industry. First of all, it led to new standards in the rating of films. When productions were sold in advance to the exhibitor, stories, expensive settings, and the names of players, directors, authors, or playwrights were important selling points. A picture to be based on a famous story or best-selling novel or "hit" play could more readily be booked with the exhibitor. If a picture was extravagant in settings, costuming, number of players, and so on, it was more costly and consequently regarded as worth more to the exhibitor. A picture featuring a popular star would bring more people into the theatres and therefore was more valuable and worth a higher rental price than pictures featuring lesser stars or no stars at all.

Besides affecting standards, the block-booking system was responsible for a number of evils in the industry. Producers sometimes did not live up to their promises. If the reputation of a star promised for a certain picture soared after the picture was contracted for as part of a block, the producer might label the picture as a "special" and give the exhibitor instead another picture with a lesser star. The "special" then was sold separately on more expensive terms. The exhibitor thus suffered from increased rental rates on desirable pictures, and his own plans were disrupted. Under the new system even the rental rates for regular pictures mounted exorbitantly, and malicious tactics to compel the exhibitor to depend upon the block-booking system became prevalent.

Animosity among the exhibitors toward block booking, and toward Paramount in particular, grew rapidly. The climax came in 1917 when a number of leading exhibitors, combining for protection, established a distribution channel of their own known as First National. Controlled by twenty-seven executives of established theatre circuits, including many important first-run houses, the new organization offered a severe challenge to the leading block-booking offender, Paramount. First National contracted with independent producers for pictures but eliminated block booking in rentals by granting sub-franchises to exhibitors. It later also established studios of its own to strengthen its position even further. A long and bitter fight between Paramount and First National for the control of distribution ensued, and some years later Paramount, in order to retain its leadership, was forced to enter the business of exhibition as well as production and distribution.

A temporary suspension of block booking was finally accomplished. Triangle, the first to compromise with exhibitors, eliminated the requirement of the advance deposit payment for pictures. Paramount itself was at last forced to relinquish block booking, this being its first concession in its battle with First National. In August 1917, *Photoplay* carried the following Paramount announcement:

An official statement by Adolph Zukor. . . . After August 5, 1917, any theatre in America can secure Paramount Pictures and Paramount Stars just as it chooses to book them. . . . The Restrictions Are Off.

In 1918 it seemed that block booking had been killed. Charles C. Pettijohn, now the defender of block booking but then a counsel for the Affiliated Distribution Corporation, declared,

The exhibitor is through with the order of things which forced him to put into his theatre pictures he didn't want, pictures his audience didn't want, in order that he might play pictures that he wanted.

The problem of distribution control, however, was still acute and still to be settled.

Meanwhile, exhibition, like distribution and production, had been expanding grandiosely because of the feature fashion. The longer pictures increased the length of programs to two hours, so that the old nickelodeon's scheme of short programs and quick turnover was no longer workable. Larger theatres became necessary, since exhibitors had to make up in capacity what they lost in turnover. Increased rates for feature-length films and the lengthening of programs from an hour to two hours meant the raising of admission prices as well.

Exhibitors for the first time were made conscious of the quality of their presentations and of the accommodations in their theatres. Already men like Hodkinson, Tally, and Fox had established a better type of motion picture theatre, successfully charging ten, fifteen, and even twenty cents admission. They had introduced the refinements of organ accompaniment, comfortable interiors, vaudeville novelties, noiseless projection, and better service.

The long features and Paramount's stress on "Selected Pictures for Selected Audiences" led to general improvements of existing theatres, and to the building of big new palaces on fashionable thoroughfares with admission prices of twenty-five and thirty cents. Such theatres presented the new features first and thus became clearly distinguished from the merely second-class houses.

The announcement in 1913 that Mitchell Mark was going to build a motion picture theatre in the heart of Broadway that would accommodate 3,000 people further spurred building activity. In February 1914 a precedent was set by the opening, in the heart of the Broadway theatrical district, of two elaborate theatres that rivaled the best legitimate theatres: the Vitagraph Theatre and the more spectacular Strand Theatre, which seated 3,000 and had two floors.

News of these "million-dollar palaces" swept the exhibition field. Within a short time many new-type theatres styled after the Strand and seating at least 1,200 had sprung up in cities throughout the nation. Exhibitors earnestly set about beautifying their theatres. Ornamental plaster relief work on walls and ceilings, elaborate lobbies, decorative cashiers' cages, rich carpeting, cuspidors, brass railings, and a thousand and one other embellishments became commonplace. By February 1916 approximately 21,000 remodeled or entirely new movie theatres were in operation, and by 1917 the nickelodeon had become an antique. Big movie theatres were the standard, significant and increasingly numerous symbols on the main streets of America.

The big theatres, making movies respectable, attracted a new type of audience. Hitherto movie customers had been chiefly of the working class; now that movie theatres rivaled the "legitimate" in presentations, comfort, ostentation, and price scales, the great middle classes were attracted. They liked the cathedral-like atmosphere of these new temples of silent drama, but they were not so gullible nor so readily pleased as the laborers had been. They would tolerate no inconveniences. Performances had to be mechanically perfect: the projection steady, continuous, and easy on the eyes. They had no patience with broken films; they disliked waiting while reels were changed. Movie houses had to be comfortable and sanitary, with upholstered seats, polite ushers, carpeted floors, clean lounging rooms. Slides advertising a neighborhood store or containing some friendly advice were no longer permissible. The peanut and candy vendor could no longer tramp the aisles, shouting his wares. Community singing was dropped, and music played by large (if third-rate) orchestras was substituted.

Refinement, in short, became the keynote of the new theatres' appeal—refinement not only of the theatres but of their customers. As a fan magazine of the day editorialized, "About the cheapest thing on earth is the man who stands on the outside of a picture theatre and tries to see the film through the opening and closing doors."

A "billion-dollar pastime," movies had become a fabulously rich giant in commerce. Production was reckless and extravagant; wanton waste was widespread in the industry. The prevalent attitude was that the only way to make money is to spend it. As K. Owen remarked in *Photoplay*,[2] "If it were not for the enormous amount of money expended needlessly—or apparently so—they would have the federal government after us for cornering the visible cash supply of the nation."

Gamblers all, many former nickelodeon owners, penny-arcade showmen, and "shoestring" manufacturers emerged by 1918 as movie magnates of million-dollar dimensions. The new millionaires' row, now calling themselves "producers" rather than "manufacturers," included William Fox, Adolph Zukor, Marcus Loew, George K. Spoor, Samuel Goldwyn, Jesse Lasky, Richard Rowland, Louis B. Mayer, and Carl Laemmle—to name a few. Actors, playwrights, and directors who had once shamefacedly bartered their dignity for some ready cash now found themselves upon pedestals of public adulation and financial splendor. No one knew exactly what had swept him into the current of fame and fortune, but everyone wanted to ride the wave. Not until the war's close did the scramble gradually subside. In the wake of its confusion was left an industry of complex and Gargantuan proportions that was to be fought over on an even vaster scale in the years to come.

Investment in production was no longer a matter of a few thousand dollars; it involved great financial resources. Movie making, closely knit with movie selling, was no longer an open field for any enterprising young man. Said *Photoplay* [3] in an editorial,

To those who observe the march of photoplay events it seems as though film history, like much of the record of human life, moves in a circle. When Edison was in the heyday of its power, moving pictures were ruled by a mighty trust. Then came the humble independents, their unbeatable energy, their progress—and today they are a virtual trust! What next?

[2] January 1916.   [3] August 1918.

By 1918 the reformed industry was functioning with reasonable efficiency and speed on an unprecedentedly large scale. Increasingly complex in organization, it had the lineaments of big business and had taken its place as one of the country's major industries. Production, distribution, and exhibition were supported by the star system, block booking, and the new cinema palaces. The struggle for the control of the rich mass market was beginning to produce gigantic interlocking organizations. Everyone realized that hereafter success in the industry would depend on the co-ordination of production, distribution, and exhibition on an enormous scale.

Before this period of extravagant growth closed, however, two sudden and almost simultaneous events nearly wrecked the seemingly topless prosperity of the industry. One was the Armistice. Surfeited with war, Americans boycotted war pictures, and many producers, left with quantities of pictures that no one wanted to see, were all but ruined. The second event that threatened the industry was the influenza epidemic. Thousands of theatres in the United States and Canada were forced to shut down for periods of from one week to two months, and losses due to closed theatres were estimated at $40,000,000. Some companies, operating under fantastically high overheads, were forced to the wall. All production in the East was halted; in California more than half of the production activity ceased. The movie industry, incredulous but fearful, faced seemingly imminent ruin.

XI

D. W. GRIFFITH: *THE BIRTH OF A NATION* AND *INTOLERANCE*

THE second period (1914-1917) of D. W. Griffith's career saw the production of his two greatest films, *The Birth of a Nation* and *Intolerance*. High points in the history of the American movie, these two pictures far surpassed other native films in structure, imaginative power, and depth of content, and they marked Griffith's peak as a creative artist. They foreshadowed the best that was to come in cinema technique, earned for the screen its right to the status of an art, and demonstrated with finality that the movie was one of the most potent social agencies in America.

Neither *The Birth of a Nation* nor *Intolerance* was an accident —a "lucky fluke" of directorial frenzy: both were the consummation of five years of intensive movie making. Griffith's Biograph apprenticeship is replete with presages of these two compositions. Ingenious organizational devices, startling compositional sketches, sentimental cameos, and high-powered episodes, which time and again had appeared in his hundreds of Biograph miniatures, reappeared in these two works with superlative effects. Without his experimental years at Biograph it is doubtful whether Griffith could have made at this time two such profound and triumphant films.

After leaving Biograph, Griffith produced for his new employers, Mutual, four films in quick succession, none of which particularly interested him: *Home Sweet Home; The Escape; The Avenging Conscience (The Tell-Tale Heart)*; and *The Battle of the Sexes*. Griffith was getting $1,000 a week salary, and he did these minor pictures rapidly to accumulate money—this time not so he could quit film making, but so he could make bigger and better films than any he had yet done. The specter of the European film successes still tormented him. He had been constantly on the lookout for a subject that would lend itself to a spectacular use of his talents and would put him ahead of his foreign rivals. But he did not yet have more than a vague sense of what he wanted.

Discussing his needs with Frank Woods, the former film critic who had become a leading scenario writer through Griffith's encouragement, Griffith learned of Thomas Dixon's successful dramatization of his novel *The Clansman*. Woods rhapsodized over the novel's motion-picture possibilities. He had already written a scenario of *The Clansman* for Kinemacolor Corporation, which had begun but was unable to finish the production. Griffith was naturally excited by the appeal of such a theme—the South and the Civil War—and the opportunity it offered for his particular talents. *The Clansman* seemed to fit his enlarged ambitions perfectly; so he bought the film rights.

In planning the story, Griffith added material from another Dixon book, *The Leopard's Spots*, and supplemented it with his own recollections of his father's reminiscences. The story he finally evolved was more extensive than any he had yet attempted. It covered the years immediately before the Civil War, the war itself, and part of the Reconstruction Period. Griffith called it *The Clansman*.

Griffith now began production on a vast scale. Big though the undertaking was, it was still the creation of one mind. Like George Melies before him, but with plans magnified a thousandfold, Griffith shouldered not only the responsibility of production but all the incidental business and financial obligations as well. Before he shot his first scene he put his company through six weeks of grueling rehearsals; then followed nine more weeks of painstaking shooting. An entire county is said to have been rented for the photographing of the rides and battle scenes. Unexpected difficulties developed when Griffith tried to get horses, which were urgently required in the war in Europe. Thousands of yards of cotton sheets had to be put on the Clansmen, and this material too was a war scarcity. Whole communities were combed for white

Theda Bara, the screen's first vamp, as Cleopatra in the film of that name (1917). The lurid display and over-decoration were typical of spectacle films during the war period.

"A-blink-in-smiles," Douglas Fairbanks personi-
fies democratic wide-awake American manhood
in *His Majesty the King* (1919).

goods. But one of the heaviest burdens was the feeding, paying, and management of the hundreds of extras.

The making of the picture was marked by an unceasing struggle for money, an unbroken series of desperate financial difficulties and day-to-day borrowings. Everything Griffith possessed—his reputation, his personal fortune, whatever money he could raise from his friends—was poured into his gigantic enterprise. Besieged by mounting debts, hounded by creditors, discouraged by associates, he pushed the production to completion. According to his cameraman, Bitzer, he remained calm throughout, kept his troubles to himself, and moved steadily forward, filled with a creative urge that had to run its course regardless of time, personalities, debts, and other restraints or obstacles.

To the wonder of everyone, Griffith proceeded with his costly venture without a "shooting script." He had combined, condensed, and charted the material in his mind without the use of a written continuity. Even the details for the settings, costumes, properties, and specific scene actions were not written down. Carrying the general plan in his mind, he depended largely upon the intuition of the moment for specific action, and improvised freely as he went along. Lillian Gish, who played the heroine, revealed years later how Griffith quickly took advantage of every dramatic opportunity he saw and how he shaped his material as he went. Said Miss Gish: [1]

At first I was not cast to play in *The Clansman*. My sister and I had been the last to join the company and we naturally supposed . . . that the main assignments would go to the older members. But one day while we were rehearsing the scene where the colored man picks up the Northern girl gorilla-fashion, my hair, which was very blond, fell far below my waist and Griffith, seeing the contrast in the two figures, assigned me to play Elsie Stoneman (who was to have been Mae Marsh).

Such impulsive decisions were typical of Griffith. His method of work was in direct opposition to the careful planning of a director like Thomas Ince, who worked from minutely detailed shooting scripts. Griffith's reliance upon his instincts in shooting for con-

[1] *Stage*, January 1937.

tinuity often explains the absurdities that sometimes crop up in his films. As Dwight Macdonald remarked,[2] Griffith was

a practical genius who can make things work but who is not interested in "theory," *i.e.*, the general laws that govern his achievements . . . his fitful talent throwing off the wretchedest as well as the most inspired productions. He grew up unaware of his own powers . . . guided only by his extraordinary flair for the cinema.

Finally completed in February 1915, the production was the longest American film yet made—twelve reels—"a frightful waste and audacious monstrosity." The conservative coterie of film producers refused to handle its distribution, and Griffith was forced to form his own distribution outlets. In a letter supposed to have been written by William DeMille to Samuel Goldwyn on February 10, 1915, one can clearly sense the short-sightedness and narrow attitude of the industry generally:

I also heard rumors that the film cost nearly a hundred thousand dollars! This means, of course, that even though it is a hit, which it probably will be, it cannot possibly make any money. It would have to gross over a quarter of a million for Griffith to get his cost back and, as you know, that just isn't being done. Remember how sore Biograph was with Griffith when he made *Judith of Bethulia* and how much money that lost even though it was only a four-reeler? So I suppose you're right when you say there is no advantage in leading if the cost of leadership makes commercial success impossible. *The Clansman* certainly establishes Griffith as a leader and it does seem too bad that such a magnificent effort is doomed to financial failure.[3]

When we think of the great fortune the film reaped, such remarks seem ironic indeed.

The first American picture to get a two-dollar top admission, *The Birth of a Nation* enjoyed such enduring popularity that its total earnings makes it one of the greatest money-makers in the history of the American screen.

The picture was first exhibited at Clune's Auditorium in Los Angeles on February 8, 1915, under the title of the book, *The Clansman*. On February 20 a print was run off in New York for

[2] *The Symposium*, April and July 1933.   [3] *Stage*, December 1937.

the censors and a specially invited group. At this showing Thomas Dixon, the author of the original book, became so excited that during the applause he shouted to Griffith that the title *The Clansman* was too tame for so powerful a film: that it should be renamed *The Birth of a Nation*. This became the famous picture's title.

From the moment of its public opening on March 3, 1915, at the Liberty Theatre in New York, *The Birth of a Nation* won phenomenal success. It was the first film to be honored by a showing at the White House: President Woodrow Wilson is said to have remarked, "It is like writing history with lightning." Critics, greeting the picture with boundless enthusiasm, called it "a new milestone in film artistry, astonishing even the most sanguine by its success, and inspiring the most dramatic new departure in dissipating the supremacy of the theatre." [4] *Variety* [5] excitedly headlined its front page with "Griffith's $2 Feature Film Sensation of M. P. Trade," going on to say,

daily newspaper reviewers pronounced it the last word in picture making. . . . Mr. Griffith has set such a pace, it will be a long time before one will come along that can top him in point of production, action, photography, and direction. . . .

and concluding its lengthy panegyric with the pronouncement, "This picture is a great epoch in picture-making, great for the name and fame of D. W. Griffith and great for pictures."

This great picture reviewed the Civil War, the despoiling of the South, and the revival of the South's honor through the efforts of the Ku Klux Klan. After a short introduction which showed the bringing of slaves to America and summarized the abolitionist movement, the story proper began with Phil and Tod Stoneman, of Pennsylvania, visiting their boarding-school chums, the Cameron boys, at Piedmont, South Carolina. Phil Stoneman falls in love with Margaret Cameron, while Ben Cameron becomes enamored of the daguerreotype of Phil's sister, Elsie Stoneman. Then the Civil War breaks out. Phil and Tod leave to fight for the Union, while Ben and his two brothers join the Confederate army. During the

[4] *Variety*, March 12, 1915.   [5] *Ibid.*

ensuing war years the two younger Cameron boys and Tod are killed; Piedmont undergoes "ruin, devastation, rapine and pillage." Ben, the "little Colonel," is wounded and becomes the prisoner of Captain Phil Stoneman. Nursed by Elsie Stoneman, Ben finally recovers. Elsie and his mother visit Lincoln, "the Great Heart," and win Ben's release.

The father of Elsie and Phil Stoneman is a leader in Congress; he agitates for the punishment of the South. Lincoln refuses to countenance revenge, but Stoneman persists with his plans and grooms the mulatto, Silas Lynch, to become a "leader of his people." After the surrender at Appomattox and the assassination of Abraham Lincoln, Stoneman swiftly gains power. With Elsie and Phil he goes to the South to carry out his "equality" program for the Negroes. He rents a house next door to the Camerons'. Elsie and Ben now become engaged, but Margaret cannot bring herself to accept Phil.

Meanwhile the Reconstruction Period and

The reign of the carpet-baggers begins. The "Union League," so-called, wins the ensuing State election. Silas Lynch, the mulatto, is chosen Lieutenant-Governor. A legislature, with carpet-bag and Negro members in overwhelming majority, loots the state. Lawlessness runs riot. Whites are elbowed off the streets, overawed at the polls, and often despoiled of their possessions.[6]

The organization of the "invisible empire" of Clansmen is thus inspired and justified. Ben Cameron becomes their leader, and when Stoneman learns of it he forces Elsie to break her engagement to Ben.

Events rapidly arouse the ire of the Clan and fill Ben with a desire for vengeance. The Camerons' Negro servant, Gus, becomes a militiaman and joins Lynch's mob. When Gus makes advances to Flora, Ben's younger sister, she flees from him through the woods until, in despair, she hurls herself over a cliff. There Ben discovers her, dying.

Later Dr. Cameron is arrested for harboring the Clansman. Phil, desperate on seeing to what lengths the carpet-baggers are going,

[7] From the Special Program Notes given out at the initial Liberty Theatre performance.

helps to rescue the doctor. With Mrs. Cameron, Margaret, and the faithful servants, Phil and the doctor find refuge in a log cabin. Here they attempt to fight off an attack by the Negro militia. Meanwhile Lynch, to whom Elsie Stoneman has come pleading that he save Phil and the Camerons, demands that she marry him, and he confronts her father with the proposal.

The climax comes when the Clansmen, headed by Ben, arrive in the nick of time to mow down the Negro militia, take the Lynch mansion, free Elsie and the Stonemans, kill Gus, and save the Camerons in the cabin just as they are about to be massacred. Thus the Ku Klux Klan heroically dispenses "justice." A double honeymoon, symbolic of the reunion of North and South, concludes the story. An epilogue rejoices that peace reigns once again:

The establishment of the South in its rightful place is the birth of a new nation. . . . The new nation, the real United States, as the years glided by, turned away forever from the blood-lust of War and anticipated with hope the world-millennium in which a brotherhood of love should bind all the nations.

The film was a passionate and persuasive avowal of the inferiority of the Negro. In viewpoint it was, surely, narrow and prejudiced. Griffith's Southern upbringing made him completely sympathetic toward Dixon's exaggerated ideas, and the fire of his convictions gave the film rude strength. At one point in the picture a title bluntly editorialized that the South must be made "safe" for the whites. The entire portrayal of the Reconstruction days showed the Negro, when freed from white domination, as arrogant, lustful, villainous. Negro Congressmen were pictured drinking heavily, coarsely reclining in Congress with bare feet upon their desks, lustfully ogling the white women in the balcony. Gus, the Negro servant, is depicted as a renegade when he joins the emancipated Negroes. His advances on Flora, and Lynch's proposal to Elsie Stoneman, are overdrawn to make the Negro appear obnoxious and audacious. The Negro servants who remain with the Camerons, on the other hand, are treated with patronizing regard for their faithfulness. The necessity of the separation of Negro from white, with the white as the ruler, is passionately maintained throughout the film.

The social implications of this celebrated picture aroused a storm of protest above the Mason and Dixon Line. Negroes and whites united in attacking the picture because of its extreme bias. In Boston and other "abolitionist" cities race riots broke out. The Boston branch of the National Association for the Advancement of Colored People issued a pamphlet against the film. President Charles E. Eliot of Harvard charged the movie "with a tendency to perversion of white ideals," [7] Oswald Garrison Villard condemned it as "a deliberate attempt to humiliate ten million American citizens," [8] and Jane Addams was "painfully exercised over the exhibition." [9] Local politicians and officeholders jumped into the arena, choosing the side that offered the most votes.

In response to widespread attacks, Griffith himself became an outraged pamphleteer and published at his own expense *The Rise and Fall of Free Speech in America*. Its text contained extracts from editorials in various periodicals—*The Saturday Evening Post*, *The Chicago Tribune*, and *The Boston Transcript*, to mention three—upholding the right of *The Birth of a Nation* to freedom of the screen. He campaigned for "the freedom of the screen," issuing statements, making speeches, and writing letters to proclaim the "fundamental rights of expression" which he held to be self-evident. He must have realized, however, the wanton injury he had done to a race, for in a subsequent picture he attempted to atone for it by showing a white soldier kissing his wounded Negro comrade. Though heartfelt, such a sentimental concession could do little to compensate for the harm done by his prejudice in *The Birth of a Nation*.

The raging controversy awakened the nation to the social import of moving pictures. But this realization was overshadowed by the great acclaim for the picture's artistry, its rich imagery and powerful construction. So advanced was the film structurally that even today it stands as an accomplishment of great stature. All Griffith's earlier experiments are here consolidated: the use of camera to build scenes, the pacing of shots, the sensitive manipula-

[7] *A Million and One Nights*. Terry Ramsaye, p. 643.   [8] *Ibid*.   [9] *Ibid*.

tion of camera devices for transitions, simultaneous action, movement of all kinds—all fused by brilliant cutting. The chief difference between this film and Griffith's past efforts lies in the intensity and scale of the application of the cinematic elements. Griffith's conception had ripened; an unerring command of the medium was now his.

The Birth of a Nation pulsates; it is life itself. From the very beginning, shots are merged into a flux. Either the actions within the shots have some kind of movement or the duration of shots is so timed that the effect is one of continuous motion. This motion creates a "beat" which accents the relationships of the separate elements of the film and produces a single powerful effect.

In the Petersburg sequences, the undercurrent of movement has remarkable variety partly because of the nature of the raw material, and it is marked by extensive and resourceful uses of cinematic principles. The passages that reach a climax in the battle itself, being basically all action, are broken down by Griffith into juxtaposed scenes of long, medium, close, and detail shots, varied in duration and so contrasting in imagery that they re-create in the spectator the excitement of the battle itself. In the hand-to-hand fighting, a group of soldiers swarming across the left side of the screen are followed by a group crossing at the right, so that the feeling of conflict is intensified. Often the contrast of numbers is brought into play: shots of individual soldiers are opposed to shots of many soldiers. There is also opposition of space relationships, as in scenes in which an extreme long shot is followed by an extreme close shot. Finally there is the expressive opposition of a still shot of a dead body to the moving shot of a soldier clambering up the ramparts to place a waving flag in position. Throughout this entire section of the film Griffith ingeniously employed these structural and dramatic oppositions, giving the picture a dynamic quality that carried the spectator away by its sheer sweep.

The Reconstruction sequences, starting with the struggle between the defeated Southerners (the impoverishment of the Camerons is significantly stressed) and the emancipated Negroes (made to appear vulgar, ostentatious, and arrogant), rises to a masterly climax in the ride of the Clansmen. Here the tension is heightened by

staccato cutting. The dramatic power is enhanced by night photography, acute angle shots, extreme long and close shots, sweeping
pans, and moving-camera shots. The movement of the whole has
a fast and uneven tempo emphasizing the excitement.

Typical of Griffith's vigorous style is the beginning of the "Grim
Reaping" episode in the Reconstruction section. In the following
excerpt from the script, made from the film by Theodore Huff of
the Museum of Modern Art Film Library, can be seen Griffith's
brilliant use of intercutting to relate simultaneous action and thus
produce high tension:

Shot No.			Footage
1107	*Full Shot*	Lynch has Elsie Stoneman alone in his office. Lynch turns to her, raises his two hands.	2 feet
	Title	"See! My people fill the streets. With them I will build a black empire and you as a queen shall sit by my side."	10½ feet
1108	*Full Shot*	Lynch raises his arms in the air. Elsie sinks on chair. Lynch kneels, kisses the hem of her dress. She draws away in horror —rises—staggers to door, turning about. Lynch follows—sits at left. Elsie pounds on door.	21 feet
1109	*Semi-Close-up*	(Circle vignette) Lynch leaning back in chair—smiles—indicates his people outside.	7 feet
1110	(As 1108)	Elsie begs him—pleads with hands outstretched to let her go.	6½ feet
1111	(As 1109)	Lynch smiles at her.	2 feet, 13 frames
1112	(As 1110)	Elsie turns away—screams.	3 feet
1113	*Long Shot*	By the barn. Two Clansmen on horses come from right.	5½ feet

Shot No.			Footage	
1114	*Fade-in*	Open country. Another Clansman dashes back.	7½	feet
	Title	"Summoning the Clans."	3	feet
1115	*Semi-Close-up*	Two Clansmen by the barn—one holding up the fiery cross—the other blowing a whistle.	3	feet
1116	(As 1113) *Long shot*	By the barn. They ride forward.	6½	feet
1117	*Fade-in* (As 1114)	Open country. Clansman calling—comes forward.	7½	feet
1118	*Iris-in* (As 1116) *Long Shot*	By the barn. Five more Clansmen (having heard signal) come forward from barn.	8	feet
1119	*¾ Shot*	Lynch and Elsie. She rushes to window, left. Lynch after her—she pulls away—he shouts at her. Elsie sees it is no use—his people are outside.	9½	feet
1120	*Medium Long Shot*	Woods. Two Clansmen with a signal dash forward.	5	feet
1121	(As 1119)	Lynch and Elsie. Lynch pounds his chest with fist, boastingly.	3½	feet
1122	*Fade-in Long Shot*	Stream of water. Two Clansmen dash up stream. Fade-out.	9	feet
1123	(As 1121)	Lynch and Elsie. Lynch arrogantly points to window.	1 12	foot, frames
1124	*¾ shot*	Inner room. Man and woman listening, furtively.	1 12	foot, frames
1125	(Back to 1123)	Lynch and Elsie. Lynch calls—Elsie is horrified.	1 1	foot, frame
1126	(As 1124)	Inner room. Man at door hears Lynch's call.	2 13	feet, frames
1127	*Semi-Close-up*	(Circle vignette) Door man—he enters Lynch's office.	1 12	foot, frames

Shot No.			Footage	
1128	¾ Shot	Office—different angle. Man comes to Lynch. Elsie rises.	3	feet
	Title	"Lynch, drunk with power, orders his henchman to hurry preparations for a forced marriage."	7½	feet
1129	(As 1128)	Office. Man goes. Lynch turns to Elsie—her hand over her mouth, shocked.	3	feet
1130	(As 1127)	(Circle vignette—door) Henchman rushes to carry out Lynch's order.	14	frames
1131	(As 1126)	Inner room. Henchman calls subordinate—sends him out, right.	10	feet
1132	(As 1125)	Elsie and Lynch. Elsie looks frantically about—rushes forward to door, left.	5½	feet
1133	¾ Shot	(Circle vignette—door) Elsie speeds to it.	2 1	feet, frame
1134	(As 1132)	Elsie and Lynch. Lynch shouts to her to come back.	2	feet
1135	(As 1133)	(Circle vignette—door) Elsie tries to open door, can't, turns terrified.	1 11	foot, frames
1136	Fade-in Long Shot	Stream. A large group of Clansmen dash forward across shallow stream.	6	feet
1137	(As 1134)	Elsie and Lynch. Lynch calls Elsie back.	1 11	foot, frames
1138	(As 1135)	(Circle vignette—door) Elsie comes forward, terrified.	3½	feet
1139	(As 1137)	Elsie comes forward slowly.	4	feet
1140	Long Shot	Crossroads. Two Clansmen stop —give signal, dash on.	8	feet

Shot No.			Footage
1141	(As 1139)	Elsie and Lynch. Elsie pushes him away—rushes back to rear door—he after her—she escapes—comes forward around chairs—he chases her.	8 feet
1142	*Fade-in Long Shot*	Army of Clansmen lined up and forming—Ben in background.	7½ feet
1143	*Semi-Close-up*	(Circle vignette) Ben on horse—surveys army (mask off).	4 feet
1144	(As 1140)	Crossroads. Several more Clansmen come.	5½ feet
1145	*Fade-in Long Shot*	Field. Joining the army, Ben salutes.	6 feet
1146	*Long Shot*	Silhouette of hill. Horsemen (tiny specks) riding along ridge.	5 feet
1147	*Medium Long Shot*	Stream and cornfield. Two signal riders dash along.	3 feet
1148	*Medium Shot*	(Moving) Two signal riders (camera on car precedes them).	13 feet
1149	(As 1141)	Lynch and Elsie. Elsie rises from chair—she tries to get back.	5 feet
1150	*Medium Shot*	Street outside Lynch's office. Horse and wagons come, followed by Negroes, etc. Two men on horses enter, also.	10 feet
1151	(As 1141)	Lynch and Elsie. Elsie falls back in faint—Lynch supports her.	3½ feet
1152	*Medium Shot*	Entrance to Lynch's office. Horse and carriage stop before it—crowd around cheering.	7 feet
1153	(As 1151)	Lynch, holding Elsie, hears—	2 feet
1154	¾ *Shot*	A carriage. Stoneman steps out.	4 feet
1155	*Medium Shot*	Stoneman goes on porch through cheering crowds.	3 feet

Shot No.			Footage	
1156	(As 1153)	Lynch and Elsie. Lynch draws Elsie closer to him.	2 11	feet, frames
1157	¾ Shot	Hall. Stoneman comes—knocks.	1 15	foot, frames
1158	(As 1156)	Lynch hears—turns to Elsie.	2 3	feet, frames
1159	(As 1157)	Stoneman is impatient—asks guard the trouble—guard doesn't know.	6	feet
1160	(As 1158)	Lynch wonders what to do.	2 12	feet, frames
1161	(As 1159)	Hall. Stoneman impatient—paces —pounds cane—asks reason for delay.	12½	feet
1162	(As 1160)	Lynch and Elsie. Lynch carries Elsie forward.	6	feet
1163	¾ Shot	Inner dining room. Lynch brings her forward (unconscious, hair streaming)—sets her in chair, left. Orderlies instructed to guard her.	10	feet
1164	(As 1151)	Stoneman starts away.	2 10	feet, frames
1165	(As 1163)	Inner dining room. Lynch leaves —crosses room.	4	feet
1166	¾ Shot	Office. Lynch goes to outside door—unlocks it.	3½	feet
1167	(As 1161)	Hall. Stoneman hears—turns back —is admitted.	5½	feet
1168	(As 1166)	Office. Lynch and Stoneman come forward—Lynch apologizes —Stoneman gives him paper.	4	feet
1169	Long Shot	Clansmen forming in field. More going—Ben waves.	7½	feet

Shot No.			Footage	
1170	(As 1168)	Office. Stoneman starts back. Lynch stops him.	5	feet
	Title	"I want to marry a white woman."	5	feet
1171	(As 1170)	Stoneman pats him on shoulder —"Sure, go right ahead"—shakes hands—smiles.	5	feet
	Title	"The Clans, being assembled in full strength, ride off on their appointed mission."	8	feet
1172	Fade-in Long Shot	Field. Several hundred Clansmen come forward (horses rearing) to Ben, who salutes them. He rides off—motions to others— they follow with banners and fiery crosses in clouds of dust.	28	feet
	Title	"And meanwhile other fates—"	4	feet

The conception in 1915 of such a remarkable cutting sequence, marked by significantly few titles, demonstrated an unusual mastery of the movie medium. As can be seen from the footage of the shots, they are trimmed down so that only one essential fact is given each time. The effect builds up shot by shot, and the suspense increases, in a manner which the great Russian directors were later to develop with amazing skill. There is, furthermore, an extraordinary audacity displayed in the cutting from one scene to another without allowing either to terminate and from one episode to another so that the threads of meaning are cunningly interwoven. The tension that develops in the spectator is not relieved until Griffith resolves both episodes. This "constant shifting of scenes" is the essence of filmic technique. Henry MacMahon was one of the first to realize Griffith's accomplishment and succinctly pointed out in *The New York Times*, June 6, 1915:

Every little series of pictures, continuing from four to fifteen seconds, symbolizes a sentiment, a passion, or an emotion. Each successive series, similar yet different, carries the emotion to the next higher power, till at last, when both of the parallel emotions have attained the n*th* power, so to speak, they meet in the final swift shock of victory and defeat.

Many other episodes could be cited to prove the excellence of the film's structure. Of the rioting of the Negroes in the streets, for example, Vachel Lindsay in 1915 said, "Splendidly handled, tossing wildly and rhythmically like the sea." [10] A typically striking use of the "switchback" occurs in the episode of Phil's proposal to Margaret. We see a medium shot of Margaret considering the offer; then the film flashes back to scenes of her brothers being killed by Northerners. The following close shot of Margaret refusing her suitor is thus made forceful to the spectator without use of words, titles, or pantomime. Again, the three-cornered chase involving Flora, Gus, and Ben in the woods is filled with fearful suspense through cumulative editing: the contrast of extreme long and close shots and Flora's zigzagging course convey to the audience the desperation of Flora in her wild, headlong run.

These impressive devices are supplemented by another celebrated one: the iris, strikingly used in the sequence of Sherman's March to the Sea and the burning of Atlanta. In the upper left-hand corner of a black screen, a small iris discloses the pitiful detail of a mother and three children huddled together. Gradually the iris opens to reveal more of the scene, and when it is fully opened we see the reason for the misery of these figures: in the valley below an army of Northern invaders is marching through the town the woman has just fled. The scene is startling in its implications; the dramatic effect is far more gripping than it would have been if, through mere cutting, the shot of the army had been placed to follow the shot of the mother and children. The iris functioned not only as a dramatic means of presenting an action and its cause, but as a transitional device to frame the sequence. A daring and masterly use of the camera for a psychological effect, it shows Griffith's precise sensitivity to the dramatic possibilities of the medium.

Besides having such prime technical devices, *The Birth of a*

[10] *The Art of the Moving Picture,* p. 49.

Nation was one of the first films to make much use of symbolism. Suitable objects and animals were introduced to heighten a mood, sharpen an inference, or delineate a character. In an ecstasy of emotion, Elsie (Lillian Gish) embraces a mahogany bedpost. (Years later Greta Garbo as Queen Christina, after being closeted with her lover for three days, plays the scene similarly.) Lynch, the villainous mulatto, is shown mistreating an animal. The "little Colonel" is shown fondling small birds (a symbol taken over notably by von Stroheim in *Greed*, and since used so often that today it is a cliché).

The Birth of a Nation also introduced the practice of accompanying movies with a specially arranged orchestral score. Although this was not actually the first time music had been so used—as early as 1908 several imported French pictures had carried musical-score sheets—Griffith had exploited the possibilities of music far beyond the ordinary practice of the day.

The cultural world rapturously hailed *The Birth of a Nation*, and Griffith was enthroned as the film's first master. The acclaim was sweet to his ears, more than compensating for the public's temporary neglect of him during the preceding year, when the sensational European films had held America's admiration. He now stood at the peak of his career, the summit of his six years of struggle to make the movie an eloquent, vital, and respectable medium for art.

The Birth of a Nation was produced less than a decade and a half after motion pictures had learned to narrate. But its technique was incomparably superior to that of its primitive progenitors. If *The Great Train Robbery* was the giant of American pictures in 1903, *The Birth of a Nation* made it seem a pigmy in 1915.

The Birth of a Nation propelled the film into a new artistic level. A high point in the American movie tradition, it brought to maturity the editing principle begun with Melies and furthered by Porter. So rich and profound in organization was this picture that for years thereafter it directly and indirectly influenced film makers everywhere and much of the subsequent filmic progress owes its inspiration to this master achievement.

The commotion produced by *The Birth of a Nation* awakened

Griffith to the effectiveness of pictures that dealt with social con-
troversies, and it influenced him to increase the dimensions of his
next film. Before the excitement attending *The Birth of a Nation*
had completely subsided, he was at work on *The Mother and the
Law*. The story for this picture was based upon the Stielow case,
then making headlines in newspapers, and upon a federal industrial
commission's report of the killing of nineteen employees by a chemical manufacturer's "Goths" (as Griffith termed the militia) during
a strike for higher wages. Griffith enlarged the original idea and
expanded his theme so that it became more than a simple exposé:
it was an elaborate condemnation of hypocrisy and cruelty resulting from prejudice—a theme that was ironic in view of his own
bigotry in *The Birth of a Nation*. To suit the magnitude of his
new undertaking, the title was finally changed to *Intolerance—A
Drama of Comparisons*. Said Griffith, "If I approach success in
what I am trying to do in my coming picture, I expect a persecution even greater than that which met *The Birth of a Nation*." [11]

Presumably in answer to the attacks upon *The Birth of a Nation*,
his pamphlet, *The Rise and Fall of Free Speech in America*, had
been published to prepare the public for the theme of this picture.
The pages of this booklet were shrewdly sprinkled with such
phrases as "Intolerance is the root of all censorship," "Intolerance
martyred Joan of Arc," "Intolerance smashed the first printing
press," "Intolerance invented Salem witchcraft." The recurrent emphasis on intolerance appears too deliberate to have been anything
but a calculated advance blast for the forthcoming picture.

In making *Intolerance* Griffith was faced with financial problems
even greater than those encountered in the making of *The Birth
of a Nation*. Although he had command of plenty of money after
the triumph of that film, his expenditures on this new enterprise
reached a fantastic high. The payroll alone amounted to as much
as $12,000 a day. Settings for Babylonian walls 300 feet high and
for elaborate streets in Paris, Judea, and New York (miniatures and
processing were still unknown), not to mention the expense of
costumes, cost thousands more. The grandiose banquet scene for
Belshazzar's feast is said to have cost $250,000. The photography for

[11] *Photoplay*, December 1916.

the picture consumed 300,000 feet of negative—a stupendous quantity even for today's epic productions. When Griffith's backers became alarmed and refused to put up any more money, Griffith bought them out, going heavily into debt to do so. When the costs were finally totaled, the figure was reported to be $1,900,000. *Intolerance* was by far the costliest production up to that time and for many years after.

The complete picture was thirteen reels long and contained three other stories in addition to the original one of *The Mother and the Law*: the fall of Babylon, the Christ legend of Judea, and the massacre of the Huguenots on St. Bartholomew's Eve. The whole was, as Griffith himself stated,[12] "a protest against despotism and injustice in every form." To tie the four stories together Griffith used a symbol: the recurring image of a mother rocking a cradle, suggested by Walt Whitman's lines ". . . endlessly rocks the cradle, Uniter of Here and Hereafter."

The scope of the theme required a most exacting and uncommon craftsmanship. A unique structural form, stemming from Porter's *The Kleptomaniac* and from Griffith's own *Judith of Bethulia*, but magnified a hundredfold, was planned. Declared Griffith: [13]

[the] stories will begin like four currents looked at from a hilltop. At first the four currents will flow apart, slowly and quietly. But as they flow, they grow nearer and nearer together, and faster and faster, until in the end, in the last act, they mingle in one mighty river of expressed emotion.

The picture opens with a statement of the theme, then the presentation of the symbol of the Mother, "Today as yesterday, endlessly rocking, ever bringing the same human passions, the same joys and sorrows." [14] Then a book—referred to when each of the other stories is introduced—opens and "our first story . . . out of the cradle of the present" begins by sarcastically depicting reformers and the evils of prohibition. Then the story switches to Babylon and its scheming priests. Next is the sequence in Palestine, in which the motivation

---

[12] In Program given out at Revival Showing, November 10, 1933, at 55th St. Playhouse.
[13] Robert Edgar Long's *David Wark Griffith*. [14] A main title in the film.

of the Crucifixion begins. Finally the spectator is taken to Paris to witness the plotting of the St. Bartholomew's Day massacre. These parts, separated in time and space, are linked through parallel and contrast editing; structural cohesion gives them a united effect. Their interplay brings out the emotional values in each and, as they progress toward a common climax, they force the audience to appreciate Griffith's message: "Each story shows how hatred and intolerance, through the ages, have battled against love and charity." [15]

The modern story was the most carefully thought out and dramatically motivated sequence of the four. It has the most "bite" and despite minor absurdities is as telling today in its ironic denunciation of reformers and profiteers, as it was then. A group of "Uplifters" obtain the financial support of Jenkins, an industrial magnate, through his sister, an embittered old maid. In order to gain more money to donate to this "false charity," he cuts the wages of his mill workers and a strike follows. The militia is called out and the strikers are ruthlessly mowed down. When strikebreakers are employed, many of the destitute townspeople are forced to leave. Among these are the Dear One and her father, the Boy, whose father was killed in the strike, and the Friendless One. All four arrive at the neighboring big city.

Here, unable to get work, the Friendless One is enticed by a "Musketeer of the Slums"; the Boy robs a drunkard and becomes a member of the Musketeer's gang; Dear One's father dies. The Boy and Dear One marry but the Musketeer "frames" the young husband who has decided to "go straight," and he is arrested and sent to prison. During his absence, Dear One has a baby but it is taken from her by the "Uplifters." On the pretext that he will get back the child, the Musketeer forces his way into Dear One's room not knowing that the Friendless One, now his mistress, is jealously spying. Just as he attacks Dear One, the Boy, who has been freed from jail, arrives. During the ensuing struggle, the jealous girl perches herself on a ledge outside the window and when the Boy is about to be overcome, she shoots the Musketeer, throws the gun

[15] From the main title prefacing the film.

into the room and escapes. In the confusion, the Boy picks up the gun and is found with it in his hands when the police arrive. Arrested for murder, he is tried and sentenced to be hanged. Dear One seeks a pardon from the Governor but is unsuccessful. At the final moment, however, the murderess confesses. There is a last-minute chase, first to get the pardon from the Governor before he leaves on a trip; then to reach the prison in time to stop the execution. The Pardon is presented as the noose is to be cut. The Boy is saved; the family reunited.

The second story depicted the fall of Babylon through the treachery of the High Priest of Bel. The tale of the Mountain-Girl's love for Belshazzar and her futile attempts to save Babylon from Cyrus and the Persians, made this the next most dramatically defined sequence. In opulence it has rarely been equaled, the scenes of the Feast of Belshazzar and the attack and counterattack on Babylon, particularly, reaching heights of unprecedented grandeur.

The third and fourth sequences or "rings," as they were then sometimes called—Christ in ancient Jerusalem and the massacre of the Huguenots in France on St. Bartholomew's Eve—were the least developed in plot.

The four stories culminate in a plea for tolerance: symbolic double exposures of angels, prison walls dissolving into open fields, children playing and kissing each other, and as a finale, after a vast multiple exposure, a close shot of the recurrent symbolic image, the Mother rocking the Cradle of Humanity.

Profound though its theme is, the commanding feature of *Intolerance* is its internal organization. Years ahead of its time (it was to become a major influence on the Soviet school of directors), *Intolerance* surpassed even *The Birth of a Nation*. The comparatively simple editing pattern of the latter film, based on one single event and story related in time and space, was in *Intolerance* expanded into a complex form with four movements, all progressing simultaneously. The film cuts freely from period to period as the theme of intolerance in each is developed. Episode is paralleled with episode. With bold, staccato cutting, Griffith interweaves the motifs of Christ struggling toward Calvary, the Babylonian mountain girl speeding to warn Belshazzar that his priests have betrayed him, the massacre on St. Bartholomew's Day by the French mercenaries, and Dear One rushing frantically to save her husband at the gallows.

These passages are vividly motivated by every means Griffith had at his disposal. A shot is cut before the completion of its action; the moving camera parallels and reinforces a movement; iris and masks are used to emphasize a significant detail or eloquently effect a transition; large detail close-ups and extreme long shots produce effects of intensity and vastness. All these camera devices are brought into play to create a rich and varied film which flows in unbroken and mounting suspense until the end. Here, as in *The Birth of a Nation*, an underlying movement creates a rhythmic beat, which increases in frequency as the four climaxes approach. There is not a moment, not a shot, that is not controlled, timed, and selected for what it means and adds to the whole.

In the climactic sequences, particularly, is Griffith's artistry supreme. Here all the opulent details of the lavish scenes are subjected to an unceasing movement, action follows action, and none is ever allowed to terminate as the rhythm sweeps along. Christ is seen toiling up Mount Calvary; the Babylonian mountain girl is racing to warn her king of the onrushing enemy; the Huguenot is fighting his way through the streets to rescue his sweetheart from the mercenaries; the wife is speeding in an automobile to the prison, with a pardon for her husband who is about to be hung.

Images whirl across the screen, startling the spectator with their pace and holding him spellbound by their profusion, rhythm, suspense. They are a visual symphony, swelling steadily until the final moment when all the movements are brought together in a grand finale. As Iris Barry wrote [16] of these passages, "History itself seems to pour like a cataract across the screen."

Individual episodes within each movement also have striking beauty of structure. At one point in the modern story for example, the reformers, whom Griffith satirically called Vestal Virgins of Reform, are shown going to workers' homes, led by a rich industrialist's wife who gives the workers charity and moral guidance,

[16] Museum of Modern Art Film Library Program Notes (III).

keeping them from drinking, gambling, and prostitution. Following this are scenes showing factory workers being shot down by militia called out by the industrialist.

This is one of the many striking episodes, and recorded shot by shot from the film by Theodore Huff, is given below in its complete form. It is a vivid instance of Griffith's cutting. By an overlapping of movement from one shot onto the next, a double edge is given to the images and strong tension is created. Each shot, moreover, is cut to the minimum; it gives only the essential point. Facts build upon one another in the audience's mind until, in the very last shot, all the facts are resolved and summarized through the introduction of another type of shot, longer than any of its predecessors and significantly different in character. Not only the cutting and treatment of the sequences, but the deliberate documentary quality of the shots themselves, are remarkable. In this episode the origins of the remarkable Soviet technique are clearly evident.

Shot No.	Title		Footage	
	Title	"Resuming our story of today— Dividends of the Jenkins mills failing to meet the increasing demands of Miss Jenkins' charities, she complains to her brother, which helps decide him to action."	17	feet
198	Long Shot	Large, bare office. Jenkins and assistant at desk. Sister hurries in from left—sits at desk—hands paper to brother.	6	feet
199	¾ Shot	Assistant getting number—hands telephone to Jenkins.	3	feet
200	¾ Shot	Factory manager answering phone.	2 4	feet, frames
201	(As 199)	Jenkins phoning to manager.	5	feet
	Title	"Order a ten-per cent cut in all wages."	2 9	feet, frames

Shot No.			Footage	
202	(As 200)	Manager hangs up telephone—surprised—nervously wipes forehead and mouth. Iris out.	5	feet
203	*Long Shot*	Iris-in of men at gate of factory.	3	feet
204	*Medium Shot*	Iris-in of gate—men posting sign ordering the wage cut.	3	feet
205	*Long Shot* (As 203)	Gate of factory—crowds agitating.	2½	feet
	Title	"A great strike follows."	2 3	feet, frames
206	*Long Shot*	Another part of the factory. Mob of workers agitating. The Boy in foreground. Man addresses crowd.	4	feet
	Title	"They squeeze the money out of us and use it to advertise themselves by reforming us."	9	feet
207	*¾ Shot*	The Boy, angry—others, also. Argues.	3½	feet
208	(As 206)	The mob.	3½	feet
209	*Long Shot*	A mound. Workers' families grouped on hill watching the strike.	6½	feet
210	*Long Shot*	A row of small houses—families standing by gates and on sidewalk, listening.	3	feet
	Title	"Hungry ones that wait to take their places."	3	feet
211	*Medium Shot*	Group of men at gate, waiting.	5	feet
212	*Long Shot*	Road by factory. Militia come forward.	3	feet
213	*Long Shot*	Strikers fleeing.	5½	feet
214		The militia come forward—set up a line across the road.	6	feet

Shot No.			Footage	
215	*Medium Shot*	The Girl's yard. She comes forward, stoops to pick up kindling wood.	4	feet
216	*Long Shot*	Militia barricade in street.	3	feet
217	*Medium Shot*	Cannon—men lying down with rifles.	2 5	feet, frames
218	*Semi-Close-up*	Rows of men and rifles—rifles are cocked.	4	feet
219	*Medium Long Shot*	Strikers shaking fists.	3	feet
220	*Extreme Long Shot*	From above—the lines of soldiers at the factory.	1 12	foot, frames
221	*Long Shot*	People on the hill—they shake their fists.	5	feet
222	*Medium Long Shot*	Cannon—they start firing.	5	feet
223	*Long Shot*	Strikers—they run back, down the hill.	2 11	feet, frames
224	*Long Shot*	Families on the hill—some run.	3	feet
225	*Long Shot*	Row of houses—people excited.	2	feet
226	*¾ Shot*	The Girl—frightened (hand to mouth)—drops wood—runs back toward house but comes forward again.	9	feet
227	*Medium Long Shot*	Cannon firing.	2 11	feet, frames
228	*Medium Long Shot*	Strikers—man in foreground bares chest, daring soldiers to shoot him.	1 12	foot, frames
229	*Long Shot*	Inside factory fence: 4 strikers beyond—factory guards in foreground.	1 12	foot, frames
230	*Medium Shot*	Manager and assistant agitated—manager runs forward.	2½	feet

Shot No.			Footage	
231	*Medium Shot*	Factory door—manager runs in.	2 2	feet, frames
232	*¾ Shot*	Office—manager runs forward to telephone. Calls Jenkins.	1 12	foot, frames
233	*Medium Shot*	Bars of fence—strikers behind, shaking fists and sticks.	1 10	foot, frames
234	*Long Shot*	Jenkins' office—he answers phone.	2 3	feet, frames
235	(As 232)	Manager at telephone, excited.	1 13	foot, frames
236	*Medium Shot*	Jenkins at telephone, answering calmly.	1	foot
237	*Another Angle*	Jenkins.	14	frames
238	(As 235)	Manager hangs up receiver—hesitates.	1 15	foot, frames
239	*¾ Shot*	Jenkins sitting at desk—staring ahead—indomitable.	2 6	feet, frames
240	(As 238)	Manager rushes back to door in rear	1 12	foot, frames
241	(As 231)	—runs out door.	1 13	foot, frames
242	*Long Shot*	Factory guards—manager comes with order—group starts back toward fence.	4	feet
243	*Medium Shot*	Strikers by fence—shake fists—a few have revolvers.	1 12	foot, frames
244	(As 242)	Factory guards firing.	13	frames
245	*Long Shot*	People on hill.	5	feet
246	(As 244)	Guards firing.	9	frames
247	(As 243)	Strikers shake fists and fire.	1½	feet
248	*Medium Long Shot*	Guards firing.	1 14	foot, frames

Shot No.			Footage	
249	¾ *Shot*	The Boy helping wounded father —others fleeing in background.	4	feet
250	(As 233)	Men sticking fists through pales of fence.	1 9	foot, frames
251	(As 249)	Others fleeing and falling. Smoke.	3½	feet
252	*Long Shot*	Group on hill—people run frantically.	4	feet
253	(As 225)	Rows of houses—people excited.	2½	feet
254	(As 226)	The Girl—frightened—puts hand over her mouth fearfully.	3	feet
255	*Extreme Long Shot*	Camera pans slowly from strikers shooting to the factory crowd firing. On the fence in background the sign, in large letters, "The same today as yesterday."	13	feet

As in its cutting, so in its details *Intolerance* had impressive originality. Huge close-ups of faces, hands, objects, are used imaginatively and eloquently to comment upon, interpret, and deepen the import of the scene, so that dependence upon pantomime is minimized. A celebrated instance is the huge close-up of the clasped hands of Mae Marsh, suggesting her anguish during the trial of her husband. Camera angles are used to intensify the psychological impact: the extreme long shot of the industrialist alone in his office (lord of his domain) characterized him better than any action, incident, or subtitle. The handling of crowds as organized units in movement, as in the firing of the militia or in the notable Babylonian sequences, heightened the dramatic intensity of such scenes. The deliberate use of artificial sky above the onrushing Persian chariots gave the panorama great depth and massiveness, heightening the sense of impending doom as no natural sky could have done, and incidentally introducing to film technique the "process shot."

The singling out of significant action on one part of the screen by lights, irises, or masks—examples of which appeared in almost every sequence—indicated Griffith's sensitive regard for the apt image. With admirable ease, he cuts daringly into the square shape of the screen and blocks out whole sections, sometimes leaving them blocked out for the duration of the scene, sometimes opening the frame to its size. But whether he uses it closed in or opened out, he rarely uses the same shape twice in succession, but contrasts them so that the eye of the spectator is kept moving. For example, if the screen opens in a semi-circle from the lower right-hand corner to the upper-left, as in the opening mass scene of Babylon, the next time, the screen opens in a semi-circle from the upper left-hand corner, then opens out and down diagonally to the lower right.

This dramatic "framing" of the image throughout the film is done with a variety and skill that has rarely been equaled. The screen is sliced down the center revealing only the middle (the great wall of Babylon), then opens out. The screen is cut across diagonally, sometimes from upper left to lower right, sometimes from upper right to lower left. Details are thus brought to our attention and yet kept part of the larger scene itself in a more precise way than the use of close-up insertions could afford. This movement and variety of screen shapes keep the image ever-fresh and vital and heighten the momentum of the whole.

If the "framing" of the screen is remarkable, no less so is the fluid and active participation of the camera. Its physical capacities for movement and dramatic angle—generally conceded to be the original contributions of the post-war German craftsmen—must have strained to the taxing point whatever was known then of camera grace and flexibility. Yet there is never a sense of striving for sheer mechanical wonder, but always a subordination of such capabilities to the subject and the point to be made. The unceasing use of the camera to drain everything that is significant out of the scene, accounts in no small measure for the overwhelming sense of lavishness and opulence that is so impressive to all. For example, we are shown the court of France, 1572, first from an extreme long-shot. The camera is stationary for a few moments as we take in the elaborate scene; then the camera begins slowly to "truck" into the court, moving in on King Charles receiving on his throne; then the camera "pans" to the right around the crowded room to pause on

the Prince-Heir, who, incidentally, is portrayed as a decadent fop
with a realism worthy of von Stroheim. Later in the film, in the
marriage market of ancient Jerusalem, the camera "pans" to the
right, showing the painted women framed in a diagonal strip across
the screen from lower left to upper right. Again, in the Temple of
Sacred Fire in Babylon, the camera plays caressingly over the white
nudeness of erotic and sensual women clothed in flimsy chiffons,
beflowered and bejeweled, by "panning" from right to left, then
from left to right; then the screen frame closes in, then moves out,
and in again with marvelous facility.

More spectacular than any of these devices, however, was the
remarkable "trucking" camera shot which traveled, without a pause
or a cut, hundreds of feet from an extreme distant view of the
entire grandeur of ancient Babylon to a huge close-up of the scene
itself. This shot, embracing immense sets, thousands of people and
animals, was unprecedented and is still an amazing piece of camera
bravura.

The film also utilized dramatically tinted film stock. Then a
comparatively common device, it was seldom used on as large a
scale or with as great variety. Night exteriors are tinted blue; sunny
exteriors or lighted rooms are in various tones of yellow; blackness
drapes the figures in the Temple of Sacred Fire; the Babylon battle
at night is highlighted by red flares. Throughout the tints attempt
to approximate reality; they show Griffith's awareness of the emotional values to be gained from the use of color.

With all its profound excellence, *Intolerance* nevertheless had
many unfortunate weaknesses that marred its complete realization.
The most obvious were Griffith's inherent sentimentality and his
tendency to overdramatize. These weaknesses had appeared in *The
Birth of a Nation* but, in view of that picture's subject and story,
were less glaring. In *Intolerance* the maudlin names "little Dear One,"
"Brown Eyes," "Princess Beloved," all hangovers from the movies'
past, are laughable. The extravagant posturing and the black-and-
white characterizations are also hangovers from the pre-war period. The massacre of the Huguenots and the Babylonian episode
are full of bloodshed and violence, which reaches a ludicrous
high when the soldier of Belshazzar cuts off the head of his enemy

so that the audience can see it topple off (a scene that had appeared in *Judith of Bethulia* and the older *Mary, Queen of Scots,* and was apparently acceptable in its day). Griffith's overindulgence in pious, highly moral, and frequently saccharine explanatory titles is another defect.

The greatest fault of *Intolerance* was what Julian Johnson, reviewing the film for *Photoplay*,[17] was the first to comment upon: "The fatal error of *Intolerance* was that in the great Babylonian scenes you didn't care which side won. It was just a great show." The overemphasis upon the spectacle outweighed the message. The formal concept ran away with the thematic; the execution was brilliant, but the point was forgotten. This discrepancy between the admirable structure and the uncertainty of the message is the reason why many people regard *The Birth of a Nation* as the greater of the two films. In that film one is forced, by the way the case is presented, to side with the South; in *Intolerance* the spectator is emotionally aroused but not as a partisan.

First shown publicly September 5, 1916, the film evoked mixed criticism. Many of the critics of the day were bewildered by the cutting style, could not follow the story from period to period, and were confused by the "interminable battle scenes" and the recurring "mother rocking her baby." They found the idea obtuse and the effects exhausting. Like other publications *Variety*,[18] giving it far less attention than that accorded *The Birth of a Nation*, called it "a departure from all previous forms of legitimate or film construction . . . so diffuse in the sequence of its incidents that the development is at times difficult to follow." Heywood Broun[19] declared that the bathing beauty spectacle *Daughter of the Gods*, starring Annette Kellerman, "has the enormous advantage over *Intolerance* that it tells a story." Years later Pudovkin, in his book *Film Technique*,[20] praised Griffith's structural innovations in *Intolerance* but thought the film "so ponderous that the tiredness it created largely effaced its effect."

At the time of the picture's release something like a war spirit was growing in the nation, and people could not reconcile the

[17] December 1916.   [19] *The New York Tribune*, October 20, 1916.
[18] September 8, 1916.   [20] P. 8.

pacific intentions of *Intolerance*—intentions which they understood mainly through its titles—with the current militarism. As the country moved closer to active participation in the war, opposition to the film grew more vigorous. Censured and then barred in many cities, the picture suffered a sad and ignoble fate. Although it stands as a milestone in the progress of the American film, for Griffith it proved to be a financial disaster of crippling proportions. Through its failure he lost his independence and, no doubt, much of his great zeal.

Modern criticism of *Intolerance* has been increasingly favorable. The film has been called "a timeless masterpiece" [21] (Richard Watts, Jr.): "the end and justification of that whole school of American cinematography" [22] (Iris Barry): "an opulence of production that has never been equaled" [23] (Frank S. Nugent). It has thus reclaimed its rightful position as a peak in American movie making, the consummation of everything that preceded it and the beginning of profound new developments in the motion picture art. Its influence has traveled around the world, touching directors in Germany, France, and Soviet Russia in particular. A testament to Griffith's maturity, it marked the end of his second and most brilliant period and the turning point in his career. Although continuing actively in movie making in the next years, and maintaining his high reputation, he was never again to equal *Intolerance*, or its predecessor, *The Birth of a Nation*.

[21] Quoted in Program given out at Revival Showing, November 1933, at 55th St. Playhouse.
[22] Museum of Modern Art Film Library Program Notes (III).
[23] *The New York Times*, March 8, 1936.

XII

TOWARD STYLE

WE have already observed how the war between the patents trust and the independent producers stimulated movie makers to try for quality in their work. A number of new influences during the war period still further advanced the artistic progress of the cinema. The establishment of features, imported foreign spectacles, Griffith's discoveries, a broader and more cultivated audience, the growing affiliation between Hollywood and Broadway talent, the giving of screen credits to individuals—all contributed to improvements in movie craftsmanship, refinements in mechanics, and higher standards of production. The war period is marked by a bolder and surer grasp of the medium, the emergence of gifted new directors with personal styles, and several significant motion pictures, the leaders among which were Griffith's. At no time since has Hollywood been so aroused by high ambitions, keen personal rivalry, and lofty aspirations.

The effort toward artistic quality in motion pictures was further quickened by the critical comments of a fan magazine of the day, *Photoplay*. Under the editorship of James R. Quirk from 1915 on, it encouraged and praised genuine artistry in films. A typical editorial [1] remarked,

> Will you think of your art as a business or of your business as an art? Will you say, "Make this picture because it will sell?" or "Make this picture because it deserves to sell?"

[1] February 1918.

Continual prodding of this sort kept the question of quality uppermost in the minds of producers throughout the war years.

The feature form particularly encouraged great strides in film making. Production became elaborate; direction, photography, screen writing, acting, and settings steadily improved as increased budgets, enlarged staffs, and longer production periods became the rule. The addition to the staffs of new professional workers—the scenario editor, the art or "technical" director, the cutter, the musical scorer—resulted in refinements in story continuity, make-up, clothes, interior decoration, and presentation. Pictures lost their old poverty-stricken air; they became groomed, even ostentatious. By 1918 they had not only acquired all the main fundamentals but that veneer which was to be cultivated in later years.

Direction, in particular, showed a marked improvement during the war period. The technical discoveries of Griffith were quickly seized upon by other directors; such innovations as the close-up, full shot, fade, iris, cutting for tempo, and suspense became more common. Movies were now rendered more and more in the film idiom and less and less like a stage play, the emphasis now being on delineation of character through detail shots and the selection of incidents. The continuity of the story was developed more logically, more dramatically, and with more unity. Significant of the general betterment of technique is the description (taken at random) of *The Ghost House:* [2]

You see a small table topple over. In a flash you see the awakened, startled, superstitious burglar. In another the terrified though less superstitious women. In five seconds you understand what a writer would need many hundreds of words to tell. So throughout the picture.

Much of their early awkwardness and self-consciousness having been overcome, directors were now self-assured and ambitious for national renown. With his enlarged responsibilities, the director, as the guiding hand, became the most important single figure in the making of a movie, dictating every phase of production. His position was distinguished, and his fame often traveled as far as that of his star player. From a job paying $25 to $50 a week directing

[2] Kitty Kelly's description in *Photoplay*, December 1917.

had advanced to the status of a profession paying $100 and more. No longer left to improvising as he went along or directing "on the cuff," the director worked with the story editor on the story, helped to plan its continuity, instructed his cameramen, rehearsed his players with a script in one hand and a megaphone in the other, and finally supervised the editing of the completed film. The finished production therefore was thoroughly colored by his personality.

Of the many new directors who emerged at this time three stood out beyond the others. They achieved distinct personal styles and supplemented the technical contributions of Griffith by devices of their own. Two centered their efforts on dramatic themes: Thomas Ince brought discipline and organization to story telling, and Maurice Tourneur contributed a pictorial imagination. The third director, Mack Sennett, specializing in comedy, introduced a unique slapstick style.

Of the three, Thomas Ince enjoyed the highest reputation. Coming to movies in 1910, he had risen so rapidly in the industry that by 1916 he headed the finest and most elaborate studio in Culver City—a studio costing half a million dollars. He was the developer of the producer-director combination concept, and he himself was the finest example of it. He developed the unit system of production initiated by Blackton, in which the director supervised a number of pictures simultaneously. First carefully planning the story and detailing every phase of its action in scenario form, Ince would then hand the manuscript to a director under him, with the stamped order, "Produce this exactly as written!" When the shooting was finished, Ince himself would edit the film. He was able to delegate the task of direction because of his aptitude in visualizing the completed film beforehand. This ability had been educated by his thorough experience in every phase of movie making. In his unpublished manuscript on the history of movies, he relates how in his earliest days at IMP he wrote, acted, and directed one film a week, cutting it at home in his kitchen with an improvised cutter.

Hundreds of movies were therefore credited to Ince. The most notable dramas were *The Wrath of the Gods, The Italian, Civiliza-*

Lila Lee, Gloria Swanson, and Thomas Meighan
in *Male and Female* (1919), the picture that set
off the Hollywood revolution in sex and sensation, introduced a new moral code for the screen,
and launched Cecil B. DeMille, its director, as the
pace setter of the early post-war period.

Mary Pickford in *Pollyanna* (1920). The good-
little, bad-little, rich-little girl with the curls
symbolized the ideal of American girlhood
during the period of the film's innocence.

tion, Vive la France!, *Behind the Door*, *The Coward*, *The Iron Strain*, *The Battle of Gettysburg*, *Extravagance*. His most famous comedy was *23½ Hours Leave*, and his outstanding William S. Hart Westerns included *The Two-Gun Man* and *Hell's Hinges*. All these films had the Ince touch—directness, a clean-cut style, and tight dramatic structure, although many were actually directed by other men.

To Ince the most important criterion of a film was its story, although it is said that he himself never read a book through in his life and, when he had to meet an author, asked his associates to tip him off so that he could discuss the author's works with him. Called the "greatest film editor the business has ever produced," "the doctor of the sick film," he ruthlessly cut out anything that did not contribute to the progress of the film story. He is said to have spent most of his time in his specially decorated projection room cutting films, with the consequence that all his productions were models of direct story telling. His severest criticism was "It wanders." Ince's stress on story and straightforward movement accounted largely for his films' great popularity, and it created a bold style in movie making.

Ince's narrative flair was enhanced by his feeling for human relationships, space, and nature. The themes he chose most frequently were, as a contemporary expressed it, "soul-fights." Many of his films did not conform to the happy-ending convention but were tragedies. Sweeping landscapes, imposing mountain ranges, desert wastes—all these he brought into play to give his films color, to heighten dramatic moods. A torrential rain fell on a desperate hand-to-hand fight; the prairie wind beat back a tired traveler; the midday sun tortured a thirsty desert prospector. Ince was proud of his technical ability in presenting spectacular catastrophes of nature; he is credited, in fact, as the first director ever to put an earthquake and a volcano eruption into pictures.

Inscrutable and dynamic, Ince was called the "enigma of picture drama." Essentially a business man, he conducted himself and his film making in businesslike fashion: his "lot" was noted for its remarkable discipline; everything was systematized; everyone knew what he was to do. Ince himself appeared on the set in workmanlike clothes—a nondescript sweater and a cap—and with a stumpy cigar in his mouth. His attitude and method, new to the industry, were far removed from the happy-go-lucky spirit that prevailed generally.

According to Thomas Ince, "Making a photoplay is something like baking a cake . . . you have to have certain ingredients and know how to blend them." It is this conception of planning and construction that makes Ince a significant figure in the history of American films. Essentially an organizer, he brought forethought and discipline to haphazard production methods. Planning in advance meant better unity of structure, less chance of uneven quality, and economy of expression.

The detailed scenario introduced by Ince was later utilized by all studios because of the economy and efficiency it made possible. In common use today, it is known as the shooting script or continuity. Ince's custom of handing completed scripts to directors with the order to "shoot as is" also was taken over by others; today it is the distinguishing trait of the producer Darryl Zanuck. Although Ince's unit system worked remarkably well in his own enterprises and was soon applied by the industry as a whole, it was not uniformly successful. For some directors it turned out to be practicable, as in the case of Mack Sennett; for others, notably Griffith, it proved unmanageable. On the whole, however, successful or unsuccessful, it gave producers and directors alike valuable ideas for the control of technique and production.

At the peak of his profession when the war ended, Ince suddenly and inexplicably disappeared from the forefront of the movie world when his company, Triangle, collapsed. In 1924 he died under mysterious circumstances.

Of entirely different temperament and talents was Maurice Tourneur, a bold and imaginative director who brought to the screen a primarily pictorial style. Tourneur's films were distinguished for their decorative quality, emphasis on atmosphere, and selection of exotic characters. Few directors had his ability or perception in such matters, and his stress on composition, lighting, costuming, and personality types educated other directors to a watchfulness and greater care with such factors in their own efforts. Tourneur was rewarded, like Griffith, with the title "David Belasco of the Screen." This was a meaningless commendation because it had become commonplace, but it does suggest the high regard which Tourneur earned in the industry.

A former stage director and producer for the French Eclair Company in Paris, Tourneur was one of the first foreign directors to come to America. Oddly enough, his first assignments were those dealing with American life: *The Man of the Hour*, *The Wishing Ring*, *Alias Jimmy Valentine*, *The Pit*. It was not until he was given a story that was related to his background and stimulated his pictorial mind that he became widely known. *Trilby*, the adaptation of the story of Bohemian Paris that Tourneur knew so well, made his name respected throughout the American screen world in 1916. He was included in *Who's Who in Motion Pictures* for that year, his work being described as "characterized by refinement and strength. . . . Photographic effects, settings, lightings, and pictorial compositions of his offerings are always artistic in the extreme."

After *Trilby*, Tourneur continued to handle various types of material. But whether he was making *The Closed Road*, *The Rise of Jenny Cushing*, or *A Doll's House* (all serious drama) or *The Hand of Peril* or *Sporting Life* (trivialities) Tourneur endowed his work with distinction and imagination. In *The Hand of Peril*, a typical melodrama of a United States Secret Service operative, for example, he ingeniously divided the screen so that nine rooms were shown at once with action occurring in each room simultaneously. After seeing *Sporting Life*, Julian Johnson [3] noted his ability to "So glorify, embroider and adorn a tawdry primitive story [that] it becomes believable. . . . The dim depths of real night in the exteriors have never been equaled. . . . Real London fog . . . breathless suspense."

As Tourneur progressed, his pictorial feeling and ability to evoke mood and atmosphere led him to devote his talents more and more to the exotic and fantastic. With such material he excelled, directing the top-ranking stars of his day; and instead of being overshadowed

[3] *Photoplay*, December 1918.

by their big names, he blazed the brighter. Elsie Ferguson's first starring film, *Barbary Sheep*, laid in the Sahara Desert, won Tourneur the label of "genius." Wrote Dorothy Nutting,[4] "Here is poetry, here mystery, here almost hypnotic handling of light and shade . . . achieved haunting desert atmosphere, the lure of Saharan mystic romance to a bewitching degree."

Of *Poor Little Rich Girl*, starring Mary Pickford, one critic said, "The camera, not Mary Pickford, should have been the star." *Exile*, which starred Olga Petrova, prompted the remark, "Tourneur is the star . . . picturesque grouping and mass movement." For *Prunella* and *The Bluebird*, starring Marguerite Clark, Tourneur was hailed as "blazing a new trail in film art."

These last two films are particularly notable. Their subject matter is delicate and philosophic, lacking the conventional situations, and their execution was novel for the screen. Conceived fancifully, they were a fresh and daring escape from the staid realism of the day. Their settings were silhouetted against black drops; costumes were highly decorative; the staging was theatricalized; the whole atmosphere was deliberately artificial. Important though they were as new approaches to film art, however, they had little immediate influence on other American directors.

Tourneur, acknowledged in 1918 as an outstanding pictorialist of the screen, made his contribution to the "era of spectacles" with *Woman*. Like other films of the period, *Woman* revealed the strong influence of Griffith's *Intolerance*. The story was based on a similar structural pattern and was executed with the same degree of grandeur, the vamp pictures being climaxed by the highlighting of four historical episodes of woman's wickedness. As with all Tourneur's efforts, the distinction of *Woman* was its unusual lighting, its photography and composition, its atmosphere and moods—qualities which Rex Ingram and Josef von Sternberg, in particular, were later to exploit further.

After the World War the same fate that had overtaken Ince overtook Tourneur: he quickly disappeared from the forefront of filmdom. In 1924 *The Blue Book of the Screen* named him as "one of the men who have brought the director into the spotlight of public

4 *Photoplay*, July 1918.

esteem." He achieved a temporary comeback in the next year (1925) with two distinguished films, both in exotic locales—*Never the Twain Shall Meet* and *Aloma of the South Seas*. When sound came, his career in America was ended and he returned to France.

Although Tourneur was an impressive pictorialist and director of talent in his day, his films did not stand the wear of time. Griffith's films, dated in sentiment, had a solid cinematic structure that gave them permanent importance and still inspires respect. Their content, moreover, was taken from life; it dealt with real problems. Tourneur's scenes of visual beauty, on the other hand, while often compensating for structural weakness, failed to cover the vast stretches of mere grandiosity and emptiness in his work. Vivid in light, shadow, composition, his films were devoid both of inner integrity and significant content. When his imagery was not overwrought, however, Tourneur did bring to the camera a splendor that affected later pictorial techniques. His importance in the history of American films, like the importance of some other pioneers, lies not so much in the work he left but in his suggestiveness to the industry. Much of the atmosphere, design, and pictorial beauty of pictures today are due indirectly to Tourneur's influence.

Ince and Tourneur, both film dramatists, dealt exclusively with the feature film; Mack Sennett specialized in the production of comedies rarely more than one or two reels long. He was the first of America's comedy directors to develop a distinct film style: slapstick. With its burlesque satire, with its action and fantasy achieved through the use of camera trickery, his method was the fruition of some fifteen years of experiment with the humorous incident and the chase situation. For a decade this type of comedy had been developing in form and broadening in content. Sennett consolidated its traits, added new ones, and gave it a unique and inimitable flavor of his own. He was the first to perceive that if a chase is funny, a riot is funnier; if a pretty girl is pleasant, a dozen pretty girls are delightful; if a cop is comic, a gross of cops are hilarious; if an action—such as a fight or a man running—when photographed at normal speed is interesting, the same action photographed at sub-normal speed or high speed (creating the effect of extra-fast motion or slow motion) is exciting. But more than this, Sennett had a feeling for pace and unity in scene progression—even though the events were in themselves mad and were improvised as the action developed—which distinguished his films from all other comedies of the day.

Years of work with Griffith as an actor at Biograph gave Sennett the conviction that, above all, movies must move, and it was this attitude applied to his own pictures that created a unique comedy style. In full command of his own studio in 1912, he made his pet subject, the vaudeville cop, a national figure. With his patrol wagons flying down the street, custard pies encountering various faces, never-ending chases, and bathing beauties swirling about the Keystone cop, Sennett created a world of absurdity which in two years made him the top comedy director. In 1916 his success and fame had become so pronounced that he became the third producer of the Triangle Corporation, sharing honors with Griffith and Ince.

Sennett's pictures were all alike, being either parodies or burlesques, with little plot and a great deal of sauciness. Mainly they "kidded" other movies. This was true of his *The Sheriff Out West, Bright Lights, A Small Town Idol, The Grand Army of the Republic*, and his detective series. Or they ridiculed noble virtues and lofty sentiments: *Bright Eyes, Mabel in the Park, Fatty and Mabel Adrift, The Butcher Boy, Fatty Makes the Conquest, A Versatile Villain*, and hundreds of other comedies. In all these films Sennett used the old props: coincidence, treachery, disguise, chivalry, superheroism, sentiment, gags—the entire baggage of the burlesque stage.

For gags for their own sake Sennett had little regard. For him the joke had to grow out of the incident. In an interview with Harry C. Carr,[5] Sennett explained his method of work:

Having found your hub idea, you build out the spokes; those are the natural developments that your imagination will suggest. Then introduce your complications that make up the funny wheel. . . . We have tried famous humorists and I can say with feeling that their stuff is about the worst we get. . . . What we want is a real idea. . . . We will add the action.

[5] *Photoplay*, May 1915.

Nevertheless many of Sennett's gags were the old "sure-fire stuff"; his guilelessness and extravagance lifted them to originality. There was the perilous situation: a man in woman's clothes, sitting on a lighted stove that burns through the dress and reveals trousers underneath. Or there was the abrupt contrast (which he used time and again): a character is about to "sock" a man smaller than himself when, suddenly, a giant of a bully appears out of nowhere to confront him. Then there was sudden rough stuff: the bouncers pouring out of a tiny door, grabbing their victim, twirling him around their heads as if he were a sack, and then casting him off into some corner lot a mile away. The incongruous was exploited: beautiful girls absurdly languishing for the love of pot-bellied, bald, ridiculously fat men; or the poor, innocent, lonely damsel in distress embracing her rescuer and at the same time stealing his watch.

Sennett is all fantastic. Ridiculous villains remove their false whiskers a dozen times throughout a scene. Guns fire hundreds of bullets at dozens of cops who chase a culprit in a flivver which mows down telephone poles, crashes through houses and fences, plunges into the river and out again unharmed, only to explode when the victim is finally caught and being taken to jail.

Sennett's most important gags were the visual ones, depending upon an admirable use of camera trickery. Like Melies, Sennett exploited the camera devices, but whereas the Frenchman used them for magical effects, Sennett employed them for nonsensical effects. Stop-motion, slow-motion, fast-motion, double exposures, were as much a part of the Sennett ménage as Mabel Normand, Fatty Arbuckle, Mack Swain, Chester Conklin, Ben Turpin, Ford Sterling, the Keystone cops, and custard pies. Cops chase their victim at a mile-a-minute-pace; fat men leap hundreds of feet in the air; the hero dashes through walls or over a speeding train with the greatest of ease; explosions send characters sailing serenely through treetops; motorcycles swoop down waterfalls; the lowly two-seater Ford ejects literally hundreds of policemen and, after the last cop is finally out, bursts into fragments. In almost all Sennett's Keystone pictures there is some bit of camera bravura to highlight the foolishness of his performers.

Sennett's performers, like his gags and situations, came out of the crazy school of burlesque. They were all distinguished by some preposterous make-up and abnormal individual characteristics. In addition to Charlie Chaplin, who left Sennett after the first year, there were "old baggy-pants," the energetic fat man (Fatty Arbuckle); the innocent damsel (Mabel Normand); the soulful nincompoop (Hank Mann); the squinting Romeo (Ben Turpin); the "dumb clucks" (Louise Fazenda and Polly Moran); the smirking cavalier (Ford Sterling); the madcap Keystone cops; and the beautiful but dumb bathing belles. It was a portrait gallery worthy of any comic strip, but far more robust and full of Rabelaisian gusto.

Despite the seemingly illogical character of his films, Sennett believed that it was not possible to be really funny without being logical. Like Ince he believed that the events even in his roughest comedies have a degree of probability and sequence, and he cut all his own films to give them a continuous forward flow. Commenting on his ruthlessness in the cutting room, *Film Pictorial*[6] said,

A Keystone is never good enough to suit this exacting man. . . . The effectual elimination of six to a dozen feet for every foot saved, is what makes [Sennett master] . . . for that one foot must be chosen to tell all that originally was in a dozen times that length.

Sennett, a prolific worker, had an entire school of writers under him, besides many directors. He always made his "gag men" tell their stories to him, so that he could visualize the action and improvise the continuity of the film as they spoke. Often during the telling of a story Sennett, trailed by the writer, would go to the corner of the studio where his locales—lakes, rooms, fire escapes, etc.—were chalked out and there work up the plan of the film, while stenographers followed to take down his directions for the script. The next day such scripts would be turned over to a sub-director who turned the chalk scenes into real ones. In this way Sennett often personally supervised the direction of ten or twelve units at once.

The best of Sennett appeared under his Keystone trade-mark dur-

[6] October 1916.

ing the years 1913 to 1916. When he relinquished to Triangle his rights to the name Keystone and joined Paramount in 1917 as a producer, his slapstick style began to become refined in the fashion of the day. His popularity, however, did not wane; he continued to prosper and, by 1921, had his own company once more. Although his pictures in 1924, 1925, and 1926 were mere shadows of his earlier efforts, he says that these were his most profitable years. His burlesque, however, had become softened; his comic flair for satire had lost most of its vitality. The new middle-class audience that had come into the movie houses since the war had gradually and subtly moved Sennett to transform his slapstick into polite comedy, at which he was unsuited, and even into the sophisticated humor that was becoming popular.

The arrival of sound stunned Sennett. Since most of his comedians were unfit for talkies, he quickly began to develop new talent, discovering Bing Crosby and rediscovering W. C. Fields. But the panic of 1929 ruined him financially; it is said he lost between five and eight million dollars.

The hardest blow to Sennett was the appearance of the animated cartoons, in particular Mickey Mouse. The immediate and tremendous popularity of these films was the touch of death to Sennett's career. A new age of comedy had been initiated by a new kind of humorist. Once the "King of Comedy," Sennett is today only occasionally active.

Sennett's pictures are remembered, however, for their startling absurdities—the extremely lean, the extra-fat, the heavily bearded, the ridiculously dressed people; the rough-and-tumble action which once started kept on; the celebrated chases which defied the laws of gravity, hundreds of bullets, steel walls, stone buildings, water, and fire. Shunning dignity and refinement, Sennett created a world of vulgarity and violence, with movement, speed, nonsense, and improvisation as the chief elements of his style. He launched an entire school of comedians—Charlie Chaplin, Fatty Arbuckle, Harry Langdon, Gloria Swanson, Wallace Beery, Carole Lombard and instituted a type of comedy known as "slapstick," which springs essentially from the film medium.

Besides Ince, Tourneur, and Sennett, there were other directors, competent craftsmen of their day, esteemed by the trade, who occasionally made an outstandingly successful picture. Of these perhaps Herbert Brenon, called the "x" in Fox and spoken of as "probably the most successful of the newly famous makers of the big films" during this period of spectacles, enjoyed the most prestige. His claim to fame rests on *Neptune's Daughter, Daughter of the Gods, War Brides, The Fall of the Romanoffs,* and *Empty Pockets.* Both *Neptune's Daughter* and *Daughter of the Gods* (1916) featured the then renowned Annette Kellerman, swimming star. These pictures, sensational aquatic revues, were frames for the mermaids. *War Brides,* featuring Alla Nazimova and produced in 1916, was a dramatic and pacifistic film provoked by the Wilsonian campaign in which "He kept us out of the war" was the most familiar note. So effective was the film that, on America's entry into the war, it was deemed unsuitable for public showing. Distinguished by the fine acting of Nazimova, mass scenes, and dramatic tension, it was probably Brenon's best effort.

Quite as spectacular was *The Fall of the Romanoffs* (1917), which was ostensibly aimed at the Kaiser, upheld Kerensky, disparaged the Bolsheviks, and tried to prove that the Czar was the dupe of the mad Rasputin. Rendered in the hysterical high key of the day, this film won Brenon an invitation from the British government to make them a propaganda film of which there is no record in this country. His *Empty Pockets* (1917) was a poignant picture of ghetto life: it contrasted conspicuously with the extravagance of his previous efforts but was nonetheless dramatic.

A "big" director, Brenon always just fell short of great stature, but he was commercially extremely successful. He was one of the few directors of the time to maintain a top-ranking position in later years, during which his outstanding successes were *Beau Geste* (1926) and *Sorrell and Son* (1927). He was selected as one of the ten best directors of 1926, 1927, and 1928. Since sound he, too, has been eclipsed by others.

J. Stuart Blackton, chief director for the Vitagraph Company, the firm he helped to found, gained during the war years his greatest acclaim. The fervent patriotism expressed in one of his pioneer efforts, *Tearing Down the Spanish Flag*, now had another definite issue on which to work. Even while America was still neutral, he became the leading film propagandist for war, producing such pictures as *The Glory of the Nation, Womanhood, The Common Cause, Safe for Democracy, The Battle Cry of Liberty, The Battle Cry of Peace*, and *Missing*. The lucid titles of these films indicate their militarism and nationalistic ardor.

Blackton was never a creative director comparable to Griffith, nor an organizer so able as Ince, although he directed longer than either of them. But he had, in addition to his flair for propaganda, a versatile ability to adapt ideas; long experience gave him a fluency in story telling. The quick, deft, and shrewd directorial hand evident in such a variety of films as *The Judgment House, World for Sale, Life's Greatest Problem, The Blood Barrier, My Husband's Other Wife*, and *The House of the Tolling Bell* suggests his capabilities. Such pictures, however, show his limitations, also, for they were only average achievements.

When the Vitagraph Company ended business in 1925, Blackton was one of the last of the pioneers still connected with pictures in a major capacity. For twenty-nine years he had been a leading although not a potent figure in the industry, and he retired a millionaire. He lost his fortune in the 1929 crash, and in 1933 he was reported working on an SERA project in California.

Colin Campbell, a leading though lesser figure in these formative years, was Selig Company's chief director. His personality, approach, and style were similar to Thomas Ince's. Not confidential with his cast, he won a reputation as a cold intellectual man, keen and abrupt, and effective as a worker. He believed like Ince that the function of the movie is to tell a good story well. More than once he expressed the conviction that wherever progress was to be made in pictures would be made toward that end. Despite the vogue of spectacles, he did not believe in their lasting appeal. He continued to produce dramatic tales which, while adding nothing to the technique of movie making, were all good renditions according to the knowledge and standards of the day.

Perhaps his best and most famous work was *The Spoilers*, which opened the Strand Theatre on Broadway in 1914. Colonel Selig declared in 1920 that he could retire with the profits he had made on that film alone. *The Spoilers*, a tense drama, contained a fight sequence which became the classic example of such action on the screen. Some of Campbell's other successes were *The Ne'er-Do-Well*, *The Crisis*, and *Sweet Alyssum*. In later years Campbell was, like the pioneer Selig Company, to be forgotten.

Others in the rising school of new directors became known because of the famous stars they directed, the material they were given, or a freak hit. In the first group were Allan Dwan, who directed Mary Pickford in many pictures (*The Foundling*, *The Girl of Yesterday*), and also Douglas Fairbanks (*Manhattan Madness*, *The Good Bad Man*, *The Half-Breed*); Clarence Badger, who made the Will Rogers pictures; and Ralph Ince, director of the Anita Stewart pictures. Lois Weber was notable for her birth-control propaganda films (*Hypocrites*, *Where Are My Children?*, *Idle Wives*), and Frank Lloyd, for screen adaptations of literary classics, which he does to this day (*David Garrick*, *Davy Crockett*, *The Gentleman from Indiana*, *A Tale of Two Cities*). Those who enjoyed temporary fame for individual successes included George Loane Tucker (*Traffic in Souls*), Rupert Julian (*The Kaiser, Beast of Berlin*), Frank Powell, the discoverer of Theda Bara (*A Fool There Was*, which set a new vogue and introduced "the vamp"), and J. Gordon Edwards (*Cleopatra*).

Still other men at this time, working in movies in one capacity or another, were to reach their full stride in the post-war years and become leaders. They included Cecil B. DeMille, Erich von Stroheim, James Cruze, John Robertson, Rex Ingram, "Mickey" Neilan, Henry King, and an entire school trained under Ince—Fred Niblo, William Neil, Victor Schertzinger, Lambert Hillyer, and Rowland Lee. These names were to become esteemed in later years, and at least two were to be numbered with the most influential directors in American film history.

Like direction, the technique of acting for the screen was now following some general screen principles. Although acting was still commonly stilted and stage-mannered, there was among directors a growing consciousness of the screen's peculiar requirements, and efforts were being made to adapt actors to those requirements. As one writer exclaimed, "How much easier folks die now!" It was learned that movements had to be slowed to a speed below normal if they were to appear natural. The establishment of the feature-length film having eliminated the need to hurry the scenes, characterization became subtler, rounder. Conventional costume symbolism was outgrown, and the trite gesture was avoided. Even the esteemed John Barrymore was criticized for belonging to the class of "eyebrow actors." Regarding the "society" actor with his skyscraper handshake, his eyebrow emotions, his soul of despair, and his "woggle-walk," one commentator protested, "He is really Young America's misleading man." It was also being realized how much the camera, under sensitive lighting and direction, could do for the actor. Even Griffith noted that "Every year actors make less and less fuss with their hands and tell more and more with their eyes."

The star system stimulated the imitation of popular personalities by minor performers, but what caused particular players to be cherished by the public was a mystery no one was able then, or has since been able, to determine. Some producers thought that the drawing power of an actor might be based on stage training and a big Broadway reputation. Stage celebrities were therefore barraged with pleas to act on the screen, and crowds of them moved to Hollywood. But box-office receipts showed that screen requirements were very different from those of the stage: actors who were distinguished in one medium were often ineffective in the other. The numerous attempts to transplant stage luminaries provided, in the end, expensive lessons. By 1918 it was conceded that screen acting demanded a technique of its own; that stage reputations were of little avail before the camera; that screen stardom had to be earned on the screen.

Prominent actresses of the period were the Gish sisters, Blanche Sweet, Anita Stewart, Alice Joyce, Theda Bara, Mary Pickford, Mary Miles Minter, Marguerite Clark, Alla Nazimova, Olga Petrova, Beverly Bayne, Florence Turner, Kathlyn Williams, Pearl White, Clara Kimball Young, Lillian Walker. The leading actors included Charles Chaplin, Douglas Fairbanks, Francis X. Bushman, William

Farnum, H. B. Warner, Henry Walthall, J. Warren Kerrigan, William S. Hart, Creighton Hale, Earle Williams.

Just as producers were for a time sure that famous stage stars were the best and most logical choices for screen stars, so they were convinced that successful plays were the most valuable sources for screen stories. Following the example set by Zukor's Famous Players in Famous Plays, movie makers spent fortunes on plays, only to find that the screen made its own peculiar demands on stories just as on acting, and that screen stories were best prepared by people who had been trained in the movie medium itself.

During this era of adaptations of plays, prices for play rights soared to absurd heights. Vitagraph paid a top figure of $50,000 for *Within the Law*. The sums paid for novels were not so great: Mary Pickford, for instance, paid $15,000 for rights to film *Rebecca of Sunnybrook Farm*. The usual arrangement was that the author should receive a royalty on the picture's returns. The highest royalty mark for a single production was the $260,000 paid to Thomas Dixon during the first year alone for his 25 per cent interest in *The Birth of a Nation*.

Despite their growing realization that "originals" might after all be the best solution to the problem of getting screen material, producers no longer engaged free-lance motion picture writers with much confidence. Neither highly paid for nor esteemed, free-lance stories and ideas were no longer sought. Having often become involved in suits for plagiarism, companies were wary of accepting stories from unknown sources. The open market that had existed for motion picture writers contracted, and it became difficult for the novice to break in.

The technique of screen writing itself, however, developed rapidly during these years, becoming more formalized and distinct from the literary and stage techniques. Screen writers became aware that above all it is necessary to think in terms of action, not description or dialogue: that the camera is the paramount consideration. Scenarists were advised to "Use 'close-ups' frequently; the directors like them and it familiarizes the audience with the characters." The plot itself had to conform to certain accepted commercial patterns: "the menace thread . . . the lovers are the mainspring . . . dramatic situation is the real basis . . . must have a woman somewhere in its plot."

Under the supervisory system of Thomas Ince, more exact care was given to the construction of the story, and the working script or "shooting" script came into use. So complete was the new type of scenario in its specifications of camera position, angle, action, and transition, that it approximated the finished film as completely as writing could. It was from the shooting script, whenever it was available, that the cutter put together the strips of film. Since a thorough knowledge of camera technique and motion picture technique generally was essential to such scenario writing, many a future director emerged from among the scenarists. There were still, of course, many directors who worked not from a shooting script but, like Griffith, from their mental plan or from a loose tabulation of scenes, place, time, and action.

One of the highest paid and most influential scenario writers at this time was Anita Loos. At the top of her profession in 1918 and called the "O. Henrietta of the screen," she specialized in satirizing everyday events. She may be credited with introducing genuine satire into films and with elevating the subtitle to "sanity, dignity," and even brilliance.

Considered the leading screen wit of the day—a sort of movie Dorothy Parker—Anita Loos, together with her director-husband John Emerson, formed one of the first and most potent director-scenarist teams in movie history. They were serious analysts of their art. In a series of articles in *Photoplay* in 1918 on the treatment and selection of subject matter for the movies, they emphasized the vital difference between a movie of plot and a movie of theme. Pure plot, they showed, is a series of incidents, one growing out of the other, as in farces, mysteries, and comedies. The plot involves a conflict which, to be effective and hold the audience, must be perfect in form. The theme movie, on the other hand, is a basic idea out of which incident, conflict, and climax issue in inevitable succession: less common, less obvious, it is more profound than the plot movie. Working on these principles, Anita Loos did much to broaden the range of screen subjects and refine the tone of movies. It was her satires, moreover, that helped to establish

Douglas Fairbanks as one of the leading figures on the American screen.

Other outstanding contemporary scenarists, who are still prominent today in various capacities, were Hector Turnball, editor for Lasky's company; C. Gardner Sullivan, scenarist for Thomas Ince; Jeanie MacPherson, for Cecil B. DeMille; Louella O. Parsons, for Essanay; and Frances Marion, for Mary Pickford.

Increasing numbers of staff writers in the studios brought subtitling under closer scrutiny and deliberation. From 1914 to 1918 many experiments were made with subtitles and many principles were evolved. The written word had always been required to clarify the course of action or to supplement it. The subtitle was used at first between scenes to explain the picture that was to follow: thus a subtitle might be "Next day Jack Jones took his wife visiting," and it was followed by a picture of Jack Jones and his wife visiting. Then it was realized that this kind of subtitle gave the story away and made the succeeding picture superfluous. Titles were accordingly shortened so that they would just cover the time gap: "Next Day." For a brief period subtitles were abandoned entirely in favor of other devices such as lecturers, who proved unserviceable. Gradually titles were accepted again as a permanent part of the film.

The expansion of the old movie form into the feature made subtitles more necessary. Directors felt they could not do without them entirely, because they were a quick, efficient means of indicating lapses of time, of giving information about events taking place before the movie had begun and for at once establishing relationships between characters, and even of aiding the development of the plot. As Stephen Bush pointed out,[7]

The perfect picture tells its story without any titles, but as there are very few perfect pictures good titling becomes a necessity. . . . The idea that titles should take the place of pictures instead of merely supplementing them is a fruitful source of mistakes.

Subtitles were made to confirm the pictorial action instead of anticipating it. The word supplemented the image, carrying out

[7] *The Moving Picture World*, October 1913.

the long-standing convention of the stage, on which the gesture is made first and the speech follows to interpret it. It was also learned that words could be related to the action without being composed like a sentence on a printed page. Succinct phrases were found sufficient to effect transitions between scenes. Concerned entirely with speedy communication, titles were freed from grammatical regulations: "Night," "Music," "Came the Dawn." Words were used telegraphically, speeches were boiled down to essentials and speeded up, so that the flow of the film would be little hindered. In time the art of title writing was developed to a high order of directness for motion pictures, still in evidence in the "trailers" or "coming attractions" advertisements of the present day.

To eliminate the retardation of tempo that inevitably resulted from title insertions, in several movies in 1915 the words were printed directly on the scene with the players, just as today English titles are added to the action scenes of talkies with foreign dialogue. This method was found to interfere with the action and was soon abandoned.

Decorative symbolic titles were tried out with *Peggy*, starring Billie Burke, and became a fad under Irwin Willat, cameraman, and M. W. Randall, artist, at the Ince Studios. In a story of big-city politics, for instance, a title would show a loving spider ensnaring a fly. Behind the opening titles of *A Gamble in Souls* was seen a tiny frieze on which living pictures acted out an allegorical prologue. Because an overabundance of decorative and symbolic titles held up the flow of the picture and distracted the spectator's attention, the fashion eventually fell into disuse. Another novelty was introduced by Walt Mason in his one-reel comedies: the rhymed subtitle. This enjoyed great popularity for a time.

Owing to the influence of Anita Loos, humorous titles became popular. The titles of her Fairbanks satires proved to be as sensational as Fairbanks himself, and soon the screen was deluged by literary "gags." "Old Patrick Spaulding was as good a golfer as his tailor could make him," and "It's sometimes hard to tell who's the spider and who's the fly," are samples of the humor that prevailed for a time. Puns, *double entendres*—especially in slapstick comedies—and wisecracks became the vogue.

During these war years the cameraman was edged into the background by the star, the director, and the scenarist. But Bitzer's camera work in *Judith of Bethulia*, *The Birth of a Nation*, and *Intolerance*, and the encouragement of various directors, awoke cameramen to the possibilities of their craft. They applied themselves energetically to experimentation—to composition, to lighting, and to developing the mechanical devices of the camera itself. In Westerns and melodramas, chiefly, it became usual to pan the camera or place it upon a moving vehicle, the train and automobile being most commonly used for this purpose. The use of masks—keyhole, opera-glass, and heart effects—and shooting through doorways, arches, and shrubbery also became popular.

Cameras themselves were being refined and elaborated. Under the stimulus of war needs, new inventions and improvements in lenses and other camera accessories for military use were numerous: for instance, more accurate view finders, more flexible tripods, longer focal-length lenses, and the telephoto lens, called the "long tow." The telephoto lens made it possible to photograph a distant scene so that the scene would appear within close range on the screen, like an image seen through a telescope. To eliminate the necessity of cranking the camera—a hindrance to war photographers—the gyroscopic camera was invented. Operated by compressed air, this camera could be swung on a strap over the newsreel cameraman's shoulder and could be held in his hand during shooting. After the war both the telephoto lens and the gyroscopic camera were modified for commercial movie use and were adopted widely in the studios. Also after the war a number of former Army Signal Corps cameramen, including Victor Fleming, George Hill, Ernest Schoedsack, Josef von Sternberg, Alan Crosland, and Wesley Ruggles, became movie directors.

The increased flexibility and mobility of his instrument turned the cameraman's attention particularly to composition. He was no longer satisfied to shoot the scene as it happened to be: he arranged objects, moving a chair or shifting a table, and placed the performers so that he could take a better picture. The camera was often shifted above or below the eye level, and occasionally to an extreme angle view. Maurice Tourneur and Cecil B. DeMille both showed that the set need not be lighted evenly all over: that light could be keyed to the mood of a scene, that atmosphere could be created by the judicious use of light tones and variations. Cameramen soon started to "place" shadows, to subdue or lighten reflections, to keep the background unobtrusive in halftone lighting, and actually to sketch their shots with light.

The first attempts to model with light—to bring out the best features of the players, to emphasize character, to reduce the prominence of irrelevant effects—were begun. Bert Glennon, Victor Milner, Sol Polito, Charles Rosher, John Arnold, and Joe August were all experimenting with the mercury-vapor lamps then in use to make them more adaptable to modeling.

Toward the end of the period cameramen were modifying their close and medium shots by diffusion, because at close or medium range the wiry-sharp lens and the orthochromatic film showed up the physical defects of players mercilessly. Gauzing the lens to soften the features of the players became, therefore, a usual practice. Alvyn Wyckoff, DeMille's cameraman, introduced a spotlight effect ("Rembrandt" lighting) to create strong dramatic contrasts; others developed the idea and began to use the spotlight for night effects, although night scenes were still usually shot in daylight and printed on blue-tinted film.

By the end of the war period cameramen had thus become sharply aware of the importance of composition and lighting in their work. During the following years they continued their study earnestly. Although Bitzer was the pace-setter, Tony Gaudio, Victor Milner, and Charles Rosher were developing distinctive styles, and such newcomers as Alvyn Wyckoff, Joe August, Clyde DeVinna, and Bert Glennon were laying the groundwork for their future high reputations.

Toward the close of the war, art directors (also known as "technical directors") became necessary members of the production staffs in the leading studios. The staging that George Melies, with his knowledge of the theatre, had first brought to the screen in 1900 was now being used extravagantly. When American directors saw poor films saved by elegant backgrounds, by "eye appeal," they began giving more attention to such matters. Make-up was, as one commentator expressed it, becoming more "humanized." Interior decoration and etiquette were stressed. Taste in ornamentation and costuming was much refined, although contemporary standards tended to encourage exaggerations in the way of ornate lamps, tables, and mantels; heavily carved chairs, bric-a-brac, and luxurious draperies, all of which were intended to signify gentility and elegance. Accuracy as well as elegance, however, was an important consideration. *The Birth of a Nation*, which had subtitles pointing out the historical accuracy of many of the scenes, did much to increase the movie world's respect for authenticity in staging.

Film cutting likewise became a specialized craft. At first the cutter's job was more or less mechanical; he merely relieved the director of the physical labor of piecing strips of film together. Gradually, however, as the scenario was broken down into full, medium, and close shots, the directors depended more upon cutters to give films unity. Many directors delegated to cutters the entire responsibility for the finished work. Soon the cutter was indispensable to the director. Later, in the post-war period, he was to give the film its final form, covering the director's mistakes, giving the film continuity and logic, and "making or breaking" a player by including or leaving out scenes in which the player appeared. Film cutting thus became a highly important, if unpublicized, operation in production.

With the enlarging of theatres and the change in the character of audiences, the music accompanying a motion picture was given careful attention. Owing principally to the successful scoring of *The Birth of a Nation*, the musical scorer became an esteemed figure in the motion picture industry almost overnight. His job was to plan the accompaniment of a picture, which was then printed in book form as a "cue sheet," exactly like the libretto of an opera. The score was rented to theatres with the picture. By 1916 only the very cheapest of movie houses did not have an orchestra instead of a pianist. The leader of the orchestra in the better theatres would synchronize the musical score with the film according to the picture's subtitles.

Famous composers were now being engaged by the studios, the most publicized of such engagements being perhaps that of the renowned Victor Herbert. The composers created themes to identify different characters and to associate ideas. Before long a number of musical clichés had resulted from this practice: Chopin's "Nocturne in E," Massenet's "Elegie," and Rubinstein's "Kammenoi-Ostrow" denoted melancholy; Grieg's "To Spring," Chaminade's "Scarf Dance," and Schubert's "Serenade" signalized joy; Rachmaninoff's "Prelude" and "The Storm" or "One Fine Day" from the opera *Madame Butterfly* presaged tragedy. As these selections indicate, the trend was toward the use of classical music rather than evanescent tunes of the day.

By 1919 the major crafts having been established, the movie's form began to show signs of maturity, and individual styles became apparent. Motion pictures had acquired all the characteristics of an art. Swift progress in the development of mechanical instruments was notable and was to become more fully apparent in post-war productions. People who worked in movies were conscious that they were early settlers and builders in the realm of a great art and prime social force. Success, money, and fame, pouring into the laps of the fortunate, stimulated all in the industry to greater efforts. The tremendous mass appeal of movies impressed those working with the medium perhaps even more than people who observed its course from the outside. At no time since the war period have the makers of motion pictures felt such responsibility and such an urge to do their best.

XIII

CHARLES CHAPLIN: INDIVIDUALIST

TO think of Charlie Chaplin is to think of the movies. Yet this unique actor, director, and producer has added little to movie technique or movie form. He has been not a technician but a pantomimist, a commentator, a satirist, a social critic. His artistic problems have not been cinematic; they have been personal, always being solved by feeling. His importance lies not in what he has contributed to film art, but in what he has contributed to humanity. If he is negligible as a movie craftsman, if he has evolved no new formal aspects to enrich the medium, he has created many moments to enrich society. Chaplin will always be known for his social outlook, his insight into human nature, his pantomimic skill, his ingenious development of the incident, and his evocation of a mood. It is these qualities rather than any plastic contributions which have made him significant as a screen artist.

In the history of the American film no other single personality has so endeared himself to the world as Charlie Chaplin. His presence is as much alive as ever in the thousands of 16 mm. revivals of his work. Every generation takes him to its heart anew. As with all great characters, one sees in Chaplin what one brings to him. Children love him for his humor; adults are moved by deeper meanings, too. Every man recognizes in Chaplin's experiences his own dreams, illusions, problems, disappointments. This little tramp does what most of us would like to do and see ourselves as doing, but yet cannot bring ourselves to do. His frustrations are mankind's; his successes, universal triumphs. When he laughs, races and nations shout with him; when he is sad, a sorrowful wail encircles the globe. So readily can his slightest gesture evoke human emotions that he can be truly called the film's miracle man.

To have such far-reaching influence a man must be extraordinary. Yet when we view him with his doleful countenance and foolish mustache, his ill-fitting derby, his absurd shoes, his gentleman's cane, his ineffectual gait, we see a child—a child playing grown-up. In this is the man's humor. An adult playing a child is merely foolish; but a child imitating his elders without understanding their world or their experiences is poignant indeed. Chaplin intuitively knows the incongruity of such behavior and employs it as the mainspring of his humor and pathos. It is the quintessence of his art.

Chaplin has been a man of position so long that it is difficult to think of him as an apprentice struggling to make his way. Yet up to the time of his first success, when he was about twenty-five (he had been born April 16, 1889), his life was anything but easy. His parents had both been obscure ballad singers. Though the two never teamed together in the same act, they had traveled with the same company, always in bitter want. As a child, all Chaplin ever really dreamed about was becoming rich.

He remembers acting for the first time at the age of five or six in London, when his mother became desperately ill and he took her place, singing an old Coster song called "Jack Jones." About this time his father died. Without means of support, and sick, Mrs. Chaplin left Charles and his brother Sydney in a poorhouse. Here, ill himself, Charles spent his days dreaming of riches, of a seat in Parliament, and of being a famed musician.

When Mrs. Chaplin recovered and was able to go back to work, Charles and Sydney were retrieved from the poorhouse—Sydney to become a sailor, and Charles to be an apprentice to his mother. Charles made his first formal stage appearance with "The Lancashire Lads," doing a clog-dancing, tumbling vaudeville routine. Turning then to dramatic roles, he received his first real notice in *Jim, the Romance of Cocaine*, by H. A. Saintsbury. This performance led to other roles and inspired his determination to become a legitimate actor instead of a vaudeville trouper like his parents. By the time he had played in *Sherlock Holmes*, however, he found himself too old for boys' parts and too young for men's. At seventeen, therefore, he returned to the variety shows, joining Fred Karno's famous English Pantomime troupe as an apprentice. He stayed with the troupe almost five years, acquiring a repertory and technique. It was this experience and schooling that laid the foundations for his remarkable pantomimic style. Many of the Karno skits, in fact, such as *The Billiard Player, Drunk Coming Home, Boxing Lessons, Behind the Scenes of a Music Hall*, were later incorporated in Chaplin's films almost without change.

When he was twenty-one Chaplin, with Karno's Number 2 company, toured the United States for three years as a drunken dress-suit comedian in *A Night in a Music Hall*. It was Adam Kessel, of Kay-Bee Bison Company, who saw in Chaplin a likely prospect for movies and sent him to Sennett's Keystone unit in 1913. At first Chaplin was reluctant to give up the stage for pictures, still considered by most actors as a foolish venture. But the increase in salary that went with the offer ($150 a week as against the $60 he was getting on the stage) and a year's guarantee of a job decided the issue. About a year later, in January 1915, Chaplin related to Gene Morgan, of *The Chicago Herald*, his feelings and experiences on going into movies:

I traveled all the way across the continent with glorious visions haunting my lower berth dreams. I dreamed that I was the great romantic actor of the age—the Ideal Romeo of the Photo-Shakespearean. When I arrived in California I prepared to don the doublet and hose of the 14th century lovers. You can imagine my feelings when I was told that the first character I would play would be a man with a limp and a backache, trying to carry a trunk and balance a scuttle of coal on his head while climbing a greasy step ladder. . . . I was indignant. I said I wouldn't play . . . and then I thought of the long trip back to Broadway and decided it was a good plan to try anything once.

When Chaplin actually saw himself on the screen for the first time, he was ready to quit: "That can't be I," he thought. Then, when he realized it was, he said, "Good night!"

Kessel, however, was impressed.

Strangely enough, I was told that the picture was a scream. I had always been ambitious to work in dramas and it certainly was the surprise of my life when I got away with comedy stuff.

Since his first screen appearance in 1913, Charles Chaplin has made history. As a whole, his career during twenty-five years has been marked by ripening ability and a steadily rising reputation. Until 1918 his pictures were experiments in technique and style, containing all the external characteristics that Chaplin was later to synthesize, and revealing his growing awareness of aims. His films during the following years were mature, rich in insight and understanding. In recent years, since the advent of the talkies, he has used his genius humorously and pathetically to reveal the sores of modern life. Intensely conscious of modern social conditions, he employs his artistry on behalf of the underprivileged, speaking out for the individual against all forms of oppression. His social conscience has been the inspiration that has transformed his outmoded silent-screen technique and kept his work contemporary and meaningful.

Chaplin began his screen career under Sennett, in the Keystone unit. Here he had difficulties. At first he met with personal opposition from the other comedians, who, being jealous, subjected him to practical jokes to discourage him. But in time their admiration, particularly for his falling technique, overcame their hostility.

More trying to Chaplin was the inconsistency between his pantomimic style and Sennett's demand for slapdash, whirlwind, action pictures. His simple gestures were strange and out of place in the Keystone burlesques: there exaggeration, speed, and the "socko" type of acting were the rule. Sennett's directors tried to alter Chaplin's delivery to conform to their standard but finally gave up in disgust. No director now wanted to use Chaplin at all. But finally Chaplin persuaded Sennett to let him act in his own way.

The famous Chaplin make-up—derby, diminutive mustache, baggy trousers, oversize shoes, and cane—did not come into existence at once. In his first pictures he wore a drooping mustache, ordinary shoes, and no derby. Noting that he could not be distinguished from the other Sennett comedians, he looked around for some individual costume. From Max Linder, the French comedian, whom he greatly admired, Chaplin took the idea of burlesquing a dandy by means of the cane, the French kick, and the derby (instead of the Homburg). A pair of Ford Sterling's old cast-off shoes supplied the ridiculous note; the mustache was cropped to resemble a brush, and an ill-fitting waistcoat gave the final touch of foolishness to the character he was to make famous.

During his year at Keystone, Chaplin appeared in a great many pictures, most of them being one-reelers, several two reels long, and one, *Tillie's Punctured Romance*, one of the first feature comedies, five reels long. In most of these productions Mabel Normand, then Sennett's star, was Chaplin's leading lady. An accurate list of the complete series is impossible, for no record was kept at the time and since then many of the titles have been changed in revivals, in abridged 16 mm. versions for libraries, and in Europe.

Making a Living
Kid Auto Races
Mabel's Strange Predicament
A Film Johnnie
His Favorite Pastime
The Cruel, Cruel Love
Mabel at the Wheel
The Star Boarder
20 Minutes of Love
Caught in a Cabaret
Caught in the Rain
Tillie's Punctured Romance
The Fatal Mallet
Her Friend the Bandit
The Knockout
Mabel's Busy Day
The Property Man
The Face on the Barroom Floor
Recreations
The Masquerader
The Baggage Smasher
The Rounders
The New Janitor
Those Love Pangs
Dough and Dynamite
A Gentleman of Nerve

His Musical Career
His Trysting Place
Getting Acquainted
His Prehistoric Past
The Dog Catcher

Chaplin's Keystone films were, in the main, rapid-fire farces, as can be seen from their titles. They were not built around Chaplin's personality but rather employed his talents to carry out the usual Sennett pattern. Incident followed upon incident swiftly, so that Chaplin's individual pantomime and subtlety were sacrificed for pace and action. These elements Chaplin was later to incorporate in his own films, but he adapted them to his personality and individual style.

From the very beginning Chaplin was singled out by public and critics alike. Movie-goers began to ask who the little fellow with the funny walk was. Inquiries poured into Sennett's office so fast that a staff was kept busy answering them. By the end of his first year in pictures, Chaplin's popularity had reached such amazing proportions that *The New York Herald* [1] declared, "The Chaplin craze seems to have supplanted the Pickford craze." *The New York Mail* [2] unequivocally announced, "Charles Chaplin stands today as one of the biggest drawing cards in the films. In many cases the Chaplin comedies are renting for bigger prices than feature films of twice their length."

Before even Chaplin could realize it, he had become the most talked-of personality in the United States. Children promised to be good all week if they could see a Chaplin comedy on Saturday. The man's face and figure began to appear everywhere—on balloons, postcards, and statuettes, in choruses of revues and vaudeville, on electrical toys, on a thousand and one novelties, just as Mickey Mouse, Shirley Temple, and Charlie McCarthy are exploited today. Unknown before 1914, by 1915 Chaplin had become America's newest idol. Yet he himself declared,[3] "I wasn't meaning to be funny then. I am not a bit funny really. I am just a little nickel comedian

[1] April 20, 1915.   [2] April 10, 1915.   [3] *Photoplay*, February 1915.

trying to make people laugh. They act as though I were the King of England."

Chaplin had left Sennett meanwhile to join Essanay as his own director, and had been given a free hand to select his own stories. His Keystone experience had been valuable. He now not only understood the technique of movie making and the elements of film fantasy, but was aware of his unique motion picture talents and of the direction he should take in the future. In an interview soon after his contract with Essanay had been signed, Chaplin told Esther Hoffman of *The Milwaukee Journal* [4] that "Comedy is really a serious study, but one must never take it seriously. To be a successful comedian there must be an ease in the acting that cannot be associated with seriousness." It was toward this ease in acting that Chaplin thereafter aspired, so that he became less a slapstick comedian and more a pantomimist.

For his new employers Chaplin made fourteen pictures. The first two were made in Chicago; the others he insisted upon making in California. He asserted his independence further by selecting a leading lady from the ranks of the inexperienced, finding her through a local advertisement in Hollywood. His choice was tall, blond Edna Purviance, who presented a striking contrast to Chaplin's dark face and delicate figure. His intuition was justified, for Edna Purviance acted with him successfully until 1925.

His year at Essanay was transitional: he was now sharpening burlesque into satire. His first effort for Essanay, appropriately titled *His New Job*, ridiculed star worship—then reaching great heights—by exposing the absurdities of a star's manufacture. In this picture Chaplin rose from a carpenter's assistant to a matinee idol. The beginnings of a style were so apparent that *The Chicago Tribune* [5] commented, "In this display he is a little nicer than he has been in Keystone, but not too nice to spoil his humorous appeal."

Chaplin's second Essanay film, *One Night Out*, was a bit of pantomimic bravura in which he repeated his Karno "drunk act," adding to it a significant bit of action: While being dragged along a path by Ben Turpin, he suddenly plucks a daisy and smells it. In a

[4] March 18, 1915.   [5] February 2, 1915.

moment the drunk is transformed into a poet; nonsense is made poignant. The unexpectedness and incongruity of this little event struck to the heart of the movie audience. It was the first of many such human touches that were, in time, to become familiar in Chaplin characterizations.

The Tramp further presaged the emotional overtones and common-man characterizations of Chaplin's later work. In this picture Chaplin, a tramp outside the pale of society, tries to improve his position by conforming to the ways of society but is frustrated at the moment of seeming victory. Having lost the material world symbolized by the girl for whom he has given up his ideal world, he shrugs his shoulders sadly, and with his peculiar childlike kick straggles off, resigned to a lonely fate. The pungency of this action went deeper than "gag" humor, and the laughter it aroused was full of pathos. Thereafter Chaplin's films were saturated with both humor and sadness, and whichever happened to predominate at a particular moment, his pantomimic skill rendered it inimitably and movingly.

The remainder of Chaplin's pictures for Essanay were a variety of extravaganzas studded with moments of satire, pathos, and fantasy. *The Champ, The Jitney Elopement, The Bank, Police,* and *Carmen* (a five-reel venture) made fun of sports, honeymooners, pillars of society, officers of the law, and opera. In these films Chaplin broke away further from the burlesque nonsense of his earliest efforts: wit supported tears in the beatings, frustrations, and heroics. *In the Park, By the Sea, The Woman,* and *Work* revealed a playful Chaplin, dilly-dallying at work and working at dilly-dallying. His attempts to become a man of leisure through the power of imagination alone strike a responsive chord in our own day-dreaming. *Shanghaied,* a return to the Sennett burlesque, and *A Night at the Show,* a bit of virtuosity reminiscent of the Karno troupe days, completed his program of pictures for Essanay.

Though these films had little narrative structure, the story being improvised as it progressed, Chaplin's pantomimic talents were fully in evidence. His smallest gesture—fixing a tie, flicking dust from his coat, twirling his cane—became of great significance. Percy Hammond [6] eulogized his "inestimable faculty of absolute unconsciousness of and indifference to his audience . . . to such an extent that the proceedings seem to be an improvisation."

Grown in stature, reputation, and facility at the end of his contract with Essanay in 1916, Chaplin was signed by Mutual for $670,000 a year, in those days so fabulous a sum that he must have been one of the most valued actors in the movies. With the Keystone and Essanay experience behind him, he now set for himself higher standards, not only to sustain his reputation but to improve it. From now on every film he turned out was to be the result of an ordeal of nervous tension, infinite and unrelenting effort, constant self-questioning. His story values, humor, ideas, everything that went into his picture, were chosen to reveal the universal in human nature. He worked tirelessly, critical of himself and of everything and everyone about him. Shooting scenes and incidents over and over again, he would use hundreds of thousands of feet of film to get two thousand feet that satisfied.

His dozen Mutual pictures, made in 1916-1917, were Chaplin's richest in inventiveness, tenderness, and gravity. From the first, *The Floorwalker*, to the last, *The Adventurer*, he piled up a roster of heartbreaking fun. All the wounds he had endured during his poorhouse days, his struggles for a livelihood, his early poverty, his yearning for beauty that had been constantly denied or constrained, were expressed in one form or another, in film after film, with high imagination and eloquence. It was the Chaplin of these pictures who became the beloved idol of millions throughout the world.

Whether a floorwalker (*The Floorwalker*), fireman (*The Fireman*), vagabond (*The Vagabond*), drunkard (*One A.M.*), count (*The Count*), pawnbroker (*The Pawnshop*), actor (*Behind the Scenes*), skater (*The Rink*), crusader (*Easy Street*), invalid (*The Cure*), immigrant (*The Immigrant*), or adventurer (*The Adventurer*), Chaplin is David confronting the Goliath who makes life miserable for the weak until he is resolutely challenged. Battered, pursued, frustrated, lovesick, through his quick-wittedness and nimbleness Chaplin finally emerges from the conflict victorious—and alone. The sparks that fly from his many engagements are touched

[6] In *The Chicago Tribune.* March 14, 1915.

with deep humor, tender pathos, bitter satire, any of which he can achieve by the use of any prop at hand—an escalator, a mannikin, a violin, a carpet, or a clock. Gems of Chapliniana, these pictures reveal his increasing social awareness. The self-consciousness and groping that marked his Sennett and Essanay films are gone; he now has self-assurance and a ripened purpose.

The Pawnshop shows how the ingenious, dexterous, resourceful Chaplin could take whatever came to hand and, by the sheer power of his artistry, make it amusing. Gilbert Seldes in his book *The Seven Lively Arts* [7] has recorded the entire film in detail; a few excerpts emphasize Chaplin's singular flair for improvisation on material immediately at hand.

[He has just been fired.] He makes a tragic appeal to be reinstated. He says he has eleven children, so high, and so high, and so high—until the fourth one is about a foot taller than himself. The boss relents only as Charlie's stricken figure is at the door. As he is pardoned, Charlie leaps upon the old boss, twining his legs around his abdomen; he is thrown off and surreptitiously kisses the old man's hand. . . . He goes to the kitchen to help the daughter and passes dishes through the clothes wringer to dry them—passes a cup twice, as it seems not to be dry the first time. Then his hands.

Most of the time Chaplin personalizes everything he touches, but on occasion he will objectively include a social comment without projecting it himself. In *The Immigrant*, for example, as the ship approaches Ellis Island, we see the Statue of Liberty, and immediately thereafter the roped-in steerage passengers being shoved about and herded like cattle.

The Vagabond was Chaplin at his most pathetic—a wandering fiddler in love with a gypsy girl he is too shy to woo. Chivalrous, kind, and extremely innocent, he wins the girl's admiration by bluffing a bully. When the girl gives Charlie her hand, he slips it into his pocket.

In *Easy Street* he is a derelict who wanders into a Bowery Mission where, on being reformed, he returns the collection plate he has stolen. He then joins the police force and is assigned to Easy Street, the city's toughest neighborhood. from which policemen

[7] P. 362.

are sent home on stretchers. In his characteristic way he soon sets things right, rescuing the mission worker who reformed him. This was one of his best and most characteristic efforts.

The close of this third year of movie making saw Chaplin pre-eminent in the comedy field, far outstripping his former overseer Sennett. Acclaimed everywhere, besieged to speak at banquets or lead parades, stopped on the streets, sent thousands of fan and crank letters, he rivaled in human interest the European war then raging.

From 1918, when he signed a million-dollar contract with First National Pictures, who were to finance and distribute his produc-tions, Chaplin worked entirely for himself. His pictures now stand distinct from his earlier efforts. After 1918 his movies are fewer and longer, ever growing in complexity and profundity but spring-ing from essentially the same sources that became apparent in his earlier years.

No longer concerned with mastering a technique, Chaplin now was free to develop his unique characterizations and subtle witti-cisms further, giving comedy emotional depth and satirical signifi-cance in his criticism of conventions, dogmas, and injustices in society. Only once did he depart from his usual form of expression: in 1923 with the single dramatic venture *A Woman of Paris*, in which he appeared only briefly as a porter.

Chaplin in these years gained a reputation as an eccentric. He was said to be sensitive to the point of melancholy and misery, beset with constant misgivings in his attempts to surpass his previous work. *The Atlanta Constitution* [8] aptly observed that "off stage he looked like a man with a burden." He labored day and night for the qualities that would make his characterizations universal in meaning. Groping for a formal method of developing ideas, he surrounded himself with interesting and talented writers and artists, not so much for what they could contribute concretely but for the stimulation they offered. A dictagraph machine was installed at his bedside to record any notions that might occur to him during the night. Everything he heard he weighed as possible material for his films. It was said he talked to himself, played the violin in the middle of the night, was a "sun dodger," did not drink, drank too

[8] February 28, 1919.

Werner Krauss as Dr. Caligari in that unique "expressionistic" picture *The Cabinet of Dr. Caligari* (1919), which made movie-goers "art film" conscious.

Two stills from Henry King's celebrated *Tol'able David* (1921), an early example of American regionalism.

much, worked only when the spirit moved him, was exceedingly generous to anyone in need, was close with money at other times—in fact, was as erratic as geniuses are generally conceived to be.

Probably all the eccentricities attributed to him had their basis in fact. But they were not affectations; many sprang from his deep concern for self-improvement. Refusing to be dazzled by his phenomenal reputation, he had the humility to question everything he did. It was this rare personal quality that made his films of this period, though basically the same in technique as his earlier pictures, particularly rich in human touches, uncommonly penetrating, and high-lighted by sure pantomimic sketches.

The first picture Chaplin made for First National release was *A Dog's Life* (1918). The title, like most of his subsequent titles, was significant and symptomatic of the social consciousness that was to permeate his future productions more deliberately than heretofore. Made soon after America's entrance into the World War, *A Dog's Life* showed Chaplin as a vagabond philosopher, a Walt Whitman of the screen, a characterization that afforded him ample opportunity to prick the bubbles of social conventions and show up humbuggeries, and that he later adopted repeatedly. Its underlying theme was also typical of Chaplin: living is, for the common man, a dog's life, but that is no excuse for not making the best of it.

"One must love," said Chaplin. And in a seething, warring world, he recognized understanding, toleration, and individual freedom as other vital human needs. Hating regimentation of any kind, he cunningly pointed the film against the most extreme form of regimentation: War, with its mother, Hate. In *A Dog's Life* the hero played by Chaplin preferred a free and independent existence to military conscription, dogmatism, and routine, even if his choice meant he had to forage for food for himself and his pet. Delluc, the French critic, said of this picture,[9] "This is the first complete work of art that Chaplin has."

His next effort, *Shoulder Arms*, was a contribution to America's war chest and was the greatest single success in his career up to that time. Chaplin's vagabond in this picture, repudiating his peaceful ideals, acquired a soldier's uniform—a symbol of his compromise

[9] *Chaplin*, J. Lane Co., 1922.

and a suggestion for others to do likewise. The soldier-philosopher laughed off the hardships of the trenches, cooties, rain, the thousand and one inconveniences of regimented life, and made the war easier to accept. Typically Chaplinesque was the eloquent scene where he tries to tell the French girl he is an American: after many vain linguistic attempts, he has a brilliant inspiration—he pantomimes the stars and stripes of the American flag, in his own deft way. At once the girl understands.

Although released too late to play a recruiting role in the war, *Shoulder Arms* served a therapeutic purpose by relieving the suffering of men in canteens and soldier's hospitals abroad, where it was widely shown. The picture was immensely popular in America, also.

After the Armistice Chaplin reverted to his favorite theme: the little man who lacks material possessions but is a person of position in his own dream world. This was the personality Chaplin cherished above all, and it was near to the heart of his audiences. His next three films, *Sunnyside*, *A Day's Pleasure*, and *The Kid*, all exploited that dream world. In these pictures Chaplin is again the gentle tramp-philosopher, leading a meager existence but dreaming of a better day. Each of the films contains wish-fulfillment dream sequences in which the vagrant achieves what society denies him in real life.

Of the three, *Sunnyside* was perhaps the most enchanting, *The Kid* the most significant. *The Kid* represented not only a mature development of Chaplin's art form—it was the longest picture he had yet made—but a culmination of everything that had gone before. Many critics considered it his masterpiece. In this modern fairy tale, a woman abandons her child, hoping it will be adopted by rich people; instead, a tramp finds and raises him. The characters are symbols in the tradition of the pre-war morality movies: the Man, the Woman, the Tramp, the Child, the Policeman. The Tramp and the Kid, social outcasts who hope for little, contrive to get along: though they exist in squalor, they live in the imagination. Society, in the person of the belligerent Policeman, finally restores the Kid to the mother, now a celebrated opera singer, and the

Tramp, a guardian angel, is asked to become the boy's father. The cherished dream thus finally comes true.

Throughout the film Chaplin's fertile imagination and social intuitions were manifested in a thousand little touches that the audience never missed, no matter how minute and seemingly trifling the touches were. Everything was fraught with meaning. The film's opening caption, "Her only sin was motherhood," was a significant poke at conventions. Chaplin as the Tramp, politely sporting his polished rags, strolls leisurely down the street, twirling his cane. He removes his fingerless gloves with the aplomb of an ambassador, opens his cigarette case—a sardine box—and, after careful deliberation, selects a butt, which he proceeds to tap down before smoking. With perfect pantomime the street gamin, refusing to be abashed by his low economic position, has caricatured the man on the other side of the railroad tracks.

The arrangement by which the Kid breaks windows so that the Tramp can mend them, and so earn money for them both to live on, is a sharp indictment of a society that ignores its less privileged members. Prudery, too, takes its share of ridicule when the Tramp finally discovers the foundling infant's sex by peeping under the blankets.

The dream sequence is significantly labeled "Fairyland." In Heaven the Tramp finds the Kid and the rest of his neighbors in Slum Street, which is festooned and garlanded. All the inhabitants, even to his mortal enemy the Policeman, fly about with white wings on their everyday clothes. It is too good to be true; the Tramp suddenly wakes up. Dazed and uncomprehending, he looks for the wings on the real cop who is dragging him off, apparently to jail. As they come to a lamp post, the Tramp, submissive and resigned to his fate, dodges back from the post to walk around it and so avoid bad luck. The move is deft; it is poignant; it is true. Then comes the climax as the Tramp is put into a limousine instead of the patrol wagon he has been expecting. As the car starts, his face is filled with fright, hope, bewilderment (such things do not happen to *him*). That, in the words of Gilbert Seldes,[10] is "a moment of

[10] *The Seven Lively Arts*, p. 51.

unbearable intensity . . . one is breathless with suspense—and with adoration." No other actor in films has the ability, or permits himself, to show such depths of feeling.

Worn out, emotionally exhausted after *The Kid*, Chaplin went abroad like other actors for a holiday—his first holiday in seven years. Asked at the time of his departure if he expected to visit Soviet Russia and if he were a Bolshevik, he answered, "I am an artist. I am interested in life. Bolshevism is a new phase of life. I must be interested in it."

A series of articles about his European tour (later put into book form [11] and said to have been ghost-written by Monta Bell) was published by *Photoplay*. Feted in his native England, Chaplin said, "I had a profound sense of humility when I saw these people who came to look at me." [12] He was decorated by the French government; he traveled without a passport, for his face was known everywhere. Photographs in *Photoplay* showed him surrounded by admiring throngs and greeted by the German star, Pola Negri, in the company of famous diplomats and dignitaries. Chaplin, the former poverty-stricken orphan, had become a world celebrity; his boyhood dreams had come startlingly, unbelievably true.

The European trip left a strong impression upon Chaplin. He saw a post-war, shattered world full of poverty and misery. The results of the ruthless war madness, apparent everywhere, moved him far more than the homage and admiration accorded him. One of the earliest observers to see at first hand the toll of war in human terms, he returned to America to make pictures with a deeper, more serious purpose.

His next three pictures revealed him as one of the few movie makers in Hollywood who dared assume a critical attitude toward society. *The Idle Class* (1921), *Pay Day* (1922), and *The Pilgrim* (1923) were thrusts at social inequalities. Sympathetic toward the working man, they tried to show that spiritual good is more likely to be found in a convict than in those who make convicts what they are. All three films were adroit expositions of Chaplin's credo, although they were not propagandistic in the common sense of the

[11] *My Trip Abroad*, Harper & Bros., 1922.   [12] *Photoplay*, December 1921.

term and did not essentially differ from the points of view of his previous films.

After *The Pilgrim* Chaplin suddenly surprised everyone by directing a dramatic film in which he did not star. It is upon this film, *A Woman of Paris* (1923), that his reputation as a great director has often been wrongly based. In direction the film was neither brilliant nor remarkable, though many claimed it to be both. Its style was elementary; it had none of the remarkable camera work of the German school, then at its best, nor any unusual insight regarding movie continuity. The film's interest lay in pyschological portraiture, in its honesty in depicting character, environment, and human relationships. What mattered most in the film was the motivation of the characters' actions—the petty quarrels and jealousies, the thinking processes. "I treated the subject," Chaplin said, "in the simplest possible manner."

The story, written by Chaplin himself, was in essentials melodramatic. In a dismal French village a French girl (Edna Purviance) is turned out of her home by an angry father for having an affair with an artist. The parents of her sweetheart refuse to take her in. With her lover she starts for Paris, but on the way they learn that the boy's father has become ill because of the elopement. The boy returns home while the girl, in desperation, goes on to Paris alone. Here poverty and her belief that she has been abandoned lead her to become the mistress of a well-to-do Parisian (played by Adolphe Menjou). When her former sweetheart later discovers her situation, he commits suicide. His distraught mother starts out to kill the girl but, finding her at her son's bedside, cannot shoot. A reconciliation between the two grief-stricken women follows, and the girl gives up her wealthy lover to find sanctuary in the country with the dead artist's mother. The film ends ironically when the girl years later, while riding a clumsy cart, is forced off the road by a high-powered motor car. In the car her former Paris lover is riding; but neither he nor the girl suspects the identity of the other.

The treatment of the story eliminated the moral tone that such a story would be expected to have. Chaplin called the film "a drama of fate": in it he tried to show the influence of circumstances upon people. He did it with, in the words of *Photoplay*, an "unrelenting realism that makes each incident seem inevitable."

So frank and sympathetic is the characterization of the girl that one reviewer exclaimed, "Any fifteen-year-old child who appreciates it should be taken home and spanked." The film's implications regarding marriage are likewise unconventional. At one time, for instance, Marie tells her lover she would like a home and babies. Pierre goes to the window and points out, in the street, a passing family: a mother slapping a child, the father carrying a heavy burden, and two more children trailing behind.

Generally praised as an outstanding film, *A Woman of Paris* was said to have inspired Lubitsch's *The Marriage Circle* and, through that, dozens of other films. Many of Chaplin's supporters, however, were shocked; they could not reconcile the comedian with "such serious stuff." James R. Quirk summed up their doubts when he wrote: [13]

Dear Mr. Chaplin: Please make more comedies. . . . Why should you enter into competition with the DeMilles, the Neilans, the Griffiths, the Niblos and the others? . . . Be yourself.

Chaplin never did repeat this venture into straight dramatic subject matter. Two years later he returned to comedy again with his celebrated *The Gold Rush* (1925).

This movie was made during a rising national prosperity, and the title was a gentle jibe at the money-madness of the nation. The story was also an autobiographical picture of Chaplin himself. It showed that wealth is illusion; that the happy moments of life are those of anticipation. (Extremely wealthy now, was Chaplin giving us an insight into his own feelings?) At the moment of striking it rich, the little prospector finds himself suddenly and completely alone. (Was there some resemblance here to Chaplin's own life?) When the prospector thinks the most beautiful girl in the world is beckoning to him, his face lights up with ecstasy, and when he realizes that she is summoning someone else, another illusion is shattered. In his happy anticipation of the arrival of his beloved at his party, he impales two rolls on forks and makes them dance:

[13] *Photoplay*, September 1923.

a ritual of joy. When his guest does not come, the bottom of his world again drops out. (Another instance of his frustrations in real life?) This scene, like the one in which he delicately eats his own boots, droll though it is, has an undercurrent of sorrow so strong that it is hard to dissociate the film from the real Chaplin whose early life had been hard and who had at last achieved riches. The cabin teetering on the edge of the abyss was another incomparable moment of satirical fantasy springing from deep experience of the real world.

Three years later, when America was rushing on to vainglorious heights of overproduction, overinflation, and overostentation, Chaplin made *The Circus* (1928). Here he reverted to the fluttering, elusive figure of the pre-Kid days. Again the wanderer, penniless, he comes upon a circus and gets his first meal at the hands of a baby hanging over the shoulders of the unsuspecting parent. He stumbles into a conjuror's tent and, like Pandora, lets loose the furies—birds, rabbits, pigs, geese, balloons, and what not, and then, with a dismay and pathos that make the scene unforgettable, tries to put things right again. His acrobatic ability is given ample play: mistaken for a pickpocket, he is chased by the police and frightened by a donkey into the big top, where his unintentional antics save the circus's prestige.

At the end of the picture all the clowning and gags are resolved into a mood only Chaplin could create. The circus wagons have gone, taking along with them the girl whom he had given up to his rival, the tight-rope walker. Charlie is sitting alone, brooding on his sacrifice; at his feet in a ring of sawdust are the remains of the clown's motley with a star on it—an empty reminder of his dream. Across his face passes a look so sad that it is almost unbearable to watch. Then, with another gesture which erases his sorrow, he is off, a tragicomic figure destined to loneliness.

Though *The Circus* added nothing to Chaplin's reputation, it was complete and unified, and contained the essence of his remarkable qualities.

Then came the "talkies" and the depression.

In the midst of all sorts of rumors and surmises as to Chaplin's future under the new movie form, he began work on the silent film with sound synchronization which appeared in 1931, *City Lights*. To *Silver Screen* magazine Chaplin had disclosed his belief that, though the talkies were having a tremendous vogue, their popularity was waning. He appeared in *City Lights* as mute as ever but surrounded by sounds—the talking of others and even, at times, sounds made by himself.

Of first importance in this film were, not Chaplin and the sound-film form, but Chaplin and what he had to say about the changed times. The theme of *City Lights* was basically a variation on what he had expressed before: protest against the crushing of the individual by social forces. But it gained added significance under the circumstances of a world-wide depression. The film opens with an elaborate scene of the unveiling of a statue of "Peace and Prosperity." As the veil is withdrawn, in the lap of the central figure one sees a tramp in blissful slumber, as if in ironic answer to all those contemporary prophets who kept reiterating that prosperity was around the corner. Later the tramp attempts to save a drunk (a broker) from committing suicide in the Thames, only to have himself almost drowned instead. The moment when Chaplin slaps his little chest and exhorts the bigger man to be brave and perk up was Chaplin's message to the nation.

Whatever Chaplin touched became alive with meaning. With the drunk he enters a night club. The instant they are seated, a waiter hands them a menu card, and Charlie and his companion rise as if to sing hymns in a Bowery mission. The broker mistakes for a shirt the napkin Charlie has tucked into his trousers. The broker thrusts the napkin deeper into Charlie's trousers, turning him around to make certain his rear is protected.

The usual Chaplin pathos occurs in the tender and pure relationship between the sympathetic tramp and the sightless girl. These sequences are built up with extremely delicate nuances of feeling; the spectator is constantly amazed at the extraordinary depth of Charlie's emotions, especially in the final scene. Here Chaplin passes the flower shop of the blind girl, now (through Charlie's generosity) cured of her affliction. He stares at her fearfully, hoping against hope that she will not recognize in this tramp her benefactor. Without knowing who he is, she pityingly gives him a flower, then jokingly a coin with which to pay for it. As she takes back the coin—Charlie hardly dares to breathe—she recognizes the familiar touch of his hand. Her eyes turn toward him in sudden bewilderment. And now is the climax: a close-up of Charlie. His face is marked by suffering of such intensity as to make the suspense agonizing. All the pathos of his intense feeling is spoken in that look.

Because Chaplin himself wrote the score for *City Lights*, much in the way of musical effects was anticipated. As it turned out, the musical accompaniment was far from the picture's strongest feature. There were several moments, however, when sound effects were satirically used. During the dedication of the statue, the bombast of the orators is rendered not in words but in ludicrous inarticulate sounds—Chaplin's witty commentary on the whole silly procedure. Later on in the film Chaplin swallows a whistle at a party. Every time he hiccoughs the whistle blows; the sound is taken up by cabs and then a pack of dogs. Such clever use of a "sound gag" was a typical instance of Chaplin's ingenuity.

City Lights was the product of three years of sporadic but concentrated effort. As with all his pictures, the emphasis lay in what Chaplin had to say and not in cinematic effects. Gilbert Seldes [14] described the film as "one of his masterpieces . . . it is a completely organized and completely created whole. . . ."

Chaplin's next film, *Modern Times* (1936), his last to date, revealed his sharp awareness of present-day conditions, as its preface indicated: "*Modern Times* is a story of industry, of individual enterprise, of human crusading in pursuit of happiness." In the prologue one sees a herd of sheep in a runway being led to slaughter, and then follows a parallel shot of a mass of workers emerging from a subway and going into a factory. Though the symbol was a cliché and was formally divorced from the film as a whole, it nevertheless presented the theme of Charlie's protest. That theme had been his since he left Sennett, and in view of the troubled times it took on fresh and sharp meaning.

Modern Times presented the shifting background of modern life: the factory, the streets, the jail, the waterfront, the hospital, Hoover-

[14] *The New Republic*, February 25, 1931.

ville, department stores, and cabarets. Its story attempted to show that suffering is caused not by individuals representing social forces but by the system itself. Chaplin, a worker in a factory which has been depersonalized by the machines and the belt system, goes mad from his monotonous and regimented job. Fleeing from the factory, he goes through one adventure after another, each time being robbed of another illusion, until at the very end he faces life in complete uncertainty and helplessness.

What *Modern Times* revealed perhaps more than anything else was the confusion of a pre-war person in a 1936 world. Events had moved too rapidly for most people. Chaplin the worker sees no relation between himself and other workers. He gets into a strike demonstration by mistake and, with no awareness of what it means, is borne forward with it helplessly. The speed-up in mass production, the use of cold television to transmit the commands of the industrial magnate, the constraint and domination of human beings by mechanical processes—as in Chaplin's terrifying encounter with the mechanical feeder and his fellow-worker's imprisonment among the rollers of a great machine—these incidents are eloquent embodiments of Chaplin's social criticism. The world has become a place of speed-ups, unemployment, starvation, riots, oppression. Even the burglars Charlie meets in jail turn out to be merely fellow-workers grown hungry. The romantic, anarchistic, earlier Chaplin, who sought beauty, peace, and enough freedom to do as he pleases, thus becomes a more concerned Chaplin, a man crazed by machinery, a bewildered job-seeker whose search is now for security.

The film has meant many different things to different people. Charmion von Weigand [15] aptly declared that *Modern Times* "has registered with the accuracy of a seismograph the confusion in the world today and particularly the confusion in the minds of the middle classes." The English film critic Ivor Montagu, pointed out [16] that it was banned by the Fascists:

The Mussolini who awarded Flaherty a gold medal, the Goebbels who declared the Aryan fairy-man, living in a vacuum in respect

15 *New Theatre Magazine*, March 1936.
16 *World Film News*, March 1936.

to his fellows and pretending the sea was his only enemy, . . . these know on which side of the barricades stands Charlie in *Modern Times*.

Whatever its technical weaknesses, the film proved that Chaplin does not become outdated so long as he retains his social awareness and purpose.

Today, in a post-Munich world arming madly, Chaplin has sent out a publicity release announcing that he is starting a film called *The Dictator*. Could any subject be more timely, more revelatory of his feelings about the modern world?

Chaplin stands out as perhaps the one unforgettable actor of the screen, the symbol of human struggle against regimentation and, now more than ever, for the rights of the individual.

Beginning as a slap-about comedian he has made himself a symbol of the spirit of the common man, readily recognized wherever mankind gathers—a humble and pathetic figure in search of beauty, the butt of jests, harassed by poverty, the law, and social forces that he can neither understand nor resist. He is the contemporary Don Quixote, venturing forth in a bewildering world to set things right single-handed, to take up the gauntlet for chivalry, honesty, beauty, and truth. The little tragicomedian is perhaps "destined by his genius," in the words of Gilbert Seldes,[17] "to be the one universal man of modern times."

[17] *The Movies Come from America*, p. 37.

XIV

MOVIES IN THE WORLD WAR

THE critical war period proved motion pictures to be one of the most powerful social agencies of modern times, especially when mobilized officially as a propaganda tool. Films of these years present a vivid and lively picture of American opinion changing from tolerance to intolerance, from progressivism to reaction, from pacifism to militarism. Not only did they reflect the rising war spirit, but they were used to intensify it, to "sell" the public on participation in the world conflict.

The outbreak of war in Europe in 1914 startled and shocked a peace-minded America. The growth of pacifistic sentiment in the United States in the preceding years had been phenomenal in speed and vigor. In 1906 Andrew Carnegie had given ten million dollars for the establishment of the New York Peace Society; in 1911 wealthy Edwin Ginn had endowed the World Peace Foundation; in 1912 the American Peace Society—the first of its kind in the world—had been revitalized. The ideal of pacifism had been carried into religious quarters by the Church Peace League. Business circles had been similarly influenced by the National Association of Cosmopolitan Clubs—the organization that was later to sail for Europe in Henry Ford's historic Peace Ship.

Despite this ascendancy of pacifism in America, pro-war sentiment began growing rapidly soon after the outbreak of war in Europe. Until now united in a firm anti-war stand, the nation found itself suddenly divided by conflicting opinions. Partisan and opposition groups hurled accusations at one another, and pacifist ideology split into a hundred inconsistent variations. In President

Woodrow Wilson the American people saw a staunch advocate of peace, and most of them for a time rallied around his neutrality policy. But during the next two years that policy was undermined. Regarded with mounting disfavor, it was finally abandoned for outright pro-war demonstrations. The transition from peaceful idealism to the violent war passion in two short years culminated, in 1917, with the entrance of the United States into the World War on the side of the Allies. Nowhere is that transition revealed more patently than in the newly found language of movies.

At the beginning of the conflict in 1914 the American movie industry was poorly prepared to act as a war-news agency for the nation. Within two months' time, however, hundreds of appropriate political and military films were ready for public showing. At first, to meet the emergency, old newsreels of military maneuvers and parades; views of Berlin, Paris, and St. Petersburg; and pictures of the Kaiser, King Albert, Franz Josef, Woodrow Wilson, Theodore Roosevelt, Taft, Poincaré, and Nicholas of Russia, were shown at random. All the nations involved in the war had equal attention on the screen and were applauded in accordance with the President's neutrality proclamation, which urged people to maintain a nonpartisan attitude. Germans were represented, on the whole, without undue animosity. The United States even imported German films that presented the German side of the war: *The Cruise of the M, The Log of U-35, Behind the German Lines. The German Side of the War*, in particular, attracted audiences of thousands. All these films were shown in American theatres as late as 1916. The tendency to sympathize with England and the other Allies, however, was apparent in the titles of otherwise objective newsreel compilations: *The Battling British, The Kaiser Challenges, The Great War in Europe, Germania, England's Menace*. The general public's attitude toward the European struggle was summed up best, perhaps, in the title of the picture *War Is Hell*.

Neutrality and pacifistic sentiment were further indicated in most of the war dramas which movie producers began to turn out as rapidly as possible. The war drama *Neutrality* pointed the lesson that in a neutral country one should be neutral. The story showed how a Frenchman and German now in the United States remained friends, despite the antagonism of their now fighting fatherlands. It did not attempt to paint the German character as villainous; rather it attempted to ease the mounting friction among the various nationalities represented in the United States.

Strong preachments against war, consistent with the public's attitude, emphasized again and again, in the spectacular style of the day, war's futility, destructiveness, and tragedy. *Civilization, or He Who Returned*, one of the outstanding pictures of the day, directed by Thomas Ince, preached peace in the lofty terms characteristic of Wilsonian idealism. In this picture the spirit of Christ returns to earth in the body of a great soldier who, insulted and persecuted while trying to restore the world to peace, finally triumphs. The film attempted a profound interpretation of the grim disaster—the bereavements, disunions, tragedies—caused by war. It was said to have helped to re-elect Wilson on his platform, "He kept us out of war."

War Brides, a distinguished film directed by Herbert Brenon, was another anti-war production which purported to show the unwillingness of the German people at large to participate in war, although the reference to Germany was veiled. The story was both strikingly conceived and strikingly executed.[1] Joan (Alla Nazimova), a vigorous young woman, begins to question the sufferings of her fellow workers in a factory town, "underpaid and overworked." Arousing them to strike, she leads them to victory and thus gains the confidence and leadership of the town. She falls in love with a farmer and marries him.

Then war is declared. Her husband goes to the front and, with his three younger brothers, is killed. The king of the country soon decrees that men shall marry all the available single girls and produce more offspring. (The girls who marry under the decree are the "war brides.") Now pregnant, Joan foresees the fate of her child in future wars, and decides to try to win over the women and stop the present war. As her campaign becomes more effective, Joan is arrested, but since she is the expectant mother of a soldier she cannot be executed. She escapes from prison and organizes the women to demonstrate before the king on his return from the front

[1] It is described fully in *Photoplay*, 1916.

to his palace. Robed in black, contrary to the law, the women greet him with anti-war chants. The king tells Joan that there will always be war. Thereupon Joan, with the shout "No more children for war!", shoots herself. The women take up her body, hold it aloft as a symbol, and with renewed courage determine to carry on their campaign.

Exceedingly well received when shown, *War Brides* was suppressed upon our entrance into the World War on the grounds that "the philosophy of this picture is so easily misunderstood by unthinking people that it has been found necessary to withdraw it from circulation for the duration of the war."

Unlike *Civilization* and *War Brides*, the pacifistic film *Intolerance*, conceived and made at a time when the national viewpoint was predominantly peace-minded, appeared at the flood of the tide of preparedness and pro-war films. Because it was perhaps the strongest outcry against the forces that lead to war, the very forces that were then being used to whip the nation into the war spirit, the film was nationally condemned and religiously boycotted. Being out of step with changed public opinion, *Intolerance* was so great a failure financially that it led to the wrecking of Griffith's (its director-producer's) career. If *Intolerance* had been released six months earlier, it would no doubt have been passionately acclaimed.

Pro-war agitation rapidly mounted despite government disapproval. Preparedness, regarded dubiously by the populace, was soon being earnestly urged by many groups. Its outstanding advocate in the movie industry was J. Stuart Blackton, always a pronounced nationalist. An old hand at patriotic propaganda, he now made some of the first flaming pro-war films: *The Battle Cry of Peace, Wake up America!, Womanhood, The Glory of the Nation.*

Of *The Battle Cry of Peace* Blackton himself said: [2]

It was propaganda for the United States to enter the war. It was made deliberately for that purpose. It was against the administration because at that time Mr. Wilson was arguing for neutrality and peace, and talking about being too proud to fight. But nevertheless *The Battle Cry of Peace* went out as a call to arms. It had collaterally associated with it Theodore Roosevelt. I lived next door to him

[2] In a lecture at the University of Southern California, February 20, 1929.

at Oyster Bay, New York . . . he and I were very good friends. We worked out a very splendid idea. We had the Army, Navy, Church and State, represented in that picture. . . . Roosevelt said, "When you have the Army, Navy, Church and State, you don't want anything else." Mr. Roosevelt would not get into the picture.

The film, based on Hudson Maxim's *Defenseless America*, emphasized an armament program for America as the only means of maintaining peace. Its treatment set the style for all future anti-German propaganda dramas. "Huns" were portrayed as leering, mustached, lustful scoundrels whose only instincts were those of rape and plunder. So incendiary was the film that Henry Ford wrathfully denounced it in full-page newspaper advertisements, pointing out that Maxim's munitions-corporation stock was on the market and that the film was merely a ruse to promote his and other war merchants' profit. But fewer people read the advertisements than saw the film. Preparedness, moreover, had become deeply instilled by this time in the national mind. In October 1916 a reader sent in the following comment to *Film Pictorial:* "Every American including Henry Ford should see *The Battle Cry of Peace.* . . . We would better be up and doing, or it will be too late. . . ."

Preparedness and pro-war sentiment, supported by Blackton, began to supersede the pacifistic and neutral attitude for which Wilson stood. Nationalist zeal was stimulated by picture slides issued by the New York Mayor's Committee in National Defense. The committee's chairman, Jesse Lasky, one of the leading producers in the movie industry, declared: "If you are an American, you should be proud to say so." More and more movie producers settled down to serving the new cause of militarism and nationalism.

Pro-war and preparedness propaganda was now subtly and astutely injected into satires, comedies, dramas, romances. *In-Again, Out-Again* jibed at the pacifist-minded sweetheart of a preparedness hero, and finally exposed the leading "pacifist" as a manufacturer of explosives. A baby-food factory was shown canning shrapnel, a wheat shreddery loading high explosives, a pill foundry making mines. In *A Man Without a Country* a pacifist was persuaded to become a recruit. *Motherhood* was eloquently summarized by a reviewer of the day as "a smug, diabetic preachment of American insular security. . . . All I can say is that it will be a mournful sugar plum for pacifists in hiding."

Battling for one's country, espionage, and other war activities were glorified and romanticized in *The Wall Between*, *Shell 42*, *The Flying Torpedo*, *On Dangerous Ground*, and *The Fall of the Nation*. How evident the strategy of the movie propagandists was, is apparent in the lengthy protest that appeared in *Motion Picture Magazine* in February 1916:

Strangely enough, these pictures have not presented to our view the actual proof of the toll of war. They have not shown us the millions of widows and the millions of orphans that are the results of this conflict. They have not proved to us the hopelessness, the despair, the hunger and suffering that have been inevitable consequences of the War. And—having failed to present these consequences . . .—these pictures have not been logical arguments in favor of Peace. They have been military—they have been martial in the extreme. . . .

Public opinion, however, was being quickly heated to a fighting temper. Anglophiles multiplied; sympathy for the Allies became the fashion. Leaders in the movement for international peace, heretofore respected as humanitarians, were regarded with increasing distrust and contempt by the man in the street. Popular emotions began to be rallied for America's participation in the War. With such noble phrases as a "war to end all wars" and "make the world safe for democracy," President Wilson finally asked Congress to take sides against Germany. The Carnegie Peace Foundation led the way for other peace organizations by announcing in the words of Charles and Mary Beard,[3] that "it could serve the ideal of its founders best by lending all its strength to the persecution of the armed conflict to a triumphant conclusion."

When the United States declared war officially on Friday, April 5, 1917, the transition from mere anti-pacifism to out-and-out prowar passion was already complete. As soon as war was declared, pacifists, socialists, Germans, and unionists became suspects. Refusal to salute the flag became cause enough for imprisonment and persecution. Mrs. Carrie Chapman Catt, the feminist leader, condemned

[3] *The Rise of American Civilization*, p. 537.

Representative Jeanette Rankin's lone vote against war as an un-patriotic stand not to be countenanced by the women of the nation. Spy scares filled the news hourly. War posters, parades, war tunes, flag waving, and singing of the national anthem on all occasions sold super-patriotism to the people and kept their excitement at fever heat. The moving pictures were immediately conscripted along with other social agencies.

Peace pictures were placed under a government ban; all anti-war films became so much junk. Movie companies zealously produced pictures in key with the emotional necessities of a warring nation and, like newspapers and other organs of propaganda, distorted, omitted, or deliberately misrepresented facts for the sake of imme-diate ends.

The Committee on Public Information, a federal organization with George Creel as chairman, created a Division of Films to sell the war to America. Two days after the war declaration, posters, slides, and slogans filled the screens. Four patriotic dramas were produced by the Division in quick succession: *Pershing's Crusaders*, *America's Answer*, *Under Four Flags*, *The Official War Review*. The Exhibitors' Branch of the National Association of the Motion Picture Industry, organized in peace times by William A. Brady, was appointed by President Wilson to organize the private pro-ducers as a fighting arm of the government. In New York City a newly organized bureau of motion pictures produced two feature pictures for recruiting purposes, showing mobilization and the life and problems of the army and navy. Fourteen sets of slides were released at once to be used daily until pictures were ready.

Motion picture theatres became centers for patriotic rallies. The populace was urged to attend; the war tax on admission prices was explained as a chance for every citizen to do his bit. The movie, a quick and vital means of communication between the government and the people, became the traveling salesman for war and war discipline. It imparted the latest "news," taught citizens how to help, shamed "slackers" and encouraged recruiting, and glorified fighting for one's country, loyalty to an ideal, heroism, and sacrifices for a great and noble cause.

The financing of the war was aided by films promoting the sale of Liberty Bonds throughout the nation. A "trailer" distributed to nearly all theatres showed President Wilson dictating his Buy-Liberty-Bonds message to the American people. Adolph Zukor lent a helping hand by distributing 70,000 slides and 500,000 feet of film which appealed for public support of the bond issue. *Sic 'Em Sam* typified the general appeal of the movies to the fighting instincts of audiences.

In teaching war discipline and war organization to citizens the motion picture was remarkably effective. Slides, shorts, and "picturettes," featuring popular favorites such as Marguerite Clark, Mabel Normand, and Elsie Ferguson, pleaded on behalf of the U. S. Food Administration for "economy for democracy." The Red Cross also found movies a lucrative means of arousing support. Hundreds of Red Cross "trailers," including *The Spirit of the Red Cross*, by James Montgomery Flagg, were displayed everywhere.

Screen players, "symbols" of American manhood and womanhood, stepped down from their pedestals to lead in the mobilization of patriotic activity. They co-operated in Red Cross drives, exhorted audiences to be loyal, became "minute men," soldiers, or nurses, and appeared on the screen to urge people to buy government bonds. Fan magazines on page after page displayed photographs of the public's favorites in uniform, buying Liberty Bonds, knitting for "the boys Over There," and training as Red Cross nurses. "Fatty" Arbuckle, in the peculiar position of having to apologize for his fatness in view of the food-conservation drive, was shown holding out his trousers to indicate how much weight he was losing in doing his bit. At a tremendous patriotic rally of motion picture people, Cecil B. DeMille was master of ceremonies, and Dustin Farnum, in uniform, passed the hat. William S. Hart, Douglas Fairbanks, and Mary Pickford were a few among many movie notables who made speeches and cross-country tours in support of Liberty Loan drives.

Having seen their sons go overseas to battle and die, movie-goers in time began to feel hostile toward prominent screen actors who stayed safe at home. Some bad public feeling was excited when J. Warren Kerrigan, answering demands that he enlist, declared that the world needed his art now more than ever. People reacted cynically; criticisms were hurled at him. Movie producers rushed to close the breach, explaining that many of the stars who appeared extremely youthful on the screen were, in reality, closer to thirty-five than to twenty-five years of age, and therefore had sound reasons for not enlisting. They assured the public that when the government was in need of them, these men would wholeheartedly do their duty. At the same time the producers pointed out that movies generally were valuable for entertainment in the camps, and that movie actresses were the sweethearts and inspirations of countless soldiers.

D. W. Griffith and Herbert Brenon were both invited to make authentic movies of the war at the front. *Intolerance* having brought down international condemnation on his head, Griffith reversed his pacifistic stand and accepted the invitation. Fan magazines now pictured him in full uniform in the trenches. The film he made abroad, *Hearts of the World*, showed German militarism as a frightful threat to civilization and demanded that it be wiped from the face of the earth.

Very little of the war "news" was authentic. Exhibitors did not hesitate to prepare war bulletins which they assumed approximated the situation abroad: these bulletins always represented the Allies as winning, and thus kept up public morale. Nationalism was inspired by glowing tributes to the American heritage, as in *The Settlement of America, Independence, World Recognition, American Achievements*. Flag waving and super-patriotism marked such films as *My Own United States, The Great Love*, and *Patria*. The last, a serial made by William Randolph Hearst, glorified not only American womanhood in the person of Irene Castle, but the Du Pont family, munitions makers. The government ordered its anti-Japanese sentiment to be deleted, since Japan was now an ally of England.

Sympathy for the Allies was intensified by films about England and France. *The Victoria Cross, Whom the Gods Destroy, An Enemy of the King*, and *Heroism of a Spy* romantically praised the Englishman and his history. *Joan the Woman* spectacularly pointed out that it was the inherited duty of Anglo-Saxons to aid France and thus expiate their part in the killing of France's savior, Joan of Arc, centuries before. *Hearts of the World, Somewhere in France,*

Daughter of France, *The Belgian*, and *For France* (which *Wids*, the trade paper, said "shows too many men being killed to please American families today") idealized France and kept the flame of kinship burning. French-produced films, such as the famous Sarah Bernhardt plea, *Mothers of France*, supported American pro-French propaganda.

While England, France, and even Russia were depicted as heroic and godly nations, Germany was painted utterly black, without a saving grace. Atrocity films that rivaled newspaper headlines in sensationalism stigmatized the whole German nation as a mass of "Kaisers." No longer was it necessary, as it had been until the declaration of war, to veil the identity of the Opposing Power. "The ruthless monarch" was now revealed as the Kaiser, "the military nation" as Germany. In the fashion established by Blackton, the "Huns" were characterized as brutal, barbaric, shameless. Nothing was too savage and uncivilized for "these primitive beasts."

A Daughter of France, *War and Woman*, *A Maid of France*, and *The Little American* were only a few of the many films in which raping, pillaging, village-burning by the Germans were featured. In *The Little American*, Mary Pickford, America's symbol of sweetness and innocence, is saved at the eleventh hour from a fate worse than death at the hands of barbaric Huns. A French spy arrested by the Germans, she demands an explanation of their savage action in raping a fellow-prisoner. The Prussian colonel, with a sneer under his waxed mustache, tells her that "My men must have relaxation."

Photoplay, reviewing *For France*, declared: [4]

There is, of course, pillaging of the farmhouse and the terrorization of people by the Hun horde—and such applause as burst forth spontaneously when the leading Hun offenders were shot! . . . *For France* means for our own homes and fire-sides.

The Kaiser became the symbol of hatefulness for the whole nation. No epithet was too vile for him. Pictures were titled *The Kaiser, Beast of Berlin*; *To Hell with the Kaiser*; *The Prussian Cur*. Charlie Chaplin in *Shoulder Arms* heaped ridicule upon this arch villain of the world. Particularly notable for its picture of the Ger-

[4] January 1918.

man ruler was *The Kaiser, Beast of Berlin,* advertised as "giving an insight into the man guiding the most horrible outrages." Rupert Julian, hated villain of the screen, portrayed the Kaiser as the "enemy of world progress," weak, insane, arrogant, and colossally conceited. He was nationally greeted with spontaneous and hearty hissing. Americans were thus conditioned to pour all their aroused spleen into one stream. In their minds the Kaiser was mercilessly burned at the stake, and the heat and light concealed, at least for a time, other possible objects of hate behind the blaze.

Other films were designed to provoke Americans to seek vengeance. *Till I Come Back to You* urged the punishment of Germany for the Belgian "atrocities." *Lest We Forget* showed the heroine defying Prussianism and preaching vengeance. Germany had to be chastised also for her designs on America, as was made clear in *Inside the Lines, The Spy, Daughter of Destiny,* and *Joan of Plattsburg.*

Perhaps the most powerful vehicles of hatred were the allegedly authentic newsreels of German cruelty. One of the most sensational of these films was *My Four Years in Germany,* based on Ambassador James Gerard's book. Supposed to be the camera record of a tour through German prison camps and courts, it pointed out that Germans now in America had the same reason for fighting their fatherland that the rest of the world had: namely, to stamp out Prussian cruelty.

The German Curse in Russia, advertised as the "inside facts" on the revolution in Russia, aroused Americans further by showing that German "lies," if given the chance to breed here, might do to America what they had done to Russia: "The world believes Russia sold out her Allies knowingly, but my camera will show that it was the German propaganda of lies that undermined this great country. . . ."

Another film dealing with the Kaiser's evil plots against America was *The Evil Eye,* compiled by William J. Flynn, Chief of the U. S. Secret Service, which showed the defensive secret warfare being waged by the government at home.

Anti-German sentiment was pitched so high that soon everything and everyone with a tincture of the Germanic were despised. So strong was this passion that Gustav von Seyffertitz, a leading player of the screen, was forced to change his professional name. According to the publicity, he had "a perfect right" to his new name, C. Butler Clonebaught, as "it belonged to his mother." But other complications created by the anti-German fashion were not so easily coped with. The greatest task was that of convincing millions of people of German extraction, now living peacefully in America, that Germany was no longer the home of friends. German-Americans had to be "educated" to hate their German relatives, to despise German culture, to be passionately loyal to their new country. *The Immigrant*, a government-made picture, taught the Americanized German-born that they owed first allegiance to the United States and must salute the Stars and Stripes.

To inspire and stimulate patriotism, films varied from plain recruiting advertisements, as in *The Spirit of '17*, *Vive la France*, *Over There*, *A Call to Arms*, and *Draft 258*, to dramas shaming the slacker, as in *The Man Who Was Afraid*, *The Slacker* (in a potpourri of American history containing tableaux of Paul Revere, Lee's surrender, Abraham Lincoln, and Nathan Hale), *The Unbeliever*, and *A Man Without a Country*.

The recruiting of women in a moral sense was just as vital as enlisting men in the army or navy. Such films as *Sweetheart of the Doomed*, *Missing*, *An Alien Enemy*, *Womanhood*, *Daughter of Destiny*, and *Betsy Ross* praised woman's heroism, bravery, loyalty, and sacrifice. Women and young girls were taught to smile and sing at home while their loved ones carried out their duty at the front. In DeMille's spectacle *Joan the Woman*, Geraldine Farrar inspired feminine militarist sentiment as Joan of Arc. This film, with its panorama of war scenes and dream effects, ritual-like in their presentation, aroused patriotism through its appeal to the richest emotional sources: love and religion.

Another film, *The Whispering Chorus*, employed the Enoch Arden theme to exploit "the religious teaching of loyalty to principle and duty as well as to flag and country." *We Can't Have Everything*, dealing with "the restless spirit of the times," advocated self-denial and self-sacrifice as ways to win the war. Like other films, this one urged women in particular to give freely, to sacrifice heroically, not to mind the tragedy of losing a son, to be brave "Gold Star mothers."

The common stay-at-home man was proved to be extremely important to the nation. *Berlin Via America* showed an unknown citizen heroically risking his life by posing as a traitor in order to make a triumphant raid on Berlin possible. *The Gown of Destiny* revealed how the poor man could be as valuable to his country as the rich man who, in exemplary fashion, celebrated his wedding anniversary by giving three ambulances to France. Mr. and Mrs. Sidney Drew in *The Patriot* comically showed how Henry and his wife decided to out-Hoover Hoover in conserving food. *For Freedom of the World*, an eighty-five minute film on doing one's bit, covered about every possible angle of patriotism. A mother gives up her son; a father leaves his child; a husband bids farewell to his wife; a slacker is converted. Enlistment, trench life, Red Cross work, and Over the Top are all exploited as themes, and an aphasia victim is cured upon seeing the American flag. In such films no avenue of appeal to human emotions was neglected.

One of the noblest reasons for America's prosecution of the war was that this was not only "a war to end all wars," but "a sacrifice for the democratization of the world." Again and again pictures showed that in the trenches all classes were leveled; the rich man's son and the poor man's son fought shoulder to shoulder. *Safe for Democracy, The Pride of New York*, and *The Battle Cry of Liberty* predicted that a wonderful sociological melioration would result from the war, that the benefits of the people's struggles and sacrifices were to be shared by everyone regardless of class and wealth, that all together were now bettering the world.

The American flag was waved on the slightest provocation. So often was it waved without apparent reason, except perhaps to lend dignity to worthless photoplays, that movie-goers in time criticized needless displays of the flag as in bad taste and insulting to the flag itself. Although such criticism was open and vigorous, the flag waving continued.

Battle scenes of every description abounded in films. Movie-goers were insatiably interested in them, perhaps because every individual, through his soldier relatives or friends, was personally concerned.

Bloody, frightful engagements in the trenches and in No Man's Land were exhibited by the thousands, and apparently the more the public saw of such films, the more they wanted to see them. Pictures were terrifying in their depiction of mysterious gases destroying cities and helpless human beings. Airplanes, machine guns, submarines, and other modern war instruments were represented with more regard for effect than for truth.

War pictures conventionally ended with the soldier boy safe behind the firing line in France. When one picture, *The Slacker*, did not follow the usual pattern, *Photoplay* (its critical faculties not altogether impaired by propaganda) commented: [5]

Mr. Cabanne [the director] had the self-restraint to send the soldier boy off to war and end the picture there instead of Inceing and Blacktoning through a reel of smoke and horror to an amorous half nelson. . . .

The movies became a sort of military textbook in which those at home could follow their sons' and brothers' experiences in the training camps. To reinforce the psychological effects of such popular songs as "Keep the Home Fires Burning," "Over There," "Smile a While," "A Baby's Prayer at Twilight," "My Buddy Lies over the Ocean," the screen showed loyal kisses, courageous good-bys and "home stuff," hospital pictures, German prisoners being brought in, and the ambulance boys at work.

In the Allied countries, no less than in the United States, pictures proved of incalculable help to the governments. Not only did they bolster public morale, but they proved valuable emotional safety valves. *Photoplay* editorialized,[6]

The reports of Mr. Hoover and his aides and successors in Belgium tell us that no matter how destitute a district, or how utterly dependent on funds from America, a portion of every family's pittance was put aside for the beloved cinema, and the oppressed Belgians went out of their troubles by going through the screen to other lands.

At the front movies were also a salve and inspiration for the fighting soldiers. Ninety feet under shell-torn Verdun crude theatres were reported to have been constructed for the army. Projector operators, exchange men, and necessary mechanical equipment for first-class moving-picture presentations were provided by both army and navy.

Army cantonments—cities with an average of 40,000 population—had theatres of their own built. It was advertised that one of the many advantages soldiers enjoyed was their exemption from paying any war tax. To relieve them of the five- or ten-cent admission price, "smileage" was invented. This was a system whereby railway mileage books, sent as gifts to soldiers, were accepted as tickets of admissions.

Ernest A. Dench in *Motion Pictures* [7] reported,

As is perhaps natural, comedy is the thing, for the soldier wants his thoughts to be taken away from the serious work ahead of him. . . . If a soldier has survived a big battle he will say, "I was in the picture show at Ypres."

One of the greatest favorites was Charlie Chaplin. Young English subalterns with a sense of humor cultivated his characteristic mustache, and cut-outs of Charlie were set up as mascots. Even the movie companies were represented appreciatively. Dugouts were named after movie trade-marks, as Keystone Kottage and Vitagraph Village.

Movies proved enormously helpful in hospitals, also. Nicknamed "The Soul Doctor," they relieved the monotony of hospital existence and helped the wounded to forget their misery. Often the pictures were projected on the ceilings so that prostrate sufferers could watch them.

American films thus carried the banner of "victory for democracy" into all the corners of the Allied countries, and helped to relieve the stress of the times wherever shown. The motion picture industry was not unaware of its powerful role in the war. Louella O. Parsons summarized that role: [8]

If German vandalism could reach overseas, the Kaiser would order every moving picture studio crushed to dust and every

[7] October 1916.   [8] *Photoplay*, September 1918.

theatre blown to atoms. There has been no more effective ammunition aimed at the Prussian empire than these pictures of German
atrocities. . . . The followers of the cinema have seen with their
own eyes how German militarism is waged against civilization. They
have seen the rape of Belgium, the devastation of France and the
evil designs against America. . . . And while these films have been
raising the temperature of the Allies' patriotism to a blood heat,
Germany has been gnashing its teeth.

Astonishingly effective for so young a medium, the movie was
among the most valuable war-time assets the United States government had at its disposal. Conversely, when the armistice was signed,
the motion picture was enlisted in the promotion of international
understanding and goodwill.

But the movies were themselves all but transformed by World
War influences, industrially, socially, artistically. The entire European continent having been drawn into the conflict, American motion pictures had the world to themselves. Hollywood became securely established as the international production center for movies.
Having become recognized as a leading agency for propaganda
and as a remarkable social therapeutic and palliative, the motion
picture was viewed with new and deeper respect. On the other
hand, given a message to deliver to the public, movie makers learned
how to deliver it eloquently and entertainingly.

By the close of 1918 the industry had grown self-assured and
was consciously directing itself as big business putting on the
screens what the populace sought in life. When the war ended,
producers feared that the motion picture's great era was done, but
a greater era was actually about to begin.

XV

GROWING SOPHISTICATION OF FILM CONTENT

TWO important developments occurred during the period 1914-1918 that profoundly influenced the character and implications of motion picture content. One was a change within the industry: the broader and new type of audience; the other was an outside development: the World War. Each carried movie content further in its development; each focused attention on the screen's power as a social agency. Together they quickened the industry to a consciousness of movie content as a social record, as propaganda, and as entertainment for the world. By the close of the war, movie content was being deliberately prepared for its three aims: to portray, to mold, and to divert twentieth-century America.

The moralism and religiousness that had characterized movies of the pre-war period found simple expression in the title of the best-selling novel and play for 1913, 1914, and 1915: *Pollyanna*. A consummation of old ideals, "Pollyanna philosophy" became the dominant note in moving pictures. It was based on the old spiritual axiom that contentment with one's lot makes for real and lasting happiness; that riches and luxuries cannot buy peace of mind, but bring disaster. It was better to be poor than rich because, as movies continued to show, the poor were always loving, kind, true, and full of virtue. The poor mother idolized her children, worked and slaved for them; the father loved the mother and seldom strayed from the happy home. Cheerfulness, optimism, love, and honesty were the essentials of well-being, and one did not need money to have them.

The Pollyanna ideal was personified first and foremost by Mary

Pickford. Her phenomenal success and popularity at this time were due mostly to her engaging spirituality. She captured the hearts of the working-class patrons because she represented them. Her charm, her sweetness, and her golden curls glorified her rags and dirt; Victorian ideals of feminine beauty were implicit in her wide-eyed innocence, her childlike, expressive mouth, her appealing eyes. Clothes, sophistication, and independence were not yet necessities for the film star.

Faithfully acting out her part, America's Sweetheart again and again turned down the rich man to marry the poor but loving beau (*Cinderella, Stella Maris, Hulda from Holland, Amarilly of Clothesline Alley*). The winsome "poor little, rich little, bad little, good little girl" brought sunshine to the world by her everlasting contentment, sweetness, and charm in every situation (*Poor Little Rich Girl, A Little Princess, Such a Little Queen, Tess of the Storm Country, Little Pal, Rags, The Foundling, Hearts Adrift, Rebecca of Sunnybrook Farm, M'liss, Daddy-Long-Legs*). As a poor, hardworking gamin, she found joys and happiness that all the money in the world could not buy.

Among other Pollyanna heroines who swept up to great heights of temporary popularity, perhaps the most prominent were Mary McAllister and Marguerite Clark. Two of their films speak for the rest. *Sadie Goes to Heaven* told the story of a girl who relinquishes the luxuries of a rich mansion rather than desert her dog: "The finale shows her just as happy in her poor surroundings." *Silks and Satins* depicted a young girl who seeks in her grandmother's diary the answer to her problem: marriage for love or for money? The answer she found was that love and contentment make for happiness; money is not necessary.

Gradually the treatment of the Pollyanna gospel changed and it was in this change that the first inkling of a growing movie sophistication appeared. Out-and-out preaching gave way to suggestive examples; obvious morality dramas were discarded for more subtle forms; the old axioms were now disseminated indirectly, by implication and inference. Instead of sympathetically portraying the poor, films turned to disparaging the rich. The well-to-do were depicted as discontented, restless, unfaithful in marriage, and neglect-

ful of the home. Children reared in wealthy homes were characterized as weak, worthless, and cowardly until a hard life regenerated
them. Charles Ray gained his first fame as a weak son of the rich
in a series of Ince's "soul-fight" pictures: *The Coward, The Only
Son, Honor Thy Name, His Father's Son, Like Father Like Son,
Playing the Game*. Such films implied that being poor was something to be thankful for. "Wealth made him a weakling; adversity,
a man."

The increased subtlety with which the Pollyanna philosophy began to be dispensed revealed a growing proficiency in movie expression, but it was in the sudden popularity of an entirely new
star, Theda Bara, that the growing sophistication of the screen was
more clearly indicated. With the rise of Theda Bara, films of un-
sullied love and innocence suddenly were rivaled by pictures of
passion and domestic intrigue. As middle-class patrons became a
more important part of the movie audience, love became a subject
of prime interest, and the "vamp" its first embodiment on the screen.

Valeska Suratt first brought the fascination of sinful love to
movies, but it was Theda Bara who in 1915 made the vamp a new
interest in American life and established sex as a dominant motif
in movies. Selected more or less perfunctorily by Director Frank
Powell to play the main role in the movie of the poem *A Fool
There Was*, being made for William Fox, Theda Bara became a
sensation.

In three years this siren appeared in forty pictures, all following the same pattern. The vamp skillfully sets her trap for a man,
only to be vanquished at the last moment by some outside force.
The outside force is introduced to point the mock moral conclusion that "forbidden paths lead but to the grave" (*The Eternal Sin,
Purgatory's Ivory Angel, Destruction, The Forbidden Path*). Actually the films placed the value of fascination on her transgressions.
Compared to the snake, patron reptile of the human vampire, she
was shown as an irresistible, half-human siren, destroying men's
lives with her wanton wiles (*The Serpent, The Tiger Woman, The
She-Devil*). She became the symbol of the alluring, heartless, coldly
passionate woman who lives only for luxury and sensual enjoyment
(*Cleopatra, Salome, The Eternal Sappho, Gold and the Woman*).

A powerful wave of publicity carried her to prodigious success. In the minds of millions she became the "fascinating and the un-fathomable, whose passion is touched with death." Her staring, sensual face, with exotic, heavy-lidded eyes, was photographed with skull and crossbones and was described as "The wickedest face in the world, dark-brooding, beautiful and heartless." Publicity stories alleged that schoolmates had shunned her in childhood; it had been whispered that she was a witch. Voluptuously swathed in black silks and satins, her white shoulders and arms left bare ("fascina-tion in their icy passion"), the dark cloud of hair encircling her white face ("spelled disaster, at the same time holding a promise of pleasure"), Theda Bara was indeed set up as the embodiment of evil. She brought to the screen a voluptuousness and sophistica-tion not there before. Hers was an impersonation alien and im-possible to the era that had borne Griffith's golden-haired virgins. She presaged the woman of the world, soon to dominate the screen, who frankly admits her desire for and her right to love and luxury.

Making the most of the vamp, movies became rife with triangle situations. Behind all such films was the code—soon to be challenged —that loyalty, faithfulness, and child rearing are natural and manda-tory in the marital relation, and that the solution to all domestic troubles is children. The "finery-loving wife who avoids mother-hood in her desire only for fine clothes and parties" caused disaster. Children brought "sunshine to the home"; they prevented husbands from falling for the wiles of another woman; they dispelled all worries and fears. Significant of the tone of domestic dramas that flooded the screen was the title of one of them—*The Blessed Miracle*.

With the close of the World War and the increasing sophistica-tion of movie audiences, the exaggerated symbolism of Theda Bara lost plausibility. Her vogue waned. But this original vamp had in-troduced to films a type of sensual interest which, later labeled "sex appeal," was to be perpetuated in ever more subtle guises. The new fashion was, perhaps, a reaction against the earlier morality dramas, a reaction the more powerful because the nation was at war.

A third sign of a new sophistication on the screen (and of the new audience) appeared in movie humor. From 1912 to 1916 Mack

Sennett was supreme as the dispenser of laughter. Gradually burlesques, chases, and slapstick were replaced by polite comedy, satires, and farces. Raw, rough-and-tumble clowning was less popular with many audiences than satire, pantomime, and gentle wit. Charles Chaplin, with his subtle social criticism, usurped Sennett's leadership. Combining Keystonery with his own inimitable pantomimic talent he satirized contemporary ideals, the rich, law and order, and soldiering. We have already observed how he pointed to discrepancies and maladjustments in society with a manner that was no less effective because it was funny and popular.

Another new comedy note was introduced by the urban Mr. and Mrs. Sidney Drew, who became leading screen comedians by politely poking fun at the foibles of middle-class domestic life. Their dignified, polite jokes depended on clever subtitles. As one writer expressed it, their stories were communicated by titles "agreeably decorated with photographs of the two interspersed." They were representative Americans—middle-aged, domestically happy, free from financial woes. Never violent, never featuring pie throwing, devoid of stunts, their comedies were light take-offs on such matters as a man's unfamiliarity with the technique of hooking his wife's gown. The titles of some of their films indicate the subject matter: *Duplicity, Cave Man's Bluff, Her Obsession, Crosby's Rest Cure, The Anniversaries, Hypochrondriacs, Henry's Ancestors, The Patriot, As Others See Us, Her First Game, His Deadly Calm*. The popularity of these pictures declined as feature-length comedies became the vogue, and came to an abrupt end with Mr. Drew's sudden death soon after the end of the war.

The quiet and refined humor of the screen lives of Mr. and Mrs. Drew became a pattern for polite drawing-room comedy and has remained with us ever since, being represented today by such teams as Victor Moore and Helen Broderick, or Mary Boland and Charles Ruggles and more recently the "Hardy" and the "Jones" family series. *Photoplay* declared [1] the Drew style to be "a step toward the development of comedy." But Gilbert Seldes insists [2] that "apart from the agreeable manners of Mr. and Mrs. Sidney Drew, nothing

[1] June 1917.　　　　　　　　[2] *The Seven Lively Arts,* p. 20.

Fritz Lang's German-made *Metropolis* (1926),
representative of European post-war stylization
at its best. In his Hollywood efforts Lang was
to abandon stylization for realism but without
relinquishing his flair for dramatic composition.

The satirical court room scene from James Cruze's *The Beggar on Horseback* (1925), treated in the post-war "expressionistic" style of *The Cabinet of Dr. Caligari* for purposes of social ridicule rather than for psychological implications.

made them successful except the corrupt desire, on the part of the spectators, to be refined."

The trend toward refinement was apparent in other short comedies as well. The George Ade, Walt Mason, and Christie films all made fun of rural or bucolic life from a sophisticated viewpoint. *Jed's Trip to the Fair* and *Mr. Jack Inspects Paris* indicate the typical subject matter used. A characteristic bit of humor is the occasion when Mr. Jack "kisses a young lady and then exhales about half a quart of face powder." [3]

Toward the close of the period the *Lonesome Luke* comedies gained popularity, with Harold Lloyd as the nice young man who gets into refined scrapes (*Bashful*, *Clubs Are Trumps*, *Love Laughs Later*, *The Flirt*). The prevalent punning was a further indication that audiences were now more literate.

By 1918 the urbanity of the Drews' short comedies and the small-town humor of the Walt Mason shorts became more pronounced in full-length comedies that paralleled on the screen the "b'gosh" school of humor in literature. Charles Ray, as the bashful, charming, naïve, and boyish country bumpkin who aspired to become a hero, became a leading screen personality, his popularity mounting steadily through 1917 and 1918 to a high peak in 1919. The titles of his pictures speak for the nature of their treatment and subject matter: *The Pinch Hitter*, *The Hired Man*, *The Clodhopper*, *The Village Sleuth*, *His Mother's Boy*, *Sudden Jim*, *Homer Comes Home*, *Crooked Straight*, *An Old-Fashioned Boy*, *Skinner's Dress Suit*. Their humor lay in a polite joshing of the "hick" who secretly longs to be a man of importance and, through a combination of circumstances, turns out to be one.

Concurrent with these comedies were the Fairbanks-Loos-Emerson satires, which ridiculed the reigning American fads with a sophistication unknown on the screen before. *American Aristocracy* burlesqued "bean-can nobility." *In-Again, Out-Again* hilariously satirized pacifism. *His Picture in the Paper* ridiculed the American's love of publicity. *Down to Earth* laughed at friends who imagine themselves with one foot in the grave. *Reaching for the Moon* joked about the vagaries of the New Thought faddists. *Wild*

[3] *Motion Picture Magazine*, September 1916.

and Woolly was a Western to end Westerns. *Mr. Fix-It* jubilantly "unstarched a stiff-necked family of aristocrats." Such films called for a degree of intellectual appreciation and their huge success at this time signifies how perspicacious both audience and film makers were becoming.

As audiences grew more critical, the thrillers which had been phenomenally popular, began to be laughed off the screens. During the early war years a vogue for pulp Westerns and supernatural hair-raisers known as "shockers," especially in serial form (the story was continued from week to week), had become established. These sensational action thrillers, modern fairy tales, enthralled uncritical spectators. Whatever skepticism they may have felt was swept aside when, threatened with death or dishonor, the heroine escaped from the trap by prodigious courage and agility, only to be caught in another trap that she would get out of next week. All movie devices for suspense, surprise, and the supernatural were exploited in such mind-twisters and nerve-tinglers as *The Diamond from the Sky, The Million-Dollar Mystery, The House of a Thousand Candles, The Circular Staircase, The Ivory Snuff Box, Mysteries of the Grand Hotel, The Breaker, The Sign of the Poppy, The Perils of Pauline.* The thrilling stunts of these pictures were often crudely faked, but to the enraptured spectators any lack of realism was unnoticeable. The physical impact, the mounting suspense, the death-defying leaps swept the audience along with the story. They stamped their feet and often cried out in the spirit of participation with the actors.

A few players in these pictures won tremendous popular followings, and it is interesting to note that they were all women: Kathlyn Williams, Helen Holmes, Pearl White, Ruth Roland. All were renowned for their stunts, physical prowess, and daring. Their exploits paralleled, in a sense, the real rise of women to a new status in society—a rise that became especially marked on America's entrance into the war, when women were offered participation in nearly every phase of industrial activity.

Before the War had ended the crudeness of the average serial with its repetitious events no longer fulfilled the emotional needs of the major portion of the movie-goers. Serials were soon relegated to the cheaper movie theatres or to those in outlying districts where audiences were largely of the uneducated. Film makers themselves responded to the increasing sophistication of the audience by ridiculing film clichés, Westerns, and melodramatic serials in such pictures as *Nut-Stuff, Her Screen Idol,* and *Wild and Woolly.* Superthrillers—with men riding on cannon balls, sitting on the moon, and chasing shooting stars—and super-Westerns heartily mocked the more implausible adventure tales. It was evident that a more intelligent audience was dictating a change in motion picture content.

America's entry into the war had a profound influence on movie content. Until our entrance into the World War the growth of the middle-class movie audience was relatively slow. But soon after our declaration of war movie-going became fashionable, and movie subject matter changed accordingly. While living on the bounty of the poor, the "first art child of democracy" (as movies had been called) had dealt with the working man's life and struggles. As the poor became less important as the mainstay of the movies, as theatres began opening on main streets, as admission prices greatly increased —particularly during 1918, with the addition of the war tax—the ideals and tribulations of the masses lost some of their importance as subject matter for the motion picture. Patrons of the better-class theatres had more critical standards, more security in life, and different interests. To please such patrons movies had to be more subtle and refined, broader in scope, not quite so simple and forthright as they had been in the earlier days. This development of sophistication was inevitable in the films' growth, but the addition of the middle class to the audience hastened the transition. Pictures began now to be devoted almost exclusively to pleasing and mirroring the life of the more leisured and well-to-do citizenry.

The entrance of America into the World War stimulated the change that was taking place in the outlook of the middle class itself. The shattering of nineteenth-century attitudes, already begun by muckrakers and reformers, was continued under war pressure. New and liberalizing ideas about personal moral problems displaced the old. Materialism superseded idealism, and the popular desire for escape from acute social problems and war put an end to enthusiastic progressivism. Morals were viewed questioningly and criticized freely. Films vividly reflected these alterations and revaluations of ideas, and noted the beginnings of new standards and conventions that were to be ascendant after the war. The fact that the screen was now a major means of entertainment and release from the hard everyday world was also significant. Movie subject matter, when it was not war propaganda, lost its lofty social purposefulness and devoted itself to amusing the individual.

The transition from the soft Pollyanna idealism to a hard materialism, from naïveté to shrewdness, quickened under war conditions. The naïve "black and white" portrayals of good and evil were being hooted off the screen by the new cynical, impatient, diversion-seeking movie-goers. Siding with the audiences, *Photoplay* [4] protested:

> One of the oldest and wickedest beliefs is that life eventually rewards virtue and punishes evil. . . . If this were true, life would be a puppet show. . . . Really great art ignores this premise, for material punishment is a matter of accident or . . . law.

Under such criticism movie makers had already begun to examine their premises regarding the values of life. Marriage as an end to romance had come under suspicion. The responsibilities of man and wife to each other were being given a different kind of treatment as early as 1914. Thus, in the closing scene of *The Vampire's Trail*,[5]

> The next moment the penitent husband was kneeling at his wife's feet. "My whole life shall be an atonement. Not till I nearly lost you did I realize how little I have appreciated your love—the love of a pure and noble woman who is as devoted a mother as she is a faithful wife." "No, Horace," replied his wife, "it is I who should ask your forgiveness. I gave all my love to the baby. I quite forgot that you were my lover. But you shall never again feel lack of companionship. I promise you that, my husband." We then see them both go off like two weary pilgrims.

With audiences growing more critical than ever, with moral "fundamentals" being questioned and even attacked widely, the movies had to begin reforming their habits. The ever-suffering wife was treated less sympathetically and the business-engrossed husband

[4] December 1917.   [5] Described in *Photoplay*, August 1914.

was censured. Movies now emphasized that it is necessary to marital happiness for the woman to maintain her love, good looks, and appearance after marriage so that her husband will be proud of her and will not turn to other women. The husband, for his part, must continue to be attentive and loving.

School for Husbands told the story of a husband who, ashamed of his plain wife, becomes unfaithful, whereupon his wife in retaliation turns into a "butterfly." When financial ruin stares them in the face, however, she faithfully gives him money that she had saved and he, recognizing his wife's virtue and good looks, gives up the other women. *Today, Who Loved Him Best, Man's Woman, As Man Made Her, The Struggle Everlasting,* and *The Moth* were all tracts in harmony with the new notion that husband and wife were equally responsible and must co-operate. The new attitude toward marriage was typified in *The Ne'er-Do-Well* (1916), "a study completely within the bounds of decorum, of the dammed-up passion of an over-healthy woman, imprisoned in a humdrum home with no attempt at white-washing or moralizing."

The mature woman of the world became a heroine in such screen dramas, and many actresses who played the part—Norma Talmadge, Alla Nazimova, Ethel Clayton, Elsie Ferguson, Pauline Frederick—became famous. Alla Nazimova, perhaps, best personified the new ideal. She came to the screen as a distinct type, later to become the vogue. Described as "the current wonder of the films," she had a pale face, dark hair, a large and eloquent mouth, and deep, "telling" eyes. She was the "well of emotion and sensitivity" that, a decade before, had been represented on the stage by Sarah Bernhardt. Nazimova was said to have been especially appealing to the women, and was the first to portray woman as a deeply emotional personality who has within her not only passion but a creativeness and intellectual depth once assumed to exist only in man. One of the most beloved of screen actresses, she had a neurotic quality, then called "bizarre," that was to be noticeable in personalities who supplanted her in popularity in the following years—Gloria Swanson, Pola Negri, and Greta Garbo.

Divorce and even birth control were taken up by the movies with ever-lessening timidity and ever-growing seriousness. Prodivorce films maintained that a woman was justified in leaving an unfeeling and deceiving mate; that divorce was not an "easy way out," but a necessary means to rectify a mistake (*The Strong Way, The Horror of Mary Black*). Films against divorce argued that it led to wantonness (*Let's Get a Divorce, The Perils of Divorce*), rash errors (*Her Second Husband*), and ill effects upon society (*Divorce and Daughter*), and above all, that divorce violated the code that a wife's duty is loyalty and devotion at all costs.

In films on birth control, now a subject of national interest, a similar conflict was apparent. Lois Weber, a leading woman director at this time, laid the issue before the public in a number of propaganda films. *Where Are My Children* rebuked "married butterflies who shirked motherhood"; *The Hand That Rocks the Cradle* was the high-water mark of the sentiment that motherhood was a sacred trust. Other pictures revealed the swift-changing streams of thought: *Hypocrites, Motherhood, Flaming Youth, We Moderns*. Bold arguments for and against the repeal of the law making abortions illegal were offered in *The Curse of Eve* and *The Unborn*. *Enlighten Thy Daughter* and *The Law of Nature* emphasized the need for popular knowledge on the subject.

The disintegration of old moral codes was evident also in films about the young modern woman and in "educational" sex dramas. The stock story of the girl who is lured to the city and victimized by the man of the world no longer closed on the familiar moral note: the girl's repentant return to the farm. Instead, the temptations to "break away" that beset the ambitious were justified; movies showed that the straight and narrow path means poverty and oppression. *The Payment, The Easiest Way, The Angel Factory, The Yellow Ticket*, and *The Lash of Destiny* were bold depictions of prostitution as a means of livelihood. *The Adventurer* portrayed the temptations confronting girls who wanted to be free of "tenement existence."

In a war-disturbed world sex was discussed more openly. The old axioms about virginity were forsaken for the slogan "If you can't be good, be careful." Films aimed at educating soldiers in sex facts, teaching the danger of venereal diseases (*Fit to Fight, The End of the Road, Open Your Eyes*) and the evils of masturbation (*The*

Solitary Sin). Other films sought to forewarn and forearm women (*The Foolish Virgin, Protect Your Daughter, The Price She Paid, The Girl Who Didn't Know, The Girl Who Didn't Think, He Was a Travelling Man*). Romanticism faltered as such public discussions which heretofore had been suppressed as "shockingly indelicate," were brought into the open.

In keeping with this new-found realistic outlook went a loss of respect for spiritual values and an increased regard for material ones. The philosophy of self-aggrandizement, the regard for elegant clothes and polished manners, the veneration of the successful business man and wealth, and the fashion of high-pressure salesmanship —all of which were to become dominant in films of the post-war period—now began receiving favorable attention on the screen. There appeared tales such as *Brewster's Millions*, "the romance of spending a million," and *Humanizing Mr. Winsby*, the story of the reformation of the town skinflint and mortgage collector into a philanthropist.

A conciliatory attitude toward those who have, rather than the bitterness of those who have not, became the new movie viewpoint. *The Jack Pot Club* showed the business man and employer as helpful and enlightened philanthropists. A poverty-stricken inventor who has been cheated out of his patent is about to kill himself when the Jack Pot Club, "composed of the town's capitalists who every week give the proceeds of a poker game to some deserving but helpless individual," come to his aid. They discover his patent is good and put the inventor on his feet by financing his enterprise.

The value of money began to be pointed out, not as a dire necessity in preventing sickness, injustice, or starvation, but as a means to power, luxury, a full life, social importance, and even as an end in itself. *Social Hypocrites* pointed out the superficiality of aristocratic titles and implied that not background, but money, counts.

Respect for the bold and aggressive character appeared in a host of films. *American Methods*, starring William Farnum and Florence Vidor, depicted the superiority of Americans in "getting results"— in this case, their superiority to the traditions and aristocracy of the old countries. *The Gift o' Gab, New York Luck*, and *A Game of Wits* were stories of the quick-thinking individual who, through sheer mental cleverness, could turn a situation to his advantage. *Skinner's Dress Suit* pointed out that regardless of what you might like to believe, people judge you at your face value, and if you "put up a good bluff, you are pretty sure of getting by."

A new conception of the film hero and film heroine naturally began to appear. The gawkiness and clumsiness, the shirt sleeves and ruffled hair, of the 1908 working man gave way to the polished, cultured characteristics exemplified in the advertising drawings of Leyendecker, Christy, Fisher, and Underwood which were then flooding the country. Movie idols were no longer the stocky, strong, slow-thinking and lumbering working man, but slim men of quick wit, chivalrous manners, and worldly ways. The rough-and-ready William and Dustin Farnum were replaced by the fashionably dressed, athletic Wallace Reid with his plastered-down hair and chiseled features, the fashion-plate J. Warren Kerrigan, the boyishly charming Charles Ray, and above all the energetic, aggressive, optimistic Douglas Fairbanks with his gay handshake and smile.

Fairbanks' alliance in 1917 with Anita Loos and John Emerson resulted in a series of witty, fast-action satires that set the fad for screen comedies and, within one year, made Fairbanks the representative ideal of the ambitious, upright, democratic American youth. In all these films Fairbanks was "the self-made man," unbeatable and undismayed. Quick intelligence and indefatigable energy always won him success in terms of money and the girl.

Combining the Roosevelt concept of the "strenuous life" and the American worship of speed, Fairbanks made "pep" the essential attribute of the new movie star. He was always brisk, blind to obstacles, deaf to fear, "ready with the left hook," strong for home life, and constantly "ablink in dazzling smiles" (*The Americano, Flirting with Fate, The Habit of Happiness, The Mollycoddle, Manhattan Madness*). A lover of slang, he made the exclamation "Gee whiz!" popular.

In 1917 Fairbanks published an inspirational pep-talk book, *Laugh and Live*. Each month, from November 1917 on, he contributed a page to *Photoplay* on wholesome living:

Be clean in body and mind. Perhaps the greatest foe . . . is strong drink. . . . Personally I have never tasted liquor. . . . It was my mother's influence . . . I promised her when eight years old that I would never drink.

The new ideal physically and mentally, Douglas Fairbanks was honored by having one of the peaks in Yosemite Valley named after him. Along with Charles Chaplin, Mary Pickford, and Theda Bara, he took his place as a leading legendary character in screen mythology, symbolic of an era.

The "self-made" hero had his counterpart in the new-type heroine who, by her spirit and ambition, wins wealth and happiness. Movies no longer married the girl to the poor but loving sweetheart; the "rags-to-riches" romance was more popular. *The Rise of Susan, Up the Road with Sallie, The Dream Girl, Common Ground,* all variations on the Cinderella theme, were then fresh and new to the screen. Wish-fulfillments all, signs of the new materialistic philosophy, they won enormous and firm popularity. Mary Pickford was now rivaled by Mae Murrays, Clara Kimball Youngs, Marie Doros —the "moderns." The Constance Talmadge types that appeared had a new, bright glint in their eyes and an alertness that was to soon be an outstanding trait of all ingénues. The heroine of this era dressed more fashionably, her manners were more polished, her conduct more ladylike.

The World War not only quickened the sophistication of film content, but established movies for once and for all as an "escape world." As early as July 1914, Thomas Curtis Clark had sent to *Photoplay* the poem called "An Effective Remedy":

> If you're feeling tired of life,
>   Go to the picture show.
> If you're sick of troubles rife,
>   Go to the picture show.
> You'll forget your unpaid bills,
>   Rheumatism, and other ills,
> If you'll stow away your pills,
>   And go to the picture show.

The tremendous effectiveness of motion picture entertainment in relieving the mind, in turning it toward a dream world where all the injustices and discrepancies of real life are adjusted, was being recognized. For a time movies continued to stress the edifying influences of morality dramas, news events, and "educationals." But after America entered the war pictures were more consciously presented as consolations and diversions from the anxieties of everyday existence. As their function as emotional safety valves for the public was understood, a flood of romances, comedies, and spectacles of every description was produced. Pictures such as *The Kleptomaniac* were no longer seen on the screen; poverty began to be ignored in a world of plenty. One of the last big realistic productions of the very poor was *Empty Pockets*:

Takes you down into the East Side, that modern Babel where crime flourishes like ragweed in a neglected garden; where hopes and ambitions are buried behind walls of misery; where beauty and purity are sold through bitter poverty; down there where "Empty Pockets" spells its worst.[6]

Though sensational in style, this movie's concern with social evils was real. In the years that followed its type was to become less familiar to movie-goers.

Visions of tranquillity, ease, and overnight conquests, a life in which everything goes smoothly and rightly, were now being deliberately presented to the public in the form of light romances. Full-length comedies and "bathing beauty" exhibitions likewise diverted people's minds from the moment. It was a definite policy of the government to encourage the entertainment of the populace during the dark war days.

Love as a boy-and-girl situation, heretofore of secondary importance, became prominent in a host of romantic films. With sweethearts, husbands, and sons away at the training camps or at the war front, the women of the country sought on the screen what they lacked in real life. Harold Lockwood, Francis X. Bushman, Earle Williams, J. Warren Kerrigan, and Wallace Reid became the lovers of the whole female population, America's "heart-throbs," in such pictures as *Red, White and Blue Blood, Indiscreet Corinne, Please Help Emily, Jules of the Strong Heart, The Countess Charming,* and *Rimrock Jones*. Becoming popular as a form of escape

[6] *Photoplay*, December 1917.

during the war years, such romantic dramas during the post-war years were to be a major kind of film entertainment, depicting a world troubled only by "lovers' quarrels."

Displays of youthful beauty became a feature attraction in the new films. Director Herbert Brenon little realized what he was starting when he made the spectacle *A Daughter of the Gods*, which, according to *Variety*,[7] "made full use of photographing Miss Annette Kellerman, the diving beauty, 'sans habillement,' on every possible occasion." *A Daughter of the Gods* brought bathing beauties to films, preparing the way for *Neptune's Daughter*, *Sirens of the Sea*, and *The Queen of the Sea*. Sennett's bathing beauties were already familiar, but lovely undressed girls now became so popular that even dramatic films were showing them. In *The Slacker*, for instance, "for no reason bathing beauties are shown frolicking on the sand in a scene when a man saves another from drowning."

The screen was filled with girls. After the war, they were to be seen in every possible stage of dressing and undressing, as the movie makers intensified their exploitation of "body appeal."

Despite attempts to get away from the problems of the everyday world, some acute public questions, besides the war issue itself, did receive attention on the screen. Agitation for the passage of the federal prohibition law was the subject of such films as *The Enemy*, *A Case at Law*, *The Drunkard*. In Wilsonian fashion some pictures exposed political chicanery and racketeering (*The Public Be Damned*, *Cheating the Public*, *Kinkaid, the Gambler*, *The Widow's Might*). The controversy over capital punishment that was arousing the country was taken up in *Who Shall Take My Wife*, and the evils of dope—an increasingly serious social problem during the war —were dramatized in *The Devil's Needle*. *The Governor's Boss* was a propaganda film that aimed to expose Tammany Hall's impeachment of Governor Sulzer of New York because of his antagonism toward that political organization. *Buy a Bale* was an attempt by propaganda to prevent the bottom from falling out of the cotton market.

In 1916 *Government in Action* represented the Democratic campaign for the re-election of Woodrow Wilson. Governor Whitman

[7] October 20, 1916.

of New York was conceded to have won the election largely because the moving pictures backed his veto of the censorship bill. A feature-length motion picture about him, supervised by D. W. Griffith, had been circulated free throughout the state.

Your Girl and Mine was one of the many movies that helped to make woman suffrage a fact. Serious labor unrest, on the other hand, provoked a number of anti-labor films such as *The Black List* and *The Strike*. Even Charlie Chaplin, in *Doughnuts and Dynamite*, made fun at the expense of strikers.

Before the United States entered the war, Negroes and characters of foreign nationalities appeared in films in a rather unfavorable light. Of all, the Negro was treated most harshly. An attempt in 1914 to star the famous Negro stage actor, Bert Williams, in films resulted disastrously. His first picture, *Darktown Jubilee*, resulted in a race riot in Brooklyn and elsewhere met an undercover boycott. Bert Williams was thus forced out of a promising motion picture career.

The most violent movie tirade against the Negro was, of course, D. W. Griffith's *The Birth of a Nation*. So passionately was it felt by its Kentucky-reared director, so effectively was it couched in the movie idiom, that protests against it were quick to appear, equaling the tempestuous acclaim it received for its artistry. Speeches, riots, newspaper editorials, stirred racial feeling to a high pitch, attesting not only Griffith's eloquence but the movies' power as a social agency. The reception given to the picture influenced Griffith's choice of theme of his next work, *Intolerance*. This was in part an apology, more or less intentional, for his prejudiced stand in *The Birth of a Nation*. The extraordinary success of *The Birth of a Nation*, however, wrought great harm upon tolerance, for other anti-Negro films soon appeared. *Broken Chains*, in typical style, depicted the Negro as a murderous and villainous agitator.

The crisis of the World War, however, led to a new policy regarding all minorities. Inspiring all to rally around the American flag regardless of their race and blood, films extolled the immigrants who became citizens (*One More American, An Alien*) and even depicted the Negro as a good soldier (Griffith's *Hearts of the World*). Likewise the "yellow peril" agitation against the Japanese and Chinese disappeared from the screen, since these groups were now with the Allies. The Japanese were represented not only humanly and sympathetically but romantically. Especially significant was the rise of the Japanese actor Sessue Hayakawa. He became one of the leading stars of the day, combining culture, sensitivity, exotic handsomeness, and refinement (*The Honorable Friend, The White Man's Law, The Secret Game*). Other nationalities, except for the Germans, also received more liberal treatment at the hands of the movie makers.

Besides being utilized for propaganda, war activities, and romantic escape, the motion picture was used by industrialists for educational and moral purposes. The railroad companies, for instance, found motion pictures excellent aids in training their workers. In 1917 they made *The House That Jack Built* (a man dreams of a wreck due to his carelessness) and *The Rule of Reason* (a lesson against drinking, in which a drinking young yard brakeman causes a bad accident). Other films dramatically showed other causes of accidents and also taught the habits of courteousness and efficiency that are essential to the success of the railroad business. One railroad company fitted up two cars as moving picture theatres and sent them touring throughout the system.

One of the first business men to see the value of movies in this light was H. J. ("57 Kinds") Heinz. In 1915 he built a motion picture theatre on the grounds of his Pittsburgh plant for the use of his employees. Other enlightened business men encouraged moviegoing, reporting that this kind of entertainment reduced drunkenness and prostitution and often increased the efficiency of employees.

The Navy Department also found movies helpful. It was reported that, except for small torpedo boats, by 1915 there was not a ship in the Navy that did not have full moving picture equipment and two or three operators. In battle practice, a cameraman on each ship took movies of shots landing near the target to help the marksmen to perfect their aim. Newsreels of Navy parades excited the sailors, so it was said, and made them eager to parade so that they could later see themselves on the screen. Shows were presented to Navy men on the ships three times weekly.

Other groups were to avail themselves of the educational advantages of movies and from now on, such visual education was to become an increasingly important factor in schools, museums, and other non-theatrical fields.

By 1918 the movies were dispensing a new philosophy of life, new standards of morals and manners. The reaction against nineteenth-century attitudes mounted steadily during the war years, and the movies supported it. As an escape medium, as a stimulant to day-dreaming, as a provider of vicarious experiences, movies had proved unsurpassed.

As early as 1916 the importance of the motion picture in the nation's emotional life had been indicated in the "Answer Lady's" column in *Motion Picture Magazine:* [8]

M. V., Kansas City: My dear child—so you and about ten others who have written me this month want Anita [Stewart] to marry Earle Williams. Why not let her enjoy her beautiful youth and give you all the benefits of her talents for a while longer? She adores babies and loves a home so much that were she also to love any one special man, she would be apt to forget any career that might be before her.

Now, in 1918, the film stars were not merely subjects of intense interest; they were objects of worship. The fan magazines showed them living like gods and goddesses in their gorgeous mansions, with their swimming pools, costly limousines, and luxurious clothes. They dwelt in the land of the public's dreams. It was no wonder that manufacturers began to persuade them to endorse their products, and that endorsements such as "Every Woman and Girl Wants a Mary Pickford Cap—Craze of the Age" were great successes.

By 1920 a dozen weekly and monthly publications, solely devoted to intimate inquiries and gossip about the personal lives of the screen stars, had sprung into existence and reached a total circulation of several millions. Rather than decreasing as time went on, they increased in number. Their clientele were now pasting up pictures of their favorites in the privacy of their homes with much more widespread enthusiasm than stage stars had ever inspired. These magazines, prophetic of the movie's new course and character, were

8 September 1916.

symptomatic of the truth expressed in a Paramount-Artcraft advertisement published in *Photoplay* in July 1918:

CASTLES IN SPAIN

Day dreams, day dreams, every man is entitled to them occasionally. They help him on, he is not a machine.

Paramount and Artcraft Moving Pictures have brought more to us Americans than we have yet realized.

Their closeness to our deepest emotion has caused us to live more vividly—to see life . . . [through] other people's eyes—to develop a more generous personal philsopohy.

Though in a large measure still inarticulate, exploited by business men for quick profits, movies had become recognized by the close of the World War in their full social significance. The power of movies in shaping public sentiment, in taking up war duties, and in reflecting the changing temper of American society, had substantiated W. P. Lawson's statement in *Harper's Weekly* in 1915: [9]

While laws are always in the long run the product of public opinion, public opinion itself is created by various humble but effective influences of which the movie . . . is . . . a most potent factor in shaping national mind and morals . . . what the movie says soaks in.

[9] January 2.

PART FIVE

INTENSIFICATION (1919-1929)

XVI

BIG BUSINESS

IN 1918 the movie industry was shaken by a serious loss of patronage because of the influenza epidemic and the absence of millions of men at the front or in training camps. The public's distaste for war films after the Armistice was also a threat to the industry's well-being. But the setback was only temporary. Recouping their losses, producers quickly resumed expansion and consolidation. Inter-organizational rivalry attained proportions that made the old trust war seem petty. Having realized its fundamental large-scale characteristics, the industry began its ten years of growth as big business—a growth to be intensified, in the closing years, by the sudden and revolutionary addition of sound.

Unrivaled by foreign films during the four war years, American films were firmly established not only at home but in all parts of the globe—even in India, western Asia, and Africa. In 1919 American motion pictures exclusively were being shown in South America; in Europe ninety per cent of the movies shown originated in the United States. Hollywood had become the unquestioned motion picture center of the world.

The post-war period was one of unrestraint in business as in life generally. To be important a thing had to be big—and so the movie became one of the biggest things in American civilization. Everything connected with it was inflated, materially and psychologically. Companies, studios, productions, theatres, salaries, sales, advertising —all took on gigantic proportions. Excesses were characteristic of the hysteria and booming prosperity of "the jazz age."

Profits, huge though they were, were not big enough to finance the vast undertakings of these years. Wall Street banking houses, issuing stock lavishly, poured millions into the laps of the merging film companies to meet their ever-expanding needs. New men from Wall Street, educated in finance, became the overseers of the motion picture business. Characteristic of the new managerial figures were two directors of a new and powerful company, Loew's: W. C. Durant, at that time also head of General Motors Corporation, and Harvey Gibson, president of the Liberty National Bank. Kuhn, Loeb and Company had already entered the field to back Famous-Players-Lasky; now the Du Ponts and the Chase National Bank undertook to finance Edgar Selwyn and Samuel Goldwyn, "the late Samuel Goldfish, not dead but legally annihilated" (January 1, 1919), in their new enterprise, Goldwyn Pictures. Loew, Pathé, and Fox listed stock on the New York Stock Exchange for public investment: this was the latest business method of getting much capital quickly. By 1925 stock issues had been floated also for Metro-Goldwyn and Universal.

Fiercely fighting for greater outlets for their productions, and to block the outlets of competitors, companies were ever at each other's throats. It was "company eat company." As the lords of finance grappled, minor companies were badly mangled. The steady expansion of the industry was marked by the continual attacks and counterattacks of First National versus Paramount versus Fox versus Universal versus Metro versus the independents. It was a new kind of warfare in the industry—large-scale economic warfare between powerful organizations for the control and monopoly of the motion picture business.

During the first years after the war the control of distribution was the major goal. Benjamin Schulberg effected the incorporation of the United Artists Company in order to distribute productions of directors and stars "too expensive for any single company to maintain on a permanent pay roll." The directors and stars were the "Big Four": Mary Pickford, Douglas Fairbanks, Charles Chaplin, and D. W. Griffith. Another distribution combination was Associated Producers, consisting of independent director-producers: Thomas Ince, Allan Dwan, George Loane Tucker, Mack Sennett, Marshall Neilan, Maurice Tourneur, J. Parker Read, Jr., and King

Vidor. This group merged in 1921 with First National as their producers, and became known as Associated First National. Vitagraph, which had bought out the pioneers Kalem and Lubin during the war, was itself bought out in 1925 by Warner Brothers, a new company, which in 1929 absorbed First National as well. Goldwyn bought out the Triangle Corporation studio in Culver City, and in 1924 formed Metro-Goldwyn-Mayer. Meanwhile William Randolph Hearst launched Cosmopolitan Productions, which distributed through Metro-Goldwyn-Mayer.

The block-booking system, broken in 1918, was re-established. The exhibitors organized in angry groups to fight it, but their struggle was on the whole desultory. Distribution became increasingly centralized within the power of the major producing companies. These companies, having fought bitterly for the control of production through distribution, carried the fight into the field of exhibition. Control of exhibition assured not only definite number of theatre outlets for productions, but a longer length of life and definite revenues on which to base future productions. Control of exhibition became a major means to keep rival productions off the screen and thus force competing companies out of business.

Just as Fox had been able to fight the Motion Picture Patents Company because of his ownership of theatres, so now First National was in an advantageous position to fight Paramount. First National, during the years 1919-1921, had some 3,400 theatres, some of them being among the largest and most important in the United States. Zukor, of Paramount, saw at once that he would have to enter the field of exhibition if Paramount was to be victorious, and he quickly began buying up theatres. Brilliant and ruthless as a business executive, he aroused increasing bitterness in his attempt to get, as nearly as the law allowed, a monopoly on movie theatres. He bought out thousands of theatres in small and large towns, and even acquired stock in the rival First National Company so that he could "bore from within." Endorsed by a national administration that believed in leaving business to its own tactics, he stopped at nothing to gain his ends.

Zukor's most formidable rival next to First National proved to be a new producer-exhibitor combination launched in 1920. This consisted of a theatre circuit that had been one of Paramount's chief customers, Loew's, and Metro, a new producing company. Paramount, Metro, and First National now fought savagely for big theatre control, squeezing many of the large independent theatre owners out of business, and forcing to the wall independent producers who had no theatre holdings. The situation was soon so acute that the independent exhibitors rose up frantically against the exhibition-distribution-production combinations. In 1921, at a national convention in Minneapolis, the independent Motion Picture Theatre Owners Association (M.P.T.O.) and the independent producers sought a way of checking monopoly operations, but their intentions bore little fruit.

The Federal Trade Commission filed complaints against Paramount and its affiliated corporation, studios, and individuals on the ground that in producing, distributing, and in addition owning from four to five hundred theatres, they were violating the trust laws. The proceedings temporarily halted Zukor's operations within First National but did not stop him from continuing his expansion policy, nor did it prevent his conquest of First National later.

Constant litigation and mutual accusation were giving the industry bad publicity and placing its leaders in a critical position. This was coming moreover at a bad time for other unforeseen factors were cutting in on the movies' soaring profits. Business conditions in general were depressed; this was not helped by the sudden strong competition of foreign films which were so far superior to Hollywood productions that many reasoned that they ought to be suppressed on this ground alone. At about the same time a wave of agitation for federal censorship of movies was gaining strength. Added to this was a series of scandals that aggravated the increasing animosity against the movie makers. For the first time in its history, the box office wavered. Many independent minor companies were forced to suspend operations under the pressure of the times. Others sought ways and means to maintain their power. The most essential item was to adjust the industrial and moral disputes amicably and thus forestall government interference or federal censorship.

In 1922 an organization was formed for self-regulation, both on the moral front and on the business front. The name of the organization, the Motion Picture Producers and Distributors Association, significantly omitted mention of exhibitors.

The industry selected Will H. Hays, a "distinguished and financially uninterested citizen," as president of their organization. Hays had first become known for his work in publicizing the Indiana State Council of Defense. An active worker and organizer in the triumphant Republican Party in 1920, he had come into national prominence as Postmaster-General in Harding's Cabinet. As head of the Motion Picture Producers and Distributors Association, Will Hays now became "the buffer between industry and the public."

The association immediately set up rules for arbitration and exhibitor units to eliminate monopoly practices and establish ethical standards. Just how far-reaching its reforms were can be judged from the fact that in 1925, three years after the association was formed, Vitagraph withdrew, on the grounds that theatres were still producer-owned.

The battle for control of exhibition continued unabated, the aim of the combinations being to acquire the best first-run houses and chain theatre circuits throughout the nation.

Mergers became the new economic order. Independent corporations and individuals were eliminated or submerged as the operations of production, distribution and exhibition became more and more interlocked and concentrated into the control of a few. Within a few years nearly all the major and first-run houses in the United States and Canada had been acquired by Paramount, Loew's, Inc. (Metro-Goldwyn-Mayer), and the large circuits affiliated with the First National group. Fox and Universal had outlets on a lesser scale. By 1927, with close to 600 exchanges in 46 key American cities, and 20,000 theatres, exhibition had become almost entirely monopolized by chain theatres, all in the hands of the major producer-distributor-exhibitor combinations. The following year Zukor was finally successful in weakening First National's control by acquiring one of its largest chains, the Katz-Balaban circuit. This was merged with his other theatre interests in the Publix Corporation, which ostensibly separated his production and exhibition activities.

The producer-distributor-exhibitor combination deeply influenced the industry's functioning. It minimized the roles of production and distribution and made exhibition the controlling factor in the industry. Producers who owned the most important chain of theatres controlled the source of receipts. This assured them in advance of an income upon which they could figure production budgets. Under the producer-distributor-exhibitor combination, the main channels of distribution and exhibition became virtually closed to newcomers or independents; for them, only the cheapest of markets remained. This control of outlets confined competition to the few major combinations. Under the new order financial dependence on Wall Street increased enormously and the vast resources now at the disposal of these million dollar movie combines led to a higher degree of extravagance and waste. Spending became the motto as never before; costs and prices reached new prohibitive highs.

In this era of extravagance producers competed intensively in building elaborate and luxurious showplaces. With a speed suggestive of the growth of the old nickelodeons, mammoth theatres accommodating thousands of people—at least three times as many as before—appeared throughout the country. In New York City the Capitol Theatre, completed in November 1919, had 5,300 seats. It had carpeted floors, costumed ushers, upholstered seats, eleven rock-crystal chandeliers, and the grandeur of Empire-period furnishings. Commented *Photoplay*, "The mezzanine floor looks as if it had been designed for eight-day bicycle races." Grauman's Egyptian and Chinese Theatres in Hollywood rivaled even this. Other New York palaces included Loew's State and, later, Roxy's, Paramount, and the Radio City Music Hall.

Expensive theatres in downtown districts of the metropolitan cities were regarded as safe investments, since the country was experiencing a building and real-estate boom in these years. Even neighborhood movie houses became luxurious. In 1928 alone, $161,-930,000 was spent on new theatres; the total number of theatres at that time was about 20,500. In hundreds of towns the moving picture theatre had become the outstanding building.

Admission prices, despite sharp competition, were forced upward. Movies were no longer "the poor man's show" but the "universal American entertainment." Downtown theatres charged from

65 cents to $1.00. *Broken Blossoms* in 1919 got a record price of $3.00 a seat for its première. Second-run houses in the neighborhoods charged 25, 35, and 55 cents. Even fifth-run houses in poor side streets now charged 10 or 15 cents. The nickel no longer gave one entrance to the movie world.

To meet competition, exhibitors added elaborate stage presentations and novelties to the regular movie program. "Roxy" set an example when he introduced "prologues" consisting of operatic soloists, seventy-five-piece symphony orchestras, and a *ballet de corps* in 1925 in the Strand Theatre. Producer-exhibitors everywhere emulated his showmanship. The practice of offering elaborate stage shows spread so rapidly that after a few years these "prologues" became despised as "poisonous clichés." Extra attractions became so long and numerous that Richard Watts, movie critic of the New York *Herald Tribune*, protested,

Heaven knows it is not my intention to cheer over-lustily for the film little theatre when you consider some of the exhibits they have offered lately; but at least they are about the only retreats left for the quaint ancients who want to see a motion picture.

Despite such animosity, "prologues" continued to flourish on a lavish scale.

Like exhibition and distribution, movie making also became a huge and extravagant undertaking practicable only for the wealthiest and strongest companies. The cost of picture making had grown from $100,000 for *The Birth of a Nation* in 1915 to millions for comparable spectacle productions. *Ben Hur*, said to have been the most expensive film ever made, cost $6,000,000.[1] The expense of the average picture likewise doubled and trebled. In 1920 the average five-reel feature cost from $40,000 to $80,000; "specials" of six to nine reels, from $100,000 to $200,000. By 1929 the average five-reeler was costing up to $200,000. To paraphrase Heywood Broun, it was not only that movies represented the views of big business; the movies now were big business.

The profits to be made from expensive pictures were obviously limited once the peak of theatre expansion had been reached. *The*

[1] According to *Variety*, April 18, 1925.

Ten Commandments, costing close to $2,000,000, netted about $750,000 as road-show profits, and *The Covered Wagon*, costing under $350,000, netted over $1,500,000 on the road. It became apparent that the really steady income was to be got from the comparatively inexpensive productions—pictures graded as "program" or "B" pictures. The costlier "specials" were to function as "prestige films," productions that would keep the name of the producing company a favorite with public and exhibitor alike.

Now that profits were soaring, extravagance pervaded the film studios. Salaries reached fabulous amounts. Outstanding directors received from $20,000 to $50,000 for one film; screen writers, $1,000 to $2,500 a week and $10,000 to $25,000 for a novel or play adaptation. Among all the individuals involved, however, perhaps the star enjoyed the biggest income. The early post-war years saw his salary mounting at an alarming pace. William S. Hart netted $900,000 in two years, and got $2,225,000 for nine productions in the succeeding two years. Goldwyn paid Geraldine Farrar $10,000 a week; Metro topped the scale with a salary of $13,000 a week to Nazimova, then at the height of her screen fame. Nazimova's contract provided for a lump sum of $65,000 to be paid in weekly installments; a limit of five weeks was placed on each picture, and for each day over that she was to be paid accordingly.

By 1923 the boom in salaries had created a new financial rating in the film world. Actor-producers—Harold Lloyd, Douglas Fairbanks, Charles Chaplin, Norma Talmadge, Mary Pickford, and one or two others—drew incomes ranging into the millions. If the salaries commanded by stars seemed preposterous, fan interest in the stars appeared to make them worth the money. It was estimated in 1919 that a quarter of a million dollars was spent annually on correspondence between stars and fans.

The standard pay for supporting players was now $600 a week and up—a big jump from the average of $100 to $200 a week in 1916. Leading men received $1,000 a week and more, less than female stars, who were considered more important. The high salary became so widely regarded as an index of a player's value that nearly everyone exaggerated the amounts received. So pronounced did this tendency become, owing to the activity of press agents, that Heywood Broun, writing in *The New York World* in 1922, was moved to remark,

When an actor tells you how much he received, you discount his figure by 50 per cent and arrive at the approximate truth. This ratio does not hold with players from motion pictures. Time is required to take their figures and work out the answer. Nobody can very well be expected to divide a given sum by 11½ in his head.

Stars began forming their own production companies. If an actor or actress incorporated, it was the sign of success. William S. Hart, Anita Stewart, Norma Talmadge, Charles Chaplin, Douglas Fairbanks, Charles Ray, Clara Kimball Young, Sessue Hayakawa, Roscoe Arbuckle, Frank Keenan, and Agnes Ayres were a few of the many notables who flung themselves into production. Because of the lack of exhibition and distribution facilities and of poor management, few of them succeeded. Having amassed fortunes as stars, many lost their wealth promptly as producers.

As costs of production mounted and control settled into the hands of Wall Street bankers, the producer-supervisor was brought into the studio to oversee production. This new kind of executive, appointed by the Eastern financiers, was to assume more and more power, making the director, stars, and other movie workers mere pawns in production, of which he assumed full charge. The producer-supervisors set about making "entertainment the public wants." They had little creative imagination and were ruled by practical concerns. "Higher quality within one's means," the adage of the best of the old producers, was changed by these new Hollywood executives into "higher means within one quality."

The reign of the director by 1926 thus came to an end. Producer-supervisors, taking over the reins of production, began to supply the ideas, select the talent, choose the director, and steer the entire policy and conception of pictures according to their points of view. Business men and executives, but not craftsmen, they began to emphasize the more obvious aspects of their commodities, telling the exhibitor—and through him the public—what to look for in a picture. Movies were analyzed for the following selling points: (1) "Names"—that is, stars; (2) "Production Value" —elaborate sets, big crowds, and other proofs of great expense; (3)

"Story Value"—the huge price paid for the original and its great reputation as a novel or play; (4) "Picture Sense"—a conglomeration of all these items; (5) "Box Office Appeal"—plenty of all the standardized values which had proved successful in years past.

All prospective films had to conform to these criteria of the producer-supervisor. He discovered that the quickest way to sell pictures in advance and to produce them rapidly was to duplicate the most recent successes. Thus what became known as the "cycle" in motion pictures, the unit of which was the "formula" picture, was born. The scheme was so "sure-fire" that producers found themselves not only aping the successful pictures of their competitors but even duplicating their own hits.

Production methods under this rigid system became mechanized; the "assembly line" appeared in Hollywood. The resulting standardization of pictures caused the downfall of the most important directors during the late twenties. The various branches of production were divided and specialized so specifically and minutely that directors had a lessening opportunity to contribute to the whole. Most directors became "glorified foremen" under the producer-supervisors.

As the director was shorn of his creative power, films became increasingly monotonous. Men with a passion for the movies and with promising talents were turned into orderlies, taking orders from superiors far less imaginative. The efforts of creative individuals to break through the limits set by the studios' new production chiefs were in most cases futile. The choice of the director himself now depended on considerations that had little connection with the movie art. As early as June 1921, *Photoplay* told the story of how executives of a company discussed a new director:

"He'll make good," insisted the chief director of the company. "But he never directed pictures," said another director a bit jealously. "What makes you think he's going to be so wonderful?" "He's the man that invented the short-vamp shoe over in Paris a dozen years ago," said the boss director seriously.

Competition as well as expensive contracts and big capital investments demanded that production be kept going at all costs. The necessity to meet schedules often forced a producer to assign a second-rate director to a certain film, although the producer knew beforehand that the film would then be mediocre. There was only a limited supply of acknowledged and experienced first-rate directors available. When a second-rate director was assigned to a film, the safest procedure was to instruct him to imitate the style of a more talented director as closely as possible. It was not uncommon for a director to be told outright to copy the effect or trick or mannerism of some more distinguished craftsman. Indeed, if a lesser director who was getting a relatively low salary could do this effectively, he was a great commercial asset to his employer. At the same time, of course, the more esteemed directors were continually asked to repeat their own successful efforts.

The result of all such commercialization was the hindrance and misdirection of motion picture progress. Bad pictures, if they made money, were held up as models of perfection, while a good film that received less notice because of its lack of "star appeal," its poor publicity, or its unusual theme was overlooked and even abhorred as "arty." As Gilbert Seldes declared,[2]

. . . on the rare occasions when a director cuts loose from his own or established moving-picture tradition and does something new his work will be taken as a dreadful warning or an enviable example, depending on the box-office receipts.

This was the state of affairs in the movie industry when an apparently insignificant event began a movement that was soon to revolutionize the business. On August 26, 1926, Warner Brothers, in a desperate effort to ward off bankruptcy, premièred a novelty, the first motion picture with sound accompaniment, *Don Juan*. Its opening at the Manhattan Opera House in New York City was made the more auspicious by Will Hays' address, recorded on the film's sound track, welcoming sound to the world of cinema. The innovation did not at first greatly alarm the industry. But the sound film was welcomed by the movie audiences, and soon Warner Brothers, surviving its financial troubles, was making real profits in its pioneering. *Don Juan* was quickly followed by *The Better 'Ole*

[2] *The Nation*, July 27, 1927.

and *When a Man Loves,* both of which had synchronized musical scores, and by a number of short sound films that featured the voices of famous singers: Schumann-Heink, Gigli, Mary Lewis, Alda.

The enthusiasm of the public for the sound film was so pronounced that the other companies got together to decide what action to take regarding this invention which they had so far ignored and, confidentially, expected to fail. The five major companies resolved to fight the "Warner Vitaphone peril" on the grounds that:

1. Present equipment would have to be discarded, and expensive talking equipment would have to be bought.

2. Such equipment could be obtained only by paying royalties to a competitor.

3. Obeisance to Warner Brothers meant loss of prestige.

4. The technique of production would have to change radically.

5. Long-term contracts with "silent" stars and directors might prove to be frozen liabilities.

If their opposition proved unavailing, these companies were prepared to rush the installation of sound apparatus for their own use. This alternative was encouraged by Western Electric, the backers of Warner Brothers, since Western Electric was eager to come to terms with the larger companies in view of the greater profits that such an alliance would make possible.

While the major companies were making up their minds about sound, Warner Brothers advanced and consolidated its position by presenting to the public, on October 6, 1927, the first feature film with synchronized speech as well as music and other sound: *The Jazz Singer.* The audience responded riotously to Al Jolson's "Come on, Ma! Listen to this . . ." in a natural, intimate voice. People were even more fascinated by his speech than by his singing. Warner Brothers immediately added "dialogue sequences" to three more sound movies then in the making: *The Lion and the Mouse, Glorious Betsy,* and *Tenderloin.*

The other companies meanwhile still hesitated to accept sound pictures as more than a temporary fad. Their situation was the more complicated and precarious because of the flood of other new inventions, each of which was hailed as revolutionary: Color, Grandeur-Screen, Three-Dimension. Each new discovery sent a new shock through the already nervous industry, and few companies wanted to jump one way or the other. For a time the only producer besides Warner that definitely accepted sound was Fox, who launched his own more flexible system, Movietone, in 1927.

Until May 15, 1928, Warner and Fox were the only two studios in the field of sound pictures. After that time the public's enthusiasm for the sound film could no longer be denied or ignored. The entire industry, now in a panic, rushed into the production of sound pictures, hoping to make up for lost time; overnight Hollywood became frantic with the mad race to catch up with Warner. The remainder of the year was full of chaos, conjecture, and confusion. As in motion pictures' earliest days, quantity alone counted. The novelty of talking and sound had enchanted the nation, and producers could not keep up with the demand for sound pictures.

Major companies at first tried to play the game from all sides. Their production schedules included part-talkies, all-talkies, sound films, and silent films, the common supposition being that eventually the talkie would merely share the screen with the silent movie. But as time went on and more theatres were wired for sound, it became apparent that the talkies were entirely supplanting the "silents." With theatre patronage mounting from 60,000,000 in 1927 to 110,-000,000 in 1929, largely because of sound, the hundred-per-cent talkie became recognized as the established form for all future productions.

The motion picture industry now proceeded to dig the grave of the silent picture. Millions of dollars having been invested in sound, all the resources of advertising, publicity, and direct appeals to audiences were used to kill the silent film and establish the talkie. The campaign was reminiscent of Paramount's earlier launching of features to replace the one- and two-reelers of pre-war times. Before long, like features in their early days, talkies became the norm. People took them for granted, and could hardly remember when talkies did not exist.

Hollywood set itself to solve as rapidly as possible the new financial and technical problems that sound posed. Technological unemployment and rapid labor turnover were prime worries. Thousands of extras were thrown out of work because of the new vogue of drawing-room talkie dramas. Musicians by the hundreds were unable to find jobs either in theatre orchestras, now eliminated, or in the studios which had formerly employed them during the shooting of scenes to induce the desired mood in players (a use of music now completely impracticable). "Gag" men and title writers were dropped from the pay rolls as playwrights and dialogue writers were added. Broadway and "Tin Pan Alley" were ransacked for talkie talent, while directors, actors, and writers who had made reputations in the "silents" were put to tests that few of them could pass. Changes in lighting equipment also eliminated a great many studio electricians; for where it had formerly taken fifty men to handle the lights on a big set, with the new incandescents only four or five men were now needed to do this work. Salaries throughout the studios decreased markedly as new and less expensive Broadway personnel were hired. Within an amazingly short time, once the new sound studios were equipped and a clearer understanding was reached as to the type of talent needed, there was a rapid readjustment in the industry.

While in the midst of these stabilization activities, the motion picture industry like the rest of the nation was shocked by the stock-market crash of 1929. Panic gripped Hollywood as fortunes were lost overnight, the building boom collapsed, and motion picture companies' big theatre holdings and real-estate investments swiftly depreciated. But despite the national turmoil and widespread fears, the box-office receipts of theatres continued the climb they had started with the innovation of sound. Wall Street gazed in astonishment at what appeared to be a "depression-proof" industry. The "resistance" of the movie to the stock-market debacle so impressed Wall Street interests that during the following years they were to struggle with more resolution than ever to gain control of the movie industry.

Thus the motion picture survived and even profited despite two acute crises within two years: the advent of sound and the onset

Charles Chaplin as few people know him. Directing a scene for his *A Woman of Paris* (1923).

Erich von Stroheim's penchant for uncompromising characterization and realistic detail is evident in this scene from *Greed* (1923), that extraordinary film which culminated twenty years of realism on the American screen.

of the depression. Its commerce now exceeded a billion and a half dollars a year. The end of the silent movie had closed an era of tremendous and fantastic expansion. Economic progress in the industry was henceforth to take the form of a greater concentration of its resources.

XVII

ADDITIONS TO FILM ART

THE international supremacy and financial success of the American movie in 1918 hid its inadequacies; constant physical refinements diverted attention from its lack of taste. But as conditions became more settled during the early post-war years, motion pictures began to rise to a higher level of development. Once again, as in the early days, the new developmental impulse came from Europe. It took the form of a wave of films from Germany, Sweden, France, and finally Russia. Just as Porter had been roused by the films of the Frenchman Melies, as Griffith had been impressed by the spectacles of the Italians, so American directors were now spurred to meet the competition presented by the foreign productions.

The post-war tidal wave of foreign films reached American shores suddenly and unexpectedly, for European studios had been thought virtually dead. Even more surprising than the unanticipated appearance of these films was their high merit, their sure and profound conception. The foreign producers' keen awareness of the medium's possibilities and their skill in executing their stories startled and frightened Hollywood. Recognizing the superiority of the foreign products, American companies imported foreign talent as soon as it appeared. The invasion of Hollywood by European movie makers and the freshened ambition of American producers led to important innovations in film technique and to an improvement of American films generally.

The greatest number of importations came first from Germany; in fact, the preponderance of German films made the "foreign invasion" really the "German invasion." The reason for the sudden spurt in German film production was political. The new German government, subsidizing movies for use as international good-will advertisements, set intelligent and able craftsmen to exploring and intensifying the film medium. The discoveries of these workers in movie technique were in many ways revolutionary; their contributions to American film tradition were numerous and far-reaching.

One of the earliest German films to circulate in America after the war was *The Cabinet of Dr. Caligari* (produced in 1919 and exhibited here in 1921). Seen by comparatively few people, it was nevertheless the most widely discussed film of the time. According to Willard Huntington Wright,[1] "It is a matter of record that no picture, not even *The Birth of a Nation*, ever created quite as much comment, argument, and speculation in one month's time as did *The Cabinet of Dr. Caligari*."

The film was conceived by painters—Robert Wiene, Walter Reimann, Herman Warm, and the architect Walther Rohrig—who were not so much interested in movies as in the forms of "expressionism" and "dadaism" then taking hold in the artistic world. As "expressionism," the film showed the adventures of a madman as seen entirely through his own eyes. The film represented "dadaism" in that sanity and insanity were proved to the spectator to be purely relative states.

The Cabinet of Dr. Caligari startled all who saw it. "It is a fantasy of terror told with the virtuosity of a poet in terms of the screen," commented the National Board of Review.[2] Its stylized rendition, brooding quality, lack of explanation, and distorted settings and lighting were new to the film world. Revelatory and challenging, "it suggested that a film instead of being a reality might be a possible reality." Not since the days of Melies had such fantastic images been seen; and now the images were twisted and made more profound by psychological implications. A few American films had attempted the psychological theme (Griffith's *The Avenging Conscience*) and stylization (Tourneur's *Prunella* and *The Blue Bird*), but these had all been treated conventionally from the viewpoint of the sane and without the pictorial perversion from

[1] Writing in *Photoplay*, September 1921.
[2] *Exceptional Photoplay Magazine*, 1921.

the norm that featured *The Cabinet of Dr. Caligari*. Although on the whole the German picture's dark neurotic tone and unrelieved seriousness were alien to American movie-goers, its execution was so fresh that even a fan magazine said, "*The Cabinet of Dr. Caligari* is as good as a week in the mountains for any movie fan tired of the conventional pictures." [3]

The film called American attention to the importance of distortion and stylization for mood by lighting, composition, setting, costuming, and acting. In the picture the actor's body leans with the chimney (to cause uneasiness in the spectator). To accent the feeling of chaos and mood, curves and dark tones are contrasted with straight lines and light tones. Compositions are carefully arranged to converge to focal points of interest. The stylized black tights and masklike make-up of the madman contribute to the ominous and tragic atmosphere and emphasize the frailty and helplessness of the white-chiffon-draped woman whom the madman carries off. The audience is led into a world of weird shapes and maladjustments without explanation, and is held there with a growing sense of horror until the very end, when a final scene discloses that all these happenings have occurred in an insane man's mind. The difference between *The Cabinet of Dr. Caligari* and American productions, remarked Will Rogers, was that the former was frankly about the ravings of two maniacs while the latter was the result of the ravings of director and star.

The Cabinet of Dr. Caligari attracted the attention of artists and intellectuals who had been indifferent to the screen. The film's embodiment of current artistic doctrines suggested to many of the intelligentsia that they were seeing an entirely new art form with great artistic potentialities and a brilliant future. On contemporary American productions, however, this strange picture had little immediate effect. Perhaps the only American movies that actually showed its influence were James Cruze's *One Glorious Day*, *Hollywood*, *Beggar on Horseback*, and Mrs. Wallace Reid's *Quicksands* and *Human Wreckage*, which included interludes showing the world as it appeared to a crazed drug addict.

In perspective *The Cabinet of Dr. Caligari* can be looked upon

[3] *Photoplay*, July 1921.

as a freak film, in the sense that it was a unique effort of its time and country and was never significantly followed up in America. It stands today as an important work in American film tradition because at a critical time it inspired a new interest in the artistry of film making and indicated the many new directions the film could take in the artist's hands.

More influential and more characteristic of the run of German films in general were the historical dramas. Since they dealt with important events in the history of France, England, and Russia, they gained immediate attention outside Germany. So skillfully were they made, so extraordinary were they in treatment and rendition, that they were acclaimed everywhere. Hollywood producers were amazed to see the American public go wild over "costume dramas," which they had ruled out since the war as strictly unpopular.

Of the German films of this type that came to America, five of the most notable were by one director, Ernst Lubitsch. Unlike many of the foreign importations, all five Lubitsch pictures—*Passion, Deception, Gypsy Blood, The Loves of Pharaoh, One Arabian Night*—were released nationally, and hundreds of thousands of Americans went to see and admire them. For his spectacular, stirring, and original work, Lubitsch was enthusiastically hailed as the "Griffith of Europe," "the great humanizer of history," "the greatest living director."

Passion (*Madame Du Barry*), the first picture of Lubitsch's to be shown in America, evoked perhaps more acclaim than any other foreign film. Featuring a striking personality, Pola Negri, the film displayed remarkable directorial craftsmanship, unusual care and devotion in the execution. The drama was, moreover, as much a depiction of Du Barry's times as a personal story. Artfully contrasted were the grandeur of court life and the barbaric poverty that existed beside it: the wealth of the rulers and the crude existence of the common people. The authenticity of the atmosphere, the details of the settings, and the costumes; and the fine taste exhibited in their application, were outstanding. The dramatic manipulation of masses and the continuity of the whole made the spectacle powerful in effect.

Passion introduced to America a director of distinguished ability. The films that followed *Passion* were equally excellent, and if they did not advance Lubitsch's reputation, they served to secure it and to convince America that an artist of no small might was putting Hollywood to shame. *Deception* (*Anne Boleyn*), *Gypsy Blood*, *The Loves of Pharaoh*, and *One Arabian Night* set new standards for astute and skillful cutting, fresh and daring camera angles, attention to minor roles, the individualization of mob scenes, suggestive and subjective treatments, the mobile use of the camera as a participator in as well as spectator of action, the subordination of stars to the film as a whole, rich contrasts, and a co-ordination and unification of all elements. In their use of unreality, of stylization, lighting, and composition alone these films would have been important. Many of the innovations they introduced are ordinary today; but in those days it was revolutionary to tilt a camera toward the sky or turn it toward an arabesque mosaic in a floor, and to see the backs of a crowd was unorthodox; quick cutting, too, was shocking. These films were more than novel: they disclosed a magic hitherto unsuspected in the movie medium.

With its light and "sexy" theme, *One Arabian Night* catered to the tastes of the American market. A fantasy, whimsical and humorous, it was certainly the most insinuating and sophisticated one yet seen on the American screens. It not only revealed Lubitsch as an ingenious director of comedy, but introduced a risqué wit that killed the heavy-handed American sex and style displays. This film presaged the flock of films Lubitsch was to make in America and was to have a lasting influence on American productions generally. After Lubitsch, it was "Good-by Slapstick, Hello Nonchalance!"

Other German films that came to America at this time and affected American films included *All for a Woman* (*Danton*), *Othello*, *Peter the Great*, directed by Dmitri Buchowetsky; and *The Golem* by Henrik Galeen and Paul Wegener. All acclaimed as "masterpieces," these German films displayed unusual cinematic understanding, sensitive fusing of substance and form, astute and skillful camera work, wise cutting, care and devotion to composition and decoration, sound architecture, vivid characterization, movement, effective lighting, the use of "unreality," and, above all, a love of the medium. They aroused American directors to a fresh awareness of their tools and set new standards of movie quality. To American directors from whose pictures (according to the cutters) mob scene after mob scene could be removed without noticeable damage to the film, these foreign pictures were models of structure and economy. If they had done nothing else, these German films would have renewed America's interest in the future of the movies as an art form.

By 1923 the German films had accomplished what they set out to do: to make a reputation. The entire film world spoke of German films with awe. So far did this veneration go that as early as 1922, in his picture *The Ropin' Fool*, Will Rogers was prompted to remark, "If you think this picture's no good, I'll put on a beard and say it was made in Germany, and then you'll call it art."

German talent, including Ernst Lubitsch, Pola Negri, Hans Kraly, Buchowetsky, and others, was imported rapidly. But no sooner had it reached American shores than new talent appeared in Germany to replace it.

In 1925 America was again aroused by a number of unusual productions from German studios. Two in particular stimulated Hollywood to emulation and had immediate and widespread influence on American motion picture technique: *Variety*, showing that the camera could be put to shocking and astounding uses; and *The Last Laugh*, emphasizing fluidity and titleless narration by means of the moving camera. Both brought a closer realism to the screen, interest in the common man, his milieu, and his feelings; both showed how the camera could be used to give psychological insight; both stimulated important innovations in American methods.

Variety put American movie-goers into a white heat of enthusiasm over film art. It became the most important movie of the day, rivaling *Greed* and *The Cabinet of Dr. Caligari* in the amount of discussion it provoked. Unlike any of its German predecessors, this film was neither stylized, spectacular, nor graced by subtle wit, but instead, to quote Evelyn Gerstein,[4] it was "a dark, stinging tale of life in variety, utterly devoid of the pale puerilities, the sterile conventions. . . ." Intensely real, even sordid, in the tradi-

[4] *The New Republic*, July 20, 1926.

tion of von Stroheim, the film dealt with the lust of people who
have nothing else. Its uncompromising depiction of a man-crazy
woman (Lya de Putti) and her victim (Emil Jannings), and the
ensuing murder and tragedy, combined horror and dread with
sensuality.

Throughout the film the camera was like a piercing eye that
sees inside the players, revealing to the spectator their psychological
make-up, unknown to themselves. Brilliantly knit sequences produced high dramatic tension; no element was presented that did
not contribute to the whole. Fluid camera transitions, skillful dissolves, multiple exposures, arresting angles and perspectives, eloquent pantomime (on occasion, overwrought), dramatic lighting,
free use of detail, and moving camera made the film an unforgettable work from which much was to be learned.

Variety demonstrated that the camera could function like cutting. We see a man in a furnished room waiting for a girl to come
down the hallway past his door. He is listening intently for her
footsteps; the moment is full of suspense. The camera moves into
a close-up of the man's ear. The ear then dissolves into feet walking
down the stairs. Without a title and without a cut, we follow the
man's action and what he hears. Such execution was novel and
fluent beyond contemporary America's technique.

The camera not only was used to tell the story, but by its use
as the eye of the character it presented the audience with the
world as the character saw it, subjectively. The camera swings on
the trapeze with the circus man so that we experience what he
sees and feels. In this way the emotional impact of the scene and
the moment was intensified and sensed physically as well as emotionally by the audience.

This fresh conception and the skillful application of the camera's
versatility opened the eyes of American producers. Already startled
by the variety of perspectives and shifts of camera in von Stroheim's
and Lubitsch's films, Hollywood was ready to appreciate and quick
to adopt the contributions of *Variety*. Camera angles already being
a commonplace, movies now indulged in dissolves and transitional
devices constantly.

Typical was Victor Schertzinger's treatment of *Forgotten Faces*

(1927), in which the German influence is clearly evident. To indicate a lapse of fifteen years, the hero is shown walking down the street with a policeman. The camera "pans down" to their moving feet, which now dissolve into other moving feet. The camera "pans up" to the bodies of the owners of these feet and we see they are convicts, filing through a prison corridor. The camera swings to a convict in a cell: he is the hero. He takes a picture from his cot, and the camera swings around so that we see the picture over his shoulder. It is of a girl baby. The hero takes out other pictures from behind the frame: these show the growing progress of the girl until she is a young lady.

Clearly inspired by *Variety*, in this picture the use of dissolves, the lack of explanatory titles, and the use of the moving camera instead of cutting revealed a cunning command of the medium and the increased ingeniousness and imagination now becoming more prevalent in Hollywood as a direct result of the German pictures.

The director of *Variety*, E. A. Dupont; its supervisor, Erich Pommer; its photographer, Karl Freund; its scenarist, Leo Birinski; were all quickly rushed to America like others before them.

The Last Laugh, like *Variety*, seemed to embody a solution of the uppermost problem in moviecraft—story telling entirely through picture progression. Subtitles in *The Last Laugh* were reduced to one. As in *Variety*, the camera moved constantly, and dissolves were used freely but precisely so that the story was unfolded by the selection and presentation of the images alone. Imaginatively conceived, sensitively executed, the film showed a keen understanding of the basic nature of the screen medium and, with *Variety*, it brought Hollywood up sharply to a realization of possibilities in technique.

The story of *The Last Laugh* was extraordinarily simple, and in this respect alone it was different from all previous films. It related the tragedy of an elderly doorman of a huge hotel who was stripped of his identity when discharged. Without any of the usual dramatic complications, without plots and subplots, the richness of characterization sustained one's interest, presenting a rounded study of a man's personal loss when he finds himself without a job and position in life. The camera traveled continually from the opening scene of a revolving hotel door, in and out of streets, up and down houses, through doors and windows, like a living organism and with amazing facility. Windows opening on a courtyard showed the city awakening. Bedding hung out to air and the sunlight moving across a dark wall told the passage of time cinematically and without recourse to words. As Kenneth White later expressed it,[5]

The pantomime everyone had thought to be the derived art of the movies was not discoverable in *The Last Laugh*. The doorman got drunk, but not in the way a pantomimic actor with subordinate properties got drunk; the camera did it for him.

Simple, unpretentious, natural, told through the camera eye and pantomime rather than subtitles, *The Last Laugh* made Director F. W. Murnau and Leading Actor Emil Jannings renowned in the United States overnight.

Other German films that continued to come to America similarly demonstrated the value of highly planned, carefully executed studio procedure. Individual and resourceful craftsmanship and emphasis upon atmosphere, architecture, and camera mobility appeared in a number of distinctive films, including among others Galeen's *The Student of Prague*, Lang's *Metropolis* and *Siegfried*, Robison's *Warning Shadows*, Leni's *Three Waxworks*, Pabst's *Joyless Street*, Berger's *Cinderella*, Czinner's *Nju*, and Joe May's *The Homecoming*. The list was brought to a striking climax in Murnau's *Faust*. These films like their predecessors, with high artificiality, psychological intensity, varied moods, and smooth realizations, nourished Hollywood's best minds and inspired them to a new creative interest in the movie medium.

Besides Germany other European countries were also contributing to world production and influencing American directors. During 1919 and 1920 the Swedish film industry was large and well organized. Such notable importations as *The Girl from Marchcroft*, *Puss in Boots*, *A Man There Was*, *The Atonement of Gosta Ber-*

[5] *Hound and Horn*, July-September 1931.

ling, although never widely circulated or so startling in their technique as the German productions, nevertheless brought a new note to movies. Opposed to the artificiality of the German films in their stress on the real world of nature, the sea and the landscape, Swedish pictures were impressive for their simplicity, realism, sensitive acting, and sincerity. The leading figures—Victor Seastrom, actor and director, and later Mauritz Stiller and his discovery and protégée, Greta Garbo—were all brought to America, as was Lars Hanson, the actor. Like the Germans these notables were to become significant workers in Hollywood and to contribute directly to the American tradition.

France, having sent to America an occasional imposing film such as *J'accuse* (1921), a spectacular fourteen-reel story of the early days of the World War, directed by Abel Gance, suddenly in the late twenties presented important innovations to the motion picture world. Unusual cinematic sensitivity was displayed in *The Passion of Joan of Arc*, directed by Carl Dreyer and distributed here in 1929; in *Thérèse Raquin* and *Les Nouveaux Messieurs*, by Jacques Feyder, which was little shown here; and in *The Italian Straw Hat*, by René Clair. These films were unlike any that had yet appeared, being different in conception and rendition from both German and Swedish efforts.

The Passion of Joan of Arc was a tense personal dramatization of the famous martyr. Unlike the German historical dramas, the rendering was unspectacular, the backgrounds were stylized, the power of the film being derived from cutting and continuous camera movement. An extraordinary emphasis upon the close-up caused in the spectator an almost oppressive tension that was in keeping with the theme; the whole picture had a tremendous emotional impact.

Feyder's films demonstrated the psychological possibilities of the movie in its remarkable characterizations. The Clair productions, on the other hand, were the work of a humorist with a flair for lampooning the conventions of the middle class and with an unusual sense of cinematic continuity and movement. Both Feyder and Clair were later to make important sound films and to grow still larger in artistic stature. All these French films, meritorious though they were, were given little attention because of contemporary excitement over the invention of sound and over the Soviet films. They did point, nevertheless, to the still untapped artistic resources of the American movie.

The Soviet films followed quickly after the German films, bursting upon the American film scene between 1926 and 1929. Hollywood had not yet assimilated the contributions of the German pictures when the brilliant films of Eisenstein, Pudovkin, and others appeared with their fresh vigor, high imagination, and profound cinematic skill. The Russian films created even more excitement and controversy than the German productions had provoked. Intellectuals and artists, not to mention producers, argued hotly and constantly about the merits of these Soviet newcomers. Cries of "propaganda" were mingled with cheers for their dynamic forcefulness. When the smoke of conflict had cleared away, it was apparent that a new era had begun in screen esthetics; a profound conception of film composition, consummating all the structural principles which had come down from Melies, Porter, Griffith, and the other Europeans, had been formulated. With the Soviet films the art of movies became clarified.

Unlike the films from other countries, Soviet movies were not made to entertain; their purpose was far deeper. State-supported, they were produced to instruct, develop, and inspire the citizens of their country for their own social, scientific, and political progress. They were educational films in the highest sense of the term. Reflecting the life and interests of a people building a new world, the themes of these pictures were not trivial but were of deep and immediate meaning. The 1905 abortive sailors' revolt, a peasant's development into a revolutionary, the ten turbulent days following the establishment of Kerensky's provisional government, a comparison of the old and new farming methods, and many similar historical and sociological events were used to sum up the achievements and ideals of the Russian revolution.

More than any others, Soviet films were saturated with reality. They were not studio-made. The cameras were put to work in the open air, the forests, city streets, mountains, plains, and vast farms

Palaces, fortresses, factories, the Russian peasant hovels, the kulak homes—these were not sets, but the real thing. Russian directors believed that the camera does best in the actual place. "Away from realism to reality," said their leader, Eisenstein. And as with locales, so with actors: "from the studio setting and . . . professional actors to the original place and person." Peasants, workers, sailors, soldiers, housewives, were the actors in these silent movies. The Russians had no use for stars or the star system; they insisted that the camera obliterates the difference between professional and novice. This stress on reality, together with deep purpose, serious subject matter, and grasp of cinematic form, gave the Soviet films a drive, conviction, and distinction that made non-Russian pictures seem petty.

Unlike the German directors, the men who made the Soviet movies had not trained in commercial studios, but were chemists, engineers, factory workers; a few had been theatre technicians. It was with a serious and analytical attitude and a long-range program that they approached movie making. They gave their problem all the rapt attention of scholars, first studying, theorizing, and experimenting to discover the values and basis of their medium: they were artisans, not business men. They maintained that in every art there is a material and a method of organizing that material according to its own nature. Finally they determined what Melies, Porter, and Griffith had sensed many years before: that in movies the basis of expression is the organization of the film pieces, which in themselves contain the elements of the larger forms and, in their relationships, give the film its unity and effectiveness.

This Russian emphasis was more profound than the German emphasis upon the camera eye and camera mobility; it was nearer the essence of film art. For through a command of cutting, a film could be made from still photographs if necessary. Cutting was most important; the camera was an essential but nevertheless subordinate tool to the cutting process. The Russians consolidated the results of their research and experimentation into a unique body of concrete principles, which have become the basis of all modern film making and which, underlying their own films, made them the most outstanding productions of the "silent" era. The summing up of the Soviet credo was the word *montage*.

Americans first heard of montage through the writings and films of the two leading Soviet theoreticians and directors, Eisenstein and Pudovkin. In the pages of *Close Up* and *Experimental Cinema*, two significant social and artistic movie magazines, can be found many of their articles explaining montage methods, purposes, and principles. Perhaps the simplest summary of the Soviet film ideology is found in Eisenstein's lecture [6] at the Sorbonne University in Paris in the spring of 1930:

We have discovered how to force the spectator to think in a certain direction. By mounting our films in a way scientifically calculated to create a given impression on an audience, we have developed a powerful weapon for the propagation of the ideas upon which our new social system is based.

Eisenstein is generally regarded as the leading genius of the montage school; Pudovkin, as the most intelligent eclectic. Eisenstein has been compared to a general because of his scientific strategy in planning, constructing, and analyzing every element of the picture according to its probable effect on the audience. Pudovkin is thought of as an artisan whose sensitive feeling guides the form of the film, although he also is adept at structural planning. Eisenstein's pictures have been called epic because of their broad theme and vast scale; Pudovkin's are called lyric because of the personal conflicts involved in them. Where Eisenstein is all mind, Pudovkin is mostly feeling.

This difference in approach has caused many observers to say that Eisenstein's films are cold and aloof, marvelous examples of mathematical structure; that Eisenstein is the formalist. Pudovkin's work is said to be warm, intimate, more closely related to the spectator's feelings; hence he is called the poet. The contrast is the more notable because of Eisenstein's use of the masses as a hero and Pudovkin's use of the more conventional individual as hero. Eisenstein, moreover, has disdained the story method: his films are built around themes and deal mainly with concepts. Pudovkin has always a story to relate: his movies show the development of an individual against a turbulent background. It is these two main channels of movie making that Soviet directors generally have followed.

[6] Reported by S. Brody in *Close Up*, April 1930.

The essence of Eisenstein's montage is movement. Movement in an Eisenstein film functions like color in a Cézanne painting. It becomes the architectural basis of composition, pervading sequence development, scene construction, shot analysis, and action of subject matter, and providing that vigorous sweep which gave Griffith's *The Birth of a Nation* and *Intolerance* their dynamic forcefulness, which is the vitality of any film, and which can be found in all great films.

Eisenstein's reputation was made with his second film, *Potemkin* (1926). His first, *Strike* (1925), had little distribution in Russia and none in America. *Potemkin* was followed by *Ten Days That Shook the World* (1927) and *Old and New* (1928). All three films are remarkable achievements, full of that unique cinematic quality, penetrating vision, and vigorous style which have made Eisenstein perhaps the greatest figure in the movie world.

Potemkin, Eisenstein's most popular film, is perhaps his most unified. It is made up, as Dwight Macdonald [7] pointed out, of three sections or major movements in which an infinite number of lesser movements prevail (motion in the frame, cutting on movement, and continuation of motion from shot to shot, all given further mobility through tempo and mounting). The introductory section starts with a moderate movement—with evenly paced shots of the flowing sea, the swaying hammocks of sailors' quarters, the sailors' morning activities—and builds gradually to the excitement of the sailors' protest over wormy meat. The tempo of the shots, which has been imperceptibly speeded up, gains force in the conflict between the sailors and officers, and is climaxed in the revolt, with a crescendo of cutting (close and angle shots) in the battle for the ship. From this high point, the movement recedes to a sequence of calm—the burial of the dead sailor, presented in extreme long shots, curving panoramic scenes, and "pans," all set to a quiet, slow rhythm.

The second section is swift and vigorous. Movement begins immediately with the gay groups on the harbor steps acclaiming the battleship *Potemkin,* now in the control of the sailors. The shots are full of motion: twirling parasols, laughing faces, hands waving, cheering, boats sailing out with food, sailors on deck. The rhythm

[7] *The Miscellany*, March 1931.

is free, and ingenious in its variety. Then suddenly and without warning this gay mood is broken by the introduction of another kind of rhythm—the steady, methodical beat of the oncoming impersonal Cossacks. The meeting of the two contrasting types of movement, underlying the opposition in scenes, urges the conflict to a nerve-racking climax in the massacre. The intensity, speed, and impact of the staccato close shots of firing soldiers, screaming victims, and careening baby carriage intercut as a point of reference with flashes of legs, steps, blood (all in ironic contrast to the scene's happy beginning), make this sequence one of the most powerful in movie history. Throughout this episode Eisenstein never allows the tension to subside, but rather increases its pitch and ends not by resolving it but by cutting it short. In this way not only is the horror of the scene implanted in the spectators' consciousness with far greater forcefulness, but they are left taut for what follows.

The third movement is tense from the very beginning. It opens with the slow movement of the crew watchfully awaiting attack; the cutting is moderately paced. Learning of the approaching Czarist fleet, the sailors act more quickly; their preparations for defense involve a rising excitement, heightened by swifter cutting and angle shots. With the appearance of the Czarist navy, the conflict has gained impetus. The rapid intercutting between the *Potemkin's* sailors and the approaching ships, the huge close-ups of the ships' pumping engines, men loading guns, shells being moved into position, cannon rising ever higher in the screen frame—all the shots set to a rapid-fire tempo—create a terrific tension.

Then comes not a climax but an unbearable suspense. As the ships approach one another with guns trained, the cutting is suddenly slowed down to a crawling pace. All movement seems to cease as the sailors on the *Potemkin* await the first shots of their adversary. The prolonged pause keeps the spectators breathless; they identify themselves with the crew of the *Potemkin* as the crew waits, motionless. When finally the climax comes, when the Czarist fleet hoists peace signals and steams past the *Potemkin* without firing a shot, the sudden scrambling of the relieved sailors is caught in a sequence of frenzied cutting that releases the pent-up feelings of the spectators. The swift movement of these shots gives a kind of exuberance to the last moment of the drama. The audience is now spent; the film is over. But the note on which it has ended leaves the spectator with a deep exhilaration.

Eisenstein's next picture, *Ten Days That Shook the World*, was a dramatization of the ten days following the establishment of the Kerensky provisional government; it appeared so real that many claimed its shots were actual newsreels of the historic events themselves. In common with its predecessor *Potemkin*, it had no hero except the revolutionary masses, and its basic structural principle was movement; but instead of centering about a single event, as was true of *Potemkin*, it dealt with a series of events. It was Eisenstein's most complex effort. Its structure is so closely knit that the film is impossible to analyze at one viewing. Shots are blended with each other with such amazing dexterity—with such intuition for the precise image, the exact pace, the best psychological angle, the perfect fluidity—that they are overwhelming. This is truly a great director's picture.

Many of the individual sequences are striking examples of Eisenstein's montage: the flight over the drawbridge, Kerensky's ascension to temporary power, the Cossack dance, the storming of the Winter Palace, the Women's Battalion, the Bolshevik leaders talking to the soldiers. Two sequences in particular might be singled out for analysis, one for its emotional power and the other for its intellectual import. Both display the startling pictorial quality as well as the dynamic continuity that gave the film a symphonic sweep.

The first of these sequences, the drawbridge episode, is perhaps the most forceful example of Eisenstein's use of intra-scene cutting for dramatic impact. Here he brings all the cinematic elements under his control into a scheme of dynamic construction which he has called "the mounting of attractions." It "consists in evoking in the spectator a series of successive thrills." People running from Czarist soldiers and a machine gunner are being shot down as they make for the drawbridge, already opening to trap those who escape the bullets. Men and women fall as they turn back in panic to the shore. Left to their fate are a horse and carriage and a dead girl, both caught on either side of the drawbridge just at the place of opening. Detail shots of the scurrying populace and the firing soldiers are intercut furiously as the desperation and excitement increase. The movements of the running people are never shown completed; they are cut short, and the rhythm is continued with another shot of a similar or opposing movement and is intercut to the point of reference—the dead girl and horse and carriage—but each time from another camera viewpoint (dependent upon the preceding shot) and in a more precarious position (to emphasize the plight of the fleeing victims). In the image of the dead girl, whose hair slips bit by bit into the opening of the rising drawbridge, and in the spectacle of a horseless carriage being lifted higher and higher on the rising side of the drawbridge, the desperateness of the situation is sharply conveyed to the spectator. Eisenstein, moreover, destroys all sense of real time through his repetition of the two images (he cuts back to the girl at least fourteen times and almost as many times to carriage); thus he extends and prolongs the suspense ("a series of successive thrills"). At last, the climax—the dead girl falls—the carriage raised aloft on the upraised span, rolls furiously down to the bottom. It is a moment of deep horror. And then the movement and the emotion of the episode are resolved.

Eisenstein's satire is displayed in his characterization of Kerensky. As Kerensky arrogantly walks up the steps of the Winter Palace, Eisenstein cross-cuts to near-by statues (ironically commenting on the would-be dictator's ambition). At the top of the steps, under a marble statue whose outstretched arm holds a laurel leaf, Kerensky pauses, a self-imagined Caesar, but Eisenstein photographs him from above to dwarf his figure and exhibit his weak, chinless head.

Inside the Czar's room Kerensky toys with the cap of a whisky flask before him; intercut are statues of Napoleon, serving as visual metaphors. When Kerensky leans forward to place the cap on the flask, the spectators suddenly notice that the cap is a miniature coronet, and that Kerensky is cherishing Napoleonic ambitions. At that very moment of realization, the film cuts to a screaming factory whistle, announcing the attack on Petrograd by Kornilov, another would-be ruler. The ambitions of the two are symbolized in statuettes of Napoleons which merge, then crash as the October Revo-

lution bursts. Such a sequence is indicative of the intellectual plane
on which most of Eisenstein's films are conceived.

More direct than *Ten Days That Shook the World* was Eisenstein's next film, *Old and New*. Like both its predecessors it showed
Eisenstein as a director of such resourcefulness that the more one
analyzes his picture the more is revealed. Its simple Russian theme
—the problem of whether to go on a collective farm and earn a
living or to remain an individual farmer and starve—was a peasant's
struggle against superstition, greed, and animosity during the establishment of a collective. In this epic of the countryside Eisenstein
pits brother against brother, the peasant against the kulak, and the
atheist against the religious man in images that are biting, satirical,
tender, dramatic. He shows the louse-ridden homes of the old
peasants in contrast to the comfortable ones of the overfed kulaks.
In a sequence with brilliant intra-scene cutting, he depicts the religious peasants with their village priests in their drought-stricken
fields, praying for rain which does not come. In another sequence
he turns the activity of a milk separator into a tense and dramatic
episode, the marriage of a bull into a hilarious ballad, the wheat-
cutting contest of a collective into a sort of music that keeps the
spectators swaying in their seats to the rhythm of his cuts. The final
sequence, in which a lone tractor pulls the collective's carts up the
hill, with the enraptured country people frolicking behind—the
whole is set to a mazurka rhythm—is one of the gayest episodes
Eisenstein has ever made.

Unlike the work of most directors, Eisenstein's pictures are so
rich in emotional overtones, so complex in montage structures, that
only by constant re-viewings can they be fully appreciated.

Of lesser stature than Eisenstein, Pudovkin has enjoyed greater
popularity. This is true because his pictures are more traditional
in their structure and ideas, and hence easier to follow. They have
a story, a protagonist, and a narrative form suggestive of Griffith,
whom Pudovkin greatly admires. *Mother* (1926), the best film of
this Soviet director, was not shown in America until ten years after
its production, and then it was not widely seen. *The End of St.
Petersburg* (1927) and *Storm Over Asia* (1928) were the pictures
that made Pudovkin famous.

The End of St. Petersburg, called by Leonard Hall "A worthy successor to *Potemkin*," was so popular that it became the first Soviet film to play in America's largest theatre, the Roxy. It was shown there for several weeks after it had completed many weeks of a two-a-day run at Hammerstein's. The film dramatized, through the eyes of a peasant, the social upheaval in St. Petersburg (Leningrad). Pictorially it had a sweep and richness comparable to Eisenstein's films, but it had less intellectual and structural complexities. Its feeling for the vastness and atmosphere of the Russian countryside (a characteristic of all Soviet films), its innumerable satirical touches (such as the shrieking Kerensky and the pompous police commissioner), and its portrait of the bewildered peasant who comes to look for work and finally emerges from perplexity to an understanding of the upheaval, are rendered in a quick, sharp style that emphasizes the intensity of the events and carries the spectator away by the sheer force of narration as much as by the facts themselves.

The execution of the stock-exchange sequence has become celebrated. Pudovkin portrays in extreme close shots the hysteria of the war profiteers, then cross-cuts to another kind of hysteria, to men in the war zone being mowed down by bursting shells, shivering in dugouts, killing and being killed, forcing the spectator to draw his own conclusion from the parallel cutting. Another example of this telling style is the recruiting sequence. A demagogue, exhorting a crowd to join the army, smashes his own top hat, explaining that the enemy made it; then he breaks his cane because that, too, is enemy-made; then he airs his admiration for a passing soldier, and calls upon the onlookers to join the army. But the crowd know this soldier as a released convict who was forced to join the army. A further satirical touch is given the scene when the soldier reveals that he is carrying, much against his will, a large portrait of the Czar. Such sequences are typical of the tenor of the film throughout.

Storm Over Asia, Pudovkin's third film, paralleled in many respects *The End of St. Petersburg*. It too has a single protagonist who, in the confusion of events, becomes socially awakened and leads his fellow men against their oppressors. In *Storm Over Asia* the hero, a Mongol who through a series of circumstances is mistaken for the heir of Genghis Khan, is prepared to be used as a dupe by British interests so that they can control his people, but upon realizing the situation he turns upon them.

The structure of the film, simpler than that of *The End of St. Petersburg*, is a good exposition of Pudovkin's film credo. His progress is from the general (long shots) to the particular (close shots). The first shots are of clouds, then distant hills, then bare lands, and gradually the camera comes to the immediate—a foreground, a hut, the inside of the hut, its inhabitants, the sick father. Finally come detail shots of the ensuing situation, a fight which starts the first episodes. The pace begins with a moderate tempo and ends with a rapid one.

The next sequence reverses the pattern: progress is from the particular to the general. The young Mongol in the hut prepares to take the fox skin to a distant trading post. As he takes his leave, detail shots of his mother, the priest, and himself gradually become medium and semi-full shots. Outside we see the mother in full shots, and the son riding off; then, from the son's angle, there is a more distant shot of his home and mother. This is followed by a still more distant shot, until finally there is only a tiny speck of a rider seen on the vast spaces of Mongolia. The pace, begun with a fast beat (the fight), ends with a moderate one (the slow, long shots of the leavetaking). The formal opposition of the two sequences creates a pattern of continuity in time which is characteristic of the whole film.

In the middle part of the film, parallel and contrast cutting are used with telling effect. A small battle between the insurgents and British is going on in a distant valley while the English commander and his wife are dressing to attend a ceremony at a Mongolian lamasery. A witty analogy is created by the intercutting of shots of the dressing Britishers and the Mongolian dancers: both don clothes, trinkets, headgear, and masks (paint, powder, and a "best smile" for the commander and his wife). The rhythm of the sequence is deft and precise. But the episode is only the preparation for a more ironic sequence. The commander, his wife, and the staff come to the temple for the ceremonies, paying their compliments to the priest gravely: "My government," the commander murmurs, "deeply regrets your recent demise" (here a flash shot of a Mongolian infant on the altar, the New Lama, playing with his toes) "and hails with joy your new birth." This is followed by a shot of the British shooting Mongols which begins a sequence of biting sarcasm.

The English entourage in the temple are all smiles; their expressions of good-will increase as the ceremony proceeds. Intercut with these shots are those of the British and Mongols fighting, so that while the general is paying his respects to the priests, his soldiers are shooting down the Mongolian peasants. By such referential cross-cutting of contrasting scenes, Pudovkin achieves a bitter irony.

The end of the film, a simple double exposure, illustrates a profound use of symbolism. The Mongol youth (mistaken heir of Genghis Khan) has fiercely fought his way out of the British headquarters and is riding across the desert, pursued by his erstwhile captors. A windstorm begins. The Mongol raises his ancient sword and cries out: "O My People!" Suddenly, as if in answer to his cry, the desert becomes alive with hundreds of mounted Mongols. Again the Mongol calls: "Rise in your ancient strength!"

The screen fills with Mongolians, riding furiously, and when the Mongol once more calls out: "—and free yourselves!" the desert storm takes on the force of a hurricane as the Mongolians sweep everything before them—the British army, trading posts, trees—in a tempestuous movement symbolical of their united strength and the imminent *Storm Over Asia*. The whole is a powerful example of the implanting of what Pudovkin calls "an abstract concept into the consciousness of the spectator."

The differences that distinguish the work of Eisenstein and Pudovkin are reconciled in a third, little-known director, Dovzhenko. His films have not had such advantages of widespread publicity and distribution as the other two directors have enjoyed, but they are in many respects equally unique and valuable. To the structural contributions of his associates he has added a deep personal and poetic insight, which not only gives his films a mystical quality but makes them utterly unusual. *Arsenal* and *Soil* are the only two of his films which were seen in America. Both are laconic in style, with a strange, wonderfully imaginative quality difficult to describe. Says Dovzhenko, "Excitement runs like a red thread through all my films." Neither of these works has a story; both spring from moods, concepts, and images of Ukrainian legends. Both contain some of the most sensitive pictorial compositions the screen has ever known, superbly related in angle, tone, and movement. So personalized are these pictures that they achieve the emotional intensity of great lyrical poems; so concentrated, rich, and unexpected are their images that Dovzhenko, perhaps more than anyone else, can be called the first poet of movies.

In addition to these "giants of the Soviet cinema" there were a group of films which, while less masterful, were nevertheless forceful and often brilliant, originating in the same principles and backgrounds. Trauberg (*China Express*), Raisman (*In Old Siberia*), Stabovoi (*Two Days*), Ermler (*Fragment of an Empire*), Tarish (*Ivan the Terrible*), Turin (*Turksib*), Kozintsev and Trauberg (*New Babylon*), all extraordinarily skillful craftsmen, showed distinct personal styles despite the similarity of their themes (various phases of revolutionary action). Many of them experimented individually to carry further the ideas of Kuleshov, Pudovkin's instructor, and Eisenstein.

Collectively these productions from the Soviet Union put the Russian film far in the vanguard of movie progress and turned American attention back again to the importance of form and structure through editing. The enormous power of the Russian films, despite their many mechanical crudities, showed Hollywood that imagination and vital subject matter could overcome other drawbacks, and that camera facility and virtuosity were not everything. Montage became the new vogue; it was synthetically inserted in films as "effects." The term was absorbed by Hollywood film language, its meaning in the main however being restricted to an impressionistic series of quick cuts or rapid dissolves used for the purpose of transition.

The Russian films also showed American directors another aspect of screen acting. They pointed the fact that, the nature of the film being what it was, for silent films the trained stage actor was not necessary. Basing their technique on a highly realistic approach, they used real characters, placing them in situations which were part of their everyday existence. By means of cunning camera compositions, significant details, and judicious cutting, they achieved a verisimilitude that was rich in characterization, spontaneous in quality, and three-dimensional in form. With the Russian examples before them, Hollywood producers began to choose their players for character parts more carefully and tried more imaginatively to build character through significant details.

Of all the Soviet directors only one was brought to Hollywood: Eisenstein, in 1930. After completing two scripts, *Sutter's Gold* and *An American Tragedy*, which were later directed by others from other scripts, he was released from his contract. Later he was independently financed to make a picture in Mexico. After he had been at work several years, his backers refused to continue the project, recalled him, took the photographed but uncut film, condensed the material according to their own viewpoint (which was not Eisenstein's), and released the film as *Thunder Over Mexico*. A great hue and cry went up led by the film magazine *Experimental Cinema* and followed by other serious film journals, film students, critics, and intellectuals in America as well as Europe. They protested against the damage done to Eisenstein's film and reputation, and a concerted effort was made to have Eisenstein cut the film himself, but it proved of no avail. Eisenstein returned to Russia.

Under the stimulus of European films and with the influx of fresh talent into Hollywood, the craftsmanship of American motion pictures steadily improved throughout the ten post-war years. The intensification and refinement of all phases of production finally culminated in the invention and adoption of sound, which resulted in a confusion that temporarily canceled all the advances of these years. Until sound came, directing, writing, photography, art direction, and acting developed in skill and subtlety. Not only had the resources of the medium been enriched but they were being exploited individualistically and with increasing complexity and variety. The content of films remained, on the whole, so shallow and cheap that most Hollywood movies, while mechanically admirable, were disdained for the level of their conception.

Directors were showing a sharper awareness of film technique, a deeper appreciation of the camera and cutting, and a desire to formalize what knowledge had become available. The advent of European films emphasized the importance of telling the story visually and by movement. Victor Schertzinger represented the attitude of the industry when he declared in 1927 that

the lens' possibilities are just beginning to be realized with the growing utilization of camera angles first tried in Germany. Now the camera has burst its bonds of immovability and has been made to follow the players. . . . If they are climbing a stairway, the camera by various devices can record their progress step by step. Dramatic effects can also be greatly enhanced by the proper use of dissolves and moving camera shots.

The new view of the camera, story value, choice of players, and art direction lifted motion picture craft to a higher average. A movie no longer was praised for good photography, as in pre-war days, but was criticized if the photography was poor. A high order of skill in all the physical and outward aspects of motion picture art—photography, settings, costumes, lighting, make-up—was now taken for granted. If a film lacked that skill, it was disdained as amateurish and suitable only for the cheaper market.

During the early twenties directors who had been connected with movies in various capacities without gaining much notice came to the fore in great numbers. The sudden appearance of this abundance of young talent was due to a combination of circumstances. First, the growth in public demand for films called for expansion of production schedules; studios' output now included hundreds of features a year, and many new men were given the opportunity to direct. Second, during the intense competition of the first post-war years, the director gained freedom to carry out his undertakings as he saw fit and to participate actively in every phase of production, from story construction and casting to the final editing. This directorial freedom lasted until the industry's entanglements with Wall Street financiers took the responsibility for a picture out of the hands of the director and gave it to the producer-supervisor whom Wall Street brought in. The producer-supervisor then, as already pointed out, selected the story, players, technicians, and art directors, and assigned the director to carry out his plans. The weakness of this new method was the fact that in most cases the producer was a business man, chosen for his executive ability and background, but having little artistic knowledge and few criteria to guide his judgments.

The most marked improvements during the first years after the war occurred first, however, not in the field of direction but in screen writing. Once looked upon as a mere hack, unadvertised, low-paid, the writer was brought out of obscurity and esteemed almost on a par with the star and the director. The day had passed when a newspaper reporter could jot down some ideas in his spare time and make money by selling them to the movies. Now that the technique of movies was becoming ever more defined and studio schedules were requiring more planning in advance, the staff writer was appreciated as a vital contributor to the business.

Samuel Goldwyn established a custom by engaging and widely publicizing such well-known authors as Rex Beach, Rupert Hughes, and Gertrude Atherton. Competition for "name" writers became fierce. Paramount was soon advertising [8] that

The greatest living authors are now working with Paramount. Sir James Barrie you know; and Joseph Conrad, Arnold Bennett, Robert Hitchens, E. Phillips Oppenheim, Sir Gilbert Parker, Elinor Glyn, Edward Knoblock, W. Somerset Maugham, Avery Hopwood, Henry Arthur Jones, Cosmo Hamilton, Edward Sheldon, Samuel Merwin, Harry J. O'Higgins—all these famous authors are actually in the studios writing new plays for Paramount Pictures, advising with directors, using the motion picture camera as they formerly used a pen.

Hollywood became the writer's Mecca. A steady stream of stories poured in from amateur plot makers throughout the world. Plagiarism suits became common; the cry of "swindling" was taken up. Soon companies refused to accept unsolicited manuscripts; only professional novelists and playwrights could now get through the closed studio doors, and "names" were esteemed as never before. Average prices paid to contemporary successful authors rose to $15,000, then $20,000 and up to $50,000, for a story. Stories were

[8] In *Photoplay*, June 1921.

used up so fast that studios had to read books even before publication.

Despite their new recognition and high wages, authors were dissatisfied, declaring that nothing was demanded of them but a formula plot. Outspoken protests piled up. "As an author," declared Rex Beach, "I say that it is bunk that you want more and better authors. . . . What you want is more mush and slush, pre-digested pap." Such was the opinion of nearly all the famous writers.

Meanwhile it became increasingly clear that a good scenarist, rather than a good author, was perhaps the greatest asset to a studio. Photoplay writing had long been recognized as a specialized profession; the skill of translating plots into visual factors remained a trade known only by a few. No matter how famous the author of an original novel or play was, what gave the novel or play substance was its working out in terms of the camera and film. The ability to do this task was not easily developed; good scenarists were uncommon. Scenario writing demanded not only dramatic training but a thorough understanding of the film's unique tools. The best scenarists in the industry were not world-famous authors but the long-experienced motion picture script writers, many of whom had been working in the industry since its earliest days. In the words of Joseph Hergesheimer,[9] "The moving pictures have learned to their sorrow that whereas a novel is valuable, a novelist is not."

The scenarists broke down the various parts of a proposed film story into the "synopsis," which outlined the story and then the "treatment," which was longer and developed the story from a definite point of view. If accepted, the "treatment" was developed into the "continuity," which was a literary transcription of the finished movie as it would appear on the screen. This final form, being the director's "shooting" or "working" script, required a highly technical understanding of the film medium if it was to be of any real service and value. Continuity writers were therefore soon recognized as the backbone of production: they saved time and trouble in addition to planning the final form of the film, from which the cost of production was computed.

Though few scenarists became publicly known, their prestige

[9] *Motion Picture Classic*, February 1927.

mounted constantly. Increasing responsibility for the finished film was laid upon them. Often, in big producing companies, the director was given little or no chance to co-operate with the writer in the story's construction; in such cases, the real director of the film was the continuity writer. It was presently realized, however, that the best results were obtained when the director and scenarist worked together.

One of the most important scenarists in motion pictures during this time was June Mathis. To her—and to Thomas Ince—can be credited the make-up of continuity as we know it today. Gaining a reputation for her stress on timely themes and her careful planning, she originated the writer-director combination which was to plan the film's action before any shooting began. The result was less waste, lower production costs, and a smoother, more rounded picture. June Mathis proved that the carefully prepared shooting script was essential to good results in an art that was becoming more and more a collective project. As head of the Metro and Goldwyn units for a time, she became a potent influence on film making. Some of her best known successes at this time were *Eye for an Eye, The Red Lantern, The Brass Check*, and *The Four Horsemen of the Apocalypse*. She is still writing continuities today.

Next to June Mathis perhaps the most important scenario writer of the day was C. Gardner Sullivan. He had been an important worker in the Thomas Ince studio, where he had written, among other scripts, *The Aryan, The Payment*, and *The Pinch-Hitter*. It is said that the downfall of Ince was due in large measure to the severance of his relations with this capable scenarist. Sullivan is still a leading figure in scenario writing.

Other important scenarists included many who had become "typewriter stars" by 1918. Anita Loos was still a major writer, her most famous film of the period being *Gentlemen Prefer Blondes*. Frances Marion, who had written most of Mary Pickford's vehicles, including *The Foundling, Rebecca of Sunnybrook Farm, The Little Princess, M'liss, Amarilly of Clothesline Alley*, and *Johanna Enlists*, was now known for her *The Scarlet Letter* and *The Wind*. Other prominent scenarists were Monte Katterjohn, editor of the first magazine for photo-playwrights, *Motopsis*, and Bess Meredyth, who, coming to movies in 1917, had written ninety features by 1919. Bess Meredyth is still one of the top-ranking writers.

Late in the post-war period others came to the fore, including such outstanding studio-trained scenarists as Howard Estabrook (*Driven to Kill, She Goes to War*), Jules Furthman (*Hotel Imperial, Underworld*), Benjamin Glazer (*The Flesh and the Devil*), and Sonya Levien (*Power of the Press, The Younger Generation*). From Europe came Hans Kraly and Carl Mayer, both of whom were the scenarists responsible for some of the most important foreign successes of these years. All these writers are important in their profession today.

Like script writing, subtitle writing steadily increased in importance. It was studied more and more, and many experiments were attempted. In *Mary's Ankle* (1920), animated titles danced to express elation. Other experiments took the form of large type, italics, and other visual means of bringing out the feeling behind the title, to make up for the lack of the player's voice. Toward the middle of the period there was a return to subtitles that were excessively literary, affected, and self-conscious. Lengthy and flowery phrases often approached the ludicrous. Even in *Greed*, as cut by June Mathis, there were many over-elaborate titles and bad literary clichés.

Two circumstances conspired to banish the fancy subtitle and bring back the succinct phrase. One was the foreign films, which had a notable lack of titles. *The Last Laugh*, in particular, was earnestly praised for its effort to eliminate the subtitle entirely. The effect of this phase on American movie makers was not lost: titles became more restrained. The other circumstance that reformed the subtitle was the change taking place in literature itself. The ascendancy of certain schools of experimental writers and poets, exemplified by James Joyce's *Ulysses*, was reflected on the screen. Observed *Motion Picture Classic*, in reviewing two of the new films,

The syntax is sinful. Verbs left out . . . literary hiccups . . . inspired by a new school of experimentistic writing. Stimulating terseness.[10]

[10] April 1928.

Something should be done forthwith toward bringing the sub-title back to normalcy. It has been taking excursions too much of late in arty pastures where the blunt phrase and the dot and dash live and have their being. . . . A good deal of the success of the Mack Sennett comedies is founded upon the wit of titles decorating them.[11]

The duties of the title writer now were much more than merely the task of phrasing the thoughts of the players and writing "catch" lines and dialogue. It was the title editor, and the film cutter in a larger sense, who together worked out the final form of the film. It was their job first to assemble, out of thousands of feet of film, a story. This work required skill, ingenuity, and considerable tact. "Fill up the holes!" was a common order for them. It meant that they had to match scenes, to insert close-ups, flashes, and titles, to create suspense, to cover up plot inconsistencies, bad acting, the absence of necessary shots, and other inadequacies—in short, to turn out a smooth-flowing narrative. In doing this, moreover, they had to avoid offending the star, the director, and the author.

The duties of the film cutter were extended and made ever more important. Besides working with the director and title writer, often he was assigned to cut down the major pictures after their first runs. In the smaller towns the double-feature program had sprung up, and so the special features were shortened. Certain narrative adjust-ments were necessary, moreover, according to the locality where pictures were to be shown. People in some localities could follow action more readily than others, who had to see more of the details of a picture to understand it.

Among the better known cutters at this time were Rose and Jimmie Smith, who under Griffith had cut *Intolerance;* June Mathis, who cut *Greed;* and Dorothy Arzner, who worked on *The Covered Wagon.* Many of the better directors refused to allow anyone to cut their films, but in the rush of commercial requirements such an attitude was regarded by studio heads as eccentric.

Along with these marked developments in direction, screen writ-ing, and cutting went developments in art direction. As a result of the invasion by foreign films, there was a renewed concern for

11 May 1928.

decoration and costuming. It was quickly realized that otherwise weak stories could be made pleasing by charming the eye with color and the picturesque. Reviewers began to comment favorably on settings as they had previously noted quality in photography: "The settings are handsome," "Pictorially the effects are admirable," "Scenically interesting." Art directors and art departments, already established in the studios, were supplemented with researchers, interior decorators, furniture makers, carpenters, drapers, and fashion designers.

The problem of costume was particularly complicated. With picture fashions being watched assiduously by women patrons, the same gown could not be used too often in the same picture, and never in another picture. Styles had to be advanced enough so that when the picture reached the theatres, months later, the clothes would not look dated or out of fashion. Often, however, the remodeling of clothes could be done economically because colors did not have to match except in black and white values. As for the styles themselves, it was observed that clinging, draped gowns and sparkling jewelry photographed most effectively. With the camera and lighting facilities of the day, the problem of color and texture was also important. It was discovered that red photographed better as black than black itself; white reflected so much light that pastel shades were used instead to give the effect of white.

Photography was affected by the increased refinements of the camera, lens, film, and lighting equipment during these years. For a time after the close of the war, there was a vogue for diffused photography. Edges were made soft and fuzzy by gauze placed in front of the lenses, this being done to achieve the quality of certain paintings and for the practical reason that, in close-ups of women stars particularly, such photography was highly flattering—it softened features and eliminated signs of age. As lighting equipment improved, experience showed that proper lighting could secure the desired effects far better. Standards in art changed and the false notion of achieving artistry by making the photograph like a painting was discarded by the more capable movie makers.

The German school especially introduced many new ideas in photography. Their lighting schemes, camera effects, and careful compositions were slavishly copied, and their camera technicians were often brought to America to work on Hollywood productions.

Perhaps the most potent factor in the improvement of photography was the improvement of the film itself. All improvements in lighting and in the camera had depended upon improvements in film sensitivity. During the years 1924 to 1925 panchromatic film was invented and put to use. More sensitive to tonal values and capable of approximating the tones of nature closer than any other type of film then known, panchromatic film made possible revolutionary changes in photography, lighting, and settings. Less light was now needed, more natural colors could be used, make-up could be closer to normal, and the picture as a whole could have greater tones and brilliance.

By 1927 and 1928 the photography of American films had advanced so far and so rapidly that pictures a year or two old seemed greatly dated. Cinematographers numbered in the hundreds, the following being the most outstanding: John Arnold (*The Wind*), Joe August (*Two Arabian Knights, Beloved Rogue*), Lucien Andriot (*White Gold, The Valiant*), George Barnes (*The Winning of Barbara Worth, Magic Flame*), William Daniels (*Torrent, Flesh and the Devil*), Tony Gaudio (*The Temptress, The Racket*), Lee Garmes (*The Private Life of Helen of Troy*), Bert Glennon (*Hotel Imperial, Underworld*), Peverell Marley (*The Volga Boatman, Silence*), Oliver Marsh (*Camille, Divine Woman*), Victor Milner (*The Way of All Flesh*), Hal Mohr (*Wedding March*), Charles Rosher (*Sunrise*), and Henry Sharp (*The Crowd*).

Under the European influence, the style of screen acting became more defined and still farther removed from the stage gestures of pre-war days. A restrained naturalism was cultivated. The Swedish director Victor Seastrom endorsed a restraint in acting and pantomime that made for a minimum of gestures. Lillian Gish, after playing under him in *The Scarlet Letter*, declared,[12]

His direction was a great education for me. In a sense I went through the Swedish school of acting. I had got rather close to the Italian school in Italy. . . . The Italian school is one of elaboration; the Swedish is one of repression.

[12] In Paine's *Life and Lillian Gish*, p. 225.

A scene from the suppressed orgy sequence in Erich von Stroheim's *The Merry Widow* (1925). The glittering decadence of these continental aristocrats offers an interesting comparison to the simple pleasures of the lower middle class family in *Greed*. Unrelenting realism and a sharp eye for richness of detail mark both.

John Gilbert going "over the top" in King
Vidor's *The Big Parade* (1925), a nostalgic review of the World War.

Actor and director alike were realizing that the camera could do even more to create a personality than any alliance with stage technique could do. Pantomime of a new kind, keyed to the camera, became the new method, but more significant than this was the fact that the actor's body could be "decomposed" by the camera so that only the important movement or gesture was shown. Griffith had already proved expert in such technique, but the German influence brought it into greater prominence. Directors like Lubitsch, Murnau, and Dupont were able to take stereotyped American players and bring out fresh and new values in their personalities because of their camera approach to screen acting. The Russians, moreover, gave a fresh importance to realistic types, character, and individuality even in bit players.

Some of the most famous players of the day were Europeans: Pola Negri, Greta Garbo, Emil Jannings, Lars Hanson, Conrad Veidt. Other new stars of the decade included Gloria Swanson, Thomas Meighan, Rudolph Valentino, John Gilbert, Mae Murray, Richard Barthelmess, Richard Dix, Rod La Rocque, Lew Cody, Adolphe Menjou, Florence Vidor, Marie Prevost, Norma and Constance Talmadge, Harold Lloyd.

The artistic intentions of the European films, furthered particularly toward the close of the period by *avant-garde* films and numerous publications devoted to the movie art, inspired many experiments in America. The interest of the experimenters was addressed to the technique of expression rather than to content. Nazimova's *Salome* was an early bold experiment in stylization. Dramatic and psychological interpretations marked Paul Fejos's *The Last Moment*, Michael Zilburg's *Breakwater* and *Olivera Street*, Charles Klein's *The Tell-Tale Heart*, Charles Vidor's *The Bridge*, and Roman Freulich's *The Prisoner*. Attempts to capture a lyrical quality featured Henwar Rodakiewicz's *The Barge*, *Portrait of the Artist*, and *The Face of New England*, and Herman Weinberg's *Autumn Fire* and *City Symphony*. Experiments in thematic composition included Ralph Steiner's H_2O and *Surf and Seaweed*, Jay Leyda's *Bronx Morning*, Irving Browning's *City of Contrasts*, Robert Florey's *Love of Zero* and *The Life and Death of a Hollywood Extra*, and Paul Strand's and Charles Sheeler's *Manhatta*.

Suddenly in 1927 the progress of motion picture technique was brought to an abrupt halt by the invention and adoption of sound. The incorporation of spoken dialogue as a permanent element of motion pictures caused a cataclysm in the industry. Technique lost its sophistication overnight and became primitive once more; every phase of the movie medium reverted to its rudiments. The interest in artistic film expression that had been stimulated by the superior foreign films, now having reached a climax, was stifled in the chaos that the advent of sound produced. The new film principles that were just beginning to crystallize seemed destined for the dump heap, and directors, stars, writers, musicians, and foreign talent who had succeeded in the era of the "silents" found themselves unwanted. Movie art was forgotten as the studio doors were flung open to stage directors, Broadway playwrights, vaudeville singers, and song-and-dance teams. Voice, sound, noise, were all that now mattered. Diction schools sprang up; everyone took singing lessons; voice tests became the rage; speech filled the ears of the movie capital.

The year 1929 was literally a time of sound and fury. What lay ahead?

XVIII

A THRONG OF DIRECTORS

THE character and quality of the films of any particular period in American movie history can be epitomized in the names of reigning directors. When the film was still a primitive instrument of magic and wonder, the leader was George Melies; when it became a story-telling medium, Edwin S. Porter was the dominant figure; when the film's own idiom was being explored and developed, D. W. Griffith dominated the scene. When, after the war, the movie makers had become self-assured and were using the medium to create "sensations," Cecil B. DeMille, mentor of erotica and display, became the leader.

From 1919 to 1924 DeMille exerted enormous influence. He was copied and envied by all, although a far greater figure—a man head and shoulders above him in talent—Erich von Stroheim, was then making extraordinary films. The man who was finally to take the crown of leadership from DeMille was not to be von Stroheim, however, but a European, Ernst Lubitsch. After 1924 he dominated American directing; like DeMille, he is still a leading figure.

During these years two other Europeans, Fred Murnau and Victor Seastrom, also became noted in American film tradition. There was, besides, a throng of younger directors, many of whom are still prominently active today, who helped to further the film in style, individuality, and importance.

Cecil B. DeMille was a showman, and he flourished at a time when showmanship was the nation's way of life. To neglect or

minimize his importance in an evaluation of the film directors of
post-war years, on the grounds that his works were superficial and
added nothing to film art, would be to ignore the standards of a
public who looked upon him as the model. Practical first, eclectic
afterward, DeMille could sense the changing temper of the times.
His success and his intrinsic merit as a director became so confused
that they were mistaken as identical. An extraordinary showman,
publicist, and business man, DeMille developed the ability to move
with the times. It was this major asset that kept him in the forefront
of movies for twenty-five years, while better talents fell by the
wayside.

DeMille came from a family of playwrights. Before coming to
movies he himself had written, among other plays, *The Return of
Peter Grimm*, *The Royal Mounted* (with his brother, William),
The Genius and *After Eve*. Having also had the enviable experience
of being associated with the "Dean of the American Stage," Belasco,
he was admired as having the "superiority of being probably the
only director who was 'in close' to the big theatres of Broadway." [1]

DeMille was one of the first to produce feature-length pictures:
these were the first indication of his ability to look ahead. In 1913-
14 he did *The Squaw Man*, *The Virginian*, *The Girl of the Golden
West*, and *The Warrens of Virginia*. But he began to become
known outside the industry only with his spectacle *Carmen* (1915),
starring the opera singer Geraldine Farrar. This movie brought him
praise for those theatrical effects which were later to become typical of him. It had genuine sets instead of the painted, flat scenery
usual at the time; the actors spoke lines (though sound had not
been invented) just as on the stage; and faithfulness to minor details,
theatrical realism, showmanship, and a concern for "production
values" that were to be his distinguishing trade-marks ever after,
were also manifest.

The following year DeMille made a significant picture which,
although it did not create much of a stir in its day, clearly foreshadowed his later famous work. *The Cheat* was one of the first of
the domestic dramas of the well-to-do in their own surroundings

[1] *Photoplay*, 1915.

and with their own problems, presented without moralizing and from their point of view. In this picture a "butterfly wife" is branded by a wealthy Japanese for not living up to her agreement to become his mistress after he has loaned her a considerable sum of money. Praised as "true to life" for its unconventional situation and ending, *The Cheat* presaged the post-war movie pattern.

Upon America's entrance into the war, DeMille turned out in swift succession a pro-Ally sermon (*Joan the Woman*), an anti-German harangue (*The Little American*), a patriotic exhortation (*The Whispering Chorus*), a sermon on self-denial (*We Can't Have Everything*), and a plea for vengeance (*Till I Come Back to You*). All these propagandist spectacles were distinguished by the biggest stage stars (Geraldine Farrar, Fannie Ward, and Elliot Dexter) and screen favorites (Mary Pickford, Wallace Reid, and Theodore Roberts), and by lavish "production values" and dazzling technical effects.

Joan the Woman gained the most attention. Its panoramas of war scenes, the ritual-like dream effects, and a striking double exposure (Joan is in Charles VII's court pleading for soldiers to save France, while dim and shadowy figures of great knights in armor plunge over them all) caused critics to compare the film with Ince's *Civilization*, "equaling but not surpassing it." The technical effects were praised as "Michelangeloing the sunshine." [2]

DeMille himself is said to have considered *The Whispering Chorus* as his best film at this time. The brutal realism that had made *The Little American* distinguished as "patriotic . . . sensible" was carried further in *The Whispering Chorus. Photoplay* [3] commented that

the final scenes are unnecessarily terrible; with awful, subtle suggestions that will drive sensitive spectators almost into hysterics. Much of the tale has been splendidly told with the shadow representatives of silent voices handled in a manner most artistic.

Before the close of the World War, DeMille's ability to look ahead again asserted itself. While other directors were still centering

[2] *Photoplay*, 1917.   [3] June 1918.

their stories on the war, DeMille turned elsewhere for subject matter. Before 1919 he made three pictures of different types and watched to see which would appeal most to the current public state of mind. One picture was a romantic "outdoor" film, *Nan of Music Mountain*, in the manner of his first production, *The Squaw Man;* another was an exotic spectacle, *The Woman God Forgot,* in the line of his biggest success, *Joan the Woman;* and the third was *The Devil Stone,* a domestic extravaganza of a sort DeMille had already attempted in *The Cheat.* The enthusiastic reception of *The Devil Stone* decided DeMille on what to do next.

From 1919 to 1924 Cecil B. DeMille made a series of pictures which were shrewdly turned out to appeal to the middle-class audience that had come into the movies with features, and to reflect the post-war changes in manners and morals. *Male and Female* (1919), *Don't Change Your Husband* (1919), *For Better or Worse* (1919), *Why Change Your Wife?* (1920), *Forbidden Fruit* (1921), *The Affairs of Anatol* (1921), *Saturday Night* (1922), *Manslaughter* (1922), *Fool's Paradise* (1922), and *Adam's Rib* (1923) all condoned the loosening of the marital ties and depicted "wild youth at its wildest and the younger generation on a rampage." These films featured sex, sensation, finery, and new standards of living in a way that fascinated the new movie-goers. They were sought in every American town for their lessons in manners and etiquette—how to order in a restaurant, what to wear on all occasions, how to conduct oneself at all times. The audiences accepted this film society as the real thing, few people having the perspicacity of Gilbert Seldes, who declared,[4] "High life in the DeMille manner is not recognizable as decent human society, but it is refined and the picture with it is refined out of existence."

A barrage of publicity made DeMille renowned as a producer of the lavish, the provocative, the daring. His films were advertised as "typical DeMille productions—audacious, glittering, intriguing, superlatively elegant and quite without heart." DeMille was a name implanted in the public's consciousness, and for a while this alone was sufficient to carry his films to financial success.

The timeliness of this movie content and the skill with which it

---

[4] In *The Seven Lively Arts,* p. 338.

was displayed tended to hide the formal weaknesses of DeMille's work.

Don't Change Your Husband was criticized as "obvious, mechanical, movieish," and was hailed as a "masterpiece as a matter of screen tone and wall decoration."

Wrote Burns Mantle [5] in his review of *Why Change Your Wife?*:

The Sennetts and the Sunshine boys may outdo Mr. DeMille as masters of the lower limb displays, but he completely outdistances them in technique of the torso.

William Haskell [6] said of *Adam's Rib:*

The picture is frankly extravaganza; its weaknesses are so camouflaged by DeMille's scenic details that they are overlooked by many, yet to this writer the picture sinned more on the score of dullness than in more external matters. It was Laura Jean Libby given carte blanche at the best shops and decorators'.

Other critics were more outspoken. Reviewing *Adam's Rib*, C. Ruth Doran [7] complained:

The silly weak story it told did not justify such expenditure—in other words, there was "much ado about nothing."

Mabel Oppenheimer [8] said flatly that *Adam's Rib* was

a star example of the kind of thing which made intelligent people laugh at the motion pictures.

E. V. Durling [9] called *Adam's Rib* a "Dangerous conception of social life."

Trivial though these films were, they had an enormous influence upon the motion picture craft and the country at large. DeMille more than any other director made the movies "production-conscious." He brought to the screen many refinements, stemming from Belasco's realistic theatrical methods but altered and adapted with exaggeration to meet the demands of the day. His films, more than any other director's, seemed up-to-date. Deportment, clothes, make-up, lighting, properties, and settings under his direction be-

[5] In *Photoplay*, May 1920.   [6] In *The Knickerbocker Press,* Albany, 1923.
[7] In *The Rochester Post Express.*
[8] In *The News Sentinel*. Fort Wayne. Indiana.
[9] In *The New York Globe.*

came of immense importance. Establishing costume departments to fashion the latest styles in clothes for his players, he brought in hairdressers from New York and Paris, ordered the newest in shoes from manufacturers, and set up a staff to design lingerie, gowns, hats, furs, accessories. Under his influence Hollywood took rank as a new fashion center, rivaling Paris, and films began to be rated according to their sumptuousness and display.

DeMille introduced "style" into films, but so far as direction was concerned his style was largely theatrical. His respect for stagecraft blinded him to the possibilities of camera use and cutting except as means for trick effects. In his films the camera simply photographed the actor and the setting; it was a wholly reproductive instrument. Unable to think in terms of images, DeMille depended upon artists to illustrate the scenario in sketches as literally as possible; he conceived of a film not as a moving and changing medium but as a series of separate pictures. All his films therefore lacked a cinematic continuity—a failing only partly compensated for by sensuous diversions.

As for DeMille's ability to direct players, one contemporary said that he was "lacking [in] Griffith's demoniac faculty of making even an extra do in a picture just what he would do in life." In an interview in 1922 DeMille said he believed in making actors do the part and never showing them how to do it. Nevertheless, he was noted for being "all over the set," always stopping the camera to illustrate an action himself. It was said he seemed to draw the work out of the actors by the force of his personality.

Of DeMille the personality much has been written. Always the showman, he was known for his silver whistle, open-throat shirt, pants, puttees, Louis XV hat, drooping pipe, and silver bugle. He created a great stir by being the first to use the megaphone, and later, when directing Feet of Clay in 1924, he became the first to use the radio loudspeaker.

The innovations in production and content that DeMille had introduced were taken up by the rest of the industry and, by 1924, were commonplace. Thenceforth DeMille's significance began to wane. His films were still in the style he had popularized, but were altered in psychology to keep abreast of the times. *The Ten Commandments* (1924), bellowing the moral that "You do not break the commandments, they break you," was DeMille's warning (he was now on a new bandwagon) against the attitude toward morals which he himself a short time ago had been condoning. *Feet of Clay* (1924), *Triumph* (1925), *The Golden Bed* (1925), *The Road to Yesterday* (1926), and *The Volga Boatman* (1927) were similarly moralizing, but were still significantly couched in sex and display. As DeMille declared,[10] "Your poor person wants to see wealth, colorful, interesting, exotic."

But DeMille was being overtaken by others who could say what he had to say with greater wit and effectiveness. DeMille's production values and showmanship were no longer exceptional qualities; spectacles had become commonplace. So DeMille now attempted to outdo DeMille. He made *The King of Kings* (1927), a religious spectacle of vast proportions based upon the life of Christ. DeMille made the picture because, as he said, a religious picture has never failed. The popularity of the film, helped no little by its display of violence and sadism, proved his business acumen, and his position as a leading director was saved.

With the coming of sound, DeMille like others had to re-establish himself by proving that he could handle the new medium. His next films, showing stage influence, were attempts to master the talkie technique. *The Godless Girl* (1929), intended to expose "the insidious propaganda teaching atheism menacing the youth of the nation,"[11] was one of the least noteworthy of his sound pictures, but it had the novelty of occasional dialogue and synchronization. Looking in it for something to praise, *Film Mercury* declared that "its sound effects are easily among the best." DeMille's first all-talkie, *Dynamite* (1929), and his second, *Madame Satan* (1930), a conglomeration of all the jazz-era bathtub antics that had made him famous, were produced to show that he could handle sound as well as silent films. But at the end of his trial in sound he was no longer the leading director in the industry although still a major one.

The stock market crash of 1929 and the ensuing critical years of

[10] *Motion Picture Classic*, November 1925.

[11] Introductory title in film, *Motion Picture Herald*, May 4, 1929.

the thirties saw DeMille respond to the changing times as acutely as ever. With his ear to the ground, all his next pictures—with perhaps the exception of *Four Frightened People* (1933)—were testimonials to his sensitivity to the changing national temper. *The Sign of the Cross* (1932) was in the words of Terry Ramsaye, "Good for audiences today, tired of sophistication, science, the pursuit of riches turned to dust, of all that is material, disappointing." *This Day and Age* (1933), timed to coincide with National Boy's Week, was a dangerous appeal to the youth to take the law in their own hands and "ride the union racketeers and gangsters on a rail to the court house." *Cleopatra* (1934), *The Crusades* (1935), were bawdy, corrupt, and spectacular concessions to the aggressive time spirit. *The Plainsman* (1936), *The Buccaneer* (1938), and *Union Pacific* (1939), dramatized important events in America's past in keeping with the nation's renewed interest in its own heritage. All these films were expensively made, expensively advertised, and starred the leading personalities of the day. All have been money makers and maintained DeMille's prestige as a sharp-eyed director whose sense of what will be popular remains unimpaired while his sense of theatrical aplomb continues to divert attention from the filmic and artistic weaknesses which mark his productions.

Why DeMille continues to outlive greater directors, and why he remains in the foreground in a constantly changing world and business after over a quarter of a century, has already been made evident. Artistically his films are of little value; indeed, his ability to make a bad film successful provoked Gilbert Seldes [12] to declare that

Mr. DeMille has never made a supremely fine film, only supremely pretentious ones. In that pretentiousness he has satisfied almost all the low esthetic cravings of the multitude—who were so unaware of having cravings . . . that they would have cheerfully accepted the best instead of the worst.

If in the artistic perspective of American film history Cecil Blount DeMille is valueless, in the social history of films it is impossible to ignore him. Almost more than any other director, he caught in his

[12] In *The New Republic*, July 1927.

films the changing temper of the times, and his creations are singularly representative of the social attitudes that inspired them. He profoundly influenced the movie industry by bringing in stage devices and by making movie makers production-conscious. He influenced the nation through his emphasis upon sex, manners, and post-war conduct, and upon clothes, furniture, homes, and living standards. Exemplifying Hollywood ideals perhaps more than any other single figure, DeMille stands out as one of the most singular personalities in the rise of the American film.

If Cecil B. DeMille dominated the movie in its post-war period, Erich von Stroheim was its most inspiring force. Von Stroheim emerges as one of the most important directors in American film history not only for what he accomplished himself but for his stimulation of other directors and for his artistic integrity. No director since D. W. Griffith had so fired the motion picture world. Praised, condemned, finally outlawed, he was the most discussed and respected director during those years when DeMille, at his peak, was the commercial model for the industry. While the rest of the movie makers tried to simulate DeMille, von Stroheim was acknowledged as inimitable, a "genius." If the industry envied and valued DeMille, it was von Stroheim of whom they stood in awe. Von Stroheim was on another plane, not perhaps so dexterous a commercial technician as DeMille but more truly the artist. In this Viennese movie people saw a man with a creative passion, whose will could not be broken and whose integrity could not be compromised.

In 1926 von Stroheim was elected one of the best ten directors in the *Film Daily* annual poll; the following year his name did not even appear among those of the one hundred eighteen directors who received honorable mention. By 1928 his career in Hollywood was over. Yet von Stroheim continued to wield influence. If his presence had created excitement, his absence brought him adulation. His genius still permeated the movie world like an electric current, sharpening the artistic awareness of movie makers and movie-goers alike. Today he is looked upon as a martyr to the great god Commerce: harassed by financiers, he fought persistently for the freedom to report and interpret and criticize life as he had experienced it in many towns and cities of the world.

Generally regarded as the American film's first realist, von Stroheim was actually the culmination of a long line of realists that ran back to Porter. Working with extreme care to achieve the realism he wanted regardless of the box office, he was castigated as an extravagant spendthrift. Had he been more willing to compromise in his attention to details, his big expenditures would have been condoned and exploited in publicity. Actually he made no more box-office failures than less worthy directors; no more money was lost on *Ben Hur*, for example, than on *Greed*. But Hollywood steered clear of von Stroheim because it was steering clear of reality and endorsing claptrap. His career, brilliant and spectacular, was climaxed in his excommunication by the very companies and individuals whom his film successes had given major stature.

Von Stroheim is said to have been born in Vienna in 1885 and educated in a military academy. Before becoming an actor and general assistant in movies in the United States in 1914, he worked as army officer, newspaper man, magazine writer, section hand on a railroad, boatman, book agent, vaudeville trouper, and playwright. His contact with all walks of life was later to be revealed in his movies.

In 1914, when war films were popular, von Stroheim's Teutonic appearance and knowledge of Europe stood him in good stead. He worked with Griffith (*Intolerance, Hearts of the World*), Fairbanks (*In-Again, Out-Again*), Ince (*For France, The Unbeliever, The Hun Within, Less Than the Dust*). But when the war ended and war films were taboo, he found himself without work, and his Prussian army uniform began gathering dust. But the prospect of obscurity only spurred his self-confidence. One night he went to the home of Carl Laemmle, stated his case, and left with Laemmle's promise that Universal (then a minor company) would produce his first directorial effort.

Von Stroheim's debut as director of *Blind Husbands* was heralded in a full-page advertisement in *Photoplay:* [13]

[13] December 1919.

In all my years as a producer of the best photoplays that the art has created I have not known more delightful entertainment than is provided by this amazingly artistic drama, written and directed to the uttermost detail by Erich von Stroheim, who, furthermore, plays the leading part.

Carl Laemmle, President

Thus began a directorial career that in less than ten years produced a remarkable roster of films: *Blind Husbands* (1919), *The Devil's Passkey* (1919), *Foolish Wives* (1922), *Merry-Go-Round* (1923), *Greed* (1923), *The Merry Widow* (1925), *The Wedding March* (1928), and *Queen Kelly* (1930). Whether or not von Stroheim's films are great works of art, as many think, is debatable, but they were at least so personal, so sincere, so serious in conception and execution, that they had monumental significance in their time. *Greed*, in particular, emerges as an outstanding achievement in American film tradition.

All von Stroheim's films were melodramas of lust—lust for money (*Greed*, *The Wedding March*), or for youth, love, or debauchery (*The Devil's Passkey*, *Blind Husbands*, *Foolish Wives*, *The Merry Widow*, *Merry-Go-Round*). Executed with a hard, unrelenting honesty, they were by turns sordid, scathing, mocking, ironic. His characterizations and viewpoint brought to the screen an individuality, a maturity, and a meaning not to be found in the pictures of the DeMilles, the Inces, or the George Fitzmaurices. He was a compendium of varied talents in an industry in which only specialists were given an ear: he was the writer and the player, as well as the director, of many of his films.

Von Stroheim's first three pictures, *Blind Husbands*, *The Devil's Passkey*, and *Foolish Wives*, were both timely and of high quality. They promulgated the post-war belief that women have a right to love after marriage and that, if husbands are indifferent, those husbands cannot blame their wives for seeking attention elsewhere. Common as the theme was, von Stroheim's treatment of it was far from common. The setting of *Blind Husbands* was high in the Alps (the original title for the film had been *The Pinnacle*), and its characters were an American surgeon indifferent to his pretty wife and a continental Austrian who appreciated the importance of love.

Unlike other triangle stories, this one was not in the pulp fashion; it was penetrating and serious, and distinguished in its realistic detail and vivid characterizations.

The same realism and uncompromising characterization that distinguished *Blind Husbands* were evident in *The Devil's Passkey* and *Foolish Wives*. The sex relationship in both was handled bluntly, and the decadence of the European aristocrat was mercilessly portrayed. Of *The Devil's Passkey* one reviewer said, "The moral problem here is . . . not of the highest order nor the most desirable," while *Foolish Wives*, the biggest money maker of all, elicited "A review of a picture that is an insult to every American . . . continual innuendoes as to American ideals; sly little thrusts at our tradition and sentiments." [14] The characteristics of these three films were to reappear in all von Stroheim's later efforts.

As von Stroheim worked he grew more certain of what he himself wanted to do. But in the midst of his fourth production for Universal, *Merry-Go-Round*, he was replaced by another director, Rupert Julian, of *Beast of Berlin* fame. The company was fearful that the cost of the undertaking as von Stroheim was proceeding would ruin them. Even more they dreaded the extreme daring of the story as he had planned it.

Meanwhile the newly merged Metro-Goldwyn Company was seeking to establish itself in the motion picture industry. Realizing that von Stroheim's pictures had placed Universal among the major studios, Metro-Goldwyn now engaged him to do the same for them. The result was *Greed*, a complete box-office failure but one of the shining achievements in American film history. Without an iota of glamour, grim and unrelenting, *Greed* was hardly likely to please the prevailing post-war taste, especially at a time when Lubitsch's *The Marriage Circle* and DeMille's *The Ten Commandments* were competing for attention. It is singular that any studio should have allowed this ex-Austrian to direct such a highly realistic dramatization of American working-class life, a dramatization certainly out of tune with the times. *Greed* was, at any rate, the last of the films about the working man in that period: the culmination of the tradition that had borne Porter and Griffith.

[14] *Photoplay*, March 1922.

As an achievement of motion picture art, *Greed* is unusually effective. How sincere von Stroheim was in this undertaking is indicated by its personal dedication, the first of its kind in the field of motion pictures—"To My Mother." Everything in *Greed* stemmed from his personality. Not so important in structure as *The Birth of a Nation* or *Intolerance*, this film nevertheless takes its place beside them because of its honesty and profundity. Those qualities compensated for the many faults and weaknesses in its form.

Before making *Greed* von Stroheim had written,[15]

It is possible to tell a great story in motion pictures in such a way that the spectator . . . will come to believe that what he is looking at is real. . . . Even so Dickens and DeMaupassant and Zola and Frank Norris catch and reflect life in their novels. . . . It is with that idea that I am producing Frank Norris's story *McTeague*.

He carried out his intention. The sordid dramatic tale was executed with painful realism. Zasu Pitts, Gibson Gowland, and Jean Hersholt—none of them important or known stars at the time—enacted drab, unsympathetic roles.

The film begins as an educational film on mining might begin. The realism and objectivity are at once so pronounced that the whole has the quality of a newsreel. In this respect alone *Greed* is a memorable achievement. As the story unfolds, the individuals and the outside world are continually placed in relation to each other so that the drama is intensified. When Mac embraces Trina at the depot, for example, a train roars by, suggesting all the suppressed passion in Mac. Again, at the wedding of Trina and Mac, a funeral procession seen through the window gives an ironic overtone to the ceremony. The marriage ceremony and feast in themselves are a masterpiece in the realistic re-creation of a cross-section of life at that time and in that social class.

The farewell of the family and friends, and Trina's overwhelming timidity on her wedding night, are most eloquent recordings of the mental attitudes of the pre-war period. Finally, the events of the

[15] *The Truth About the Movies*, p. 355.

world are made to intensify the personal situation in the sequence in which Mac murders Trina for money. The Christmas tinsel hanging in the house provides that sardonic irony for which von Stroheim was well known.

Von Stroheim's stress on realistic detail was not a fetish; it was based on dramatic necessity and characterization. There was abundant evidence throughout the picture that he could be richly suggestive and unrealistic in style when he wanted to be. The murder is built up psychologically, the mood being heightened by deep, dramatic shadows and weird shafts of light. We see Mac and Trina struggle from one dim room to the next, then back out of sight, their figures vague in the darkness. Suddenly we see Mac in the light, walking away from the shadow: we know at once that Trina is there, dead.

Another instance of the careful von Stroheim style is the scene showing Trina at work as a scrubwoman. We see only her on the floor at work; her dark dress and hair are in black shadows. We don't know what kind of house it is, or if it is a house at all that she is working in. That kind of detail would have had no significance; indeed, it would have diverted attention from the mood the scene was to arouse.

The characterizations of the three central figures of the story are full and rounded, uncompromising and consistent throughout. The idiosyncrasies of Jean Hersholt in the role of Marcus made him true and unforgettable. Such details as his picking at his ear and nose, his chewing gum, his sporty clothes and wise-cracks— these made him alive. Zasu Pitts, as Trina, is at one moment as appealing and soft as a bird, then a scheming, hard woman, filled with hatred for the husband who, by biting her finger, forced her to give him money.

So consistent were the characterizations that at times their realism was startling. Take, for instance, the scene in which Mac, starved and homeless, returns at night and begs Trina to take him in. He appeals to her sympathy (and the audience's) by pleading that he has not eaten for a whole day, that even a dog should be fed. But Trina, miserly, unrelenting, crushes him (and the audience) by sharply holding up the finger he once bit and retorting, "Not a dog that bites you."

Another moment that shocks because of its profound revelation of character and its lack of sentimentality occurs when Mac comes home drunk. He has been treated to some drinks by a friend, after having walked all day in the rain looking for a job because Trina had refused him carfare. Mac fights with Trina and finally falls onto the bed. We feel a surge of sympathy for Trina as she sits down at the table, sore, hurt, pitiably weak after the fight. Our sympathy quickly turns to bitterness, however, when we realize that her only thought is about where Mac got the money for the whiskey.

That von Stroheim had been a careful student of Griffith is evident throughout the film. The use of large close-ups, details, camera angles, dramatic lighting and composition, the iris-out, the mask-in— all stemmed from Griffith. Even more suggestive of the Griffith influence were the symbolism, the style of acting, the characterizations themselves. A person's rough treatment of a bird or cat, so familiar in Griffith's films, was used here to indicate that person's character. At the wedding we see a large close-up of Jean Hersholt's hands, clasped behind his back in jealousy. This was reminiscent of Griffith's close-up of hands clasped in anguish at the trial in *Intolerance*. The fragility and innocence of Zasu Pitts, her fluttering delicacy, were all very close to the traits of the Griffith heroines in the Lillian Gish school.

Whatever else *Greed* may have been, it had the virtue of being unforgettable down to the last moment, when the two men are dying in the desert. The constant repetition of the theme, the hammering away at the idea, may have been burdensome to the watching spectator, but it produced an after-effect, rare in films. The picture was deeply impressed upon one's mind. As Harry Carr declared,[16] "Von Stroheim . . . gives you a sense of seeing beyond the picture. . . . He digs deep into humanity."

In its original form *Greed* was said to be forty-two reels long, taking ten hours to show. June Mathis, the most esteemed scenarist in Hollywood and perhaps the person who was most influential in persuading Metro-Goldwyn to engage von Stroheim, was put to

[16] *Motion Picture Classic*, November 1925.

the task of making the film wieldy for commercial exploitation. The film was trimmed down to ten reels, and this version was then released.

Significantly enough, this depletion and editing of von Stroheim's work by another mind did not vitally affect it. His films are not based on the editing principle but on the piling up of detail within the scenes. In the scenes themselves he did everything that another director would do by cutting; his continuity and story were within the scene itself, and did not depend for meaning upon a particular combination and organization of shots. Details, action, and comment were selected and brought into the camera's scope without any changing of the shot. Hence someone else could edit von Stroheim's films without destroying the essential von Stroheim: the edited version was not so effective as the original, but it was still powerful.

Von Stroheim's lack of knowledge and power in editing account for his films' faults and high expense. His ability to see a scene only in terms of its independent existence gave his work an elephantine and blundering quality. Partly for this reason his films all lacked variety. *Greed*, for instance, had the inevitable weaknesses of monotony—an unchanging level of dramatic intensity that made it a tiring and exhaustive work to witness.

Reducing *Greed* to ten reels created a jerkiness that necessitated a great number of subtitles. The first part, particularly, was laden so heavily with literary titles that the picture became at times mere verbal representation. The burden of the story's continuity itself was carried almost entirely by the titles, which, written in a heavy style, connected not only whole sequences but individual scenes. Especially faulty because of this dependence on titles was the sequence in the beginning of the film, when we suddenly find that Mac, who is giving ether to Trina, has—for no apparent reason—fallen passionately in love with her. Also faulty were the editor's insertions of highly fantastic, static scenes of treasures and gold, glittering and stylized, in strong contrast to the drab reality of the story itself. According to the original von Stroheim plan such insertions were to play a large part in the film, but as it turned out only two of them were used, and these seemed arbitrarily placed and were repeated with apparently little relevancy or reason.

Despite such weaknesses *Greed* was an important contribution to movies in general. Von Stroheim's very incompetence in editing forced him to enrich the scene. This achievement was appreciated by other movie makers and emphasized the importance of utilizing, for effects, whatever comes within the scope of the camera.

Greed having been a dismal box-office failure, von Stroheim made his next film, *The Merry Widow*, a box-office triumph. He said in an interview,[17]

When I saw how the censors mutilated my picture *Greed*, which I did really with my entire heart, I abandoned all my ideals to create real art pictures and made pictures to order from now on. My film *The Merry Widow* proved that this kind of picture is liked by the public, but I am far from being proud of it and I do not want to be identified at all with the so-called box-office attractions. So I have to quit realism entirely. . . . When you ask me why do I do such pictures I am not ashamed to tell you the true reason: only because I do not want my family to starve.

It is reported that *The Merry Widow* cleared about four million dollars.

Despite von Stroheim's attitude toward it, *The Merry Widow* had an intensity no other director could have achieved, and it revealed a growth in his own ability and skill. He utilized the camera with keener awareness, discretion, and sureness, although this film like the others lacked dynamic continuity. Its entire conception and treatment was in the tradition of his *Foolish Wives*, having the Continental flavor that American producers cherished but could not imitate. Fearless like Lubitsch in dealing with sex, von Stroheim gave the film a hard, cynical undertone that made it true and serious. Taking a typical risqué Hollywood "hokum" story, von Stroheim lifted it to importance.

Throughout the film von Stroheim displayed that same keen outspokenness which amounted to shock, but was yet full of nuances and a clarity at times so masterful that the audience was disarmed. The love scene between the prince and the dancer in a nondescript

[17] *Film Daily*, reprinted from *Film Kurrier*.

hostelry is perhaps bolder in its insinuations than any other incident of its kind on the American screen. Neither Lubitsch nor DeMille ever approached it for frank sensuality and passion.

It was *The Merry Widow* that clinched von Stroheim's reputation as the greatest spendthrift the movie industry had known. In trying for a desired effect he used endless reels of films. His recklessness regarding expense was not due to sheer willfulness, however, nor did he use more film than such men as Chaplin and Griffith. None of these men worked from a planned script, and therefore their story developed largely as it went along. Despite *The Merry Widow*'s success, von Stroheim was censured for his "waste" and was forced out of the company for whom he made it.

Now Paramount engaged von Stroheim, and he went to work on his memorable *The Wedding March*. After two years the film was finally cut (by von Sternberg?) and released in 1928. It was typical of his productions generally. Bold and realistic, the massing of its details created a unique, powerful effect, with strong, ironic undertones. Characteristic of the rendition is the sequence in which the aristocrat (von Stroheim) and the vulgar millionaire tradesman are groveling on the floor of a brothel. In their stupid, drunken orgy they sign a marriage contract to unite their children. The cynicism of von Stroheim is here uppermost.

The Wedding March can be regarded as von Stroheim's last directorial effort to date, for it was his last production to be distributed, although he was at work subsequently on other films. By this time the industry's fear of him had reached a peak. As he himself later remarked,[18]

> They said I was crazy. Nasty and malicious stories were told about me. I could take no action; they knew I had no money. But I didn't want to anyway; it would mean putting myself on the same level as themselves.

A marked man, von Stroheim went about among whispers such as "Here is a man who spends money on films without regard for profits." *Motion Picture Classic*,[19] at a time when von Stroheim was already classified as "the autocrat of directors," spoke of him as "demoted but not defeated."

A turnover among executives after the stock-market crash and the coming of the talkies put von Stroheim back temporarily in a director's seat. J. P. Kennedy, a banker, on coming to the industry in 1930, engaged him to make a musical film starring Gloria Swanson, who had just made her singing debut in the movie *The Trespasser*. Von Stroheim wrote, directed, and acted in the new film, *Queen Kelly*, but it was shelved. No one has since seen or heard of it; no explanation for its shelving has appeared in print.

So once more von Stroheim was without work. A few years later, Fox engaged him to direct *Walking Down Broadway*, but in the midst of work he was again called off. Perhaps the producer who had engaged him had himself been fired by the company. At any rate that was the last event in von Stroheim's directorial career in Hollywood. He has since returned to acting in French films, winning fresh acclaim as a performer. "Perhaps," he says,[20] "one day I will direct a picture again. In France or in England."

The troubled career of von Stroheim has left in its wake fabulous tales of his personality and his method of work, his strong will power, his steadfastness, his thoroughness. To relate the various tales of his towering rages, the extravagant lengths to which he went in having the silk underwear of soldiers in *The Merry Widow* marked with the coat of arms of the mythical country, in paying $10,000 to have special medals designed for an imaginary army, in installing in a prop hotel in *Foolish Wives* a complete electric bell system that was never to be seen—this is not to indicate the talent of the man. It only suggests his urgent sincerity, his intense desire to make the entire scene real and to impress his cast with the reality of what they were doing. The use of genuine props has never in itself resulted in a fine film.

But von Stroheim's insistence upon what might appear to be trifles was important to him. It was not that he wished to dazzle, nor even that he lacked imagination, but that he demanded that everything be provided for to the smallest detail so that he could proceed confidently. If he had all the details of a scene at hand,

[20] *World Film News*, September 1937.

he felt free to eliminate and select. This was his virtue and his failing, his strength and his weakness; he lived by it and he fell because of it.

The influence of Erich von Stroheim on American directors was not so apparent or so marked as the influence of Cecil B. DeMille, who as a showman was far more successful. There were, however, a few who appreciated von Stroheim's love of the medium and his integrity, and who were inspired by it to explore the possibilities of realistic film drama. Some of the early works of King Vidor, William K. Howard, Josef von Sternberg, and Karl Brown, bear the definite stamp of von Stroheim's influence.

Meanwhile the European invasion had established three new leading directors in the American film industry: Ernst Lubitsch, who became the new pace-setter for Hollywood, supplanting DeMille; Fred Murnau, a man with a passion for movie art; and Victor Seastrom, who, perhaps the least publicized, was one of the most sensitive of directors.

Of all foreign talent coming to Hollywood, Ernst Lubitsch adjusted himself most readily. Arriving in 1922, preceded by his acclaimed German productions, by 1925 he had outstripped DeMille as the leader in American directing. In the ensuing years he sustained his reputation, identifying himself more and more with the American film; indeed, he never has left Hollywood to make pictures elsewhere. With their Continental and sophisticated humor, his films displayed such a distinct command of the medium that he stands out as a major director; his activities to this day merit attention.

Before coming to Hollywood, Lubitsch had been in the movies thirteen years. When he was a young man his ambition had been to become a great actor; in his teens he knew the plays of Sudermann, Shaw, and Wilde better than he knew his father's clothing business. After a two-year apprenticeship at the Berlin Bioscope Studio (1909-1911), where he did everything from acting to taking care of props and helping with the camera and lights, he joined Max Reinhardt's company as an actor. Later he became a leading player in the play *Sumurun*. His success in this role put him as the star into a four-reel film, which enjoyed such popularity that late in 1914 he was promoted to the status of actor-director. He now turned out two-reel comedies steadily, writing as well as directing them. In 1915 he began to direct features. After the war he produced his celebrated *Passion*, and then, in the next two years, four more films which were imported to America and proved so exceptional that he was called to Hollywood and welcomed enthusiastically.

All the American-made Lubitsch films have been distinguished by a personal style and craftsmanship. His flair for witty imagery gives his pictures a laconic and yet scintillating quality. His swift, deft plotting is enhanced by the rapierlike "comments" of his camera, which have become known as "the Lubitsch touch." Throughout his career he has displayed an uncanny ability to get the most out of his actors, too. His naturally sharp perception, made keener by the fact that he was working in a foreign land, gave him such insight into the traits and demands of America that his films, made with extraordinary technical skill, were often more penetrating than those of native directors in the twenties. With two exceptions his pictures have all been comedies of manners, centering entirely among well-bred, sophisticated, upper-class people. He delineates their fads and foibles with a Continental suavity that has made them fresh and fascinating to American movie-goers. His cultivation of this field may yet prove to be his downfall.

Before making his first American film Lubitsch shrewdly studied other American pictures. In an interview [21] with Helen Howe in 1922, he disclosed that he considered Chaplin the great American artist, admired Harold Lloyd, thought Lillian Gish in *Orphans of the Storm* almost supreme, and regarded von Stroheim's *Foolish Wives* as a masterpiece in detail but the story as inadequate for the man's great talents. "The American public—the American public with the mind of a twelve-year-old child, you know—it must have life as it ain't." [22]

His first job was to direct Mary Pickford in a costume drama,

[21] *Photoplay*, December 1922.   [22] *Ibid*.

Rosita. In view of the works that had made him famous, *Rosita* was undistinguished and disappointing. It is significant that Lubitsch did not again undertake to direct a famous American star like Mary Pickford, but chose unknown players, or players he had already directed in Europe, until he was well established.

As sensitive as DeMille to the times, and as shrewd a showman, Lubitsch forsook the serious historical subjects that had won him fame in Germany. He took instead Chaplin's *A Woman of Paris*, DeMille's *Forbidden Fruit*, and Cruze's *Always Audacious* as models for his next efforts. In the risqué, bantering vein he had already introduced in *One Arabian Night*, he directed a series of films of such sophistication, wit, and cinematic brilliance that he soon became the dominating figure in the movies, his cigar rivaling De-Mille's whistle. He was emulated by everyone, equaled by few, acclaimed by all as the latest "film wizard."

Three Women, Kiss Me Again, Lady Windermere's Fan, So This Is Paris, Forbidden Paradise, The Marriage Circle—all had the common distinction of sophistication, nonchalance, and a new kind of elegance and wit. They achieved what few other pictures had, the film equivalent of an epigram, stemming from Lubitsch's reading of Wilde and Shaw.

Perhaps the most brilliant of these efforts was *Forbidden Paradise* —although it was *The Marriage Circle* which won the most acclaim and was seriously compared to Arthur Schnitzler's works. *Forbidden Paradise* was a satire about Queen Catherine (Pola Negri) for whom love-making was a means to forget the trials of her responsible position. The sweetheart of one of her ladies-in-waiting, a young soldier (Rod La Rocque), wins her fancy and is promoted to Captain of the Guard. When he discovers he is only one of many in the queen's favor, he revolts. She threatens to execute him but relents on becoming intrigued with another. Graustarkian as the story was, its treatment was insinuating and subtle, spiced with sophisticated satire. Typical was the scene of the revolutionary uprising when the chancellor (Adolphe Menjou) calmly confronts the rebels. As one of them reaches for his sword, Menjou reaches for his hip-pocket as if to draw a gun but pulls out instead a check book and proceeds to buy off the revolutionists. Many observers regarded this scene as a jibe at Hollywood's practice of silencing dissension by money. Throughout the film every opportunity was craftily taken advantage of to inject witticisms on sex, political diplomacy, and court etiquette.

Everything in the picture was big, smartly finished, richly ornate, indicating how closely Lubitsch had sensed the American spirit of the day. In a restrained style and with better taste than DeMille could show, Lubitsch emphasized a new kind of spectacle—the spectacle not of crowds but of space. Spacious, shining floors; massive, tall columns; long, sweeping draperies, towering doors, and great staircases—all produced an effect of spaciousness and depth that American directors had seldom achieved. Lubitsch's exquisite taste for detail and atmosphere, his feeling for elaborateness and decoration, set off the comedy of manners with new brilliance. "Sexy," mocking, *Forbidden Paradise* was one of the best of this new type of comedies and like *The Marriage Circle*, it served as a source picture for a circle of younger directors, notably Frank Tuttle, Mal St. Clair, Monta Bell, Harry D'Arrast, Wesley Ruggles, and Lewis Milestone, who were modeling their efforts on Lubitsch's.

Having found his forte in domestic philanderings and risqué whimsies, Lubitsch now broadened his themes. In 1927, assigned to a romantic drama of the Cinderella variety, *The Student Prince*, he revealed his usual skill in making the best of banal material; he endowed its sentimentality with a color, glamor, and sophistication that made it a first-rate work. The film proved to be one of his most popular efforts.

The following year saw Lubitsch's first dramatic effort in Hollywood, *The Patriot*. Made from Alfred Neumann's play about the mad Czar of Russia, Paul the First, and featuring Emil Jannings, this film represented a fusion of Lubitsch's German spectacles and his American-acquired frippery. Superior in technical virtuosity to his German historical pieces, showing increased cunning and dexterity, *The Patriot* nevertheless had less vitality than his German-made *Deception*. Like that film it attempted to "humanize" a monarch by high-lighting intimate details. The Czar, for instance, is constantly putting his mistress's dog out of his room, and later, when slapped by his mistress several times, he suddenly realizes that he is her monarch and forthwith "socks" her in the jaw. The emphasis upon such gags kept the film from becoming the profound effort it might have been.

Interviewed at this time by Herman G. Weinberg,[23] Lubitsch significantly expressed great admiration for the Russian school of directors, mentioning *Potemkin* as "the greatest film ever made." In view of Hollywood's disdain for Soviet films at this time, Lubitsch's high regard for them indicates his own keen understanding of motion picture art.

The development of sound pictures put Lubitsch, like all others, to the test. More astute than most directors, he did not rush into talkies but bided his time. When sound technique had outgrown many of its early crudities, when Lubitsch had had an opportunity to examine the first fumbles and mistakes of others, then he gave the waiting movie world three musical-comedy films in a row—each one a distinct achievement, proving that Lubitsch was not only the most inventive of Hollywood directors but the most versatile.

Structurally as well as technically, Lubitsch's first sound films put their contemporaries in the shade. Faced with the problem of handling music, dialogue, and songs, he gave mobility to the until then static microphone, blending sound and image in a casual but extremely interesting fashion. The camera at that time was still imprisoned in a soundproof booth. But Lubitsch kept the camera moving freely and, with the same dexterity he had exhibited in making "silents," gave the images, dialogue, and songs a fluidity which kept both the eye and the ear amused. In these musical comedies there was little to remind one of the conventionalities of a *Broadway Melody* or *Paramount on Parade*. The conception was rather on the plane of the stage operetta in which song and story move steadily along without the use of a chorus "leg line."

Of the first of these musicals Alexander Bakshy said,[24] "The most surprising thing about *The Love Parade* is not Chevalier, but its more telling comedy produced by deft juxtaposition and contrast of scenes provided by Lubitsch." *The Love Parade* became a

[23] *Movie Makers*, September 1929.   [24] *The Nation*, February 5, 1930.

model for other musicals, even as *Forbidden Paradise* had been a model for the silent sophisticated comedies.

Monte Carlo (1930) and *The Smiling Lieutenant* (1931), employing the most recent innovations in sound, were no less witty, polished, and cunning. As repetitions of *The Love Parade's* success they proved that Lubitsch's skill was consistent. *Monte Carlo* in particular, with its "Blue Horizon" sequence, in which Jeanette MacDonald's song is deftly mounted with shots of the speeding express train and a chorus of peasants at work, showed the movie world how music and visual effects could be integrated so as to advance the action and develop the situation.

The same ease and brilliance with which Lubitsch overcame the problems of film musicals were apparent in his handling of a dramatic talkie, *The Man I Killed*, released as *Broken Lullaby*. The anti-war theme involved an unusual psychological approach. A sensitive French soldier is tortured after the war by the memory of the young German he killed in the trenches. Praised for his deed by the priest (a sardonic Lubitsch touch), he goes to the dead boy's family to confess and ease his conscience. There his intention is frustrated by the family's belief that he was their son's best friend, and by his growing love for their daughter.

Broken Lullaby revealed little new development in Lubitsch's directorial skill. Because of the vital content, however, it was very forceful. The best moments of the film—the old Germans in their beer gardens recalling their past glories, with the camera gliding over their faces; an Armistice Day parade, photographed through a one-legged ex-soldier; and particularly the last scene, with the camera anticipating each expression as it moves from the boy playing his violin to the waiting girl and to the watching old couple— were executed entirely by the lens. An ironic touch was the scene in the church where the camera moves past the praying officers and reveals their guns beside them. Though such accomplishments were nothing new for Lubitsch, the deeper meanings to which his skill was applied made it more significant.

With its serious characterizations and pacifistic overtones, *Broken Lullaby* was not a financial success according to Paramount standards, and so Lubitsch went back once more to the gay, romantic musical, making a sound version of his most popular silent picture, *The Marriage Circle*. Debonair and sophisticated as only he could make it, *One Hour with You* (1932) was the most effervescent of his sound comedies. Remembering his "Blue Horizon" sequence in *Monte Carlo*, with its integration of music and story, Lubitsch expanded the idea and gave his dialogue the form of couplets. Rhythmic dialogue not only blended better with the smooth pictorial continuity (in many moments delightfully counterpointing it) but gave the film a freshness and lilt. In keeping with the informality of the whole idea Lubitsch had Chevalier, during his lovemaking, address the audience directly time and again, taking the audience into his confidence and thereby heightening the intimacy of the film. *One Hour with You* has been perhaps the most thoroughly Lubitschian film since the advent of sound.

Since then Lubitsch has made only straight, sophisticated, drawing-room comedies (with the exception of a farcical sequence in *If I Had a Million*), all in the vein of his first Hollywood efforts. His style has undergone a gradual change; his content begins to appear dated because of changes in American tastes. His pictures have grown more refined in qualities, situations, characterizations, and continuity, and although still extremely skillful they show a significant loss of vitality and timeliness. Lubitsch has centered his camera almost entirely upon nuances of pantomime, subtle inflections, and double meanings, so that his films seem static. Such a tendency had already become apparent in 1925, when Matthew Josephson commented,[25]

. . . He seems to depart steadily from the true character of motion pictures. . . . Here the people stay in a room, the tempo is slow, everything is reduced to little smiles and grimaces or hand waves that move back and forth to each other.

This slowing down of Lubitsch's pictures has grown more pronounced in recent years and has cost him his leadership in the motion picture directorial field.

Beginning with *Trouble in Paradise* (1932), a story about an intrigue among sophisticated jewel thieves, Lubitsch narrowed his range of expression to pantomime, *double entendres*, and suggestive

[25] *Motion Picture Classic*, March 1925.

continuity. This has been apparent in all his succeeding films: *Design for Living* (1933), a Noel Coward triangle, *Desire* (1936), which he supervised (it was another picture about jewel thieves); *Angel* (1937), a story about blue-blooded philanderers, and *Bluebeard's Eighth Wife* (1938), a film dealing with high-society marital difficulties. These films are compendiums of such subtleties as a look, a gesture, a tone. The acting and situations have become over-refined, the cinematic treatment confined. Lubitsch's technique now has been reduced to a scheme of construction based upon elimination of intervals in the continuity. He himself has described this scheme in explaining his technique: [26]

I have confidence in the intelligence of audiences . . . in *Bluebeard's Eighth Wife*, audiences will see him (Gary Cooper) entering her (Claudette Colbert's) hotel room in a furious temper. They'll see and hear him slam the door violently. Now, instead of following him into the room with the camera, I dissolve from the slamming of the door to a night club, where the audience will next see them dancing together romantically. I'll let the audience figure out for themselves what happened behind the closed door, and only show the result.

Clever and ingenious though this method is, it has been used only as a trick.

Lubitsch was and is still a great talent. His analytical mind always shows an awareness of the richness of the movie medium. His films have the great virtue of simplicity; nothing is too slight to be put to use. Specializing, however, in the sophistication and realism of promiscuous sex relationships, a theme in keeping with the old post-war days, his most recent films do not show that he is keeping abreast with the swiftly changing times. Yet, as one of America's most skillful directors, he still stands out as one whose every effort is of interest, if not of much importance, but the leadership he enjoyed during the pre-talkie era has been lost; his influence today is of minor proportions.

Unlike Lubitsch, who adapted himself to Hollywood at once, Fred Murnau, coming from Germany about three years after, had

[26] *The Daily News* (New York), November 9, 1937.

difficulties. He took the commercial demands of the movie business lightly; his few American efforts before his sudden and untimely death were marked by integrity and purpose. So strong were his stylization, his emphasis upon mood, and his acute awareness of the function of the camera, that what is Murnau and what is Hollywood in his films can be easily distinguished. His last film revealed that he was developing in new directions, but his unfortunate death leaves us able only to speculate on what he might have achieved.

Murnau's first American film, *Sunrise* (1927), was his best Hollywood effort. Based on a story by H. Sudermann of two country sweethearts, the intrusion of the sophisticated woman, and a near tragedy, the first half was characteristically Murnau. It was featured by camera fluidity and by mood and stylization rendered through extreme studio artificiality—mists, double exposures, and soft, unreal lighting. This half had a lyrical quality and was removed from the real world. It approached the universality of a fable—Murnau's aim.

The second half, obviously suffering from Hollywood interference, was completely different. Its mood was realistic; the lyricism was dissipated by comic relief; the universality was destroyed by melodrama. C. Adolph Glassgold pointed out [27] "the discomforting mixture of contradictory types of directing and filming" due to these qualities in the second half of the film.

Plastically *Sunrise* stood out from the rest of Hollywood films not only for what it achieved but for its implications. An earnest believer in the "camera eye," Murnau attempted to tell the story completely in camera terms. The camera roved everywhere: through the forest, into the city, over the lake. Not only did the camera move, but the action within the camera's range moved, so that action played against action. So pronounced was this effect that Louise Bogan declared,[28]

Not since the earliest, simplest motion picture . . . has there been such a joy in motion as under Murnau's direction. . . . When the rare shot shows human gesture against a static background, the stillness is an accent.

[27] *The Arts Magazine*, Fall 1928.   [28] *The New Republic*, October 26, 1927.

Often the camera took the place of the character so that the audience saw everything through his eyes and participated directly in the story, being identified with the player. Murnau was interested always in arriving at the mind behind the action. He pointed out,[29]

We have our thoughts and also our deeds. James Joyce, the English novelist, demonstrates this very well in his works. He first picturizes the mind and then balances it with action.

Sunrise throughout was built by moods. Lighting, pace, the carriage and movement of actors, and the camera were all applied to create the dominant mood of each sequence. The opening sequence of multiple exposures presented holiday excitement in terms that were, in that day, fresh and dazzling. Trains and steamboats loomed up and disappeared in flashes, suggesting the journeys being taken by the many vacationists. In sharp contrast was the quiet sensuality of the seduction scene. The overhanging mists, the dew, the full moon, the sinuous and constant movement of the camera— all combined to create a dark, somnolent mood. Again, the trolley car bumping along through the countryside into the city expressed vividly the high excitement of the two frightened country people riding on it. The amusement-park sequence was another instance of glittering dissolves and "gliding" cameras that reproduced all the color and feeling of the place.

Cinematic skill was further revealed in the editing. Details were combined to communicate an idea, an action, a sound. For example, at one point we see a huge shot of a horn and then a large close-up of a woman shouting through cupped hands; thus the effect of a sound is given. This was expressive of Murnau's conviction—he was a staunch advocate of titleless and silent films—that symbols are the best means of obviating the need of literary devices. This synthesis of all factors to create a particular mood for a scene or a sequence imbued *Sunrise* with a psychological intensity and a rare style.

Murnau was deeply affected by the innovation of sound. Still in a speculative frame of mind, he continued working in the "silent" tradition with his next film, *The Four Devils,* a saga of circus per-

[29] *Theatre Magazine,* January 1928.

formers. It was as though another director had attempted to make an American version of the German picture, *Variety*. The film revealed a Murnau who was repeating *Variety* under strict orders; it had none of his individual manner.

Murnau must have sought a way to overcome Hollywood interference with his methods, for on his next assignment, *Our Daily Bread*, he insisted on working away from the studio in the wheatfields of the Dakotas. Further complications, however, seem to have developed. The film was never finished, and Murnau with Robert Flaherty, director of *Nanook of the North*, left the United States to do a picture in the South Seas.

At that time the confusion caused by the advent of the talkies was at its height. Murnau, refusing to recognize the possibilities of sound as an ally of a swiftly developing medium, stated before he left: [30]

The only point on which I would assert myself is that the ordinary picture, without movietone accompaniment, without color, without prismatic effects and without three dimensions [all these were being spoken of at once as new additions to moving picture art], but with as few subtitles as possible, will continue as a permanent form of the Art. Future developments may give birth to other forms but the original form will continue with an identity of its own.

The film that resulted from Murnau's South Seas sojourn was *Tabu* (1931). A lyrical salutation to the simplicity of primitive life, it had exquisite photography and an unusual idyllic mood. But disagreement between Murnau and Flaherty regarding the film's conception injured its unity. This was Murnau's first outdoor work. How strong an influence it might have been on his future efforts will never be known, since shortly after his return to Hollywood he was killed in an automobile accident.

Murnau's methods aroused Hollywood. Perhaps more than any other German director at this time, he awoke in American producers a realization of the boundless opportunities yet to be investigated in the silent film. His own deep personal interest and constant groping for new forms of expression, as much as his films, stimu-

[30] *Theatre Magazine*, January 1928.

Harold Lloyd in *The Freshman* (1925), typify-
ing the breezy, devil-may-care, super-charged
collegian, during the raccoon coat generation.

A pictorial style, stemming from Maurice Tourneur and the German school, distinguished
Rex Ingram's flair for atmosphere and architecture. (*The Magician*, 1927.)

lated others to a new respect for the medium. His own words [31] express best what he stood for and what he sought:

Real art is simple, but simplicity requires the greatest art. The camera is the director's sketching pencil. It should be as mobile as possible to catch every passing mood, and it is important that the mechanics of the cinema should not be interposed between the spectator and the picture. . . . The film director must divorce himself from every tradition, theatrical or literary, to make the best possible use of his new medium.

Kenneth White has truly remarked [32] that

The value which Murnau's work might have for a student director, if it were accessible over a long period of time, is inestimable. For the problems which Murnau stated in all of his pictures are problems persistent in the making of good movies.

Murnau emerges as a man of stature in a transitional period of motion picture development. High integrity, deep sincerity, and insight into the possibilities of the film set him aside from ordinary directors. He was one of the few in Hollywood of whom it can be said that he wanted to do great things in films not because of fame or fortune but because of a real personal enthusiasm for the medium.

Like Murnau, Victor Seastrom, the Swedish director, aimed to express a universality in films, and to do it with simplicity and sincerity. He, too, depended upon the creation of mood. In approach, however, these men were widely different. Murnau was subjective, interested mainly with the camera eye; Seastrom, more objective, concerned himself with characterization through acting and with the forces of nature. In Seastrom's pictures, as in von Stroheim's, the work of the camera is not particularly noticeable; the cutting is academic. It is the relevant details placed within the scene as a whole that makes the film significant. Watching a Murnau picture, one is always aware of the amazing technique involved; it is only after seeing a Seastrom film that one becomes fully aware of its power.

One of the first foreign directors to come to Hollywood during the "foreign invasion," Victor Seastrom had been a leading figure

[31] *Ibid.*   [32] *Hound and Horn*, July-September 1931.

in the outstanding Swedish cinema since 1912. Although achieving little public renown in the United States, he made a number of notable productions, of which one in particular—*The Wind*—is one of the finest achievements among silent American films. In technique, Seastrom was a director of distinguished talent; in subject matter, a man of keen social outlook. Though perhaps only *The Wind* was fully representative of him, all his pictures had a lyrical approach, the strength of honest characterization, and social awareness. The theme of his films was always man in conflict with society and nature; it dealt in the larger emotions, and the whole was rendered simply and lyrically. The titles of his efforts indicate Seastrom's concern with man's struggle with man and natural forces: *Name the Man* (1923), *He Who Gets Slapped* (1924), *Confessions of a Queen* (1924), *The Tower of Lies* (1924), *The Scarlet Letter* (1926), *The Wind* (1928). Never spectacular or sensational, his films did not get the attention they deserved. What Tamar Lane, the critic, said of *The Tower of Lies*, one of Seastrom's earlier American efforts, was true of most of his work. "One of the finest [films] of the past decade—seems doomed to fade silently into motion picture oblivion, unheralded and unsung." [33] In 1927, however, Seastrom was finally singled out—because of *The Scarlet Letter*—as one of the ten best directors in Hollywood.

The Wind, overlooked at its release because of the new excitement over sound, was his best American effort. Unrelieved by a romantic love story, the film was a fine study of the effects of rough climatic conditions and hard living on a sensitive girl unable to adapt herself to such circumstances. A young, refined, homeless girl from the East (Lillian Gish) comes to a hard-bitten household in the West. The gaunt, coarse, and insensitive woman of the house, worn out by the struggle to gain an existence from the soil, resents the additional burden of keeping the girl and is irritated by her delicacy and refinement. The woman's husband, trying to ease the girl's position, only succeeds in making his wife jealous and more determined to get rid of her. Having no place to go, the girl is forced into marriage with a cowhand (Lars Hanson) whom she neither knows nor loves but who can supply her with a home.

[33] *Hollywood and the Movies*, p. 56.

Fearful of married life, revolted by the coarseness of the husband and the surroundings, she is further depressed by the unceasing wind and endless dust, which seem to penetrate into her very being. She becomes horrified by the thought that her life will be warped and meager like that of the woman whose household she has left. The climax arrives when, during a rising windstorm, she is attacked by a former acquaintance, and maddened by the wind and her terror, she commits murder.

Throughout the film Seastrom emphasizes his theme: human lives molded by the elements. It is the wind that brings about the young girl's meeting with a man who subsequently violates her; it is the wind that forces her into an unwanted marriage; it is the wind that finally drives her to madness and murder.

The wind became the physical expression of the emotional struggle of the characters as, in Murnau's *Sunrise*, the bouncing trolley car expressed the excitement of the two country visitors. The arid heat of the prairie was caught in the wind, the dust, the sand, cloudless skies, and vast, unbroken space. The outstanding quality of the film was its documentary realism (much of it was actually photographed in the Mojave region), which had much in common with *Greed*. Like *Greed* it penetrated into the psychology of its characters by means of an objective treatment of their environment. Dealing with a grim subject, Seastrom was as uncompromising as von Stroheim in depicting it.

Seastrom achieved effects with a technique similar to that of *Greed:* the use of details within the scene itself rather than the building of the scene with an assemblage of detail shots. In one scene, for example, the woman cuts a carcass for food and is covered with blood. The girl, who is going for an iron to press her clothes (here is an ironic contrast between purposes), sees the blood and draws away in revulsion. This incident was depicted in the whole scene with a minimum of cutting. Again, the scene where the wind sweeps through the house, breaking the window pane, forcing the doors open, rattling shelves, turning over the lamp so that it sets fire to the tablecloth—during which confusion Lillian Gish makes futile attempts to keep the wind out—was rendered with a similarly sparse use of cutting. If Seastrom was limited in the command of his medium, he nevertheless had a profound compensating insight into character.

The Wind brought to American films a style that, while typically Swedish, was closer to American feeling than any of the German film styles. Seastrom displayed a restraint, seriousness, and grimness in keeping with the Midwestern character. A small-town drama of small-town people, close to the soil, confronted with the difficulties of living and their own conventions, *The Wind* was direct in narration, strong in drama, and realistic in style.

Subsequently Seastrom lost his footing in Hollywood. He was forced to subordinate himself to the star, Greta Garbo, in *The Divine Woman* (1928), to studio demands in *Hell Ship* (1928) and *Masks of the Devil* (1928), and to the talkie cycle of drawing-room dramas in *A Lady to Love*. Of this, his last American film, a reviewer in *Film Spectator* [34] commented, "I don't think it would be possible for Victor Seastrom to make a poor picture. If he had nothing to start on he probably wouldn't start."

At present Seastrom is, ironically enough, back where Hollywood first found him—acting and directing in Swedish pictures.

Victor Seastrom was one of the best of the silent-era directors, but he has had very little influence on the American screen. His propensity for psychology, realism, and the rendering of the characters of people close to the soil had little popularity in the late twenties, and what contributions he may have made to American films were obscured by the regard for commercial values. Seastrom was nevertheless a rare director, whose work, in the words of Robert Herring,[35] "gives us state of mind more clearly than purely psychological interpretation would. Tricks, dissolves, all that. . . . [His films may not be] true, pure cinema; but the cinema there is in them is pure, and their own, which is why they breathe a nobility unlike any other films' nobility."

During these years a number of minor director-craftsmen stood out because of a particular, if not profound, flair for certain material. None achieved von Stroheim's stature or Lubitsch's popularity, but a few created works of genuine significance. Of this

[34] March 15, 1930.   [35] *Close Up*, January 1929.

group those who emerged as notable were Robert Flaherty, J. Stuart Robertson, Henry King, James Cruze, and Rex Ingram.

Robert Flaherty was the first to venture into a new realm opposed to the story film: the thematic film. Rightly enough, he was not a motion picture director originally, but an explorer. The first movie he made, a film dramatizing man's struggle with nature, was done under unconventional conditions. Revillon Frères, a fur company, financed him to make an advertising film while he was on an expedition to Canada. The result, *Nanook of the North,* not only changed Robert Flaherty's future but added a new province to the domain of motion pictures. With his film was launched what was later to be known as the "documentary" form.

Nanook of the North documented and dramatized the Eskimo's fight for existence in a land where getting food is a major problem. It had no plot in the dramatic sense, nor was it fictional in the literary sense. It was a photographic description of the real life of Eskimos in their own haunts, made without artificial properties or professional actors. Its fidelity alone made it fresh, honest, and far more moving than any studio-enacted film could have been. The sensitivity of its director and his selection and arrangement of material made the film utterly different from and superior to the old-time travelogues.

Although untrained and inexperienced in movies, Flaherty conceived, directed, edited, and realized the entire film himself. His results showed that honesty, intelligence, perception, and vital material are the prime elements in movie production.

Impressed by the success of *Nanook of the North,* Paramount hired Flaherty to direct a documentary film of life in the South Seas. This venture resulted in *Moana of the South Seas* (1926). In a beautifully photographed record, the Samoan tribes were revealed in all their inherent charm and simplicity, without the usual South Sea sex story. Paramount, sorely disappointed, let Flaherty go.

Two years later Flaherty again went to the South Seas, this time for Metro-Goldwyn-Mayer, who had sent him off with a Hollywood script and another director, W. S. Van Dyke. After trying vainly to reconcile his own views with Hollywood's, Flaherty dropped his part in the production and allowed Van Dyke to finish the film himself: *White Shadows in the South Seas* (1928). There are several notable, photographically beautiful sequences in the film, typically indicative of Flaherty's sensitivity; as a whole, however, the picture was of minor significance.

In 1930 Flaherty made a third trip to the South Seas, now in association with the German director, Fred Murnau. Once again two opposing personalities clashed, and although the resultant film, *Tabu* (1931), had distinguished moments and a lyrical mood, characteristic of each director's style, it cannot be considered representative of Flaherty.

Since these unfortunate experiences with American studios, Flaherty has been working in Europe, making the type of picture he was not allowed to do here. He cannot rightfully be considered any longer a part of the American film world. But he is today famed as "the father of the documentary." Although his influence has been greater in Europe, especially in England, his methods have recently been applied with new vigor to non-commercial American films, most notably, perhaps, in the work of Joris Ivens, Paul Strand, and Pare Lorentz.

Flaherty brought to movies an interest in the contemporary drama of man's struggles with the forces of nature, a feeling for the significance of facts, an objective approach to contemporary life and a new kind of realism. More and more in recent years, owing to profound social changes that are taking place, these contributions have taken on increased value and have become criteria for the fictional as well as the thematic film. If Flaherty's works are not in themselves great filmic accomplishments, they nevertheless broadened the scope of motion pictures and pointed the camera toward new horizons.

John Stuart Robertson came to the movies in 1915 and made over a dozen minor films before achieving a major success. The film that brought him into prominence was *Dr. Jekyll and Mr. Hyde* (1920). Since then Robertson has been an unspectacular but notable director. His films are marked by the sensitivity and sincerity of his cultured, quiet temperament. Called the "best-liked director in Hollywood," he is a man of fine tastes, intelligence, and dignity. Having been trained in the academic tradition of the theatre, he has been able to turn out a picture smoothly and intelligently, to distinguish it with atmosphere, local color, and characterization, despite the fact that he has never been given subject matter with large implications.

During a period when DeMille's involved domestic intrigues were considered "top notch," Robertson's films were notable for their simplicity. The drama of *Dr. Jekyll and Mr. Hyde* (1920), the delicacy of *Sentimental Tommy* (1921), the rich suggestiveness of *Captain Salvation* (1921), the tenderness of *Tess of the Storm Country* (1922), and the poignancy of *The Bright Shawl* (1923) lifted those films above their subject matter. From a simple human story Robertson was able to achieve the maximum of emotion with the minimum of effort. His renderings seem artless. His characters and their relationships, as in a good book, spring from their environment and so have a roundness and credibility rare in Hollywood movie fiction.

Robertson worked in his own production unit from 1925 to 1927. In 1928 and 1929 he was with Metro-Goldwyn-Mayer and, unlike many of his co-workers, was able to survive the upheaval caused by the new talkies. Since the advent of sound, Robertson has been catalogued by Hollywood as the man to handle human-interest stories of the sentimental school. His keen perception and sincerity, however, have often enabled him to compensate for the shortcomings of his material.

In 1930 and 1931 Robertson was assigned such melodramas as *Night Ride*, *Madonna of the Streets*, *Beyond Victory*, and *The Phantom of Paris*. In the small scenes and isolated sequences, his sensitive direction can be seen trying to overcome the banality of the material. *One Man's Journey* (1933) and *Wednesday's Child* (1934) offered more opportunities in characterization. In the former an old man, and in the latter a sensitive young boy, were made moving, quietly effective, and real by Robertson's directing talent. His more recent efforts, *Grand Old Girl* and *Our Little Girl* (both 1934) and *Captain Hurricane* (1935) were all machine-made plots.

Robertson's career has been overlooked for the most part. A director for twenty years, he has had little written about him; the usual publicity interviews somehow are lacking. Although he has contributed nothing new to movie technique, he stands out for the insight, care, and sincerity he has displayed, particularly in his silent efforts.

His task has been to salvage the sentimental and to render it with poignancy. He has been a sort of American Seastrom: his films have delicacy and refinement, are quiet and unpretentious but sincere and moving. His reticence in both his personality and his work, in an industry which believes in self-advertisement, has caused him to remain in the background. If he has been little noticed, however, he nevertheless is a distinct and valuable figure in American film history.

Henry King has many of the qualities that distinguished Robertson, and others besides. Reticent like Robertson, he had for years been an actor (for Lubin, Balboa, and Pathé) and a director (working for Ince, among others) before achieving his first big success. This was Tol'able David (1921), one of America's celebrated pictures. It revealed King as a director with an unusual taste and talent for cinema values and methods. Though destined never to become a dominant leader like Griffith, Ince, or DeMille, or a fiery revolutionist like von Stroheim, King became one of the most respected and esteemed directors because of his delicate and moving artistry and technical command of the medium.

In an interview with Delight Evans,[36] King expressed his basic tenet: "You have got to tell a story if you want to make a good picture. You've got to think in terms of pictures. Films demand different treatment from the stage."

This understanding has been evident in all King's efforts.

Having been reared in a Virginia village (Christiansburg), Henry King endowed stories of small-town American life with a naturalism uncommon on the screen. Tol'able David, shown to an unsuspecting audience with a minimum of advance publicity, made its mark immediately as a small-town masterpiece. During a year when the industry was undergoing its first major depression, when people were staying away from the "scandalizing" Hollywood products,

[36] Photoplay, December 1922.

Victor Seastrom's *The Wind* (1928), an important silent film obscured by the arrival of sound.
Seastrom, like von Stroheim, emphasized significant detail and characterization.

Sunrise, directed by Fred W. Murnau. His stress on atmosphere and on mood as prime elements of a film is readily apparent.

when panicky producers were making more and more lurid "sexy" pictures to attract customers, the public flocked to see this simple, unextravagant, sincere, and moving tale of Southern life.

Tol'able David was what is known as a smash hit. Its subject matter—the tale of a poor mountain boy—was fresh and unstereotyped; its setting was real; its characterizations were honest and rounded; the narrative was simple and unmelodramatic; the whole picture was frank and pungent rather than sentimental. Years later the noted Russian director Pudovkin, in his book *Film Technique*, selected several sequences from *Tol'able David* as vivid examples of the correct use of plastic material. In the sequence in which a new character, a tramp who is a brutal escaped convict, comes into the action, King achieves characterization swiftly and entirely through the use of incident and shot arrangement, as the following summary from Pudovkin's book, indicates: [37]

1. The tramp—he is about to enter a house, but stops, his attention caught by something.
2. Close-up of the face of the watching tramp.
3. What the tramp sees—a tiny, fluffy kitten asleep in the sun.
4. The tramp again. He raises a heavy stone to kill the animal but is prevented from doing so only by the entrance of another character into the house.

Simply, pictorially, convincingly, the man's cruelty is depicted in four shots.

This scene, like King's technique throughout, stemmed from Griffith. Whether or not King was conscious of this influence is hard to say; but his leading man in *Tol'able David*, Richard Barthelmess, had been discovered by Griffith and used by him in *Broken Blossoms* and *Way Down East*. The Griffith influence was so marked, in fact, that Paul Rotha [38] has declared, "King robbed Griffith of all that was good, combining the spoil with his own filmic knowledge."

King's next films, regional depictions of small-town American life, were distinguished by the same sound cinematic structure, unpretentiousness, and realism: *Sonny* (1922) and *Fury* (1923), both starring Richard Barthelmess. Hollywood rewarded King for these

[37] *Film Technique*, p. 28. [38] In *The Film Till Now*, p. 131.

efforts by giving him "tear-jerkers" of elaborate proportions, and King did them lavishly. These were a religious tragedy, *The White Sister;* a Roman historical spectacle, *Romola;* and the mother-love drama *Stella Dallas,* "one of those rare films that rested on treatment alone." [39] Despite the sentimental quality of the material, King managed it with such sympathy and skill that the films were above the ordinary, and King himself was brought to the front rank of directors.

During the early days of sound films King's work declined. As a disturbed reviewer of *Film Mercury* [40] remarked, all had "something wrong" with them. Before long, however, King emerged once more as an assured and distinctive director. He has recently been in the forefront with such pictures as *State Fair* (1932), *Marie Galante* (1934), *The Country Doctor* (1936), *In Old Chicago* (1938), and *Jesse James* (1939). A serious and earnest craftsman of the Griffith school, Henry King is still a prominent talent.

James Cruze, who had become a film actor in 1908, starring in the Thanhouser serials in 1910, directed his first picture in 1918: *Too Many Millions.* Since then he has directed about one hundred fifteen feature-length pictures. It is as the director of the renowned *The Covered Wagon,* a historical spectacle of the pioneers' westward trek, that he is popularly remembered today, but it is Cruze's flair for satire and domestic comedies that has made him a notable director. At his best he had a style that was direct, light, bantering, and breezy, and he turned out picture after picture with facility and ease. Cruze never reached real importance because the early promise he showed as a screen satirist faded as he became merely another maker of pot-boilers. He himself declared that his main fault was an overanxiety to please, and that he had "no guts." In his heyday, however, he did evidence a talent that was original and might have continued to produce significant films if he had been less compromising. Cruze's films of the post-war period, like DeMille's and Chaplin's, are said to have been the models that Lubitsch studied when he came to America.

His Wallace Reid pictures in 1919-1921—*The Valley of the*

[39] In *The Film Till Now,* p. 131. [40] August 31, 1928.

Giants, Hawthorne of the U. S. A., The Roaring Road, The Dictator, The Lottery Man, and *The Charm School*—brought Cruze into notice as a director of fast-action romantic comedies and revealed his feeling for humor and pace. He then directed a series of "Fatty" Arbuckle features—*Crazy to Marry, Gasoline Gus, Dollar-a-Year Man,* and others—which, although brought abruptly to an end by a scandal that caused Arbuckle to be ostracized by the screen, developed his technique and established him as a prominent director of comedies. Arbuckle had been trained in Sennett slapstick, and from the experience of working with him Cruze acquired a feeling for spontaneity, improvisation, and satire. His next films, with one exception, were characterized by an increasing knack for light satire and dexterity in technique.

One Glorious Day (1922), originally planned for Arbuckle but given to Will Rogers when the fat man unwillingly retired, was the first indication that Cruze had the makings of a distinctive director. This story of Ek, a spirit from Valhalla who comes to earth and inhabits the body of Professor Botts for one day, was a clever satire debunking politics and spiritualism. The Exceptional Photoplay Committee of the National Board of Review praised the picture for its "exceptional grasp of the possibilities of screen in the realm of imagination." Cruze, who had written the story himself, had executed it with wit and fantasy, with a touch of stylization that was said to have stemmed from *The Cabinet of Dr. Caligari.*

One Glorious Day, however, was considered a failure at the box office, and Cruze was put to other tasks. After quickly directing a farm story, *Old Homestead,* he was assigned a "sure-fire" Western. His employers had originally bought the story for the star, Mary Miles Minter, but she and three directors had already declined to do it. The story, published in *The Saturday Evening Post* and written by Emerson Hough, until then unknown to movies, dealt with the hardships and struggles of pioneers in their trek across the prairies and mountains to Oregon and California.

The Covered Wagon became the biggest popular triumph Cruze was to enjoy and one of the largest money makers of film history. Described by Robert Sherwood [41] as "the one great American epic

---

[41] In *The Best Moving Pictures of 1922-1923,* p. 72.

that the screen has produced," it was "epic" only in those parts that were stripped of fictional elements. As a reconstruction of the hardships of the journey, showing the grim faces of those pioneer men, women, and children, revealing the vast unpopulated spaces, containing long panoramic shots of the wagon trails winding endlessly into the unknown and of the cattle fording the rivers, *The Covered Wagon* was forthright, impressive, and vigorous. It injected a freshness into the jazz-ridden film world.

So authentic had Cruze tried to make the film that he declared,[42] "There wasn't a false whisker in the picture. The dust raised by the wagons was real dust, the Indians were real Indians, the beards on the pioneers were real beards." But opposed to such plein-air documentation was the weak and illogical story; the heroine who remains ridiculously clean despite desert winds, snowstorms, and Indian attacks; the inconsequential and interminable romance, sprinkled with spurious villainy; and the conventional Wild West Indian fights. The brutal murder of an Indian at the ferry by one of the pioneers is not shown to be in any way responsible for the subsequent Indian attack on the wagon train. Such faults kept the picture from really being what it might have become—an honest, profound, and moving social document on a heroic scale. The awkward attempt at fiction doomed, from the start, whatever epic proportions the film might have attained.

The phenomenal box-office success of *The Covered Wagon* and its general freshness obscured its weaknesses and led many to believe they were seeing a masterpiece. It did have unusual qualities in its representation of the old West—the broad countryside, the vast sky and earth, the abundance of space and air—which, together with its realistic execution, stamped the film as distinctive. But it was very far short of a masterpiece.

Even before *The Covered Wagon* was released, Cruze had already started on another picture, *Hollywood*, about a scandalous subject then in the limelight. Here the traits that commonly distinguished Cruze were paramount. The film's story—partly satirical, partly straightforward—of the small-town girl who does not make good in Hollywood was probably the truest picture of the industry

[42] *Op. cit.,* p. 73.

yet made. Day after day the heroine trudges from studio to studio, looking for work vainly, while her grandfather, home on the hotel veranda, is picked up by a director as the "right type" for the role of an extra. An allusion to the current Arbuckle scandal was the pointed scene in which the heroine seeking a place in a crowded line before a casting director's window, is politely given room by a fat man. She is rejected at the casting window, and then he applies. The window slams in his face: upon it is the word "Closed." The fat man turns to the camera: he is "Fatty" Arbuckle, outlawed from further movie activity.

Cruze's talent for satire and comedy was evident in the imaginative treatment he gave the dream sequence, in which the hero imagines himself a knight-errant in a twentieth-century Babylon, his mission being to rescue his girl from the "dread dragons of cinema." He rows through congested Los Angeles streets in a boat, pounces on an Arrow Collar man in B.V.D.'s who is shaving before the mirror on a chewing-gum machine, catapults into an enchanted garden where film stars, fully dressed, are diving backwards out of a swimming pool. Various well-known stars appear from moment to moment, dressed as aristocratic roués, sheiks, apaches, clubmen, and bathing girls; ludicrous costumes are used to ridicule them. This was an imaginative and telling rendition in which Cruze employed the camera devices of slow and fast motion and double exposure to make the comment forceful. Such "take-offs," done simply but ingeniously, proclaimed Cruze's real forte.

After *Hollywood* Cruze turned out a series of satires distinguished by the same light and imaginative touch. *Ruggles of Red Gap* (1923) poked fun at the Englishman's idea of America as a wild, Indian-infested country and brought to the fore a comedian whom Lubitsch was later to make famous: Edward Everett Horton. *Beggar on Horseback* (1923), taken from the stage play of the same name, was a skillful thrust at the *nouveau riche*. This film, handled throughout with distinction, was regarded by Cruze as his best effort. Although the expressionistic settings and grotesque exaggerations of the play (immensely popular in the experimental theatre of the early twenties) were carried over directly into the film, Cruze's direction deserves credit. Opposed by a literal-minded

Hollywood, he tried to capture the play's unique quality of stylization. His imaginative use of the movie medium, capable enough in *Hollywood*, was here developed farther. The camera showed people unnaturally large or small, overdressed, overjeweled, stuck to chairs. Rooms appeared absurdly large; ostentatious settings were greatly exaggerated; the courtroom scene was stylized and fantastic throughout; actors' movements and gestures were sharp and grotesque. Such features made the satire an outstanding movie that still looks meritorious today. Despite the fact that the *Beggar on Horseback* was never a great box-office success, it was perhaps more creditable in its way than *The Covered Wagon*.

His next films continued in this satiric vein. *Merton of the Movies* (1924), taken from the novel of the same name, made fun of the aspiring young movie-struck hero and lampooned the motion picture world, not so boldly as *Hollywood* but with the same breeziness and forthrightness. *The Fighting Coward* (1924), from Booth Tarkington's *Magnolia*, again showed Cruze's flair for humor in its exaggeration of the fire-eating Southerner of pre-war days. A contemporary critic credited Cruze with furnishing "more satire and more laughs than Tarkington did."

Now at the peak of his career, noted for his working speed—he is said to have completed a major full-length feature in eight days, still considered a Hollywood record—Cruze had become one of the highest-paid Hollywood directors, earning $6,000 to $7,000 a week. In the next few years he turned out a series of domestic comedies that caused him to be hailed for his "razzing" of American foibles. The witty *The Goose Hangs High* (1925), the adroit *Marry Me* (1925), the sharp *Waiter from the Ritz* (1926), the facile *We're All Gamblers* (1927), the wise *On to Reno* (1927), and the hardboiled *City Gone Wild* (1927) were all expressive of Cruze's talents. By this time, however, Lubitsch had taken the field in sophisticated humor; his quiet innuendoes were prized, and Cruze's accomplishments were not receiving much attention.

In 1927, in an attempt to duplicate the success of *The Covered Wagon*, Cruze undertook his longest and most lavish production job: *Old Ironsides*. This film on an American historical subject proved to be a dismal failure. It was now clear that such material was entirely unfit for Cruze and that his success with *The Covered Wagon* had been a flash in the pan.

When sound became the big topic of controversy in Hollywood, Cruze was among those who were heartily against it. "This is a passing fad," he is reported to have said. After several years of inactivity, during which sound became established, Cruze came back to direct a number of films, none of which was outstanding: *The Great Gabbo* (1930), with Erich von Stroheim in the leading role, *Washington-Merry-Go-Round* (1931-1932), *I Cover the Water Front* (1933), *Helldorado* (1934), and *Sutter's Gold* (1936). All these were swiftly done in a stereotyped manner, and Cruze's reputation declined. Presently he became a director in a minor company, Republic, turning out *The Wrong Road* (1937) and *Prison Nurse* (1938). Like his other efforts since 1930 these action pictures gave him small opportunity to display his old ability in satire and light comedy. Today Cruze is rarely heard from: he is a director whose spark of creativeness seems to have been quenched.

A cynic to whom film making was easy, Cruze seldom exerted himself to produce anything superior to what was demanded. He was best at domestic comedy, having a particular bent for satire and the imaginative use of the movie medium. Remembered chiefly for *The Covered Wagon, Beggar on Horseback,* and *The Goose Hangs High,* Cruze lacked the integrity of a von Stroheim (one of his best friends, whom he greatly admired) and was unable to make any valuable contribution to American films. Still, in 1928 he had the acumen to protest that bankers and supervisors were having a bad effect on the movies: "If supervisors are good, they should direct; if no good, they should be shot." Always a competent craftsman and a prolific worker, Cruze remains a minor figure whose talents were unrealized.

About the same time that James Cruze was emerging into prominence, Rex Ingram came to the fore as a notable director. A stylist in the minor school of Maurice Tourneur, he achieved in his films an individuality and personal quality through his sensitivity to pictorial composition and atmosphere. Earlier, as an art student, he had studied sculpture at Yale. Partly for this reason, perhaps, as a director he depended upon light and shade rather than plot to create mood. A fertile imagination for the pictorial, an alertness for scene composition and the beauty of the shot, made his films striking, although they were often without dramatic form and devoid of solid film structure.

In 1921, at the age of twenty-nine, Ingram won sudden world fame with his *The Four Horsemen of the Apocalypse*. His experience in movies dated from 1915, when he had acted in Vitagraph and Edison pictures. After going to war as an aviator, he had returned to take up his career where he had left off, developing from actor to scenarist and finally to director. At the time of his first major hit, he had already been well schooled in moviecraft, having directed a number of minor and unnoticed pictures: *The Great Problem, The Chalice of Sorrow, Broken Fetters, The Reward of the Faithless, Under Crimson Skies, Hearts Are Trumps*.

The unexpected and phenomenal success of *The Four Horsemen* made the reputation of Rex Ingram as a director; put the company which produced it, Metro, into the major class; established Rudolph Valentino, an unknown actor, as a star; and brought recognition and praise to June Mathis, its continuity writer and cutter. The film, based on the Ibañez novel, was a pro-war picture showing the awakening of an Argentinian to his duty to his father's country, France. Although its story was drawn out, the characters were undefined, and the attitude toward war and the Germans was still soured by the bigotry of World War days, *The Four Horsemen* was distinguished by pictorial beauty and an uncommon exotic atmosphere. Many hailed the film as a magnificent work of art. In technique it displayed the influence of Griffith and of the current German importations. Animals and birds were used to point a situation humorously; the symbolic sequences of the Four Horsemen—War, Plague, Famine, Death—galloping through clouds over a battletorn world were reminiscent of Griffith; the spectacular mass scenes suggested the German films. The whole was blended of exotic settings, striking compositions, dramatic lighting, and colorful if sordid atmosphere.

In a preface to the book *Pictorial Beauty on the Screen* (1923), by Victor O. Freeburg, Rex Ingram explained his credo: "A motion picture must be composed of scenes that have certain pictorial qualifications, such as form, composition, and a proper distribution of light and shade."

The Four Horsemen exemplified this viewpoint and presaged the style of all Ingram's subsequent efforts.

His next film, a story from Balzac, *The Conquering Power* (1921), displayed the same feeling for the mood of a scene and the same eye for the pictorial. The use of suggestion through the selection of detail further set the film apart. It was a picture maker's picture, the work of a man who believed that

fine atmosphere and characterization are of more vital importance than incident, for nine times out of ten it is the characters and the mood in a great novel that we remember—rather than the plot.[43]

After a nondescript effort, *Turn to the Right* (1922), which moved skeptics to say that his scenarist, June Mathis, had been the creator behind his former films, Ingram made some of the biggest hits of the day: *The Prisoner of Zenda* (1922), *Where the Pavement Ends* (1923), and *Scaramouche* (1925). Like *The Four Horsemen* all these films were romantic dramas laid in exotic locales and marked by spectacles. All, and particularly *Scaramouche*, revealed Ingram's indebtedness to Griffith. Made after Griffith's *Orphans of the Storm*, *Scaramouche* showed many similarities in its crowd scenes, tableaux, and the use of significant detail for atmosphere. The colorful material of these films—the imaginary kingdom in *The Prisoner of Zenda*, the South Seas in *Where the Pavement Ends*, and the French Revolution in *Scaramouche*—gave Ingram full opportunity to exploit his flair for the pictorial. Whenever possible he high-lighted his films with interesting close-ups of eccentric types. This device, which gave a local-color touch to his stories, was to be adopted years later by von Sternberg.

Having reached the top of his profession in 1925 and 1926, Ingram left Hollywood to settle in Nice as an expatriate and produce for himself. There he made four more notable and commendable pictures before the invention of sound halted his activities. *Mare Nostrum* (1926), a melodrama about espionage, abounded in striking camera compositions inside submarines, where much was made

[43] Quoted by Peter Milne in *Motion Picture Directing*, p. 67.

of the machinery by means of dramatic lighting. *The Magician* (1927) contained a sequence of a surgical operation which pictorially was as impressive as any of the celebrated photographic effects coming from the German studios at this time. *The Garden of Allah* (1927) and *The Three Passions* (1929) stressed locales and again showed striking photographic effects. *The Garden of Allah* was especially outstanding photographically because it was one of the first movies made on panchromatic film. All his pictures had a natural tone that was subtle and satisfying: seldom shooting a scene in direct sunlight, he worked from four to five-thirty in the afternoon, when the light was soft, mellow, diffuse. This emphasis upon photographic beauty affected the form of his work.

In direction he followed Griffith (from whom, as he openly declared, he like all others had learned the rudiments) and J. Stuart Robertson, a director who not only rivaled Ingram in achieving pictorial quality but had a broader understanding and surer sense of values as well.

Since sound pictures became established Ingram, living in almost complete obscurity in Nice, has contributed nothing to motion pictures. In his day, however, he brought to Hollywood a sensitivity for composition, atmosphere, lighting, and pictorial mood.

Never a major figure in movie history, Rex Ingram will be best remembered for his development of the contributions of Maurice Tourneur to motion picture art.

During the same period there were, in addition, a horde of commercially prized directors of big reputations, many of whom are still active today, who had a knack for particular material. Among them were Frank Lloyd, known for his adaptations of novels; Tod Browning, who had a propensity for dealing with the world of people warped in mind and body; Marshall Neilan and Allan Dwan, with their flair for human-interest material; and Fred Niblo, George Melford, and George Fitzmaurice, who showed ability in directing romantic and exotic tales.

In the latter half of the period emerged a number of more significant directors who displayed unusual talents and achieved notable productions: King Vidor, Josef von Sternberg, Lewis Milestone,

Frank Borzage, and William K. Howard. These men now were looming up as distinctive film makers, but it was in the next period that they were to reach their prime.

Of the numerous talents that came to Hollywood during the "foreign invasion" not all were to survive there. Benjamin Christiansen, who had come from Denmark, dropped out of the movie world after making one picture, *The Devil's Cargo* (1926).

Mauritz Stiller, invited to America with Greta Garbo and Lars Hanson because of the success of his *Atonement of Gosta Berling*, from the very beginning clashed with Hollywood. In his first assignment, *The Temptress*, he was replaced by Fred Niblo. His next assignment, *Hotel Imperial* (1926), starring Pola Negri, exhibited—especially in the first half—some of the realistic qualities of his Swedish films. After his next film, *The Street of Sin*, a banal story, Stiller died.

E. A. Dupont, whose sensational *Variety* brought him to America, never again made any picture comparable to it. Lothar Mendes, after directing *The Prince of Tempters* (1928) and *Interference* (1929), returned to Europe. Jacques Feyder, sensitive French director of *Thérèse Raquin*, left after making *The Kiss* (1930), starring Garbo. Paul Fejos, the Hungarian, came into prominence with his independently made *The Last Moment*, which was derivative from the German technique, but after *Lonesome* (1928), *Broadway* (1929), and *The King of Jazz* (1930), his best effort, he too was no longer heard of.

Paul Leni, having become famous for *The Three Waxworks*, continued with his flair for the macabre in *The Cat and the Canary* (1927), *The Man Who Laughs* (1928), *The Chinese Parrot* (1928), and *The Last Warning* (1929). Leni suddenly died after directing the last of these pictures.

XIX

THE DECLINE OF D. W. GRIFFITH

THE third period of D. W. Griffith's career is bounded by the financial fiasco of his masterpiece, *Intolerance*, in 1916 and his hurriedly recalled swan song, *The Struggle*, in 1931. Fifteen years separated these two films—one the finest expression of craftsmanship on the American screen in its time, the other a sorrowful example of ineptness. Between these dissimilar efforts Griffith's career as a director steadily fell back to make way for Griffith's career as a business man: both careers came at last to an obscure end. Preeminent in the American movie world in 1918, achieving international acclaim in 1919, by 1931 Griffith was out of movies altogether. Newcomers who knew better how to keep up with the swiftly changing times had supplanted him.

The reasons for Griffith's decline were twofold. First, he lost interest in films as such, and with each new picture he became farther out of touch with the altered post-war audience. Secondly, an increasing regard for wealth and success compromised his integrity. That spirit of inquiry and humility which had once been his outstanding trait was replaced by a spirit of self-aggrandizement and ostentation. He began to concentrate upon exploiting his personality and reputation; it made no difference what he did, so long as the name "Griffith" appeared in print. He prophesied the future of pictures; he planned seventy-two-reel movies, and a chain of Griffith theatres from coast to coast that would show only his pictures; he spoke before chambers of commerce about the blessings of the movie trade; he criticized the government income-tax rate; he railed against censorship; he took public credit for every artistic advance made in movies. And all the time his films were becoming worse.

Revolutionary changes in moral attitudes during these years were irreconcilable with Griffith's nineteenth-century orthodoxy. He clung to a moral code which was disdained and mocked as "old-fashioned." Even when he chose up-to-date themes, his outmoded and deep-seated prejudices were obvious; all his films appeared stilted, forced, ludicrously colored by pre-war ideals. Griffith's great weakness was his inability to move with the times.

Even after the financial debacle of his *Intolerance*, Griffith was regarded as the "dean of American screen art"; no other director was so renowned or esteemed. When the federal government mobilized the motion picture industry on America's entrance into the World War, Griffith was one of the first to be recruited. Feted and acclaimed, he was sent to England to produce two propaganda pictures, one to arouse anti-German sentiment and the other to show "the regeneration of British society through its war activities." These pictures were made with the earnest co-operation of the officials of the Allied governments. England put all her stage, screen, and society notables at Griffith's service, and the French and Belgian governments conducted him on a tour of their battle fronts. No financial or artistic restraints were placed upon him. Thus, allowed unlimited resources and assured of the widest distribution governments could provide, Griffith made *Hearts of the World* and *The Great Love*.

Hearts of the World depicted the German occupation of a French village. Germans were shown, in the fashion of the day, as "Huns"—as plunderers, debauchers, and horsewhippers of beautiful French girls. Such titles as "Month after month piled up its legend of Hunnish crime on the book of God" may have been, as one critic of the day [1] put it, "A powerful stimulus to patriotic emotions," but they certainly served the film in no other way. This is the film in which Griffith, to compensate for his anti-Negro prejudices in *The Birth of a Nation*, deliberately inserted a scene showing a white soldier kissing a dying Negro soldier who is crying for his mother. Though perhaps an honest gesture, this was out of place

[1] *Variety*, August 11, 1919.

and certainly could not make up for his bigoted portrayal of the Negro race in the older film. Altogether maudlin and biased, *Hearts of the World* had the faults of Griffith's sentimental style at its worst.

Much was expected of Griffith's English war film, *The Great Love* (circulated exclusively in England). This too proved to be a mediocre effort. Numerous shots of royal personages and scenes of important places so overburdened the film that it evolved as nothing more than a glorified newsreel of Who's Who and What's What in war-time England. After the remarkable structure and fine humanity displayed in *Intolerance*, *The Great Love* no less than *Hearts of the World* seemed like a picture made by another man— by anybody but Griffith. Both of these war pictures, written by Griffith himself under pseudonyms, were devoid of that formal distinction which had made his previous efforts so startling; both were rabidly militaristic and revealed little comprehension of the great issues at stake. In a statement to reporters on his return to America, Griffith revealed his superficial understanding of the war by remarking that his sets for *Intolerance* had been more impressive than anything he saw in war-torn France and Belgium. "Viewed as drama," he said, "the war is in some ways disappointing." [2]

The Armistice found Griffith, like most movie makers, unprepared for peace. While waiting to see what type of stories the public wanted now—war pictures became a drug on the market— Griffith recut *Intolerance* into two pictures, *The Fall of Babylon* and *The Mother and the Law*, and in addition quickly made a number of typically pre-war idylls: *True-Hearted Susie*, *The Romance of Happy Valley*, *The Greatest Thing in Life*, and *The Girl Who Stayed at Home*.

To the Babylonian picture were added many love scenes which had been omitted from the *Intolerance* version. They caused one critic to comment,[3] "The picture is given a velvety touch which was originally lacking, as it is it appeals not only to the eye but to the emotions."

The Mother and the Law was released as "An indictment of the conditions that permit the oppression of the poor through the medium of 'Uplifters' who work for self-aggrandizement; also a plea for tolerance in law."

The other films, the titles of which were symptomatic of a past day, were released in 1919 to a cynical and sophisticated audience who had just come through a war. The films were greeted with snickers and laughter. This was the first clear indication that Griffith's unchanged moral outlook had become dated.

Griffith was now floundering in the commercial revolution the industry was undergoing. New companies were springing into existence; mergers were changing the status of older firms; great new studios were being built; huge and elaborate movie theatres were appearing on the nation's main streets; thousands of additional people of varied talents were being drawn into the feverish activity that characterized the movies' post-war boom days. Before Griffith found a secure berth, he made two pictures for two different companies: *Scarlet Days* (1919), a Western melodrama of Joaquin Murieta, and *The Greatest Question* (1919), dealing with spiritualism. Neither was released at first because they were of such poor quality. When finally exhibited, they were widely criticized as mediocre efforts, unworthy of a great director.

In the fall of 1919, Griffith and three other leading Hollywood figures—Charles Chaplin, Mary Pickford, and Douglas Fairbanks—formed a producing-distributing company, the United Artists Corporation. The prestige of the names of this "Big Four" assured financial support and made the firm a potential force in the new order of things. Griffith, like each of the others, was to direct and supervise his own productions, relying upon the pool for distribution and exhibition. While this seemed a perfect arrangement for a craftsman like Griffith, in reality it soon proved to be a great hindrance. For when Griffith became a member of United Artists, he became a part of that circle of producers whose only criterion for movie art was the box office. Hereafter all his efforts were directed toward getting the dollar; he made pictures on a strictly business basis, relying upon his prestige and associations to sell them. His new ambitions were power, fame, and money.

This change in Griffith, dictated by the pressure of the times and the vast capital investments in the business, paralleled the change in national attitudes. Movies having become big-scale operations, necessitating large returns, there was no longer room in the industry for independence or daring. Deviations from a closely knit manufacturing system involved great risks. In short, Griffith could no longer take chances.

The first picture made for United Artists was his last outstanding cinematic achievement, *Broken Blossoms* (1919). This picture, his most successful and most acclaimed effort since *The Birth of a Nation* and *Intolerance*, supported his sagging reputation. A distinguished if not a great work, the film contained a number of features that were deliberately chosen for their publicity value and revealed Griffith's growing esteem of showmanship: the racial issue (a Chinaman in love with a white girl); the unusual locale (the Limehouse district of London); "impressionistic photography" (gauzes and soft-focus effects, then new enough to be startling); and the novelty of tinted sequences and beams of pastel-colored lights, thrown from a projector while the picture was in progress to endow the sequences with additional emotional overtones. All these elements were reasons for the stir and admiration that greeted the film on its release.

Broken Blossoms, based on Thomas Burke's *Limehouse Nights* and in particular on "The Chink and the Child," is a poignant, romantic tragedy of the love and care of a Chinaman for a mistreated girl. Its mood is set by a pseudo-poetic preface which ends, "It is a tale of tears." This note is sustained throughout the leisurely but dramatic unfolding of the story. Despite its lapses into sentimentality, the whole has a reality and plausibility that represented Griffith at his best, from the opening scenes in the streets of the Orient with the carousing American sailors and the religious solemnity of the Chinamen, to the fog-drenched docks of Limehouse and the lurid interior of the smoking den.

Impressive as the atmosphere is, it is equaled by the characterizations. Richard Barthelmess as the Chinaman appears as sensitive and fragile as the story wants us to believe. Slender and pale, with his tilted head, his withdrawn, curved body, and his dreamy countenance emphasized in large close-ups time and again, he is a vivid

The dynamic movement of this still marked the whole of Sergei Eisenstein's monumental *Ten Days That Shook the World* (1927).

The individual against the mass in King Vidor's
sociological film *The Crowd* (1928), one of the
outstanding American silent pictures.

character in contrast to the large, restless, energetic Brute (Donald Crisp).

There are many splendid moments in the film that suggest Griffith's faculties in their prime. There is, for example, the beating of the waif by the Brute—subtly edited so that one does not see the suffering girl during her torture; or the intensely dramatic closet scene in which the terrified Lillian Gish, knowing that there is no escape for her, spins despairingly around and around in the small space as the Brute pounds on the door; or the suspense up to the climax, when the spy tells the Brute the girl has gone to live with the Chinaman.

The fine execution and cutting of these scenes were supported by a sustained use of the camera to evoke moods, feelings, pictorial qualities. The "soft-focus" suited the tenderness of the tale. Altogether *Broken Blossoms* was a brilliant culmination for the "sweet-and-innocent" era in American movies, already dying and being succeeded by the sophisticated, daring "triangle" era.

Griffith's own press books are full of the glowing praise critics heaped upon *Broken Blossoms*. *The New York Evening Telegram* [4] declared, "It is as if Dickens had spoken by means of the camera." According to the *Chicago News*,[5] the film was "an eloquent and decisive flight beyond the speaking stage," while the *Literary Digest* [6] concluded that ". . . on that night [of the opening] the screen jumped five years . . . with the showing of *Broken Blossoms* a new art arrived, an art as important as music or poetry." Said *The New York Morning Telegraph*,[7] more effusively,

Such art, so real one can think only of the classics, and of the masterly paintings remembered through the ages; so exquisite, so fragile, so beautifully and fragrantly poetic is *Broken Blossoms*.

The conservative *New York Times* [8] was no less enthusiastic:

All his mastery of picture making, the technique that is preeminently his by invention and control, the skill and subtlety with which he can unfold a story, has gone into the making of *Broken Blossoms*. It is a masterpiece.

[4] Griffith Scrapbooks at the Museum of Modern Art Film Library.
[5] *Ibid.*   [6] *Ibid.*   [7] *Ibid.*   [8] October 19, 1919.

Not even *The Birth of a Nation* had aroused such widespread adulation. Once called the "Belasco" of the screen, Griffith was now acknowledged as "the Shakespeare of the movies."

With his head in the clouds, Griffith sent out a series of lofty pronouncements. His next picture was to be the world's largest film, consisting of seventy-two reels; he was going to build his own theatre, "The Griffith"; he was going to build a chain of theatres all over the country to show only his films. Imperious, affiliated with money interests, powerful, he began to lecture, prophesy, advise, find fault with the industry and the nation at large. He assailed the income tax:

The income tax . . . is one of the most unjust systems of taxation known to modern civilization. . . . The income tax does not weigh upon the rich in any way as heavily as upon the workers and creators. . . . With the crash of nations falling before the menace of Bolshevism around the world, we believe it is very good time to pause and take thought about the matter. Bolshevism in the old days had small chance of gaining a foothold in America because the American worker . . . knew that the rich of America had begun just as he had . . . but we believe that the income tax makes it impossible to feel the same in this regard and gives a potent reason for discontent.[9]

About this same time he released *The Greatest Question* (1920), which he had made before *Broken Blossoms* and which he now hoped would benefit by that picture's success. In connection with the new film a singular event occurred which placed Griffith's name on the front pages of newspapers throughout the country. At the moment when the picture which "tried to answer the question whether communication with the dead was a fact or fancy" appeared, word was received that Griffith and his party, on board the yacht *Rosanda* en route to the Bahamas to film some scenes for his next production, had disappeared. The news was headlined on the front pages of all the New York papers on December 13, 1919. That afternoon thousands of people stormed the Strand theatre, where *The Greatest Question* was playing, and even overflowed into the Rialto and the Capitol, besieging the managements of those neighboring theatres for details of Griffith's whereabouts.

[9] *Los Angeles Times Magazine Section*, October 26, 1919.

During the next few days the press continued to feature the story, made the more exciting now by the intervention of the United States government, which had dispatched Navy planes, a submarine chaser, and Coast Guard cutters to search for Griffith along the Florida coast. Finally, a week later, word was flashed that Griffith and his entire crew had been found safely cruising off the coast. The nation heaved a sigh of relief, and Griffith presently came home, a national celebrity.

Soon, however, the air was filled with angry insinuations that a hoax had been perpetrated. This was vehemently denied by the Griffith office. But an editorial in *The Baltimore Sun* [10] diplomatically summed up the matter, commenting that

the most expert press agent of all stagedom could not have invented a more thrilling and effective publicity stunt had he worked a year on it, than this wholly unpremeditated one.

There was no disputing Griffith's showmanship thereafter. The new role of producer-director pleased him immensely. Everything he touched for the next five years received widespread publicity. His activities were always colorful copy. The old ambition to become a famous writer had long since disappeared; he was more famous than the best of writers.

If fame was welcome to Griffith, the business of making pictures was rapidly becoming a burden. After twelve years in the industry, during which he had made several hundred films, he found the effort no longer exciting. Though the rewards had greatly increased, picture making had become more and more a hard discipline, even though Griffith now had a staff of directors under him to carry out his plans. Gradually he lost his passion for movies and concentrated more intently on his career as a business magnate.

The pictures Griffith produced during the next few years were costly but were formula pictures with out-of-date themes; they were sold on his past reputation and showed a steady decline in his directorial faculties. *The Idol Dancer* (1920), which he went to the Bahamas to make, and *The Love Flower* (1920) were both criticized as "unworthy of the master." *Way Down East* (1920),

[10] December 18, 1910.

which got great publicity because of the $175,000 paid for the story, turned out to be a stilted treatment of an outdated social problem with little meaning during these rebellious years. *Dream Street* (1921) was a weak attempt to repeat the success of *Broken Blossoms*. Declared *The Baltimore Sun*,[11]

One doesn't expect these things from the most loudly lauded director-producer of the day, nor does one take kindly to such a plentiful evidence of crude, amateurish acting, such wholesale symbolism, such mawkish sickening sentimentality. Where is the D. W. Griffith of yesteryear?

Griffith's next film, *Orphans of the Storm* (1922), was the work of a man who was no longer influencing the movies but being influenced by them. A drama of the French Revolution, it clearly bore the marks of the German historical dramas then the rage.

Griffith was rapidly becoming a "back number." Pictures had taken over the attributes and point of view of a jazz-conscious world. It was DeMille and Lubitsch, with their sophisticated films about marital infidelity, bathtubs, and forbidden paradises, who were now the leaders. Even other men who had trained under Griffith were beginning to supersede him in popularity. The time was not far off when DeMille's forecast, recalled to Harry Carr years later,[12] was to become fact: "Some day Griffith would take a hard bump—due to his refusal to take ideas from the trend of the day."

At a time when the country was fast breaking its prohibition laws, winking and drinking recklessly, rejoicing in the daily stock-market rise, throwing traditional morals to the winds, Griffith made a number of futile attempts to regain his foothold in the industry. *One Exciting Night* (1923) was a melodramatic mystery, "jumbled and pointless."[13] He sent out notices that he was having great difficulty in finding the right sort of material. Tamar Lane, West Coast film critic,[14] attacked him as being unable "to get away from the situation of the attacking, raping, or wronging of the defenseless girl," in almost every one of his screen stories of the past few years.

The White Rose (1923) was so hopelessly pre-war in outlook

---

[11] *May 24, 1921.*
[12] *Cinema Digest, May 1932.*

[13] *Photoplay, January 1923.*
[14] *What's Wrong with the Movies*, p. 63.

that F. J. Smith, in *Photoplay*,[15] remarked: "Somehow he seems to us to be a great man living within a circle of isolation, surrounded by minor advisers, genius out of touch with the world, as it were."

This lack of touch with the times was notable also in his next film, *Isn't Life Wonderful* (1924-1925). Simple to the point of bareness, it appeared drab and out of place beside the films of glamour and elegance then in vogue. Although it was moving and honest in its theme—the tragedy in Germany during the war—and was adroitly constructed, it was received unsympathetically. People of the twenties were concerned chiefly with physical sensations and had little time for honest appraisals of social conditions: Griffith was blindly bucking the tide. His succeeding film, *America* (1924), scarcely improved his position; absorbing bits of realism culled from his research, years before, in soldiers' diaries, it was undoubtedly inspired by the phenomenal success of *The Covered Wagon*.

The end was not far off. By 1925 Griffith was no longer his own producer. At Paramount he became merely one of a large staff of directors. Here he was subjected to the commercial pressure he had always abhorred: he had to make pictures on schedule, to stay within the budget, to turn out "program" features.

A minor director now, he made a series of romantic films which attempted to capture the time spirit. *Sally of the Sawdust* (1925), a circus tale, was slow in a fast age, pre-war in temper. *That Royle Girl* (1926), despite "clever touches," remained a Victorian melodrama. *Sorrows of Satan* (1926-1927), an obvious imitation of the day's outstanding sensation from Germany, *Variety*, emerged as a hackneyed morality tale. The industry whispered that Griffith was "through."

For the two and a half years thereafter, Griffith made no films. What he was doing, what he was thinking, no one knew. All sorts of rumors circulated, but he did nothing. Then in 1928 he suddenly returned to United Artists—in which he still held stock—and once more resumed motion picture directing. Expectations of a brilliant comeback were put to an end after his production of *Drums of Love* (1928), based on the Paolo and Francesca legend; *The Battle of the Sexes* (1928-1929), a rehash of his 1913 film; and *The Lady*

15 August 1923.

of the Pavements (1929), a romantic melodrama to which sound was added.

Into his first all-talking film Griffith poured a great deal of effort. Choosing a story and background he knew well, he filmed *Abraham Lincoln* (1930). As one of the earliest of the all-talking films, it was typically static and had no feeling for the movie medium. There were so many moments of absurd sentimentality—the death of Ann Rutledge and the pardon of the boy soldier, to mention two glaring instances—that the whole carried little weight.

Griffith has made only one film since then: *The Struggle* (1931). Independently financed, a half-hearted effort, it was recalled from exhibition after a few showings: a sad finishing touch to Griffith's career. Sound had confirmed Hollywood's conviction that Griffith was an "old-timer."

So fast has the motion picture world moved in thirty years that today Griffith is in the peculiar circumstance of being regarded as an "old master," although he is still alive. Notwithstanding all his great contributions and his early talent, he has unquestionably declined since the war. As soon as he was no longer moving forward, he disintegrated as an artist. The profound film form of which he achieved mastery could not sustain or compensate for the superficiality of content and the commercial motives revealed in his postwar work. His romantic leanings, inbred prejudices, and moral inflexibility, while serving him well in their day and age, at last became millstones around his neck. Of this misfortune he apparently was unaware, since he became absorbed in high finance and the personal glories of success. The name of Griffith, nevertheless, has come to signify American motion picture art: his contributions to it enriched its traditions and gave it vital momentum.

FILMS OF THE POST-WAR DECADE

THE movies produced between 1919 and 1929 are eloquent social documents on a lively era in American life. So thoroughly does the spirit of the decade saturate the films that they are distinguished perhaps more for their innocent reflection of contemporary life than for their technical advances, remarkable though these were. This is true even in the case of such important directors as Erich von Stroheim, Fred Murnau, and Ernst Lubitsch. While valuable innovations in the motion picture craft were coming into being in Europe, Hollywood was content almost exclusively with titillating the senses of the increasingly prosperous American movie-goer.

The addition of the middle class and well-to-do to the movie audience, already apparent on America's entrance into the World War, was now complete. After 1919 motion pictures with rare exceptions—notably Charlie Chaplin's comedies—were made to please the middle class. The working man as a subject for films disappeared after the war, reappearing only when the depression reawakened interest in his milieu. It was the leisure class that now became the focus of the cinema: their life was mirrored on the celluloid slickly and ingratiatingly.

Recovering from the excitement of the Armistice, the public soon became aware that the so-called victory was an empty honor; the war, a business maneuver. The shattering of principles, the loss of confidence in leaders, the liberals' lack of resolution at the crucial time all induced a contempt for political progressivism. Prohibition became a federal law; the "Red scare" reached unprecedented extremes in the Palmer Raids; intolerance was rampant.

Assailing the objectives of the war, denouncing the atrocity stories as myths, salving an embittered and tired populace with the slogan "back to normalcy," Warren G. Harding—staunch Rotarian and dark horse, of whom Alice Longworth once said, "Harding was not a bad man. He was just a slob"—replaced Woodrow Wilson, the broken idealist, as President of the United States in 1920. The government was now in the hands of the business men. Extreme conservatism replaced progressivism as the cynical nation eschewed political embroilments of any kind and began to ride high on prosperity.

The end of the war saw violent reverses in manners and morals. "The license of war time, trench coarseness and materialism, the sex life of great masses of young males held long without feminine companionships of the better kind, the atheism and pessimism bred in camps," to quote Fred Lewis Pattee,[1] now bore their fruits. Changes in morals already begun as a result of the new scientific discoveries and attitudes were speeded by the popularity of Freudian psychology and the growing economic independence of women. The lust for thrills, excitement, and power, the recklessness and defiance of authority condoned by governmental policy, and a general social callousness due to the war, all combined to produce a moral uncertainty and laxity unprecedented in American history.

Two social currents therefore ran parallel at this time: reactionism in political and economic life and revolutionary attitudes in ethics. Belief in the old order of things having been undermined, idealism fell back before materialism; respectability and gentility became old-fashioned. Most of the post-war generation, impatient and bitter, wanted above all to be free of the old dogmas. Disdainful of anything that smacked of the past, they constantly rebelled against tradition and convention.

Restrained as life had been during the war days, it was now unbridled. Sexual promiscuity, faithlessness in marriage, divorce, bad manners, the hip flask, and general cynicism became popular as millions of people attempted to escape from responsibilities of all kinds. Americans surrendered themselves to fads and sensations: Emile Coué's "every-day-in-every-way" philosophy, the tabloids, the radio,

[1] The New American Literature, p. 461.

The Patriot (1928). Ernst Lubitsch's feeling for space, grouping, and camera composition which made his German films outstanding were again emphasized in his first synchronized sound film.

Lewis Milestone's *All Quiet on the Western Front* (1930), one of the more serious war pictures, showed the comradeships as well as the horrors of war.

Mah Jong, the Leopold and Loeb "thrill murder," Freud and the Libido, crossword puzzles, the Dayton trial, Florida and the building boom, golf, Eskimo pies, speakeasies, night clubs, roadhouses, bathing-beauty parades, Lindbergh, Ford's new Model A automobile, the stock market, Al Capone and gang rule in Chicago. All the while King Jazz titillated the nerves of the nation and gave the era its name.

Movies, like the Supreme Court, followed the election returns. They took up the cause of business, grew cynical, and participated in the repudiation of pre-war conventionality. Like the tabloids of the day, hundreds of films specialized in speed, spice, and spectacle. "Jazz films" by the middle of the period had superseded the last of the pictures in the pre-war tradition, substituting materialism and freedom for the old idealism. Popular directors of the previous era, such as Porter, Blackton, and even Griffith, could no longer satisfy the national appetite, just as popular novelists of the past— Hall Caine, Marie Corelli, Laura Jean Libby—were now "old stuff." These producers and writers were all moralists, and the public was tired of morality. People wanted to shock and be shocked.

Films attacked the genteel tradition with ever-increasing boldness, mirroring a nation that was recklessly experimenting, experiencing, asserting its right to live its own life regardless of age, class, or tradition. Hollywood movies pivoted almost exclusively on sex and sensation. Toward the close of the period the critical realism that had been evident in the works of literary rebels began to be manifested on the screen and to portend a change. The main traits of these ten years as reflected in films, however, were indifference to social responsibility and absorption in the "individual."

The reaction from progressivism was sharply revealed in film attacks on labor, liberalism, and Bolshevism. In the fright over the recent successful revolution in Russia, intolerance was running high. The business man's government unofficially enlisted the motion pictures, now that their war duties were ended, to do their bit in upholding capitalism. The government condoned Red scares, Palmer raids, race riots, and the expulsion of Socialist assemblymen in New York State, and sought to end the post-war tide of strikes in the building trades, shipping, stockyards and shipyards, subways, the shoe industry, communications, mines, and railroads. At the same time it had the task of pacifying the men returning from France. A "gentlemen's agreement" was soon concluded between the national administration and the motion picture industry. It was reported in *The New York Times* for January 12, 1920:

The movies will be used to combat Bolshevik propaganda as the result of the conference held yesterday. . . . Mr. Lane [Secretary of the Interior] emphasized in his address the necessity of showing films depicting the great opportunities which industrious immigrants may find in this country, and of stories of poor men who have risen high. He suggested that the industry organize immediately to spread throughout the country the story of America as exemplified in the story of Lincoln.

Movie makers earnestly set about to do their duty. Pictures painted Bolshevism in the blackest terms and declared that Americans would not for long ". . . tolerate or be misled by such foreign ideas." *Bolshevism on Trial*, based on Thomas Dixon's *Comrades* and advertised as an impartial representation of all sides of the question, was in reality a violent denunciation of the "impracticability of idealism, the eternal selfishness of human nature," and "the lunacy of free love." *The New Moon* caricatured the Bolshevik as indolent, lustful, cruel, vile. *Dangerous Hours* demonstrated how Bolshevism victimized everybody—the dreamer, siren, fanatic, coward, good-natured dupe, misguided student, bully, street woman, sneak, and old lady. *The Uplifters*, a film based on Wallace Irwin's book, satirized parlor Bolshevism. *The Undercurrent*, a variation on a favorite theme, told of the returned soldier who, "misled," becomes embroiled in "Red plots," only to perceive the danger at the last moment and turn on "the destroyers."

A steady and emphatic stream of movies pointed out the need for the laborer and employer to get together and co-operate against their mutual foe, Bolshevism. *The Right to Happiness* posed the question, "Which would you rather have in this country—destruction under the Red flag or construction and co-operation under the American flag?" *Democracy, The Vision Restored* urged capital and labor "to kiss and make up." *The Other Half* showed that the man from the "classes" as well as the man from the "masses" has his problems. *A Child for Sale* suggested that striking laborers and profiteering capitalists were both responsible for the prevalent industrial unrest. *Paid in Full* told the tale of a clerk who "thought the world owed him a living" and of "the wife who saved him from his own folly." *The Little Church Around the Corner* depicted angry coal miners striking for better safety conditions. (The minister, performing the miracle of curing a deaf-mute before their eyes, convinces the workers to return to their mines and arbitrate their differences with the employer, who has also been chastened by the miracle.) *The Dwelling Place of Light*, boldly advising wealthy mill owners not to pursue working girls, was one of the few films to indicate that strikes may be caused by injustices.

These pictures clearly indicate the post-war antagonism between capital and labor, but as the years advanced, the issue lost some of its urgency. With a rising bull market, with prosperity seeping through the nation, labor was placated, industrial unrest diminished, and confidence in business rule became entrenched. The "gentlemen's agreement" between the government and Hollywood no longer demanded action. Hollywood was learning, in fact, that the populace was more interested in sensations than in politics or economics, and desired above all to escape social controversy. The screen therefore devoted itself to meeting these new demands.

At this time the pre-war type of movie, with its emphasis on religion, parental love, self-sacrifice, duty, devotion to home and family, and contentment with one's lot, was making its last stand in such pictures as *Humoresque, Madame X, The Little Shepherd of Kingdom Come, Way Down East, Broken Blossoms, Over the Hill*, and *Eyes of Youth*. These films were holdovers of pre-war sentimentality. Their values were based upon virtues soon to be mocked and openly defied, upon a code of loyalty soon to be completely broken up.

The new materialistic standards and the rebellion against outmoded dogmas were first manifested on the screen in two signal "hits" of the blundering post-war year of 1919: *The Miracle Man* and *Male and Female*. *The Miracle Man* frankly and shockingly depicted the hero (Thomas Meighan) as a racketeer and crass materialist who seeks only easy graft. It openly acknowledged sex magnetism and the "sheer brute instinct which holds Rose to Burke." Such outspokenness and emphasis on sex were indicative of the new frame of mind, which dealt in "essentials." The exposure of racketeering, a new phenomenon in American life, with its exploitation of honest people for selfish ends, was in itself a significant disclosure of popular interests. Despite the spiritual note on which the film closed, *The Miracle Man* was a portent of the new, hard order of things in which principles were being discarded for material things.

Even more suggestive of the new era was the significantly titled *Male and Female.* A modernization of James Barrie's *The Admirable Crichton*, it related the intimate adventures of a lady (Gloria Swanson) and a butler (Thomas Meighan) on a desert isle, emphasizing the supremacy of sex over class barriers and condoning marital infidelity, "spice," and sensation for their own sake. More daring in its subject matter than any other picture Hollywood had produced, bolder in its attack on the genteel tradition, this film ushered in the new movie showmanship. Throughout it played on the audience's senses with luxurious settings, cave-man love scenes, sensual display. As DeMille, the director, pointed out,[2] "The ruined woman is as out of style as the Victorian who used to faint."

DeMille's quip found ample support in fact during the following years. Hundreds of films, like *The Miracle Man* and *Male and Female*, attacked the genteel tradition, flaunted sex, advocated new morals, condoned illicit and illegal relationships, set up new ideals, established a new tempo in living, and broke down pre-war class distinctions with the new emphasis on money, luxuries, material success. Refinement went out as aggressiveness came in. Films set the pace for the nation as cynicism and disillusionment marked the gradual decline of an old order and the upsurge of a new.

The breakdown of the old order on the screen was signalized first and most markedly by the pictures of Cecil B. DeMille, condoning the loosening of marriage bonds and questioning responsibilities until now conceded to be necessary in home life. The promiscuity and new attitude toward marriage presented in *Male and Female* were carried further in his series of domestic dramas that

[2] *Photoplay*, December 1919.

reversed the previous moral order. *Don't Change Your Husband* (1919) told how a young and beautiful wife (Gloria Swanson) goes to the seashore to arouse her neglectful business-engrossed husband (Elliot Dexter) to remember her. There she meets a "home wrecker" (Lew Cody) and divorces her husband to marry him, only to discover he nags at her continually. Five years pass and they are in bad financial circumstances. Her former husband, on the other hand, has gained greater success. On meeting, they become reconciled and remarry. Ostensibly an argument against divorce, the film predicated the new notions that a woman had a right to break her marriage bonds as she saw fit.

For Better, For Worse (1919), *Something to Think About* (1920), *Why Change Your Wife* (1920), *Forbidden Fruit* (1921), *The Affairs of Anatol* (1921), *Fool's Paradise* (1922), *Saturday Night* (1922), *Manslaughter* (1922), *Adam's Rib* (1923), formed a glittering array of DeMille problem plays of sex intrigues among the wealthy. They disregarded the sanctity of the home and of woman's duty, at all costs, to be a loyal wife and mother, and subordinated all problems to the new major interest of the post-war age, Sex.

Reinforcing these DeMille films were the hundreds of domestic dramas by others that stemmed from these. All emphasized the importance of love in marriage and woman's rights to independence. Wives became the heroines in all sorts of situations. Movies taught them to keep up their appearance and "style" after marriage, convinced them that they had a right to love and attention after marriage, and finally began to suggest that legal bonds should not prevent wives from having an independent life of their own—a prerogative heretofore looked upon as exclusively the property of husbands. *The Amateur Wife*, *The Misfit Wife*, *Poor Men's Wives*, *Behold My Wife*, and *Old Wives for New* all eloquently lectured on "the frump who learns it is important to remain stylish and good-looking after marriage." *Blind Husbands*, *The Devil's Passkey*, *Don't Neglect Your Wife*, *Foolish Wives*, and *The Merry Widow* pointed out that wives and mature women have a right to love after marriage and that business-engrossed husbands cannot expect to hold their "love-starved" wives. *Virtuous Wives*, *Flapper Wives*,

Bluebeard's Eighth Wife, *Other Men's Wives*, *Scrambled Wives*, *The Married Flapper*, *Week-End Wives*, and *Miss Bluebeard* all mirrored the increasing daring and independence of the woman who engaged in flirtations and was growing ever more astute in using "her chastity as a fence between her and men."

As we already know, a new note in Continental sophistication and marital laxity was brought to the screen in the films of von Stroheim. These were sly thrusts at traditions and sentiments, and their gleeful acceptance by the public indicated how rightly attuned they were to the national state of mind—despite *Photoplay's* prim remark,[3] regarding *Foolish Wives*, that it was "an insult to every American." Von Stroheim did not treat sex so frivolously as other directors; the underlying tone of even his lightest works was earnest. His insistence upon sex as a serious matter to be openly acknowledged rather than mockingly and teasingly exhibited was one of the reasons for the vast amount of antagonism—and praise—that his films inspired.

As the importance of love in marriage grew and sex became ever more predominant, pictures began to emphasize that disappointment and repression in marital relations (here Freud's influence was plain) were valid reasons for a married woman to have a fling at love and romance. Marriage became an open sesame to freedom rather than a responsibility. Elinor Glyn became the popular author of the day, and her novels were transposed regularly to the screen. *Three Weeks*, perhaps the most renowned of the movies based on her work, told the story of a queen who, bitterly disappointed in marriage, allows herself one romantic interlude. Hundreds of similar tales swamped the screen, thumbing their noses at "Victorian" codes as they justified adventures outside the bounds of marriage.

In the prevalent post-war disillusionment most people sought "escape." The movies obligingly offered substitutes for life in the form of exotic and erotic costume dramas, all affording vicarious satisfactions and extravagant visual magnificence. The phenomenal success of *The Sheik* (1921) climaxed the series of exotic "red-hot romances" begun toward the close of the war and started a cycle of dramas of the "great, throbbing desert": *Arabian Love, Burning*

[3] March 1922.

Sands, One Stolen Night, When the Desert Calls, Tents of Allah, Sons of the Desert. The men in all these films were passionate and aggressive lovers who, casting aside all prudence, swept the women off their feet. Films of this sort waned toward the middle of the period as dramas in the jazz spirit became ever more daring.

Serving the same yearning for escape into dream worlds in the early twenties were the excessively sentimental and nostalgic adventure tales of by-gone days. Douglas Fairbanks reached the high peak in his career as a swashbuckling hero in *The Thief of Bagdad, Robin Hood, The Mark of Zorro,* and *The Three Musketeers,* being rivaled by the dashing Ramon Novarro of *The Prisoner of Zenda,* the heroic Milton Sills of *The Sea Hawk,* and the chivalrous John Barrymore of *Beau Brummel.* Sentimentally expressing the "back to normalcy" nostalgia were the sweet Norma Talmadge of *Smilin' Through,* the old-fashioned Marion Davies of *When Knighthood Was in Flower* and *Little Old New York,* and the endless series of films about imaginary kingdoms with imaginary kings winning imaginary queens: *The Bohemian Girl, Young April, Bardelys the Magnificent, If I Were Queen, Valencia*—Graustarkian fables all. These pictures catered to the public desire to forget the brusque, hard world of the moment in a make-believe world of grand romance.

Such story-book films grew fewer in number as the years of prosperity wore on and America grew more hardened and reckless. The farcical treatment of situations that would have been tragedies in pre-war days no longer appeared shocking, and movies had to become ever more daring if they were to titillate their audiences. Marital fidelity was now even ridiculed; adultery and philandering among mature married people were not only frankly condoned but made fashionable and attractive.

Lubitsch's films in particular were attuned to this attitude. In risqué and teasing terms his films all dealt with the flirtations and playfulness of the rich and carefree. His characters were always mature men and women of the world who engaged in their little games with full knowledge of what they were doing: sinfulness was now a spicy social sport rather than the road to a dire fate. *The Marriage Circle, Forbidden Paradise, Kiss Me Again,* and *Lady*

Windermere's Fan were high-water marks of this movie fad. *The Marriage Circle* with its humor and its sophistication, portraying the promiscuity in high society between other men's wives and other wives' husbands, all engaging freely in the interplay, became a model for other movie makers and even for the national way of living.

Hollywood offered advice liberally in such films as *Don't Tell Everything, Secrets, Should a Wife Tell?* (the answer was *No*), and recommended philandering in *Honeymoon Flat, Husbands for Rent, Breakfast at Sunrise*. One film bluntly called *Sex* moralized, "Don't do anything to another woman's husband that you would not have done to your own," and included the usual scenes of "wild" dinner parties, amorous adventures, and—despite prohibition—drinking orgies.

In such films marriage as an institution broke down utterly. Desires for family life and its responsibilities were looked upon as old-fashioned. The woman in the home became a whimsicality, and wide-eyed Mary Pickford an emblem of the past. People on the screen lived in apartments, ate out, gave up the home life their elders knew. Childbearing was disapproved, as in *The Very Idea* and *Children Not Wanted*, and the new vogue of adoption was discussed, as in *Married People*. "Companionate marriage," "modern marriage," "free love," terms that rang through the nation, filled the screens: *Affinities, Man and Wife, Modern Marriage, Is Matrimony a Failure?*

Marriage being regarded as a license for escapades, divorce was viewed as the path to even greater freedom. Divorcees and widows, like wives, were considered far more fascinating than young girls. The new pictures time and again showed divorcees victorious in their lives despite their unconventional position in society, as in *The Impossible Mrs. Bellew* and *Divorce Coupons*. Divorce was offered as an excuse for frivolity and excitement in such films as *On to Reno, Reno Divorce, The Merry Widow*, and *Beware of Widows*.

Once marriage and the home had broken down on the screen, there was a breakdown in morals all along the line. Impropriety, promiscuity, illicit sex relations, and bad manners generally were shown as prevailing among married and unmarried alike. Movies reflected the vogue of hip flasks, cocktail parties, speakeasies, petting parties, necking, and recklessness and defiance of all laws, written or unwritten. Morality having been proved to be a useless asset, lovemaking and golddigging and excitement for its own sake became the chief pursuits of the nation—at least in the nation represented by films.

Thus began that remarkable series of jazz-age pictures exemplified in DeMille's works, which, speaking for the hedonism of a nation on the wave of prosperity, helped to set new styles in social behavior and reflected the new standards of living. The old order now crumbled away entirely. The screen world became crowded with dancing mothers, flaming youth, jazz babies, cake eaters, flappers. Revolutions in etiquette, culture, and conduct generally broke out in this new film domain of electrified apartments, Bagdadian bathtubs, seductive boudoirs, hilarious speakeasies, night clubs, and petting parties. Movies, like the tabloids and the confession and sex magazines, now booming, gave their all to the task of giving America sensations.

The screen was invaded by hordes of "hot mammas," bathing beauties, and Volstead violators, as each movie tried to outdo its predecessor in daring licentiousness. Modesty and virginity became absurd as lovemaking took on the appearance of a wrestling match. The movie woman was now thrown around, carried off, flung on the couch by her man in the holocaust of primitive passion. Bedroom farces and other teasers were multitudinous: *The Gilded Lily, Lying Lips, Mad Love, Temptation, Passion Flame, More Deadly than the Male, Love Is an Awful Thing, One Week of Love; Parlor, Bedroom and Bath; La, La, Lucille; Twin Beds.* Movies glorified the smart set (*The Smart Set*), the Long Island set (*Upstairs and Down*), the country-club set (*Darling of the Rich*), and the "very rich, moral and very human humans of the Rolls Royce set" (*The Fighting Chance*). They depicted the *Wildness of Youth, Madness of Youth, Risky Business*; asked *Has the World Gone Mad? Why Be Good?*; and captured the hysteria of *The Jazz Age, The Plastic Age, Flaming Youth, Reckless Youth, Our Dancing Daughters, Children of Divorce, Children of the Ritz*, and *Modern*

Maidens. The sermonizing with which such films ended was mocked by the attractiveness with which they portrayed sin. When F. Scott Fitzgerald's *The Beautiful and Damned* was filmed, it was said that

If he depicts life as a series of petting parties, cocktails, mad dancing and liquor on the hip, it is because he sees our youthful generation in these terms . . . it is our youthful fascisti possessing its measure of money and knowledge, fighting against the swing of the pendulum which has brought us the you-must-not era.[4]

Married men and women were shown keeping up with the wild parties and recklessness of their children: *Dancing Mothers, Paid to Love, Love Mart, Man and the Moment, Gigolo. The Mad Whirl* (1925), adapted from Richard Washburn Child's "Here's How," depicted the new family life:

11 A.M. is Bromo-Seltzer hour, when three servants march to the rooms of father, mother and son, who have been out carousing the night before, as well as every other night. The mother "does at 40 what she was not allowed to do at 20." The father has [the] "Jazz microbe at 60." And the subtitle calls him "an expert at squeezing the hand that feeds him." At breakfast table mother dates up with another man and father with another woman, and the servants take advantage of the situation by asking for afternoons off; otherwise they might divulge the secrets. They drink till daylight. Lying around [on the] floor in each other's arms. Girl so drunk the son carries her home, and so the fun goes on.[5]

Middle-aged men and women were advised "to make hay while the sun shines." *Only 38* told the tale of a widow's quest for lost youth. *The Dangerous Age* was a society drama of a husband who runs wild at forty. *The Young Diana* proved that even an old maid can become young if she has the right spirit.

Films featured the lust for youth (beauty packs, bobbed hair, and short skirts were essential in pictures), flattered the masses' new taste for finery and culture (films were notable for interior decoration, travel, sophistication), fed the romantic desire for "freedom" (speakeasy gods and goddesses gamboled in and out of parties), and stumped for the mercenary business psychology of the day by

4 *Photoplay*, February 1923.   5 *The Educational Screen*, May 1925.

demonstrating the great American dogma that any man can achieve success by high-pressure salesmanship, aggressive scientific business methods, and football-conference huddles.

The mockery of ethics, of the old "inner goodness" of the film heroes and heroines, was paralleled by the new regard for material things. A burning ambition to be identified with the rich, a deep reverence for material goods, characterized American attitudes. Silk stockings, silk underwear, furs, automobiles, phonographs, elaborate furniture, servants, apartment houses, electrically equipped kitchens, hotels, night clubs, country clubs, resorts, sports, colleges—these were paraded across the screen in exaggerated splendor. *Brown of Harvard*, *The Quarterback*, *The Flirt*, were typical of dozens of films of the "higher learning" variety, all featuring raccoon coats, roadsters, and swank fraternity parties. Money alone talked; clothes were an index of position in life; aggressiveness and ruthlessness were the real virtues; material success alone mattered.

A Slave of Fashion, *Ladies Must Dress*, *Pretty Clothes*, *Fashion Madness*, *Let's Be Fashionable*, and the equally blatant *Charge It*, *Madame Peacock*, *Gimme*, *Extravagance*, *The Thirteenth Commandment*, reflected the contemporary passion for clothes and fineries.

Forbidden Fruit (1922), one of DeMille's biggest successes, dramatized the current goals to reach society and to be identified with the rich. A seamstress wife (Agnes Ayres) of a "worthless" husband, poses for a rich woman as one of her dinner guests in order to "vamp" a rich man to delay his departure. At the dinner party, the scene of her hesitation as to which fork to use for the different dinner courses, is said to have amazed Ernst Lubitsch. The importance given such a detail—which had little to do with the plot itself —no doubt served to give him an insight into American psychology. Such an incident mirrored a common predicament of the day, for every shopgirl longed to be accepted as the heroine of the film, into the social circles of the rich, and sought a knowledge of table etiquette, how to dress, how to be introduced, how to order, and how to conduct onself in general.

Eloquent of the new materialistic credo were such titles as *Look Your Best*, *It Pays to Advertise*, *Go and Get It*, *Do and Dare*, *The*

Go-Getter, If You Believe It, It's So, Putting It Over, Success, Get-Rich-Quick-Wallingford, The Three-Must-Get-Theirs, The Miracle of Money, and *Money, Money, Money.*

Such films encouraged respect for, and even envy of, the expensively "kept" woman, the high-class prostitute. The motto *Ladies Must Live* was proved by silks and satins. The "sisterhood of those that toil not, neither do they spin" were objects of admiration in such films as *Outcast, Rouged Lips, Trifling Women, Pretty Ladies, Lilies of the Field, Ladies of Ease, Bought and Paid For, The Joy Girl, Silk Legs, The Rag Doll.* The harlot and the adventuress were no longer hussies but women to esteem and emulate (*Lady of the Night, A Woman of Paris, A Woman of Affairs*). Money and luxury were presented as major goals in life to be gained at all costs.

This worship of money, hard-boiled materialism, irresponsibility, living for the moment, callousness toward human life, and violent lust for excitement formed a background for the large-scale racketeering and other criminal activity that broke out after the war. The Volstead Act itself made lawbreaking fashionable. The bootlegger, the highjacker, the gangster, and the racketeer flourished as drinking became "smart," as speakeasies and gambling rooms replaced the old saloons, as bars were set up in glamorous surroundings. Colorful entertainment in these establishments where men and women drank freely covered the cheapness of the underworld, investing it with an air of splendor, wealth, and luxury, and above all a spirit of adventure. The illegal liquor and drug traffic thus built a new underworld that was patronized by the respectable; it created a new stratum of life for American society.

At first movies featured racketeering and crooks for their dramatic possibilities, blaming crime on personal afflictions, animosities, and the desire for thrilling adventure. *The Penalty* displayed Lon Chaney as "the legless wonder" who has sworn revenge on society because both of his legs were amputated by a careless doctor after an accident. Bitter and violent, he becomes ruler of the underworld. The removal of a blood clot from his brain by a surgical operation finally restores him to decency. Ridiculous though such a solution appears to us today, in the light of more recent realism regarding crime, it was accepted as plausible then.

In a stream of films Lon Chaney became famous for his characterizations of the underworld ruler: *Partners of the Night, Black Shadows, The Girl in the Rain, Kick In, One Million in Jewels, Dollar Devils, Boston Blackie, Outside the Law*, and the celebrated *The Unholy Three*.

The sinister, ruthless criminal of these films gradually was transformed in succeeding pictures. The underworld became inhabited by the smart set, "the right people"; the gangster was revealed as an enviable hero, quick and intelligent, refined, influential politically and powerful financially. Movies like the tabloids glorified his life, showing it full of exciting adventure, beautiful women, and plenty of money. Although gangsterism was becoming a national scandal, gangsters were not yet popularly regarded as a vicious group of public enemies.

By 1925 Chicago, considered the world center of crime and the Mecca of gangsterdom, had become the cynosure of the nation's attention, and movies were following the tabloids and the stage in reflecting the racketeering and gangster rule prevalent in that metropolis. One of the most popular and revelatory of the films was *Chicago*, adapted from the play of that name. It drew an uncompromising picture of the jazz-mad wife of a simple worker who is unable to supply the luxuries she demands. Failing to get those luxuries, she goes out with a playboy who, by her dispassionate order, is subsequently "bumped off." The ensuing publicity is far from distasteful to her; she revels in the new-found excitement and importance. The outraged husband comes to her defense in court. Sympathy, however, is not with him, but with the luxury-loving wife.

As gangsterism became a more critical national problem toward the close of the twenties, an increasing number of gangster films reached the screen. They were now more realistic. *The Big City, Tenderloin*, and *Chicago After Midnight* emphasized the fact that the complexities of city life make racketeering possible. *The Street of Forgotten Men*, in a tale described as "sordid," exposed the street beggars' racket. Josef von Sternberg's series—*Underworld, The Drag Net, The Docks of New York, Thunderbolt*—and Roland West's *Alibi* acidly depicted the underworld as aggressive and ruthless, as a plague in society. Lewis Milestone's *The Racket* attempted to expose the perfunctory activities of the police against the big city rackets with frankness and seriousness—an attitude soon to become pronounced. It is notable that the hardness and realism introduced in these films were to become the dominating tone in the next period.

The revolution in morality and manners that was taking place had introduced new ideals of personality. The modern girl evolved from flirt to flapper, to jazz baby, to baby vamp, to salamander, and finally to the sophisticated, colorful woman of the world. Wanda Hawley, Julia Faye, and Constance Talmadge were typical of "the young rascals whose bite was more dangerous because it was hidden behind innocent eyes" (*A Virtuous Vamp, Dangerous Business, The Love Expert, In Search of Sinners*). Colleen Moore, Clara Bow, Sue Carol, Madge Bellamy, Louise Brooks, and Joan Crawford typified the "frivolous, promiscuous, mocking type" with "a hard body and long, exposed legs, bobbed hair, bold eyes" (*The Perfect Flapper, Flaming Youth, It, Daughters of Pleasure, Get Your Man*). Gloria Swanson, Pola Negri, Norma Shearer, and Greta Garbo were the prototypes for the ultra-civilized, sleek and slender, knowing and disillusioned, restless, over-sexed and neurotic woman who "leads her own life" (*Flesh and the Devil, A Woman of the World, The Single Standard, Lady of Chance*).

Short skirts, boyish figures, silk stockings, step-ins, cigarettes, and drinking not only emancipated the modern girl from "woman's passive role" but freed her for masculine pursuits as well. The new girl was shown in airplanes, roadsters, and petting parties, with rolled stockings, hip flasks, bobbed hair, and bold aggressiveness. The advertisement for DeMille's *Adam's Rib* prated: [6]

The modern girl in a new light. . . . With all the luxury of beautiful gowns and magnificent sets that are an integral part of C. B. DeMille's art, *Adam's Rib* reveals the modern girl in her true color, and in a story crammed with action, interprets her impulsive heart to all who wish to appreciate her for what she is.

Provocative, tantalizing, beautiful, the modern girl was further imbued with a fascination that lay in her frank flaunting of sex. Sex

[6] *Photoplay*, February 1923.

appeal became the ultimate criterion of personality. Elinor Glyn's "It" was now an idiom of the American language.

Independent, level-headed, ambitious, the new movie girl used her femininity to obtain a good living, ease, pleasure. In *Soft Living* the stenographer finds it easier to get alimony than to work for a living. *The Taxi Dancer* and *Love 'Em and Leave 'Em* were two of dozens of films showing the emancipated working girl who was out to get what was coming to her. When *Gentlemen Prefer Blondes* reached the screen, *Photoplay's* editor declared, "If you don't want to see this film version . . . something is wrong with you." *The Golddiggers, The Exciters, The Flapper,* were stories of money hunters, thrill hunters, and sensation mongers.

Typical of contemporary films was *Manhandled,* the story of Tessie McGuire, a little shopgirl whose sweetheart, a shop mechanic, has an invention for a new carburetor. Tessie is invited by the boss to a wild party, where she "plays with fire." Finally she tires of the men she encounters on the boss's level and returns to her old love—now, happily, a millionaire. This story, endorsing the woman's right to sow her wild oats, gave the word "manhandled" to the American vernacular.

The Cinderella tradition of feminine modesty, in which woman is a vassal-in-waiting, was thus supplanted by the post-Ibsen concept of a "devastating," aggressive creature, attractive, smart, seductive, independent, daring, fast. Prince Charming, for his part, was transformed into a dynamic, pursuing, commanding Atlas, crammed with sex appeal, lasciviously bouncing into every parlor, bedroom, and bath of female America. The gods of the screen were no longer spoken of as matinee idols but as great lovers. At first the vogue for the exotic, passionate, Latin man of the world brought to the forefront such personalities as Antonio Moreno, John Gilbert, Ricardo Cortez, Ramon Novarro, Gilbert Roland, and most sensational of all, Rudolph Valentino. Later the American ideal became the energetic, clean-cut, high-pressure go-getter, the apostle of postwar speed and pep—the wise-cracking William Haines (*Brown of Harvard*), the hard-drinking, cynical Richard Arlen (*Rolled Stockings*), the bouncing Douglas MacLean (*A Man of Action*), the self-assured William Boyd (*Two Arabian Knights*), the dynamic

George Walsh (*Dynamite Allen*), and the "natural-born world-beater" who summed up all the qualities of this type, Harold Lloyd.

Lloyd, whom Gilbert Seldes [7] called ". . . a man of no tenderness, of no philosophy, the embodiment of American cheek and indefatigable energy," was the particular ideal of the younger generation. The titles of his pictures summed up admirably the philosophy of his apostles: *Never Weaken, Now or Never, Why Worry?, Speedy, Get Out and Get Under, Welcome Danger*.

Screen villains were streamlined into "gigolos." They were attractive, nonchalant, sophisticated, witty, "humanly wicked." Lew Cody, Adolphe Menjou, Earle Fox, Roy D'Arcy, Rod La Rocque, Stuart Holmes, Nils Asther, Lowell Sherman, William Powell, and most strikingly Erich von Stroheim, were the fascinating menaces, the hated, envied men of the world.

Although DeMille's films held the limelight in this period and set the pace, tone, and temper of the movie medium during these gay twenties, a reaction against middle-class materialism began slowly to appear. The first indication of a critical attitude appeared in the work of literary rebels. With the publication of Sinclair Lewis' book *Main Street*, the dominance of the business man's values was challenged. *Main Street* was soon reinforced by other blasts against American civilization, notable among which were H. L. Mencken's book *The American Credo*, Theodore Dreiser's *An American Tragedy*, and John Dos Passos' *Manhattan Transfer*. A bevy of radical magazines such as *Gargoyle, Broom, The Little Review*, and *transition* provided further ammunition for the attack. The flight of intellectuals and artists to Europe to work in an atmosphere "free from Puritan inhibitions," and the publication of that collective cannonade *Civilization in the United States: An Inquiry by Thirty Americans*, called attention to a growing if still localized dissatisfaction with contemporary American life.

The critical realism of the literary vanguard was taken up by various film makers sporadically. Stroheim's brutally realistic *Greed*, Cruze's domestic satires, Vidor's *The Crowd*, Seastrom's sensitive *The Wind*, King's and Robertson's attempts at naturalism, and Chaplin's social satire were all significant. These signs of a serious

---

[7] In *The Seven Lively Arts*, p. 15.

concern with reality suggested that the broad social outlook that had been coming into being before the war had not been entirely lost.

Auspicious was the popular welcome given to the "documentary" films—factual records of man's struggle with his environment. The first of the "documentaries," Flaherty's *Nanook of the North*, appeared in 1922 in the midst of the deluge of "jazz" films. Its popularity was remarkable in view of the fact that the interest of the nation was at that time in escape, thrills, and personal sensations. *Nanook of the North* initiated a style for motion pictures which has only recently been revived with new vigor. Within the eight years that followed Flaherty's hit a dozen and more such efforts appeared in whole or partly fictionized treatments, notably *Grass*, *White Shadows in the South Seas*, *Moana*, *Tabu*, and *Trader Horn*.

Allied in spirit to the semi-documentary films were the realistic regional dramas, appearing concurrently, that dealt fictionally with contemporary life in various regions and of many classes. These were intended to portray actual social conditions realistically. Some of the stories centered on personal conflicts (*Stark Love*, *White Gold*, *Sunrise*), some on social struggles (*The Barker*, *The Crowd*, *The Vanishing American*), others on the battle with nature's forces (*Down to the Sea in Ships* and *The Wind*) and still others with man's own nature as conditioned by himself (*Greed* and *The Tower of Lies*). A few were accurate appraisals of regional life (*Driven* and *Tol'able David*).

Other films openly began to mock the false standards of materialism. *Beggar on Horseback* ingeniously travestied the *nouveau riche*, while *The King on Main Street* lightly jeered at the smug small-town life and popular secret societies that had rooted themselves in America. The latter picture shocked one reviewer into exclaiming, "Imagine that two years ago!" Other films such as *Babbitt*, *Proud Flesh*, and *The Goose Hangs High* derided the inanities and vanities of the social standards people were trying to live up to. A number of films exposed the peculiar twists and idiosyncrasies of people who were concerned only with making money, using it as a yardstick in all their judgments. *The Four-Flusher*, *The Show-Off*, *The Nervous Wreck*, *The Snob*, *The Idle Rich*, are self-descriptive.

Will Rogers' film *Don't Park There* satirized modern progress and the big city. He finds horses so out of date that he acquires a Ford, but he has to travel over the country trying to find a parking space and, in doing so, gets into the toils of the police. *A Poor Relation* was the story of an empty stomach and the high hopes of poverty. Raymond Griffith, the sophisticated humorist, ridiculed sophistication itself in such parodies as *Paths to Paradise, Hands Up, Wet Paint, You'd Be Surprised, Waiter for the Ritz.* Buster Keaton's satires (*The General, The Navigator*) poked fun at conventions and pomposity, Buster being the weakling lost in a world of gigantic he-men. All such travesties pointed out the weaknesses in contemporary living and, like the gangster films, were to become increasingly common in the next period.

Toward the end of the twenties, the country was riding along merrily on a rising bull market. At no time had wealth appeared so abundant nor was the stampede for a share of it more pronounced. Misgivings and criticisms of the business men's rule were left largely to the literary vanguard and the "ex-patriates." Movies, acquiring sound, burst forth in lavish musicals and when the stock market catapulted in 1929, were out-dazzling each other with ever more spectacular effects.

The national craving for thrills, excitement, escape, and experience during the twenties was manifested by the tremendous patronage movies enjoyed. By 1926 the United States had 20,000 theatres, attended by 100,000,000 Americans weekly. The effect of motion pictures upon the very people whose desires it was attempting to satisfy had increased enormously in thirty years. When Willard Huntington Wright, the noted art critic, observed in 1919 [8] that "The motion picture industry's staggering and far-reaching effect on American life has not yet been given proper recognition by historians and scientists," he hardly imagined what vast social territory the American film would yet encompass. In hundreds of towns the moving picture theatre had become the outstanding building—according to Charles Pettijohn,[9] "a civic monument pointed

[8] *Photoplay*, December 1919.   [9] *The Motion Picture* (pamphlet).

out with pride by citizens, a place of culture where good music and good taste were being cultivated and reading encouraged."

Films during Porter's day, in reflecting reality, had made audiences more receptive and more reflective. Now films were helping people to forget, helping them to avoid reflection. Knowledge and awareness of the real world were rarely dispensed by the screen. Movies were framed to assist people to escape their personal problems, their frustrations, their unhappiness. The Lynds reported in their book *Middletown*, the classic record of the post-war decade, that movies quickened life for the

youngsters who bulk large in the audiences, for the working man, for the wife and for the business class families who habitually attend. . . . At the comedies Middletown lives for an hour in a happy sophisticated make-believe world that leaves it, according to the advertisement of one film, "Happily convinced that Life is very well worth living."

The American film had thus become by 1929 a more powerful social agency than ever. Reflecting current states of mind, it also deeply influenced them. Its persuasiveness won not only natives of America but Europeans, Asiatics, South Americans, and even Africans. Hollywood, nationally and internationally supreme, was very nearly Americanizing the world. What Maurice Maeterlinck [10] had said at the beginning of the period was, at its end, generally recognized to be true:

. . . at no time in history has there been such a means of influencing the spirit of men and particularly of women and children. . . . All ideas of duty, justice, love, right, wrong, happiness, honor, luxury, beauty, all ideas regarding the goal of life . . . are ideas implanted by movies.

[10] *Photoplay*, 1921.

PART SIX

MATURITY (1929-1939)

X X I

NEW AFFILIATIONS AND CONSOLIDATIONS

THE ten years from 1929 to 1939 have been dire ones economically for the world at large and for the motion picture industry in particular. The industry's two major events in 1929—the stock-market crash and the acceptance of sound—had far-reaching effects upon industrial and financial organization in the movie world. Although they were radical in effect, they did not alter the character of movie making as big business, but rather extended its scope and concentrated its capital into a higher peak than ever before. Sound gave the medium its maturity, and the depression gave the industry its modern financial rank.

The merging and remerging of companies into fewer and larger producer-distributor-exhibitor corporations had gone on merrily in the post-war decade, the bulk of power being centralized more and more in Wall Street. Upon the advent of sound, the enormous expense of installing sound equipment and undertaking the production of talking films required a further concentration of capital and put the motion picture industry, after a long and bitter battle, under the indirect control of the two dominating financial groups in the United States today—the Morgan group (telephone interests) and the Rockefeller group (radio interests). Between these two financial powers now rests the control of the motion picture industry.

The fight for theatres as the key to control of the market—a fight that had been raging since the war—came to a climax in 1929 when First National, completely weakened with the loss of its major theatre circuits to rivals, finally expired after Warner Brothers acquired its only remaining valuable circuit, the Stanley group. In

1928, however, there had been formed a new and powerful organization more than capable of replacing First National. This was the Radio-Keith-Orpheum Corporation (RKO). Organized to make talking films, it was formed by the combination of Radio Corporation of America (RCA), American Pathé, and the Keith-Albee theatre circuit. RKO was supplied with sound equipment by RCA and for a while was the only major producing company dealing with RCA. The other companies, in a panic over Warner's head start, and desperately anxious to get their own talkies on the market, had signed so-called "suicide" contracts with Electrical Research Products, Inc. (ERPI), the marketing subsidiary of Western Electric.

At first there was no serious attempt by Wall Street to get control of the industry. But financiers soon noticed that the depression which had prostrated most businesses had hardly touched the movies. This was astonishing, for from its earliest days as a one-man business to its establishment as a huge industry, the motion picture had been regarded as a speculative investment—as a business which, although steadily growing, was full of flagrant inefficiency, waste, and extravagance. Now that most industries were facing a sharp slackening of demand and the movie industry was experiencing a rush of orders and a box-office boom, Wall Street awoke to the fact that what had been regarded as a shaky business was proving to be the safest of all. A new fight, more bitter and for higher stakes than ever before, began as the Morgan and Rockefeller interests went after the sound-film business with a firm determination to control it.

The first objective in the campaign was to obtain the most important American patents in sound equipment, now divided between Warner (Vitaphone) and Fox (Movietone). The struggle with Warner entailed lengthy court proceedings, with Vitaphone bringing suit against ERPI. The litigation was finally settled in 1935, the Morgan interests winning the victory. ERPI acquired Warner's patent rights and a release from further obligations in consideration of the payment of back royalties.

At the same time the more violent struggle to wrest the patent rights from Fox came to an end with a victory for ERPI. Fox had been in a stronger position than Warner, since he had retained personal control of the company and personal ownership of the patents. Western Electric sought first to break his control of the company: while lawsuits raged, they kept him from getting financial backing, tried to throw him into receivership, and filed antitrust charges against him because of the Fox-Loew merger. In 1935 the Supreme Court, reversing the findings of all the lower courts, annulled William Fox's patents, and Fox was forced to sell out his voting stock for $18,000,000.

These developments placed the most important American patents in sound equipment in the joint control of Western Electric Company and RCA Photophone. Western Electric, a manufacturing subsidiary of the American Telephone and Telegraph Company (organized by Morgan and still under his control, a minority interest being owned by Rockefeller), markets its sound film equipment through its own subsidiary, Electrical Research Products, Inc. (ERPI). RCA Photophone is the manufacturing subsidiary of the Radio Corporation of America which, incorporated in 1919, in 1930 came under the control of Rockefeller interests through Chase National Bank, when Rockefeller gained control of that bank as well. The entire motion picture industry, therefore, through patent ownership is indirectly under a monopoly control far beyond the early aspirations of the Motion Picture Patents Corporation. That control is "never for one moment basically deflected by the unceasing obbligato of government anti-trust actions that enlivens its progress."[1] The peak figures in American finance, Morgan and Rockefeller, either indirectly through sound-equipment control or directly by financial control or backing, now own the motion picture industry.

Competition in the motion picture industry today has narrowed down to a fight between the two major financial interests of the country for the balance of power within the eight major studios and their affiliated theatre and distribution channels.

The past few years have seen RCA gaining in the rivalry between the Morgan and Rockefeller interests in supplying sound equipment. *The New York Times* in June 1936 reported that, because ERPI has failed to improve theatre equipment, RCA has been gaining

[1] *Money Behind the Screen*, F. D. Klingender and Stuart Legg, page 79.

supremacy in the battle for studios and theatres. RCA is supplying, in addition to RKO, former Morgan-controlled companies including 20th Century-Fox, Warner, and Columbia, and two new companies, Republic and Walt Disney, and has a chance of acquiring Metro (Loew) and Paramount in the future. Despite this rivalry, however, it must be pointed out that both Morgan and Rockefeller have interests in each other's enterprises.

An industry once made up of many individual independent enterprises has thus resolved down to eight gigantic companies, which today control the most important positions in production, distribution, and exhibition:

1. Paramount Pictures
2. Metro-Goldwyn-Mayer (Loew's, Inc.)
3. 20th Century-Fox (merged in 1935)
4. Warner Brothers (absorbed First National Distributors in 1929)
5. RKO (launched in 1928)
6. Universal
7. Columbia
8. United Artists (distributing organization of independent producers and stars)

None of the pioneer film executives is any longer in control of his company. The last to lose his grip was Carl Laemmle, who in 1936 sold his stock in Universal.

During this economic evolution in the industry, the depression was making itself felt in the movie business. For two full years after the stock-market crash, the box office had been unaffected, still thriving on the wonder aroused by the novelty of sound. The "all-talking, all-singing, all-color" pictures had been entertainments that even a distraught and shorn public found money to pay for. As the advertisement for *King Kong* (March 1932) blurted, "NO MONEY—Yet New York dug up $89,931 in four days (March 2, 3, 4, 5) to see *King Kong* at Radio City." By 1933, however, the novelty had worn off, the depression had deepened, the public was in a more critical state of mind, and slackening patronage was worrying the movie makers. The dangerous year for Hollywood, as it turned out, was not 1929 but 1933.

The industry now went through an experience it had never before known—the experience of falling profits, falling demand, and a public becoming critical. According to an estimate made by *Film Daily*, by midsummer in 1933 approximately 5,000 of 16,000 regularly operated theatres in the United States were closed. "De luxe" houses which charged high prices and were burdened with heavy overhead were particularly hard hit. Real-estate losses mounted, theatre chains collapsed, companies went through bankruptcies and reorganizations.

The friendly atmosphere that had prevailed in the industry when profitable mergers were common, and when financiers had found it easy to float stock issues, vanished as business slipped down into the red and motion picture stocks became a drug on the market.

Hurried conferences among executives resulted in the decision to cut expenses to the bone, since production had to continue at all costs. The cut affected every studio. Wages were halved and whole staffs disbanded. For eight weeks the salaries of all motion picture employees were reduced. The general strike called by the International Alliance of Theatrical Stage Employees (IATSE) was the first aggressive labor action in an industry until then without weighty labor troubles. Warner Brothers announced they were trying out a plan to speed and economize production by setting an eighteen-day limit for shooting.[2] Irving Thalberg, leading executive of M-G-M, ascribed the high costs of production to excessive distribution charges and the overseating of theatres. (In 1932 an enormous theatre had been opened in Radio City: Radio City Music Hall—a gigantic failure, unsuited in size for the requirements of talking pictures.)

Fear and retrenchment along all fronts paralyzed producers, and new and bitter animosity arose among them. Stabilization methods which had been depended on since 1910 were proving ineffective. The star system and the formula picture both were being repudiated by the public at large at the box office. *Variety* reported that the number of film stars who maintained their personal box-office value in 1933 was, at most, ten. The market, both domestic and foreign, was further upset by the sudden competition of meritorious British productions financed by the British government. Foreign

[2] *The New York Herald Tribune*, February 3, 1933.

markets generally, because of political alignments, had shrunk
alarmingly.

The necessity of doing something concrete about the country-
wide depression had meanwhile caused a change in the economic
outlook of the nation. The progressive principles of Roosevelt as
embodied in the New Deal platform resulted in his election and in
the National Industrial Recovery Act. Government co-operation
was offered to the motion picture industry, as to other industries,
to facilitate its recovery. John T. Flynn, who had been in charge
of the Liberty Loan propaganda in theatres during the war, was
chosen to create machinery whereby the movie industry, under the
National Industrial Recovery Act, could establish a legal code of
conduct for its business.

"All hail collapse!" wrote Dalton Trumbo in *The Hollywood
Spectator*.[3] He voiced the general opinion that the public and the
industry were being purged by the depression and would emerge
intellectually, socially, and economically improved. A fresh awareness of producers' social obligations, of companies' dependence upon
workers, of workers as the capital of the nation, of fair practices in
floating stocks and in producing better commodities for the con-
sumer-public—this lent credence to Trumbo's remarkable comment.

The Literary Digest reported on January 6, 1934, that "Motion
Pictures Move into the New Deal. President Declines to Establish
Federal Censorship as the Nation Spends Over $1,000,000,000 at
the Movies and the Industry Reaches Transitional Period."

An NRA code, drawn up for recovery and reform, applied to
the motion picture producers and distributors of America and to
independents as well, was to prevent block booking and blind buying of films, eliminate advertising reels, prohibit price cutting, regulate the employment of extras, and arrange for the equitable distribution of pictures. The President was to receive a "full report on
excessive salaries or other emoluments, both as to artists and as to
executives and their families." But however constructive and important it was or might have been, the NRA code was short-lived.
Hardly had it been established when, in 1936, it was repealed.

The federal government's subsequent attempts to relieve de-

[3] June 23, 1933.

pressed conditions through the Works Progress Administration, the Public Works Administration, the Agricultural Adjustment Act, and other emergency agencies and measures, supplying subsistence and work for those unable to find employment in private enterprises, saw a certain amount of the money spent find its way into the movie box office. Said *The New York Times*,[4]

It is calculated now that the cash registers in the nation's movie houses are clicking to the tune of some 80,000,000 admissions a week . . . general recovery has reached the point where the average person is now able to seek a little entertainment.

The motion picture business improved steadily, and 1937 proved to be the best and most profitable year it had known since the depression started. Following the government's financial retrenchment in the early part of 1938, however, movies suffered a marked slump along with the rest of the nation's business. Today the industry is facing less prosperous times. Its era of expansion is at an end; the problem now is to keep the public going to the movies.

The depression, shaking the self-assurance of the movie world, brought new developments in production, exhibition, public relationships, and government regulation. The desire to tempt the public with "sure hits" has increased with the vicissitudes the business has undergone since 1933. Production, called the "lifeblood of the business," today represents an investment of over two and a half billion dollars in the United States alone. A vast enterprise, it involves two hundred seventy-six different arts, professions, and vocations—a far cry from Porter's day, when all that was required was a cameraman, a camera, and a few feet of film. Naturally the enormous investment and tremendous overhead involved in production have reinforced the belief that the only way to make money is to spend it. Not only do producers strive to outshine their competitors, but they have learned that high-priced pictures usually get high rentals, since the expensive picture brings exhibitors more patronage. One good million-dollar picture, it appears, is more profitable than two lower-priced films. Under the circumstances producers prefer to minimize the risk rather than decrease

[4] September 24, 1936.

the cost. They willingly pay for expensive stars, directors, writers, and cameramen because of the assurance that these talents will draw the public and are more apt to turn out a hit.

The vogue of expensive pictures has lifted the cost of many films to a million dollars. *The New York Times* on October 24, 1937, announced:

Five years ago million-dollar films were so rare the trade papers gave editorial ravings to their announcement. Today they get no more than a few lines on an inside page.

Terry Ramsaye has prepared a cost chart for *The Motion Picture Herald* [5] showing how the million is spent:

Cast	$250,000
Director	100,000
Extras	50,000
Assistant directors	20,000
Camera crew	15,000
Lights	20,000
Makeup	9,000
Teachers	2,000
Labor	12,000
Story preparation	70,000
Story	50,000
Costuming	20,000
Sets, Art director	125,000
Stills	4,000
Cutter	10,000
Film negative	10,000
Tests	12,000
Insurance	20,000
Sound	31,000
Publicity and transportation	20,000
Indirect costs	150,000
	$1,000,000

Because of the limited returns now possible for a picture, costly productions often do not realize their investments. Today, therefore, the backers of movie producers are demanding the control of expenditures. But despite a warning to producers from Wall

[5] July 10, 1937.

Street, "from all exterior signs," says *Variety*,[6] "that's as far as the warning has gone. Not a single studio has made a move the scope of which would impress the trade." About $165,000,000 will be spent on the supply of films for 1938-1939—four hundred fifty features, twenty of which are in color, and about forty of which will cost over $1,000,000 each.

Despite the vogue for million dollar productions, during the first half of 1938, when the "recession" was growing worse, studio overhead was steadily cut down. "Junior writers" were hired at the reduced wage scale of $35 to $75 a week to replace the more experienced and higher-priced writers. Unknown, cheaper players were signed to take the places of known, expensive ones. A corresponding readjustment followed all along the line, publicity departments, extras, press agents, and utility workers also being subjected to measures of economy. Stenographers and other office help were reduced in numbers, and skeleton crews carried on production. In March 1938 the Central Casting Bureau announced that work for extras had been cut almost in half, the working days having been cut to the lowest figure in three years. Said a fan magazine, *Screen Book*,[7]

There is no relief organization sponsored by the industry . . . to which they [extras] can turn for assistance. More than 18,000 registered extras in Hollywood . . . average yearly . . . $250 . . . only two earned last year more than $2,000.

Leading producers nevertheless bemoaned the high salary scale in the industry. Samuel Goldwyn voiced the opinions of his associates when he denounced the overpayment of writers, actors, and directors.[8] A month later *The Hollywood Reporter*,[9] a trade paper, followed up with a red-bordered advertisement, signed by the Independent Theatre Owners Association of New York, condemning many of the highest-paid stars as box-office "poison" and advising producers to make good pictures. "We are not against the star system," complained the Association, "but we don't think it should dominate the production of pictures . . . we want them [the stars] when we get value. . . ."

[6] January 4, 1939.   [8] *The New York World-Telegram*, April 2, 1938.
[7] June, 1938.   [9] May 4, 1938.

This advertisement was a bombshell: the metropolitan newspapers took up the hue and cry, and Hollywood became panicky. Sharp-eyed observers, however, aware of conditions in the industry, believed that the hubbub was instigated by the producers themselves, who now had the best of chances to cut stars' salaries without bringing blame upon themselves. It is significant that a second advertisement of the ITOA of New York a week later, calling for the elimination of double features and "B" pictures, demanding the abolition of "factory-product, run-of-the-mill films turned out quickly and half-baked in order to keep up with double-feature requirement," was little publicized.

The moving picture editor of *The New York World-Telegram* commented that "It looks as if more were wrong than the salary scale. The squawk hasn't been a bad stunt, however."

P. J. Wood, secretary of the ITOA of Ohio, declared that "the high cost of pictures is . . . due . . . to the fantastic salaries paid some of the New York executives and Hollywood studio directors of the producing companies." He gave as an example the published [10] payroll of Metro, which began with Louis B. Mayer's income of $956,000 and ended with a $154,000 figure. Darryl Zanuck, he pointed out, received $5,000 a week, $500,000 a year with bonuses.

Others pointed out that the noisy publicity campaign was part of a concerted drive by producers not only to lower wage scales but to destroy agreements with the movie guilds. Labor unionization in the industry had proceeded rapidly, particularly during 1937. Each trade and craft and each of its subdivisions had established locals, some stronger than others. The International Alliance of Theatrical Stage Employees (IATSE), affiliate of the American Federation of Labor covered almost all workers except actors, who came under the Associated Actors and Artistes of America (AAA) of the Actor's Equity. (Recently a movement has begun to bring the actors also under the IATSE.) The technicians likewise had been well organized.

Despite the disapproval of the producers, the Screen Writers Guild of the Authors League of America was established by the National Labor Relations Board after Hollywood studio workers

[10] *The New York Times,* May 22, 1938.

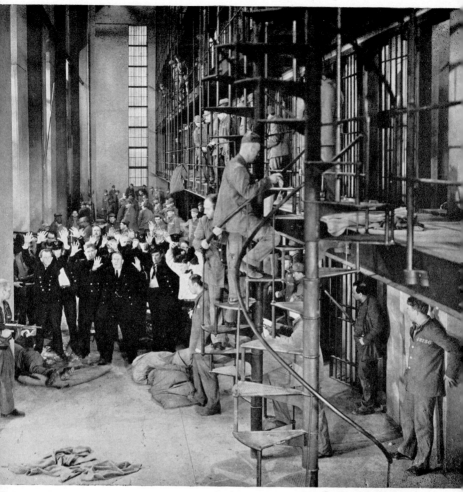

The Big House (1930), typical prison picture exposé reflecting the critical attitude and loss of respect for authority.

Greta Garbo, shown here in *Susan Lennox, Her Fall and Rise* (1931), has for more than a decade represented the ultra-sophisticated, neurotic woman of the world who lives only for love.

were given the opportunity to choose their union. The poll, the first of its kind in Hollywood, designated the Screen Writers Guild as the bargaining agency for writers. In spite of the election results, *Motion Picture Herald* [11] said:

It is expected that the producers will refuse to negotiate with the Guild, that course having been indicated when the studios refused to supply the Labor Board with copies of their payrolls as of June 4th and announced they would fight the Board decision in the courts. . . . The producers have indicated they will carry the fight to the Supreme Court if necessary.

Unexpectedly in March 1939, the producers did accept the Guild as the writers' legitimate bargaining agency. This action followed the precedent set by the acceptance of the recently formed Screen Directors Guild as the legitimate bargaining agency for directors. Unionization is rapidly becoming a part of the huge industry.

Throughout the tribulations of these years exhibitors, the first to feel the effects of the slump, were devising new ways of their own to mitigate the box-office depression. Exhibitors found they would have to reduce their prices or play to empty houses. The higher-priced chain and first-run houses, charging about twenty cents more per ticket than second-run neighborhood theatres, found receipts dwindling rapidly. Because of their thin pocketbooks people no longer cared to see movies in their first run. The second-run chain houses were forced to reduce their prices further, so that the difference between their prices and those of the neighborhood theatres was narrowed down to about five cents. The third-, fourth-, and fifth-run houses had either closed their doors or lowered their admission prices so far that it was difficult for them to make a profit.

Cuts in admission prices, however, were not enough. Theatrical presentations—vaudeville and stage shows—having been given up, the double-feature program, begun by the small neighborhood houses years before, became generally adopted by the major theatres. On September 9, 1935, *The New York World-Telegram* ran the announcement that all Loew and RKO theatres (except the

[11] July 2, 1938.

State and Palace, which still presented stage shows) would thereafter show two feature films. But by that time the double-feature
scheme had already become common practice.

As the double features came to be taken for granted, and as bad
economic conditions persisted, movie houses resorted to other in-
ducements to keep the customers coming in. Games with premiums
and cash prizes—"Screeno," "Banko," "Bingo," and the like—came
into vogue. Individual pieces of china and silverware were given
away free to women on certain nights so that, by steady patronage,
a woman could collect a complete set. *The New Republic* [12] reported that this allurement resulted in an increase of twenty to
twenty-five per cent in female patronage. Prizes ranging from one
dollar to hundreds (for the jackpot) were offered on cash-prize
nights, which, commencing on a once-a-week basis, had become
by 1936 and 1937 a daily offering in many of the smaller houses.

The popularity of such schemes was so widespread that by the
end of 1936, as *Motion Picture Herald* [13] reported, Chicago exhibitors alone were giving away six million dollars a year. Disdaining
such methods at first, the chain theatres too were soon forced to
incorporate such attractions: "Prosperity Night," "Movie Sweep-
stakes," "Treasury Night," and so on. By 1938 about half of the
nation's theatres were using some sort of incentive other than the
movie presentation to lure customers.

So desperate did the box-office depression become that, in the
fall of 1938, for the first time in motion picture history, a concerted and most spectacular drive was initiated by producers and
distributors to resell the movies to the critical and impoverished
public. Under the slogan "Motion Pictures Are Your Best Entertainment," a $1,000,000 fund was appropriated (one-fourth being
contributed by the exhibitors) to advertise the benefits of movies
in a nationwide Movie Quiz Contest offering prizes to perspicacious
movie-goers. In a huge newspaper campaign and on the screens of
the nation, institutional advertising brought the slogan and the
contest directly to the patrons.

The scheme proved for the most part a failure. William Boehnel
of *The New York World-Telegram* [14] remarked:

[12] May 6, 1936.   [13] December 5, 1936.   [14] January 7, 1939.

. . . we don't think much of the artificial respiration known as the $200,000 Movie Quiz Contest, which was part of Motion Pictures' greatest year. It is generally agreed that the motion pictures' greatest year was not a success.

Motion Picture Herald [15] called the "greatest year" campaign "blind buying."

Hostility to the distributor-producer-exhibitor organizations has intensified because of the uneasy box-office conditions. Monopoly charges have been brought against the motion picture industry by independent exhibitors and by the federal government. Independent exhibitors have raised funds to fight for the separation of production, exhibition, and distribution and for relief from trade malpractices, percentage pictures and designated play dates, evils that were prevalent in the trust war back in 1908-1912.

On February 27, 1937, *Motion Picture Herald* headlined, "Legislators Open Attack on Industry in 13 States." Six of these states proposed the divorcement of production and distribution from exhibition.

In Congress the Hobbs Bill proposed an investigation of the Hays organization and various monopoly charges. The Dies Bill, supplementing this, covered questions of monopoly, unfair trade practices, cutthroat competition, wages, and interlocking directorates in exhibition, production, and distribution, recommending investigation to determine whether the interlocking directorates tended to monopoly. *The New York Times* on March 9, 1938, reported the introduction of the Neely-Pettengill Bill to prohibit compulsory block booking and blind selling. This bill is still pending; meanwhile the industry is continuing with self-regulation.

In July 1938 the heads of the eight principal movie corporations, accompanied by Will Hays, met with President Roosevelt. The ensuing announcement declared that a special committee had been designated to consider a program and code for revised trade practices. This committee is to effect self-regulation in the industry while the government is proceeding with its monopoly investigations of industries in general (including the motion picture business).

[15] January 14, 1939.

With antitrust suits in the offing, with the possibility of self-reform through government co-operation and trade-practice codes, and with the rise of unionization, public good-will campaigns, double features, and "give-aways," the problems now besetting the movie industry are those of a mature commerce.

The depths of depression in 1932 and 1933, the temporary NRA code, the recovery, and the succeeding slump have raised for the industry new problems involving, as we have seen, not only trade practices but labor, the government policy, and public relations. With the end of its "talkie boom" and the concentration of its economic functions, the industry has been faced, moreover, with the realization that economically the movie as a mass-entertainment form has reached its commercial zenith. Future developments are not in the line of expansion so much as in that of refinement.

Whatever the economic course movies will take in the future, production policy must take into account the fact that the eighty million people who go to movies today are no longer made up of one group or level of intelligence. Says Albert Lewin,[16] producer for Paramount:

I believe we're coming to the point where intelligent adults will gravitate more and more to the small theatres that have no double features. And more and more, they will go to see foreign-made films, because those films are adult, mature, made for people who think.

16 The New York World-Telegram, January 14, 1939.

XXII

REFINEMENTS IN TECHNIQUE

THE years 1930-1939 have seen an earnest study of the relationships of the motion picture medium and attempts to bring the medium to a completeness of expression equal to its artistic and physical possibilities. Science has steadily increased the means of expression by constantly improving the tools and adding the elements of sound and color. Today movies have all of their mechanical needs and basic technique ready-made; their further progress will lie in the refinement and intensification of expression by craftsmen and in the grade of material to which this is applied.

When the first complete talkie, *Lights of New York,* appeared in 1929, the consensus was that moving picture art had, with the addition of sound, forgotten everything it had so recently learned. This relapse was so rapidly corrected during the next two years that today such a criticism—along with the first talking film—would seem absurd. Sound proved to be only a temporary setback to motion picture technique. But its effects on every phase of movie making were profound and far-reaching: it altered some techniques completely, modified others, quickened progress in all. It freed the director from the clumsiness of titles, gave more directness to the medium, enriched the reality of the story, increased the intimacy of the audience with the characters and situation. Sound was not only a business man's ruse to build up movie attendance; it represented a logical advance in motion picture expression.

Most directors favored sound from the start. They felt that it would not profoundly change the primary elements of motion picture expression but would release the medium from the impediment of titles and make it more interesting by the addition of the human voice, noises, and music. Long before sound came, Erich von Stroheim had lamented its absence. F. W. Murnau, although championing the silent screen, had himself attempted by devious means to do away with titles. Carl Dreyer, director of *The Passion of Joan of Arc*, bitterly regretted not having dialogue with which to work. Lubitsch hailed the new invention at once and never lost an opportunity to talk of its superiority. In October 1928 *Closeup* published a statement signed by three leading figures in the Soviet film industry—Eisenstein, Pudovkin, and Alexandrov—the opening sentence of which was "The cherished dream of a talking film is realized." The statement went on:

Sound, treated as a new element of the mounting (as an item independent of the visual), will inevitably introduce a new and enormously effective means for expressing and solving the complex problems with which we have been troubled, owing to the impossibility of solving them by the aid of cinematography operating with visual images alone.

These men felt that the new technical discovery would solve the problems of film text and explanatory items, and would hold in check attempts at overloading the picture with montage effects.

If directors welcomed the new invention, the critics and a majority of intellectuals were belligerently antagonistic toward it. Viewing the static pictures of the early days of the talkies, steeped in the traditions of the silent movie and disliking the prospect of re-education, critics were grief-stricken. Throughout 1927, 1928, and 1929 newspapers and magazines were filled with their discussions about the comparative merits of the sound and silent films. Judging the talkies by silent-film standards, without taking into account the mechanical changes and readjustments that had yet to be made, most critics could see little in the future of the talkie. Only Alexander Bakshy, writing in *The Nation*, seemed to keep a clear head:

When the talking-picture mechanism is made perfect the really important development . . . will definitely direct the talking picture away from the stage and toward a new, authentic motion picture drama. This evolution is inevitable. It is dictated by the inner logic of the medium.[1]

[1] February 20, 1929.

Much of the criticism launched at the first talkies was justified, for moving pictures retrogressed markedly after the introduction of sound. The immediate effect of the invention was that dialogue supplanted the camera. Movies became merely static reproductions of stage plays.

This failing was conditioned by two factors, both temporary. One was that the public, fascinated by the novelty, wanting to be sure they were hearing what they saw, would have felt that a trick was being played on them if they were not shown the words coming from the lips of the actors. Movement for the time being was therefore forgotten: talking and singing became paramount.

More important was the second factor: the mechanical drawbacks and new problems of the yet crude and unfamiliar invention. The microphone not only was immobile and unselective, but it picked up all noise mercilessly, just as the camera lens ruthlessly records every detail it sees. This meant that shooting had to be conducted in silence, and the moving picture camera, which made a good deal of noise (at first almost impossible to eliminate), had to be kept in a soundproof booth. So imprisoned, the camera lost all its recently acquired mobility, and action was rigidly restricted to playing areas within the camera's range. The immobility of the microphone, moreover, required the actor who was speaking to remain comparatively still if his speech was to be recorded clearly; hence the scenes became even more static. The complete shifting of camera, microphone, and electrical apparatus, a time-taking procedure required for almost every "set-up," further limited the talkie medium. Movies thus shrank to a minimum number of shots, as a stage play is restricted to a limited number of scenes. Synchronization of sound and image was a highly exacting task, curtailing the director's freedom; and editing itself returned to the rudimentary level of pre-war days.

The pacing of the scenes also was unduly slow because of the adjustment that had to be made in the speed of the camera. Sound, to seem normal, had to be taken at ninety feet a minute. The silent-film camera, which photographed a scene at sixty feet a minute, had to increase its speed to ninety feet a minute in order to synchronize the image with the sound. This increased shooting speed made the players' actions appear unnaturally slow; scenes dragged. Not until the actors were instructed to move faster than they had moved before the silent camera did their actions appear normal. To give the scene a faster pace and more realism, dialogue was also quickened.

Pictorial composition of the scene had to be abandoned for a time. The set had to be prepared and lighted so that several cameras at different angles could be going at once to obtain a single vocal record. The composition of three or more players in the scene was difficult when long shots were taken simultaneously with close shots. Presently it became a practice to take "wild shots"—shots without the microphone, sound being added later. This ruse led to the use of special scenes (as for musical numbers and singing) which, being synchronized only after they were photographed, made possible an increased control and manipulation of the film.

Sound itself was crude, and the principles of its use were still unformulated. Almost from the first, for instance, it was known that sound could be distorted; the "mixer" in the "mixer booth" could amplify it. The mixer could switch from one microphone to another to bring out weak voices and quiet loud ones, just as radio engineers do, but this was a new and highly technical craft and in the beginning there were few men skilled in it. Again, the cutting of sound pictures was risky: in comparison with the "silents" they were inflexible, permitting little manipulation.

Under the sudden onslaught of the sound invention, all movie crafts underwent necessary modifications. Directors felt suppressed and confused. They had to learn to direct in silence and hence perfect a scene in rehearsal before shooting it. No longer could they shout directions while the camera was grinding, or use incidental music to enhance the mood, or allow the player to improvise as he went along. Special dialogue experts were called in from the stage to supplement the director's work (they persist in Hollywood to this day). Engineers became the overlords of production, and those silent-movie directors still retained in the industry were forced to subordinate everything they knew about film artistry to sound and talking.

For a time Broadway playwrights, next to the engineers, became

The cold-bloodedness, violence, and lawlessness of the gangster-racketeer era climaxed in *Scarface* (1932).

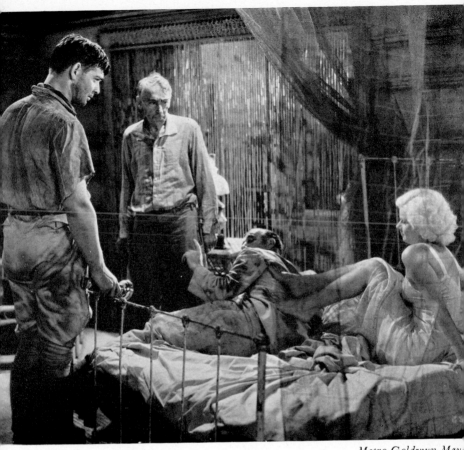

Platinum-blond Jean Harlow, representative of
the hard-boiled and uninhibited woman of the
thirties. Photograph from *Red Dust* (1932).

the most respected participants in movie production. The vogue for Broadway names forced some silent-film scenarists out of the industry and injured the standing of others. For a while, therefore, film continuity suffered, because, as movie makers soon were to discover, dialogue was not an entirely new problem; it merely enlarged an old one, made it more pronounced. Action was eliminated to provide enough time for speeches; consequently scenes lasted longer, and the cuts were relatively fewer. The continuity of the story itself was made dependent upon the dialogue, and the visual abilities of the film to tell a story were disregarded.

Now that dialogue was what mattered, the scenario writers were in a gloomy frame of mind. For years they had been learning how to present a story by means of the camera, and now "speeches" were asked of them. Soon the problem of writing the talkie had produced two schools of thought. One believed in taking the stage dialogue and emphasizing the action; the other, in taking the screen action and emphasizing the dialogue. Many agreed with Alexander Bakshy that "if the talking picture could do no better than 'can' the masterpieces of theatrical presentation, it would still deserve every praise for making these masterpieces accessible to large masses of people." [2]

Under the mechanical and technical handicaps of the new and crude sound apparatus, the first talkie pictures were poor and quite naturally disheartened critics. Like the first silent movies they represented the experimental gropings of all who had a part in their production. Besides, in the desperate effort to produce a large quantity of pictures, it was considered safest to repeat past successes in silent films and operettas, revues, or stage dramas that had achieved popularity on Broadway. The result was such imitative sequels of old hits as *The Cockeyed World*, *Madame X*, and the first Western in sound, *In Old Arizona*.

Operettas soon became the rage, largely because the problem of recording and synchronizing speech was far more complicated and difficult than that of handling music. Many of the early revues attempted to combine musical sequences with short dramatic skits. One picture would include Beatrice Lillie and Bull Montana, John

[2] *Theatre Arts Monthly*, February 1929.

Barrymore rendering a soliloquy from Shakespeare's *Richard III*, or such a combination as Gus Edwards' chorus doing "Singin' in the Rain" and Norma Shearer and John Gilbert (in color) performing the balcony scenes from Shakespeare's *Romeo and Juliet*.

Photography was conceived as an accompaniment to dialogue, illustrating it, much as years ago the pictures had been used as tableaux to illustrate titles. These early talkies first showed the event; then characters described it and commented on it. Stage plays were transplanted from Broadway and photographed almost without alteration, the playwrights, casts, and scene designers being transported wholesale to record the plays for the camera and microphone.

Some of the new Broadway talent, such as Rouben Mamoulian in direction and Ann Harding and Fredric March in acting, were to show decided ability in the film medium; others—Arthur Hopkins and George Abbott, stage directors, and Ina Claire, the renowned stage star—were entirely out of their depth. Foreign talent such as Pola Negri, Emil Jannings, and Conrad Veidt sailed away to Europe. Many of the famous American silent stars also were dropped, the producers finding in poor voices a good pretext to get rid of players no longer considered worthy. On the other hand, such players as Conrad Nagel, Lionel Barrymore, John Barrymore, and Dolores Costello enjoyed a boom in their reputations merely because their voices and enunciation had proved acceptable on the sound track.

Though the first consequence of sound was to send the movies back to 1910 methods, once sound was permanently accepted the progress made in perfecting its instruments and in learning its artistic functions and principles was amazingly swift. The revolutionary changes in the medium soon looked promising rather than disastrous. The very difficulties involved in sound were incentives to the refinement of the equipment, and they stimulated the imagination of directors, who now began to see new possibilities of expressiveness in their medium. Even Richard Watts, Jr., one of the leading die-hards, was finally forced to admit the overwhelming evidence in favor of talkies. He wrote in *Film Mercury:*[3]

[3] August 1, 1929.

As one who fought despairingly in the barricades against the coming of audibility, I must keep on admitting—as I have for several months—that it would be absurd, even if it were possible, to do away, at this period in the photoplay's progress, with the new invention.

The year 1929 has been generally recognized as the most important epoch in the movies' technical history. Tools, materials, and every phase of production were rapidly developed and altered to meet the new critical demands of the talkies and to free the director from mechanical restrictions. Films improved steadily as the dependence of the camera upon the microphone was relieved and as the microphone was given the mobility of the camera. The creative possibilities of sound were also gradually disclosed.

The camera was no longer necessarily and invariably focused on what was heard: the image and the sound began to be separated. In *Broadway Melody* (1929) a girl is seen on the screen while one hears the car she has just left drive off. Such separation of sound and image opened up a world of opportunities for contrast, counterpoint, and psychological effects. In *Strange Interlude* (1932) we hear the subconscious thoughts of the characters. In Gregory La-Cava's *Private Worlds* (1935) and *Stage Door* (1937) the audience is forced to identify themselves with the player and to experience her emotional crisis because it hears what is going on in the upset girl's mind.

Mamoulian's *Applause* (1930) was among the first films to demonstrate that the camera need not be leashed to the microphone. Mamoulian restored mobility to the camera by putting it on wheels and demanding that the microphone follow; if necessary he used many microphones on the set so that the visual flow of the picture would be uninterrupted. Sound was thus given fluidity and perspective, and the director was once again empowered to control the elements of his film. A further divorce of visual elements from speech was evident in Lewis Milestone's *The Front Page* (1931). Here the dialogue was rapidly paced and scenes were cut short during speeches. Not only was pace given to speech, but cutting was freed from dependence on dialogue. Editing, no longer hindered by sound, once more became an important operation in production.

The stress on dialogue was much reduced as the dramatic values of silence, sounds in nature, and music became apparent. One of the first films to show a richer sound technique was the successful and notable *Alibi* (1929), directed by Roland West and, significantly enough, written by that experienced ex-Ince scenarist, C. Gardner Sullivan. The film was reviewed as

One of the most important works in the development of cinema audibility. Significant because it first showed the value of sound as opposed to speech and with high conclusiveness demonstrated the importance of silence in the midst of vocal.

In this film silence, used to create tension and suspense, proved its strength as a dramatic ally of sound.

King Vidor's *Hallelujah* (1930) brought out the emotional values of natural sounds. In the swamp sequence one man is being trailed by another, and all that is heard is the labored breathing of the man, the swish of the grass, the rustle of the branches, the lapping of water, bird and insect noises. These natural sounds heightened the terror of the fugitive and the tension of the chase. Gangster films brought into play the dramatic world of sounds in city life. Here dialogue was set in relief by automobile sirens, gunshots, the ticking of clocks, smashing glass, and running feet on pavements, all of which played on the nerves of the audience.

Musical accompaniment as a means of eliminating or enhancing dialogue was explored in Lubitsch's and René Clair's musical films and Walt Disney's animated cartoons. All three directors revealed how music could be blended with the cutting of images so it became a part of the total effect. Sound not only illuminated characters and situations but intensified the effect of the images by matching them or by being in contrast to them; often music made a witty comment out of an otherwise trivial scene. The musical films of these directors showed, moreover, that a picture's movement need not wait on vocal renditions; that songs and music could be a natural and integral part of the whole, neither forced upon it nor made paramount in it.

At first, the physical task of cutting the synchronized sound was a puzzle which even the mechanics could scarcely solve. But once engineers perfected sound movieolas, by which the sound track could be cut and pieced together, sound could be edited like silent scenes. A new world was thus opened up for the manipulation and distortion of sound for sharper effects. For a musical number, for example, the singer may make forty vocal recordings, just as a scene may be photographed over and over again. Then the best moments of each recording are taken (just as the best shots in the scenes are selected) and put together so that what is finally heard is a rendition perfect beyond human capabilities. In this way a singer can be made to hold a note on the screen longer than is actually possible. One of the first films to achieve good results through such manipulation was *One Night of Love* (1934), with Grace Moore.

The tendency in sound recording has been toward more naturalism and informality, so that speech and the noises of nature in films are very close to real life. *The Thin Man* (1934), directed by W. S. Van Dyke, set a high mark in realism with the ease, spontaneity, and intimacy of the actors' speeches and the flow of images and talk generally. The camera did not wait on the sound, and the conversation did not seem to be aware of the microphone's presence. In the house-party scene the informality and realism were heightened by the subdued snatches of conversation, the mingling of voices, and the occasional high-lighting of some "wise-crack." The whole scene was maintained at a natural pitch and tone without any "microphone consciousness."

As the creative potentialities of sound have been explored, engineers have been steadily improving the instruments so that the directors will have greater power and freedom in their work. Besides increasing the adaptability and portability of equipment so that the microphone does not restrict camera mobility, scientists have been attempting to extend the recordable range of the mechanism and to refine the quality of projection. Sound men have been co-operating with cameramen with remarkable results. The latest advance has been in "stereophonic sound," or the "push-pull" method of recording and reproducing: the characters can be followed by the microphone as they move about the scene, so that their voices seem to issue from their lips wherever they are instead of from a central stationary point. *The Great Ziegfeld* was a notable experiment in the use of this method. Today it is a common practice.

Recent years have seen developments in the manipulation of sound for dramatic purposes by editing and by the discovery of devices inherent in the sound-recording instrument. An art of sound devices now parallels the art of camera devices: the elimination of all but one voice or sound on the sound track parallels the camera close-up; the mingling of voices or noises corresponds to the double exposure; the traveling of sound is like panning or dollying of the camera; the elongation of sound beyond normal parallels a lengthy "still" shot. The dissolve and the fade, the stop-voice and the play-back—these are other sound devices which approximate devices of the camera.

In the prison-cell scene in Mamoulian's *City Streets* (1931), for example, we see the girl and learn what she is thinking through an impressionistically mounted sound flashback. In *Dr. Jekyll and Mr. Hyde*, synchronized with the scenes of the character's transformation was an unearthly sound achieved by the combination of recordings of rapid heartbeats. The sound track was artificially made by extreme high-frequency vibrations, which created a pitch impossible by any other method, and by the sound vibrations from a bell: the assemblage of sounds producing a strange tonal quality emotionally attuned to the supernatural transformation going on. Jean Cocteau's French-made *Blood of a Poet* (1931) shows a striking use of the unnatural prolongation of a single high note, which has the effect of suspending time and subjecting the spectator to an excruciating tension. The documentary films by Pare Lorentz (*The Plow That Broke the Plains* and *The River*) have pointed the way to a lyrical blending of narration and music, and to a contrapuntal relation of sound and image.

It was Walt Disney's animated cartoons, and particularly his Silly Symphonies, that revealed how richly and imaginatively sounds could be manipulated and fused to intensify the image. Disney's films from the outset have been a resourceful exploitation of the sound medium. His music and sound effects give reality to the world of Mickey Mouse and Donald Duck, to its flowers and trees and animal life, and in their originality and ingenuity they have contributed more than any other films to the development of the sound medium.

Many contributions to the development of the art of sound have come from European movie makers. English documentaries have shown how narration, song, and speech can be mounted in manifold ways for subtle, provocative, moving effects (*Night Mail, Song of Ceylon, We Live in Two Worlds, Shipyard*). Alfred Hitchcock, the brilliant English director, revealed an imaginative and dramatic flair for sound as early as 1920 with *Blackmail*, and he has since given the movie world striking examples of the use of sound for transition, association, contrast, characterization. In *The Thirty-Nine Steps*, for example, a woman discovers a dead body. She opens her mouth to scream—and we hear the shrieking whistle of a train speeding into a tunnel. The whistle both voices the alarm of the woman and, at the same time, carries the spectator into the next scene, where the story is to develop further. At another point in the film the rhythmic noise of the train's wheels becomes a disembodied voice which keeps repeating, "He mustn't, he mustn't, he mustn't," heightening the drama of the situation in a way possible only with sound synchronization.

Many Russian sound films have also displayed provocative and effective instances of the counterpointing of sounds with images. Pudovkin, the leading exponent of this technique, in his first sound film, *The Deserter* (1932), showed throughout how strips of sound could be mounted like film strips and given a unity which in form is independent of the image, but for meaning depends on its relationship to the image. In his book, *Film Technique*,[4] Pudovkin summarizes his basic principle:

Every strip of sound, speech or music may develop unmodified while the images come and go in a sequence of short shots, or alternatively, during images of longer duration the sound strip may change independently in a rhythm of its own. I believe that it is only along these lines that the Cinema can keep free from theatrical imitation, and advance beyond the bounds of Theatre. . . . The slogan *Cut* remains equally imperative now that the sound film has arrived.

[4] Enlarged edition, New es, 1933, p. 168.

One of the finest Russian sound films, *The Last Night*, directed by Yuri Raisman, offers an impressive instance of how tense silence can become and of how a naturalistic sound can be used symbolically. In one scene the Red soldiers await a train on which they think the enemy is coming. As they peer out of the waiting room, there is a taut silence. Then the low puffing of the train is heard as it pulls slowly toward them into the station. The soldiers awaiting it are mute, guns ready. The train, inside the shed, continues its labored puffing, seeming to voice the soldiers' tension and anxiety, and creating extreme suspense. When put to such uses, sound adds much to dramatic tension and increases the emotional impact of a film.

The exigencies due to the presence of the microphone have quickened advances in other factors of film making—lights, scene designing, raw film stock, lenses, make-up, art direction, and miniature and process effects. The use of incandescent lighting, explored by Peter Mole and Elmer Richardson and stimulated by the introduction of panchromatic film, was made imperative by the addition of sound. Whereas the old arc lights caused sound trouble because of their vibrations, the incandescent bulb was silent. Lighting technique was soon, therefore, revolutionized. Incandescents were made in all sizes and labeled accordingly: as "baby" and "giant"; when on wheels, as "rifles"; when they were lights mounted on top of the camera booths, close to the action, as "inkies." Later the side floodlighting and the front lighting gave way to selective and controlled lighting.

Incandescent lighting has resulted in superior photography. Color is illuminated without being falsified; make-up therefore does not have to be so heavy or so artificial as under the blue-white arc lights. Interiors of Hollywood sets now have fine, graduated color tones with subtle variations that increase their visual beauty and make for sleek grooming.

Accompanying refinements in raw film (high-speed emulsions of very high sensitivity—Super Pan, Super X, Super XX—and special-effects emulsions) and faster lenses and specially sharp lenses for process photography, and trick-effects lenses, have reduced the light necessary for both interiors and exteriors. This minimization of lighting not only has facilitated work but has made for subtle tonal values closer to nature.

Progress in scene designing has been much affected by the refinements in lighting, sound, and film stock. Sound raised the most acute problem because of the absorption or reflection of sound by the set. Changes in film and lighting led to the use of white sets, whereas previously white had been the worst color for the screen. Photographing white had been difficult because it had produced a dazzling effect; whenever white was wanted, pastel pink or green had been used instead. White interiors now became practicable and popular, reaching a high point of effectiveness in *Dinner at Eight*, in which remarkable luminosity and softness was achieved. Under the leadership of such men as Cedric Gibbons (art director of M-G-M since 1924), Van Nest Polglase (RKO), Hans Dreier (Paramount), Anton Grot (Warner), Steven Gusson (Columbia), D'Agastino, and Howard Miles, scene designing has advanced notably.

With the coming of sound came the problem of what to do when scenes were taken in noisy places such as streets. The process background which had been used sporadically now came into widespread use, and because of its economy its use has been popularly continued. Special-effects departments have doubled in size, and their work includes a number of ingenious devices. These have become increasingly skillful through a pact made in 1936 by major producers. A cross-licensing agreement which provides for the pooling by major producers of all existing patents on special processing, and provides for licensing under future patents, is now in effect. Producers who are not parties to the agreement also can obtain licenses.[5]

From the outset of movie making color, like sound, has been regarded by some people as a natural ally to motion pictures. In the very first days of movie projection, films were hand-tinted and colored. About 1910 Charles Urban brought to American shores a film of the Durbar at Delhi in full color. The Motion Picture Patents Company, however, made a deal with him which aborted

[5] See *The American Cinematographer*, December 1936.

any immediate future color might have had. In the twenties a number of color films appeared, but were so crude that the public found them distasteful. Most companies no more desired to use color than they wanted to use sound, and they did nothing to develop or encourage either.

The overnight success of Warner's first talkies, however, created a panic among producers and spurred them to obtain rights to other available inventions so that they would not be caught unprepared again. Color was at once seized upon as an invention with a future. Warner Brothers pioneered again with the first all-talking, all-color picture, *On with the Dance*. Still crude, color appealed little to audiences and critics. Other attempts were made in color films— *The Song of the West* (1930) and *The Vagabond King* (1930)— but they were only indifferently successful, and it looked as if once again color would be abandoned.

Scientists were not discouraged, however, and in 1932 Technicolor (in existence since 1917) developed a successful three-color process (red, blue, and yellow instead of red-green) which was successfully used by Walt Disney in *Flowers and Trees* and *Three Little Pigs*. In the following year Pioneer Company produced the first three-color process film of a dramatic subject, *La Cucaracha*, which was unique in that an artist and scenic designer as well as a scientist had overseen the colors' execution. Although short, the picture was notable and impressive in its demonstration of the dramatic value of color. Then appeared the full-length feature *Becky Sharp*, equally provocative in its development and application of color. Since then color pictures have been made by almost every company with increasing success, and an increasing number of them are scheduled for future programs. Color today is taking its place as a permanent addition to film resources.

The problem of color is being solved much more slowly than the problem of sound. Color technique has hardly reached the same stage of excellence as sound technique, although it has been practically available for a much longer time. Two reasons account for this lag: one is economic; the other, artistic. The urge to survive and compete against a rival firm when sound came inspired all companies to co-operate to improve sound methods; scientists were given every opportunity to pool their ideas so that progress could be (and it was) made as rapidly as possible. Again, sound was applied by artists: special writers were employed to write dialogue, and special directors to direct it; cameramen, sound men, directors, players—all worked together to apply sound as artistically and perfectly as craftsmen and scientists could.

The conditions affecting the progress of color are different. Most of the companies have a financial stake in Technicolor, so that there is little fear of competition to hurry Technicolor's development. Moreover, since these companies do not wish to relinquish the patent rights to the Technicolor process as Warner and Fox had to give up their rights to the electrical companies, and since they would dislike being faced by a competing color process, all scientific research in color is done in complete secrecy. There is little co-operation among laboratory workers; what knowledge there is about color is held by a few. As in the early days when attempts were made to keep the movie projector in the hands of the few, today Technicolor equipment cannot be bought; it can only be rented with operator and crew. Negatives are processed behind the guarded doors of the Technicolor laboratory by Technicolor technicians.

The American Cinematographer [6] has sharply criticized the policy of keeping the color process surrounded by mystery. It declares that if the cameramen and studio technicians who know the basic principles of color photography were given a free hand, they could produce as good a color picture as the specialists, who are trying to create "a mystic fraternity with a language unintelligible to the lowly uninitiated":

If the color enthusiasts would turn over their processes intact to practical studio production men, they might be able to iron out the kinks from a practical angle and develop color's commercial application. . . . Reports mainly have it that current color processes have all too definite limitations in reproductive capabilities under actual production conditions, that too little now is known about the play of light on colors, that cameras need design improvement and a wider range of performance, that processing is done

[6] Quoted in *Motion Picture Herald*, November 14, 1936.

behind barred doors, that costs are needlessly high, that the whole subject is smothered in uncalled-for pseudo-theory and technicalities and that young blades from science academies are not necessarily picture producers.

Within the past few years, however, Technicolor has changed its policy of supplying cameramen for color work. It now turns over the responsibility to the studio's regular black-and-white cinematographers. Henceforth progress in color should be more rapid.

With the exception of Robert Edmond Jones—who today is inactive—artists and designers with a knowledge of the esthetics of color have not been called in to add their perceptions to those of the scientists. Indeed the general attitude today is to "rarefy" color; that is, to use it as unobtrusively as possible, so that clashing of tones will be minimized and the audience's eyes will not tire. This policy is based on the general reaction against all the early color films, in which colors were flashy and disharmonious, and distracted attention from the story.

Although more subtlety in the handling of color is necessary and closer relationships between color and film are urgent, the dramatic value of color in enriching a film is not to be denied or disdained. A considerable part of the future of motion pictures depends on advances in color science. Studio technicians are today trying to reproduce the color tones in nature just as the black-and-white cameramen endeavored to develop natural tones without color. As soon as the tremendous amount of light still needed in color photography (as in the early days of black-and-white photography) can be reduced, general difficulties with color will diminish accordingly.

Since their inception, all progress in movies has been toward achieving a more effective reality. The film's two new allies, sound and color, have freed it from certain mechanical restrictions and brought it closer to the world of fact. All sounds can now be reproduced; speech has given a new dimension to the shadow players; color brings to the monochrome black-and-white movie world all the hues of nature. These additions have not changed the basic principles of film structure, but only qualified them. Direction, writing, photography, acting, art direction, make-up, cutting—all have acquired through sound and color a subtlety and richness of expression once impossible.

In the movies' first stages, when the business was a small venture, the cameraman had been considered the most important single figure in production. As soon as the film's dramatic form developed, the director became the pivot in movie making. Rivaled at times by the star or author as the business grew commercially, the director nevertheless remained the guiding spirit. When the movies became big business, a new figure took over the reins of production, the associate producer, and before long he had usurped many of the director's functions. Today, with Wall Street controlling the companies, it is the associate producer who is chiefly responsible for production. Not only is he the executive in charge of the budgeting and financing of a film, but he decides what story shall be made, how it shall be treated, and who shall direct and act in it, and often he contributes directly to its realization by offering "suggestions."

Producers who often leave their stamp upon their productions include Pandro S. Berman (*Of Human Bondage*), Samuel Goldwyn (*These Three, Dodsworth, Wuthering Heights*), Arthur Hornblow, Jr. (*Ruggles of Red Gap; Swing High, Swing Low*), Albert Lewin (*The Good Earth*), Robert Lord (*Bordertown, Black Fury, Oil for the Lamps of China*), Kenneth Macgowan (*Little Women, Topaze*), Joseph Mankiewicz (*Fury*), Joseph Pasternak (*Three Smart Girls*), David O. Selznick (*A Star Is Born, Let Me Live*), Robert F. Sisk (*The Plough and the Stars*), Hunt Stromberg (*The Thin Man, The Great Ziegfeld*), Hal B. Wallis (*Little Caesar, The Story of Louis Pasteur*), Walter Wanger (*The President Vanishes, You Only Live Once*), and Darryl F. Zanuck (*The Public Enemy, Les Miserables, Lloyds of London*).

Although most progressive producers work hand in hand with their directors, the director's part in the execution of the film has been minimized. John Ford [7] has declared that the director is ordered to do a picture, having been neither consulted about the

[7] *New Theatre*, April 1936.

script nor asked how he feels about it. On arriving at the studio, he is given a few pages of straight dialogue or final calculated action; often he does not know any more about the full story than the players know. Everything has been made ready for shooting; he has little to say, no opportunity for choice. Allowed an hour to study his day's job, he then proceeds to stage the scene. When it is over, he goes home with little or no idea of what he will do the next day. Under such circumstances direction has become depersonalized and synthetic.

If the producer sets the course of the film, and sound and camera engineers are its overlords in production, the director and the writer still remain the chief creative agents in the treatment of the film. The script itself—the dialogue and the scenes—is fully detailed before the shooting begins. The scenarist, therefore, is a figure whose importance is pronounced. Often he is the real director and creator of the film, for he actually plans the continuity and editing before it is shot.

Sometimes as many as fifty writers work on one script. The policy of combining the talents and ideas of various individuals has, in fact, been exaggerated so often that its original purpose has been destroyed and the film has frequently been incoherent, inconsistent, without integrity. Few writers express any satisfaction over working this way; most prefer to work in close collaboration with the director.

Important as scenarists are in the creation of a film, few have achieved personal recognition outside the industry; few have been as publicized as they deserve. Outstanding today are many scenarists who made reputations in the silent era. Among the many talented new ones are Dudley Nichols (*The Informer, The Plough and the Stars*), Robert Riskin (*It Happened One Night, Mr. Deeds Goes to Town*), Oliver H. P. Garrett (*City Streets, One-Third of a Nation*), Talbot Jennings (*Mutiny on the Bounty, The Good Earth*), Waldemar Young (*The Plainsman, Love Me Tonight*), Aben Finkel (*Black Fury, The Black Legion, Jezebel*), Jo Swerling (*No Greater Glory*), J. L. Mankiewicz (*Million-Dollar Legs, Manhattan Melodrama*), John Twist (*A Man to Remember*), Sid

Buchman (*Holiday*), Dalton Trumbo (*Road Gang*), John Huston (*The Amazing Dr. Clitterhouse, Juarez*), Dore Schary (*Boys' Town*), and John Howard Lawson (*Blockade, Algiers*).

Cameramen today grapple less with engineering problems than with those of pictorial design and photographic values. Many have gained reputations not only as skillful craftsmen but as artists in their own right; a few have a style which often is the outstanding merit of a film. Cameramen work in groups of three: the first composes the lights and scene, the next, the operative cameraman, actually shoots the scene, and the third assists him. Often pictures employ several crews at one time.

Of the hundreds of cameramen active now, many of the leaders have come up from the "silent" days. New talents that have emerged are Karl Freund (*The Good Earth, Camille*), Karl Struss (*Sunrise, Dr. Jekyll and Mr. Hyde*), Leon Shamroy (*You Only Live Once*), James Wong Howe (*Viva Villa, The Thin Man*), Rudolph Maté (*The Passion of Joan of Arc, Dodsworth*), Theodore Tetzlaff (*My Man Godfrey; Swing High, Swing Low*), Gregg Toland (*We Live Again, Wedding Night*), Ernest Haller (*The Journal of a Crime, The Key*), Ray June (*Arrowsmith, Treasure Island*), Joe Valentine (*Three Smart Girls, One Hundred Men and a Girl*). Other prominent cameramen are Ernest Palmer, Arthur Miller, Arthur Edeson, Floyd Crosby, Sol Polito, Leo Tovar, George Folsey, Joe Walker. Not a cameraman, but a specialist in the creation and direction of camera "montage effects" is Slavko Vorkapich.

Today Hollywood cameramen can reproduce practically anything in nature, as well as anything the imagination can conceive. The miniature technique has manufactured fire, rain, snowstorms, and earthquakes as well as Frankenstein, Dracula, Tarzan, Topper, and various magical effects. The earthquake in *San Francisco*, the pestilence in *The Good Earth*, the icebergs in *Spawn of the North*, the hurricane in *The Hurricane*, are some recent examples of extraordinary skill in the realistic reproduction of the phenomena of nature. James Basevi is the best known of such special effects directors.

Tools in abundance now exist for the art. The medium has a creative tradition. Artistry now moves toward deeper subject matter, subtlety in expression, rounder characterizations, truer relationships. The motion picture, in its mechanical maturity, is steadily becoming more meaningful in our lives.

Paul Muni as the hunted man in Mervyn LeRoy's *I Am a Fugitive from a Chain Gang* (1932), a forceful exposé of corruption and brutality in the penal system.

The exotic pictorialism and symbolism of this
still from *The Scarlet Empress* (1934) are characteristic of Josef von Sternberg's talent.

XXIII

CONTEMPORARY DIRECTORS

DIRECTION today, as we have already seen, is so hampered by commercial demands and economic incumbrances—to say nothing of pressure from special interests regarding movie content—that artistically the director is sadly fettered. Many directors must do a picture they dislike so that later they will be allowed to make one they think is worth doing. Because of the appalling amount of money needed for a sound film and because of distribution problems (theatres being controlled by producers), it is practically impossible for a director to do a picture on his own. The art of moving pictures is so dependent for its livelihood on commerce that directors enjoy less freedom than artists in any other media.

Despite these disadvantages of their profession a few directors have achieved fine individuality and style. Walt Disney stands out as the most distinctive and advanced of directors since the adoption of sound. He takes a position beside his forerunners—George Melies, Edwin S. Porter, D. W. Griffith, the Germans and the Russians —as an important innovator and a great contributor to movie tradition. Though active only in the sphere of the animated cartoon, he nevertheless is more significant as a film artist than any of his contemporaries.

In the dramatic field, directors of notable distinction in approach, style, and personal interest in the medium are King Vidor, Fritz Lang, Josef von Sternberg, Rouben Mamoulian, Frank Capra, and John Ford. All command the highest commercial respect, receive the fullest resources of their studios, and are in a position to insist on certain material. At the same time, of course, their reputations and

the costliness of their productions deprive them of the full freedom
they would like. The financial investment entailed in their pictures
is so huge that any experimentation is considered too speculative
to be undertaken. On those occasions when they have been interested in their assignments they have made distinguished motion
pictures that are more than merely good commercial art.

King Vidor has stature not so much for his brilliancy of rendition or profundity of filmic conception as for a certain sincerity
and viewpoint that has, time and again, lifted his films out of the
regular run of entertainment trivialities and made him a notable
director in the late twenties of the silent era when von Stroheim,
Seastrom and Lubitsch were the American screen's major figures.
A social conscience, a mind quick to absorb advanced ideas, and a
belief in honesty and realism have repeatedly brought him to the
forefront during the past fifteen years after long intervals of semi-
obscurity as a director of "pot-boilers." When Vidor's efforts have
been motivated by his beliefs, they have been uncommonly good;
when the reverse is true, his films have been marked by a plodding
if intelligent cinematic style. Significantly his last effort, *The Citadel*, has once more given him prominence and reveals him not as
a man who has seen his day but as a director who will continue
in the forefront of his contemporaries by the earnestness of his
social outlook.

Before becoming a full-fledged director, Vidor had been prop-
boy, writer, cameraman, and assistant director. Training in these
various capacities of movie making gave him a practical knowledge
of the medium; experience in directing added sureness and a high
level of competency; worth-while themes have more than once
aroused him to strike out in an individual manner. At its best, his
style is marked by a more subtle use of the resources of the medium,
a skill in handling material realistically, and a flair for characterization.

Vidor has believed from the first that a picture must have something of social import to say. His earliest obscure efforts in the
early twenties were colored by this interest; they comprised most
of the few realistic films about the common man and his struggles

during the post-war deluge of "sex" and "jazz" movies. *The Turn of the Road, Better Times, Poor Relations, The Other Half, The Family Honor, The Jack-Knife Man*, and *Dusk to Dawn* stressed characterization, local problems, economic issues, relation of capital to labor, social conditions generally—elements Vidor was to employ again and again and to make his own. These pictures won regard for him as a sincere and promising talent but no one thought when he directed *Proud Flesh*, an unusually deft satirical comedy, that his next film would lift him to fame and prove to be the biggest box-office sensation since *The Covered Wagon*. That next film was *The Big Parade* (1925). It was intended to scoop the screen adaptation of the year's biggest stage hit, *What Price Glory*, and this it did by one whole year; but its success was due to scores other than timeliness.

The phenomenal success this film enjoyed brought forth exaggerated praise; the picture was hardly as worthy or artistically significant as it was declared to be. A romantic depiction of America's part in the World War, *The Big Parade* was on the whole a superficial, if impressively executed, production. At moments however, there were flashes that revealed a perception and directorial ability above the average. In the opening, men and women are shown being stirred to war, without knowing why, the men seeing in it a chance for heroics, the women for romance. Later in the film, the scenes of the soldiers' evacuation of the French village for the front was made an impressive sight with the endless lines of troops and trucks, the airplane convoys, village streets fading into country lanes and forest footpaths in the "big parade" to the battle field provoking an uncanny sense of impending disaster. Perhaps the most outstanding sequence cinematically was the one in which the soldiers advance through the woods in silent, fearful formation, while the unseen machine gun of the enemy thins their ranks. Here the cutting of the shots to a march time created an arresting and powerful impact.

Distinguished by colorful characterizations, high-lighted by many fresh incidents, the film nevertheless was based in sentimentality. This weakness kept it from being a profound achievement. Vidor himself, talking about the film years later, admitted his deliberate compromise: [1]

People still talk to me of that scene in *The Big Parade* where poor Renée Adorée ran after John Gilbert as his army truck was taking him away to the front. The film showed her grasping at his arms, his trouser legs, his shoes, as she gradually saw him slipping out of her life. It was a scene designed to "jerk a tear," and it did it, I may say.

The Big Parade gave King Vidor a reputation, but it was *The Crowd*, three years later, that consolidated his repute in the critical world and revealed him at his best. With this film Vidor reached his peak of eloquence as a silent film director; he has surpassed it since only with *The Citadel*, produced some ten years later.

The Crowd was an ironic story of two ordinary middle class people seeking love, marriage and a simple happiness but frustrated in their desires by the struggle to exist. In theme it was opposed to every Hollywood convention and its depictions of the drab realities of unemployment, the petty dickerings, the futile dreams, the oppression of the individual who tries to break out of the crowd, the endless frustrations sinking the characters deeper into the morass of a system which was mangling them, was in sharp contrast to the prevalent ideas about "Coolidge prosperity."

The depth of the theme stimulated Vidor to a more exciting and imaginative technique than he had yet displayed. Its rendition was strongly influenced by the recent innovations of the German school, most apparent in the roving and subjective use of the camera, and in the many symbolic touches. Vidor brought out the immensity of the city, its speed and indifference, by sweeping the camera over the metropolis, up skyscrapers, through crowded streets. The camera selects a majestic skyscraper, the symbol of the modern city, tilts up, up, up, moves across an interminable façade of windows, trucks through one into an office where hundreds of regimented clerks, all looking alike, are all engrossed in the same kind of work behind identical desks and selects one clerk in particular, the protagonist of the story who attempts to rise out

[1] *The New York Times*, March 17, 1935.

of the crowd. It was a highly effective presentation, setting the keynote for the theme in a fresh and striking manner.

Throughout the picture there were instances attesting to Vidor's grasp of filmic means. A subjective treatment distinguished the Coney Island sequence. Here the camera became the actors and the audience experienced their thrills in riding the shutes, whirling on the revolving floor, speeding through the "Tunnel of Love." Most graphic were the scenes depicting the degeneration of the household. The bold treatment of the neglect of the home, and the increasing estrangement between husband and wife, as their need for money grows more desperate were reminiscent of similar scenes in *Greed*, and displayed Vidor's adeptness at realism. The relationships between the young couple made poignant through intimate details, showed Vidor's talent for characterization. Most dramatic perhaps was the episode in which the father maddened by the city noises which he thinks are preventing his dying child from recovery, attempts to quiet the crowds, the taxicabs, the fire engines. He moves arms upraised against the mass of people in the streets who sweep past him indifferent and impervious to his anguish. Outstanding as these single instances were, the film as a whole lacked unity and a too even level of narration impaired its dramatic impact.

The Crowd despite enthusiastic recognition from critics proved a financial failure. Jazz-preoccupied and hard-boiled, Americans preferred light pictures in the Lubitsch vein; *The Crowd*, with its sharp disillusionment, made them uncomfortable. To recover his commercial position, Vidor directed two Marion Davies comedies, *Show People* and *Patsy*. While he was doing these, sound arrived.

Vidor undertook the new form at once. As with many other directors, sound and dialogue gave him additional power and stimulus. With his first talkie venture, *Hallelujah* (voted by *The Film Daily* one of the best ten of 1929), Vidor again proved himself to be a significant director. For one thing, he risked a feature film with an all-Negro cast, itself a historically important event in the cinema. Appalling though this seemed to the movie industry, it is not so surprising when we recall that one of the biggest successes Broadway was then experiencing was the all-Negro production *Porgy*. Vidor undertook to do its counterpart in *Hallelujah*, spying a grand opportunity for song and music in the new sound form. He believed that sound should be used imaginatively rather than realistically or literally. He declared at this time in many interviews with the press that he intended to record noises into patterns and formalize the sound background. An admirer of the animated cartoons, he believed much was to be learned from them. At the same time Vidor expressed the desire to adapt for the screen the views and manifestations featured in the work of modern artists such as Leger, Picasso, Matisse, and Chirico. He pointed out that painters got extraordinary effects by distortion and that the same could be done in the movies, adding that the way Hollywood was making pictures was not necessarily the only way.

In undertaking *Hallelujah*, Vidor also said he was primarily interested in showing the Southern Negro as he is. The deed fell short of the intent. The film turned out, however, to be a melodramatic piece replete with all the conventionalities of the white man's conception of the spiritual-singing, crap-shooting Negro. But whatever its sociological faults, and it had many, its technique reflected a thinking director. Utilizing knowledge gained in the silent movies, Vidor used sound effects well and allowed only a minimum of dialogue. Refusing to be sidetracked by the excitement over the talkie instrument, he kept the camera foremost in importance (letting down surprisingly, however, in the singing sequences). At a time when most directors were confused about the relationships between film and sound, he conceived his movie largely and properly in terms of movement enforced by sound. The film therefore had far more fluidity than the usual static pictures of the day, although it never did achieve the stature critics claimed for it.

During the next five years Vidor turned out a group of box-office hits: *Dulcy* (1930), *Billy the Kid* (1930), *Street Scene* (1931), *The Champ* (1931-1932), *Bird of Paradise* (1932), *Stranger's Return* (1933). None of these helped his reputation. Even *Street Scene* which offered him material to which he was sympathetic, was no more than an adequately rendered Hollywood production. His next film, however, a box-office failure, *Our Daily Bread* (1934), called "the achievement of a courageous mind," re-established him as an individual director.

Impelled by his sociological interest, as he had been in his silent film, *The Crowd*, in *Our Daily Bread* Vidor sought to use the screen more vigorously and imaginatively than he was wont to do with his frankly commercial pictures (he paid for *Our Daily Bread* out of his own pocket). But the theme, dealing with the problem of unemployed, an issue with which the whole nation was then concerned, was never adequately resolved. Vidor's conclusion, that in a return to the farm men will solve their unemployment problem, was not logically thought out and contained dismal implications. Either because Vidor "pulled his punches" at the resolution or because like a good many others he was confused, the film never achieved the force it might have had. It never achieved the stature, even in its last and best sequence, of the minor Soviet film *Turksib*, to which the rhythmic cutting for the irrigation sequence was indebted. It is for this reason that the film did not prove a box-office success, not because it was too "artistic" or had too much "propaganda," as Hollywood averred. It was nevertheless another serious, forward-looking, and courageous effort by one who, time and again, had turned away from rubber-stamp movies. It was important for what it attempted. Vidor wanted to do a profound thing, and his boldness in an industry that does not stop at blacklisting deserves praise.

At the time *Our Daily Bread* was being shown on Broadway, King Vidor revealed in an article in *New Theatre* [2] the conditions that hindered creative direction in the Hollywood studios:

> The final decisions are made by business men, not artists. . . . The supervisor, with his lack of visual imagination, is unable to fill in the gap between the scenario and the finished article. Consequently the order that each detail of the script be so obvious and overwritten that . . . the ultimate whole is all too obvious and dull.

These remarks immediately raised a question: was the intent of *Our Daily Bread* radically modified in production, which, though

[2] September 1934.

financed by Vidor, had to have the approval of a national distributor, United Artists?

After this "escapade" Vidor returned to the Hollywood fold. Awarded a gold medal by the League of Nations for *Our Daily Bread*, he was now engaged by Goldwyn to direct a two-million-dollar investment, Anna Sten, in *The Wedding Night* (1935). This story attempted to lift itself above the commonplace by means of a tragic ending. At times, particularly in the relationship between Tony and Manya, Vidor's restraining hand kept the film from becoming the usual movie banality. The scenes of the Polish village customs transplanted to Connecticut, though few, gained for the story weight and believability. But the more the film unreeled, the more compromises were made. The final result was that Vidor had momentarily, in the words of André Sennwald, "refreshed and dignified a routine love story by austerely excluding all the infantile convolutions to which Hollywood has accustomed us in dramas of this kind."

Vidor's next efforts, *So Red the Rose* (1935-1936), a false picture of the South; *The Texas Rangers* (1936), a glorified Western; and *Stella Dallas* (1937), an outdated tear-jerker, may have reassured Hollywood but at the same time they alienated his admirers. When he sailed for Europe after making *Stella Dallas*, he went not as the "white hope of the American film scene" but as a "has-been." But when he returned from England with a picture he had made there, *The Citadel* (1938), he not only regained his old stature but topped it. Considered the best American film of 1938, *The Citadel* fulfilled the promise of *The Crowd* and *Our Daily Bread* and portended a new development in Vidor's growth, thematically and cinematically.

The Citadel was a story of a young doctor, his fight against ignorance and bigotry, the dangers of occupational diseases, the hostility of industry toward disclosure of such facts and independent research, and the difficulty of maintaining ideals in a profession where being "fashionable" brings greater reward than honesty or knowledge. The film pleaded eloquently for a progressive system of socialized medicine and hospitalization for the masses.

Deeply felt and absorbing in content, the film was handled with

Paramount Pictures

Fritz Lang's *You Only Live Once* (1937). Composition, lighting, and camera angle exploited to create a dramatic unity, characterize Lang's talent.

John Ford (*seated*) directing Victor McLaglen
in a scene from *The Informer* (1935), one of the
best of American sound films.

an intelligence and sensitivity too infrequently seen on the American screen. The first half, dealing with the Welsh mining communities, the drab lives of the people, the workingmen's circles, the selfish, hypocritical wife of the chief doctor whom the young physician had come to assist, the smug company medico, and the simple courtship of the doctor (Robert Donat) and the school teacher (Rosalind Russell), showed a genuine grasp of the material and achieved considerable force. These sequences were as solid, as real, as Joris Ivens' *Borinage*, or von Stroheim's *Greed*. Here was evidenced Vidor's penetrating social viewpoint, his keen observation and care in characterization, and sharp ear for pungent dialogue. In such dramatic episodes as the doctor's struggle to breathe life in a still-born child ("Thank God I'm a doctor!"), his droll proposal to the school teacher ("I don't suppose you'd want to marry me, would you?"), the plotting and blowing up of the sewers, the miners' debate over the new doctor and later their diplomatic dismissal of him, were all shaped with economy and restraint, but imbued with tension and vigor. None the less sharp were the disclosures of medical quackery in the fashionable hospitals, the callous physicians at their golf.

In technique, *The Citadel* revealed a feeling for documentary objectivity and dramatic understatement. It was not the cutting that mattered but the uncompromising tone of the content. This made for a persuasive and straightforward style as powerful and clean as a newsreel. The questions arise, was Vidor, once away from Hollywood, given the opportunity to make a film the way he always wanted to? Had he seen Grierson's English school of documentary films of the same regions? The answers to these two questions would still not account entirely for the high seriousness and intelligent rendering of the picture. Perhaps more than any other of Vidor's films, *The Citadel*—for its integrity even more than for its form—brought the old Vidor to a new frontier.

Throughout his long career, Vidor has been able to maintain a position of importance while other directors more gifted have been forgotten. He has risen above the commonplace because of his repeated attempts to deal with important themes, and an eagerness to try the resources of the medium. Never brilliant or facile in technique, he is often more sound in other respects. Attuned to the times, his belief that a picture should say something worth while, may still lift his form higher than it has ever been and give him a value superseding many greater craftsmen.

An equally keen awareness of society and in addition a genuine talent for original film expression are possessed by Fritz Lang, German director of *Destiny, Siegfried, Metropolis, Spies, Dr. Mabuse,* and *M*, which brought him to America. By virtue of only three efforts in Hollywood, Lang has become one of the country's most significant film makers. *Fury* (1936), *You Only Live Once* (1937), *You and Me* (1938), paradoxically though it may seem, had more American local color and a keener perception of national characteristics than films by Americans dealing with similar subject matter. These pictures are the work of an older craftsman who, despite his transplantation to a new country—or perhaps because of it—has reached out successfully for new powers of expression and social penetration. The first two, in particular, are in execution far above the standard. Lang has not only been steeped in the best traditions of the medium but contributed to those traditions himself even before his arrival on American shores.

Like the eminent contemporary English director, Alfred Hitchcock, Lang has a flair for dramatic intensity and terseness of rendition. Often his imagery and cutting, especially in his sound and dialogue, are so succinct that much of their brilliance is overlooked in a first viewing of the picture. His keen sense for fluidity of movement, apparent even in the longest of his scenes (he uses whatever elements there are in the shot to continue the flow), gives his cutting and sound a kinetic quality that is the envy and admiration of other directors. Also like Hitchcock he gets the maximum effect out of his materials. In Lang's films everything on the set—props, actors, background, sound—is utilized to enrich the scene, delineate character, heighten the mood. Such economy makes for simplicity of a high order. Perhaps more than any other man in Hollywood today Lang is the "director's director."

The story of *Fury* is, like all Lang's work, simple but compelling. Joe Wilson, a gasoline-station owner, while driving to meet the girl he expects to marry, is arrested as a kidnapper on the outskirts of a small town and is taken to jail by a sheriff's deputy to await an investigation. (Joe is, of course, innocent.) Rumors spread through the town that the kidnapper has been caught, and by nightfall the citizens have become an unruly, lynch-minded mob. They storm the jail, beat the sheriff aside, and, unable to reach the prisoner, set the building on fire. The prisoner, however, has miraculously escaped from the building. Later, when the law steps in to punish the mob leaders for killing an innocent man, Joe Wilson listens to the trial over the radio, vengefully keeping his safety secret so that his "killers" will be convicted of murder. Later in the film the emphasis on the guilt of the mob is shifted to Joe's guilt—his "maniacal" desire to see his would-be murderers punished by death. Even Joe's girl turns against him, pleading for the lynch mob: "Oh, Joe! A mob doesn't think, doesn't know what it's doing. . . . You might as well kill me, too, and do a good job of it!"

Despite this final concession to the box office (for which Lang cannot be blamed) *Fury* was a memorable film, in theme as well as in rendering. Lang's acute direction built up a frightening tension. Everyday events and people suddenly took on tremendous and horrifying proportion; even the most insignificant details had a pointed meaning. All converged into a bitter denunciation of mob action. From the quiet beginning, when Joe Wilson is picked up on the road, to the scenes of the hysteria of the mob and the burning jail and to the trial of the hypocritical townspeople, Lang's camera piled detail upon detail from the point of view of the spectator, the victim, the community, and the law, making them an inspired commentary upon bigotry, provincialism, and intolerance.

An example of sharp characterization is the scene where Joe is being questioned by the sheriff while the slow-witted "Bugs" behind him is nabbing flies—a background motif which, incidentally, carries on the internal movement of the scene as a whole. Again, during the burning of the jail we see a woman holding her child aloft to get a better view, a moronic adolescent hanging on to a vantage point and crying out gleefully, "I'm Popeye the sailor man

—tweet, tweet!", and a gaping boy biting into his hot dog as he shifts about for a better look at the conflagration.

It is the courtroom scenes, however, that are the high-lights of the film. The fidelity of portraiture of the hypocritical citizens, and the prosecutor's ingenious use of the newsreels which, taken on the night of the fire, show the righteous woman (now on trial) murderously whirling a firebrand, are eloquent. As Howard Barnes of the New York *Herald Tribune* [3] pointed out, *Fury* "remains a compelling and terrifying document."

If *Fury* indicted mob violence, Lang's next film, *You Only Live Once*, a harrowing study of terror, challenged the society which condemns criminal offenders to ostracism. A picture which in other hands would have degenerated into a raucous melodrama, Lang turned into an absorbing, tense, and tragic social document.

Eddie Taylor, with three convictions on his record, has just been released from prison, has married his girl, and is determined to go straight. But he is fired from one job after another, and is finally blamed, because of his record, for a bank robbery and murder: a hat bearing his initials has been found at the scene of the crime. Sentenced to die and imprisoned, he escapes from the death house only to be trapped in the prison yard. Here a priest pleads with him to lay down his gun, telling him that his innocence has been proved and that he has been pardoned. Thinking this a ruse, Taylor makes the priest his hostage, gets out of the yard, and then kills him in making his escape. Now wanted for murder, Taylor gets his girl and flees. Dogged from town to town, both of them are finally shot dead by police.

Cinematically the film was conceived on the same ironic note as *Fury*. Lang's camera was seldom still, and it became subjective as well as objective by turns (the characters' point of view at one moment, the spectators' the next). His sound was equally versatile, recording dialogue, a heartbeat, night noises, and the imaginings of the pursued couple, without any disunity or self-consciousness. His use of nature to build mood and individualize the scenes—rain during the bank holdup, swirling fog for the prison break, night and the frog pond for the idyllic love scene, and the muddy embank-

[3] June 6, 1936.

ment for the bloody ending—was resourceful and gripping. Throughout the cutting was swiftly paced, economical, urging the story to its savage conclusion.

You and Me, Lang's last picture, was his least important, although it too was a bold attempt to break away from Hollywood formulas and to experiment, particularly with sound. In this unconvincing story a jailbird marries a girl who is trying to reform him, not knowing that she herself is out on parole, and then on discovering her past he reverts once more to a life of crime. The story had moments of novel treatment. The beginning was in the form of a prologue rendered with chants and asides and accompanied by a "montage effect" of jewels, furs, bathing beauties, airplanes, and furniture, pointing out that nothing in life is free. Although novel, this was unrelated to the rest of the film's treatment, and in itself was insufficiently executed. There were, however, many striking camera bits, and there was the same pungent characterization and moodiness that was evident in Lang's first two films. As a whole the picture was slow in development, lacked conviction, and showed a failure between intent and achievement.

Today Lang is without doubt one of our ablest film makers. A careful planner, he blends the resources of camera, light, sound, and cutting in an individual, compact, imaginative style. To pictures he brings a deep understanding of character and society. All his material is from everyday life; its drabness is made dramatic by his masterly depiction of the social net in which the average person is caught. His integrity, command of the medium, and desire to make films as he sees fit, should produce work of profound and lasting importance.

Markedly different from Fritz Lang in approach, style, and purpose, Josef von Sternberg also emerged in the silent era and has always shown himself to be a serious craftsman. All his films, no matter how lame, have personal characteristics that lift them above the average. This director's distinguishing trait, more pronounced with each new film, is his sensuous pictorialism. His flair for composition, lighting, and photography is evident even in the poorest of his pictures; his credo appears to be that the movie is a painting in motion.

So ardently has von Sternberg devoted himself to the pictorial that this feature in his films has superseded story, characterization, and cutting. There is no better pictorial craftsman in Hollywood. He achieves mood through a chiaroscuro that is the envy of other directors, and continuity through an interrelationship of tonal values, not of the content or the montage. His movies have become increasingly precious examples of photographic craftsmanship, remote from reality and very close to museum pieces in character.

Von Sternberg came into prominence with his first picture, *Salvation Hunters* (1925). Behind its production is the story of a man who, to prove his talent, struggled against odds to raise credit and to make a film on his own. *Salvation Hunters*, which it was said von Sternberg considered his best work, was made soon after von Stroheim's *Greed* and, like other movies stimulated by that picture, it had the same realistic approach but with individual touches that were later to be characteristic of von Sternberg's pictures.

The story told of an embittered and cowardly man and his wife who leave their mud-scow home when they find an abandoned child. A procurer gives them lodging in the hope of obtaining the services of the wife; when the procurer mistreats the child, the husband is aroused to beat him up and change his way of life. A grim, lumbering portrait of the waterfront and its derelicts, it opened with scenes of a cat at a garbage can, a sea gull flying, and a patch of beach strewn with wreckage—sure indications of von Sternberg's pictorial and symbolical leanings. Shadows of the dredge were used throughout as a psychological symbol to haunt the characters. The emphasis upon sordid atmosphere, the lack of action, the pictorially posed characters, and the many symbolical references were the particular concerns which were to continue to dominate von Sternberg's work.

Salvation Hunters was bought by United Artists and distributed by them. Charles Chaplin next engaged von Sternberg to make a film called *The Sea Gull* with Edna Purviance, but this was never released. Those who have seen it say that it is a lovely collection of photographs but has little story value. His next effort, *Escape* (*Exquisite Sinner*), made for M-G-M, aroused no comment. Finally in 1927 von Sternberg surprised everyone by making for Paramount what was generally conceded to be one of the most outstanding films of the year, *Underworld*, which won a $10,000 bonus from the studio for being the most successful picture shown at the New York Paramount Theatre that year.

Underworld was one of the first and best of the Chicago gangster pictures. Written by Ben Hecht, the plot was compact, dramatic. Von Sternberg brought to it a realistic atmosphere, striking lighting effects and compositions, characterization expressed through deft angle close-ups and selection of types, a sense of timing and economy of means (the jewelry store hold-up was shocking in its impressionistic effect—a pistol shot smashes a clock in a jewelry store; a frightened clerk turns; a hand gathers diamonds from the case; a crowd collects), and above all a freshness and discipline that made the melodrama outstanding. Unquestionably a new director had "arrived" in this picture.

Von Sternberg continued in the same melodramatic vein with a series of underworld vignettes: *The Dragnet* (1928), *Docks of New York* (1928); and *The Last Command* (1927-1928), the last an Emil Jannings portrayal of a Russian general who had become a Hollywood extra. Each of these productions moved farther away from dramatic compactness and more toward visual slickness. *The Case of Lena Smith* (1928-1929), showing von Sternberg's still-growing interest in the pictorial, climaxed his career in the "silents." The casualness of its plot and subject matter, sacrificed for colorful characterization, gloomy backgrounds, novel atmosphere, and an unbroken rhythm obtained by a continuously moving camera, was to become typical of his later style.

By the close of the silent era von Sternberg had become a significant directorial figure. Though his genuine artistic integrity was under suspicion, though he was neither respected like von Stroheim nor envied like Lubitsch, he had won a reputation for being "different" and for his determination to carry out his own ideas. More than ever a pictorialist, with a penchant for photography, lighting, and composition, he was to refine his aptitudes further despite the innovation of talkies.

Von Sternberg made his first sound film, *The Blue Angel* (1930), in Germany under Pommer's supervision. Based on a novel by Heinrich Mann, the picture was a psychological study of a sex-starved professor, a sort of characterization for which the star, Emil Jannings, had already become known. Opposite Jannings was an obscure music hall singer, Marlene Dietrich, subsequently to become, as Dwight MacDonald put it, Sternberg's *femme fatale*. This technically superb picture had all the qualities Sternberg was to overemphasize in his later efforts: luminous chiaroscuro of a deep, low tone, remarkable camera angles and composition, elaborate background details, a smooth and easy blending of sequences through dissolves, and music and song which moved with the images. Such features gave the film a sensuous elegance.

Though none of his films which followed equaled *The Blue Angel*, all were profoundly indebted to it. *Morocco* (1930), *Dishonored* (1931), *Blonde Venus* (1932), *Shanghai Express* (1932), *The Scarlet Empress* (1934), and *The Devil Is a Woman* (1935), all starring Marlene Dietrich, attested to von Sternberg's high seriousness and misdirected purpose. Made up of ravishing pictorial effects, peppered with lewdness and suggestive symbols, set in a macabre, unreal world created solely for the senses, these films trace the gradual withering of a talent who has withdrawn into a cinematic ivory tower. They abound in madonnaesque close-ups, background symbolism, striking lighting effects, exotic atmosphere, and continuous dissolves, all at the expense of other organizational devices. They are tonal tapestries, two-dimensional fabrications valuable only for their details.

Four attempts by von Sternberg to escape his shadowy world—*Thunderbolt* (1929), *An American Tragedy* (1931), *Crime and Punishment* (1935), and *The King Steps Out* (1936)—were ineffectual. Their virtues, due to his pictorial eye, were canceled out by their faults.

Despite his dramatic failings Josef von Sternberg is distinct from the horde of motion picture directors because he "has never directed a film indifferently." His talent cannot be denied. Although oblivious to the import of content, drama, and the deeper aspects of structure, he has the best pictorial imagination among contemporary Hollywood directors.

The rush of stage directors to the movies on the coming of sound brought a man who from childhood had been associated with the theatre: Rouben Mamoulian. Reared by cultured and theatrically active parents, schooled in Paris, he struggled long to gain a foothold in the theatre. At an early age he founded a theatre in his home town, Tiflis, near the border of Georgia, Russia. Soon he was directing in London, and from there he came to America to direct the American Opera Company of the Eastman Institute in Rochester, New York. The next steps in his career followed logically: the Theatre Guild, the Metropolitan Opera House, the Paramount Company, Hollywood.

Intelligence, an experimental willingness and aptitude, and an understanding of pictorial and sound effects (which springs both from his operatic experience and from his studies of other craftsmen) have raised Mamoulian into the first rank of directors. His awareness of pace, rhythm, movement, and music has made his musical films his best; in these more than in his dramatic pictures he has blended the cinematic elements into an excellent whole.

Mamoulian's first movie, *Applause* (1930), revealed a director who recognized the difference between stage and screen. In a day of readjustments, when the proper relation between the film and the microphone was being groped for consciously or, in many cases, unconsciously, *Applause* spoke in favor of camera mobility first, talk second. Audiences sat up and took notice; critics could not ignore the film's cinematic implications. Mamoulian's use of mobile sound was then novel: for instance, a chorus starting a song is left by the camera for a second scene, and the music continues through this second scene, being modulated so that a conversation can be heard above it. The camera moved freely, daringly, and even enthusiastically—sometimes, in fact, too much for the spectator's comfort.

One of the most effective moments in *Applause* comes when the lover of the fading burlesque queen tells her she is old, ugly, finished. The camera hovers for an instant over Miss Morgan's face, moves slowly to the framed picture of her in her lovely youth, and then comes back to her. The movement of the camera and the continuing bitter voice over it combine to intensify the effect enormously. In another scene, as the dancer's daughter in a restaurant lifts a glass of water, the music fades slowly and the picture dissolves to the identical movement of her mother's arm, lifting a glass of poison to her lips. Obvious though such touches appear now, they were uncommonly good in the early days of sound.

In *Applause* Mamoulian endeavored to blend light, shadow, and sound imaginatively and dramatically, and whenever possible he introduced nature to heighten the mood. His love scenes were exquisitely lyrical, presaging those in all his later works. His young lovers on top of a skyscraper were played against the sky and the wind; later, in *City Streets*, his lovers were placed in a setting against the sea; many of his later films show them in the rain. Such scenes, stemming from his thorough knowledge of the stage, are indicative of Mamoulian's forethought and awareness of the dramatic elements at the disposal of a director.

Mamoulian's daring and perspicacity in moving the camera, while other directors' cameras were literally hand-tied, contributed much at the psychological moment to the mutual adaptation of sound and camera. Although *Applause* was a sensitive venture in the right direction, however, the lack of restraint in Mamoulian's use of the camera suggested immaturity, defective discrimination, a lack of understanding of filmic continuity. Harry Alan Potamkin [4] later cautioned Mamoulian against allowing his ingenuity to "become a routine of excess mobility and other fallacious devices."

Mamoulian's second undertaking, a melodramatic gangster film, *City Streets* (1931), displayed a firmer control of the medium. The film demonstrated Mamoulian's awareness of sound's possibilities and his intelligent application of the contributions of other directors (traits he has manifested ever since). In the episode where Sylvia Sidney is in jail, the audience hears in a sound flash-back a garbled repetition of her earlier conversation with her lover. The influence of Russian and German films is strongly evi-

[4] *Vanity Fair*, March 1932.

denced in the symbolic use of inanimate objects to suggest or accent a character. Birds flying through the prison windows make the cell seem more confining than ever; the snuffing out of a match by a character just before he murders his rival portends the killing; the statues of cats in scenes of the jealous girl sharply point her characterization. Since *City Streets* such symbolism has become pronounced in Mamoulian's work. The cutting of this film on the whole showed a more balanced conception of the film medium.

Mamoulian's next assignment was a melodrama offering unusual opportunities: *Dr. Jekyll and Mr. Hyde*. In the silent films this story had already shown itself to be powerfully adaptable to the screen. Mamoulian brought to it his flair for the moving camera, eerie compositions, and unusual sound effects. His superior taste, feeling for mood, sense of the theatrical, and use of symbolism in this film were very pronounced, lifting the story well above the *Frankenstein* class if not into the class of the distinguished.

After these tries at melodramatic material, Mamoulian turned his hand to a musical film. He had directed opera and was well versed in sound accompaniments. Perhaps his outstanding merit as a film director, thus far, had been his intelligent and often original use of sound. Given Maurice Chevalier and Jeanette MacDonald (erstwhile Lubitsch stars), Charles Ruggles, Charles Butterworth, and Myrna Loy, Mamoulian produced *Love Me Tonight* (1932). By this film a true appraisal of Mamoulian can be made, for it brings to light at its best his outstanding talent. In *Applause* that talent was suggested; in *City Streets* and *Dr. Jekyll and Mr. Hyde* it was approved; in *Love Me Tonight* it was acclaimed.

Love Me Tonight was in every way a delightful musical fantasy in real movie terms. So directly was it derived from René Clair and Lubitsch that had either of those names been affixed to the film no one would have been surprised: it was charming, fanciful, witty, sophisticated. The opening sequence, a symphonic montage of a city awakening; and the deer-hunt episode, a Disneyesque tour de force, were high-lights of a brilliant movie. Mamoulian has never equaled it; neither Lubitsch nor Clair ever surpassed it.

Having directed four pictures, of which at least three—*City Streets, Dr. Jekyll and Mr. Hyde,* and *Love Me Tonight*—were accomplished works, Mamoulian subsequently made a series of films which, if they were the only ones to his credit, would hardly earn him a reputation. *Song of Songs* (1933) glorified Marlene Dietrich; *Queen Christina*, made the same year, starred Greta Garbo; and *We Live Again* (1934) attempted to put Anna Sten in their class. None of these pictures compared with his previous efforts.

In 1935 Mamoulian made his first color film, *Becky Sharp*, the first full-length dramatic photoplay done by the Technicolor process. That Mamoulian was selected to direct this initial Technicolor feature was a signal recognition of his position. As a film it followed close upon the static style of his previous two pictures; as a color experiment, it had many exciting moments that presaged a brilliant future for color in films. The most outstanding instance was the device of using color dramatically for an emotional overtone. In the scenes of the ball, the color is at first somber; then, as the roar of the cannons is heard, the color intensifies with the excitement of the dancers, until at last, as the officers rush off to battle, it is vivid scarlet. Although it was considered by André Sennwald as, "coloristically speaking, the most successful [film] that ever has reached the screen," its endless talk and tableaux weakened it.

In 1936 Mamoulian once again showed himself to be a distinctive director with another musical film, *The Gay Desperado*. Under no obligation to be serious, he had gone seriously to work to produce a clever, satirical, flowing film that would be exceptional and more original than *Love Me Tonight*. A gay and colorful comedy about Mexican outlaws who ape the slang and tactics of American gangsters, it was exactly the type of satirical fantasy at which he excels. The behavior of Leo Carrillo (the bandit with a soul for music), the kidnapping of Nino Martini, and the hold-up of the radio station were satire of such excellence as to place the film far above its musical contemporaries. The interweaving of song, music, and story was imaginative, fresh, and structurally sound, and proved that *Love Me Tonight* was no accident.

Mamoulian's most recent film, *High, Wide, and Handsome* (1937), was a spectacular and lavishly produced show which, while it had many qualities typical of his best work, was as a whole a second-rate concoction. Newspaper notices reported that Mamoulian had gone to Pennsylvania to absorb its atmosphere and become acquainted with the oil industry. But the film itself had conflicting aims in trying to present, at the same time, a social and industrial development and a spectacular operetta of "atmosphere and songs." The best parts of the picture were those showing the early Titusville oil drillings; the worst were those of the ensuing battle between the railroad crowd and the circus, which arrives like the marines at the last minute and, with the aid of elephants, gets the pipe line through. The lively subject matter of the film was never co-ordinated: it was operatic one moment, serious the next, and confused the third.

Mamoulian has resolved his technique into musical rhythm, just as von Sternberg has resolved his into pictorialism. He believes that anything can be put to music, and apparently he is intent upon proving it in his movies. When his philosophy coincides with his material, as in *Love Me Tonight* and *The Gay Desperado*, we get a good musical film; when it is forced upon dramatic material with undue and unnatural emphasis, as in *High, Wide, and Handsome,* the result is not so successful.

One of the most thoughtful of Hollywood craftsmen, Mamoulian has described himself as a director of high-budget pictures who really wants to do a low-budget one so that he can be left alone to do what he likes: "I want to straighten up my back and fight. Why must we make all pictures alike?" He thinks that with a "B"-picture budget he would be freer to experiment and make something fresh. He voices the sentiments of many other directors who have expressed a willingness to gamble on a share of earnings provided they are allowed to make a picture the way they see fit. In Mamoulian's case, as in a few others, such a chance would be worth taking.

Frank Capra is undoubtedly one of the most valued of Hollywood directors. We feel that his films mean something to him; that they are not merely jobs, as they might be to many of his contemporaries. His own remarks show that he is eager and zealous about his problems:

I like to break the rules. To my mind plot is unimportant. . . .
I am interested most in characterizations. The people must be real.
. . . Fitting the actor to the character is fifty per cent of the battle
in creating good pictures. If they are not twin personalities the
story itself loses conviction.[5]

This underlying credo has made Capra the success he is and explains the individuality that marks his productions. Back in the
twenties a minor independent company, Columbia Pictures, gave
Frank Capra his first job in movies—that of making Screen Snap
Shots. Less than ten years later Columbia Pictures and Frank Capra
had become leading influences in the motion picture industry, rank-
ing with the best. Their gradual climb from obscurity to fame and
fortune was possible largely because of their association, Capra
being as important to the commercial success of Columbia Pictures
as D. W. Griffith had been to Biograph.

Sicilian-born, Los Angeles-reared, Capra as a youth in 1915
entered California Tech, yearning to be an engineer. (These were
the days when The Birth of a Nation was taking the country by
storm.) Upon the entrance of America into the World War two
years later he became an instructor in the Army. After the war
ended he continued to teach in the Army for a time, but before
long his practical mind and imagination had turned to the movie
industry that had so swiftly arisen in California and had already
attracted many ambitious men and women. Soon Capra was among
the thousands knocking on the doors of Hollywood.

After a first try with struggling Columbia Pictures, he landed a
job as assistant director with Paul Gerson Company in San Francisco, producers of Toonerville comedy shorts; he also worked for
Christie Comedies on two-reelers. As a result of a one-reel comedy
he wrote, directed, made, acted, and cut for Walter Montague (the
film was released by Pathé), he was given his first big chance as a
"gag man" for Hal Roach and Mack Sennett.

He now began climbing. His next important association was with
Harry Langdon, whom he assisted in his first feature production,
Tramp, Tramp, Tramp (1926). Proved successful, their affiliation
was continued in the production of The Strong Man, one of

[5] Stage, December 1936.

the best comedies of the year, and *Long Pants*. Graduating from slapstick, Capra won the directorship of *For the Love o' Mike* for First National, a picture starring the newly recruited Broadway actress, Claudette Colbert. After this undistinguished picture was finished, Colbert returned to the Broadway stage and Capra was let out at First National.

But it had been a significant film for Capra. Recalling those days in 1936 for *Stage*,[6] he pointed out: "The fault I know now was with the story. It was Hollywood formula No. 1 and was catalogued under Rules for Romance. I am deeply grateful for that picture now. It started me thinking."

Since 1927 Capra has insisted on fresh and carefully prepared story material.

Harry Cohn of Columbia Pictures, which was now expanding and on more solid ground, re-engaged Capra to make a program picture called *The Certain Thing* (1928). As a result of its success Capra was given a long-time contract, and the Columbia-Capra alliance was launched. Capra soon became the backbone of the company with his series of successes: *The Donovan Affair, Flight*, Joe Cook in *Rain or Shine, Ladies of Leisure* (1930), *Dirigible* (1931), Jean Harlow in *Platinum Blonde* (1931), Barbara Stanwyck in *The Miracle Woman* (1931), and *Forbidden* (1932). He finally emerged as a major figure in the movie world with *American Madness, The Bitter Tea of General Yen*, and *Lady for a Day*. Almost every year thereafter has seen at least one Capra hit: the famed *It Happened One Night* (1934), which won him the award as the best director of the year; *Broadway Bill* (1934), *Mr. Deeds Goes to Town* (1936), *Lost Horizon* (1937), and *You Can't Take It with You* (1938).

Capra's best pictures are marked by a sense of humor, an awareness of American life, and a shrewd use of topical events, all these being traits developed from his early association with screen-comedy specialists. *Lady for a Day* depicted in a light vein a 1933 phenomenon of the depression: Apple Annie. *It Happened One Night* exploited the latest American innovation in living—bus travel and tourist camps—for a romantic tale. The witty *Mr. Deeds Goes to Town*

6 *Ibid.*

pitted happiness against money before a semipolitical American background.

In all of these pictures Capra has shown himself to be a professional craftsman more interested in what he has to say than in the way it is said. Cutting, composition, and rhythm in the more profound sense are rarely seen in his work. His forte is humorous characterization, the light incident, local color, and sentiment. When he has a more serious story that demands strong imaginative treatment, such as *Lost Horizon*, he is out of his realm. Gags, ingenious pieces of business, novel story twists—these are his main tools in trade. Perhaps more than any other director he could be called the O. Henry of the screen.

Lady for a Day was the first film in the Capra idiom. It is significant that Capra worked on this in association with Scenarist Robert Riskin, who is as much Capra's backbone as Capra is Columbia's. (The close association of Capra and Riskin is, next to that of John Ford and Dudley Nichols, the foremost example of that co-operation between director and writer which is fast becoming a practice in Hollywood.) *Lady for a Day* was the frank, unashamed, sentimental, straightforward kind of film that, with its homely incidents, skillful pacing, and apt dialogue, has built the Capra reputation. The story of Apple Annie's devotion to her daughter was not fresh in Hollywood story annals, but the way Capra and Riskin rewrote it it was, if not brilliant, most assuredly fresh.

The success of *It Happened One Night*, perhaps Capra's most popular picture, disconcerted Hollywood. For it was the audience that spread the praises of the picture—spread them so enthusiastically that the picture became the industry's biggest sensation, was shown again and again to a captivated public, and still enjoys occasional revivals. Despite all the Hollywood axioms, the film had little of the appeals usually regarded as prime necessities for a hit: "production value," spectacle, gorgeous clothes. It did have other qualities, such as a well-constructed story based on simple human sentiments, fresh locales, witty adult dialogue, intimacy, informality; and above all it was devoid of much of the usual Hollywood affectation. Its success, causing considerable soul-searching in Hollywood, influenced contemporary production as widely if not so deeply as the German and Russian films had in the days of the "silents."

Mr. Deeds Goes to Town, charming and homely like its predecessor, was more significant because its hero moved in a real world of economic disturbances. Mr. Longfellow Deeds, a small-town native, inherits a fortune of two million dollars from an eccentric uncle who has been killed in an auto crash in Italy. Coming to the city to control his legacy, Deeds is made a laughingstock by newspapers and especially by the star reporter, Jean Arthur, with whom he falls in love. Bitter on learning that she is mocking him, he is about to return to the country when a dispossessed farmer breaks into his house and begins to berate him for not using his fortune to help the starving. Deeds thinks the man is just another swindler trying to get some of his money. The desperate farmer suddenly pulls out a gun, but as he is about to shoot Deeds he is overcome by his emotions and breaks down weeping, apologizing for his moment of insanity and explaining his distress.

After talking with him, Deeds decides to spend his fortune on farm lands for the unemployed. For attempting to do this he is accused of being insane and brought to trial by the men who control his money. In a final, ingeniously written sequence, Deeds proves his sanity with several amusingly pointed remarks. He does it so amusingly, in fact, that the significance of the social project which motivated the scene is completely forgotten.

The merit of the film is in its characterizations and incidents. The hero is witty, whimsical, socially conscientious. His two old-maid aunts are clever caricatures; their description of Deeds as a "doodler" gave a new word to American slang. The common human habit of scribbling while in thought is cleverly utilized to show that the judge in the court is a doodler, too. The novel twists and surprises in the film are of the kind that have made Clarence Budington Kelland beloved of *Saturday Evening Post* readers, and the local color, the trial of Deeds as insane because he wishes to give away his money, and the victory of the small-town American over Big Brains from the city all appealed equally to the instincts of American audiences.

Lost Horizon was in almost every possible way opposed to the sharp human deflections that made its predecessors so popular. Where the latter had homely wit and common sense, *Lost Horizon* had a sophomoric philosophy; where they had whimsey in characterization, *Lost Horizon* had fantasy of unfantastic proportions; where they had simplicity and warmth, *Lost Horizon* had pretentiousness and vulgarity. Shangri-la itself—the mythical kingdom of the Tibetan lamas, where perfection exists through the idealization of the "middle course" and the elimination of extremes—was absurdly represented in vast, cool marble palaces and gardens suggestive of Versailles, with none of Versailles' reasons for being, and certainly in contradiction to the lamas' own philosophy of moderation.

You Can't Take It with You, Capra's latest film, an adaptation of the Pulitzer prize play, reproduced all the bland Capra touches that were so popular in his previous films. Its story of a working girl who wins the boss's son is invested with many incidents of contemporary interest which are cunningly related to the romantic progress of the stars. Crazy things such as the Big Apple impromptu with the children in the street, the fireworks episode, the harmonica playing, the gadgets and inventions, the dancing and writing—all expressive of the self-indulgent eccentricities of the Vanderhof household—all appealed to the audience's sympathies. The impassioned speeches of Lionel Barrymore against "isms" and the income tax also indicate the film's shrewd catering to the popular topics of today. All of these elements are loosely strung together cinematically even though they are ably plotted. In this picture, as in all of Capra's, the unity is created by ingenious character touches, novel twists and catch phrases, meandering and charming incidents.

Frank Capra is a fully experienced and mature director: his technique is formulated, his purpose is clear. He knows what he wants to do and what he is after. Integrity in the selection of his material, seriousness of approach, simple and unpretentious rendition, and emphasis on fresh incident, characterizations, and clever twists—these make his efforts easily appreciated, readily understood, widely enjoyed. His aims and interests fortunately coincide with commercial standards; so well, indeed, that his success has obscured his weaknesses and made a virtue of superficiality. His films, like O. Henry's stories, will be enjoyed as pastimes by millions, and as such are undeniably important.

John Ford is best known today as the director of the celebrated picture *The Informer*. Until 1935, when that film was made, Ford was hardly known outside the trade; yet for twenty-one years he had been directing, turning out good, bad, and indifferent films, changing his style in each to meet the demands of his employers. Extremely versatile and efficient, he has been regarded as a commercial asset by the studios and given all sorts of stories. In the past ten years, however, he has become more purposeful, attempting again and again to get subjects that will reflect his sincerity and craftsmanship. When such subjects have been available, he has turned out interesting pictures. *Four Sons* (1928), *Men Without Women* (1930), *Arrowsmith* (1931), *The Lost Patrol* (1934), *The Informer* (1935), *The Prisoner of Shark Island* (1936), *The Plough and the Stars* (1937) have, in varying degrees, recorded his attempts to say something important and say it well.

John Ford can be said to have found himself in his association with Dudley Nichols, the writer. In complementing each other to the best advantage they are like Frank Capra and Robert Riskin. John Ford alone made merely commercial box-office successes; the John Ford-Dudley Nichols combination, after a few desultory efforts, made above-the-average films.

The first picture of note produced by Ford and Nichols was *The Lost Patrol* (1934), a story of a small band of British cavalrymen who are lost in the Mesopotamian Desert during the war days and, one by one, die at the hands of their unseen Arab enemy. This pulp adventure film depended on the suspense of one situation and upon characterization for effect: it showed that Ford could make a film from the barest of material provided he was moved by it. One reviewer went so far as to say that it was a "virile poem, a short, impressive saga of man's courage."

This picture had many of the qualities that were to distinguish Ford's later work: a single strong situation, unity of time, place, mood, vivid characterization, colorful locale, suspense. Ford and

Nichols strove to achieve that "wholeness of mood and effort" which has been their professed aim ever since.

It was reported at the time *The Lost Patrol* was made that Ford waived his salary in favor of a percentage agreement on the film's actual earnings because he wanted so much to make it. Such zeal suggested that at last John Ford had awakened from his indifference and intended to make films about which he cared. Direct, unembroidered, without a love story, *The Lost Patrol* no doubt surprised the producers when it turned out to be a success—a success created, one might add, not by advance ballyhoo but, as in the case of *It Happened One Night*, by word-of-mouth advertising. Its enthusiastic reception spurred Ford and Nichols to undertake a story they had been trying for five years to induce the studios to make: *The Informer*. This film proved to be one of the most important contributions to films since sound. "Unrivaled in the 1935 cinema," Sennwald said of it in *The New York Times*.[7]

Known as a "sleeper"—the trade jargon for a film that is made and released without even the studios being aware of it—*The Informer* was more or less sneaked into production by Ford and Nichols. Instead of salary Ford took a percentage of the profits. The production is said to have cost $218,000, a relatively small sum; $5,000 was paid for the rights to Liam O'Flaherty's novel. The picture took only three weeks to shoot, and Ford declared it was the easiest he ever made. And no wonder: he says he dreamed of the film for five years.

The story was not "Hollywood," to use a descriptive adjective used by Ford himself. It depicted the events during one night of the Sinn Fein rebellion against British imperialism in 1922. Gypo Nolan (Victor McLaglen) betrays his friend, Frankie McPhillip, for twenty pounds, and the consequence of the betrayal is McPhillip's death. To protect himself, Gypo accuses another man, then blusteringly tries to forget while spending the blood money on whiskey and his "friends." Taken before a rebel court of inquiry, he finally breaks down, but he succeeds in escaping from the court and hides in the room of the girl for whom he got the money, a street-walker. But she has no respect for an informer—". . . you'll never know what you've done to me." When he falls asleep, she goes to the commandant of the revolutionary organization, pleads unavailingly for Gypo's life, and unwittingly gives him away. He is sought out by the revolutionaries, pursued, and, mortally wounded, finally drags himself into a church to die.

Under Ford's compact direction the film was the tragedy of a stool pigeon told in a somber key, dark shadows, muffled voices, carousing, night sounds. Mood, pace, character, and sound are blended into a fluid unity which, from the first scenes of fluttering newspapers to the last scenes of the shooting and death of Gypo, holds the spectator taut. Image moves into image succinctly, at the right time and with the right tone, through the rhythm of the direction. A slow, restrained tempo in acting and cutting deepens the sense of tragedy and ominousness; tension and suspense are built on mental rather than physical excitement and action. The heaviness of the slow pace is enforced by the photography and emphasized by the shadowy, dense Dublin fog and the night that envelops and pervades the film throughout. The nightmarish sequence of Gypo's carousing about the town with his blood money was, as Herman G. Weinberg pointed out,[8] "reminiscent . . . [of] Joyce's famous night-town sequence in Ulysses."

Ford's selective control over the camera is always apparent. There is, for instance, the visual presentation of the police notice offering a reward for Frankie (it is not read aloud); then the suggestion of what is going to happen, as the notice flutters along the pavement until it clings to Gypo's feet; finally the eloquent symbolism of the sight of it burning, curling up and distorting the picture of Frankie's face.

The subjective approach to Gypo's character is an uncommon achievement of the objective camera. Most directors can visualize only an objective use of an objective medium; this accounts in part for the stereotyped presentation of material by most Hollywood directors. In The Informer we see Gypo standing outside a tourist office, looking at the advertisements there. We follow his eyes as they lower to the model of a liner. This image dissolves into the deck of a real ship on which are Gypo and Kate, dressed as bride-

groom and bride. Everyone understands instantly the secret dream
transpiring in Gypo's mind. At another time in this film Gypo
returns to the place where, from the poster on the wall (which is
now bare), he first got the idea of betraying his friend. We are
carried along with his emotions, as we see the poster take shape on
the wall, with the face of Frankie now accusing and angry. Again
we see into Gypo's mind when, drunk, he approaches a girl, a
stranger, whose features (through double exposure) change and resolve into Kate's.

The use of sound is one of *The Informer's* most vital features:
noises as well as monologue are imaginatively used. Ford, in fact,
uses sounds not only to intensify the drama but for cinematic transitions. For example, after Gypo informs on his friend, there is suddenly heard the ticking of a clock: we have a prescience of relentless evil. The ticking continues into the next shots: Frankie at home
with his mother and sister; there another clock continues the sound
and thus welds the transition structurally. Later the tapping of a
blind man's stick when Gypo is escaping from the rebels' headquarters once more takes up the sound, in this way recalling an earlier
sequence of McPhillip's betrayal. Through the sound repetition, the
association of ideas is dramatically and instantly communicated.
Moreover the rhythmic flow of the whole is sustained.

Inner monologue is cinematically used with effect, less as a stunt
and more as a necessity. As we see Gypo looking dreamily at the
model of the steamship, we hear Frankie's voice warning him that
he is lost, that without the aid of his friend's brains, Gypo is helpless. Such a subjective use of monologue is profound in its implications, for it opens up a whole new sphere in the application of
sound.

Symbolism, a device too often avoided entirely or used so bla-
tantly as to be ineffective, was utilized in this film in a subtle and
striking manner. Dudley Nichols [9] explained,

> Symbolism is only good when the audience is not aware of it.
> So when we had to deal with a character like Gypo, who was a
> traitor out of ignorance, out of smallness of mind, we thought we
> would make it the state of his mind . . . as the story progresses

[9] *National Board of Review Magazine*, March 1936.

he is overtaken by conscience slowly working up out of his uncon-
scious mind. We gave that a symbol of a blind man. So that when
Gypo first gets his money, his 20 pounds, as he starts away, as
he comes out he sees the blind man, seizes him by the throat and
realizes he is blind. It is as if he has seen his own conscience. He
passes his hand over his eyes and hurries away and always the
tapping of the blind man's stick is behind him. I dare say nobody
was aware that it was a symbol, but it very definitely was.

Every small item in the picture is used to intensify the moment;
nothing appears that is not made significant. A richness resulting
from economy is the paradoxical result.

The film failed only at those points where Ford allowed the
dialogue to take precedence over visual movement. This accounts
for the relative weakness of the last court-martial scenes and the
sequences in Kate's room. Here words were substituted for pictures,
and a let-down was the result. As a whole, however, *The Informer*
was a distinguished effort and was unanimously named the best film
of the year by the film critics in New York. "No movie of equal
seriousness and sincerity has appeared during the year" was the
remark of James Shelley Hamilton in the *National Board of Review Magazine*.[10]

Now in the limelight as a distinguished combination, John Ford
and Dudley Nichols subsequently collaborated in other productions,
Mary of Scotland (1936), *The Plough and the Stars* (1937), and
Stagecoach (1939). John Ford has also made, without Nichols, *The
Whole Town's Talking* (1935), *The Prisoner of Shark Island*
(1936), *Four Men and a Prayer*, *Hurricane*, *Wee Willie Winkie*,
and *Submarine Patrol* (all last four, 1938). These efforts were pot-
boilers all, only *The Plough and the Stars* and *The Prisoner of
Shark Island* being at all provocative and interesting.

The Plough and the Stars, an adaptation of O'Casey's play, was
an honest attempt to create something vital and profound, but it
was unfortunately aborted by the pressure of commercial interests
and professional censors. Some understanding of Ford's struggle
against these insensitive but powerful forces can be gleaned from
Emanuel Eisenberg's interview [11] with him before the picture was
made:

[10] January 1936.   [11] *New Theatre*, April 1936.

We [Nichols and Ford] did *The Informer*. Does that make it easier to go ahead with O'Casey's *The Plough and the Stars*, which we want to do after *Mary of Scotland?* Not for a second. They *may* let us do it as a reward for being good boys. Meanwhile we're fighting to have the Abbey Players imported intact and we're fighting the censors and fighting the so-called financial wizards at every point.

The result was compromise on both sides. In return for starring Barbara Stanwyck, Ford got Barry Fitzgerald and Dennis O'Dea of the Irish Abbey Players. The social point of the original was destroyed; a "free" transcription was used. It was said that Ford steadfastly refused to see the picture after he was through with it, for the studio had inserted more "love interest." As Robert Stebbins [12] observed, "To all intents and purposes Ford and Nichols have yet to make *The Plough and the Stars*."

Many moments in the film, nevertheless, had the flavor of *The Informer* and showed Ford's individual ability. Scenes dealing with group events—the shifting from tenement to tenement, the post-office barricade, the funeral procession, and the flight over the housetops—were executed skillfully, although appearing too generalized and even stylized to be consistent with the realism of the rest. Some moments, such as the activity in the pub and the drunken looting, were eloquently humorous, while the panorama of Irish characters—peppery Fluther, the Socialist Covey, the idealistic leaders, housewives on the barricades, boys sniping—were saturated with virility and native Irish spice. The film was, on the whole, a mixture of some good Ford and some bad Hollywood.

The Prisoner of Shark Island, a melodrama in which Dr. Mudd, the innocent doctor who repaired Booth's leg after he had shot Lincoln, is railroaded to the prison on Shark Island, also had some of the qualities of *The Informer*. The murkiness, the suspense, the swift movement that characterized the Irish film also pervaded this one, although its unity, relationships, and characterizations were far more forced to fit the Hollywood mold. Many scenes were made vivid by Ford's feeling for unusual compositions. He is not afraid to shift the camera viewpoint from the eye level, to shoot from

12 *New Theatre*, June 1937.

below or above, to move into a scene and around characters, and to light a set for the mood and realism. This knack with the camera, lighting and composition, saved a film that otherwise would have been one more stereotype.

Ford himself is most aware of how good or bad his films are. Like Lubitsch and some others, he cuts his pictures whenever he is allowed. When he inserts in a film something he does not believe is right, it is because he must compromise. Ford knows so well the medium in which he is working that he rarely leaves the composition, camera angle, lighting continuity and editing to highly skilled technicians as almost all other directors do. Whenever possible he participates in all phases of production and believes that from first to last the picture must be seen through by the same group of workers. He expressed some of the difficulties facing the director in the Hollywood studio: [13]

. . . it's a constant battle to do something fresh. First they want you to repeat your last picture. . . . Then they want you to continue whatever vein you succeeded in with the last picture. You're a comedy director, or a spectacle director, or a melodrama director. You show 'em you've been each of these in turn, and effectively, too. So they grant you range. Another time they want you to knock out something *another* studio's gone and cleaned up with. . . . There's a new kind of public that wants more honest pictures.

From his own words and from the material he has chosen to deal with, it can be seen that John Ford looks upon the world today with a new social viewpoint that has given his film work fresh drive and inspiration. The acclaim that greeted *The Informer*, proving that there are always audiences for serious artistic efforts, has heartened him considerably. In association with Dudley Nichols, Ford looms as one of the most promising motion picture directors in Hollywood today. He has not only King Vidor's earnestness, versatility and craftsmanship but as sincere a purpose and social awareness of the times. He has displayed a distinct flair in the use of the camera, care in composition, a feeling for mood, a deft cutting style, an appreciation of movement as the prime element of the movies, an eye for colorful characterization, and a great ease in the manipula-

[13] *New Theatre*, April 1936.

tion of all these elements that is the mark of the accomplished. Not yet a great director, but always a proficient and once exceptional, John Ford may yet produce a great picture.

Other contemporary directors, no less commercially proficient and who occasionally also produce arresting pictures, are Mervyn LeRoy, Lewis Milestone, William Dieterle, Michael Curtiz, Rowland Brown, William Wyler, William Wellman, William K. Howard, W. S. Van Dyke, Gregory La Cava, Frank Borzage, George Cukor, and Sidney Franklin.

Mervyn LeRoy, one of the most prolific, turns out films swiftly and competently. He has a vigorous style that deals only in essentials, and this style, when it works on material of real import as in *Little Caesar* (1931), *I Am a Fugitive from a Chain Gang* (1932), and *They Won't Forget* (1937), shows strength and conviction. *Little Caesar* was a tight, well-knit portrait of an egomaniac, bleakly realistic. Its straightforward, economic cutting, with each sequence growing out of a particular detail, provided an organizational unity that only a first-rate craftsman could achieve. Excellent in its feeling for pace (dialogue was kept terse, images were cut to the essentials) and sharp in characterization (Edward G. Robinson has ever since been tagged as a gangster), the film was one of the best of the gangster cycle, making LeRoy's reputation as well as its leading performer's.

I Am a Fugitive had the same succinct quality: it spoke simply and to the point. Its scenes of brutality, the road gangs, the escape of the convicts, the sterling character work by Muni, were all notable. There was, too, its unforgettable last shot, in which Muni in the half-darkness, replying to his sweetheart's question "How do you live?", hisses, "I steal!" and then recedes into blackness. The film's deep social message, its unrelenting singleness of purpose, its elimination of all comic concessions, and the general high tenor of its exposé made it a genuinely moving production and established LeRoy as a genuine talent.

They Won't Forget was even more forthright. A grim and scathing portrayal of prejudice, intolerance, and mob fury in the deep South, its story progresses with a newsreel objectivity that gives its incidents the reality if not the intensity of Lang's *Fury*. The depiction of Redwine, the terrified Negro janitor who discovers the body of the murdered girl in the school's elevator shaft, is one of the few instances in American films in which the fear and oppression that fill the life of the Southern Negro is strikingly told.

Other outstanding touches are the concluding scenes. Hale, the framed victim, is being rushed by train from the lynch mob in the Southern city to a place of safety. But a lynch posse board the train, overpower Hale's guards, and drag him to their waiting cronies. As he shrieks for help, another train speeds by, its rumble and roar drowning out Hale's cries.

This kidnapping scene is followed by one in which symbolism is used most expressively. The shot reveals a mailbag suspended from a crosstree beside the railroad tracks. At the moment of the lynching of Hale, a train roars by, emitting an unearthly shriek as a steel hook extended from the mail car catches the mail sack and whirls it away. So the unseen horrible deed is summed up far more tellingly than would be possible in an actual scene of lynching. Such imaginative touches reveal LeRoy at his best.

Never a strident director, always an efficient one, "as good as his script," Mervyn LeRoy can produce good films when he is given good stories.

Although he had served in every production capacity in Hollywood since 1919, it was not until 1930 with his *All Quiet on the Western Front* that Lewis Milestone became acknowledged as a prime American film talent. The film was one of the few serious attempts at a realistic approach to the World War. The "girl-meets-boy" clichés that had cheapened *The Big Parade* were non-existent; the drama was kept within the bounds of its theme: a critical recapitulation of the slaughter of innocents. Sincerity and integrity shone through the artificial settings and photography, the lengthy and oftentimes over-repetitious rendering. Many instances were eloquent and moving indictments of the emotional and physical destructiveness of war: the sequence of the dead boy's cherished boots being taken over by his comrade, and the celebrated closing scene of the hand of the young soldier reaching out from the trenches for a butterfly only to fall limp on being shot. Such laconic and mature comments on a serious subject were symptomatic of the emotional qualities of the film as a whole.

The film appeared at a time when sound was still new and film makers were groping for a correct application of the added element. It is to the credit of Milestone that he conceived *All Quiet on the Western Front* on a visual basis; he subordinated dialogue to the image and used sound effects simply, fluently and realistically. A flair for cutting that he was later to exploit more cunningly, was also apparent in the film, especially in the machine-gun episode. Here Milestone intercut moving shots (taken from a crane) of soldiers being shot down as they run across a field, with still shots of the machine gunners. The repetition of moving and still shots created a rhythmic visual pattern which, when combined with the rhythmic rat-tat-tat of the guns, made for an intensity of effect.

The vital theme and impressive technical range of the film overwhelmed critics of the day: contemporary movies were for the most part vapid in content and static in treatment. Not as great as many claimed it to be, *All Quiet on the Western Front* stands out as a noteworthy achievement in the roster of more serious Hollywood efforts.

Previously to this sound film, Milestone's picaresque *Two Arabian Knights* (1927-1928) and his bootlegging exposé *The Racket* (1928) had called attention to him as a competent and resourceful director with a penchant for acid, realistic touches and rowdy characterizations. All these qualities came to the fore in 1931 in his second sound film, the rapid-fire newspaper melodrama, *The Front Page*. This, like *All Quiet on the Western Front*, was one of the first talkies to recapture the spirit and movement of the silent film. So artfully paced was its dialogue, so swift were its cuts, that Harry Alan Potamkin declared [14] that with this film Milestone became "the second American director since Griffith to advance a major strategy." Exaggerated though the tribute was, it nevertheless indicated Milestone's directorial abilities. A robust film if not a great one, *The Front Page* excelled most of the talkies of its day by sheer treatment. The speedy delivery of lines and business and the re-emphasis upon cutting as a prime structural element—dialogue is

[14] *Vanity Fair*, March 1932.

clipped, curt, direct, faster than normal, as are the players' gestures and movements—made the film a model of mobility for confused directors who did not know yet how to handle sound.

Since *The Front Page* Milestone has turned out a number of unimportant pictures with only scattered touches of interest. *Rain* (1932) had some of the hard-boiled quality of his *Two Arabian Knights*. *Hallelujah, I'm a Bum* (1933) experimented with rhythmic dialogue but lacked the finesse of a Lubitsch to "pull it off." *The Captain Hates the Sea* (1934), *Paris in Spring* (1935), and *Anything Goes* (1936) were all routine. With *The General Died at Dawn* (1936), however, Milestone's knack for crisp dialogue, robust characterization, and movement values was once more apparent. Melodramatic as the film was for the most part, it disclosed again his feeling for camera play, composition, and mounting, and proved again that he has ability if he has the right sort of material. Competence alone, without the spirit of strong themes, soon degenerates. Like many directors Milestone needs subject matter that is real and that he can believe in.

William Dieterle and Michael Curtiz are two of the foreign directors who like Lang have gained places in America since the arrival of sound. Both are serious film makers, extremely able and versatile; their pictures often have something to say and are marked sporadically by genuine discernment and feeling. Dieterle's *The Last Flight* (1932) and *Fog over 'Frisco* (1933) showed a rousing command of the medium; *The Story of Louis Pasteur* (1936), *Emile Zola* (1937), and *Blockade* (1938) showed, in addition, deep social purpose. Curtiz's *Cabin in the Cotton* (1932), *Black Fury* (1935), and *Four Daughters* (1938) were adroit, and their content for the most part was of social consequence. Both directors' work, with its forthrightness and economy of means, is best characterized by Dieterle's own advice to directors: [15] "Get the audience like a lion! Pounce upon them and hold them fast. Don't tease and lie with them. . . ."

Rowland Brown, another competent director, appeared full-grown in the film world with his first film, *Quick Millions* (1931). In this picture his freshness, intelligence, and surprising grasp of

[15] *The New York Times*, September 26, 1937.

cutting technique overshadowed the work of most contemporaries of longer repute. *Quick Millions* was highly compressed, swiftly paced, alert in its treatment of the gangster against a social background, and extraordinarily adult in its conception, editing, and appeal. Rowland Brown was singled out as "a cinematic talent who will be exciting to watch."

His second film, *Hell's Highway* (1932), was awaited eagerly but, although timely in its attack on outrages in convict camps, failed to come up to the promise and standard set by *Quick Millions*. A subsequent film, however, *Blood Money* (1933), showed again Brown's devastatingly honest character depictions (especially bold was the nymphomaniac), his cutting for intensity and movement, and his knowledge of gangsterdom, which could spring only from actual experience.

Since then Brown has written several scripts of note that have been mishandled by other directors, including *The Devil Is a Sissy* and *Boy of the Streets* (1937). Again and again reported in the news as the director of forthcoming pictures, he is invariably removed from the directorship before their completion. All sorts of rumors have therefore sprung up regarding Brown's unique capabilities and his insistence on doing things his own way or not at all. Although there is no question about his talent, it has not been seen since *Quick Millions*.

The films of William Wyler, William Wellman, and William K. Howard are always good, rarely touched with stage conventions. These directors are notable for their seriousness, economy, efficiency, and straightforwardness; they show little concern for dialogue as such, and their method is closely related to the silent technique. Their films are marked by facility and versatility, and when they have topical material they treat it forcefully.

William Wyler, one-time assistant to von Stroheim, not only is a proficient film maker but has an eye for characterization and human relationships. His films steadily grow in stature: his content becomes deeper, his execution more thoughtful, his problems more vital and relevant. Purposefulness lifts his films higher and higher out of the ordinary. *Counsellor-at-Law* (1933), *Dodsworth* (1936), *These Three* (1936), *Dead End* (1937), *Jezebel* (1938), and *Wuth-*

ering Heights (1939) reveal his increasing social awareness, sharper sensitivity and penetration into character, and conscious effort at organic unity that springs from a real and serious interest in the film medium. Wyler is a director of whom one expects a really exceptional film some day.

William Wellman came out of the property ranks and into prominence with *Wings* (1927), but it was *The Public Enemy* (1931) that first proved him to be a stimulating, even dynamic director. His *Wild Boys of the Road* (1933), although inferior to its Russian inspiration, *Road to Life*, was hard-hitting. *The President Vanishes* (1935), the third in his topical efforts, was daring; its high point was a visual parallel between the munitions makers and vultures. *A Star Is Born* and *Nothing Sacred* (both 1937) were satirical, swift-moving, and at moments vigorous. Terse and breezy, his films have a journalistic zest that is always stimulating.

A director of more serious purpose is William K. Howard. Since his *White Gold* (1927), which stamped him as a director of talent, and *The Valiant* (1928), he has been identified with restraint in treatment and a bristling eagerness for significant material. Unafraid to speak out, he has stated time and again since 1930 that "Hollywood . . . is . . . like one of the old feudal states. . . . We're built over the same cesspool of politics, intrigue, lies and fashion." [16] This is the protest of every director who is more than a hack, who can turn out significant films when he is given the opportunity. Howard's *Transatlantic* (1931) and *The Power and the Glory* (1933), indicating an intelligent competence in construction and emotional conviction, were both uncommon films.

W. S. Van Dyke and Gregory La Cava have directed every sort of story from Westerns to musicals and are considered skillful if not too inventive craftsmen. They are adaptable, and whatever they undertake is certain of an interesting though too often a casual rendition. Each has made a few outstanding pictures but seems too willing to compromise his talents. Their facility has given their best efforts a spontaneity which has kept them at the movie forefront.

W. S. Van Dyke's best efforts perhaps have been *White Shadows in the South Seas* (1928, in collaboration with Flaherty), *Eskimo*

[16] *Film Spectator*, November 8, 1930

(1933), and *The Thin Man* (1934). He is a swift worker, and each of these pictures has had a racy, straightforward, apparently effortless style. A light touch has been associated with Van Dyke's name ever since.

Gregory La Cava, ex-cartoonist and one of the pioneer animators of the screen, rose into prominence with the heavily sentimental *Symphony of Six Million* (1932). (He already had dozens of pictures to his credit.) But it was *The Half-Naked Truth* (1932) that first did justice to his knack for fast-moving light comedy. *Gabriel over the White House* (1933) and *Private Worlds* (1935) showed him to be equally adroit with serious material. *My Man Godfrey* (1936) and *Stage Door* (1938) secured his reputation as a screen humorist and moved comedian W. C. Fields to concede that, next to his own, La Cava had the finest comedy mind in pictures. Regardless of what may be said of that comparison, La Cava is best as a light-comedy director; to such comedy he brings a naturalness that arises from his impromptu methods. Perhaps more than any other director except Chaplin, La Cava makes up his pictures as he goes along. He begins with a general idea, like Sennett, and develops the scene and situation on the set. Such a procedure, he feels, gives his films freshness and verve.

Clarence Brown and Frank Borzage are the screen's leading romanticists. In pictures for over twenty years, they are hard-boiled about film making and go about it rather conventionally. They believe story is the first and main essential of a movie, and they depend considerably upon their performers for effects. "Big directors" of little films, they are perhaps more "sure-fire" than other directors. Their budgets are invariably large, their stories expensive, their stars Hollywood's most important; and "production values" make their pictures seem more impressive than they are. Yet each director has occasionally made better-than-average films. Called "Garbo's Man Friday" since his *Flesh and the Devil* (1926), Clarence Brown has also directed *Night Flight* (1933) and *Of Human Hearts* (1938). All three pictures were notable for their freshness, aptitude for characterization, and utilization of cinematic fundamentals. Frank Borzage's best films, *Seventh Heaven* (1928), *Bad Girl* (1931), *A Farewell to Arms* (1933), *No Greater Glory* (1934),

James Cagney as the idol of the "Dead End" kids, in the picture, *Angels with Dirty Faces* (1938-39), directed by Michael Curtiz. Ruthlessness and violence expressive of the attitude of the 1930's are at the roots of this film.

American Documentary Film

The City (1939) an argument for city planning, significant of the new interest in the documentary form and the new tendency to combine entertainment with enlightenment.

American Documentary Film

and *Little Man, What Now?* (1934) also displayed a sound knowledge of movie making and a flair for the poignant—which, in his lesser work, too often descended to bathos. These men have let their potentialities go unrealized. Borzage's statement in an interview [17] in 1937 clearly sums up their artistic credo:

The trouble with most directors is that they take the whole thing too seriously. . . . Making a motion picture consists merely of going onto a set, training a camera on competent players and letting them enact a good script.

Although George Cukor has been directing pictures only since sound and Sidney Franklin practically grew up with movies, the qualities of these directors are fairly similar. Their productions are carefully planned and lavish, but marked by theatricalism. Like Brown and Borzage they get only the highest-priced story or play material, the biggest stars, the most expert technicians; no expense is spared to make their enterprises outstanding. It is, however, only by their fine taste and attention to acting that their films are distinctive. Their renditions are for the most part static, suggesting the stage plays and stage tradition from which their style stems.

George Cukor, who came to movies as a dialogue director for Milestone in *All Quiet on the Western Front,* has made such successful pictures as *A Bill of Divorcement* (1932), *Our Betters* (1933), *Little Women* (1933), *Dinner at Eight* (1934), *David Copperfield* (1935), *Romeo and Juliet* (1936), *Camille* (1937), and *Holiday* (1938). All have gentility; all show painstaking care with dialogue, characterization, details of setting, costume, and movement of plot; in technique all are scrupulously traditional. The same can be said about Sidney Franklin's *Smilin' Through* (1932), *The Guardsman* (1933), *The Barretts of Wimpole Street* (1934), and *The Good Earth* (1937). Although both directors are meticulous workers, their elaborate approach is narrow and confined, with only occasional feeling for the movie medium as such.

There are in addition to these directors a large number of other able commercial craftsmen who show talent for a particular type of story: Leo McCarey (*Love Affair,* 1939), Wesley Ruggles (*True Confession,* 1938), Mitchell Leisen (*Midnight,* 1939), and Henry

[17] *The New York World-Telegram,* April 3, 1937.

Koster (*Three Smart Girls*, 1937), for light romantic comedy; Richard Wallace (*John Meade's Woman*, 1937), John Cromwell (*Algiers*, 1938), Anatole Litvak (*Confessions of a Nazi Spy*, 1939), Edmund Goulding (*Dark Victory*, 1939), and Jack Conway (*Too Hot to Handle*, 1938) for straight dramatic pictures; Edward H. Griffith (*Café Society*, 1938), George Stevens (*Vivacious Lady*, 1938), and Robert Florey (*King of Alcatraz*, 1938) for romantic drama; Frank Lloyd (*Wells Fargo*, 1937), for historical costume dramas; and Victor Fleming (*Captains Courageous*, 1937) for "action" pictures.

Since the twenties, which brought such directors as Lubitsch, Murnau, and Seastrom to Hollywood, there has been no new concerted "foreign invasion." Hollywood, with more talented directors than any other country, believed for a time that foreign films can teach it little. After the coming of sound it was doubted that even first-rate foreign directors could direct players in a language with which they have little acquaintance. But on both scores recent events have proved the contrary. The European studios were completely revitalized with the coming of sound; not since before the World War have they been so fruitful as they are today. England, particularly, and more recently France, have made pictures of such high merit that Hollywood has once again become fearful of foreign competition. Between the two English-speaking countries an amazing amount of talent has been exchanged. For a time it became customary for American players and directors to go to England and make at least one picture a year. Outstanding films by Hitchcock, Victor Saville, Anthony Asquith, and Robert Stevenson are appearing in America with regularity and are setting high standards. France in the past few years has produced a number of important if not great directors and pictures, among the former being René Clair, Anatole Litvak, Jean Renoir, Benoit-Levy, and Julien Duvivier. Only Litvak and Duvivier have come to Hollywood to work on films; Litvak with good results (*The Sisters, Confessions of a Nazi Spy*). Germany, Austria, and Sweden have not produced any directors or films of note, but Soviet Russia continues to send over excellent sound pictures.

The vast capital necessary to make a sound film has restricted individual experimentation and has kept the movie in America almost entirely a commercial undertaking. Since sound, however, a few films have made daring explorations of the medium and have touched on more profound subject matter than Hollywood will usually risk. In the vanguard are Joris Ivens of Contemporary Historians and Paul Strand, Leo Hurwitz, Lionel Berman, John Howard Lawson, Robert Stebbins, David Wolf, Eugene Hill, and Irving Lerner of Frontier Films. Within the short period of their operations they have already produced seven films of most progressive tendencies: *The Spanish Earth, The 400,000,000,* by the former, and *Heart of Spain, China Strikes Back, People of the Cumberland, Return to Life,* and the as yet untitled film about civil liberties called *Production No. 5* by the latter.

Prominent in the educational realm for their attempts to project esthetic values as well as information are Pare Lorentz, with his government-sponsored *The Plough That Broke the Plains* and *The River;* Oscar Serlin, Ralph Steiner and Willard Van Dyke and their city planning film, *The City;* Leo Seltzer and Elaine Basil, with their study of social hygiene, *From Hand to Mouth;* Nancy Naumburg, with *Taxi;* Julian Roffman, Robert Del Ducca, and Victor Kandel, with their series *Get Your Money's Worth;* Lewis Jacobs, with *Hopi,* a documentary of the Hopi Indians, and *Tree Trunk to Head,* a study of a sculptor at work.

Other directors more frankly experimental include J. Sibley Watson, with his two notable pictures *The Fall of the House of Usher* and *Lot in Sodom;* Josef Berne, with *Dawn to Dawn,* which attempts a mood reminiscent of Sherwood Anderson; Mary E. Bute and Ted Nemeth, with their "seeing-sound synchronies": *Anitra's Dance, O Evening Star,* and *Parabola;* Emlen Etting, with his *Oramunde,* "a cinematic poem"; and John Flory and Theodore Huff, with *Mr. Motorboat's Last Stand,* a satirical fantasy.

XXIV

WALT DISNEY: VIRTUOSO

OF all the directors in motion pictures today, Walt Disney is perhaps the most renowned and acclaimed. Undaunted by Hollywood superstitions, undeterred by money needs, Disney has brought to American films a personal touch, a zeal for quality, an appreciation of artistry, and a disdain that is almost a fear of the "formula" picture. That his convictions have been matched by a distinct talent has been aptly and fortunately proved.

Disney has made his animated cartoon perhaps the finest expression of motion picture art in contemporary America: this despite the fact that so far only one of the hundreds of Disney cartoons has been of considerable length. His pieces have brought unanimous praise from artists, intellectuals, children, workers, and everyday people the world over, being singled out even above superior dramatic films. As a humorist in *The Saturday Evening Post* [1] put it, "Americanism: Spending millions of dollars to make spectacular movies; sticking through them to see Mickey Mouse."

In the realm of films that combine sight, sound, and color Disney is still unsurpassed. The wise heir of forty years of film tradition, he consummates the cinematic contributions of Melies, Porter, Griffith, and the Europeans. He has done more with the film medium since it added sound and color than any other director, creating a form that is of great and vital consequence not only for what it is but for what it portends. He is the first of the sight-sound-color film virtuosos, and the fact that he is still young and still developing makes him an exciting and important figure to watch.

[1] May 21, 1938.

Disney not only is the pace setter in his own particular specialty, cartoon animation, but in skill and imagination he outranks even the craftsmen in the realistic story-telling business. His remarkable ability to produce hit after hit without repeating himself or consolidating his successes into clichés speaks for his integrity as well as his ambition. No one knows how far, under the circumstances, Disney may yet go—or if, perhaps, he now is in his prime.

When Melies was being acclaimed for his "magical effects," Disney was in kindergarten. At the time Griffith was making momentous innovations in film expression, Disney was a young man working in Kansas City as an obscure commercial artist. When Melies had long been forgotten and Griffith was in his decline, Disney began turning out advertising slides for theatres. It was this occupation in 1920 that suggested experiments with animation. He now decided what he wanted to do, and he started doing it. Thereafter his career was comparatively quick and direct in development.

With several Kansas City cartoonists Disney made his first series of animated cartoons—fairy-tale pictures: *Little Red Riding Hood, Jack the Giant Killer, The Town Musician of Bremen, The Three Bears, Goldilocks, Alice in Cartoonland.* These were sold and distributed non-theatrically. With the money saved from these first ventures, Disney went to Hollywood. For the next two years he made animated cartoon series about Alice and Oswald the Rabbit, which were released with Universal pictures by an independent distributor. Finally deciding to push out in new directions, Disney asked the distributor for additional money. On being refused the money, he acted with the dispatch, daring, and independence he has shown ever since: he broke relations with the distributor and launched out entirely on his own.

Disney and his wife, a former cartoonist, now began the creation of the new character that was to bring him world fame. With little artistic self-consciousness, working in a field that was generally disdained, Disney and his wife patiently completed two pictures starring Mortimer Mouse. But just now a revolution was taking place in the movie industry as a result of the synchronization of Al Jolson's voice in *The Jazz Singer.* The animated cartoons were, consequently, overlooked. Undiscouraged, Disney made a third Mortimer

Mouse cartoon, to which he added sound: *Steamboat Willie*. When it was presented at the Colony Theatre in New York in September 1928, it won immediate success. Disney thus was launched as a new American director of importance, and Mickey Mouse—for so the name had been shortened—began to build his reputation as an international figure.

In the next three years Disney, growing ever more skillful and inventive, made ninety pictures. To the Mickey Mouse series he added the *Silly Symphony* series and many new characters. When three color process became practicable he was one of the first to use it, and instead of hampering him color brought new values to his inimitable style and, like sound, intensified his form. His swift rise since then is common knowledge. He won the Motion Picture Academy Award for distinction in his field six years with *Flowers and Trees* (1932), *The Three Little Pigs* (1933), *The Tortoise and the Hare* (1934), *Three Orphan Kittens* (1935), *The Country Cousin* (1936), and *Snow White and the Seven Dwarfs* (1938). Such a record has never been approached by any other director. In 1938 he received honorary degrees from the University of Southern California, Yale, and Harvard, and in 1939 the New York Metropolitan Museum of Art finally endorsed his artistry by displaying an original water color from one of his films.

When one speaks of Disney, it is his chief creation, Mickey Mouse, that most readily comes to mind. Although Disney has created an entire menagerie of characters, including dogs, ducks, squirrels, insects, birds, and flowers, Mickey is still the world's favorite. In the eleven years of his existence he has played gaucho, deckhand, farmer, impresario, teamster, musician, explorer, swimmer, cowboy, fireman, convict, pioneer, taxi driver, castaway, fisherman, cyclist, Arab, football player, inventor, jockey, storekeeper, camper, sailor, Gulliver, boxer, exterminator, skater, poloist, circus performer, plumber, chemist, magician, hunter, detective, clock cleaner, Hawaiian, carpenter, driver, trapper, horseman, whaler, and tailor.

Always a conquering hero, Mickey has accumulated the greatest army of followers in the world. Whether he is called Michael Maus (Germany), Michel Souris (France), Miki Kuchi (Japan), Miguel Ratoncito (Spain), Topolino (Italy), Mikel Mus (Greece), Musse

Pigg (Sweden), El Ratón Miguelito (Central America), or El Ratón Mickey (Argentina), he is the one universal movie idol besides Chaplin that has captivated through laughter the hearts of the world. Thrown out of Yugoslavia for conspiring against a throne (part of his adventures in a comic strip), and barred in Hitler Germany because he was accompanied by a brigade of animals wearing Uhlan helmets—considered a reflection on the Nazi German army— he could not be kept out of even these countries for long. His popularity outranks that of kings and dictators; he is the best-known figure of the twentieth century.

Disney is the modern Aesop. Like the ancient sage, he deals in fables, often reshuffling Aesop's own but more often using the older tales to create something more contemporary. Today, when the real world is full of ruthless conflict, it is significant that Disney's films more than anyone else's (perhaps because he is the ablest of all) are full of ruthless conflict. Their violence, reaching extremes of destruction in *Mickey's Polo Game* and *Who Killed Cock Robin?*, finds its counterpart in the brutality of the modern world. Mickey is almost pure physical force. Although he is kindhearted, he is all nerves and muscle; he bangs, knocks, punches, mutilates, annihilates every obstacle in the path of his desires. In this respect he resembles Popeye the Sailor, his lesser rival in films. Of late it has been said that Donald Duck, of the inflammable temper and vicious tongue, is gradually usurping the popularity of Mickey. Is this happening because Donald's desperation is closer to the time spirit than Mickey's triumphant aggressiveness?

It is disturbing to find such reflections of the real world in the fantastic realm of Disney's characters, but the paradox is not so strained as it might seem. Though Disney's scene and characters are mythical, the events that transpire in his cartoons have their basis in actuality. In an age in which might is so widely condoned, respected, and even glorified, the element of force is manifest in all contemporary mores. As the world-wide popularity of his films proves, Disney is a most acute if unwitting interpreter of the violent spirit of the times. Declares Jay Franklin,[2]

[2] *New York Evening Post*, February 22, 1938.

If Charlie Chaplin's pathetic "little guy" was the symbol of the last 20 years of social confusion, Walt Disney's animated fables may well supply a key to our progress during the next 20 years.

Despite his clear mirroring of the time spirit, Disney depreciates the insinuations of his films. He has emphatically denied that they have any ulterior motives, any philosophy of life, any hidden political beliefs, or any of the social or psychological intentions. But in view of their parallels to human behavior, it seems impossible to regard them as unrelated to contemporary society.

Take one celebrated instance of Disney's contemporaneity. *The Three Little Pigs*, appearing at the low point of the depression, was at once associated with the economic situation. To many people this film suggested that only by building an "impregnable house" can the "big bad wolf" of hunger and fear be kept out. In a time of spreading bank failures, bankruptcies, and unemployment, the message of *The Three Little Pigs* was emphatic, especially after Roosevelt's famous appeal to Americans to stick together and not give up hope. The picture's theme song, "Who's Afraid of the Big Bad Wolf?" became a national anthem overnight. Originating as a popular child's fairy tale, the film became by force of circumstance and the time spirit a heartening call to the people of a troubled country.

But whether we have Donald or the Three Little Pigs or Pluto or even the *Silly Symphonies*, the form of a Disney film is always the same. He has standardized his construction of the formal elements into a semi-dramatic pattern. Two opposing forces are established: they come into conflict, there is a crisis, a chase, complications, a higher crisis, a last-minute climax, and a swift resolution. So skillfully does he manipulate his material that the similarity of the underlying structures of his different films is never obvious. His formal mastery frees him from any technical difficulties and leaves him only the problem of new ideas. With his theme selected, all he has to do is to divide it into the various parts—beginning, middle, and end—and allot so much time for each.

Comparatively simple though Disney's structural design appears, it is of a high esthetic order. His images move rapidly and blend smoothly, rising from point to point without a wasted frame, mov-

Columbia Pictures

"I-Like-to-Break-the-Rules" Capra getting his cast of *You Can't Take It with You* in an appropriate mood for the climax of the picture.

(*Below*) The scene as it appeared in the film. Capra believes in giving his players "plenty of business" to make their characterizations uncommon.

Columbia Pictures

Terrorized sharecropper. From the re-enacted documentary based upon the findings of the La Follette Civil Liberties Committee, produced independently by Frontier Films. Representative of the new trend toward non-fiction films.

ing on to an ever higher tension, increasing interest, arousing excitement, provoking laughter, building suspense, always advancing with remarkable fluidity and imagination to a last-minute crescendo and a final hilarious and unexpected resolution. It would be as impossible to cut a scene in a Disney film without destroying its flow as it would be to expect a man with one leg to walk as well as one with two. Succinct structural form marks all Disney's pictures and makes other animated cartoons, no matter how ingenious they may be, look pallid.

Disney like all gifted directors employs movement as the basis of his structure. Sound and color have not impeded his structural movement, but have themselves become integrated with it. Sound and color both function as mobile units. Sound is expanded or condensed to parallel the movement of the image from scene to scene; animals, birds, plants, machines, furniture, carry on an unbroken rhythm of sounds and music with as many aural variations as pictorial ones. Every accessory in movement also has its sound key and rhythmic pattern.

The color, especially in the *Silly Symphonies*, is seldom static. As the characters fly, dance, run, or evolve into other shapes, the color too is animated, becoming sinister, gay, sanguine, or merely decorative, but always taking on a new hue with each of the emotional developments and moving with the images and sound. The North Wind blows through the autumn forest, and as he does so the entire tonal scheme changes from golden red to icy blue, while the sound accompanying the transformation changes from an autumnal lyric to a wintry blast. Perhaps a more amusing example is the one in which Pluto, lost in the Alps, is found frozen blue by the faithful St. Bernard, who after forcing a whiskey down Pluto's throat watches the warm color slowly seep back into the dog's body as he thaws out. Here, too, the sound paces the return to life with an increasingly lively tempo.

Disney is unexcelled among directors in his exploitation of the full resources of his tools. An unlimited technical range of effects marks his structure: his camera swoops, glides, shoots, zooms, rides, bounces, and uses other movements that would be impossible in conventional studio pictures. And as with his camera, so with his sound. He disdains dialogue, fabricates an unreal world of sounds in unheard-of combinations. Sometimes the effects are created by the junction of actual sounds, and at other times by the use of light vibrations synthetically applied to his sound track to produce intensities and tones impossible to achieve from nature. His color, too, is wild, fantastic, subtle, or merely literal, for it depends not upon the real colors of objects but upon the pigmentation dictated by his imagination. Not bound to imitating nature, he distorts it as he likes: a piano is instantly turned into a grand-opera singer, a daisy into a chorus girl. His unlimited technical means he merges into a style so mobile, vigorous, and terse, so accomplished altogether, that his structure far surpasses any yet achieved by his contemporaries.

On occasion the structural elements have become the basis for a story. *The Four Seasons*, for instance, stemmed entirely from the seasonal color changes in nature. *The Battle Between Classic and Jazz* would never have been done if there had been no sound synchronization: the conflict between the two islands of music is expressed entirely through musical opposition, the camera being used to heighten the aural effects.

Disney's structure is enriched by a fertile imagination compounded of many elements. Fantasy, humor, satire, sentiment, violence, and mystery are blended, one or another sometimes predominating. At all times they are produced through strictly visual means, then enforced through the use of color and sound.

Being an imaginative man, Disney disdains the obvious, deliberately avoiding the "wise-crack" and the spoken dialogue gag. He says: [3]

Proper comedy for the screen is visual. Films try to get too many laughs out of dialogue. We use pantomime, not wise-cracks. . . . Portrayal of human sensations by inanimate objects such as steam shovels and rocking-chairs never fails to provoke laughter. Human distress exemplified by animals is sure-fire. A bird that jumps after swallowing a grasshopper is a "natural." Surprise is always provocative. We try to create as many laughs by visual means as possible in a sequence and then give the situation a quick twist . . . we

[3] Interview with Douglas W. Churchill, *The New York Times Magazine Section*, June 3, 1934.

don't bother with a formula. We make the characters as human as we can so that they will seem logical to the audience.

The most ambitious of all Disney's efforts has been his first feature-length production, the fairy tale *Snow White and the Seven Dwarfs* (1938). Representing a culmination of ten years of labor to make the animated cartoon an impressive as well as a solid structure, *Snow White*—three years in the making—was his most ambitious enterprise. While this film is not his best or his most unified (in it his problems were increased tenfold), it embodies all the principles of his shorter efforts. There are the same uncanny camera effects, rhythmic cutting, mobile sound, and kinetic applications of color; the same imagination, taste, and humorous characterizations that have made his style unique.

The story of *Snow White*, from the Grimm brothers' fairy tale, is familiar. The wicked Queen, jealous of Snow White, attempts to have her murdered. Snow White escapes, through the kind-heartedness of the Queen's huntsman, and is adopted by the Seven Dwarfs in the forest. After eating a poisoned apple given her by the Queen, who is disguised as an old hag, Snow White dies, only later to be revived by the kiss of Prince Charming. Well known though such material is, Disney's treatment of it abounds in beauty, freshness, and lyricism.

The best qualities of the picture represent Disney's style at its best. Snow White's flight through the forest has powerful effects like those in *The Cabinet of Dr. Caligari*. The housecleaning sequence, with the squirrels using their tails as brushes and dusters, the swallows scalloping pies with their feet, the fawns licking the plates clean, the chipmunks pulling cobwebs free, the birds flying with sheets to dry them, the tortoise offering his back to the rabbits as a scrubbing board, is as artlessly sophisticated as any Lubitsch touch. The music-hour episode, with the penguins acting as organ pipes, their ventholes stopped with clappers which Grumpy whacks shut by hand, and particularly the transformation of the Queen, her flight, and her death (with an eerie use of kinetic color, extending the principle introduced in *The Three Little Pigs*, where the wolf blows himself blue in the face), were also high points. All these sequences represent an astonishingly fine blending of imagination and mathematical organization. Image, sound, and color are mounted into a rhythmic ensemble that moves from incident to incident with wit, fantasy, beauty, and precision.

In *Snow White* basic musical themes are identified with each of the characters. Snow White and the Prince have their own variations of love ballads; each of the dwarfs has his own musical motif; even the turtle has an identification theme in a plodding, grave movement. The envious, wicked Queen is announced by a sinister motif. Sequences as well have their particular melodic accompaniments: the mirror scenes, a *mysterioso* of eerie quality; the plotting and witch's brew episode, a grim tonal foreboding, which develops into a dramatic *furioso* that hurls the Queen over the precipice in a hurricane of sound.

The film's most obvious fault was the attempt at making the human characters realistic, and the awkward relationship between the realistic three-dimensional background and the unrealistic two-dimensional figures. When Disney leaves stylization to attempt realism, the limitations of animation become sharply apparent. Though Snow White and the Prince are supposed to be realistic, they are indifferently good drawings of the "cute" school of art, and move (because we associate them with real people) choppily. We cannot believe in them. This criticism does not apply, of course, to the dwarfs, who are grotesquely realized, or to the animals; here Disney did not attempt to make his figures natural but kept them flat and decorative. They were done in his best manner, and we accepted their actions, no matter how far-fetched, as plausible in that realm of fantasy in which they dwell.

Despite its minor lapses, *Snow White* was a notably successful experiment and a gigantic financial coup. It is said to be grossing more money than any other picture in the history of movies, and it has encouraged Disney to start two new full-length pictures, *Pinocchio* and *Bambi*. These undertakings will undoubtedly eliminate the minor faults in *Snow White* and achieve a more integrated use of Disney's talents in this longer form.

With all his success, Disney is first and last a craftsman. In article after article he has stressed that, unlike most Hollywood producers, he is not interested in what money he can make at the moment. His is a far-seeing policy that is based on group co-operation:

I want to build a permanent organization that will allow for continual and expanding work. Money is important indirectly; experimentation comes first. Quality is the thing we have striven most to put into our pictures.[4]

Disney has repeated that over and over again.

. . . I don't favor much commercialization. Most producers think it is better to get while the getting is good. We have not operated that way. Because we own our business we can dictate our policy.[5]

This integrity accounts for Disney's continued growth and explains the lasting freshness of his films. Pandering to no conventional notions, he is motivated entirely by the feelings of his fellow artists and by his own. Because he prizes originality above all else, his outstanding films are remarkable for their new ideas. Like Chaplin, Disney is less concerned with what the public is supposed to want than with what pleases his staff and himself. He is never satisfied with any one of his efforts until he is certain that it is the best he can do. That is why his films, perhaps more than those of any other director, have been consistently superior and unexcelled as entertainment.

Walt Disney, today, stands as the virtuoso of the film medium. The technical dexterity and remarkable command of the medium that are his, gives all his efforts a brilliancy of rendition that makes even the least of them dazzling. Added to this is his constant flow of fresh ideas and keen observation of contemporary foibles. These qualities easily make Disney the peer of present day film makers. In the rise of the American film however, he will stand out, not only as a master craftsman in his times but as a contributor to film traditions. His contributions in the application of sound and color to movement have added new concepts—still to be formulated into principles—to the body of film knowledge on which the medium will now progress further.

[4] *Ibid.*   [5] *Ibid.*

XXV

SIGNIFICANT CONTEMPORARY
FILM CONTENT

THE turbulent course of national events since 1929, complicated by an increasingly acute European situation and directly touching the lives of all Americans, has made social, political, and economic issues of paramount interest to the common man. The flight from reality has come to an abrupt halt; the vogue of social irresponsibility, random self-indulgence, and escape into the "ivory tower," which prevailed in the twenties, has been abandoned. Most people have become social-minded and have developed a more realistic attitude toward life's problems. The desperateness of economic conditions, the need for equitable treatment and conditions for all, the menace of war and fascism, have produced an intense popular interest in current events, history, biography, social studies, facts, brought to us by legions of news magazines, topical and factual digests, reviews of all kinds, radio news commentators, and public debates. Government conservatism in the twenties has given way to progressivism (which is now being threatened once again by political reaction), and indiscriminate rebellion against moral conventions has been succeeded by an earnest search for moral norms. If cynicism still prevails, it is a new kind of cynicism, marked not by individualistic retreat but by a militant group spirit.

This quick transformation of American attitudes has been reflected in the content of American motion pictures during the past ten years, not only in fictionized films but in newsreels and documentaries. Movies reveal the change as it has progressed from the suspicion that something is wrong, to the exposure of corruption, to an awareness of widespread injustices and economic discrepancies, and to the search for a new code of individual and social values. The threatening rise of fascism in Europe has spurred the films to take up such questions as war, nationalism, democracy. We have today a revival of the progressive spirit that was so marked at the beginning of the century, and this spirit has affected the screen, even if infrequently, with an unprecedented urgency.

As always in critical times, the capacity of movies to mold opinion is put to use by those who control them. Sometimes the use of the motion picture as propaganda is unintentional; but when those who control pictures have a stake in the issues—such as when labor problems or the threat of fascism is involved—the use is deliberate. During the crisis of the thirties the participation of the movie in public discussion has been pronounced. Sometimes the producer's point of view is directly expressed; often it is only indicated by evasion or by tardiness in taking up the question at issue. Evasion and dilatoriness in the movies in such times as these is vitally harmful because public attention is diverted from important problems when it is most necessary that they be known and aired in discussion.

However, the movies' responsibility to society has been taken lightly.

Although movies are today mirroring the times with a realism not seen since the World War, their treatment of story material is still for the most part superficial, and in fact most pictures are still devoted to trivialities. J. P. McEvoy [1] offered one reason for this state of affairs when he remarked, "I know that no writer in Hollywood is as free to give the best in him as a writer of books or plays. . . ." Another reason is the powerful and unceasing censorship, moral, political, international, that is brought to bear on the movie industry. The Hays organization, the Legion of Decency, state and city boards, political and special-interest groups, educators, and other influential organizations or persons are constantly attempting to control the course of movies, sometimes for good, sometimes for evil. Dudley Nichols, as President of the Screen Writers Guild, [2] pointed out the necessity for breaking through such restrictions:

[1] *The Saturday Evening Post*, December 24, 1938.
[2] Radio speech broadcast, January 1939.

Hollywood, in its fear of losing profits by making enemies, in its mad desire to appease the prejudices of every group, has submitted to an ever-tightening censorship under which it becomes impossible to deal [honestly] with reality.

For almost two full years after the stock-market crash, Hollywood maintained a "hands-off" policy regarding discussion of the deepening depression. Films continued to emphasize sex, sophistication, and spectacle, although the jazz era was distinctly dead. This policy was partly due to the fact that the public as a whole hated to acknowledge the reality of the economic debacle. National leaders persisted in declaring that the crisis would be short-lived; President Hoover, in July 1930, declared that it was already over. The invention of sound and talking, moreover, not only maintained interest in movies for their own sake but, despite the nation's thinning pocketbook, increased it. Fascinated by the novelty, curious to hear the vocal ability of silent motion picture favorites, the public found the new film form exciting even if its subject matter was stale.

Photoplays after 1929 presented entertainment that grew ever more incongruous with the national temper: escape via the senses was still the standard offering of the screen. The extraordinary success of *Broadway Melody* in 1929 set a vogue for musical shows that flourished until 1933 and still persists today. Picture after picture, replete with song and dance shows, showed the miraculous rise of some unknown vaudeville actor to Broadway stardom. These films diverted the public from the disturbing times and kept them from realizing the full import of what was happening. The popular motto of the nation in 1930 was expressed in the titles of three films of those post-stock-market-crash days: *Let Us Be Gay, Strangers May Kiss, A Free Soul*.

Bedroom farces, illicit adventures, and sinful tales of the sophisticated woman of the world reached a climax in *The Last of Mrs. Cheney, The Divorcee, Paris-Bound*, and *Merrily We Go to Hell*. The disillusioned neurotic who flings herself into passion, luxuries, and a "free life" was played over and over by Constance Bennett (*The Easiest Way*), Tallulah Bankhead (*Tarnished Lady*), Greta Garbo (*Susan Lennox, Her Fall and Rise*), Norma Shearer (*Strange Interlude*), Joan Crawford (*Letty Lynton*), Marlene Dietrich

(*Blonde Venus*), Katharine Hepburn (*A Bill of Divorcement*), and others.

It was not until the close of 1930 that movie makers began to sense that audience's interests were changing. The box office began to gather dust as the national crisis deepened and the novelty of talking films faded. The feeling spread that something basic was wrong with America and with pictures. Cecil B. DeMille voiced the prevailing attitude in 1931 before leaving on a trip to Europe and the Soviet Union.[3]

I am not a radical but now things are a question of right and wrong. The public have been milked and are growing tired of it. It is not speculation alone. There is something rotten at the core of our system. We have to get back to the simple true principles that our government was founded on.

As unemployment spread and the depression deepened in the early thirties, disillusioned Americans turned a more realistic eye on the social evils around them.

The new realistic attitude was reflected first in a stream of gangster films. Gangsterdom was not news to the public or to movies. By 1927 organized crime had become "big business," and its leaders men of envied financial and political strength. Movies had already depicted the underworld and racketeering in 1927 and 1928. But the populace in those days of the booming stock market had been only mildly interested in crime. It was the murder of Arnold Rothstein in 1928, the St. Valentine's Day massacre in Chicago in 1929, the indictment of Al Capone, the thirty-one-year-old "Big Fix," in 1931, and above all the economic collapse, that jarred the nation out of its indifference, put an end to smug security, turned people to reality, and thus prepared them for the "crime wave" from Hollywood.

One of the first to act on the public's changed frame of mind was Mervyn LeRoy, then a comparatively obscure director of gold-digger comedies. Recognizing the import of the success of W. R. Burnett's book *Little Caesar*, a story of the rise of a gang leader, he is said to have induced First National to allow him to direct it free of the usual "front office" interference. Darryl Zanuck, later

[3] *Variety*, June 1931.

to become famous as producer in his own right and to win a reputation for his choice of timely material, was supervisor; Hal B. Wallis, soon to be known for his leadership in producing social exposés, became its producer; and Edward G. Robinson and Glenda Farrell, new types of "hard-boiled" players, were cast in the leading roles. The result was a film which, coming at the psychological moment, became the herald of the new vogue, just as DeMille's *Male and Female* had heralded a fashion in the previous decade.

Little Caesar (1930) realistically and uncompromisingly depicted the rise of an egotist through aggressiveness, ruthlessness, and organized, large-scale racketeering. It was shocking, it was hard, it was not pleasant, but it was real. Lack of sentimentality, brutal assault on the nerves with gunplay, violence, chases, tense struggles over big stakes, callousness toward human feelings, appealed to a public suddenly insecure in their own lives, faced with a desperate struggle for survival and menaced from all sides. Despite its reformist conclusion, *Little Caesar's* condonement and even glorification of rule by force reflected the cynical state of mind, the belief in the power of force over ideals, that had taken hold in America. In this gangster film the audience saw the tough, fighting world where the question of right is thrust aside for the supremacy of might—that world of naked, crude essentials by which they themselves were threatened. Reviewed as "the most penetrating study of the modern gangster, not very entertaining," *Little Caesar* was an overwhelming success, making the reputation of all who worked on it and becoming the pattern for succeeding films.

Of the cycle of gangster films that followed, even the worst were received with significant enthusiasm. Relentlessly honest in their depictions, these pictures showed

a certain section of America to itself against the background of pool-rooms, stale beer, cigarette smoke, alleys, bare electric-light bulbs, cities at night. Exaggerated and single-tacked . . . there was never any doubt that the setting was an American city of the prohibition period.[4]

They manifested consideration and sympathy for the courage, daring, and loyalty of gangsters according to their own code.

[4] Museum of Modern Art Film Library Program Notes, Series IV, No. 8.

Realistically and objectively presented, without apology or white-washing, the criminal leaders were in a sense exalted and their methods condoned.

"Little Caesar" was an Italian motivated by sheer vanity and personal desire for power; succeeding movies characterized the gangster as a typical everyday American turned hero. In *The Public Enemy* (1931) James Cagney personified the tough young leader whose hardness and fearlessness get him "on top." Gary Cooper in *City Streets* (1931) is the tall, good-looking Midwestern man whose quick wits and courage win him success in the desperate underworld. The hero of *Quick Millions* (1931) is likable Spencer Tracy, who upholds the philosophy that the "smart guy" can get away with anything, and the more you can steal, the more reputable you can become. In the picture he says he is too nervous to steal, too lazy to work, but his brains can organize others to carry out his schemes. Such emphasis upon brains as a means of getting by the law was marked in other films such as *Blonde Crazy*, *Smart Money*, *Two Seconds*, and *Blood Money*. They all inspired admiration for the "guts" of the gangster who defies the law and lives luxuriously; they all exploited the current psychology of aggressiveness ("You can dish it out and I can take it!"), power ("big shot"), and ruthlessness ("Take him for a ride!").

In bringing the gangster into esteem these films paralleled the literary school of cruelty, vulgarity, and terror of which Ernest Hemingway was the leader and James T. Farrell's *Studs Lonigan* the perfect expression. What Henry Seidel Canby has said [5] about this literary school applies with equal relevance to the movie school: it presents "a post-war world where sensitive disillusioned spirits strike out before they are struck and drink in order to forget."

Repudiating the Cinderella romance and the DeMille sex fantasies, these films acknowledged the new, hard world where values were relative, unstable; admitted the inhumanity of man toward man; upheld the admiration for the strong, the daring, the ruthless; provoked disdain for the weak and the spiritual. Might became right in a constantly changing world where values, attitudes, beliefs seemed to reverse themselves overnight.

[5] *The Saturday Review of Literature*, May 22, 1937.

The Public Enemy (1931) told of two boys, brought up together, who become bootlegging leaders. One night the boys'
mother, who does not know of their racketeering, goes to the front
door to answer the bell. The door opens and, to her horror, the
bandaged corpse of her "bad" son falls into the room. (The boy
has been killed in a gang war.) The brutality of this scene summed
up the brutality of the gang world. Another significant moment
comes when the "bad" son, James Cagney, mashes half a grapefruit
on the face of his "moll": in that action the myth of Prince Charming was overthrown.

Scarface (1932), "the gangster picture to end all gangster pictures," with relentless realism depicted the career of Al Capone,
the St. Valentine's Day slaughter, the shooting of gangster "Legs"
Diamond in a hospital, the siege of "Two-Gun" Crowley by officers
—all the violence and barbarity of gang rule and the underworld.

These films were intended to expose the underworld, but
scarcely to explain its causes. Audiences were interested in the
events of the criminal world for their own sake. The pictures,
presented with the "So what?" attitude of the day, were advertised in the same fashion as the pre-war films and carried such
prefaces as "Every event shown in this film is based on actual
occurrence . . . all characters are portraits of actual persons, living
or dead."

Gradually this indifference to the social implications of gang rule
was replaced on the screen by intimations that society was responsible for crime and should do something about it. The foreword
and afterword accompanying pictures reflected a growing realization of the social seriousness of racketeering. The title of *The Public Enemy*, for instance, implied that gangsters, though heroic, are
social evils, and a preface in dubious words pointed out that the
conditions shown are problems the country must solve. At the
close of the film it was suggested that business men and the public
generally, district attorneys and judges, must bear the responsibility of eliminating those conditions. Although this was a superficial
conclusion it was indicative of the trend. The producer's bolder
prefatory statement to *Scarface* voiced the growing public protest
against gangsterism: "This is an indictment against gang rule in

America and the careless indifference of the government. . . . What are you going to do about it?"

After *Scarface* a number of startling events climaxed the issue of gangsterism and resulted in the decline of gangster films. The spectacular gang killing on February 7, 1932, of Vincent Coll, "baby killer," by machine-gun fire in a drugstore in New York City; the kidnapping of the Lindbergh baby on March 1, 1932; and the million-dollar robbery of the Koch and Company real-estate office in Chicago in September, outraged the public. Advocates of censorship attacked crime pictures as incitements to lawlessness, encouraging brutality, violence, glorification of the criminal, the lust for easy money and the luxury of the gangster's life. The agitation finally culminated in the formation of the Legion of Decency in 1934. The public had, moreover, become surfeited by the overproduction of gangster films, and racketeer-bootlegging had been decreased by the repeal of the prohibition law in December 1933. Perhaps more influential than any of these reasons for the decline of the gangster films was the deepening depression, which turned people's minds to political, economic, and social issues more important to their immediate welfare.

The gangster theme gradually became rarer on the screen until 1937, when it was revived in a new vein. Now, as the titles of the pictures signified, the gangster was bitterly denounced and deprecated. Pictures manifesting the new attitude included *Crime Does Not Pay*, a series of shorts which occasionally went to the extreme of depicting union organizers as racketeers; *20,000,000 Years in Sing Sing*, *The Wrong Road*, *The Petrified Forest*, which condemned gangsters; and *Show Them No Mercy*, a denunciation of kidnappers, wherein a girl, in heroic and exemplary style, kills the ruthless gangsters with a machine gun (greater force overcoming force). Others were *Public Hero No. 1*, praising the G-Man; *Dangerous to Know*; and *The Last Gangster*.

Recent years have seen the desire to correct social evils applied to the crime problem. Films have blamed crime on deep-rooted social conditions and on the World War, which taught a man to shoot and think nothing of it (*They Gave Him a Gun*); on slum conditions (*Dead End, Boys of the Streets*); reform schools (*Crime School*); and bad environment (*The Devil Is a Sissy*).

A recent film, *Angels with Dirty Faces* (1938), made a bolder attempt to interpret the crime problem by pointing out many different causes of crime, stressing lack of the sense of social responsibility and the sorry condition of a world in which ethics seem worthless and rule by force prevails. The swift opening cavalcade, showing the development of the slum boy who finds in reform schools real butter on both sides of his bread, and who in post-war prohibition days learns how to make easy money, reflected the newer tendency to seek out the sources of events. The gang leader (James Cagney) is the ruthless tough guy who can "dish it out," whose axiom is "Don't be a sucker," and whose greeting is a mingling of belligerence and friendliness—"Waddya hear, waddya say?" The other "big shots" in the racketeering underworld are the corrupt lawyer and the boss who shrewdly maneuvers to make the law do his work. The gangster is fearless; he says himself that he is heartless; but withal he is an endearing person, arousing pity rather than animosity.

The church is shown participating in the correction of social conditions that breed crime. The spiritual ideal is represented as bringing more compensation than power and worldly success. However, no matter how often the priest reiterates that conscience is most important, actual incidents and the power the gang leader attains refute him. The priest himself in the film asks, "What is the use of preaching honesty when, all around us, you can see dishonesty winning out?"

One sequence significantly indicated our present-day respect for violence. The slum kids engage in a basketball game with a rival team, and their slugging, kicking, and breaking of rules, and the physical torture endured by all alike, cannot be controlled by the priest. But then Cagney steps in, and by sheer physical force he not only subdues them but wins their admiration as well. The sequence itself is swift and brutal, not unlike a Disney cartoon in which a dozen Donald Ducks slam away at each other. The triumph of force and daring is further drawn in the moments when James Cagney wins by bluffing his opponent—once when he saves himself by lying to the "boss," who has him trapped; and again when he saves himself by threatening to kill the priest if he is not set free. All these examples of the effectiveness of bluff, violence, fearlessness, are symptomatic of our times.

The gangster film introduced into American life a new type of hero, personified in James Cagney. He is tough and aggressive in everything, including lovemaking; danger and sex are his everyday life. Women are not adored by him, but are treated without sentiment and are accepted for what they have to offer. James Cagney of the motion picture sizes every woman up from only one point of view—sex. This frankness provides a certain fascination which, combined with his own physical appeal—his brisk movements, agility, nervous energy, and hard muscular body (he does not have a particularly good-looking face)—has made him enormously popular. He is a man of shrewdness, a man of action, a tireless talker, an indefatigable fighter—and a simple man of the streets whom anyone might know. Some titles of his films are vivid descriptions of his personality: *Taxi, Smart Money, The Crowd Roars, Blonde Crazy, Hard to Handle*. Lincoln Kirstein has said of Cagney: [6]

No one expresses more clearly in terms of pictorial action the delights of violence, the overtones of a semi-conscious sadism, the tendency towards destruction, toward anarchy, which is the basis of American sex-appeal.

By 1932 Hollywood, no longer able to ignore the economic depression, was turning its cameras upon it. Although its treatment of the crisis was not profound, it at least was a recognition of the acute problems that were touching the life of every American citizen. Becoming gradually bolder, movies dramatized the crash of 1929, hinted at its causes, suggested methods of reconstruction, and, in 1933, participated in the launching of the New Deal and in cheering on the populace.

The bankrupt world faced by young men and women of the day was mirrored in *Gentlemen Are Born* (1932). In a simple, straightforward style the film traced the paths of four men after they graduate from college, showing that they could get no legitimate means of livelihood commensurate with their training and

[6] *Hound and Horn*, April 1932.

ability. The film ended with the protest of youth; no cure or happy ending was proffered. *Wild Boys of the Road* (1933-1934) showed how, under economic stress, young people were forced out onto the edge of society to live by their wits.

Movies blamed the course of events on the nation's desire to make money easily and quickly (*The World Changes*, 1933), promulgated the theory that depressions are inevitable in business cycles after a period of prosperity (*Conquerors*, 1933), claimed that organized crime and "dirty politics" had brought on the disaster (*The World Gone Mad*, *Washington Merry-Go-Round*), and traced the vast unemployment to machines (technocracy was then enjoying a vogue as an economic philosophy).

Four major remedies for the depression were offered by movies in 1933 and 1934. One was family loyalty and "all pulling together" (*This Side of Heaven*, *Looking Forward*, *The Poor Rich*, *In the Money*, *Three-Cornered Moon*). Another was an American brand of dictatorship, suggested in *Gabriel over the White House*. In this picture a new President, after inauguration, turns out to be just another politician. But after being in an auto wreck he has a vision, fires his Cabinet, and becomes a dictator. He organizes the unemployed into an army and thus solves the unemployment problem; he takes gangsters to Governors Island and, by shooting them, solves the crime problem; he takes the conference delegates out and shows them his naval and air force, and thus solves the foreign debt situation. This film, in pointing out the advantages of a dictatorship or a similar form of rule, was significant, coming at a time when conditions were critical.

The third remedy suggested was a return to the soil (*State Fair*, *Beloved*, *Our Daily Bread*, *Stranger's Return*, *As the Earth Turns*). Will Rogers in *Dr. Bull* and *Mr. Skitch* pointed out the virtues of small-town farm life. The fourth remedy, comically advanced by Marie Dressler and Polly Moran in *Prosperity*, was to put all the idle to helping themselves by working the materials lying idle.

The election of President Roosevelt and the launching of the NRA, put into action a New Deal Program to alleviate conditions. Films set about endorsing the new experiments and trying to dispel the rising despair and fear that paralyzed the nation. They pre-

Warner Brothers

In this production still from *Juarez* (1939) can be seen the large technical crews and elaborate machinery needed for today's production standards.

The group method of film making. Walt Disney
and members of his staff discussing a sequence
for one of their films.

dicted that united action would bring the nation "out of the dumps," and emphasized the prediction with a flood of "pep-talk" sequences in spectacular musicals. In a "depression tableau," *Moonlight and Pretzels* (1934) eulogized the Roosevelt administration and the NRA. *Footlight Parade* was climaxed with a pro-NRA demonstration. In *Stand Up and Cheer* a Department of Amusement was established to sell laughter to America. This picture also ended with an NRA parade.

In 1933 appeared the cheerful Walt Disney cartoon *The Three Little Pigs*, with the theme song "Who's Afraid of the Big Bad Wolf?", which set the whole nation whistling to keep up its spirits. This helped to turn the tide of pessimism toward optimism and strengthened the hope that co-ordinated action would pull the country out of its slump. During the next years the screen

committed itself and the nation [as one observer noted] to a smug belief in the return of prosperity, the continuance of democracy, and the maintenance of a social-political system which guarantees life, liberty, and the pursuit of romance. . . .

Indeed, according to Will Hays,

no medium has contributed more than the films to the maintenance of the national morale during a period featured by revolutions, riot and political turmoil in other countries. It has been the mission of the screen, without ignoring the serious social problems of the day, to reflect aspiration, achievement, optimism and kindly humor in its entertainment. Historians of the future will not ignore the interesting and significant fact that the movies literally laughed the big bad wolf of depression out of the public.[7]

By this time strong public animosity toward banks and bankers had been aroused by widespread bank failures, in which the savings of thousands had been suddenly and mysteriously wiped out. Movies took up the defense of the financier by either significantly avoiding the issue or by presenting the banker as a high-spirited public servant (*American Madness*). The integrity of bankers in national and international dealings was eulogized in *The House of Rothschild* (1934), which William Troy [8] described as "almost a lyrical tribute

[7] Quoted by Rose R. Terlin in *You and I and the Movies*, p. 24.
[8] *The Nation*, April 4, 1934.

to the nobility, self-sacrifice and unwavering patriotism of that group of international bankers." To the later *Lloyds of London* (1937) the same comment would apply.

Since the movie industry itself is big business, the conflict between organized labor and capital—grown ever more serious since 1929—was represented in movies mainly from the viewpoint of the employer. Unionism was smeared, strikers slandered, the causes of industrial conflict identified with personal jealousies. *Red Dust* and *Riffraff* denounced organized labor action no matter how justified it might be. Strikers were presented as "Reds," as ugly, foreign, dirty, troublemaking drunkards; their leaders were shown as gangsters or racketeers. If the hero was in a strike, he was "ignorant" or guileless, and finally "awakened." In *I Believed in You* a liberal who has taken the part of "scoundrelly" unionized coal miners is "saved" by his girl.

Black Fury (1935), dramatizing a strike among mine workers, gave no explanation of what a strike actually means to the worker. The strike was portrayed as a shameless revolt of workers inspired by outside gangsters. There was little indication of the workers' privations during a strike and the workers' grievances themselves were stated by men obviously supposed to be villains. That the movies chose to depict a mine strike and a drab mine town at all was indicative of the new interests of the nation-at-large.

The working man's point of view regarding unionism has gained access to the screen mainly in productions made independently of the moving picture industry proper. *Taxi, Millions of Us,* and *The Wave* showed the unemployed man's awakening to the reasons for organized action in strikes and to the meaning of "scabbing." These films aimed to educate workers in the benefits of a union, the harm of strikebreaking, the power of united action. *People of the Cumberland* showed the advantages accruing to a backward American community through organized social enterprise. The counter-effect of such pro-labor films against pro-capital films has been, however, very limited, since the former are not presented in major theatre chains and, generally, have a much narrower distribution than the Hollywood made films.

In Hollywood's minor ("B") pictures there has been apparent

more recently, concurrent with the growing public acknowledgment of the rights of labor, a more sympathetic attitude toward organized workers. *Sinners in Paradise* (1938) showed a rich girl who is made to wash dishes after an airliner has crashed: she threatens to "strike"—and simultaneuosly, back home, the workers in her father's place are striking for the same reason. *The Jury's Secret* (1938) depicted the strike leader favorably, touching on the intolerable conditions that may be the causes of a strike. Few and slight though such sympathetic pictures are, they do reveal a new, less bigoted attitude toward the worker's problems.

In a few pictures the worker has been portrayed as an obscure hero who often follows his line of duty under exacting, dangerous conditions. *Tiger Shark* (1932) related the drama of the worker in the tuna-fishing industry. *Oil for the Lamps of China* (1935) revealed the employee as a courageous and loyal if unrecognized hero who, in the face of personal griefs and hardships, carries on his job in a huge enterprise. *Slim* (1936) depicted the heroic self-sacrifice and death of the power-line worker in the course of his job. Stunt men were the heroes in *Lucky Devils*; sign painters in *The Face in the Sky*; airplane hostesses in *Air Hostess*; and stokers in *Pacific Liner*. *She Loved a Fireman* was reviewed by *The New York Times* [9] as "oppressively plebeian as some other productions are offensively upper-class." In all such films the working man or woman is honest, sincere, courageous, and conscientious, American in aspect, simple in his ideas, and filled with the conviction that his job is extremely important.

An unconventional picture of outstanding significance regarding labor was Charlie Chaplin's *Modern Times*. As we have already seen elsewhere this picture showed, from Chaplin's extremely individualistic viewpoint, the regimentation and bewilderment of millions of workers in modern industry.

The industrialist and big business man, on the other hand, is no longer represented as the "arrived" power who finds relaxation in beautiful women, country clubs, and golf, but as the man who works as hard as any of his laborers, who learned his business from the bottom up, who has struggled hard for success and must continue

[9] January 1, 1938.

struggling to keep it. He is beset with financial worries, labor problems, personal disappointments. Like the banker, the corporation executive is depicted as a leader fighting single-handed to help the people. *Working Man*, for instance, featured George Arliss as a shoe manufacturer who is himself a hard worker. The rugged, fair-minded, hard-working industrialist has been epitomized in the actor Spencer Tracy: he is intelligent, human, a man whom any one of us might know. Through hard work, character, and integrity he rises from the ranks (*The Power and the Glory, Mannequin*).

Another personification of the big business man is the hearty, aggressive, rich Edward Arnold. Heavy-set, as quick to laughter as to battle, in the words of Frank S. Nugent "Mr. Arnold is getting to be to industry what George Arliss was to history; a general utility man." Typical of his sympathetic portrayals of the successful business man who fights upward from the ranks with his philosophy of "all's fair in love and business" were *Come and Get It*, a drama of the rise of a lumber king, and *The Toast of New York*, a glorification of the magnate Jim Fiske.

Such films reflect new methods in industry's campaign to gain the good-will of the populace. In effect they are like institutional advertising campaigns designed to prove that big industry and utilities benefit their workers and the community at large, and that all of us, poor and rich alike, workers and bosses, are working equally hard to serve society. This psychology has become more prevalent with acute economic conditions.

Unemployment and insecurity as they confront the average man have gained respectful attention. Such films as *One More Spring, Little Man, What Now?; 100 Men and a Girl, My Man Godfrey* and *Mr. Deeds Goes to Town*, no longer showed the out-of-work citizen as a "tramp" or a sluggard but a victim of circumstances; however, he is still finally rescued by the benevolence of some socially minded rich person or family. A more realistic view of insecurity was apparent in *Make Way for Tomorrow* (1937), which dramatized the necessity for an old-age security system by showing the unfortunate circumstances of an elderly couple who are too old to get work, are unwanted by their married children, have no income, and lack means of self-support and independence. Had this picture been called *Why?*, with its moving presentation of the predicament of a middle-class couple who all their lives have been people of position but at last find themselves without the means of a livelihood, it would have been denounced as blatant propaganda.

The futile struggle of the farmer and the economic discrepancies responsible for it have rarely been touched upon by the movies. Here is a signal instance of the intentional neglect of social material of the utmost importance. The few films about the farmer that have appeared reveal only too clearly how desperate, how deep-rooted and many-sided, his problem is. *Cabin in the Cotton* (1932-1933), one of the first pictures to recognize it, showed the plight of Southern planters, tenant farmers, and the poor whites of the South. A foreword stated that the picture did not take sides, but the conclusion of the film clearly favored the landowners. Biased though it was, it did expose the conditions and acknowledged the importance of the issue of tenant farming. *Golden Harvest* (1937), approaching the farm problem from another angle, pictured the hard-working farmer at the mercy of wheat-pit speculators, and *White Bondage* (1937) portrayed the struggling existence of sharecroppers. But these few recognitions of the plight of people on the land are trivial and ineffective as compared with films that divert attention from it. Most pictures, nostalgic and idyllic in feeling, show the farmer happy in rural community life, far more fortunate in his opportunities than the city dweller (*State Fair, Stranger's Return, As the Earth Turns*).

Of extreme significance on this score are two government-made documentary films revealing how crucial the farm problem is and what is being done about it. *The Plough That Broke the Plains* (1936) explained the disintegration of the wheat country, showed the tragedy of those families impoverished by annual droughts, and pointed out how the Resettlement Administration is adjusting this condition. *The River* (1938), a "tragedy of land twice impoverished," depicted the effects of erosion caused by the Mississippi floods and showed the work of the Farm Security Administration in rehabilitating the land and the lives of people in the Mississippi Valley. Such cognizance of the economic maladjustments of the country gives films a new vitality and makes them more important to our lives.

Paralleling the films that depicted the economic tribulations were films boldly exposing public officials and authorities, racketeering in businesses and professions, that have a responsibility to society. Politics and politicians were debunked. Thus *Washington Masquerade* (1933), paralleling the exposé of ex-President Harding's personal life in the popular book *The President's Daughter*, showed how an honest Senator was seduced by a woman into corruption and disgrace. *The Dark Horse* and *Convention City* (both 1934) exposed in cynical terms the politicians who manipulate the national government for their personal advantage. *The President Vanishes* (1934) revealed the "money interests" behind the national scenes and the extent to which they will go to get their way.

I Am a Fugitive (1932), an adaptation of an authentic experience widely publicized in book form (*I Am a Fugitive from a Georgia Chain Gang*), exposed chain-gang tyranny, brutality in the treatment of convicts, and the callous detachment of officials in regard to the suffering of their fellow men. This film produced a tremendous public response despite *Hollywood Filmograph's* prediction, after seeing a preview of the film, that the public would never want to see such a picture—that people wanted escape from depressing things. So strong was the public's indignation about chain gangs, in fact, that the picture *Hell's Highway* was hurriedly made to counteract it. At the conclusion of the film the governor of Georgia appeared to prove, as Pare Lorentz pointed out,[10]

that our penal systems are really managed by kind old gentlemen, and that crooked, mysterious contractors are responsible for all the cruelty and sadism which the Wickersham Committee has discovered in our prisons.

Mayor of Hell (1933-1934), turning to another aspect of the crime-correction problem, boldly revealed a reform school run by grafters and racketeers. These scoundrels are run out by organized protest, and the reform school is given democratic self-rule under the guidance of an "understanding" warden.

[10] *Vanity Fair*, 1932.

Many motion pictures have been distinguished by strong sympathy for men and women caught in the net of crime and punishment. Humane treatment of the imprisoned lawbreaker was demanded back in 1930 and 1931 in such films as *The Big House*, *Ladies of the Big House*, and *The Last Mile*. *San Quentin* (1937), *Penitentiary* (1935), and *Alcatraz Island*, *Blackwell's Island*, *Women in Prison*, and *Condemned Women* (all 1938) treated prisoners not as self-made criminals but as products of social evils. An awareness of the responsibility of society to eliminate prison conditions which make criminals worse, and of the problem of ex-convicts who are unable to go straight and rehabilitate their lives after being released, was evident in *Mary Burns, Fugitive* (1937) and *You Only Live Once, You and Me, Parole, Girls on Probation* (all 1938). Such depictions of the criminal, throwing the brunt of the problem on society, are further manifestations of the new critical attitude.

The ruthlessness of big-business journalism, with its battle for circulation and frequent irresponsibility to the public at large, was also exposed in *Five-Star Final* (1931), *The Front Page* (1931), and *Big News* and *The Power of the Press* (both 1931). *Hi Nellie* (1934) and *Exclusive* (1937) elaborated on various traits of yellow journalism, racketeering in publishing, and newspapers as a tool in the hands of big business men (a theme in such recent books as George Seldes' *The Freedom of the Press*). *Variety* [11] reported that the

Newspapermen screen cycle portrayed the business in a light that is calculated to do the [motion picture] industry no good with the average editor. In a recent tour of several states in the east to discuss pictures with editors, a representative of the Motion Pictures Are Your Greatest Entertainment campaign was astonished to learn how much the average Horace Greeley resented the manner in which newspaper life was Hollywood-handled.

The social irresponsibility of some circles in the medical fraternity, and more recently the need for socialized medicine and hospital care, have become common picture subjects. In this sphere Hollywood has been stimulated by growing national agitation for various socialized institutions and by the federal government's at-

[11] January 4, 1939.

tack on the American Medical Association as a trust. From *Arrow-smith* (1931), the story of the rise of a small-town physician and of the medical scientist's dilemma of a choice between the immediate relief of sufferers and the eventual immunity from disease for all mankind, movies have advanced to *Bedside* (1934) and *Internes Can't Take Money* (1937), which exposed the seamy side of medical science and the racketeering prevalent in some medical quarters.

A Man to Remember (1938) recounted the life of a small-town doctor who is confronted with bigotry and lack of understanding support: despite his practical human experience, because of his lack of a degree he cannot continue his investigations. *Men in White, The Young Dr. Kildare, Yellow Jack, Dr. Monica, Main Street,* and *Of Human Bondage* revealed other professional, economic, and ethical problems faced by the doctor. *The Life of Louis Pasteur* re-evaluated the great scientist's work in the light of social and political pressure that was exerted to frustrate him. The culmination of the exposures of the medical profession came with *The Citadel* (1938), in which not only a protest against injustice but a demand for a new order of things was clearly voiced.

Other films exposed a number of other important social and political issues. *State's Attorney* (1932), *Counsellor-at-Law* (1932), *Attorney for the Defense* (1933), and *The Mouthpiece* (1933) led dozens of similar films in dealing with problems in the legal profession. Other pictures lifted the veil from racketeering in money lending (*I Promise to Pay*, 1937) and in football (*Rackety Rax*, 1933). *Mountain Justice* (1937), based on Edith Maxwell case headlines about a hill-billy girl's killing of her father because of his tyrannous bigotry, mirrored the contemporary issues of child marriage, the backwoods health clinic, and lynching. *I Am the Law* (1938) focused attention on Mayor Hague's political dictatorship over New Jersey and Jersey City in particular. *The Marked Woman* dramatized the exposure of "Lucky" Luciano's prostitution ring, then filling the headlines, while *Confessions of a Nazi Spy* (1939) dealt uncompromisingly with the Leon G. Turrou exposé of Nazi espionage in America.

The urge to seek out the underlying causes of present-day social troubles has been manifest in films that reflect and resurvey facts according to the new, more socialized outlook of Americans. It is a far cry from DeMille's plea in *This Day and Age* (1934) for youth to organize into lynch mobs and clean up gangsters to the more recent films condemning mob hysteria. Three outstanding successes, *Winterset* (1936), *Fury* (1937), and *They Won't Forget* (1937) bitterly censured lynching, "legal" or illegal. Political ambitions, inefficient police forces, and the press's appetite for circulation were blamed in these pictures for the victimizing of the innocent for selfish ends. In their realism and strong protest against social attitudes and institutions that condone injustice, all three films stand out.

Winterset, adapted from the stage play by Maxwell Anderson, was an acid dramatization of the conviction and execution of Sacco and Vanzetti because of their liberal activities. It pleaded for the necessity of fair play for all. *Fury* exposed the blind, insistent brutality of a mob which, without a shred of evidence to support its conviction that a certain man is a kidnapper, attempts to kill him by burning the jail in which he is held prisoner.[12] With shocking honesty the film bared the lust for violence and blood that can burst forth in the quietest of small towns among the most respectable people (a woman holds up her child to see the conflagration). *They Won't Forget* likewise struck out at the persecution of innocent men by mobs in the South. As its title suggested, the film showed that communities where such events can occur have farreaching influence, and implied that their guilt can be covered up but never expiated. This "crusading" film, as it was called, told the story of how sectional bigotry, exploited for personal ends by a prosecuting attorney and by newspapers, results in the lynching of a Northerner. The *National Board of Review Magazine* [13] clearly pointed out the picture's purpose:

> The indictment here is not against the lynching of an innocent man, but rather against the dreadfulness which is lynching itself and against the fierce and uncontrolled hatreds that make lynching possible.

These three films are indicative of the resurgence of the progressive spirit that was quenched by the World War. They plead for

[12] See page 463. [13] October 1937.

toleration, social justice, peaceful methods of dealing with community problems.

The realistic interpretation of present-day social conditions, has brought a more realistic scrutiny of history to the screen. Apparent in some movies has been the intent to re-survey the past in its bearing on the present and, in so doing, to search out facts rather than romantic legends. An approach like that of *Time* magazine, which not only reports current happenings but summarizes events leading up to them, has been reflected in various movies based on historical figures and events and on new adaptations of literary classics.

Historical figures who have been dramatically reappraised include the former ruling heads of various European countries: Russia (*Rasputin and the Empress, The Scarlet Empress, Catherine the Great*), Sweden (*Queen Christina*), Great Britain (*Mary of Scotland*), and France (*Conquest*). Such films portrayed people heretofore regarded as demigods with a significant lack of respect. Although history itself was grossly distorted and the rulers favorably romanticized often at the expense of truth, such individuals of rank were portrayed as having many of the weaknesses of ordinary people and hardly the superior beings they were supposed to be. This was particularly true of the English importation *The Private Life of Henry the Eighth*, which was notably popular. The more recent *Marie Antoinette*, on the other hand, provoked strong criticism because of its romantic unreality.

Like ruling figures, less known individuals who have had a hand in historical events have been reviewed with a determination to expose social injustice and even to justify popular rebellions (parallels in our own times often being suggested). *The Prisoner of Shark Island* related the story of an innocent doctor who, suspected of implication in the assassination of Lincoln, was railroaded to the horrors of the old federal prison on Shark Island. The Irish rebellions, in particular, have been dramatized with a growing sympathy for the rebels. In *The Informer* (1935)[14] this sympathy is clear: Gypo Nolan, who turns stool pigeon during the desperate Sinn Fein rebellion against the British for the sake of twenty pounds, is

[14] See page 480.

a character molded by the times and by his social status. *The Plough and the Stars* (1937) told of the Dublin uprising of Easter Week, 1916, and its failure. Here, too, the Irish rebels were shown to be justified. In *The Beloved Enemy* the English heroine informs on the British not only because of her love for the Irish leader but because of her desire to see Ireland established as a separate entity. Sympathy for another sort of rebel appeared in *Mutiny on the Bounty* (1935), in which the crew of the ship revolt against the tyranny of Captain Bligh.

Perhaps the three most notable biographical films were *The Life of Louis Pasteur* (1936), *Emile Zola* (1937), and *Juarez* (1939). All exposed treason in high places; all were predominantly social in outlook and realistic in interpretation; all suggested strong parallels in our own times. *The Life of Louis Pasteur* was more than the biography of a scientist; it was an allegory of the battle for progress that is going on every day in countless occupations. In the words of James Shelley Hamilton,[15]

To have taken a life story of this kind, so far removed from the romantic tangles and physical activities of the usual popular entertainment, and made it vivid, engrossing and thrilling for the mass audience, is a step that may lead the motion picture along a path some of its best friends have long wished to see it tread.

Emile Zola, on the other hand, was strong enough to inspire newspaper editorials. Said the *New York Post*,[16]

The Dreyfus case was a forerunner of the Reichstag fire trials . . . the movies are taking on a new stature. . . . Hollywood resisted the temptation to make a spy thriller out of social conflict.

Juarez, the most recent of the trio, has aroused huzzahs from all because of its unequivocal partisanship on the side of democracy and because in the interpretation of a historical figure, and his country, a direct parallelism of the past with our times was deliberately injected. As Frank S. Nugent[17] aptly pointed out,

. . . Warners have written between the lines of Benito Juarez's defy the text of a liberal's scorn for fascism and nazism.

[15] *National Board of Review Magazine*, February 1936.
[16] September 4, 1937. [17] *The New York Times*, April 26, 1939.

The approach taken in these biographies is most significant; equally vital is the growing concern in the nation at large, apparent in these reappraisals of past events and figures, toward international social and political issues, and what shapes them.

Events in Europe—the rise of fascism, Japanese aggression in China, the Spanish civil war, and the Munich pact, all seeming to hold the threat of another World War—are changing people's attitudes on the issues of war, nationalism, and democracy, now more urgently in the public mind than ever before.

The hatred of war which had been mounting since the conflict "to save the world for democracy" has become increasingly apparent on the screen. A number of films in the early thirties exposed war, in no mincing terms, as futile, horrible, destructive. *All Quiet on the Western Front* (1930) stressed the useless destruction of war and, incidentally, depicted the Germans sympathetically. (It was proposed that the producer of the film, Carl Laemmle, be awarded the Nobel Peace Prize.) *Journey's End* (1930) and *Dawn Patrol* (1930) revealed the barbarous killing of humanity for no good reason. *The Man I Killed* (*Broken Lullaby*) in 1932 emphasized the emotional warping of soldiers due to war experience. *Doomed Battalion* (1932) and *The Lost Patrol* (1932) followed the hardships of soldiering. *The Man Who Reclaimed His Head* (1933) exposed munitions manufacturers as the unprincipled salesmen for war. Sad accounts of human suffering made up the anti-war stories in *A Farewell to Arms* (1933-1934) and *The Eagle and the Hawk* (1933-1934), while *Private Jones* (1934) satirized war.

By 1936 a strong anti-war sentiment, voiced in President Roosevelt's contemporary declaration "I hate war!", had filled Americans. But as international events were shaped more and more by the aggressions of dictators, the beginnings of another attitude came into prominence on the screen. In 1937 and 1938, a time of rising tension throughout the world, the screen took a boldly militaristic stand. Pictures of the Army and Navy reappeared with a new glamour and a martial spirit. The anti-war films were replaced by a stream of romantic patriotic spectacles: *Annapolis Farewell, Flirtation Walk, West Point of the Air, Navy Blue and Gold, Shipmates Forever* (dedicated to the Naval Academy). Other films such as *Come On, Marines; Here Comes the Navy, Tell It to the Marines, Follow the Fleet, The Singing Marines,* and *Wings of the Navy,* acquainting audiences with the various branches of the service, were pre-recruiting sales talks.

While the international crisis was growing worse, *Motion Picture Herald* [18] announced that the government had set new rules for the filming of the U. S. Navy and that there would be a stronger censorship of news and fiction. The National Council for the Prevention of War soon afterward [19] condemned the Navy Department's practice of allowing motion picture producers the free use of ships and personnel, on the ground that this stimulated militaristic propaganda, spent taxpayers' money for private profit, and was unfair to professional movie actors. Since the President and Congress acceded to the War Department's request for a bigger budget in 1938, and since national feeling has been rising against "aggressor nations," the militaristic emphasis of films has seemed likely to continue. Declared the advertisement for *Spirit of Culver:* [20] "It's better to die on your feet than live on your knees!" The film, *Men with Wings* (1938), a cavalcade of aviation, had its pacifistic ending changed on the advice of the War Department so that America's air-preparedness was emphasized and the men who build bombers, glorified. The threat of a rising fascism and the tendency of America to take a militant stand on those things that are worth fighting for are becoming more pronounced; pacifism seems already to have become a philosophy of the past.

The two wars abroad, however, received little recognition in American movies up to 1939. The only serious Hollywood film based on the war in Spain was *Blockade* (1938). In this picture the factions in the civil war were not actually named, but the sympathy expressed was clearly on the side of the Loyalist (democratic) government. The film ended with an appeal to the "conscience of the world" and a protest that the conflict was "not war but murder."

Besides *Blockade,* several independently produced (non-Hollywood) dramatized documentaries appeared: *The Spanish Earth, Heart of Spain,* and *Return to Life.* All depicted Loyalist Spain's

[18] March 27, 1937.   [20] *New York Post,* March 7, 1939.
[19] *Daily Worker,* April 29, 1937.

heroic struggle against Europe's fascist nations. Two of the most forceful political documentaries were the more recent *The 400,-000,000*, showing the background and forces behind China's defense against Japan's aggression, and *Crisis*, telling the tragic story of Czechoslovakia's dismemberment after the Munich "betrayal."

Except for these films movies have merely capitalized on the interest in Europe by using Spain and China as backgrounds for melodrama: it has been hoped that the wars would give the pictures timeliness. *Exiled to Shanghai* (1937) was a story of newsreel men in China, and *Daughter of Shanghai* (1938) a melodrama of a smuggling ring. *International Settlement* and *West of Shanghai* (1938) were based on news of the bombing of Shanghai. *The General Died at Dawn* (1936), attempting to go a little further, was a spy story revealing the treachery of war lords and making a plea for the oppressed and downtrodden. The war in Spain became a fictional stepping-off point for *The Last Train from Madrid* (1937).

Under the threat of a spreading fascism, democracy has once again become a rallying point around which national sentiment is consolidated. In 1934 appeared the film *Are We Civilized?*, an impassioned demand for freedom of thought, speech, and press, and for international peace and understanding. Independently made, it was countered by blatant Red-baiting films produced in Hollywood, *A Call to Arms* and *Red Salute*, which attacked the student movement against war and fascism and ended with the heroine marrying the Army man instead of the young radical. Here were vivid instances in which a fundamental issue, presented presumably without bias, was distorted for purposes of propaganda.

The threat of fascism in America was made clearer, however, by the dramatic exposure of secret political organizations in Detroit, by the killing of Charles Poole. The affair was in newspaper headlines for weeks and roused the entire nation. Activities of such organizations were mirrored in bold social dramas: *The Legion of Terror* (1936) and *Black Legion* (1937). Although prefatory statements to these films declared that no actual incident was being depicted, there was little question in anyone's mind as to the source and truth of the material. Such pictures, together with the more recent and already mentioned *Confessions of a Nazi Spy*, helped to bring their existence sharply to the attention of all Americans.

The deepening international crisis in Europe has made the problem of maintaining democracy more urgent than ever. The President of the United States has urged a pruning of democracy in America so it can surpass the alleged efficiency of a dictatorship. Movie makers have launched a cycle of films preaching democracy and allegiance to the ideals upon which the United States was founded. *Let Freedom Ring* (1939) was an exuberant lesson in patriotism with a flag-waving finish and singing of "My Country 'Tis of Thee." Unusual enthusiasm has greeted a series of Technicolor shorts, begun during 1938 by Warner Brothers, including *The Declaration of Independence, Lincoln in the White House, The Bill of Rights, Sons of Liberty. The New York Times* [21] reported the plan of RKO-Pathé News to produce a feature-length picture, tentatively titled *United We Stand*, dealing with "the trend of Americanism today." Outside Hollywood Frontier Films has already completed a feature-length picture dramatizing America's heritage of freedom, the Bill of Rights, in terms of modern America.

Pride and interest in America's history are becoming more pronounced in movies. The trend was evident as early as 1931 in *Sutter's Gold* and *Cimarron* and in 1932 in *Silver Dollar*. More recent spectacular films about America's past include *Wells Fargo* (1937), *The Texans* (1938), and *Union Pacific, Dodge City, Stagecoach,* and *The Oklahoma Kid* (all 1939).

The emphasis upon Americanism seems to be increasing daily. Many theatres have begun the practice of opening and closing their shows with chorus singing of "The Star-Spangled Banner" as the flag waves on the screen. Film Audiences for Democracy, one of the first organizations of its kind, supports progressive, anti-fascist movies.

This rising tide of "Americanism" with its accompanying endorsement of democracy, has brought new vitality to the screen and fresh respect to producers. It has led many to hope that Hollywood will participate actively in strengthening progressive forces and in retarding the ever-threatening forces of reaction.

The spirit of revaluation expressed in such films of this period is

[21] December 30, 1938.

apparent also in the revaluation of domestic and personal relation-ships. Under more realistic and non-sentimental examination, love and sex became less passionate and less exotic, less neurotic and "escapist"; it became rather a funny business, a healthy affair, to be enjoyed readily and viewed lightly. The covert philandering and teasing of the jazz age was gone from pictures. Sin was taken out of sex; fun put in its place. Love was interpreted as a natural endowment of both sexes, to be openly enjoyed or ignored, now a pleasant passion rather than an upsetting one.

The pre-war generation had its vamp, Theda Bara; the post-war jazz period had its woman of the world, Gloria Swanson, and its flaming youth, Clara Bow; and the depression gave birth to Mae West. In Mae West is summed up the same absence of senti-mentality, the same hardness, violence, and vulgarity that is per-sonified in James Cagney. In her way she symbolizes, in sexual terms, the state of mind of the post-war, post-Freud, intra-depres-sion generation. Waving aside the old convention that sex is the handmaid of sin—the basis of all man-and-woman films since Theda Bara days—she has represented the common denominator of atti-tudes toward sex in the thirties.

Mae West has neither inhibitions nor illusions. When she wants love, she goes after it. Direct, aboveboard, without subtlety, she goes no further in innuendo than "Come up and see me sometime." But her tone, her roving eyes, her large bosom and swaying hips, make the invitation gleeful, unsentimental, and plain. She is as far removed from Pollyanna innocence as she is from the suffering "pain-of-it-all" school.

At their peak of fame in 1933 and 1934, almost all Mae West's films were significantly placed in the Gay Nineties. The titles indi-cate the plane of her interests: *Diamond Lil* (*She Done Him Wrong*), *It Ain't No Sin* (changed to *Belle of the Nineties*), *I'm No Angel, Going to Town, Every Day's a Holiday*. Her pictures culminated women's assertion of their rights and status in love.

Mae West averred that women get just as much pleasure out of sexual contact as men; that a man need no longer run after the heroine and cajole her into his arms, but that the female can reverse the old custom and cajole the male. How much distance separated

Mae West from the clinging-vine heroine of yesterday has been indicated by Mary Pickford's shocked exclamation: [22]

I passed the door of my young niece's room—she's only about 17 and has been raised, oh, so carefully—and I heard her singing bits from that song from *Diamond Lil*—I say "that song" just because I'd blush to quote the title line even here.

Mae West eyed a man from head to foot. All the time you knew she was evaluating him in terms of virility, as James Cagney eyed a woman. Neither had any use or time for camouflage, "cuteness," flirtation. Both knew what they were after, let you know it, and were intent in their playfulness. In the words of Mae West, "I like a man who takes his time."

At the same time that Mae West rose to popularity a somewhat similar actress became prominent: Jean Harlow. First publicized in *Hell's Angels* as the "platinum blonde," Jean Harlow came to represent the young, hard, unabashed American girl who resolutely takes care of herself. Like Mae West, she was down to earth, comic, and agreeable: "I'm human after all!" She came from the other side of the tracks but had more than enough warmth, vitality, and sex appeal to compensate for her lack of "refinement." In *Red-Headed Woman* she gave a striking portrayal of the brisk, snappy, "chiseling" gold-digger. In *Bombshell*, *Dinner at Eight*, *Hold Your Man*, and *Libeled Lady* she developed into the clear-eyed, lusty young woman who knows what she is after.

Just as the post-war audiences laughed the morality tales off the screen, so Mae West and Jean Harlow mocked prudery out of existence. Their honesty helped to debunk not only the innocent heroine of the pre-war days but the neurotic vampires of the twenties. Because of their presence on the screen modern woman was invested with a new and bolder attitude.

Sex and love in other interpretations have been found to be funny, amusing, "cute." *Bad Girl* (1931) has become *Easy Living* (1937); *Back Street* (1932) has changed to *Wife vs. Secretary* (1936). Films have upheld a woman's right to use whatever open strategy she can to get a man. *Man-Proof* told the story of a woman determined to win her friend's husband. *Motion Picture Herald* [23]

[22] *Motion Picture Herald*, August 19, 1933.   [23] July 27, 1937.

said of *Wine, Women and Horses*, "Other titles for this might be 'It Pays to Gamble' or 'Virtue Doesn't Always Triumph.'" *Three Blind Mice* (1938) followed three girls on a husband hunt. In *Mr. Deeds Goes to Town* the heroine runs after the hero. Unvarnished realism about love is suggested by such film titles as *Woman Chases Man, Love on the Run, It's Love I'm After, Love Is a Racket*.

But when a picture can bring out into the open the movie formula of boy-meets-girl, and laugh at it, that formula can no longer be taken too seriously. *Boy Meets Girl* voiced the growing cynicism regarding conventional love plots by deliberately spoofing them. Surprised *Stage* [24] exclaimed, "Whatever happened to Love?" Again, in reviewing *Four's a Crowd* B. R. Crisler pointed out [25] "its unblushingly superficial attitude toward romance (you never care who's going to marry who). . . ."

Marriage has also been overhauled, and domestic life is seen as a stepping-off point to more fun rather than a settling down. When *The Thin Man* made its great success, the hero and heroine were nothing other than a married couple—the sophisticated William Powell and Myrna Loy. Now the intimacy and companionship of married life were high-lighted. Husband and wife began to be treated as clever young people who continue to be in love after marriage as before, their post-wedding-day battles being on the friendliest of terms. The sense of humor of both remained their chief asset. *Vacation from Love* suggested that people "love, honor, obey and have fun." Arguments of married couples were lightly taken in *Fast Company*.

Today the triangle situation is only of minor importance. The "other woman" is no longer a vamp, the wife no longer a butterfly or a frump; it is now wit against wit, the struggle to keep a household going. The menace to marital bliss, when in the form of a beautiful female, is no longer a black-hearted Salome but a woman of charm and friendliness.

The real menace to domestic happiness, according to films, is inability to support a home. *True Confession* and *The First Hundred Years* showed a wife's attempt to help carry the expenses of a home and the husband's anxiety to meet the problem by himself.

[24] October 1937.   [25] *The New York Times*, August 12, 1938.

Such a view of domestic situations is significant. It is one more indication of the screen's attention to the everyday problems of its audiences.

Cinderella, like Pollyanna, is distinctly out of style and even incredible. *Rich Man, Poor Girl* (1938) was criticized as "trite"; films that show the heroine stepping from gutter to penthouse (*Mannequin, The Bride Wore Red*) are no longer convincing. Remakes of former domestic triangles such as *Bluebeard's Eighth Wife* (1938) and *Angel* (1937), with the philandering and faithlessness on which they pivot, seem old-fashioned and dated—unreal. Neither of these films, although rehashed and redressed, was acceptable to movie audiences. *Zaza* (1939), a remake of the story of a demimondaine who relinquishes her married lover for the sake of his child, was greeted with jeers. Said Helen Harrison [26] of such pictures,

If the past four years have done no more for movies than to kill off the whole royal cinema family from Daddy Babbitt down to the little Pollyanna herself, the step is certainly 5,000 light years nearer to adultism.

The loss of credibility in former values, the breakdown of the smugness and self-confidence of the jazz era, the growing bewilderment and dissatisfaction in a "crazy" world that does not make sense, has been reflected in the revival of comedies of satire and self-ridicule. These are best epitomized perhaps in the title of one of them: *Nothing Sacred*.

"Daffy" comedies became the fashion. Here the genteel tradition is "knocked for a loop": heroes and heroines are neither ladylike and gentlemanly. They hit each other, throw each other down, mock each other, play with each other. *It Happened One Night* (1934) was the first successful example of this school. *20th Century* (1934), *My Man Godfrey* (1936), and *Theodora Goes Wild, Topper, True Confession; Live, Love and Learn;* and *The Awful Truth* (all 1937) similarly lampooned the dignified and accepted. These films were all sophisticated, mature, full of violence—hitting, falling, throwing, acrobatics—bright dialogue, slapstick action—all imbued with terrific energy.

[26] Reprinted from *Debate* by *Motion Picture Herald*.

In these films the rebel, the individualist, is once more respected. The artist, the eccentric, the unaccountable, who was once a poor and lazy good-for-nothing in films, now is the sane person in a chaotic world. *Bringing Up Baby*, *Merrily We Live*, and *Nothing Sacred* accordingly exalted individuality and painstakingly avoided conventionality.

Emblematic of this new regard for the "wacky" are new hero and heroine types. Among the women Carole Lombard is the most outstanding in her "screw-ball" activity. Beautiful, frustrated, she asserts intense dissatisfaction with existing conventions and deep bewilderment in seeking justification of her desires. A description of Katharine Hepburn by Ruth Suckow [27] applies to Carole Lombard and the host of others of the same school:

In her willfulness, her tomboyishness, her piquant face, her tinny little voice, in her very eccentricities, there might be found a concrete definition of the intense individualism of the spoiled little rich girl of this era.

Among the men perhaps the most representative of the rebels are Fred MacMurray, Cary Grant, and Melvyn Douglas. These men are seekers of one sort or another; they point to maladjustments by pretending with childlike simplicity that they do not exist. They enter into conspiracies with themselves or comrades, telling long stories or building up long situations which are unconventional but which seem right. In *Holiday* Cary Grant turns cartwheels, with perfect English and restraint tells the heroine and the rich and dignified where to go, and dashes off and on the scene with a complete disdain of conventionality.

The same traits are exaggerated in comedians who are "out-and-out crazy": the Ritz brothers, the Marx brothers, W. C. Fields, and Mischa Auer. In their films action and conversation follow the lines laid out by the Marx brothers themselves: what is said has little relevancy to the action. One word suggests another; this suggests a third, and so the conversation spins along swiftly until something entirely irrelevant to what was originally said brings the climax. This seeming improvisation is not out of keeping with this era of "swing" and protest against regimentation of the individual.

[27] *Harper's Magazine*, July 1936.

The newsreels, no less than features, have reflected the tribulations and uncertainties as well as the foibles of the decade. Today events are photographed at the moment they occur; the addition of sound makes these records doubly valuable and has increased their scope so that their forcefulness has greatly increased. Newsreel journalists have not only recorded such "spot" news as the *Hindenburg* disaster, the British coronation, the *Panay* bombings, but documented important speeches of international figures on world important topics.

An important innovation in newsreels is the *March of Time*, inaugurated in 1934. World issues and events are presented by dramatic re-enactment in essay form so that a more rounded and more potent picture of the subject is obtained. Sensationally popular, this new approach has broadened the range and increased the power of newsreels enormously. They cover political, economic, and social issues with a deeper penetration than heretofore possible and mirror the maladjustments, uncertainties and quick march of events with a new vitality.

In general, newsreels try to avoid controversial subjects for sports, bathing beauties, fashions, and disasters but a certain percentage of political, economic and social issues are shown. In these spheres, the objectivity of newsreels has officially cleared them from censorship at all times, national and international. Nevertheless various forms of editing or omission by producers has made it possible for newsreels to propagate a particular point of view. The commentator can twist the meaning of the accompanying pictures; the proximity of certain news items can by inference comment on a particular situation; the deletion in part or whole of some important event can have a distorting effect on the news for propaganda purposes. A glaring instance of bias, for example, was the shelving of the pictures of the industrial riot and massacre in the Republic Steel Corporation strike in Chicago, June 1937. During political campaigns in particular, the partisanship of newsreels is greatly in evidence. At such times the omission or emphasis on pictures of one candidate over another has a definite propaganda effect. The impartiality of newsreels, as can be seen, is readily destroyed; the facts can be so selected as to present a particular side of a story.

This capability to manipulate facts so as to distort the event gives the movie journalists a dangerous power.

The unprecedented popularity of newsreels since sound and the depression indicates vividly the widespread concern at the present in the march of current events. This great popular participation in world news is in marked contrast to the general indifference that prevailed in the previous decade and is still another indication of the serious outlook of the times. In fact, the very popularity of newsreels today makes them a far more potent factor in shaping American thought than they have ever been before. Moreover, because their images are so obvious, their message penetrates more easily than that of the story films; because they are generally accepted as the unalloyed truth, their effect is far reaching.

The graveness of the past ten years has seen the content of movies take on a more serious tone. A depression-hit America has focused the movies' attention upon social corruption, economic discrepancies, political maladjustments, and has started a search for a code of personal and social values that will not rest entirely on sex and affluence. A fascist-threatened world has brought to films, as to the nation, a respect for force and an intense interest in war, nationalism, democracy. Responding as always to the time spirit, movies have returned to reality but under the various pressure-groups, their treatment of this reality has been for the major part, so inadequate as to render it at times meaningless. Nevertheless the movies are showing a tendency to participate more openly in world issues with a new fearlessness and with a maturity of thought that augurs a great future.

Nearly a half-century of American life could not slip by without affecting the motion pictures; nearly a half-century of motion pictures could not pass before the public gaze without affecting American life. Under the guise of entertainment movies have always not only reflected but instilled ideas and attitudes. Their power and subtlety of expression have intensified, their scope has broadened, and a widening audience has made their influence ever more potent. While being the "mirror of history," as Will Hays has said, this young art—in 1896 "another toy for Thomas Edison" —has shaped the thought and course of twentieth-century America.

Within the span of our own lifetime the American movie has come up from a minor nickel novelty to one of the foremost industries of the world whose investments total billions of dollars yearly and whose markets extend throughout the world. Beginning as a mechanical form of amusement, without any pretensions to art, the movie has enlisted all of the older arts, has developed artists within its own realm, and has discovered its own distinguishing characteristics and standards as a unique medium of expression. At the same time the moving picture has grown from a limited and comparatively simple recording device to a subtle and complex social instrument so vast in range and powerful in effect that it has become one of the most influential agencies of modern times.

This phenomenal rise has been brought about by the interaction of business man, artist, and scientist. Each has contributed with varying degrees of potency to the movie's development in every stage. After almost half a century of progress, the American film has achieved a degree of maturity. It now moves forward toward a more profound destiny. Its future lies in the creation of new forms of expression, in the deepening of its content, and in the elevation of its integrity and its point of view.

BIBLIOGRAPHY

FOR the historical background of the times, I have made special reference to the following books:

Adams, James Truslow, *Our Business Civilization*, A. & C. Boni, N. Y., 1929

Allen, Frederick Lewis, *Only Yesterday*, Blue Ribbon Books, Inc., N. Y., 1931

Beard, Charles A. and Mary R., *The Rise of American Civilization*, Macmillan Co., N. Y., 1936

Calverton, V. F., *The Liberation of American Literature*, Charles Scribner's Sons, N. Y., 1932

Cowley, Malcolm, *After the Genteel Tradition*, W. W. Norton, N. Y., 1937

Greenan, John T., *American Civilization Today*, McGraw-Hill Book Co., Inc., N. Y., 1934

Hendrick, Burton J., *The Age of Big Business*, Yale University Press, New Haven, 1919

Hicks, Granville, *The Great Tradition*, Macmillan Co., N. Y., 1933

Lynd, Robert Staughton and Helen, *Middletown*, Harcourt, Brace & Co., N. Y., 1937

Neumeyer, M. H. and E. S., *Leisure and Recreation*, Chapter XIV, "Motion Pictures," pp. 223-233, A. S. Barnes & Co., Inc., N. Y., 1936

Orton, William Aylott, *America in Search of Culture*, Little, Brown & Co., Boston, 1933

Overton, Grant (editor), *Mirrors of the Year, 1926-1927*, Frederick A. Stokes Co., N. Y., 1927

Parrington, Vernon Louis, *The Beginnings of Critical Realism in America*, Volume 3 of *Main Currents in American Thought*, Harcourt, Brace & Co., N. Y., 1930

Pattee, Fred Lewis, *The New American Literature*, D. Appleton-Century Co., 1935

Paxon, F. L., *Recent History of the United States, 1865-1927*, Houghton Mifflin Co., 1937

Shippee, Lester Burrell, *Recent American History*, Macmillan Co., N. Y., 1924

Seldes, Gilbert, *The Years of the Locust (1929-1932)*, Little, Brown & Co., Boston, 1933

Sullivan, Mark, *Our Times*, Vol. 1, "The Turn of the Century"; Vol. 2, "America Finding Herself"; Vol. 3, "Pre-War America"; Vol. 4, "The War Begins—1909-1914"; Vol. 5, "Over There—1914-1918"; Vol. 6, "The Twenties"; Charles Scribner's Sons, N. Y., 1933-35

Van Doren, Carl, *The American Novel*, Macmillan Co., N. Y., 1921

Walker, Stanley, *The Night Club Era*, Frederick A. Stokes Co., N. Y., 1933

Ward, A. C., *American Literature*, Oxford Press, N. Y., 1935

Wilson, Edmund, *The American Jitters*, Charles Scribner's Sons, N. Y., 1932

Woodward, W. E., *A New American History*, Farrar & Rinehart, N. Y., 1936

These film books were used throughout most of the periods:

Bardèche, Maurice, and Brasillach, Robert, *The History of Motion Pictures*, translated and edited by Iris Barry, W. W. Norton & Co., Inc., and The Museum of Modern Art, N. Y., 1938

Hampton, Benjamin, *A History of the Movies*, Covici-Friede, N. Y., 1931

Ramsaye, Terry, *A Million and One Nights*, 2 vols., Simon and Shuster, N. Y., 1926

Rotha, Paul, *The Film Till Now*, Jonathan Cape, London, 1930

Seldes, Gilbert, *An Hour With the Movies and the Talkies*, J. B. Lippincott Co., Philadelphia, 1929

    The Movies Come From America, Charles Scribner's Sons, N. Y., 1937

1896-1903

BOOKS

Dickson, W. K. L. and Antonia, *The Life and Inventions of Thomas A. Edison*, Thomas Y. Crowell & Co., N. Y., 1894

    History of the Kinematograph, Kinetoscope and Kinetophonograph, Albert Bunn & Co., 1895

Dyer, Frank Lewis, *Edison, His Life and Inventions*, 2 vols., Harper & Bros., N. Y., 1910

Grau, Robert, *Theatre of Science*, Broadway Publishing Co., N. Y., 1914

    The Business Man in the Amusement World, Broadway Publishing Co., N. Y., 1910

DOCUMENTS

Letter from George Melies to Jean A. LeRoy, in possession of the Museum of Modern Art Film Library

CATALOGUES

Edison Catalogues   *George Melies' "Star" Catalogues*
Kleine Optical Co. Catalogues   *Riley Brothers' Catalogues*

PERIODICALS

Leslie's Weekly   *The New York Journal*
The New York Times

1903-1908

BOOKS

Talbot, Frederick A., *Moving Pictures; How They Are Made and Worked*, J. B. Lippincott Co., Philadelphia, 1923

CATALOGUES

Edison Catalogues   *George Melies' "Star" Catalogues*
Klcine Optical Co. Catalogues   *Vitagraph Catalogues*

PERIODICALS

Film Reports   *New York Clipper, The*
Harper's Weekly   *Scientific American, The*
Independent   *Views and Film Index*
Moving Picture World, The   *World To-day, The*

SPECIAL ARTICLES

"Actorless Theatre," *Current Literature*, November, 1904

"Making of Moving Pictures," by G. Brabin, *The Scientific American*, July 11 and 18, 1908

"Moving Picture Drama for the Multitude," by G. E. Walsh, *The Independent*, February 6, 1908

"Moving Pictures ad Nauseam," *The Review of Reviews*, December, 1908

"Nickel Madness," by B. W. Currie, *Harper's Weekly*, August 24, 1907

"Nickelodeon," by L. F. Pierce, *The World To-day*, October, 1908

"Plays Without Words," *Scribner's Magazine*, July, 1909

1908-1914

BOOKS

Agnew, Frances, *Motion Picture Acting*, Reliance Newspaper Syndicate, N. Y., 1913

Ball, Eustace Hale, *The Art of the Photoplay*, G. W. Dillingham Co., N. Y., 1913

Drinkwater, John, *The Life and Adventures of Carl Laemmle*, G. P. Putnam's Sons, N. Y., 1931

Gauntier, Gene, *Blazing the Trail*, MS. in possession of the Museum of Modern Art Film Library, N. Y.

Grau, Robert, *The Theatre of Science*, Broadway Publishing Co., N. Y., 1914

Griffith, Mrs. D. W., *When the Movies Were Young*, E. P. Dutton & Co., N. Y., 1925

Harrison, Louis Reeves, *Screencraft*, Chalmers Publishing Co., 1916

Hulfish, David S., *Cyclopedia of Motion Picture Work*, American School of Correspondence, Chicago, 1911

Lindsay, Vachel, *The Art of the Moving Picture*, Macmillan Co., N. Y., 1915

Motion Picture Annual for 1912, Moving Picture World, N. Y., 1913

Rathbun, John B., *Motion Picture Making and Exhibiting*, Charles P. Thompson Co., Chicago, 1914

Sargent, Epes Winthrop, *The Technique of the Photoplay*, Moving Picture World, N. Y., 1913

Who's Who in the Motion Picture World, Who's Who in Pictures Publishing Co., N. Y., 1916 (?)

CATALOGUES AND PRESS SHEETS

Biograph Catalogues and *Press Sheets*

Edison Catalogues

Essanay Catalogues and *Press Sheets*

General Film Co. Catalogues

Kalem Catalogues and *Press Sheets*

Kleine Optical Co. Catalogues

Vitagraph Catalogues and *Press Sheets*

I. M. P. Catalogues and *Press Sheets*

PERIODICALS

Billboard, The

Biograph, The

Dramatic Mirror, The

Eclair Bulletin

Edison Kinetograms

Essanay News

Everybody's

Exhibitor's Times

Film Pictorial

Good Housekeeping

Harper's Weekly

Independent, The

McClure's

Movie Pictorial

Moving Picture World, The
Motion Picture Story Magazine
Munsey's Magazine
New York Clipper
New York Morning Telegraph

Outlook, The
Stage (1911 Anniversary Issue; September, 1935)
Woman's Home Companion

SPECIAL ARTICLES

American Magazine, "Ubiquitous Moving Picture," July, 1913

Benson, A. L., "Edison's Substitute for Schoolbooks," *World To-day*, March, 1912

Beranger, C. F., "Photoplay—A New Kind of Drama," *Harper's Weekly*, September 7, 1912

Berlyn, A., "Plague of Pictures," *Living Age*, April 25, 1914

Berry, G., "Bridget of the Movies," *The Bookman*, August, 1914

Brewer, C. B., "Widening Field of the Motion Picture," *The Century Magazine*, May, 1913

Bush, W. Stephen, "History on the Screen," *The Moving Picture World*, February 22, 1913

"Lecture on Three-Reel Production," *The Moving Picture World*, October 7, 1911

"New Functions of the Motion Picture," *The Moving Picture World*, July 6, 1912

"The Film of the Future," *The Moving Picture World*, September 26, 1908

"The Flag and Baby Picture," *The Moving Picture World*, November 30, 1912

"The Moving Picture and the Press," *The Moving Picture World*, March 8, 1913

Coffin, H. L., "Movies on the Move," *Everybody's Magazine*, October, 1912

Collier, J., "Film Shows and Lawmakers," *The Survey*, February 8, 1913

Current Opinion, "A New Art," June, 1914

"Moral Havoc Wrought by Motion Pictures," April, 1914

Davis, H. R., "Breaking Into the Movies," *Scribner's Magazine*, November, 1914

Dial, The, "Cinematographic Craze," February 16, 1914

Dunbar, O. H., "Lure of the Films," *Harper's Weekly*, January 18, 1913

Eaton, W. P., "Canned Drama," *American Magazine*, September, 1909

"Menace of the Movies," *American Magazine*, September, 1913

"New Epoch in the Movies," *American Magazine*, October, 1914

Fisher, B., "Motion Pictures to Make Good Citizens," *The American City*, September, 1912

Fox, L., "Bringing the Talkies to Your Home," *The Technical World*, August, 1913

Frohman, D., "How to Write a Moving Picture Play," *Woman's Home Companion*, July, 1914

"Movies and the Theatre," *Woman's Home Companion*, November, 1913

Fulk, J. R., "Effect on Education and Morals of the Moving Picture Shows," *National Educational Association*, 1912

Grau, R., "Actors by Proxy," *The Independent*, July 17, 1913

"Fortunes in the Moving Picture Field," *The Overland Monthly*, April, 1911

"Movies Encroaching on the Stage," *The Overland Monthly*, November, 1913

"Moving Picture Show and the Living Drama," *The Review of Reviews*, March, 1912

"Talking Pictures and Reality," *Lippincott's Magazine*, August, 1913

"Talking Picture and the Drama," *The Scientific American*, August 12, 1911

Halliday, C., "Motion Picture Teacher," *The World's Work*, May, 1913

Hamilton, Clayton, "Art of the Moving Picture Play," *The Bookman*, January, 1911

Harrison, Louis Reeves, "Apostles of Nothingness," *The Moving Picture World*, May 3, 1913

"Both Entertaining and Educational," *The Moving Picture World*, September 7, 1912

"David W. Griffith, the Art Director and His Work," *The Moving Picture World*, November 22, 1913

"Don't Bore the Audience," *The Moving Picture World*, August 24, 1912

"Economy of Attention," *The Moving Picture World*, June 7, 1913

"Historical Photoplays," *The Moving Picture World*, May 17, 1913

"Melodrama," *The Moving Picture World*, May 13, 1911

"New Fields," *The Moving Picture World*, December 14, 1912

"Photoplay Principles," *The Moving Picture World*, September 13, 1913

"Pictured Action, or Acted Pictures," *The Moving Picture World*, November 2, 1912

"Plots," *The Moving Picture World*, August 1, 1911

"Realism," *The Moving Picture World*, December 6, 1913

"The Elusive Quality," *The Moving Picture World*, Auugst 20, 1910

"The Fascinating Criminal," *The Moving Picture World*, April 26, 1913

"The Pictural Drama as a Fine Art," *The Moving Picture World*, November 19, 1911

Hibbard, D. O., "Moving Picture—The Good and Bad of It," *The Outlook*, July 13, 1912

Howe, F. C., "What to Do With the Motion Picture Show; Shall It Be Censored?" *The Outlook*, June 20, 1914

Howells, W. D., "Cinematographic Show, Its Essence and Influence," *Harper's Magazine*, September, 1912

Independent, The, "Birth of a New Art," April 6, 1914

"Drama and The People" (editorial), September 29, 1910

"Frozen Movies," March 2, 1914

Inglis, W., "Edison and the New Education," *Harper's Weekly*, November 4, 1911

"Morals and Moving Pictures," *Harper's Weekly*, July 30, 1910

Johnston, W. A., "Silent Stage," *Harper's Weekly*, November 13, 1909

Kallen, Horace M., "The Dramatic Picture Versus the Pictorial Drama," *Harvard Monthly*, March, 1910

Lanier, H. W., "Latest Business Gold Rush," *The World's Work*, June, 1914

Lawrence, Florence, "History of Moving Pictures," *Photoplay*, October, November, December, 1914

Leupp, C. D., "Motion Picture as a Social Worker," *The Survey*, August 27, 1910

Literary Digest, The, "Bernhardt in Motion Pictures," August 3, 1912

"Hope in Movies," June 13, 1914

"Monopoly and Motion Pictures," August 31, 1912

"Motion Picture as Educator," February 10, 1912

"Recruiting by Motion Pictures," June 28, 1913

"Sacred Subjects," November 30, 1912

"Solving the Cinema Morals," August 8, 1914

McKeever, W. A., "Primary School for Criminals," *Good Housekeeping*, August, 1910

Marcosson, I. F., "Money and the Movies," *Collier's*, July 18, 1914

Michelson, M., "Immortality in the Films," *Collier's*, April 12, 1913

Middleton, P. H., "Movies Speed Up Labor," *The Technical World*, April, 1913

Musson, B., and Grau, R., "Fortunes in Films," *McClure's*, December, 1912

Nation, The, "Democratic Art," August 28, 1913

New York World-Telegram Metropolitan Week-End Section, The, Interview With J. Searle Dawley, January 2, 1937

Outlook, The, "Motion Pictures of Tomorrow," June 27, 1914

"White-Slave Films," February 14, 1914

Palmer, L. E., "World in Motion," *The Survey*, June 5, 1909

Review of Reviews, The, "Cultural Value of Motion Pictures," July, 1914

"Motion Pictures and National Character," September, 1910

Rothacker, W. R., "Industrial Use of the Moving Picture," *The Scientific American*, June 5, 1912

Survey, The, "Moving Pictures to Be Social Workers," May 6, 1911

Tevis, C. V., "Censoring the Five-Cent Drama," *The World To-day*, October, 1910

Townsend, E. W., "Picture Plays," *The Outlook*, November 27, 1909

Vorse, Mary H., "Picture Show Audiences," *The Outlook*, June 24, 1911

Willey, D. A., "Theatre's New Rival," *Lippincott's Magazine*, October, 1909

Wooley, E. M., "Story of D. W. Griffith, the $100,000 Salary Man of the Movies," *McClure's*, September, 1914

World's Work, The, "Theatre with Five Millions," May, 1910

1914-1918

BOOKS

Bakshy, Alexander, *Path of the Modern Russian Stage* ("The Kinematograph as Art"), Cecil Palmer and Hayward, London, 1916

Bertsch, Marguerite, *How to Write for Moving Pictures*, George H. Doran Co., N. Y., 1917

Blackton, J. Stuart, Lecture in book (mimeographed), *Introduction to the Photoplay*, pp. 6 to 20; University of Southern California and Academy of Motion Picture Arts and Sciences, Los Angeles, 1929

Croy, Homer, *How Motion Pictures Are Made*, Harper & Bros., N. Y., 1918

Delluc, Louis, *Charlie Chaplin*, translated from the French by Hamish Miles, John Lane Co., London, 1922

Eastman, Max, *Enjoyment of Laughter*, Simon & Shuster, N. Y., 1936

Faure, Elie, *The Art of Cineplastics*, translated from the French by Walter Pach, Four Seas Co., Boston, 1923

Fowler, Gene, *Father Goose*, Covici-Friede, N. Y., 1934

Freeburg, V. O., *Art of Photoplay Making*, Macmillan Co., N. Y., 1918

Goldwyn, Samuel, *Behind the Screen*, George H. Doran Co., N. Y., 1923

Hannon, William Morgan, *The Photodrama; Its Place among the Fine Arts*, Ruskin Press, New Orleans, 1915

Ince, Thomas, *History of the Motion Picture*, MS. in possession of the Museum of Modern Art Film Library, N. Y.

Jones, B. E. (editor), *How to Make and Operate Moving Pictures*, Funk & Wagnall Co., N. Y., 1916

Lowrey, Carolyn, *The First 100 Men and Women of the Screen*, Moffatt, Yard Co., N. Y., 1920

Muensterberg, Hugo, *The Photoplay*, D. Appleton & Co., N. Y., 1916

Nathan, George Jean, *The Popular Theatre*, Alfred H. Knopf, N. Y., 1918

Paine, Alfred Bigelow, *Life and Lillian Gish*, Macmillan Co., N. Y., 1932

Phillips, Henry A., *The Photodrama*, Stanhope-Dodge Publishing Co., Larchmont, N. Y., 1914

Seldes, Gilbert, *The Seven Lively Arts*, Harper & Bros., N. Y., 1924

Wagner, Robert, *Film Folk*, Century Co., N. Y., 1918

Welsh, Robert E., *A.B.C. of Motion Pictures*, Harper & Bros., N. Y., 1916

Woods, Frank, *History of the Motion Picture; Introduction to the Photoplay* (mimeographed book published by University of Southern California and Motion Picture Academy of Arts and Sciences, Los Angeles, 1929)

PAMPHLETS AND DOCUMENTS

Pamphlets

National Association for the Advancement of Colored People, The, *Fighting a Vicious Film; a Record of Protest Against "The Birth of a Nation,"* Boston, 1915

Griffith, D. W., *The Rise and Fall of Free Speech in America*, Los Angeles, 1916

Long, Robert Edgar, *David Wark Griffith*, D. W. Griffith Service, 1920

Potamkin, Harry Alan, *The Eyes of the Movies*, International Publishing Co., N. Y., 1934

Documents

Scenarios of D. W. Griffith's *The Birth of a Nation* and *Intolerance*, furnished by Theodore Huff

Original program for first public showing of *The Birth of a Nation*, N. Y. Public Library

Original program for first public showing of *Intolerance*, N. Y. Public Library

Program for revival showing of *Intolerance*, 1933

Museum of Modern Art Film Library program notes for *The Birth of a Nation* and *Intolerance*, by Iris Barry, Series I, Program 3

PERIODICALS

American Magazine, The	*Motography*
Bookman, The	*Moving Pictures*
Collier's	*Moving Picture World, The*
Crisis, The	*Nation, The*
Current Opinion	*New Republic, The*
Dramatic Mirror, The	*Outlook, The*
Everybody's Magazine	*Photoplay*
Film Pictorial	*Review of Reviews, The*
Independent, The	*Script*
Living Age	*Survey, The*
Lippincott's Magazine	*Variety*
Motion Picture Classic	*Wids*
Motion Picture Story Magazine	*World's Work, The*
Metropolitan Magazine	

SPECIAL ARTICLES

Allen, L. A., "Making Americans by Motion Pictures," *The American City*, September, 1914

Blackton, J. Stuart, "Yesterdays of Vitagraph," *Photoplay*, July, 1919

"In the Director's Chair," *The Motion Picture Director*, September, 1926

Blaine, H. B., "An Open Letter to the Editor Concerning 'The Birth of a Nation,'" *The New Republic*, May 8, 1915

Bush, W. Stephen, "Belasco on Motion Pictures," *The Moving Picture World*, June 13, 1914

"Jack London, Picture Writer," *The Moving Picture World*, January 31, 1914

"War Films," *The Moving Picture World*, September 19, 1914

Croon-Johnson, A., A Report on the Showing of Griffith's Film at the Scala Theatre, London, *The Review of Reviews*, December, 1915

Current Opinion, "Camera Drama versus Spoken," December, 1915

"Millions of Feet of Movie Films for the Soldiers," September, 1918

Dench, Ernest A., "Following the Movies to the Firing Line," *Motion Picture Magazine*, October, 1916

Denlinger, Sutherland, "We Go to War," *New York World-Telegram Metropolitan Week-End Section*, April 12, 1937

Eaton, Walter Prichard, "Class Consciousness and the Movies," *The Atlantic Monthly*, January, 1915

"The Birth of a Nation," *The Boston Transcript*, March 31, 1915

Emerson, John, and Loos, Anita, "How to Write Photoplays," *Photoplay*, February, March, April, June and July, 1918

Ennis, Burt, "The Happy Days; The Vitagraph Years," *Motion Picture Classic*, October, 1926

Gavin, Arthur, Jr., "Making Cartoon Movies," *Photoplay*, June, 1917

Gilbert, Douglas, "Came the Dawn," *New York World-Telegram*, June 23, 24, 25, 1936

Gish, Lillian, "Birth of an Era," *Stage*, January, 1937

Grace, R., "Early Days of the Motion Picture," *Photo Era*, March, 1915

Gregory, Thomas B., "The Birth of a Nation," *New York American*, March 5, 1915

Griffith, D. W., "Pictures versus One Night Stands," *The Independent*, December 11, 1916

"What I Demand of Movie Stars," *Motion Picture Classic*, February, 1917.

Hackett, Francis, "The Birth of a Nation," *The New Republic*, March 20, 1915

Hamilton, J. Shelley, "Putting a New Move in the Movies," *Everybody's Magazine*, June, 1915

Harrison, Louis Reeves, "Alas, Poor Yorick!" *The Moving Picture World*, March 28, 1914

"Big Changes Taking Place," *The Moving Picture World*, January 3, 1914

"Five Reels," *The Moving Picture World*, February 7, 1914

"The Art of Criticism," *The Moving Picture World*, January 31, 1914

Lawson, W. P., "The Movies: Their Importance and Supervision," *Harper's Weekly*, January 2, 1915

Lescarboura, A. S., "Generals of Shadowland Warfare," *The Scientific American*, May 5, 1917

Lindsay, V., "Photoplay Progress: Professor Munsterberg's Book, The Photoplay," *The New Republic*, February 17, 1917

Literary Digest, "Fake War Movies," November 13, 1915

MacMahon, Henry, "The Art of the Movies," *The New York Times*, June 6, 1915

Macgowan, Kenneth, "Beyond the Screen," *Seven Arts Magazine*, December, 1916

"Crossroads of Stage and Screen," *Seven Arts Magazine*, April, 1917

Mackaye, Milton, "The Birth of a Nation," *Scribner's Magazine*, November, 1937

Matthews, B., "Are the Movies a Menace to the Drama?" *Current Opinion*, May, 1917

National Board of Review Magazine, "A Revaluation of 'The Birth of a Nation' in Reissued Version"; reprinted from *Variety* (December 24, 1930), January, 1931

New Republic, The, "The Editor Speaks Editorially on 'The Birth of a Nation,'" June 5, 1915

O'Hara, Kenneth, "The Life of Thomas H. Ince," *Photoplay*, June, 1917

Peet, Creighton, "The Birth of a Nation; review, including account of cost and earnings," *The Outlook and Independent*, January 7, 1931

Rumbold, Charlotte, Letter to the editor concerning "The Birth of a Nation," *The New Republic*, June 5, 1915

Scientific American, The, "Artisans of the Motion-Picture Films," September 2, 1916

"Have Motion Pictures Changed Us?" January 13, 1917

Sherwood, H. F., "Democracy and the Movies," *The Bookman*, May, 1915

Smith, Frederick James, "The Evolution of the Motion Pictures," *The Dramatic Mirror*, 1913, volume 69, number 1792

Soule, George, "After the Play," *The New Republic*, September 30, 1916

Stearns, Harold, "Art in Moving Pictures," *The New Republic*, September 25, 1915

Tourneur, Maurice, "The Movies Create Art," *Harper's Weekly*, April 29, 1916

Tully, Jim, "The King of Laughter," *Esquire*, June, 1937

Wilkinson, N.. "Shakespeare of the Movies," *Harper's Weekly*, January 15, 1916

1919-1929

BOOKS

Balázs, Béla, *Der Geist des Films*, Wilhelm Knapp, Berlin, 1930

Barry, Iris, *Let's Go to the Movies*, Payson & Clarke, Ltd., London, 1926

Betts, Ernest, *Heraclitus, or The Future of the Movies*, E. P. Dutton & Co., N. Y., 1928

Bloem, Walter S., *The Soul of the Moving Pictures*, E. P. Dutton & Co., N. Y., 1924

Blue Book of the Screen, 1924 (?)

Bollman, Gladys and Henry, *Motion Pictures for Community Needs*, Henry Holt & Co., N. Y., 1922

Buckle, Gerard Fort, *The Mind and the Film*, George Routledge & Sons, Ltd., London, 1926

Chaplin, Charlie, *My Trip Abroad*, Harper & Bros., N. Y., 1922

Carter, Huntly, *The New Theatre and Cinema of Soviet Russia*, International Publishers Co., N. Y., 1925

Dressler, Marie, *My Own Story*, Little, Brown & Co., Boston, 1934

Ellis, Don Carlos, and Thornborough, Laura, *Motion Pictures in Education*, Thomas Y. Crowell Co., N. Y., 1923

Emerson, John, and Loos, Anita, *Breaking Into the Movies*, James A. McCann
    Co., N. Y., 1921
Ernst, Morris, and Lorentz, Pare, *Censored*, Cape & Smith, N. Y., 1930
Faure, Elie, *The Art of Cineplastics*, translated from the French by Walter
    Pach, Four Seas Co., Boston, 1923
Fawcett, L'Estrange, *Films, Facts and Forecasts*, Geoffrey Bles, London, 1927
Franklin, Harold B., *Sound Motion Pictures*, Doubleday, Doran & Co., Inc.,
    N. Y., 1929
Frazier, Marion Howard, *Stage and Screen*, M. H. Frazier, Boston, 1920
Freeburg, Victor Oscar, *Pictorial Beauty on the Screen*, Macmillan Co., N. Y.,
    1923
Freeman, Joseph; Kunitz, Joshua, and Lozowick, Louis, *Voices of October*,
    Vanguard Press, N. Y., 1930
Goldwyn, Samuel, *Behind the Screen*, George H. Doran, N. Y., 1923
Green, Fitzhugh, *The Film Finds Its Tongue*, G. P. Putnam's Sons, N. Y., 1929
Hart, William S., *My Life East and West*, Houghton Mifflin Co., 1929
Hays, Will H. (compiler), *The Photoplay from a Critical Viewpoint*, 1929
    See and Hear, Motion Picture Producers and Distributors, 1929
Hughes, Laurence (editor), *The Truth About the Movies*, Hollywood, Cali-
    fornia, 1924
Huxley, Aldous, *Essays New and Old* (*Where Are the Movies Moving?*),
    George H. Doran Co., N. Y., 1927
Irwin, Will, *The House That Shadows Built*, Doubleday, Doran & Co., N. Y.,
    1928
Jones, Charles Reed, *Breaking Into the Movies*, Unicorn Press, N. Y., 1927
Kennedy, Joseph P. (editor), *The Story of the Films*, A. W. Shaw Co., Chi-
    cago, 1927
Klingender, F. D., and Legg, Stuart, *Money Behind the Screen*, Lawrence &
    Wishart, London, 1937
Klumph, Inez and Helen, *Screen Acting*, Falk Publishing Co., N. Y., 1922
Lane, Tamar, *What's Wrong With the Movies?* Waverly Co., Los Angeles,
    1923
Lejeune, C. A., *Cinema*, Alexander Maclehose & Co., London, 1931
Lescarboura, Austin C., *Behind the Motion-Picture Screen*, Scientific American
    Publishing Co., N. Y., 1921
Lubschez, Ben Z., *The Story of the Motion Picture*, Reeland Publishing Co.,
    N. Y., 1920
Mencken, H. L., *Prejudices*, Sixth Series (Appendix from Moronia), Knopf,
    N. Y., 1927
Milne, Peter, *Motion Picture Directing*, Falk Publishing Co., N. Y., 1922
Messel, Rudolf, *This Film Business*, Benn, London, 1928
Motion Picture Directors of Hollywood, 1926-1927
Nathan, George Jean, *Art of the Night* (*Notes on the Movies*), Knopf, N. Y.,
    1928
Oberholtzer, Ellis Paxson, *The Morals of the Movies*, Penn Publishing Co.,
    Philadelphia, 1922
O'Dell, Scott, *Representative Photoplays Analyzed*, Palmer Institute, Holly-
    wood, 1924
Paine, Albert Bigelow, *Life and Lillian Gish*, Macmillan Co., N. Y., 1932
Patterson, Frances Taylor, *Scenario and Screen*, Harcourt, Brace & Co., N. Y.,
    1928
Platt, Agnes, *Practical Hints on Acting for the Cinema*, E. P. Dutton & Co.,
    N. Y., 1923

Powell, A. Van Buren, *The Photoplay Synopsis*, Home Correspondence School, Springfield, 1919

Pudovkin, V. I., *Film Technique*, translated from the Russian by Ivor Montagu, George Newnes, Ltd., London, 1929; enlarged, 1933

Richter, Hans, *Filmgegner von Heute—Filmgegner von Morgen*, Herman Reckendorf, Berlin, 1929

Sherwood, Robert E., *The Best Moving Pictures of 1922-1923*, Small, Maynard & Co., Boston, 1923

Seabury, William M., *The Public and the Motion-Picture Industry*, Macmillan Co., N. Y., 1926

Talbot, Frederick A., *Moving Pictures*, J. P. Lippincott Co., Philadelphia, 1923

Talmey, Allene, *Doug and Mary and Others*, Macy-Masius, Inc., N. Y., 1927

Taylor, C. W. (compiler), *Masters and Masterpieces of the Screen*, P. F. Collier & Sons Co., N. Y., 1927

Van Zile, Edward S., *That Marvel—The Movies*, G. P. Putnam's Sons, N. Y., 1923

Williamson, Alice M., *Alice in Movieland*, D. Appleton & Co., N. Y., 1928

BOOKLETS, PAMPHLETS, ETC.

Fletcher, John Gould, *The Crisis of the Film*, Seattle, 1929

Kaufman, Nicholas, *Filmtechnik und Kultur*, Berlin, 1931

Lane, Tamar and Annabel, *Hollywood and the Movies*, Mercury Publishing Co., Hollywood, California, 1928

L'Art Cinematographique, No. IV (Paris), 1927; No. VII, 1930

Monosson, L. I., *The Soviet Cinematography*, N. Y.(?), 1930 (?)

Moussinac, Leon, *Naissance du Cinema*, Paris, 1929

Mouvement, Revue Mensuelle, No. 1 (Paris), June, 1933

Pettijohn, Charles C., *The Motion Picture*, N. Y.(?), 1923 (?)

Pfeiffer, Heinrich, *Das Deutsche Lichtbild Buch*, August Scherl, Berlin, 1930 (?)

Rambova, Natacha, *Rudolph Valentino*, Jacobsen-Hodgkinson Corp., N. Y., 1927

The Silver Sheet (press sheets, bound volume), The Studio Publication of the Thomas H. Ince Studios, 1923

Weinberg, Herman, *Scrapbook for 1925-1928* (collection of newspaper reviews, publicity stories, interviews, etc., on foreign films)

PERIODICALS

Cinema Art	*Moving Picture World, The*
Close Up (London)	*Movie Makers*
Dial Magazine, The	*National Board of Review Magazine*
Education Screen	*Nation, The*
Film Daily	*New Masses, The*
Film Mercury	*New Republic, The*
Film Spectator	*Photoplay*
Hound and Horn	*Screenland*
Judge	*Shadowland*
Ladies' Home Journal, The	*Theatre Arts Monthly*
Life	*Theatre Guild Magazine*
Motion Picture Classic	*Theatre Magazine*
Motion Picture Magazine	*Vanity Fair*
Motion Picture Monthly	*Variety*
Motion Picture News	

SPECIAL ARTICLES

Anisimov, Ivan, "The Films of Eisenstein," *International Literature* (Moscow), No. 3, 1931

Bajan, M., "Dovjenko, Soviet Cinema Director," translated from the Russian by Claire Brody, *New Theatre*, April, 1934

Bakshy, Alexander, "A Knight Errant," *The Dial Magazine*, May, 1928
"Character and Drama," *The Nation*, April 18, 1928
"Drama and the Screen," *The New York Times*, January 13, 1929
"Introducing the Dramatic Accent," *Movie Makers*, December, 1928
"Notes on Sound and Silence," *Theatre Arts Monthly*, February, 1929
"Russian Contribution," *The Nation*, July 25, 1928
"The Artistic Possibilities of the Cinema," *National Board of Review Magazine*, November, 1928
"The Future of the Movies," *The Nation*, October 10, 1928
"The Language of Images," *The Nation*, December 26, 1928
"The Movie Scene," *Theatre Arts Monthly*, February, 1929
"The New Art of the Moving Pictures," *Theatre Arts Monthly*, April, 1927
"The Road to Art in the Motion Pictures," *Theatre Arts Monthly*, June, 1927
"There Are Silent Pictures," *The Nation*, August 21, 1929
"The Talkies," *The Nation*, February 20, 1929

Barr, Alfred H., Jr., "The Researches of Eisenstein," *Drawing and Design*, London, June, 1928
"Sergei Michailovitch Eisenstein," *The Arts*, December, 1928

Bell, Monta, "The Director, His Problems and Qualifications," *Theatre Arts Monthly*, 1929

Blackton, J. Stuart, "The Movies Are Growing Up," *Motion Picture Magazine*, February, 1925

Buchwald, Nathaniel, "Film Propaganda," *Soviet Russia To-day*, 1932

Carr, Harry, "Hollywood's One Real Genius—'Von,'" *Photoplay*, May, 1928
"Von Stroheim," *Motion Picture Classic*, November, 1925

Condon, Frank, "Cruze, Director," *Collier's*, March 28, 1936

Dreiser, Theodore, "Interview with Sennett," *Photoplay*, August, 1928

Eisenstein, Sergei, "An American Tragedy," *Close Up* (London), June, 1933
"Autobiography," *International Literature* (Moscow), October, 1933
"Cinema with Tears!" *Close Up*, March, 1933
"Detective Work in the GIK," *Close Up*, December, 1932
"Doing Without Actors," *Cinema*, June, 1930
"Filmic Art and Training," *Close Up*, March, 1930
"Film Form 1935," *Life and Letters Today* (London), Spring, 1935
"Film Forms: New Problems," *New Theatre*, April and May, 1935
"Mass Movies," *The Nation*, November 8, 1927
"Open Letter to Dr. Goebbels," *Film Art* (London), Winter, 1934
"Program for Teaching the Theory and Practice of Film Direction," *Life and Letters Today*, Winter, 1936-7
"The Cinema in America," *International Literature* (Moscow), July, 1933
"The Cinematic Principle and Japanese Culture," *transition*, June, 1930
"The Difficult Bride," *Film Art*, Spring, 1934
"The Dynamic Square," *Hound and Horn*, April-June, 1931
"The Enchantment from the Pear Garden," *Theatre Arts Monthly*, October, 1935

"The Epic in the Soviet Films," *International Literature No. 10-11* (Moscow), 1937

"The Fourth Dimension in the Kino," *Close Up*, March and April, 1930

"The Intellectual Cinema," *Left No. 2*

"The New Language of Cinematography," *Close Up*, May, 1929

"The New Soviet Cinema," *New Theatre*, January, 1935

"The Mistakes of Bezhin Lug," *International Literature*, November 8, 1937

"The Principles of Film Form," *Close Up*, September, 1931

"The Sound Film: A Statement from USSR," *Close Up*, October, 1928

"Through Theatre to Cinema," *Theatre Arts Monthly*, September, 1936

Ferguson, Otis, "Pudovkin and the Little Men," *The New Republic*, June 20, 1934

Gerstein, Evelyn, "Four Films of New Types," *Theatre Arts Monthly*, April, 1927

"Potemkin," *The New Republic*, November 20, 1926

"Russia's Film Wizard," *Theatre Guild Magazine*, February, 1930

"Symbols of Silence," *Boston Evening Transcript*, November 23, 1929

"Three Russian Movies," *Theatre Guild Magazine*, October, 1929

Glagolin, B. S., "Creative Path of Soviet Films," *The New York Times*, April 30, 1931

Glassgold, C. Adolph, "Backgrounds in the Moving Pictures," *The Arts*, October, 1927

"Movie Magic," *The Arts*, December, 1927

"The Films, Amateur or Professional," *The Arts*, January, 1929

"The Films, Canned for Eternity," *The Arts*, October, 1928

"The Films, More Talk," *The Arts*, April, 1929

Goodman, Paul, "Bad 'Nature-Impressionism' in Eisenstein," *Trend*, March-April, 1934

Grierson, John, "Flaherty," *Cinema Quarterly* (London), Autumn, 1932

"Flaherty, Naturalism and the Problem of the English Cinema," *Art Work* (London), Autumn, 1931

Griffith, D. W., "The Movies a Hundred Years from Now," *Collier's*, May 3, 1928

"History and Development of Motion Pictures," *Mentor Magazine*, July, 1931

"The Greatest Theatrical Force," *The Moving Picture World*, March 26, 1927

"The Motion Picture To-day and To-morrow," *Theatre Magazine*, October, 1929

Hecht, Ben, "My Testimony to the Movies," *Theatre*, June, 1929

Heiman, Beatrice, "Eisenstein, Russia's Genius of the Cinema," *Theatre*, July, 1930

Herring, Robert, "Film Imagery, Seastrom," *Close Up* (London), January, 1929

"The Films," *Drawing and Design* (London), July, 1927

Hutchison, Barney, "Hollywood Still Leads . . . Says Ernst Lubitsch," *American Cinematographer*, March, 1933

Jacobs, Lewis, "Introduction to Eisenstein," *Experimental Cinema No. 3*, 1932-33

Josephson, Matthew, "Masters of the Motion Pictures," *Classic*, August, 1926

"Super-Realism in the Movies," *Classic*, April, 1926

Lasser, David, "The New Art of Talking Pictures," *The New York Times*, January 13, 1929

Leger, Fernand, "The Cult of the Closeup," *The Arts*, May, 1931

"A New Realism—The Object," *Little Review*, Winter, 1926

Lorentz, Pare, "The Stillborn Art," *The Forum*, 1928

Lozowick, Louis, "The Soviet Cinema," *Theatre Arts Magazine*, September, 1929

Lubitsch, Ernst, "Lubitsch Demands Beauties," *The New York World-Telegram*, October 13, 1937

Macdonald, Dwight, "Eisenstein, Pudovkin and Others," *Miscellany*, April, July, 1931

Maeterlinck, Maurice, "The Spiritual Future of America and the Movies," *Photoplay*, March, 1921

Murnau, Fred W., "The Ideal Picture Needs No Titles," *Theatre Magazine*, January, 1928

Nurenberg, Thelma, "Russia Finds Uses for the Cinema," *The New York Times*, February 21, 1932

Peet, Creighton, "The Jumbled Talkies," *The Outlook*, October 23, 1929

Potamkin, Harry Alan, "The Close-Up's the Thing," *Movie Makers*, September, 1929

Seldes, Gilbert V., "Art in the Movies," *The Nation*, July 29, 1925

"Camera Angles," *The New Republic*, March 9, 1927

"Chaplin and Some Others," *The Nation*, November 11, 1925

"How to Save the Movies from Stage Blight," *Theatre*, November, 1925

"Russian and American Movies," *The New Republic*, August 7, 1929

"Talkies Progress," *Harper's Magazine*, August, 1929

"The Abstract Movie," *The New Republic*, September 15, 1926

"The Movie Director," *The New Republic*, May 27, 1925

"The Path of the Movies," *The Nation*, April 29, 1925

"The Mobile Camera," *The New Republic*, October 30, 1929

"The Movie Commits Suicide," *Harper's Magazine*, November, 1928

"Theory About Talkies," *The New Republic*, August 8, 1928

Stearns, Myron M., "The Movies Talk!" *The Ladies' Home Journal*, November, 1928

The Film and Photo League, "History of the Soviet Film" (mimeographed programs), 1933

Tully, Jim, "D. W. Griffith," *Vanity Fair*, November, 1926

"James Cruze," *Vanity Fair*, December, 1927

"Cecil B. DeMille," *Vanity Fair*, April, 1926

"Ernst Lubitsch," *Vanity Fair*, December, 1926

"Erich Von Stroheim," *Vanity Fair*, March, 1926

Watts, Richard, Jr., "D. W. Griffith, Biography," *New Theatre*, November, 1936

"Soviet Cinema Art," *Research Bulletin in the Soviet Union*, May 15, 1936

"Tumbrels Are Heard by a Critic," *New York Herald Tribune*, July 3, 1932

Weinberg, Herman, "The Cinema Discovers the Professor," *The Institute Magazine* (Columbia University), December, 1928

"Lubitsch Views the Movies," *Movie Makers*, September, 1929

"Erich von Stroheim," *Film Art* (London), Spring, 1937

"Motion Pictures as a Social Force," *Current History*, April, 1925

White, Kenneth, "F. W. Murnau," *Hound and Horn*, July-September, 1931

"The Style of Ernst Lubitsch," *Hound and Horn*, January-March, 1931

Woolf, Virginia, "The Movies and Reality," *The New Republic*, August 4, 1926

Wright, Willard Huntington, "Romance of the Third Dimension," *Photoplay* September, 1921

BOOKS

Adler, Mortimer J., *Art and Prudence*, Longmans, Green & Co., N. Y., 1937

Anderson, Milton, *The Modern Goliath*, David Press, Los Angeles, 1935

Arnheim, Rudolf, *Film*, Faber & Faber, London, 1933

Arosev, A. (editor), *Soviet Cinema*, V.O.K.S., Moscow, 1937

Bennett, Alfred Gordon, *Cinemania*, Jarrolds, Ltd., London, 1937

Bower, Dallas, *Plan for Cinema*, J. M. Dent & Sons, London, 1936

Brundidge, H. T., *Twinkle, Twinkle, Little Star*, E. P. Dutton & Co., Inc., N. Y., 1930

Brunel, Adrian, *Filmcraft*, G. Newnes, Ltd., London, 1935
   Film Production, G. Newnes, Ltd., London, 1936

Bryher, W., *Film Problems of Soviet Russia*, Territet, Switzerland, 1929

Buchanan, Andrew, *The Art of Film Production*, Sir Isaac Pitman & Sons, Ltd., London, 1936
   Films, Sir Isaac Pitman & Sons, Ltd., London, 1932

Burnett, R. G., and Martell, E. D., *The Devil's Camera*, Epworth Press, London, 1932

Cahill, Holger, and Barr, Alfred, Jr. (editors), *Art in America in Modern Times* (Chapter VI, "The Motion Picture," by Iris Barry, pp. 91-93), Reynal & Hitchcock, Inc., N. Y., 1934

Carter, Huntly, *The New Spirit in the Cinema*, Harold Shaylor, London, 1930

Charters, W. W., *Motion Pictures and Youth*, Macmillan Co., N. Y., 1933

Cooke, Alistair (editor), *Garbo and the Nightwatchmen*, Jonathan Cape, London, 1937

Cousins, E. G., *Filmland in Ferment*, D. Archer, London, 1933

Croy, Homer, *How Motion Pictures Are Made*, Harper & Bros., N. Y., 1918

Dale, Edgar, *How to Appreciate Motion Pictures*, Macmillan Co., N. Y., 1933
   The Content of Motion Pictures, Macmillan Co., N. Y., 1935

Davy, Charles (editor), *Footnotes to the Film*, Oxford University Press, N. Y., 1937

Dench, Ernest A., *Making the Movies*, Macmillan Co., N. Y., 1915

Doyle, G. R., *Twenty-five Years of the Films*, Mitre Press, London, 1936

Educational Film Directory, *Motion Pictures of the World*, Boston, 1937

Fawcett, L'Estrange, *Writing for the Films*, Sir Isaac Pitman & Sons, Ltd., London, 1932

Film Daily Directors' Annual and Production Guide for 1929, 1930, 1931

Film Daily "New Deal" Edition (5th Anniversary Number), 15 Years, 1918-1933

Gregory, C. L., *Motion Picture Photography*, Falk Publishing Co., N. Y., 1927

Hacker, Leonard, *Cinematic Design*, American Photographic Publishing Co., Boston, 1931

Handibook, The (directory), Hollywood, 1934

Herring, Robert, and Bower, Dallas, *Cinema Survey*, Brendin Publishing Co., London, 1938

Hunter, William, *Scrutiny of Cinema*, Wishart & Co., London, 1932

Hill, Edwin C., *The American Scene* (1932), Witmark Educational Publications, N. Y., 1933

Kallen, Horace M., *Indecency and the Seven Arts*, Horace Liveright, N. Y., 1930

Kiesling, Barrett C., *Talking Pictures, How They Are Made and How to Appreciate Them*, Johnson Publishing Co., 1937

Klingender, F. D., and Legg, Stuart, *Money Behind the Screen*, Lawrence & Wishart, London, 1937

Knepper, Max, *Sodom and Gomorrah*, Hollywood, 1935

Knowles, Dorothy, *The Censor, the Drama and the Film, 1900-1934*, London, 1934

Krows, A. E., *The Talkies*, Henry Holt & Co., N. Y., 1930

Lambert, R. S. (editor), *For Filmgoers Only*, Faber & Faber, Ltd., London, 1934

Lane, Tamar, *New Technique of Screen Writing*, Whittlesey House, N. Y., 1936

Lewis, Howard T., *The Motion Picture Industry*, D. Van Nostrand Co., Inc., N. Y., 1933

London, Kurt, *Film Music*, Faber & Faber, Ltd., London, 1936
  The Seven Soviet Arts, Faber & Faber, Ltd., London, 1938

Lutz, Edwin G., *The Motion Picture Cameraman*, Charles Scribner's Sons, N. Y., 1927

Martin, Olga J., *Hollywood's Movie Commandments*, H. W. Wilson & Co., N. Y., 1937

Miller, Max, *For the Sake of Shadows*, E. P. Dutton & Co., N. Y., 1936

Moley, Raymond, *Are We Movie Made?* Macy-Masius, N. Y., 1938

Montagu, Ivor, *The Political Censorship of Films*, Victor Gollancz, London, 1929

Naumberg, Nancy (editor), *We Make the Movies*, W. W. Norton & Co., N. Y., 1937

Nicoll, Allardyce, *Film and Theatre*, Thomas Y. Crowell Co., N. Y., 1936

Nilsen, Vladimir, *The Cinema as a Graphic Art*, Newnes, Ltd., London, 1937

Ortman, Marguerite, *Fiction and the Screen*, Marshall Jones Co., Boston, 1935

Peters, Charles, *Motion Pictures and Standards of Morality*, Macmillan Co., N. Y., 1933

Perlman, W. (editor), *Movies on Trial*, Macmillan Co., N. Y., 1936

Pitkin, Walter B., and Marston, William M., *The Art of Sound Pictures*, D. Appleton & Co., N. Y., 1930

Pudovkin, V. I., *Film Acting*, translated from the Russian by Ivor Montagu, George Newnes, Ltd., London, 1933

Quigley, Martin, *Decency in Motion Pictures*, Macmillan Co., N. Y., 1937

Ramsaye, Terry (editor), *Motion Picture Almanac*, Quigley Publishing Co., 1935-36

Rand, Helene, and Lewis, Richard, *Film and School*, D. Appleton-Century Co., N. Y., 1937

Rideout, Eric H., *The American Film*, Mitre Press, London, 1937

Rotha, Paul, *Celluloid, The Film Today*, Longmans, Green & Co., N. Y., 1931
  Documentary Film, Faber & Faber, Ltd., London, 1936
  Movie Parade, Studio Publications, Inc., N. Y., 1936

Seabury, William Marston, *Motion Picture Problems*, Avondale Press, Inc., N. Y., 1929

Sinclair, Upton, *Upton Sinclair Presents William Fox*, Los Angeles, 1933

Spottiswoode, Raymond, *A Grammar of the Film*, Faber & Faber, Ltd., London, 1935

Stearns, Harold, *The Stage and the Movies in America, A Reappraisal*, Hillman-Curl, Inc., 1937

Vreeland, Frank, *Foremost Films of 1938*, Pitman Publishing Corp., N. Y., 1939
Watts, Stephen (editor), *Behind the Screen*, Dodge Publishing Co., N. Y., 1938

BOOKLETS AND PAMPHLETS

Eastman, Fred, and Ouellette, Edward, *Better Motion Pictures*, Pilgrim Press, Boston, 1936
Film and Sprockets Society of City College, *Documentary*, N. Y., 1938
Gale, Arthur L., and Holslag, Russell C., *Making Better Movies*, Amateur Cinema League, N. Y., 1932
Gordon, B., and Zimmet, J., *The Technique of the Film*, Film and Sprockets Society of City College, N. Y., 1937
Herring, Robert, and Bower, Dallas, *Cinema Survey*, London, 1938
Jacobs, Lewis (editor), *Film Writing Forms*, Gotham Book Mart, N. Y., 1934
Leiva, Augustin Aragon, *La Ciencia coma Drama*, Hecho Mexicano, Mexico, 1935
Lord, Daniel A., *The Motion Pictures Betray America*, The Queen's Work, St. Louis, Mo., 1934
Paramount Pictures, *Biographies of Paramount Players and Directors; 1936-7 Edition* (mimeographed), N. Y.
Sterner, Alice P., and Bowden, W. Paul, *A Course of Study in Motion-Picture Appreciation* (outline mimeographed), New Jersey, 1936
Terlin, Rose R., *You and I and the Movies*, Woman's Press, N. Y., 1935
University of Southern California, *Masters and Masterpieces; History of Cinematography as a Technique and an Art* (mimeographed), California, 1937

PERIODICALS

American Cinematographer, The (Hollywood, Cal.)
Arts Weekly
Billboard, The (Cincinnati, Ohio)
Boxoffice
Christian Century
Cinema Arts
Cinema Progress
Cinema Quarterly (London)
Ciné World (London)
Close Up (London)
Cue
Daily Variety (Hollywood, Cal.)
Direction
Educational Screen, The (Chicago, Ill.)
Esquire
Experimental Cinema
Fight
Film Art (England)
Film Bulletin
Film Daily
Film Daily Year Book
Film Front
Film Survey
Harrison's Reports

Hollywood Filmograph
Hollywood Reporter (Hollywood, Cal.)
Hollywood Screen World (Hollywood, Cal.)
Hollywood Spectator (Hollywood, Cal.)
Interciné (Rome)
International Cinematography
International Film Review
International Photographer, The (Hollywood, Cal.)
International Review of Educational Cinematography (Rome)
Judge
Life
Life and Letters Today (England)
Little Magazine
McCall's
Motion Picture Daily
Motion Picture Herald
Motion Picture Monthly
Motion Picture Review Digest
Movie Makers
Nation, The

National Board of Review Magazine
New Masses, The
New Republic, The
News Letter
New Theatre
Scholastic (Motion Picture Issue),
   Nov. 21, 1936
Scenario (England)
Screen Pictorial (England)
See (England)

Sight and Sound (England)
Stage
Tac
Theatre Arts Monthly
Theatre Workshop
Time
Today
Vanity Fair
World Film News (England)

SPECIAL ARTICLES

Adler, Nathan, "The Screen," *The New Masses*, February 6, 1934
American Cinematographer, "Technical Progress in Industry during 1936,"
   December, 1935
Bach, Julian S., Jr., "In the Soviet Cinema," *The New York Times*, November
   24, 1935
Bakshy, Alexander, "As You Were," *The Nation*, January 22, 1930
   "Concerning Dialogue," *The Nation*, August 17, 1932
   "Hollywood Tries Ideas," *The Nation*, June 22, 1932
   "New Dimensions in the Talkies," *The Nation*, December 24, 1930
Barnes, Howard, "Hollywood's Struggle With the Facts of Life," *New York
   Herald Tribune*, June 26, 1938
   "One Knows When Hollywood Is at its Best," *New York Herald Tribune*,
   January 16, 1938
   "Slim Pickings for Hollywood on Broadway Stages," *New York Herald
   Tribune*, April 17, 1938
   "The Story of a River, by Name the Mississippi," *New York Herald
   Tribune*, February 6, 1938
   "The World Is Too Much With Us," *Hollywood*, December 4, 1938
Belázs, Béla, "Films into Fascism," *New Theatre*, October, 1934
   "The Film of the Bourgeoisie," *New Theatre*, August, 1934
Black, C. M., "Man with a Megaphone," *Collier's*, July 16, 1938
Boehnel, William, "Super Pictures from Simple Lives!" *Screen Magazine*,
   August, 1938
Bond, Kirk, "Color and the Cartoon," *the little magazine*, August, 1936
   "Film as Literature," *Bookman* (London), July, 1933
   "Notes on the Modern Cinema," *Europa*, October, 1933
Brody, Samuel, "The Revolutionary Film: Problem of Form," *New Theatre*,
   February, 1934
Brokaw, Clare Boothe, "Mary Pickford: The End of an Era," *Vanity Fair*,
   August, 1932
Business Week, "Came the Movie Dawn," November 9, 1935
   "Movies Hit Prosperity Trail," November 21, 1936
Butcher, Harold, "An International Mouse," *The New York Times*, October
   27, 1934
Canby, Henry Seidel, "The Threatening Thirties," *Saturday Review of Lit-
   erature*, May 22, 1937
Capra, Frank, "Sacred Cows to the Slaughter," *Stage*, July, 1936
Carroll, Roger, "How Disney Does It," *Motion Pictures*, April, 1937
Chapin, John R., "Charlie Chaplin in *Modern Times*," *New Theatre*, Novem-
   ber, 1935
   "Hollywood Goes Closed Shop," *The Nation*, February 10, 1936

Chartier, Roy, "*Variety* Anniversary Issue," April, 1936

Churchill, Douglas W., "Disney's 'Philosophy,'" *The New York Times Magazine*, March 6, 1932

"Walt Disney Sighs for More Whirls," *The New York Times*, January 9, 1938

"Ecole de Custard Pie," *The New York Times*, March 6, 1938

"Hollywood Seems Shocked by the Smart Set," *The New York Times*, November 6, 1938

"How Mickey Mouse Enters Art's Temple," *The New York Times Magazine*, June 3, 1934

"Everybody's Language," *Collier's*, October 26, 1935

Clair, René, "Cinema," *Europa*, June-August, 1934

Conway, Jack, "My Four-Star Circus," *Screen Pictorial* (London), April, 1937

Crowther, Bosley, "Cartoons on the Screen," *The New York Times*, February 13, 1938

Crichton, Kyle, "The Lives of a Hollywood Director," *Screen Pictorial* (London), April, 1937

Crisler, B. R., "A Theory of Criticism," *The New York Times*, August 28, 1938

De Mille, Cecil B., "I Break Into Hollywood," *Answers* (London), October 2, 1937

"No Fight on the Edge of a Cliff," *Stage*, January, 1937

Dieterle, William, "Views on Historical Movies," *New York World-Telegram*, October 13, 1937

Disney, Walt, "Mickey Mouse—How He Was Born," *Windsor* (London), October, 1931

"The Life Story of Mickey Mouse," *Windsor* (London), January, 1934

Drabble, Derek, "Dietrich Is the Svengali!" *Film Weekly*, September 7, 1934

Dreiser, Theodore, "The Real Sins of Hollywood," *Liberty*, June 11, 1932

Eastman, F., "Chances the Movies Are Missing," *Christian Century*, May 12, 1937

Eisenberg, Emanuel, "John Ford: Fighting Irish," *New Theatre*, April, 1936

Ellis, Peter, "Fascism Marches On" (2nd article on "March of Time"), *The New Masses*, September 3, 1935

"Folk Lore and the Cinema," *The New Masses*, August 11, 1936

"Let's Build a Ditch" (article on Vidor's review of "Our Daily Bread"), *The New Masses*, October 16, 1934

"Review of 'Black Fury' and note on 'social films,'" *The New Masses*, April 23, 1935

" 'The Informer,'" *The New Masses*, May 28, 1935

"Robert Flaherty's Escape," *New Theatre*, December, 1934

" 'The March of Time,' " *The New Masses*, July 9, 1935

"What Happened to 'Fury,' " *The New Masses*, June 30, 1936

"Dovjenko's Frontier," *New Theatre*, January, 1936

Erskine, John, "Color! So What?" *Stage*, August, 1935

Faith, Joel, "Hollywood's 'Riff Raff,' " *New Theatre*, October, 1935

"Will Hays: Film Enemy No. 1," *New Theatre*, December, 1936

Ferguson, Otis, "Artists Among the Flickers," *The New Republic*, December 5, 1934

"Walt Disney's Grimm Reality," *The New Republic*, January 26, 1938

"Two New Pictures," *The New Republic*, January 5, 1938

Forsythe, Robert, "Mae West: A Treatise on Decay," *The New Masses*, October 9, 1934

"Three Times Risen," *The New Masses*, November 20, 1934

"20° Cooler Inside," *New Theatre*, September, 1934

Fortune, "Metro-Goldwyn-Mayer," December, 1932

Fortune, "Survey; Moving Pictures," April, 1936

Franklin, Jay, "We the People," Column on Disney in *The New York Post*, February 22, 1938

Garnett, Tay, "There's Profit in Sharing Profits," *The New York Times*, September 11, 1938

Gerstein, Evelyn, "Musical Talkies," *The Nation*, October 14, 1931

"What's Wrong with the Talkies?" *Film Spectator*, May 23, 1931

Gessner, Robert, "Massacre in Hollywood," *New Theatre*, March, 1934

"Movies About Us," *New Theatre*, June, 1935

Gibbons, Michel, "Von Sternberg," *Film Mercury*, January 2, 1931

Grierson, John, "Feelthy Peectures," *Everyman's* (England), April 27, 1923

"One Hundred Percent Cinema," *Spectator* (London), August 23, 1931

"Review of the Year's Films," *Art Work* (London), Winter, 1931

Griffith, David Wark, "An Old-Timer Advises Hollywood," *Liberty*, June 17, 1939

Hager, Alice R., "Movies Reflect Our Moods," *The New York Times Magazine*, April 22, 1934

Harmer, Paul R., "Motion-Picture Personnel and Production Expense," *The International Photographer*, September, 1934

Harrison, Paul, "Mervyn of the Movies," *New York World-Telegram Metropolitan Week-end Magazine Section*, March 6, 1937

Herring, Robert, "A Fresh Start for the Cinema," *Life and Letters To-day* (London), December, 1935

"Art in the Cinema," *Creative Art Magazine*, May, 1929

"Black Shadows," *Close Up* (London), August, 1929

"But Something Quite Different Is Needed," *Close Up* (London), August, 1930

"Comedy in the Cinema," *Life and Letters To-day* (London), Summer, 1936

"Time Lurches On," *Life and Letters To-day* (London), Winter, 1936-7

Hitchcock, Alfred, "Close Your Eyes and Visualize," *Stage*, July, 1936

"Director's Problems," *Living Age*, April, 1938

"How Movie Epics Are Born," *New York World-Telegram*, July 31, 1937

Howard, William K., "Stage and Screen Acting Are Almost Alike," *New York World-Telegram*, January 21, 1939

Hurwitz, Leo, "Hisses, Boos and Bouquets," *New Theatre*, July-August, 1934

Irby, Franklin S., "Recent and Future Economic Changes," *Journal of the Society of Motion Picture Engineers*, May 5, 1930

Jacobs, Lewis, "A Preface to Film Form," *Experimental Cinema*, February, 1930

"Color and the Cinema," *The New York Times*, March 17, 1935

"Decomposition," *Experimental Cinema*, June, 1930

"Dovzhenko," *Experimental Cinema*, November 5, 1934

"Eisenstein," *Experimental Cinema*, November 3, 1931

"Primer for Playwrights," *Hollywood Reporter* (anniversary issue), October, 1936

"Since Griffith," *The New York Times*, Part 1: October 20, 1935; Part 2: October 27, 1935

"Stage and Screen Directing," *Film Art* (London), Autumn, 1935

"The Filmic Image," *the little magazine*, May 25, 1935

"The Films of René Clair," *New Theatre*, February, 1936

Johnson, Alva, "Capra Shoots as He Pleases," *The Saturday Evening Post*, May 14, 1938

Johnston, John LeRoy, "Quiet, More or Less, on the Western Front," *Theatre Magazine*, March, 1930

Kallen, Horace M., "Pseudo-Mediaevalism and the Movie," *Opinion*, October, 1937

Kellogg, Arthur, "Minds Made by the Movies," *Survey-Graphic*, May, 1933

Kirstein, Lincoln, "Cagney and the American Hero," *Hound and Horn*, April, 1932

Knight, Eric M., "Your Theatre—Morality and Movies," *Variety*, January 5, 1938

Koslenko, William, "The Animated Cartoon and Walt Disney," *New Theatre*, August, 1936

Krutch, J. W., "Not So Hopeless Movies," *The Nation*, May 6, 1936

Lerner, Irving, "The Situation Now," *The New Masses*, August, 1933

Leyda, Jay, "Animated Films," *New Theatre*, January, 1935

Littell, Robert, "A Glance at Newsreels," *American Mercury*, November, 1933

"Pigs and Sheriffs," *The New Republic*, November 15, 1933

Literary Digest, "Christian Talkies to Avert War," December 27, 1930

Living Age, "Versatility of Mr. Lubitsch," June, 1936

Lorentz, Paré, "The Screen," *Vanity Fair*, 1933

Macdonald, Dwight, "Notes on Hollywood Directors," *Symposium*, April-July, 1933

Macpherson, Jeanie, " 'C.B.,' " *The Motion Picture Magazine*

Maltz, Albert, " 'Black Fury,' " *New Theatre*, April, 1935

Martin, Peter, "Montage," *New Theatre*, March, 1934

Messel, Rudolf, "Let's Laugh at War," *The New Clarion* (England), May 6, 1934

Milestone, Lewis, "First Flight," *Stage*, October, 1936

"The Reign of the Director," *New Theatre*, March, 1937

Mullen, S. M., "A Twentieth-Century Art," *Scholastic*, April 18, 1936

Nathan, G. J., "What Hollywood Does to Playwrights," *Scribner's Magazine*, November, 1937

New York Herald Tribune Editorial, "Love in Hollywood," August 24, 1938

Norden, Louis, "Luck Comes to the Proletariat," *New Theatre*, May, 1935

O'Sullivan, J., "Voice Comes Into its Own," *Motion Picture Herald*, February 12, 1938

Pabst, G. W., "My Quarrel With the Censor," *Screen Pictorial* (London), December, 1937

Page, Quintus, "Disney's Five-Year Plan," *Screen Pictorial* (London), January, 1938

Palmer, Gretta, "The Orphan Newsreel," *Today*, December 28, 1935

Parkhill, F., "Bank Night To-night," *The Saturday Evening Post*, December 4, 1937

Peet, Creighton, "Politics on Screen," *Stage*, May, 1933

Pegler, Westbrook, "Fair Enough," *New York World-Telegram*, January 15, 1938

Penfield, Cornelia, "Ace Directors of Hollywood," *Stage*, February, 1936

"Hollywood Helmsmen," *Stage*, April, May, June, 1936

"In Hollywood's Seats of the Mighty," *Stage*, March, 1936

Platt, David, "Sin and Cinema," *New Theatre*, July-August, 1934

"The Movie Front," *New Theatre*, January, 1935

Potamkin, Harry Alan, "Field Generals of the Film," *Vanity Fair*, March, 1932
  "Hollywood or Lenin Hills?" *New Theatre*, April, 1934
  "The Year of the Eclipse," *Close Up* (London), 1933
Pring, Beryl, "Shakespeare and Russian Films," *The Adelphi* (England)
Pringle, Henry F., "All for Art (Profile of Von Sternberg)," *The New Yorker*, March 28, 1931
Pudovkin, V. I., "Sound and the Future of the Cinema," *New Theatre*, March, 1934
Ramsaye, Terry, "Mistress Mary Asks Producers to Try Discovering America Again," *Motion Picture Herald*, August 19, 1933
  "Monopoly," *Motion Picture Herald*, July 9, 1938
Renoir, Jean, "Gorki in Celluloid," *The New York Times*, September 5, 1937
  "Mr. Renoir Speaks of War," *The New York Times*, October 23, 1938
Ross, Betty, "Russian Movies Use Untrained Actors," *The New York Times Magazine*, 1928
Rorty, J., "The Dream Factory," *Forum*, September, 1935
Russell, Herbert, "L'Affaire Mickey Mouse," *The New York Times Magazine*, December 26, 1937
Seldes, Gilbert, "Disney and Others," *The New Republic*, June 8, 1932
  "Motion Pictures," *Scribner's Magazine*, April, 1937
  "Motion Pictures," *Scribner's Magazine*, November, 1937
  "Motion Pictures," *Scribner's Magazine*, March, 1938
  "People and the Arts," *Scribner's Magazine*, April, 1937
  "No Art, Mr. Disney?" *Esquire*, September, 1937
  "Quicksands of the Movies," *Atlantic Monthly*, October, 1936
  "Screen and Radio," *Scribner's Magazine*, August, 1937
  "Sugar and Spice and Not So Nice," *Esquire*, March, 1934
  "The Movies in Peril," *Scribner's Magazine*, February, 1935
  "The Unreal Newsreel," *To-day*, April 13, 1935
Sennwald, André, "Josef von Sternberg, Stylist," *The New York Times*, September 23, 1934
  "King Vidor and 'Our Daily Bread,'" *The New York Times*, October 7, 1934
  "A Word With Ernst Lubitsch," *The New York Times*, October 14, 1934
  "The Screen Comes to Grips With Life," *The New York Times*, December 16, 1934
  "A Spotlight for the Film Writers," *The New York Times*, March 10, 1935
  "Second Thoughts on 'Wedding Night,'" *The New York Times*, March 17, 1935
  "Coal Mine, Melodrama," *The New York Times*, April 7, 1935
  "Upon Being Merely Clever," *The New York Times*, May 5, 1935
  "Close-Up of a Judas," *The New York Times*, May 12, 1935
  "The Future of Color," *The New York Times*, June 23, 1935
  "The Truth or the Illusion," *The New York Times*, August 11, 1935
  "The Screen Dramatists," *The New York Times*, September 1, 1935
  "On the Anatomy of Americanism," *The New York Times*, October 6, 1935
Stallings, Laurence, "How Good Is 'The Good Earth'?" *Stage*, June, 1937
  "'The Empire State Express' and Some Later Films," *Stage*, July, 1937
Stebbins, Robert, "Fritz Lang and 'Fury,'" *New Theatre*, July, 1936
  "Hollywood's Imitation of Life," *New Theatre*, July, 1935
  "Love 'Em With Bullets," *New Theatre*, March, 1936
  "The Films Make History," *New Theatre*, September, 1936
  "The Movie," *New Theatre*, March, 1936

Stebbins, Robert, and Leyda, Jay, "Cinema Becomes a Serious Art," *Magazine of Art*, July, 1938

Sterling, Philip, "Billy Bitzer, Ace Cameraman," *New Theatre*, April, 1937

Sterling, Philip, and Dannen, Dorothy, "Who Owns the Movies?" *New Theatre*, September, 1936

Suckow, Ruth, "Hollywood Gods and Goddesses," *Harper's Magazine*, July, 1936

Sugrue, Thomas, "The Newsreels," *Scribner's Magazine*, April, 1937

Sweeney, James Johnston, "Leger and Cine-esthetics," *Creative Art*, June, 1932

Theisen, Earl, "The History of Animated Cartoons," *Journal of the Society of Motion Picture Engineers*, September, 1933

"The History of the Cartoons," *The International Photographer*, March, 1933

"The Photographer in the World War," *The International Photographer*, November, 1933

Thompson, Lovell, "American's Day-Dream," *The Saturday Review of Literature*, November 13, 1937

Time, "Bank Night," February 3, 1936

"Hollywood Barricades," June 14, 1937

"Mouse and Man," December 27, 1937

Troy, William, "Academy of the Film," *The Nation*, November 22, 1933

"By Any Other Name," *The Nation*, June 12, 1935

"Eclecticism and Vision," *The Nation*, April 5, 1933

"Movie Cant and Criticism," *The Nation*, February 8, 1933

"Films: 'Picaresque,' " *The Nation*, March 14, 1934

"Pictorial Journalism," *The Nation*, February 20, 1935

"Propaganda and Beauty," *The Nation*, March 1, 1933

"Values Once Again," *The Nation*, May 10, 1933

Trumbo, Dalton, "Stepchild of the Muses," *The North American Review*, December, 1933

Tully, Jim, "Frank Borsage," *Vanity Fair*, February, 1927

"Clarence Brown," *Vanity Fair*, April, 1928

"Josef von Sternberg," *Vanity Fair*, July, 1928

"King Vidor," *Vanity Fair*, June, 1926

Van Doren, Mark, "Melodrama in Celluloid," *Stage*, July, 1937

"Stationary War," *The Nation*, September 26, 1936

Van Dyke, W. S., "Rx for a Thin Man," *Stage*, January, 1937

Vidor, King, "From a Vidor Notebook," *The New York Times*, March 17, 1935

"Rubber-Stamp Movies," *New Theatre*, September, 1934

"Technicalities Be Damned!" *Tac*, December, 1938

Von Weigand, Charmion, "Little Charlie, What Now?" *New Theatre*, March, 1936

Walker, Stanley, "Sex Comes to America" (a chapter from *Mrs. Astor's Horse*), *Harper's Bazaar*, November, 1935

Warner, Jack L., "Jack Warner Traces Origin of Talkies," *New York World-Telegram*, October 13, 1937

Watts, R., Jr., "A Denunciation of the Sense of Humor," *New York Herald Tribune*, April 3, 1932

"Films of a Moonstruck World," *Yale Review*, December, 1935

"Hollywood Sees Pink," *New Theatre*, November, 1934

"Philip Barry as a Motion-Picture Playwright," *New York Herald Tribune*, February 7, 1932

"Saint Cinema and the Dragons," *New York Herald Tribune*, May 1, 1932

"Seeing 'Cavalcade' With America in Mind," *New York Herald Tribune*, June 19, 1932

"Sight and Sound: The Fight Game," *New York Herald Tribune*, November 19, 1933

"Sight and Sound: Holiday Retrospect," *New York Herald Tribune*, December 24, 1933

"The Brotherhood of Man Gets a Break," *New York Herald Tribune*, November 13, 1932

Weatherwax, Clara, "Ain't Hollywood Romantic?" *New Theatre*, June, 1936

Weinberg, Herman, "Composing Each View," *Movie Makers*, June, 1934

- "Prelude to a Criticism of the Movies," *Close Up* (London), March, 1931

"Psychopathia Cinema Sexualis," *Film Art*, Autumn, 1936

White, Kenneth, "Animated Cartoons," *Hound and Horn*, October-December, 1931

Winter, Ella, "Hollywood Wakes Up," *The New Republic*, January 12, 1938

World Film News, Erich Von Stroheim (interview with), September, 1938

PICTURE INDEX

565

NAME INDEX

GENERAL INDEX

Associated Actors and Artistes of America, 428

Acting, 26, 59, 61, 105, 106, 120, 125, 127-129, 203, 216-218, 256, 304, 311, 323, 324, 330, 332, 333, 349, 354, 361, 365, 448, 481, 493

Animated Cartoon, 213, 440, 442, 453, 496, 497-498, 499, 501, 503, 514

American Mutoscope and Biograph Company, 98

Art, 3, 21, 22, 32, 35, 50, 51, 95, 117, 120, 133, 134-135, 171, 187, 208, 225, 296, 307, 310, 312, 313, 325, 333, 334, 336, 345, 347, 358, 364-365, 380, 382, 394, 433, 452, 453

Arcades, 4, 5, 6, 7

Art direction, 223-224, 330-331, 445, 448

"Artificially Arranged Scenes," 22, 24-28, 32

Associated First National, 289, 291

Atmosphere, 101, 110, 125, 206, 207, 208, 209, 304, 305, 310, 320, 357, 371, 379, 380, 381, 388, 467

"Bicycling," 54, 62

Biograph, 8, 9, 28, 57, 58, 59, 60, 81, 82, 86, 88, 98, 99, 100, 101, 102, 103, 105, 106, 107, 109, 111, 112, 113, 114, 115, 116, 117, 118, 122, 160, 171, 174, 210

"Block-booking," 165-166, 289

Camera, 8, 9, 10, 22, 23, 25, 27, 306, 307, 308, 309, 310, 312, 313, 318, 321, 324, 325, 326, 327, 331, 333, 340, 350, 351, 354, 355, 358, 359, 360, 361, 365, 370, 378, 389, 435, 439, 441, 456, 457, 458, 464, 465, 467, 470, 481, 484, 485, 501, 502; Angles, 306, 308, 317, 321, 323, 325, 349, 468, 485; Devices, 27, 36, 49, 186, 308, 325, 363, 377; Effects, 26, 31, 503; Eye, 310, 313, 363, 365; Mobility, 310, 313, 315, 358, 439, 441, 469

Censorship, 62-66, 77, 124, 136, 148, 155, 290

Color, 363, 364, 357, 433, 445-448, 449, 472, 498, 501, 502, 503, 504, 505

Columbia Pictures, 422, 474, 475

Composition, 125, 206, 207, 222-223, 304, 306, 312, 315, 323, 324, 331, 333, 349, 379, 380, 381, 382, 436, 465, 467, 468, 471, 476, 484, 485

Construction (Story), 36, 315, 317, 325, 328, 361, 491

Contemporary Historians, 495

Continuity, 25, 35, 38, 98, 103-110, 114, 122, 126, 173-174, 203, 204, 206, 305, 311, 317, 321, 327, 328, 340, 350, 360, 437, 485

Copyright, 61, 122, 129

Cutting, 37, 98, 103, 110-111, 112, 115, 179, 180, 185, 191, 197, 203, 224, 306, 309, 311, 313, 315, 316, 317, 319, 320, 321, 324, 325, 330, 340, 365, 367, 439, 440-441, 448, 455, 459, 461, 462, 465, 466, 471, 481, 486, 488, 490, 503; Inter-cutting, 98, 105-106, 180, 316, 321

Dialogue, 330, 334, 341, 358, 360, 434, 437, 438, 439, 440, 462, 476, 483, 486, 488, 489, 490, 493, 502

Dies Bill, 431

Directing, 59, 60, 120, 203-216, 324, 325-326, 354, 355, 362, 382, 448, 449-450

Distribution, 32, 52-54, 66, 83, 90, 94, 120, 161, 164-167, 170, 288-293, 315, 322, 453

Dissolves, 24, 49, 308, 309, 323, 325, 363, 368, 468

Documentary Films, 369, 370, 413, 443, 461, 495, 506

Double Exposures, 24, 49, 211, 322, 337, 377;—"Dream Balloons," 101, 105; Multiple Exposures, 308